Changing Families

RELATIONSHIPS IN CONTEXT — Canadian Edition

Anne-Marie Ambert
York University

Contributing Author
Catherine Krull
Queen's University

PEARSON

Toronto

Library and Archives Canada Cataloguing in Publication

Ambert, Anne-Marie
    Changing families : relationships in context / Anne-Marie Ambert.

Includes bibliographical references and index.

ISBN 0-205-41547-4

1. Family—Textbooks. I. Title.

HQ560.A34 2005   306.8   C2005-901270-6

ISBN 0-205-41547-4

Vice-President, Editorial Director: Michael J. Young
Acquisitions Editor: Patty Riediger
Executive Marketing Manager: Judith Allen
Senior Developmental Editor: Joel Gladstone
Production Editor: Charlotte Morrison-Reed
Copy Editor: Julie Fletcher
Proofreader: Karen Alliston
Production Manager: Wendy Moran
Manufacturing Coordinator: Susan Johnson
Page Layout: Janet Zanette
Photo Research: Sandy Cooke
Art Director: Julia Hall
Cover and Interior Design: Anthony Leung
Cover Image: Emily Shur/Getty Images

Statistics Canada information is used with the permission of the Minister of Industry, as Minister responsible for Statistics Canada. Information on the availability of the wide range of data from Statistics Canada can be obtained from Statistics Canada's Regional Offices, its World Wide Web site at http://www.Statcan.ca and its toll-free access number 1-800-263-1136.

4 5 6 DPC 08 07 06

Printed in Canada

Brief Contents

Contents

Preface   xx

2 Historical and Cross-Cultural Perspectives on Family Life — 31

3 Contemporary Issues in Family Life — 58

PART 2 SOCIAL AND CULTURAL FAMILY CONTEXTS   85

4 Cultural Diversity and Adaptation: Canada's Ethnic and Immigrant Families   86

5 **Effects on Families of Economic Changes and Inequalities** 117

6 Impacts of Neighbourhoods and Environments on Family Life

7 Roles of Education and Religious Participation in Family Life   172

PART 4 COUPLE AND FAMILY RELATIONSHIPS 299

11 Spousal and Partner Relationships 300

12 The Parent-Child Relationship and Child Socialization

13 Sibling Relationships and Situations 358

PART 5   FAMILY CHALLENGES AND SOLUTIONS   387

14   Divorce and Remarriage   388

15 Family Violence, Abuse, and Child Neglect 420

16 Family Futures and Social Policies 453

Preface

The field of family studies has recently benefited from an injection of innovative research from other areas of sociology as well as from other disciplines, particularly demography and psychology. *Changing Families: Relationships in Context* is the first family textbook, whether Canadian or American, to integrate this new body of knowledge—which also includes additional theoretical perspectives—in such a comprehensive manner. It follows that this book is different from others in terms of some of its contents. As well, some aspects of its format and organization are distinct.

CONTENTS

Although *Changing Families: Relationships in Context* includes all of the relevant information traditionally found in family textbooks, it also contains several chapters and many sections that are entirely innovative and even "outside the box" in the family textbook market. This is particularly evident in Part 2, where we look at how various aspects of the changing economy, neighbourhoods, and educational institutions affect families and human development within these families. The contents of these chapters reflect the fact that the best scholarly journals in sociology, family studies, and child development now regularly publish articles in these domains. This is probably the only family sociology textbook on the market that focuses on these areas combined, including the role that religiosity plays in marriage and child socialization. The media as a sociocultural context for family life is also discussed more fully than is done traditionally (in Chapter 3).

Furthermore, an entire chapter is devoted to siblings: their relationship, how they grow up to be different, and how they relate to their parents. The book also includes substantial sections on adoption, foster families, reproductive technologies, the impact of children's peers on the family, same-sex-parent families, ex-spouses' relationships after divorce, and the role of pets in family dynamics. These topics tend to be ignored or underdeveloped in other texts. Thus, this text contains a more complete overview of families and a greater diversity of domains relevant to family dynamics.

In the same vein, I have introduced a wide range of theoretical frameworks. In addition to the better-known theories, such as structural functionalism and symbolic interactionism, others, including social constructionism, are much in evidence. For instance, interactional-transactional theories are used in the chapters in which the parent-child relationship is discussed. Not only do we look at the socialization of children by parents but we also examine how children affect their parents' ability to raise them within specific environments—in other words, how parents, children, and their environment interact. Furthermore, I have borrowed from the field of behaviour genetics in order to acquaint students with new concepts, ideas, and explanations that are now regularly encountered in the area of family research and even in the popular media: the interaction between nature and nurture. Students can examine behaviour genetics within a critical sociological framework alongside interactional-transactional theories and even symbolic interactionism.

Therefore, although the results and theories from several other fields of inquiry are presented, they are placed within the analytical framework of sociology; a sociological perspective informs the text. Moreover, the interplay between the macro- and microsociological levels of analysis is evident in all chapters. For instance, family members' human development, both children's and adults', is studied within a great variety of larger contexts, whether the economy, neighbourhoods, schools, or immediate contexts such as family structure and dynamics. This intimate interplay between sociological and personal levels is generally missing in Canadian family textbooks. The disciplinary wall erected between the sociology and psychology of families prevents us from acquiring a more holistic perspective. Thus, the interdisciplinary nature of this book makes it suitable for classes in the sociology of families, family studies, and the psychology of families. This book constitutes what the publishing industry refers to as a "cross-over" text in the sense that it can benefit more than one discipline and opens avenues for cross-fertilization and exchange of perspectives in what has become an overly specialized and often narrow academic world.

Certain themes and theories that predominate in some areas of sociology and other disciplines pertaining to the family are emphasized. These themes—for instance, those of social inequalities, gender roles, and the effective community—link the various contexts together within an integrative framework. The themes give this text its theoretical individuality.

It is equally important to point out that most chapters in *Changing Families: Relationships in Context* focus on the nuclear family, broadly defined, rather than on the couple. This text is centred on the intergenerational axis rather than on adult "intimate" relationships in general. Although four chapters discuss couple formation and couple relationships nearly exclusively, most of the contents of the remainder of the text look at nuclear families as a unit constituted by parents and children or one parent and children. In other words, this is a book on families at the intergenerational level within various contexts, as well as on social policies that could enhance family life, including child socialization.

FORMAT AND RESEARCH

The text of this book includes a great deal of qualitative sociology in the form of quotes, case studies, and summaries from my fieldwork. This qualitative material serves several functions. It provides lively, illustrative material supporting the statistical information presented. In other instances, it helps explain statistical results or it provides more in-depth material. In some chapters, the qualitative data constitutes the only information that is available in the literature on some topics. The latter is the case when we discuss serial divorces and ex-spouses' as well as new spouses' social networks after divorce and remarriage. Unlike other textbooks, where qualitative material tends to be presented separately in boxed inserts as anecdotes, here it is an integral part of the contents.

I present a great deal of information, both quantitative and qualitative. Furthermore, how this information is obtained and research is carried out are important issues to me as an instructor. As a result, I have included at least one Family Research insert in most chapters; these inserts illustrate various research methods that will allow students to get a better idea of the range of methods that are used in family studies, both qualitative and quantitative. In other words, the Family Research features say, "Here is how various researchers do it, and how they get their information on family life."

While I focus on Canadian research, it should be kept in mind that, in several domains, the majority of studies on families have been carried out in the U.S. Hence, for many topics, the only research available is American (or British or New Zealander) and, when it applies to the Canadian situation, this research is herein included. In fact, many Canadian researchers publish Canadian data in U.S. journals. Thus, while this textbook focuses on Canadian families, it also contains material from other societies, particularly the U.S., because this is the society that is the most relevant to the daily lives of Canadians—via its economic supremacy, media colonization, and general cultural and historical interchanges.

ORGANIZATION

Changing Families: Relationships in Context is divided into five parts. Part 1, Foundations of Family Study, introduces definitions, perspectives, and issues pertaining to families. This includes theoretical perspectives, a historical and cross-cultural overview, a discussion of current concerns about family functions, and contemporary developments. Part 2, Social and Cultural Family Contexts, focuses on the macrosociological settings and conditions that affect family life and structure. These include the ethnoracial diversity of family life in Canada; the changing dynamics of the global and technological market economy; neighbourhoods; and schools and religious participation. The contents of Part 3 reflect its title, Patterns of Partnering and Family Formation, but also focus on sexual relations. Part 3 also introduces the developmental stages of family life before moving on to successive chapters on the spousal, parent-child, and sibling relationships in Part 4 entitled Couple and Family Relationships. Part 5, Family Challenges and Solutions, begins with a chapter on divorce, widowhood, and remarriage. It then examines violence, abuse, and neglect within the family. The last chapter reexamines the themes that have linked the contents and then focuses on future family trends and addresses social policies designed to prevent or ameliorate problems faced by families.

PEDAGOGY

Each chapter begins with a detailed outline. Throughout the text, many concepts and themes are bolded or italicized in order to help students memorize key concepts and ideas and to note emphases. Concepts that might need additional explanation are further defined in the Glossary at the end of the book. This Glossary contains fewer but lengthier definitions to serve as a reference for students who have never taken a sociology course before. Each chapter has a clearly identified but brief conclusion that serves an integrative function. As is the convention, chapters end with a Summary, a list of Key Concepts and Themes, Suggested Readings, as well as Suggested Weblinks. However, the usual Study and Review Questions have been replaced by Analytical Questions. This feature should encourage students to examine different perspectives, seek answers that may not be available in the text, draw additional conclusions from the research material that space limitations have excluded, and establish links between various parts of the text.

SUPPLEMENTS

The following instructor supplements are available for downloading from a password-protected section of Pearson Education Canada's online catalogue (vig.pearsoned.ca). Navigate to your book's catalogue page to view a list of those supplements that are available. See your local sales representative for details and access.

Instructor's Manual: This manual contains a variety of additional instructor resources, including:

- **Additional Class Material** expands upon or clarifies topics introduced in the text.
- **Chapter Linkages and Modules** help point out to students how various sections and themes in one chapter relate to their counterparts in other chapters.
- **Guidelines for Analytical Questions** help with those questions placed at the end of each chapter.
- **Suggestions for Discussion, Projects, Papers**
- **Short Essay Questions.**

Test Item File: Available in Microsoft Word / Adobe Acrobat format, this test bank includes almost 1,000 multiple-choice, true/false, and essay questions.

ACKNOWLEDGEMENTS

I want to acknowledge the contribution by Catherine Krull, from Queen's University, who wrote Chapters 2 and 4. The following colleagues and reviewers have provided comments and suggestions on various chapters. These comments have served as a basis for major structural and contents improvements. I first wish to thank two colleagues from York University—Nancy Mandell and Cliff Jansen—who have read previous drafts and have provided many helpful suggestions. The following reviewers are acknowledged: Paula Chegwidden, Acadia University; Debra M. Clarke, Trent University; Patience Elabor-Idemudia, University of Saskatchewan; Scott Kline, St. Jerome's University, University of Waterloo; Stephen Riggins, Memorial University; Noreen Stuckless, York University; Franc Sturino, York University; Alison M. Thomas, University of Victoria; Vappu Tyyskä, Ryerson University; and Mike Wahn, University of Winnipeg. These reviewers together have made me rethink and rework many sections and I am most grateful to them. I hope that I have done justice to these colleagues' thoughtful input.

I also acknowledge the advice of Martina van de Velde and Joel Gladstone, Senior Developmental Editors at Pearson Canada; and the efforts of Charlotte Morrison-Reed, Production Editor, and Julie Fletcher, Copy Editor. Furthermore, the continued interest of Jessica Mosher and Patti Riediger, Acquisitions Editors, was invaluable.

My ability to be productive in terms of publications has been greatly enhanced by the moral support I have received from two people who have been key elements in my life in the past 25 years. First, Jean-Paul—I would need pages to do justice to the support he gave me, which in turn provided me with the strength and latitude to engage in my constant research activities. His premature death in 2001 has left an enormous gap in my life. The second acknowledgment is more unusual in the sense that few people think of their mothers-in-law in this respect. But who would not enjoy being for her mother-in-law the daughter she always dreamt of having? Mothers are too often vilified. It is therefore fitting that I am grateful for having had two mothers: one for childhood and one for adulthood. Astrid died peacefully in her sleep at the end of the year 2003, several hours after one of our usual lengthy overseas phone calls.

Last but not least, I wish to acknowledge my daughter Stephanie's help. She is now a Child and Family Clinician and has worked on my various books, both authored and edited, since age 12. This time, she entered the reference section and helped with the indices at the end of the road. My books all pertain to families and children, so they form the basis of a "family business" in more ways than one.

I am especially indebted to the hundreds of couples as well as parents who have given so generously of their time and their hospitality for my various research projects over the past decades. Quotes and case studies from these families have greatly enriched this text, as has the material gathered from the over 1,500 students who wrote semi-structured autobiographies in my classes for 30 years. Most of my research ideas and theoretical revisions throughout my career have been influenced by this spousal, parental, and student contribution to my knowledge of real life as lived by others in their diverse family situations.

Anne-Marie Ambert

PART 1

Foundations of Family Study

This book focuses on two interrelated levels of family studies. First, it looks at the internal dynamics of families, such as how they are formed and the ways they adapt, as well as the relationships that take place within them: between partners, parents, and siblings. The parent-child relationship and the socialization of the child-adolescent occupy salient places in this analysis. At the second level, this book examines the contexts that shape family dynamics, influence family structure and the quality of relationships, and ultimately affect socialization processes.

I am particularly interested in the challenges that families encounter in terms of dynamics, relationships, life courses, and socialization outcomes given that their environments are often less than supportive. Consequently, families' contexts are discussed with an eye to social policies that could prevent or remedy the difficulties faced by families, parents, as well as children and adolescents.

Chapter 1 defines the various types of families and situates their study within a sociological perspective that is complemented by a multidisciplinary analysis. The main theories that inform family research are introduced and linked to the themes that run throughout the text. Methodological research considerations are also discussed.

Chapter 2 places Canadian families within their historical context and also presents a cross-cultural perspective.

For its part, **Chapter 3** focuses on contemporary developments, including the role played by more recent technological changes such as television and the Internet. The chapter also examines various issues pertaining to the family, particularly the functions it fulfills and the lack of societal support it receives.

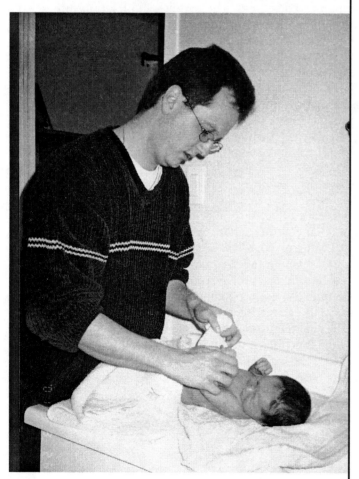

CHAPTER 1

Theoretical and Methodological Perspectives in Family Studies

My publisher suggested that I begin this chapter by answering a personal question: What in my own family life has led to my becoming interested in family studies? Simply put: I do not think that my early family life had much to do with this interest, although it certainly influenced my personal choices later on. Rather—and this may at first appear to be a strange answer coming from a sociologist—I am convinced that my interest was intrinsic to who I was (am) and stemmed largely from my genes, because I clearly recall being fascinated by family matters as young as age 6 and this interest has remained to this day. When I was small, there was no environmental reason for this interest, for my family life was then uneventful. Furthermore, the sociocultural climate of the time and place in which I lived was certainly not conducive to fostering the curiosity I was developing. Finally, it bears mentioning that my own family life course, either as a child or as an adult, does not have much to do with the topics I ended up studying or the theoretical perspectives I have used, with the exception of one (discussed in Chapter 13).

Overall—and I will return to this point in the last chapter—what has most influenced my scholarly perspectives on family life, apart from readings, has been the fieldwork I have done for my research: learning about the lives of the hundreds of children, adolescents, parents, and couples I have interviewed and observed throughout the years. Furthermore, as the reader will see at the end of this chapter, many of my students have written about their families in autobiographies. These lives, put together, have shown me that the questions that were asked in family research, especially about the parent-child relationship, and now about cultural differences ("family diversity"), were often not the right ones. The theories were too limited and did not always fit the facts I was discovering. This is what has led me to search for and consider a wider range of theoretical perspectives.

Notice that the title of this book contains the word *families* rather than *the family*; indeed, several types of families exist under one rubric. Despite this diversity, families can be analyzed as an institution. In fact, families are the most basic institution of any society, because it is within their folds that citizens are born, sheltered, and begin their socialization. **Socialization**[*] is the process whereby a child learns how to think and behave according to the ways of the society and the group in which he or she is born. Children are not, however, passive recipients in this process: they respond according to their personalities, needs, and accumulated experiences. They accept, reject, or transform the cultural messages that they receive from parents and others. It is thus through

[*]Words are bolded to accentuate key concepts and themes or to serve as additional subtitles within a section. Therefore, these words do not necessarily appear in the Glossary.

the process of socialization that a society transmits its culture, with some or many modifications, to the next generation. It is also through socialization that a society perpetuates its gender, racial, and economic structure as well as the roles that flow from it.

Why are families called an institution? An **institution** is a recognized area of social life that is organized along a system of widely accepted norms that regulate behaviours. The elements of organization and norms contribute to the predictability of life: People know what to expect—it is a shared culture. Over time, each society evolves a set of norms or rules that dictates the behaviours of family members toward each other and toward other institutions. Other key institutions in a society are the religious, educational, economic, as well as political contexts. We will study these institutions as they pertain to families in subsequent chapters, particularly in Part 2 and Chapter 16.

When a society is small and there is a great deal of consensus on values, norms, and behaviours, an institution such as the family can benefit from this stability. Life scripts do not change much over the generations and the level of continuity is high. By the same token, such a high level of stability can also contribute to the lasting subordination of women, for instance, or the rejection of alternative types of families. In Canadian society, which is a large one constituted by people from many different backgrounds, there is less consensus about family norms and behaviours as well as less stability. Change has become a part of the institution of the family, as it is in nearly all large societies of the world, and, as we see in Chapter 3, this situation leaves many people uncomfortable about the future of the family and raises concerns in their minds about its fragility.

HOW CAN FAMILIES BE DEFINED?

The task of defining what families are is a difficult one these days because our society is experiencing many changes and, consequently, experts do not all agree in this respect. Some want to eliminate the institutional aspect from the definition and replace it with a focus on close and sexually intimate relationships, however temporary. Others include networks of friends as a kind of family (e.g., Weston, 1991). The emphasis is on the voluntariness ("chosen") and the relational aspects of the relationships. For the purpose of the census, Statistics Canada broadened its definition in 2002 in order to reflect some of the current processes. For instance, Statistics Canada's definition (2002a) includes a couple, of any sexual combination, with or without children, married or cohabiting, as well as "a lone parent of any marital status, with at least one child living in the same dwelling," or a grandparent raising a grandchild. The Vanier Institute of the Family also includes a couple in its definition of families.

In this book, the definition adopted reflects current changes but also retains the institutional aspect and focuses on the intergenerational dimension of families. Indeed, recent changes such as cohabitation are becoming institutionalized although, for many others, families are still in the process of developing their own norms, as is the case for same-sex-parent families. Therefore, family is a social group, an institution, and an **intergenerational** group of individuals related to each other by blood, adoption, or marriage/cohabitation. The minimum requirement to meet this definition at the nuclear level (see Table 1.1) is the combination of two generations in one household, or the nuclear family.

TABLE 1.1 | **Typology of Unions and Families**

Type	Description
Families	
Nuclear family	At least one parent and one child living together
Conjugal	Husband, wife, and child(ren) Cohabitants with child Same-sex parents with child
Single parent	One parent and his or her child living together
Grandparent/grandchild	One grandparent or two grandparents and grandchild living together
Reconstituted	Remarried spouses or cohabiting spouses when at least one had a child from a former union
Horizontal	Sisters or brothers or cousins living together without the parent generation
Extended family	All the members of a family, including child, parents, grandparents, and other ascendants, plus uncles, aunts, and cousins (by blood, adoption, or marriage)
In one household	Generally involves three generations: at least one parent and his or her child living with another relative, usually the child's grandparent or aunt or uncle
In multiple households	Members of a family, including child, parents, grandparents, and other ascendants, plus uncles, aunts, and cousins (by blood, marriage, or adoption) living in separate dwellings and interacting on a regular basis
Unions	
Legal marriage	Socially/legally/religiously sanctioned union, which is generally heterosexual but could also be of same-sex partners, depending on the jurisdiction involved
Cohabitation	Consensual union that is not legally (common-law) sanctioned but is legally protected in Canada: it can involve same-sex or opposite-sex partners
Living apart together (LAT)	Union in which the two partners maintain separate residences
Monogamy	A legal marriage or cohabitation involving only two partners
Serial monogamy (serial polygamy)	Sequence of spouses or partners over time as in the sequence of marriage, divorce, and remarriage; spouses or cohabitants succeed each other
Polygamy	Multiple partners or spouses at the same time
Polygyny	One man married to more than one woman at the same time
Polyandry	One woman married to more than one man at the same time

Nuclear Families

A parent and his or her children as well as two parents with their children form the most elementary type of family—often referred to as the nuclear family. When a person or a couple has a child, whether by birth or adoption, a nuclear family of **procreation** is formed. What is important is not whether the offspring are biological or adopted but that a new generation is added. Under this definition, a grandmother who raises her grandson also constitutes a nuclear family and so does a single man who is fostering a boy, provided they live in the same household. However, a husband and wife, a cohabiting couple, and a same-sex couple fall under the category of *couples* (see the lower panel of Table 1.1). They constitute a nuclear family only upon the arrival of their first child. These couples are, however, members of their own families of **origin** or **orientation**. That is, they "belong to" or originate from their parents and their parents' families.

This said, however, who constitutes a nuclear family and under what circumstances calls for some flexibility. For instance, when young adults move out of their parents' house and set up a new *household*, are they still part of the parents' nuclear family or do the parents become their extended family? One has to consider the fact that parents and their adult children who live apart may still consider themselves a nuclear family. Similarly, in a situation of divorce, children may experience what is termed a **binuclear** family; that is, half of their nuclear family is constituted by themselves and their mother and the other half by themselves and their father whom they occasionally visit. When brothers and sisters share a household together without their parents, this is often referred to as a **horizontal** nuclear family because there is only one generation involved—but this generation originates from that of the parents.

Extended Families

Other relatives constitute the *extended* family or *kinship* group: grandparents, aunts, uncles, cousins, as well as in-laws. There is much fluidity between nuclear and extended families. It is not an either–or category (see upper part of Table 1.1). Most people belong to an extended family as well as to a nuclear family. Contrary to what is often believed, extended families living together under one roof (*multi-generational households*) have never been the norm in Canada, except among certain Native groups. English and French people arrived here with a tradition of nuclearity, in great part because life expectancy was too short for such a pattern to emerge on a large scale (Gee and Mitchell, 2003). Even then, rural Quebec was an exception rather than a rule when, in the 19th and early 20th centuries, most elderly parents lived with one of their many children when widowed or ill (Fortin, 1987). Such households were also more common among the poor in Quebec. Interestingly enough, three-generational households have increased substantially in Canada from 1986 to 1996, largely as a consequence of immigration from Asia and the return home of adult children with their own children (Che-Alford and Hamm, 1999). The majority of these extended families live in cities and in 48 percent of the cases, such families contain one or two grandparents with a single parent and his or her children. Yet, despite this increase, in 2001, only 4 percent of Canadians lived in multi-generational households (Milan and Hamm,

2003). Such families are least common in Quebec where they account for only 1.6 percent of all individuals. It is estimated that only about 7 to 10 percent of adult children in Canada live with an *elderly* parent (Mitchell, 2003).

Thus, generally, only a minority of individuals actually share a household with members of their extended family, although quite a few people live near relatives. Therefore, the level of exchange taking place between the nuclear family and the extended family varies by coresidence, proximity of neighbourhood, and even for emotional reasons. In North America, most relationships between members of an extended kin system are optional. For example, if two brothers and their wives or children do not get along, they are not forced to see each other, particularly if they live at a distance. Of course, the extended family is still fairly institutionalized in the west, at least at the normative level, so that it "looks" better if all the members appear to get along. Furthermore, as we will see in Chapter 4, most newly arrived families are more kinship oriented than are average Canadian-born families. Among the former, the extended family is more institutionalized: They often entertain higher values of reciprocity and have more exact rules of behaviour concerning their extended kin (Barrow, 1996).

In some ethnic groups—of Latin American descent, for instance—friends may be assimilated into the family as they become godparents to children. This is the system of *compradazgo*. When a father's friend is a frequent visitor to the house, he may be called an uncle *(tio)* and a mother's friend becomes an aunt *(tia)*, thus creating what some researchers call **fictive kinship** bonds. For many individuals who belong to a large extended family group living in close proximity, there is often less of a necessity to make friends outside the family, as all interactional needs are met within this system. This situation is further explained by a student belonging to a "white ethnic" family:

> *"We've always lived near my grandparents and several uncles and aunts on both sides of the family so I grew up with a very secure feeling of belongingness. There was always someone to play with or talk to and we never had to kill ourselves making friends at school because we had so many cousins."*

The extended family, generally in its separate households, has been the basic social unit in most societies of the western world until industrialization. Furthermore, the kinship group is still a key organizational unit in many African and Asian societies today, as we will see in Chapters 2 and 4.

Types of Union and Marriage

As indicated in Table 1.1, there are several types of union and marriage in the world, only some of which are legally recognized in Canada. Although the only type of marriage that is legally accepted in Canada today is that between a man and a woman—that is, two persons of the opposite sex—six provinces and territories have legalized same-sex marriage in 2003 and 2004. Polygamy in the form of **polygyny** (a man with two or more wives) became illegal in 1878 both in Canada and the U.S. However, an unknown number of polygamous Mormon families still exist today in the U.S. and even in western Canada, although they are not recognized by the mainstream Church of Jesus Christ of Latter Day Saints. Polygyny is widespread in Africa and Asia, particularly in Muslim countries, and is more easily maintained among the well-to-do in rural areas. **Polyandry** (a woman with two or more husbands) is less frequently encountered across the world and tends to be localized in smaller societies. It often occurs within the context of one woman being married to husbands who are brothers.

In 1993, Canadian cohabitational or common-law unions were given the same rights and obligations as marriages for income tax purposes, property held in common, and health benefits, generally after two to three years of coresidence, in all provinces except Alberta. In fact, in most provinces, long-term cohabitants are legally expected to support their children and each other after a breakup (Dranoff, 2001). However, we do not know to what extent cohabiting individuals take advantage of these rights/obligations because their relationships generally end informally rather than legally. Such breakups are not included in divorce statistics. Furthermore, a number of couples cohabit to avoid the responsibilities of marriage so that they may be less than interested in these conjugal rights afforded by the legal system.

Another type of union may become slightly more prevalent in the future: It consists of couples who **live apart together** or LAT. These couples, who maintain separate households, may or may not be married (Borrell and Karlsson, 2002) and, as a reviewer noted, some may be simply "dating." In 2001, eight percent of Canadian adults lived in LAT unions (Milan and Peters, 2003). Although most (56 percent) occurred among the 20- to 29-year-old age group, another 11 percent were found among those older than 50. Some may live with their respective parents (Nault and Bélanger, 1996). Others are older and widowed and this arrangement protects their children's inheritance; others are professionals whose careers cannot be accommodated within the same geographical area.

According to Villeneuve-Gokalp (1997), nearly two-thirds of LAT couples lead this lifestyle because of family duties or work requirements, while the other third mention the need to retain their independence as a reason. Levin and Trost (1999) found that nearly half of these persons expected eventually to cohabit with their partner, but only a minority of those older than 50 held such expectations (Bawin-Legrow and Gauthier, 2001). The latter may prefer to retain their own residence and ways of living (Caradec, 1997).

Persons who choose this lifestyle hold less traditional ideas concerning the importance of having long-term relationships than either married or cohabiting persons (Milan and Peters, 2003). Unfortunately, the studies do not tell us what proportion, even though small, of such couples are actually married to each other, and even living in separate cities, countries, or continents—closely resembling what has often been referred to as "commuter marriages." However, indications are that, when young couples have to be separated for work reasons, they may choose to cohabit rather than marry, at least for the duration of the separation period (Binstock and Thornton, 2003).

This phenomenon of extraresidential unions is widely found in the Caribbean region as an adaptive response to the socioeconomic conditions which require women to head households with very little or no economic support from their mate(s) (Barrow, 1996). In Canada, LATs are found across all income levels but especially more so among those who earn less than average.

Relevance of Definitions

The typology of families presented here does not include unrelated single people living together, even though they constitute a **household** unit or share an address. Such persons are members of their families of origin or of procreation but do not themselves constitute a family. Although this definition is restrictive in terms of what constitutes a family (not a couple, not roommates sharing a house, not friends), it is quite inclusive as to the number and sex of parents present and takes recent social changes into consideration. In contrast, traditional definitions of the nuclear family do not include unmarried mothers or same-sex-parent families, for instance.

This definitional distinction is important, not only in terms of accuracy but also because it carries family policy implications (O'Brien and Goldberg, 2000). For example, one often reads that children are born more and more "outside of the family." Such a statement is accurate when a traditional definition is applied, but is inaccurate as soon as one accepts a mother and her child as a type of nuclear family. Furthermore, in terms of policy, if a same-sex couple and their children are not accepted as a family, they will not receive benefits meant to help low-income families (Eichler, 1997).

As mentioned, some critics opt for a much broader definition of the family. This definition includes any person one wishes to recognize as such or feels close to or shares a household with. Thus, best friends can become a family, and so can neighbours who help each other a great deal, as well as former partners, ex-spouses, and friends' relatives. The emphasis is on "intimate relations" which, it is claimed, are more egalitarian and inclusive than families. This broad inclusiveness as to what constitutes a family is quite problematic for analytical and social policy purposes.

To begin with, such an inclusive family group overlaps with the concepts of social networks and support networks. Second, if we so broaden the definition of the family, it runs the risk of becoming useless. Social policies designed to facilitate family life do need a modicum of definitional precision. Third, as O'Brien and Goldberg (2000:136) so well put it, membership in a family is an ascribed status while friendship networks are acquired. "Status ascription is one of the reasons that family relations tend to be enduring, whereas friendships change over time, especially when significant changes take place in a person's life." Similarly, married or cohabiting couples often break up and may become estranged. In contrast, a family is enduring and when separating couples have children, each ex-spouse remains part of their children's families as parents. The children then have a binuclear family and remain in both extended family systems. Basically, if we choose to include anyone we are close to at any point in time as a family member, the concept of family will become so elastic that it will be meaningless. It is actually possible that, at the ideological level, it is exactly the outcome that some seek. Thus, Jamieson (1998) questions whether we are not simply exchanging one idealized version of the family (heterosexual two-parent families) as central to human life for another one ("intimate" or "chosen" families). By using an intergenerational perspective, this text repositions procreation and related linkages as central to the definition of families—no matter the gender or number of parents.

WHY IS A MULTIDISCIPLINARY APPROACH HELPFUL?

The topic of the family is a complex one and recourse to several disciplines is essential in order to obtain a more complete and refined perspective. Although a sociological perspective informs this text, the results and theories from several other fields of inquiry are placed within its analytical framework. That is, the results from other disciplines are integrated within a sociological framework. At the same time, theoretical perspectives from other disciplines help complement and even balance the sociological knowledge of the family.

Sociology itself tends to be divided between two poles: macrosociology and microsociology. **Macrosociology** studies large-scale phenomena and developments in a society, such as its social structure and organization. Macrosociology deals with economic forces, social class, gender and racial stratification, as well as cultural contexts, such as religion and value systems. It places the family within its broader historical and sociocultural context and examines how global forces combine to shape both family structure and, at a more intimate or micro level, family dynamics.

Microsociology focuses on the interactions between individuals within smaller contexts, such as a family or a group of friends. Microsociology examines relationships between family members as well as the impact of these relationships on human development, both for children and their parents. Two remarks are necessary. First, there is too much concern in sociology in maintaining these two levels of analysis separately. The reality is that, when dealing with families, there is a constant *interaction* between macrosociology and microsociology. One begins to see that they are not opposite poles after all. The interplay between the two levels is reflected within the chapters of this book. Second, family studies had in the past by and large emphasized the micro aspects (Eichler, 1988) to the detriment of research on the larger societal contexts that affect family life (Goode, 1963). However, more recently, Canadian family sociology has somewhat ignored the micro aspects. It is to remedy both situations that Part 2 has been introduced in this text: Not only is it macrosociological but it also studies how the psychological aspects of family life and human development are affected by their larger contexts.

Table 1.2 presents the various disciplines that constitute this text, more or less in order of importance in the contribution they make to the understanding of families within a sociological perspective. Some of these disciplines operate more at the macrosociological level, such as demography and economics. Others integrate themselves within a more micro context, particularly psychology, child development, and biology. Still others straddle both dimensions of sociology—for instance, anthropology, history, social work, and criminology, and even some aspects of demography and anthropology. Thus, a multidisciplinary approach helps link together *all* levels of sociological inquiry. What is important to retain is that no one single field of study can adequately cover the complex topic of the family—neither can a single level of sociological analysis. A multidisciplinary approach is essential and several levels of analysis are necessary.

TABLE 1.2	**Disciplines That Contribute to a Better Understanding of Families within the Framework of Sociology**

Disciplines	What They Help Us Understand about the Family
Sociology	Global sociocultural context that shapes families
	Community organizations that impact on family diversity and life
	Evolution of family structure and functions
	Family as a dynamic system
	Roles (fathers, mothers, children, breadwinners)
	Interactions within the family
Psychology	Interpersonal relations; feelings and emotions
	Family members' psychological processes and characteristics, such as temperament
	Child, adolescent, and adult development
Economics	How economic reorganization affects family life
	Impact of poverty on family structure
	The family as a unit of consumption
	Economic diversity among families
Demography	Trends in cohabitation, marriage, births, deaths, divorce, remarriage, residential patterns, intermarriage, immigration
Child (human) development	Human development from birth to death
	The contribution of the family to human development
History	Changes in family life, structure, definitions, and roles of women, men, and children over time
Biology and genetics	How genes and the environment (nature *and* nurture) interact to produce human characteristics
	Biological factors that affect family life
	New reproductive methods and contraception
Anthropology	Families in other cultural contexts
Social work	Problems encountered by families
	Social policies to help families and promote family life
Criminology and juvenile delinquency	Illegal behaviours of family members, their origins, and their consequences

WHAT THEORETICAL PERSPECTIVES INFORM FAMILY STUDIES?

In this section, some of the main theoretical perspectives that are encountered in the sociological study of the family are examined. To these are added three others that, although psychological in origin, are sociologically oriented and inform several discussions in this text. Each theory that follows explains certain aspects of family life, but no theory alone explains family life in its entirety. Often, two or three theories combined provide a more thorough explanation of reality; some theories are complementary. But, overall, despite a reasonably large number of theories, many aspects of family life are excluded and left unexplained at the analytical level. One can think here of family consumption, space, and time (Daly, 2003). However, this text tries to fill these gaps by introducing these topics within its various chapters.

Structural Functionalism

Structural functionalism analyzes a society's organization, its structure, and the linkages between its various systems (Merton, 1968). Within this perspective, the family is an important unit that fulfills key **functions** for society, such as reproduction and child socialization. In turn, a society's social structure provides the overall cultural and organizational contexts that influence family life. The analogy is organic: An organism (the society) is a system with many subsystems that collaborate or function together to optimize its success. The various systems fulfill functions or do things for each other.

The sociologist responsible for the propagation of structural functionalism was Talcott Parsons (1951). Structural functionalism was, to some extent, a conservative theory with assumptions of consensus or equilibrium. It left little room to address and redress inequalities in the social structure, because these inequalities were perceived to be fulfilling necessary functions for the entire social system. Thus, structural functionalism was not sufficiently flexible to analyze family developments. The changing role of women, for instance, could not be adequately examined because, under this perspective, the "liberation" of mothers threatened the family's equilibrium.

As well, the differentiation along gender lines between the **instrumental role** (father as the breadwinner and the parent responsible for linking the family to the society at large) and the **expressive role** (mother who cares for children, maintains relationships, and does the housework) was not sustainable with the return to paid employment of a majority of women and the changes in gender role ideologies (Eichler, 1988). Furthermore, subsuming all the instrumental tasks carried out by mothers under the rubric of the "expressive" realm did not do justice to reality (Luxton, 2001a). Nevertheless, if one rereads Parsons and Bales's *Family, Socialization and Interaction Process* (1955), much of their analysis of the family as a system is still relevant today. Particularly important is the view that, as agents of socialization, parents must "interpenetrate" other systems in order to be successful in their role (p. 35), a perspective that is linked to the discussion of family functions in Chapter 3 and of the linkages between the family and schools in Chapter 7.

Structural perspectives have since emerged to explain social inequalities based on the organization of society. This **social structural** orientation is evident in this text when inequalities between families are discussed, particularly in Part 2. In this respect, it is similar to a political economy approach to the family (Baker, 2001). Families' living conditions are analyzed through political, economic, and even cultural arrangements of society rather than through individuals' deficits or merits. This interpretation does not defend the status quo; rather, it suggests the necessity for change at the global level.

Functionalist terminology has persisted and has been utilized in family research without its original, consensual focus. The concept of **dysfunction**, now widely used both in sociology and in psychology, refers to situations, characteristics, or behaviours that prevent the various parts of the system from working well together. At the individual level, a dysfunctional characteristic, such as hyperactivity, is one that prevents a child from doing well at school or from integrating himself or herself within the peer group. A dysfunctional family is one that is so disorganized or debilitated by conflict, incompetence, and various deficiencies that it is unable to care for its members and socialize its children. However, as we will see later in this text, a majority of "dysfunctional" families have become dysfunctional or are so labelled because they have been socially marginalized by poverty or discrimination.

Social Exchange and Rational Theories

Both social exchange and rational theories are the product of the sociocultural environment of the 20th century and were influenced by the discipline of economics. For its part, exchange theory could not have been developed without the influence of the philosophical perspective of utilitarianism, which is based on the assumption of individual self-interests (White and Klein, 2002:33). Resources occupy a key role in both these perspectives.

Social Exchange Theory

The early proponents of exchange theory were the psychologists John Thibaut and Harold Kelly (1959) along with sociologists George Homans (1961) and Peter Blau (1964). Homans and Blau agreed that all the parties involved in an exchange should receive something which they perceive to be equivalent, otherwise imbalance will occur; one person will have power in the relationship while the other will be at a disadvantage. In this context, Homans used the term "distributive justice" while Blau referred to "fair exchange." However, Blau saw exchange as a more subjective and interpretive phenomenon than did Homans.

The basic assumption behind social exchange theory is that people interact and make choices so as to *maximize* their own *benefits* or rewards and to *minimize* their *costs*. In the market metaphor of exchange theory, **resources** and **power** occupy a central position—a perspective anticipated in Blood and Wolfe's (1960) research design in the mid-1950s. As explained by Sabatelli and Shehan (1993:386), "Each spouse's resources and each spouse's dependence on the relationship must be taken into account, for example, when attempting to study marital power." The spouse who has alternatives outside a marriage weighs the advantages of these alternatives against those secured in the current marriage (Levinger, 1976). This theory has also given rise to the equity model or the perception of equity (see Sprechner, 2001).

Exchange theory has been particularly useful in explaining gender relations, the household division of labour, and why people enter into, remain in, or leave relationships (see Chapters 8 and 11, for instance). As well, decisions concerning separation or divorce are affected by the relative resources of the spouses as well as the perceived alternatives outside the relationship. Social exchange theory focuses on rational choices; its focus on resources, which is called capital in rational theory below, brings an element of commonality between the two theories.

This market or economic orientation to human relations presents some difficulties for researchers whose values may be more altruistic and collectivist. In other words, it is difficult to believe that parents make so many sacrifices for their children on the basis of the expectation of rewards. In fact, there is often an imbalance of power in favour of children when parents raise adolescents who are particularly difficult (Ambert, 2003d). This, in itself, flies in the face of another tenet of exchange theory: that social groups such as the family exist and endure because they allow individuals to maximize their rewards. Another critique of this orientation resides in the fact that people's choices are not always made purposively.

Rational Theory

As mentioned, resources are also a key element of rational theory, which is currently used in the study of certain domains of family life. James Coleman (1990a) has been at the origin of this theoretical interest in family research. What I have excised from this theory for the purpose of this book are the concepts of social and human capital, which are used extensively to explain the socialization outcomes of children of various social classes, for instance (Coleman, 1988, 1990b). These concepts are particularly evident in Chapter 7. In this sense, rational theory is more one of capital and community than one of choice by individuals, as is the case for exchange theory described earlier.

Human capital refers to abilities, skills, education, and positive human characteristics inherited or acquired by a person. **Social capital** refers to resources that individuals or families are able to secure on the basis of memberships in social networks (Portes, 1998; Statistics Canada, 2004n). These resources enhance families' sense of belonging, child socialization, and the acquisition of human capital (Coleman, 1990a). Social capital is especially evident when parents cooperate, agree, and share authority. This allows their children to learn norms more effectively. The same results occur when the parental role is supported by a community. In both cases, *social closure* exists; that is, social networks are closed so that children are less subjected to conflicting norms. Furthermore, Coleman and Hoffer (1987) have been the proponents of the **effective community**, which I have adopted as one of the themes of this book. An effective community exists when neighbours are willing to take responsibility for all the children in their community (Sampson et al., 1999). This situation, whereby parents share a particular prosocial set of values, enhances parents' social capital and contributes to the monitoring of all children (Aird, 2001). It allows for social closure and constitutes an element of *collective socialization*.

Symbolic Interactionism

Symbolic interactionism is a popular theory in family research (White and Klein, 2002). It is favoured by qualitative family researchers and, as such, constitutes both a theoretical perspective and a methodological orientation (Eshleman and Wilson, 2001). It is a sociopsychological theory in which the **self**, social self, and **role** occupy a singular position, as do societal contexts whose meanings and structures are perceived by individuals while interacting with one another. People develop their self-concepts and the definition of the roles they occupy through other people's views of them—the concepts of "reflected appraisals" and the "looking glass self" were originally used by Cooley in 1902 and Mead in 1934. Basically, an individual acquires his or her self-definition through interaction with **significant others**—that is, people who play an important role in that individual's life, such as parents. Parents, teachers, peers, and even sports figures and movie stars may become **reference groups** for children as they grow up and learn the roles they are playing and will play as adults. This means that children look up to these individuals and groups and use them as role models or as points of reference to guide their own behaviours, develop their sense of self, and interpret social contexts.

Of the theoretical perspectives herein presented, symbolic interactionism is probably the most suitable for the study of personal and familial phenomena that have not been sufficiently researched. As Daly (2003:775) points out, "Emotions are rarely foregrounded in our theories about families, and yet much of the everyday rhetoric of living in families is about love, jealousy, anger, disappointment, hurt, tolerance, and care." Families construct an environment based on the reflections of self and on the perceptions of significant others, all key themes of this theory. Families constitute their own symbolic world through myth and rituals (Gillis, 1996).

Both symbolic interactionist and interactional perspectives view the child as a social actor who coproduces his or her development. A mother can teach her child to read, for instance, only with the child's cooperation and active participation.

Symbolic interactionism views socialization as a process whereby children participate in the formation of their identities (LaRossa and Reitzes, 1993:149). The more recent perspective on the **child as a social actor** has been inspired by symbolic interactionism (Corsaro, 1997). In this text, symbolic interactionism is utilized mainly in Chapters 11 through 15, where relationships and challenges are examined, generally in conjunction with interactional theories and behaviour genetics, a combination of perspectives that constitutes a precedent in a sociology textbook. Indeed, interactional theories, which constitute an extension of symbolic interactionism, are growing in importance in the study of child development and family relations.

The best-known symbolic interactionists are George Herbert Mead (1934), Herbert Blumer (1969), and Erving Goffman (1959). Symbolic interactionism encompasses two orientations (White and Klein, 2002). The first focuses more on family processes. The second focuses more on roles, is more structural, and has been heavily influenced by Goffman, who probably became the most popular symbolic interactionist upon the publication of his *The Presentation of Self in Everyday Life* (1959), perhaps in great part because he focused on dramaturgy (using theatre or drama terms such as *roles, actors, frontstage, backstage,* and *setting*). This orientation indicates that role strain is reduced when individuals perceive greater consensus in the expectations surrounding their role. One can think of the role of parents here. If parents perceive that their role is well defined, they are less likely to feel insecure about it and role strain will be reduced. This will become important in Chapter 12 on the parent-child relationship.

Interactional-Transactional Perspectives

The interactional-transactional framework posits that an individual creates his or her own environment, at the interpersonal level, at the same time that he or she is being shaped by this environment (Maccoby and Jacklin, 1983). This theory is particularly useful in the study of the parent-child relationship: It corrects the biases or flaws inherent to earlier socialization and child development perspectives whereby children were seen as the passive recipients of their parents' actions. Instead, the child is studied as an active social actor with individual characteristics, as are parents (Ambert, 2001). *Interactions* between parents and children *feed back* on each other. Similarly, the socialization process involves the interaction between children's personalities and parental teachings (Ambert, 1997). The child actively participates in the socialization process, albeit often unconsciously so. The child becomes **coproducer** of his or her own development (Lerner, 1982). Although this dynamic was recognized as early as 1968 by Bell, it has been largely ignored in the design of research projects.

The interactional causality model is multidimensional and bidirectional. It flows *both* from parents and children interacting with and reacting to each other and responding to the environment that impacts on them (Magnusson, 1995). Thus, the interactional perspective is also *transactional* in the sense that it involves a multiplicity of causality; in other words, it involves transactions between a child, his or her parent, and their environment within a feedback model (Sroufe, 1996). Interactional-transactional perspectives are very sensitive to the diversity of a family's environment, including culture and ethnicity (Sameroff et al., 1997). This theory applies equally well to other interactions within the family, such as between spouses or between siblings. Several chapters are informed by the interactional-transactional perspective, particularly Chapters 11 through 15.

Interactional theories are often developed within an ecological framework whereby the various levels of a child's or a family's environment influence development and interactions (Lerner, 1995). In other words, whereas children are coproducers in their development, both parents' and children's actions are enhanced, limited, and constrained by the larger environment in which they are situated (Bronfenbrenner, 1979, 1989). This is also a tenet of transactional theories and is a guiding principle in this textbook. Within sociology, these perspectives are located at the intersection of the macro- and microsociological levels.

Developmental (Life-Course) Perspectives

As White and Klein (2002) point out, family development theory is the only socio-logical theory which was created specifically for the study of families. Paul Glick (1947) and Evelyn Duvall (1957) were the first to propose a developmental sequenc-ing to family life. This is the aspect of family **life stages** that largely informs Chapter 10 and structures Chapter 12 on the parent-child relationship. In this text, however, I propose that families have a *life course* or trajectory but that it is now more fluid than in the past; as well not all families follow the same sequencing of events (Las-zloffy, 2002). Developmental theories are both micro- and macrosociological. At a more micro level, families are viewed as long-lived groups with a history of internal interactions as well as transactions with the rest of society. At the macro level of analy-sis, families are considered within the historical context of their society. Not only do families change and adapt but they do so under the influence of more global social changes (McDaniel, 2002). The effect of technology on family life is a case in point (Chapter 3) as is the economy in general (Chapter 5).

One key contribution of the developmental perspective has been to present a more **longitudinal** or long-term framework for research on families (Aldous, 1996). Longi-tudinal studies follow individuals or families over time as opposed to interviewing them just once. Furthermore, as illustrated in the opening section to Chapter 10, the devel-opmental perspective examines the careers of families within their particular socio-economic context, and takes into consideration the dynamics between the various trajectories and life stages of its members (Elder, 1998). Developmental theories rec-ognize that individual life courses at times do not mesh well with those of other fam-ily members, such as when an adolescent has a baby and this transition forces her own young mother to become a grandmother at a time when she is still raising small chil-dren (see Chapter 10).

This theory has been particularly useful in the study of intergenerational phenom-ena and relations in the context of different historical periods (Elder, 1991; Hareven, 1987). The concept of role recurs in this perspective as each individual's role evolves when additional members arrive, as children age and enter the economic system or de-part to form their own family units, and as grandchildren are born.

Dynamic concepts include transition or passage from one stage to the next as well as individual transitions within a particular family stage, such as when an older child moves out but another child who is younger remains at home. **Timing** is a key concept that is also encountered in the sociology of adult development (Clausen, 1986; Ra-vanera et al., 2004). Today, normative timing includes a 26-year-old woman who mar-ries and has her first child two years later. Less normative is the 17-year-old who has a baby. The first woman is "on time," whereas the second is "off time" (that is, too young according to the norms of society). Similarly, a 45-year-old woman who gives birth to her first child is considered to be off time, although such delayed transitions are becoming more common (Beaujot, 2004). Transitions may also include changes in family structure, such as the occurrence of divorce.

Developmental perspectives allow us to see how family cycles often, but perhaps unavoidably, overlap with parents' own life course as it follows their aging process or even the length of their union. For instance, a couple who has their first child at age 28 compared to another one who is 40 to 50 when this event occurs are at the same cycle in terms of family development but belong to two cycles in terms of individual development. This difference has consequences on how they live this experience, on family dynamics, and even child development, as seen in Chapter 10. It also means that the life course of the older couple's family may be less complex and contain fewer generations. Thus, mid-life is a particularly diverse life stage in individual development because it cuts across several different family life cycles (McDaniel, 2003).

Social Constructionism

There is some diversity within constructionist positions (Crotty, 1998; Potter, 1996), some of which are more psychological than sociological. In this text, I adopt a more sociological approach whereby knowledge is a social construct (McCarthy, 1996). Social constructionism has its roots in the classical sociology of knowledge, from Karl Mannheim's *Ideology and Utopia* (1936) through the better known Berger and Luckmann's *The Social Construction of Reality* (1966). The theory argues that various phenomena that are taken for granted and seem natural are actually culturally defined or socially constructed. A case in point is childhood, which has been redefined throughout the centuries according to prevailing socioeconomic changes (Ariès, 1962). In a now classic article, William Kessen (1979) explained how children are socially constructed by psychologists. He described the U.S. child and psychology as two cultural "inventions," or social constructs. A **social construct** is a socially accepted definition of a situation. It is a cultural creation or interpretation. In this respect, Gergen et al. (1996) analyze the discipline of psychology as a western product.

Another example is that of motherhood when it is described as "instinctive" and "natural." These two adjectives are synonymous with destiny and presuppose a lack of change in the way motherhood is practised. Therefore, these terms are used to ensure the stability of gender roles (men as breadwinners and women as stay-at-home mothers) and the perpetuation of *patriarchy* (masculine dominance in the major spheres of social life). This social construction of motherhood is not valid because, in actuality, motherhood includes practices and roles that differ from society to society and from century to century.

The concept of the nuclear family itself, as defined in North America, is partly a social construct. How we define what family is does not necessarily apply universally, as illustrated in the next chapter. But, as Fox and Luxton (2001:29) point out, the power of this social construct, along with the legal practices and the economic organization that surround it, contributes to "recruit people to produce children, share their resources, raise their children, and care for each other."

Family life is socially redefined according to the socioeconomic needs of a society at any point in time (Ferree et al., 1999). This social construction of family life generally comes from those who are in power as well as from experts who produce the knowledge that is valued by a society at a particular time in its history (McCarthy, 1996). Such valued knowledge can be religious, medical, psychological, or even legal expertise—all of which have evolved from a masculine power base. It is not surprising, then, that social constructionism is related to feminism (D. Smith, 1993). Both emphasize culture as an explanation for the definition of gender roles as well as masculinity and femininity. Both approaches present a critique of certain aspects of society (Calixte et al., 2004). Furthermore, this critique can be used to alleviate certain social conditions created by the constructs, whether it be motherhood, adoption, or adolescence, as examples.

Behaviour Genetics

The framework of behaviour genetics, which was casually introduced in my autobiographical opener, is not well known by sociologists. It should not be confused with sociobiology, which has much to do with explaining human behaviours and social institutions on the basis of evolution. Nor should it be equated with approaches that foster the notion of inequalities based on presumed genetic inferiority versus superiority between racial groups, for instance. Rather, the field of behaviour genetics studies *within*-family phenomena to explain how **nature and nurture** (or genetics and environment) *combine* and *interact* to produce personalities, parent-child interactions, the home environment, how parents raise their children, and why children grow up to be who they become (Plomin et al., 1998).

Parents influence their children, not only through their behaviours and attitudes, but also through the genes they transmit to their children and the indirect effect of their own genes on the family environment (Rutter, 2002). Parents' genes are expressed through their personalities, their socialization practices, and the lifestyle choices they make for their families, all of which are even more influenced by their environment (Turkheimer, 1998). A parent's environment includes his or her economic and cultural situation and relationship with the other parent; it also includes his or her children, their personalities, and their behaviours, which in turn affect the parent and his or her socialization practices. In other words, in a family, each person is part of the other's environment. Behaviour genetics, then, is closely related to the multicausality model of interactional and transactional theories.

Because of their different personalities, siblings in the same family do not experience their **shared environment** in exactly the same way (see Chapter 13). The shared environment consists of family events and circumstances in which everyone partakes, such as family outings, dinners, parental teachings, and even divorce (Booth et al., 2000). Therefore, depending on their own temperament, birth order, and spacing, siblings experience the shared environment differently. (There is a link with symbolic interactionism here in terms of the development of different meanings attached to experiences.) If one adds other experiences that children in the same family do not necessarily share—such as illnesses, classrooms, and peers (the **nonshared environment**)—it is not surprising that siblings grow up to be different to some extent (Plomin et al., 2001).

The closer the genetic link between two persons, the more similar their personalities and personality-driven behaviours. Thus, identical twins raised together resemble each other more than fraternal twins. Furthermore, the closer the cultural link between two persons, the more similar their behaviours become. Therefore, identical twins raised together resemble each other behaviourally more than identical twins raised separately (Kendler, 1996). Genes and the environment constitute the two engines that guide human development—*not* the environment alone and not genes alone. As such, behaviour genetics represents an important perspective for sociologists because nearly all the research on families has ignored the fact that human beings are biochemical entities that affect and are affected by their environment. Behaviour genetics *complements* sociological perspectives.

WHY IS FEMINISM A PARTICULARLY IMPORTANT PERSPECTIVE?

There is a great deal of philosophical diversity within feminism ranging from liberalism to radicalism (Calixte et al., 2004; Duran, 1998). Basically, feminism is an interdisciplinary set of perspectives and theories united by a common analysis of the patriarchal organization of society. This social structure privileges male attributes and male morality and leads to unequal gender roles in all social settings, beginning with the family (Gilligan, 1993; Thorne, 1992). Feminist scholars, however, vary in the extent to which they emphasize some of these elements over others (Luxton, 2001a).

There have been several waves of feminism in North America since the 19th century (Chunn, 2000), but ultimately feminist theories are woman-centred and aim at documenting and explaining the feminine experience (Osmond and Thorne, 1993). Feminist scholars have highlighted the fact that women's and men's experiences of life are largely different and unequal—a theme that has a multitude of ramifications for family life (Eichler, 1988) even if feminists by and large, as Hilda Nelson (1997:3) points out, have neglected family issues other than the division of labour. Notable exceptions are Margrit Eichler, Bonnie Fox, Meg Luxton, and Nancy Mandell (Mandell, 2001).

The Analysis of Gender Stratification and Gender Roles

Gender roles represent the social definition of what, in a society, is constructed as appropriately masculine or feminine in terms of behaviour. **Gender roles** are norms or rules that define how males and females should think and behave. They have the result of making men and women accept their proper place in society according to the dictates of the overarching structural arrangement by gender (Lorber, 1994). The transmission of gender roles occurs at the interface of macro- and microsociological levels.

At the macro level, gender roles are supported by the masculine, patriarchal organization or **stratification** system of the society that provides more resources, authority, opportunities, and autonomy to men than to women (Ferree and Hall, 1996). In other words, men in general have more *power* and, at the micro level, this affects the way they think and behave—differentiated gender roles. Girls and boys are socialized to occupy different roles in society, to think and feel differently, beginning with a preference for separate toys and activities. This process of socialization is so subtle that it is taken for granted as normal or as a result of nature, thus unavoidable. Consequently, on average, boys and girls grow up along divergent developmental paths and experience relationships as well as family life differently, even as adults (Bernard, 1972). This fact is particularly relevant in the study of families (Coltrane, 1997). Feminist theories have influenced researchers who study men as well as the development of boys (Messner,

1997). For instance, there is a great deal of concern over the problems created and encountered by boys as a result of their masculine socialization emphasizing toughness, emotional distance, and even bravado (Garbarino, 1999).

Feminist theories also contribute to the examination of social inequalities and diversities in general (Allen and Baber, 1992); as such, they are useful in the domains of state and social policies (Eichler, 1997; Luxton, 1997b), particularly with regard to racism (Dua, 1999; Rezai-Rashti, 2004; Weedon, 1999). In this respect, feminist theories have made it possible to examine the patriarchal structure of society from the perspective of anti-racism so as to study the impact of this double stratification on the lives of women of colour and on their families (Das Gupta, 2000). The phenomenon of immigration has been examined, including that of foreign domestic workers in Canada (Bakan and Stasiulis, 1997) as well as the role played by gender in the cultural adaptation of immigrant families (Dion and Dion, 2001).

Feminist Analyses of the Family

Families cannot be understood outside of the forces in society that are dominated—at the political and economic levels—by a gendered as well as a racial structure (Collins, 1990). The resulting division of labour by gender, both within society at large and within households, is a fundamental focus of feminist analyses (Bradbury, 1996; Luxton and Corman, 2001). Thus, feminism emphasizes the fallacy of the family as an entirely private world that is untouched by society's inequities. In this respect, there is a kinship to structuralism as used in this text. Feminists see the division of individuals' lives between the public and the private spheres as analytically flawed (Smith, 1987). Not only is the private domain affected by the public (culture, economy, polity), but the private becomes a political issue. For instance, the notion that family relations, including wife battery, are purely a personal matter has been challenged by feminists and successfully placed on the social policy and legislative agendas. As well, private decisions—such as a woman's choice to have fewer children as a personal adaptation to having the major responsibility for those children—carry important social consequences (Beaujot, 2000).

Feminism also analyzes motherhood as a social construct rather than as a purely natural product. Therefore, many aspects of feminist theories are related to social constructionism and have enlarged as well as informed this theoretical perspective (D. Smith, 1974). Marriage is seen as an institution that generally contributes to feminine inequality and perpetuates it in private life, including the bedroom. The gendered nature of marriage is particularly evident in the division of labour concerning household work and child care, one of the topics in Chapters 6 and 11. Other analyses examine the gap in parenting, what Jensen (1995) has called the "feminization of childhood," which leads to a discussion of how in our type of society the interests of women and children may be at odds (Presser, 1995).

However, feminist theories have been underutilized when studying older persons and their families (Chappell and Penning, 2001). Furthermore, feminist analyses have not sufficiently included women (and men) who might choose to be full-time parents to the exclusion of paid employment (Marks, 2004) or those who have too little education to be competitive on the labour market and instead remain as homemakers

(Evans, 1996). In a sense, feminist analyses have been developed by career oriented women within an economic system of paid employment controlled by men and within a technology designed by men to serve the capitalist economy. These existential conditions have affected theory and research and have unwittingly devalued "feminine" qualities and overvalued the male structure of work (Ambert, 1976).

WHAT ARE THE MAIN THEMES IN THE TEXT?

Within the several theoretical perspectives just described, this book emphasizes several themes. These are topics as well as explanatory models that link the contents of chapters and provide the distinct conceptual framework and flavour of this text. Social class or socioeconomic status (SES), gender, and race or ethnicity, which are key demographic variables or "social addresses" in sociological analyses in general, are woven into this multiple thematic framework.

The first theme of **social inequalities** is the dominant perspective of Part 2 and other chapters. This theme is informed by structural and ecological theories as well as by social capital or rational theory. Based on their economic situation and their ethnicity, families have unequal access to the key resources of their society. A feminist analysis informs us that gendered inequalities cut across economic and ethnic stratification: Men and women have a differential access to societal resources and opportunities within these social addresses. This is reflected at the micro level in an unequal division of labour at home (see Chapters 5 and 11) and a differential impact of children on women compared to men (see Chapter 12).

A second theme is related but not limited to the first one: **family diversity**—that is, diversity in structure, culture, and inequalities. Therefore, inequalities and diversity are the two overarching themes guiding Parts 1 and 2. My concerns about *social policies* pertaining to families flow from these two themes as well as from family functions. Social policies are intended to prevent and remedy familial difficulties created by social inequality (i.e., poverty) as well as diversity (i.e., one- versus two-parent families). Overall, diversity also includes class, ethnicity, and religion (Biles and Ibrahim, 2005) as well as ideologies leading to distinct lifestyles—whether "conservative" or "alternative."

The third theme, which will be initially examined in Chapter 3, focuses on **family functions**; it is related to structural functional theories. The text will document that, not only has the family not lost its functions, as is commonly believed, but it has actually acquired new ones. The family has become more specialized in the functions it fulfills for its members and for society as a whole. Above all, the book will document how individual families are too often ill-equipped to fulfill their functions, in part because of a lack of social investment in families—an important social policy critique that recurs and is expanded upon in the final chapter. We will also see that many more functions are actually expected of mothers than fathers.

A fourth theme running through the text is that of the **effective community**, particularly the role it plays or can play in child socialization and the successful integration of families in society. This theme, which is inspired by rational theories, emphasizes how effective communities constitute social capital that supports families. In turn, this social capital allows children to develop their own human capital: positive qualities, socially acceptable behaviour, and school completion and achievement, among others. An effective social community should also help in the care of frail elderly family members and of those with special challenges so that women are not unavoidably the chief occupiers of this role—particularly women who are already caring for their nuclear family (Beaujot, 2000). Same-sex-parent couples also often choose to construct an effective community of kin and friends in the support of their family structure.

A fifth theme revolves around the **cultural context** and includes a recourse to *social constructionism*. The social construction of reality, within the broader cultural context, is often used to show how it impacts on family dynamics. A good example of this is the social construction of adoption and how it can affect children's development (see Chapter 9). As well, the cultural context involves the audiovisual media and its impact on family interaction and child socialization. This theme of *media influence* first appears in Chapter 3 but is mentioned in several other sections of the text. Not only have the media restructured family time but they have also offered social constructs of reality that affect adults' and children's mentality. The cultural context also joins the theme of diversity inasmuch as families belong to a wide range of religious, ethnic, and ideological spectra.

The sixth theme in this book is especially important for Parts 4 and 5 and has a double theoretical focus. First, it emphasizes the **interactional** aspect of family relations as opposed to the traditional models that, for instance, tend to explain children's problems strictly through their parents' negative socialization approach. The interactional theory, as we have seen earlier, implicates feedback between the environment, the parents' characteristics and behaviours, and the children's characteristics. Second, this theme points to the complementary importance of paying attention to family members' **genetic inheritance** and the interaction of genetic inheritance with the environment in creating personalities and family relationships.

Finally, the seventh theme of **structural gender inequalities** and consequent **gender roles** originates from feminist theories as well as social constructionism. Boys and girls as well as men and women experience family life differently because of their unequal situation in the stratification system and because of their respective socialization trajectories. The theme of gender roles forms the cornerstone of several specific discussions throughout the text, particularly the domestic division of labour, relationship maintenance, and kin-keeping.

WHAT METHODS ARE USED IN FAMILY RESEARCH?

Let's briefly return to the matter of theory. A **theory** is a set of interrelated propositions that explains a particular phenomenon. A good theory can be tested against facts with a set of hypotheses. A **hypothesis** is a testable proposition or sentence. For instance, exchange theory can give rise to the following hypothesis: Employed wives are less happy with their marriage when they perceive inequity in the household division of labour (Lavee and Katz, 2002). In methodological language, marital happiness is the *dependent variable*—it depends on the wives' perceptions of inequity. Inequity then becomes the independent variable, the one that will make marital happiness change. The independent variable (perceived inequity) is one of the presumed sources of the dependent variable (marital happiness).

Theories inform the questions that researchers ask about families and provide explanatory models. **Methods** are the means or tools utilized to answer researchers' questions or obtain information. The methods utilized in family research are those of sociology, psychology, and demography in general. They are summarized in five categories in Table 1.3. This table will be useful throughout the following chapters where these methods are mentioned or are described in conjunction with various results found by researchers on a wide variety of topics. Furthermore, one or several special Family Research boxes on methods of particular interest appear in most subsequent chapters.

TABLE 1.3	**Methods in Family Research**
Surveys	Questionnaires given in groups (such as a classroom)
	Questionnaires distributed to homes (includes Canadian census)
	Face-to-face interviews in homes or elsewhere
	Phone interviews
Observations	Observation in natural settings (at homes, public places, village centre, streets)
	Participant observation where the researcher plays a role in the life of the respondents
	Laboratory observations (particularly of mother/child interactions) and one-way mirror; events are recorded as they occur
Experiments	"Natural" experiments: the study of families before and after a social event or a natural phenomenon occurs (introduction of the Internet in the home, for instance; earthquakes)
	Laboratory experiments (observations, questionnaires, interviews) before and after a variable is introduced or while the dynamics of an interaction are ongoing
Evaluative research	May involve any of the above methods in order to study the impact of social policy initiatives and clinical interventions
Content and secondary analyses	Content analysis of public documents, media programs, newspapers, books
	Content analysis of archives and personal documents such as diaries for historical research
	Content analysis of diaries and autobiographies
	Secondary analyses of surveys, census, and other statistical sources (*secondary* refers to the fact that the researchers who do the analyses were not the ones who had designed the original study or data gathering)

The matter of methods is a serious one with great consequences: The utilization of inappropriate methods simply creates useless and even misleading or false results. In turn, false or misleading results could lead legislators to enact family policies that might have negative consequences. One such example is the belief, particularly in the U.S., that welfare availability has been a main cause in the past of rising rates of single motherhood. This belief, based on poor and inherently flawed research, has recently led to a severe curtailment of help to poor families in the U.S. and in most Canadian provinces, with potentially damaging consequences for children in the future.

Qualitative and Quantitative Methods

Methods are generally separated into two large categories: quantitative and qualitative. *Quantitative methods* are based on numbers, percentages, and averages; they are shown in tables and charts and are expressed in statistical tests of significance such as regression analyses and time-series analyses or, at a more basic level, correlations. In contrast, *qualitative methods* are not based on numbers. Rather, in order to describe and explain various family phenomena in depth and to arrive at conclusions, qualitative researchers report what family members say, write, and do in the form of extracts, quotes, case studies, and summaries (Denzin and Lincoln, 1994). The reader will find many examples of such reports throughout the text, particularly in terms of quotes from students' autobiographies, excerpts from conversations with parents during interviews, and various case studies from my fieldwork. Above all, the methodological basis of qualitative methods focuses on a more holistic perspective, on letting respondents express their realities, and on informing theory. Statistical designs, in contrast, generally begin with a set of hypotheses and usually consist of multiple-choice or "close-ended" questions. Nevertheless, qualitative researchers also use the information they have gathered and summarize it numerically. For instance, they may present averages and percentages to provide an overall view of the themes and situations that have emerged in their qualitative material. This is particularly useful when large samples are involved and can lead to more sophisticated statistical analyses.

A distinction has to be made between qualitative data and "anecdotal" material. Qualitative research follows rigorous methods of information gathering. In contrast, anecdotes are gathered casually. For instance, every individual has stories to tell about his or her life that may hold great emotional and personal meanings for that person. But these have limited *sociological* value because they reveal no information about general trends and do not explain where each anecdote is situated along a continuum of life experiences on a given topic. In other words, although one life incident can be the source of a sociological analysis, it does not generally form a sociological perspective.

In this text, the quotes presented throughout are part of rigorously designed studies seeking to obtain a wide range of family experiences so as to offer larger perspectives that lead to conclusions. An example of anecdotes, in contrast, can be found on p. 336 of Chapter 12, where I report conversations overheard accidentally. But, because they are guided by a researcher's theoretical framework—in this case, the interactional perspective—these anecdotes can constitute *exploratory data*. These are insights gathered informally that are then used to design state-of-the-art qualitative or quantitative studies later on, particularly with the goal of testing hypotheses.

Qualitative and quantitative research methods are *equally scientific* and complement each other (Ambert et al., 1995); they are found within all five categories summarized in Table 1.3. In other words, both sets of methods can be used in surveys, observations, experiments, evaluative research, and content analysis. The latter includes historical documents (Schvaneveldt et al., 1993). Both groups of methods can also be utilized to test hypotheses based on most theories described earlier. However, sociologists who favour symbolic interactionism and feminism often prefer qualitative methods, whereas structural researchers, demographers, and behaviour geneticists generally have recourse to quantifications. The latter are often referred to as positivism, and there is a great deal of ideological debate concerning the merits and demerits of positivism versus postpositivism. This dichotomization is not fruitful (White and Marshall, 2001). Rigid ideologies as a basis from which to choose a methodology do a disservice to family research and narrow the scope of inquiry.

Rather, family sociologists should be concerned with choosing a research approach that can best describe the human reality they wish to study *within its social context*, whether it is a qualitative or quantitative approach or a combination of both. Methods should be selected depending on what is being investigated. For example, if one wants to study the well-being of children in a country, then clearly a large sample is required and statistical analysis is needed. The Canadian National Longitudinal Survey of Children and Youth is a good example (Willms, 2002a). Statistics Canada's various General Social Surveys are another. At the same time, however, one might want to inject more human texture and depth into the statistics by including qualitative information. This can be achieved by intensive interviewing of a small subsample of the larger one to allow the interviewees to talk at some length about the issues raised, their experience, and feelings. As well, certain aspects of spousal interaction may be difficult to approach with methods based on statistics derived from surveys, and may be more fruitfully grasped by qualitatively informed approaches, such as observations in a naturalistic setting or lengthy conversations.

An Example of Qualitative Methods: Students' Autobiographies

As pointed out in the Preface, one key source of qualitative material for this book is the research I have done from my students' autobiographies. This type of research falls under the rubrics of surveys and content analysis in Table 1.3. This material is used in the text to complement or clarify statistical studies. In other cases, it is the only material that exists on some topics. Throughout the years, undergraduate students in some of the sociology classes I have taught have written autobiographies that were semi-structured (i.e., in response to a set of **open-ended questions**). Open-ended questions allow respondents to say anything they want; they are the opposite of multiple-choice questions. This project was first initiated in the academic years 1972–74 when a format was tested on several hundred students. By the year 1974–75, the students' responses had confirmed that the questionnaire was nonsuggestive (I was not putting words into their mouths), easily understood, and yielded answers that could be analyzed into themes. From 17 questions in the 1974 schedule, there were 31 by

1990 and 27 by 2004; thus a few have been added and some deleted throughout the years. Over 1,500 autobiographies have been collected.

The core of the autobiographies resides in the following questions: "When you look back on your early childhood (0–5 years), what is it that you like best to remember about it? (What made you the most happy?)" In a second question: "And what is it that you remember being most painful to you? (What above all else made you unhappy?)" These two questions are repeated for the 6–10, 11–14, 15–18, and current age brackets. Initially, I worried that students might resent an intrusion into their recent personal lives, so I did not go beyond the 11–14 age bracket. This ethical concern was superfluous, however, as students were actually quite happy about the entire exercise. Consequently, in future years, I added questions to cover later ages and let each student choose where he or she wanted to stop his or her personal narrative.

A great proportion of the autobiographical pages are devoted to these core questions as students utilize them to narrate the main themes of the story of their lives. Other questions whose answers are used in this textbook result in descriptions of students' neighbourhoods and their relationships with parents, siblings, and peers within each age bracket. Students are at some point asked about their values as well as those of their parents and peers. They are also queried about their personality. At the end, they are requested to project themselves into their future and predict where they think they will be in 10 years from the time of writing. No question is asked about age, race, ethnicity, religion, or marital status, as these could help identify individual students. Nevertheless, most students provide this information somewhere in their narratives.

The autobiographies (as well as all other papers and tests) are submitted *anonymously*. Students are instructed to write their university identification number on the cover page only. After the autobiographies are read, I tear off the cover sheets, bring them to class and enter the grades on the class list in front of students. The autobiographies are an option: the other is a traditional research paper. Each year, only one or two students choose the conventional research paper. Many students elect to write well beyond the required minimum of 12 single-spaced pages. Students always know from the very beginning that they are working for a research project and they are keenly interested in seeing "their" work published. A formal 1990 evaluation of this assignment indicated that students not only trusted the anonymity of the procedure but also felt that they generally had benefited from the experience (Ambert, 1994a).

Students have been reliable or truthful in writing their autobiographies—a factor of great importance to a researcher. How do I "test" for truthfulness? First, I total up a few answers every other year or so and compare the results to statistics and research available for the population of students and parents. The students' profile on these questions matches that of available statistics. Second, the data provided by students on parents' marital happiness and relationship with peers replicate other research evidence. Finally, answers to several different but related questions produce a congruent profile, with the same themes recurring within a particular autobiography, thus assuring authenticity (Brown and Sime, 1981). Furthermore, students' answers indicate that they have tried very hard to project themselves back into the particular age brackets. A frequent remark is, "Of course, when I think about this now, I laugh, but it was really a terrible problem for me at that age."

To protect students' and other respondents' confidentiality, names found in the text are fictitious. At times, when a case study or a quote is so descriptive of sensitive material regarding a specific individual or family, certain demographic facts are altered. In such instances, it is customary to use one or more of the following techniques: change the gender of some of the children, their number, their place of residence, and particularly the exact occupations of fathers and mothers.

CONCLUSIONS: UNITY IN DIVERSITY

Families are tremendously diverse but they are united under the rubric of the family as an intergenerational institution. The theories used to study and explain the family are numerous but they form a totality that allows one to see the family in its entirety—to study families in the plural and yet to find important similarities among them. Furthermore, the various theories discussed in this chapter have illustrated the point made earlier: The family is an ideal phenomenon for a linkage, rather than a polarization, between the macro and micro levels of sociological analysis. Thus, some of the chapters that follow have a macrosociological framework, specifically Chapters 4 through 7 on ethnicity, the economy, neighbourhoods, and educational institutions, as well as religion. Yet, family interactions and dynamics (micro level) are discussed in terms of how they are affected by these larger forces.

On the other side of the coin, some chapters have a microsociological framework. Cases in point are the "relationship" chapters in Part 4 and much of the "problems" chapters in Part 5. Yet, these relationships and problems are situated within their larger context and, in part, are explained in terms of macrosociology. Similarly, the themes that form the basis of this text, although diverse, are unified because, when placed together, they present a holistic view on family life. This view can then be translated into social policies pertaining to supporting the family as an institution and consequently supporting individual families.

Summary

1. The family is defined as an institution and an intergenerational group of individuals related by blood or adoption. The nuclear family is generally enclosed in an extended network of kinship. The study of the family is interdisciplinary and amalgamates the macrosociological and microsociological levels of analysis.

2. The main theoretical perspectives informing family research are as follows: (a) Structural functionalism emphasizes global forces in society that affect family life, with a focus on the functions fulfilled by social systems and their subsystems. (b) Resources occupy a central position in social exchange and rational theories. Social exchange theories see people interacting so as to maximize their own benefits and minimize their costs. Rational theory also focuses on resources in the guise of social and human capitals in the area of child socialization. The concept of the effective community is also important. (c) Symbolic interactionism focuses on shared meanings, self-concept, reference groups, and roles. (d) The interactional-transactional perspective explains how family members create their environment at the interpersonal level while also being shaped by this

environment. It considers bidirectional feedback between parents and children; the latter are coproducers of their development. This perspective fits well within the ecological framework of environmental influences. (e) Developmental or life course perspectives emphasize the longitudinal approach, transitions, timing, as well as the personal and historical contexts in which family stages evolve. (f) Social constructionism argues that social phenomena that are taken for granted and seem natural are actually culturally defined or socially constructed. (g) Behaviour genetics studies within-family phenomena to explain how genes and environment combine and interact to produce personalities and the home environment, and how they affect parent/child relations as well as child socialization.

3. Feminism is a particularly important theoretical perspective in family studies because the intimate world of the family is guided by gender roles that are supported by the patriarchal organization of society at large. Important aspects of feminism include the transmission of gender roles, the social construction of motherhood, and the study of the family from a female perspective.

4. This text emphasizes seven themes that recur throughout the chapters: social inequalities, family diversity, family functions, the effective community, the cultural context and social constructionism, interactional and behaviour genetics perspectives, and structural gender inequalities and roles.

5. Qualitative and quantitative research methods in family research are equally scientific and complement each other. Qualitative methods are distinguished from mere anecdotes. Qualitative researchers do in-depth interviewing or observation. Quantitative methods use statistics. The description of students' autobiographies used in this text is presented as an example of a qualitative study.

6. The chapter concludes by emphasizing the unity that exists amidst the diversity of levels of analysis and theoretical as well as thematic approaches to the study of the family.

Key Concepts and Themes

Child as coproducer of own development, p. 16
Child as social actor, p. 15
Collective socialization, p. 14
Cultural context, p. 23
Effective community, pp. 14, 22, 23
Extended family, pp. 5, 6, 7
Family diversity, pp. 22, 28
Functions, pp. 12, 22
Gender roles, pp. 20, 23
Gender stratification, p. 20
Human capital, p. 14
Institution, pp. 3–4
Interactions, pp. 10, 16
Interactional, pp. 16, 23
Intergenerational, pp. 4, 9
Life course, pp. 17–18
Life stages, p. 17
Longitudinal, p. 17
Macrosociology, pp. 10, 28

Methods, pp. 24–27
Microsociology, pp. 10, 28
Nature and nurture, p. 19
Nonshared environment, p. 19
Nuclear family, pp. 5–6
Open-ended questions, pp. 25–26
Power, p. 13
Qualitative methods, pp. 25–26
Quantitative methods, pp. 25–26
Resources, p. 13
Shared environment, p. 19
Social capital, p. 14
Social construct, pp. 18, 21
Social inequalities, pp. 21–22
Social policies, p. 9
Social structural, p.13
Socialization, p. 3
Theory, p. 12
Transitions, p. 17

Analytical Questions

1. Many instructors prefer to teach "Intimate Relations" rather than Families classes; some say that teaching about "families" is obsolete. How can you respond to this position?
2. Which of the theories described in this chapter interests you the most? Be prepared to make a reasoned case for your response.
3. What are the main themes of this book? Link each one to a theoretical perspective.
4. How do qualitative and quantitative methods differ and complement each other? What are their respective limitations for the study of families?

Suggested Readings

Boss, P. G., et al. (Eds.) 1993. *Sourcebook of family theories and methods: A contextual approach*. New York: Plenum Press. This large text presents an overview of family theories and methods. The authors detail the historical development of each theory and methodology, as well as its assumptions and its major concepts, and present sections on research examples and other applications.

Eichler, M. 1988. *Families in Canada*. Toronto: Gage. This overview of the study of families remains a classic in this field in Canada.

Gilgun, J. F., Daly, K., and Handel, G. (Eds.) 1992. *Qualitative methods in family research*. Newbury Park, CA: Sage. This collection of articles presents an accessible introduction to qualitative methods in the domain of family life. Various family settings serve as contexts and topics.

Mandell, N. (Ed.). 2004. *Feminist issues: Race, class, and sexuality*, 4th Ed. Toronto: Pearson Education. The articles in this book are original writings and contain important discussions exemplifying how feminism relates to race, class, and sexuality.

Nelson, A., and Robinson, B. W. 2002. *Gender in Canada*, 2nd Ed. Toronto: Pearson Education. The authors present a feminist analysis of several aspects of family life.

White, J. M., and Klein, D. M. 2002. *Family theories*, 2nd Ed. Thousand Oaks, CA: Sage. The authors focus on five theoretical perspectives in family research: exchange, symbolic interactionism, family development, systems theories, and the ecological perspective.

Suggested Weblinks

Two websites which present different perspectives on family are **Council of Contemporary Family,**

www.contemporaryfamilies.org

and the **Institute for American Values,**

www.Americanvalues.org

Femimist Majority Foundation is a U.S. site that presents news from the entire world on women's issues and includes a list of feminist journals.

www.feminist.org

Judith Butler's UK site on feminist theory, including her own work, also presents much material.

www.theory.org.uk/ctrbutl.htm

CHAPTER 2

Historical and Cross-Cultural Perspectives on Family Life

Chapter by Catherine Krull, Queen's University.

"My name is Charlie Jones and I am hereditary chief of the Pacheenahts. My father, like his father, was Chief of our band. In a Chief's family—and I can name seven generations back in our family—the oldest son or brother always takes over as chief, when the existing chief dies or retires. It is important to maintain the succession from father to eldest son, as the office of Chief has always been hereditary in our tribe. It is also important for the Chief to teach his eldest son the duties and responsibilities which are a part of being Chief.

"I wasn't always called Charlie Jones.... The name of my family is Queesto, a name which means Chief Over All Chiefs. When the Catholic missionaries set up the first church in Port Renfrew, they took away our Indian names, gave us all white man's names, and baptized us as Catholics. My older sister's name was Kawa-shop-utlch, my older brother's name Cit-ka-dub, I am Chicajes, and my younger brother and sister were Ta-o-wey and Kwyanitza. Each name had its own meaning, but it has been so long since we used our names that I have forgotten what they were supposed to mean. We got into the habit of calling each other Ann and Willie and Charlie and Joe and Kathy. My name is Jones, instead of Queesto, but it was the white man's idea, not mine.

"It was exactly the same with our language: The missionaries and the government discouraged us from using our own language and made sure that all our children were sent to the white man's schools and educated in his language and his ways. My sons do not know how to speak our language, and I have forgotten half of it myself. They tried to eliminate our way of life, like our potlatches, just because they did not understand it. A potlatch is a special kind of party; joyous songs are sung and many dances are performed while the gift giving goes on. [They made] potlatches against the law for many years—they did many things to break the native way, the native law. Just imagine, [going to jail just] for having a party!"
(Pacheenaht Chief Charles Jones, Port Renfrew, B.C., 1876–1990, as quoted to his great-granddaughter, Catherine Krull, this chapter's author.)

Chief Jones's remarks about his boyhood offer stark contrast between the family structures of two of Canada's founding nations. His remarks provide an excellent example of the diversity of family structures and experiences in Canada's past and present (Eichler, 2001). Furthermore, Canadian society is not unique. When using a comparative approach, it is clear that family structures and functions differ across societies and over time within a specific society. What works in one society or in one time period may not work in another.

In order to understand families of the past, it is important to analyze family life within the context of the time period in which it takes place. Moreover, a comprehensive understanding of contemporary family life necessitates an understanding of families of the past because so much of what characterizes family life today is anchored in the history of tradition and societal systems (such as economic, religious, and political systems). It is equally important to acknowledge and appreciate family diversity across cultures. A comparative perspective allows for such understandings and highlights the fact that the nuclear family is but one amongst a multitude of family arrangements.

CANADIAN FAMILIES OF THE PAST

Thus, this chapter examines the structure and functions of families in the three founding nations of Canada: the Aboriginal First Nations, the French, and the British. It also discusses the family life of a small but important black community early on in Canada and the large-scale immigration of Europeans, Chinese, and American Mormons after 1867 to western Canada. The chapter then contrasts the Canadian historical situation with cross-cultural analyses of family life in the People's Republic of China, India, and revolutionary Cuba.

Early First Nations Families

The first families in Canada were those of the Aboriginal First Nations. When Europeans "discovered" the Americas in the 1490s, First Nations people in what is now Canada numbered about 200,000. The most densely populated areas were in the woodlands along the St. Lawrence River and the Great Lakes and in the forests and coastal regions of future British Columbia. The nations in these regions were both hunter-gatherers and horticulturalists. They lived in settled villages and engaged in some trade. In the other regions of what is now Canada, especially in the Prairies and the north, Aboriginal nations were almost exclusively hunter-gatherers and followed a nomadic existence because of the need to pursue migrating game. As the term "First Nations" implies, the various nations—more than 300 in North America by the 1490s—possessed unique histories, cultures, laws, levels of economic development, languages, and dialects.

While some Nations such as the Pacheenaht on Vancouver Island were **patrilineal**—that is, they recognized descent and inheritance through the father's line—others such as the Iroquois in the St. Lawrence Valley were **matrilineal**, whereby descent and inheritance were through the mother's line. Nonetheless, the basic social unit of all First Nations was the family. In contrast with nuclear families, First Nations' families were extended ones within clans, tribes, and bands. These families were communal, and the concept of sharing responsibilities and resources—everything from childrearing to food—dominated their lives. Although early First Nations families shared many similar characteristics between nations, there was also a great deal of diversity amongst them. Two case studies are helpful.

Plains Cree Families

The Plains Cree were a nomadic people, and their society tended to be patriarchal (men ruled) and patrilineal. Families united to form a band in order to better protect themselves against attack and to facilitate communal hunting (Mandelbaum, 1979; Rogers and Updike, 1969). Varying in size from 80 to 250 persons, bands normally comprised a male chief, his parents, brothers and their families, plus other families that may or may not have been related (Binnema, 1996). Informal councils composed of male members advised a chief, and band unity was provided by the chief's prestige and power (Christensen, 2000). Yet, while band leadership was founded on consensus-building among families, band membership was not fixed (Binnema, 2001). If individual disputes occurred, young men could join another band, perhaps even marrying within it. If a band as a whole encountered difficulties, say by the death of the chief, entire families could leave and unite with other bands. If a family decided to leave, it would probably move to another band that contained some of its relatives (McLeod, 2000; Sharrock, 1974).

A traditional division of labour structured gender roles (Friesen, 1999). Men hunted, cared for horses, and served as warriors in defending the band and its territory. Women reared children, prepared food, and made clothing and domestic implements. The band provided for needy members, especially the elderly and widows who could not hunt, and older people were at times adopted by younger families. Within the band, orphans and boys whose families were in difficult straits could live with the families of the chief or other men of high rank. They were considered members of these families, and in return for work, were given food and clothing. Like the other male children, they received instruction in hunting and warfare; female children were taught the domestic lessons needed for band survival. With the difficulties that confronted hunter-gatherer societies, this changeable band structure allowed for the survival of families in relatively difficult conditions determined by climate, geography, and competition with other bands and nations.

Iroquois Families

In contrast to the Cree, the Iroquois were a settled people. By the beginning of the 14th century, the Iroquois had embarked on intensive agriculture. Their tribes were matrilineal: Women owned all property and determined kinship (Danvers, 2001; Dauria, 1994). Therefore, when marrying, a man moved in with his wife's family and, when children were born, they became members of their mother's clan. All clan members were responsible for childrearing. Iroquois settlements were defensive fortifications and contained a series of longhouses, one for each clan, which were often more than 100 feet long; these settlements served as the political and economic centres of each tribe (Abler, 1970). Although the Iroquois were not nomadic, they would abandon their settlements periodically, either because their farmland ceased to be productive or they looked to improve their defences (see Starna et al., 1984). It was these two elements of social survival—producing food and defence—that saw gendered divisions of labour among the Iroquois. In terms of food production, since women possessed clan land, they worked the fields that produced crops such as corn (Brown, 1970). Men hunted and fished (Recht, 1997). Warfare was the principal vocation of men.

But warring societies require political organization. Given the matrilineal nature of Iroquois society, women chose the male leaders or sachem from amongst warriors in the settlements (Shoemaker, 1991). When the individual Iroquois nations coalesced into the Iroquois League, influential clan mothers continued this tradition by determining their nation's representatives within the governing council of the league (Fenton, 1998). Peacetime chieftainships were lifelong, although poor performance or mismanagement of a nation's affairs could lead to dismissal. In times of strife, however, temporary war chieftains were selected on the basis of skill and experience in military affairs and held office for the duration of a war.

Family life in Iroquois society, therefore, was based on the concept of gender equality, with men and women each having a range of specific responsibilities and rights (Brandáo, 2003; Englebrecht, 2003). By the time of their contact with the Europeans, the First Nations were political, social, and cultural expressions built around families and kinship and marked by varying degrees of complexity. Both nomadic and settled First Nations had developed sophisticated family structures by the end of the 15th century. These families' various forms—extended families, clans, tribes, lodges, bands—allowed for the nurturing and development of a series of unique societies in northern North America.

Families of New France

Significant change in the history of Canadian families began in 1535, when French explorers led by Jacques Cartier discovered the lower St. Lawrence River Valley. This territory only became part of France's overseas empire in 1608, when an expedition of fewer than 30 people headed by Samuel de Champlain established the colony of New France at what is now Quebec City. Champlain encouraged small waves of French pioneers to cross the Atlantic. By 1663, New France contained more than 3,000 colonists. A century later, in 1763, when the English regime began in Canada, 70,000 French-speaking people lived in North America. Of these, approximately 60,000 lived in the St. Lawrence Valley (Beaujot and McQuillan, 1982; Henripin and Péron, 1972). This growth constituted an extraordinary rate of population increase; it came from a very high rate of childbearing within a nuclear family structure. These 60,000 people descended from about 10,000 French immigrants, who travelled to North America over a 150-year period.

The first French-Canadian colonists were fur traders, or *coureurs de bois,* who constructed a frontier society while confronting many difficulties: extreme weather, conflict with the Iroquois, and intermittent warfare against the English colonies to control the fur trade. Harsh conditions in New France meant that the colony's survival depended on the labours of everyone irrespective of gender or social position. Until the mid-1600s, there were very few European women in New France. Apart from Roman Catholic churchmen who came to minister to the colony and convert the First Nations to Christianity, French male colonists were involved in the fur trade, military service, and administration. A significant number took First Nations women as wives—called *les femmes du pays*—in unions outside of the Church. As marriage partners, these women played an important role in the early development of New France because of their domestic skills and also because they could contribute to the fur trade their knowledge about skinning animals and preserving fur pelts, their ability in using First Nations languages, and their peoples' traditions as traders (Jamieson, 1986).

However, the nature of French Canada's economy and society changed over time and this affected families: The importance of the fur trade began to weaken, and perhaps more important, intermarriage between French colonists and First Nations women declined. As the Roman Catholic Church worked to enforce a traditional European patriarchal society in New France, colonists were encouraged to marry Métis women—those of mixed French and First Nations ancestry—and, later, white women. Between 1663 and 1673, France sent almost 800 young women, called *les filles du roi* (the King's daughters), to the colony to marry bachelor settlers; they had an enormous impact on marriage rates. Men were still involved in colonial administration, the army, missionary work, farming, and the fur trade. The new women immigrants initially found themselves freed from the traditional and confining roles common in France. They founded religious institutions and even became merchants, administrators, and missionaries (Clio Collective, 1987:49). Yet despite the earlier Aboriginal-European marriages and the advent of the Métis, New France was a society of transplanted Europeans structured around the political, social, and religious institutions of monarchical France. In this context of economic and social change, families had increasing importance in the development of New France.

By 1700, four major events had combined to relegate women to traditional female roles and promote family life. The first event was economic and pertained to the demise of the fur trade and the coinciding rise of agriculture. Although women had some freedom (Noël, 2001), a nuclear family structure became essential to settled life in farming communities. Large families were preferred since farm life required numerous workers. Under French law, a seigneur—akin to France's minor nobility—owned the land, and tenant farmers worked it. The number of land concessions worked by a tenant family depended on the number of sons a couple could have. As farmer-husbands required wives to produce families to work and perpetuate control of the concessions, marriage and family life became viewed as a means of stability for the colony.

The second event was a strategic consideration: Government policy promoted large families to strengthen the colony against British advances (Krull, 2003). Rather than encouraging massive immigration from France, the French Crown promoted high fertility to increase its colonial population. As marriage rates went up and nuclear family life became the norm, single women in non-traditional roles became a social anomaly. Women's options for economic security were quickly reduced to either marrying or entering the convent.

The third event influencing family life concerned the expanding authority of the Roman Catholic Church. As farming communities emerged and parishes increased, the Church gained more power and influence over the colonial population. By controlling education, for instance, the Church developed a gender specific curriculum: Girls were taught to be good wives, mothers, and servants of the Church. Although also instructed to serve the Church, boys were largely tutored in the ways of the world. The Church played a major role in implementing the Crown's pronatal agenda (Krull and Trovato, 2003a).

The fourth event, a peace settlement with the Iroquois in 1701, produced a more secure agrarian society. With the family as the base of this society, continued population growth remained the order of the day.

With the arrival of *les filles du roi*, couples in New France married at a much younger age than elsewhere (Beaujot and McQuillan, 1982). This tendency was reinforced by government policies that gave monetary rewards to females who married under the age of 16 and males under 20. Policies were also in place to strengthen people's desire to have large families by offering monetary rewards to couples with at least 10 legitimate children. As early as 1659, colonial authorities actually forbade celibacy (Peters, 1990). Marriage was viewed as a natural state that all colonists would eventually enter and in which they would remain until their death. And since family solidarity was thought to be more important than marital happiness, husbands and wives tended to stay together come what may. Consequently, divorce was almost unheard of. While there were many family types in New France, many early colonial families shared several characteristics such as sex-segregated roles, pronatalist attitudes, a neolocal nuclear household, self-selection in mating (but with parental approval), and kin interaction (Nett, 1993:102).

Families during British Colonial Rule

British Families

For more than two centuries after Cartier's expedition of 1535, the French were not alone in bringing different family institutions to North America. The British did so as well. However, before Britain's conquest of Quebec in 1759, the British colonial presence in what is now the United States had surpassed the French in terms of both population and wealth. Although the original purpose for Britain's presence mirrored that of France—commercial pursuits centring largely on the fur trade—its demographic superiority lay with London's policy of populating its Empire by massive immigration from the British Isles, including Scotland, Wales, and Ireland (Games, 1999). Entire families were a large part of this emigration. As in New France, British colonies before 1759 witnessed a transition from fur trading to settled agriculture and, tied to military success, this opened more territory for settlement. After the American Revolution of 1776–1782, the British presence in North America remained through control of Lower Canada (Quebec) and the loyalist colonies in the Maritimes—(New Brunswick and Nova Scotia)—and Upper Canada or modern southern Ontario (Reid, 1990).

Families in Upper Canada and the Maritimes during the period of British colonial rule, which lasted until 1867, were different from their counterparts in Quebec. Given their greater population, these British colonies experienced relatively faster urbanization and more rapid industrialization than in Quebec, and major towns emerged: Halifax, York (now Toronto), Kingston, Fredericton, among others. Because British colonists had the right to own private property, there was also another economic transition, this time from a preindustrial agricultural economy to a capitalist and industrial one.

Reflecting British society during this time—reinforced by the arrival of a significant number of Loyalist families who fled the new United States after 1782—these developments saw social stratification as classes of merchants, professionals, artisans, farmers, and labourers emerged. But even in these cases, the nuclear family structure remained (MacDonald, 1990; Potter-MacKinnon, 1993). Moreover, also reflecting British society, there was an aristocratic element in Britain's English-speaking Canadian colonies, as British noblemen and their families came to Canada to govern, lead the army and navy, and establish estates. In this context, and in that of the upper middle classes, a distinction existed between families and households. Households included domestic workers, servants, and labourers and their families who worked for and were supported by the patriarch's family (Hoffman and Taylor, 1996). In all classes in the colonies, therefore, there was an intimate connection between family life and production. As Tilly and Scott (2001:78) have pointed out, "the household was the centre around which resources, labour, and consumption were balanced."

Families in Upper Canada and the Maritimes

British families in Upper Canada and the Maritimes were nuclear ones built around Christian principles and founded on the same legal patriarchy as those in England. In these colonies, there was no central religious power equivalent to the Roman Catholic Church in New France: The several Protestant religious authorities included Anglicans, Methodists, Quakers, Puritans, Presbyterians, and others. However, as in New France, there was a strong connection between these religious authorities and the colonial governments. Christian notions that fathers and husbands owned property and were responsible for subservient children and wives underpinned colonial society in British Canada. Having custody of their families' moral character as well as their economic well-being, men worked outside the home. More importantly, British common law gave legal rights to men as the heads of their families. Women were restricted to the home as cooks, cleaners, and caregivers for their children and, sometimes, for elderly parents. In some circumstances, however, they could take a leading role within households (Smith and Sullivan, 1995). On a husband's death, for example, widows could inherit land and manage their families' interests on their own. Divorce in Upper Canada was only possible after 1839, but when it happened, men received better treatment from the law, including retaining custody of their children (Johnson, 1994).

Within the working class, children were crucial for the economic survival of families. After receiving rudimentary education, they worked to help support the family (McClare, 1997). Most working-class boys learned farming, logging, and, in the Maritime colonies, fishing, while others apprenticed in trades like carpentry and blacksmithing. Orphaned and abandoned colonial children, including some sent from Britain, were placed in willing homes where their life and education centred on becoming apprentices to a trade (Neff, 1996). Within the upper classes, male children had access to good schooling, including university, to prepare them to enter the professions and government. With some exceptions (den Boggende, 1997), upper-class females received a general education that prepared them to take their place in society. At lower levels, girls entered domestic service as young as 10 years, and remained there until they either became financially independent or married (Conrad, 1986). Overall, children only married when their contribution to the family was no longer essential; this translated into the age of marriage being higher in Upper Canada and the Maritimes than in Quebec (Krull and Trovato, 2003).

"Women's work" played a significant part in the development of British Canada (Errington, 1995). Women's contributions to social stability as wives and mothers were crucial to the strength and expansion of the economy. As much as there was a distinctive male culture in British colonial Canada built around men's social and political roles, there was also a distinctive female culture. Colonial women of all classes shared a common experience centred on the family. On one hand, there were the uncertainties of marriage and the ever-present dangers attendant on childbirth; on the other were the efforts made to meet the various needs of their families. This common experience had diverse roots. Stemming from the differing ways in which colonial women discharged their social and economic responsibilities—something determined by age, marital status, urban or rural residence, class, and changing expectations—women and family life were fundamental to the development of a distinctive British colonial society (Morgan, 1996).

This society was increasingly individualistic, a function of its capitalist and property-owning nature. One result was that for very poor families, who had no home and no income, begging was not uncommon (Hoffman and Taylor, 1996). In this individualistic society, charity from well-to-do families rather than from the government helped less fortunate ones. Because colonists from particular regions in Britain also tended to settle in the same places in the Maritimes and Upper Canada—and to name their new communities with their places of origin in the British Isles, for instance, Durham in Ontario and Liverpool in Nova Scotia—social integration existed in Upper Canada and the Maritime colonies tied to kinship and the colonists' place of origin (Clarke, 1991; Withrow, 2002).

Quebec under British Rule

In the period between the British conquest of Quebec (1763) and Confederation (1867), when Upper Canada, Quebec, and the Maritime colonies joined together to form an independent Canada, French Canadians in Quebec developed a distinct society with the family at its core (Berthet, 1992). The British governed post-conquest Quebec and dominated the upper levels of its economy. But to keep their new French-speaking colony stable, the British let the Québécois use their language rather than English; they put no strictures on the Roman Catholic Church; and they allowed French civil law to continue to be used. The result was that beneath the English-dominated political and economic leadership in Quebec, a Catholic, agrarian, and French-speaking society continued to exist as before. The family was very important in Quebec during the period of British colonial rule: Surrounded by the growing Protestant and anglophone colonies, Quebec required an increasing population. Since it was impossible to build that population with immigrants—which was not the tradition in Quebec—this requirement translated into the continued need for large families.

Accordingly, marriage in French Canada not only remained as the natural state for every colonist, it was seen as essential for the survival of Quebec's distinct culture and society (Krull and Trovato, 2003b). French-speaking government officials and the Church promoted family growth, which also meant promoting the patriarchal family system. And as old French seigneurial law had not been replaced, more sons were needed to ensure control of tenant-controlled land. Divorce remained extremely rare, as family solidarity was more important than marital happiness. In this way, the nature of Quebec families did not change despite the British conquest. The established pattern of marrying at an early age continued; large numbers of children were the norm; sex-segregated roles for husbands and wives and boys and girls were reinforced; and family life formed the basic component of a preindustrial society and economy that continued even after Confederation. Of course not everyone could or would marry. Little by little, some women and men chose not to or failed to marry. They generally stayed with their families and, in the case of older daughters, often remained to care for elderly parents.

Montreal became one of Canada's major industrial cities, with a growing immigrant population from Europe seeking employment (Papillon, no date). But the majority of 19th-century Québécois lived outside of Montreal; and because Quebec's population was expanding and its best farmland was occupied, some Québécois saw the possibility of a better life for themselves and their families outside of the Canadian colonies. Beginning during British rule and increasing after Confederation, Québécois families began moving south to find jobs in industry and in work like logging. Between 1840 and 1940, 900,000 Québécois settled in the U.S., from Maine to Michigan (Lavoie, 1981).

First Nations Families under French and British Rule

Although built on the same general Christian and patriarchal precepts, British and French families in Canada developed differently over the almost four centuries separating Cartier's discovery of the lower St. Lawrence and the early years of Confederation. Important for the survival of New France and the protection of francophone culture from the English-speaking majority surrounding them, large extended families became the foundation of an agrarian and preindustrial society in Quebec. In English-speaking Canada, the society was socially stratified and increasingly urban and industrial, and smaller nuclear families were the norm. But regardless of the differences between them, Christian and patriarchal British and French society dominated in Canada by the early 20th century.

First Nations families were extended and often shared a common dwelling in which all the generations lived in close and constant proximity. This communal life meant that all family members were responsible for the rearing of children. They formed an effective community.

In this way, contact with both the French and British brought great changes to the First Nations and their families, which proved to be fragile in the face of European contact. These changes began with the fur traders who exchanged food, alcohol, and European goods for Aboriginal furs, creating an economic dependency amongst the First Nations people on the British and the French colonizers. Diseases such as small pox, measles, and tuberculosis, which were brought over by European settlers, also decimated the First Nations people. But even more devastating was the calculated plans by both the French and British colonial governments and Christian missionaries to eradicate First Nations' culture: "When France and Britain entered what is now Canada they wanted more than the natural resources and land, they wanted to change forever the people of these lands by assimilating them into the Euro-Canadian society. To do so meant changing family values and structures and gender relations to mirror those of the dominant society" (Fiske and Johnny, 2003:182).

The European educational system played a pivotal role in colonizing Aboriginal culture. The Jesuits in New France opened schools to "properly" educate Aboriginal children about religion and French culture. The British did the same in terms of their culture. By the end of the British colonial period and the early years of Confederation, every region in Canada had boarding schools for Aboriginal children, their objective being the children's assimilation through a European-focused curriculum and an authoritarian power structure (Harrison and Friesen, 2004:191). Children were alienated from their families and stripped of all identifiers of Aboriginal culture. They were forced to take Christian names and forbidden to speak their mother tongue. Their hair was cut and their clothes were replaced with uniforms. One Aboriginal woman recalls that:

> "When I got into school, everything changed for me all at once. My parents didn't have a say any more in the way my life went. When I came in off the land, the people with any type of authority were Qallunaat [non-Aboriginal].... They treated us like we belonged to them, not to our parents.... They taught us a new culture, a different culture from our own, they taught us that we have to live like the white people. We had to become like the white people," (Emberley, 2001:61)

Many children were physically and sexually assaulted. Thus, it is not surprising that the residential schools have had lasting negative consequences both for the individuals who attended them and their families. "Generations of depression, alcoholism, suicide, and family breakdown are the legacy of such traumatic experiences and are described as the 'residential school syndrome' by native people themselves" (Das Gupta, 2000:152).

Some academics have argued that British colonial relations with Aboriginal peoples were for the most part based on a patriarchal domestic model that also ultimately "structured the proper meaning of 'the family' for aboriginal cultures" (Emberley, 2001:60). In this context, the First Nations people were treated as unruly children and the government as the benevolent father. Beginning in 1870, a series of *Indian Acts* reinforced the concept of the British nuclear family model by forcing First Nations people to change their traditional family structures. These changes ranged from "marriage practices, adoptions, and residence rights to an inability to bequeath property according to established custom" (Fiske and Johnny, 2003:183). As Das Gupta (2000:150) notes, "the European colonialists, with the help of the Church, adopted a strategy of biological and cultural assimilation of Native Peoples.... Through conversion to European religions, sacred rituals and practices to ensure socialization of succeeding generations [were] no longer employed."

Early Black-Canadian Families

First Nations families were not the only ones in Canada whose family structures and social institutions were affected by the racism and patriarchal imperatives of the French and British. Even before the conquest of Quebec, a small but important black community lived in what is now Canada. Slavery was legal in the French Empire. Consequently, a small number of black Africans were brought to New France in the century after 1650 to serve as house servants for the French religious, military, and commercial elite; thus, about 1,000 black slaves were in New France during its existence (Fabbi, 2003). Taken from their homes and families in west Africa, a rudimentary family life in New France was possible for them; but because their owners determined almost all facets of their lives, the formation of permanent family structures was delayed.

After 1763, colonial British Canada also contained a small black population. Before the 20th century, there were three general waves of black immigrants in British North America. The first were slaves brought to work in what is now the U.S. after the mid-1650s (Simms, 1993). The numbers in Upper Canada and the Maritime colonies were quite small before the American Revolution. Slavery was curtailed in Quebec in 1793 with legislation making it illegal to bring people into the colony to become slaves. Still, slavery existed in what is now Canada until the British Parliament passed the *Slavery Abolition Act* in 1833. The second wave was a mixture of free blacks and slaves who came north after the American Revolution. The free blacks were Loyalists and the slaves belonged to white Loyalists who fled the new United States (Grant, 1973). The third wave consisted of American slaves who escaped their bondage before the 1860s and made their way to Canada (Sharon, 1995).

As occurred in New France, the institution of slavery severely weakened the concept of family among slaves in Upper Canada and the Maritimes as, legally, blacks had no marital or parental rights (Ingersoll, 1995; Nicholson, 1994). Loyalist blacks and former American slaves who reached Canada did not have an easy existence because they were free: Racial discrimination and social prejudice by the dominant white society was a fact of life (Winks, 2000). In one example, Loyalist blacks in Nova Scotia received few land grants after coming north, and the land provided them was marginal at best (Calliste, 2003). In another example, in Ontario, although official policy after 1833 was to treat blacks as free citizens equal with whites before the law, they encountered general hostility from white officialdom (Martin, 1974). Although there was a strong abolitionist movement in Ontario before the American Civil War (Stouffer, 1992), British officials made some adaptations to slavery through efforts to send both fleeing American slaves and some resident Upper Canadian blacks and their families to the West Indies.

Given their lesser economic status, black husbands and wives commonly worked outside the home, men labouring and women in domestic service. Consequently, there was a reliance on the extended family to help in childrearing through a tradition of taking relatives and others who were destitute into family homes; they could help with domestic chores or could earn money. There was a reverence for elder blacks who could also join households to help themselves and the family with which they lived (Dunaway, 2003). In this context, older blacks would have adoptive titles like "Aunt" or

"Uncle" to show that they were part of these extended families. Importantly, given that black men could not always find employment, "many [black] families practised gender interdependence and reversals of traditional gender roles in the division of labour" (Calliste, 2003:203). What this meant in practical terms was that, when black wives and mothers worked in domestic service and other areas at the lower end of the economy, their unemployed husbands stayed home, minded the children, and did what they could to keep their families together.

These developments in family life were an amalgamation of their west African traditions, which survived slavery, and newer ones derived from living in British Canada. All of these tendencies in family life produced a more communal way of life for black Canadians in which bonds of kinship became extremely important for their physical and spiritual survival as an identifiable minority. Thus, black Loyalist families differed from the nuclear ones of white Loyalists: Black Loyalist households could include neighbours, orphans, members of the local church, the widows or widowers of friends, and so on (Walker, 1976). Indeed, in some places, both in Upper Canada and, later, when western Canada was being settled, entire black communities were founded. Amber Valley in Alberta was such a community, established in 1911 by 90 black American families from Oklahoma. The problem was that the white majority was prejudiced against black rural settlers, so that not every effort by blacks to build family life in Canada was successful (Shephard, 1997). In other places such as the Africville area of Halifax (Clairmont and Magill, 1999), black urban communities evolved as a result of both segregation and black leaders' efforts to organize themselves for mutual assistance, property ownership, and providing education. Black women also played a significant role in these efforts to reinforce their communities by strengthening the family (Fingard, 1992; Yee, 1994). Again, although these efforts at organization were not always successful (Pease and Pease, 1962), a distinctive family structure within a distinctive black culture emerged in Canada by the early part of the 20th century.

Industrialization and Settling the West

As the above discussion indicates, the 19th century was a period of industrialization for parts of Canada, chiefly Upper Canada and the Maritimes. In this context, urbanization was also a new element of social and economic development; it affected the family and related social constructs. By the 1840s, the concept of "childhood" began to emerge; urban social reformers became concerned about childhood employment in dangerous and unsanitary conditions. Reflecting ideas that children were actually innocent beings who needed to be protected and educated, laws were passed to restrict child labour and allow for better educational opportunities. As this was also the highpoint of the Victorian period, middle class notions of women as being naturally endowed to provide the moral education of their children and to nurture their sensitivities became widespread (Hoffman and Taylor, 1996:41–91). In the realm of men, no matter their class, the demands of employment took them daily and increasingly away from the home. There was a heavy emphasis on masculinity (Moss, 1998). The result was that the division of labour within a marriage became even more differentiated, especially within the middle classes. Husbands provided the necessities of

In poor households, children contributed to their families' economic survival well into the 20th century. Thus, the social reconstruction of children's roles did not reach all social classes simultaneously.

life; wives looked after the household and mothered children. Bolstered by the law, Christian tradition, and the rising strength of middle class values, nuclear families in industrializing Canada were being transformed.

The Beginning of Multiculturalism

By the middle of the 19th century, what is now western Canada was a large area inhabited by a very few white people, principally British and French, engaged in fur and other trading with the First Nations. After Confederation in 1867, the new federal government decided that the western regions of Canada should be populated as quickly as possible, and with the U.S. expanding westwards, federal leaders wanted to ensure Canada's sovereignty over its territory. This policy had several strands. A transcontinental railway was begun in the 1870s to link the west with the eastern regions of Canada. A police force, the North West Mounted Police, was created and dispatched to the Prairies to ensure law and order. Finally, when possible, the western territories were to be given provincial status to make the Confederation stronger. In this process, there was a conscious effort by Ottawa to encourage immigration from Europe to populate the west, the idea being that a growing population could strengthen Canadian sovereignty and the economic life of the country.

Thus, unlike the Maritimes and Upper Canada, which were populated almost exclusively by British immigrants, and Quebec, which contained a relatively homogeneous francophone and Catholic population, the Canadian west came to be settled by large groups of non-British and non-French peoples. Of course, the majority of the non-First Nations population in the west was from the British Isles, and the anglophone elite controlled business and government. But increasing numbers of new Canadians arrived from northern, central, eastern, and southern Europe along with a significant Chinese population that was brought to Canada from China to work on the railway. Thus, as the railway pushed westwards linking the emerging western provinces with central and maritime Canada, groups of Swedes, Germans, Ukrainians, Italians, and other nationalities settled in the west (Farnam, 1998; Loewen, 1994; Stambrook and Hryniuk, 2000). Mainly Christian Europeans, they imported the social structures of their homelands, especially nuclear family structures.

Initially, these new Canadians created an agrarian society built around ranching and grain growing. Nuclear families in the west worked together as a unit to ensure both their livelihood and the success of their farms and ranches. Based on British law, and bolstered by patriarchal traditions brought from their homelands, men were property owners and responsible for their wives and children (Darlington, 1997; Cavanaugh, 1993). Men worked outside the home tending land and herds; women were responsible for the home and for all domestic chores like cooking and childrearing (Gagnon, 1994; McManus, 1999). In the early period of settlement, access to education was limited. Hence, male children helped their fathers as soon as they were physically able; female children acquired domestic skills from their mothers. Once education was available, children had a few years of learning before working on the family farm or ranch. However, nuclear families did not live in isolation from one another. Community development evolved rather quickly, as groups of immigrants with the same ethnic background or even from the same region of Europe settled close together (Bennett and Seena, 1995; Voisey, 1987).

Settled areas populated by families with the same traditions and backgrounds, plus marriage among families in these new communities, reinforced traditional family structures. Within a generation of the railway being built, urbanization and industrialization emerged in a few places: in larger cities like Winnipeg and Edmonton, and in a host of smaller towns like Brandon, Prince Albert, and Red Deer. As a result, social stratification in urban areas began to develop with the emergence of classes of professionals, civil servants, merchants, and workers of various types. As occurred in Upper Canada, western urban families began to experience different levels of education, labour, and social status. As time passed, groups of immigrants from the same place in Europe—for instance, Italian immigrants in Calgary and Polish ones in Edmonton—began to live in particular parts of these urban areas (Aliaga, 1994; Lukasiewicz, 2002). Some of this movement to cities and towns occurred through the movement of younger Canadian-born people from the countryside to seek new professions and industrial work; the rest came about by immigrants from Europe moving directly to urban areas. As had occurred in rural areas, British law and the particular backgrounds of these ethnic peoples saw the strengthening of traditional family structures within developing communities (Bright, 1992). Little doubt exists that British political and social traditions, including that of the family, dominated western Canadian society during the period of settlement and after because British Canadians formed a majority of the population (White, 1994). However, as discussed in Chapter 4, because of large-scale immigration, western Canadian society (and that of Canada as a whole) began transforming into a multicultural society with a variety of ethnic traditions and family structures.

Chinese Families in the West

Among east Asian immigrants who in the late 19th century settled chiefly in British Columbia and the Prairies were Chinese men and women referred to as "sojourners" rather than immigrants because they did not intend to settle permanently in this country. Their purpose was to supplement their incomes in their home countries where their families still lived; married sojourners were prohibited from bringing their spouse and children to Canada. Male sojourners worked in railway- and road-building, in the lumber industry, and in mining, to name a few of their generally dangerous, unskilled, and low-paying jobs. Asian female sojourners were recruited to work as domestics in this country (Das Gupta, 2000:158). However, the Chinese faced discrimination from the moment they arrived. In 1885, to limit Chinese immigration, the federal government imposed a head tax of $50 on each Chinese entering the country. The head tax was raised to $100 in 1902 and to $500 in 1903. In 1923, the federal government passed the *Chinese Immigration Act,* also known as the "Chinese Exclusion Act"; until its annulment in 1947, it barred new Chinese immigrants from entering Canada. Thus, the wives and children of many Chinese-Canadian men were prevented from coming to Canada. Furthermore, all Chinese in Canada, including those born here, had to register with the authorities. These and other racist policies by the federal government were echoed in provincial statutes that remained in place until after the Second World War.

By 1947, the injustice of these policies by the white majority began to be called into question, especially since Chinese Canadians had served in the Canadian armed forces during the Second World War. By the early 1950s, East-Asian Canadians were given the right to vote in federal and provincial elections; the Exclusion Act was rescinded; and East-Asian Canadians were allowed to work in professional fields heretofore closed to them, such as accountancy, the law, and pharmacy. With the passage of the 1967 *Immigration Act*, the Chinese received the same rights as other groups of immigrants and began to reunify their families in Canada.

Mormon Immigration to the West

Besides seeing the settlement of different ethnic groups, the west also saw the arrival of religious groups as pioneers. One of the most important groups was the Mormons, who played a pivotal role in settling western Canada. The prophet Joseph Smith founded the Mormon Church, known officially as the Church of Jesus Christ of Latter Day Saints, in 1830 in upstate New York. Smith believed that polygamy (having more than one wife at the same time) would increase the solidarity of his group; contrary to Christian belief that marriage lasted until the death of one spouse, he argued that Mormon plural marriages were for eternity. However, New York officials and society at large perceived the polygamous practices of the group as a threat to the Victorian nuclear family ideal. Smith was ultimately murdered by a mob, and Brigham Young, who became the next leader, moved the group to Salt Lake City, Utah.

Fleeing from anti-polygamy laws and anti-Mormon persecution in the mid-1880s, many Mormons left Utah and sought refuge in Canada. The largest number settled in southern Alberta. Canadians had mixed feelings about the new Mormon settlements (Palmer, 1990). As Mormons were said to be industrious, zealous, and well behaved, federal officials who wanted immigrants to settle the land welcomed them. However, having been exposed to American anti-Mormon propaganda, other Canadians, especially Canadian newspapers, were not as receptive. Mormons were "cast in the roles of defiers of the state because of their resistance to American law... and [were] adamantly opposed...because of their belief in polygamy" (Palmer, 1990:112). Mormon leaders asked permission from Canadian officials to bring their plural families into Canada but they were denied; Canadian laws against polygamy were strengthened to criminalize such unions (Hardy, 1990). In 1890, the Mormon Church officially forbade polygamous marriages, and by the beginning of the First World War, the anti-Mormon movement had dissipated in western Canada.

Although polygamy has been illegal in North America for some time (anti-polygamy laws were strengthened in the U.S. in 1882 and in Canada in 1890), there still exist polygamous Mormon fundamentalist families who live underground in both countries (Kilbride, 1994). Despite their self-identification as Mormons, the Church of Jesus Christ of Latter Day Saints does not recognize these families; indeed, the Church has not permitted polygamy since 1904.

CROSS-CULTURAL PERSPECTIVES OF FAMILIES

Family structures and functions have differed across societies and, within a specific society, over time. Cross-culturally, there is a wide variety of family forms and quite an extensive range in the functions they perform. As well, different economic, religious, social, and political systems can exert influence on family dynamics. Thus, understanding family diversity in the past and across cultures is key to the realization that the nuclear family is but one amongst a multitude of family arrangements.

The Marriage Law and the One-Child Policy in China

For almost 2,000 years, China's family life was shaped by tradition and Confucian ideology. Marriage was a contract between two families, and marriage partners were chosen based on family needs and values rather than on attraction and love (Engels, 1995). It was common practice for parents to negotiate a marriage contract when their children were young; some children were even betrothed before they were born. The groom's family was expected to pay a **bride price** and the bride's family was to provide a **dowry**. The traditional Chinese family was patrilineal, **patrilocal**, and **patriarchal**, and overwhelmingly favoured sons. Prior to the founding of the People's Republic of China in 1949, women were barred from participating in public life, had few employment opportunities, and 90 percent were mostly illiterate (State Council Information Office, 2000). Few resources were spent on daughters. Custom dictated that a son reside with his parents after he married but that daughters depart to live in their husband's home. Not only could adult daughters not live with their parents, they were not allowed to provide economic support or care for their parents in old age (Fong, 2002). The marriage of sons was considered more important than the marriage of daughters, and it was not uncommon for poor families to sell daughters into servitude to pay the bride price for a son's wedding. Once a marriage contract was negotiated, daughters were unable to get out of the marriage, even upon her fiancé's death: "If the betrothed man died before the wedding, the bride had to go through a marriage ceremony with a wooden figure, a wooden or stone tablet, or a rooster; and then she was expected to remain single for the rest of her life" (Engels, 1995:60). It was also customary for upper-class men to have concubines, whom they purchased and then supported financially.

Families underwent tremendous changes in 1949 as the Communist government attempted to create a classless society. A year after the People's Republic of China was created, the government passed a marriage law meant to destroy traditional family structures, such as the feudal marriage system, and replace them with a democratic marriage system. Change did occur: Arranged and coerced marriages were abolished, monogamy became the norm, and the rights and interests of women and children were protected through law (State Council Information Office, 2000). However, China was still plagued by its considerable and rapidly growing population. Even though contraceptive technology was officially approved in 1954, fertility rates remained high. In 1970, each woman was having an average of six children, a rate well above that of western countries. But a large population was thought to be an impediment to progress. Therefore, to promote modernization, the Chinese government needed a strategy to reduce the number of people who would be competing for resources (Fong, 2002). The solution came in the form of a one-child-per-family policy in 1979 and a new marriage law in 1980.

This new law imposed many changes on marriage and family relations. The customs of a bride price and dowry were forbidden. Marriage was no longer a contract between families, but rather between individuals. Article 4 of the law stipulated that: "Marriage must be based upon the complete willingness of the new parties" (Engels, 1995:60). The new law also prohibited men from having a concubine or more than one wife. Child betrothal was abolished; men had to be 22 years old and women 20 years before a marriage could be contracted. Moreover, the law discouraged the traditional patrilocal residence custom: "The woman may become a member of the man's family, or the man may become a member of the woman's family, according to the agreed wishes of the two parties" (Engels, 1995:65). This meant that daughters, at least in the eyes of the law, were just as important as sons in providing care for aging parents. The goal was that China's population not exceed 1.2 billion people by the year 2000.

The implementation of the one-child policy has varied by region and over time. For example, great resistance to the policy emerged in the countryside because rural parents depended on their children, especially sons, to work on farms and support them in old age; thus they continued to have more than one child. In the 1980s, the government revised the policy so rural couples could have two children but urban couples were still restricted to one child. These various policies were enforced at the provincial level by rewarding individuals who complied and punishing those who did not. Pregnant women having an approved birth received free obstetric care and could obtain better housing, extra food rations, and cash subsidies as an incentive to have no further children (Short and Fengying, 1998). However, couples who had an unapproved birth not only paid for their prenatal care, they also faced substantial fines, usually ranging from 20 to 50 percent of a family's annual income. In some regions, fines have exceeded the average annual income (Short and Fengying, 1998).

Much has been written about the negative impact of these policies. For example, Doherty et al. (2001) found that women who had an unapproved birth, and thus were not eligible for free obstetric care, were more at risk of prenatal complications and even maternal death than women who had approved births. The medical costs of unapproved births were not the only deterrent to seeking prenatal care; attending a clinic resulted in the registration of the unapproved birth and ultimately a substantial fine. Arguing that the policies reinforce the traditional preference for sons over daughters, critics point to the unusually low number of female babies being born in comparison to male babies (Logan et al., 1998). Demographers have speculated that this gender imbalance, currently 1.17 males for every female born, may be the result of female infanticide, parents' refusal to register daughters, parents' abandonment or lethal neglect of daughters, sex selection through selective abortion, or some combination of these factors (Li and Peng, 2000; Coale and Banister, 1994). Moreover, women have been deprived of being able to choose their family size and have been subjected to a number of intrusive enforcement tactics, including coercive sterilization programs and mandatory IUD insertions and abortions (Short and Fengying, 1998).

Despite these negative outcomes, the policies have also generated some positive results. Two years after implementing the one-child policy, fertility decreased dramatically to two children per woman. This figure has more or less remained stable for over two decades; today, a Chinese woman has on average 1.9 children. By the year 2000, China had more or less reached its population target with a population count of 1.27 billion people (Fong, 2002). Moreover, it has enabled women more choices by freeing them from heavy childbearing and childrearing responsibilities. This is particularly true for women living in urban areas where opportunities for educational and career advancement exist.

China provides an important case study because it shows how demographic policy can greatly influence family structure. Chinese families today, especially in urban areas, tend toward gender equality and have become **neolocal, bilateral,** and **bilineal.** It would seem that earlier predictions for the Chinese family are becoming realized, at least in eastern cities: Son preference is being substituted for an equal preference for sons or daughters, and an emphasis on the needs of the adult children is replacing filial piety as the basis for intergenerational relations (in Logan et al., 1998). As Fong (2002:1102) has observed: "Parents whose love, hope, and need for old-age support are all pinned on just one child tend to do whatever is necessary to make that child happy and successful, regardless of the child's gender." Studies are also showing that, at least in cities such as Beijing and Shanghai, daughters help their elderly parents. Nevertheless, the preference for male children has not entirely disappeared, especially in rural areas, and numerous orphanages exist to shelter abandoned baby girls. As we see in Chapter 9, thousands of western couples and single women adopt these infant girls.

Arranged Marriages in India

Arranged marriages predominate in India. Even though "love-marriages" have been legal since 1872, they continue to be rare and are viewed as lustful (*vasna*), illegitimate, and unholy. "Marriage then, is not concerned with whether or not the couple are 'in love'; in fact, in the case of Hindus (who comprise 80 percent of the population in

India), it is geared around the assumption that ideally the girl and the boy are strangers to each other and that it is their obligation to their parents that makes them sometimes reluctant, though consenting, parties to the marriage" (Mody, 2002). In the case of Muslims in India, for whom marriage can take place between first cousins, the bride and the groom pretend that they are strangers to one another on the day of their marriage. "Hence the construction of the relationship between love and marriage is that love should never precede marriage; but equally, marriage does not preclude the possibility of a loving and intimate relationship" (Mody, 2002:225).

The arrangement of a marriage is taken very seriously by Indian parents. There are strict criteria used to determine an appropriate partner for one's child. For example, the future bride and groom need to be matched in terms of caste position, age, socio-economic status, education, and of course, religion (Sastry, 1999). Arranged marriages within the community (endo-recruiting) are thought to strengthen that community. Emphasis is placed on social compatibility and duty to parents and ancestors rather than on individual compatibility and personal desires for love and intimacy (Sastry, 1999:136). On the other hand, love-marriages threaten community solidarity because, in choosing their own partners, individuals are in fact showing disrespect for their parents and for the caste system, which forbids marriage outside of one's caste (Dumont, 1998). Indeed, both Muslims and Hindus view the obligation to marry within the group as the most essential characteristic of the caste system (Mody, 2002).

As we see in Chapter 8, romantic love and individual choice characterize the decision to marry or to live common-law in western societies, but collective solidarity is the important criterion for marriage in India. The societies also differ in that emotional fulfillment, support, and well-being are largely derived from the husband-wife relationship in the west. In India, the parent-child relationship is considered the most intimate and fulfilling familial relationship, with support deriving from the entire extended kin network (Dion and Dion, 1993). Although marriage may not play the role that it does in western societies, it would be wrong to assume that the relationship between husbands and wives in India is weak or deficient: The few studies that exist on this topic have revealed little linkage between a lack of emotional or sexual intimacy and the quality of marriage in India (Pothen, 1989; Yelsma and Athappilly, 1988). However, when Indian families immigrate to Canada, they are exposed to a social construction of marriage that emphasizes romantic love and companionship. Two results can follow. First, many established couples experience marital strain, at least as perceived by their children. As one woman explains in her autobiography:

> *"I would rate my parents' marital satisfaction differently, with my father's being high because he has what he needs which is a traditional Indian marriage while my mother is so lonely for just a bit of attention from him...and also because she sees that her cousins who came here before get along better and have a good relationship. It's very hard on my mother and it will be terrible when my father's mother eventually moves here from India to be with us."*

Second, although most Indian women university students still undergo some form of arranged marriage—and some even expect to be sent to the U.S. for this purpose—most will have a greater say than would have been the case "back home." One married woman student was introduced to her future husband,

"...But my mother made it clear to me, him, and my father that I had to like him. So he visited me at my home several times and I really liked him; he was so nice and brought me and my mother little gifts. I asked him all kinds of questions. Then, after several weeks, we went out with my brother who left us alone most of the time, we held hands at the movies and he even asked my brother if he could kiss me and my brother said 'go for it' and here I am, married, and pretty happy.... I think that when arranged marriages work out, they're great because your parents do all the preliminary work for you. It's a great tradition to this extent."

In a comparative study, Sastry (1999) examined the impact of family relationships on psychological well-being and home satisfaction in India and the U.S. He found that in India, socioeconomic factors such as income, education, and full-time work were more important than marriage in determining how satisfied people were with their home life (home satisfaction). Conversely, being married (or living together as married) was the strongest predictor of satisfaction with home life in the U.S. Accordingly, marriage significantly reduced psychological distress for men and women in the U.S., but it did not have a similar impact for men and women in India. Rather, high income or high education was more likely to reduce distress and increase satisfaction for Indian men and women. According to Sastry, this finding indicates that "although marriage is important to Indian men and women in terms of meeting their commitment to tradition and fulfilling cultural obligations, marriage is secondary to other more practical concerns such as earnings and status attainment capabilities" (p. 149). Furthermore, Sastry discovered a positive association between the presence of children and home satisfaction for Indian women but a negative association for American women. This latter finding indicates "support for the contention that due to more rigidly defined social roles in India, women will receive more satisfaction from fulfilling traditionally ascribed duties such as bearing children and caring for them" (p. 145).

Motherhood is of utmost importance in India because it can be a key source of power for Indian women. According to Kohler Riessman (2000:112), who spent time doing fieldwork in south India, motherhood is a sacred duty—a value preserved in religious laws for Hindus, Muslims, Sikhs, and Christians alike. She argues that having children offers several benefits: "A child solidifies a wife's often fragile bond with a spouse in an arranged marriage and improves her status in the joint family and larger community; and with a child, she can eventually become a mother-in-law—a position of considerable power and influence in Indian families." Moreover, older women rely on their children, particularly on their sons, to support them in old age. On the other hand, childless women are disadvantaged. They are publicly ridiculed even if their childlessness is due to their husband's inability to impregnate them. And since India has few governmental social welfare programs, they often face extreme poverty in old age. Thus, there is strong societal pressure on women to have children.

Women's roles are very much constrained in India. Parents have tremendous authority over their daughters, especially their sexuality. Women are for the most part subservient to their fathers and then to their husbands; their behaviour throughout life is strictly regulated. However, gender roles and family structures in India, as elsewhere, are not static. Although arranged marriages are still the dominant form, couples are having more say about their marriages, including when to marry and how many children they want. Nuclear families are also increasing in number as more young people are drawn to the cities. Women's roles are opening up in many parts of India as opportunities for education and careers are made available to them, especially in information technology and call centres. This alone can have a tremendous impact on women's status. Future families in India will likely continue to be a mixture of continuity and change as women find ways to renegotiate their roles, both inside and outside family life.

Family Solidarity in Cuba

Cuba provides a very good example of how macrosociological change can have an enormous impact on family life. Since the 1959 revolution, Cuba has experienced dramatic changes to its political and economic systems, which had been offshoots of Spanish and U.S. colonialism. Prior to 1959, the majority of Cuban families were impoverished, illiterate, and malnourished. The average education of the working majority was at a Grade 3 level, and in 1953, life expectancy was only 58.8 years (Catasús Cervera, 1996), reflecting the abhorrent living conditions in which the majority of Cubans lived. Infant and maternal mortality rates were high. A rigid division of labour demarcated Cuban society: Women's place was in the home (*casa*) and men's was in the street (*calle*). In terms of employment, only nine percent of women were economically active in 1953, compared to 57 percent for males (International Labour Office, 1970). Of those women who were employed, approximately 70 percent worked as unsalaried domestic servants (Lutjens, 1994). Excluded from official labour statistics were more than 150,000 women who worked as prostitutes (del Olmo, 1979).

The 1959 revolution initiated rapid and immense political, social, economic, and cultural change. Under the leadership of Fidel Castro, Cuba adopted a communist regime. Based on the principles of socialism, Castro wanted to create a new society with equality for all Cubans, regardless of class, race, or gender. In 1960, the Federation of Cuban Women (FMC) was founded to ensure women's full participation in all developments of the revolution. Free education, a national literacy campaign in 1961, and an increase in the number of women admitted to post-secondary schools resulted in a sharp rise in education levels for both sexes. Unprecedented in Latin America, Cuba's illiteracy rate plummeted to only 1.9 percent by 1983, from 23.6 percent in 1951 (González, 1999). In 1975, a Family Code legalized gender equality in household and childcare responsibilities. Free daycare was also established to assist working mothers. Free universal health care markedly lowered infant mortality rates (still one of the lowest rates in the world) and significantly increased life expectancy. Indeed, Cuba boasted demographic indicators similar to or superior to those of developed countries (Krull, 2002a,b). By 1979, prostitution had all but been eliminated through noncoercive reforms and legislation. Affirmative action saw women move into professional, political, and technical occupations and receive equal pay for equal work. Although not necessarily resulting in equality, particularly on the domestic front, these changes brought significant improvements for most women.

The early 1990s produced sudden and debilitating changes for Cuban families. The collapse of the U.S.S.R. (Cuba's main trading partner) and a strengthened U.S. blockade generated an exceptionally serious economic crisis, known as the "Special Period." Another shattering blow came in 1996, when the U.S. strengthened the embargo and isolated Cuba from much of the world. Consequently, Cuba's state services were drastically reduced and the standard of living plummeted (Dilla, 1999). Even though the monthly quantity of food and commodities provided by the state rationing system has improved recently, the quantity does not last a month as it did prior to the Special Period. Essential items such as soap, meat, cooking oil, and painkillers, once provided by the state, can now only be bought with U.S. dollars, to which most Cubans do not have access since their salaries are paid in pesos (Behar, 1998). Transportation difficulties and blackouts are a regular experience, and the sex trade is again flourishing as women search for ways to obtain dollars. In addition, medicines and medical supplies are scarce, significantly affecting the quality of health care (Argüelles, 1999).

With few resources to build or repair houses, one-half of Havana's dwellings are considered substandard or beyond repair (Argüelles, 1999). There is also a severe housing shortage, especially in Havana, which has resulted in almost one-half of Cuban households comprising three or more generations. Today's multigenerational family households have more to do with economic necessity than with cultural tradition. It is nearly impossible for a newly married couple to leave their parents' home and live on their own. During an ongoing study by Krull and Kobayashi, a 49-year-old Cuban woman explains that

> *"...Before the Special Period, the government was constructing houses at a very good pace. But after the Special Period, it was impossible to continue. Now there are many generations in the houses. It is good because there are more people to help survive in these difficult times, but it is a problem because the different generations think differently. For example, my son asked me if his girlfriend could live here with us. I said yes because she lives very far and it is very difficult for her to go home by the bus. My mother does not like this because they are not married."*

Multigenerational households are not the only family form that has resulted from the housing shortage. Because so many individuals are living in dilapidated or extremely crowded housing, there is a high demand on the state to assign people new housing. This means that many divorced couples, who do not have family members they can move in with, are forced to continue living together. Divorced couples have to find ways to cooperate. A 57-year-old economist talks about divorce:

> *"Divorce is a problem here because of the housing shortage. It is difficult to move to a different house when you divorce. I live with my ex-husband. He is not a good man but we divided the house so that he has his room, I have mine. We share the kitchen but we use it at different times. It is not easy. I have a boyfriend but how do I bring him to my house when my ex-husband lives there?"*

Women have been particularly affected by the Special Period. Indeed, it is primarily women who stand in long lines for food, who take care of sick family members, and who decide how to make do with very little food or money. Because of a shortage of daycare places, severe transportation difficulties, and the expectation that women are responsible for housework, which has become more laborious with much fewer resources, some women have left paid employment to become domestics in their own households (López Vigil, 1999). In one community of Havana, employed women spend an average of eight and a half hours at their place of employment and seven hours on domestic work each day (Krull et al., 2003). The role of the mother is paramount in the Cuban family, with Mother's Day considered the most important holiday of the year. In fact, all women are congratulated on Mother's Day, not just mothers, because it is a day to recognize the sacrifices that all women have made for Cuban children. These sacrifices have been multiplied during the Special Period. A 52-year-old teacher explains:

> *"During the Special Period there has been little food, yet mothers have to figure out how to make very little last the month and to make sure that their family has good nutrition.... Grandmothers are also very important for us right now. I have many female friends who could not do what they do if their mothers didn't take care of their children, help with the cooking and the domestic work, and stand in the lines for the rations."*

It is customary for adult children to look after their aging parents, and a person is viewed badly if he or she has a parent who resides in an institution or retirement centre. To facilitate the lives of working women who are also looking after an aging parent, the government created *Circulo de Abuelos*, which is similar to daycare centres in North America but which looks after older people rather than children during the day. This allows a woman to drop off her parent in the morning on her way to work and to pick the parent up on the way home from work. The centre organizes a number of activities every day and provides meals and exercise classes. Older individuals enjoy having the opportunity to interact with people of their own generation.

The Special Period has had an enormous impact on family organization in Cuba: high divorce rates; the necessity of multigenerational households; divorced couples cohabiting; adult children dependent on their mothers for assistance in their households; women's roles being redefined within the domestic realm, even if they are employed; and a renewal of the sex trade, mainly by women. Rodríguez Calderón (1993:354) points out that "the Special Period has made the daily life of Cuban women political—in the spirit that informs it and in its influence on the family and on society."

CONCLUSIONS: PERSPECTIVES ON FAMILY CHANGE AND DIVERSITY

Families are diverse social and economic institutions. Family diversity exists across time, cultures, and within societies. Regardless of the society, change to the family is inevitable. Sometimes change occurs very quickly, as it did in Cuba and China, and at other times families evolve slowly, as in the case of Canada and India. The nature of economic development has a major impact on the structure of families, their size, and their nature. No doubt exists that prior to contact with the British and French, First Nations families were complex social and economic institutions that allowed for survival of people in a difficult and dangerous land. Contact with the colonizers destroyed the structure of those families. For their part, the British and French brought their own forms of family structure, transplanted them to Canada, and over time, as modernization and industrialization brought economic and social transformations, colonial Canadian families also changed. The settlement of the west diversified families as other peoples from Europe and east Asia populated this vast region of the country. But even these families evolved as a result of the urbanization and industrialization that came to western Canada by the early decades of the 20th century.

However, what was true for Canada historically is also true for the institution of the family in other places and cultures. Change has been a constant factor when looking at cross-cultural family experiences. Different economic, religious, social, and political systems affect marriage and families. Ancient family traditions existed long ago in China and India. Yet when the People's Republic of China was formed in 1949, revolutionary policies were introduced to provide gender equality and eliminate feudal practices concerning marriage and family. Although not all problems in China have been resolved—the attitude toward female children is a case in point—there has been noticeable change in that country because of government decisions. And what is true for China is also the case for Latin American countries such as Cuba, where macro reforms at the societal and economic levels are producing new attitudes toward marriage and family. In India, on the other hand, which has been modernizing since its independence in 1947, the traditions of the past have not receded to the same degree. Change to the economy has not necessarily translated into large-scale social change concerning marriage and family. All these cases show that no family form necessarily predominates, and what exists is a social institution that can change and adapt depending on time, place, and socioeconomic and cultural circumstance.

Summary

1. It is important to acknowledge and appreciate family diversity across time, place, and culture. Historical and comparative perspectives allow for such understandings and highlight the fact that the nuclear family is but one amongst a multitude of family arrangements.

2. Whether patrilineal or matrilineal, Aboriginal families have historically been distinguished by communal living and the practice of sharing responsibilities and resources. The Plains Cree and Iroquois families are described.

3. New France was a society of transplanted Europeans structured around the political, social, and religious institutions of monarchical France. In the context of economic and social change, nuclear families had increasing importance in the development of both colonial New France and in British-controlled Quebec after 1763. For religious, cultural, and social reasons, marriage was the norm and the number of sons determined the land concessions a tenant family could work. Large families thus predominated.

4. Colonial British Canada—Upper Canada and the Maritimes—evolved from a preindustrial agricultural economy to a capitalist industrial one. Legal and religious traditions imported from the British Isles reinforced a traditional nuclear family structure that made patriarchy dominant.

5. Both French and British colonial governments—and the government of Canada after 1867—worked to assimilate the First Nations into the dominant European Christian traditional and patriarchal society. Assimilation resulted in a loss of language and culture, and a weakening of Aboriginal family structures built around communal living and shared responsibilities.

6. Black Canadians developed a communal and extended family life by the early 20th century—an amalgamation of their west African traditions that survived slavery, and newer ones that derived from living in British Canada.

7. The 19th century witnessed industrialization and modernization for parts of Canada, chiefly Upper Canada and the Maritimes. Along with urbanization, these economic changes affected the family, especially in terms of the social constructs of childhood, the role of mothers, and the repositioning of men's employment away from the home. Divisions of labour within marriage became more pronounced, especially in the middle classes.

8. The development of western Canada brought new European immigrants: Germans, Ukrainians, Italians, and others. The vast majority of new Canadians brought with them family structures derived from their various homelands. With the addition of family traditions brought by Chinese immigrants, family life in western Canada became as diversified as its peoples.

9. Not all family structures were determined by ethnic and racial traditions. In one important case, immigrants from the U.S. who adhered to the Mormon faith, including some who continued polygamous marriage, settled largely in western Canada.

10. In terms of cross-cultural perspectives on family, the People's Republic of China provides an important case study showing how demographic policy can influence family structure. China has introduced tough laws to ensure one-child families. There have been both negative and positive results, including consequences of traditional values favouring sons over daughters, and women's rights within the family being strengthened by the abolition of dowries. Marriage is now a contract between individuals rather than families.

11. In other modernizing states, older family traditions remain in place. For instance, in India, arranged marriages continue to be the norm for both Hindus and Muslims. Motherhood is a sacred duty. However, in modernizing India, despite the continued dominance of arranged marriages, many couples are having more say in when to marry and how many children they want. Nuclear families are increasing in number.

12. A good example of how macro change can have an enormous impact on family life is seen in modern Cuba after 1959. In the context of the extended family, the traditional Cuban family changed as women gained civil and economic rights. But the collapse of the Soviet Union in 1991 ushered in the Special Period, which resulted in high divorce rates, multigenerational households, divorced couples cohabiting, adult children dependent on their mothers for assistance in their households, and women's roles being redefined within the domestic realm, even if employed.

Key Concepts and Themes

Analytical Questions

1. Compare family structures amongst the early Iroquois and Plains Cree people: What accounts for the differences found between these two groups? Why were Aboriginal women important to the development of New France?
2. What can explain the development of communal and extended family life among black Canadians by the early 20th century?
3. How is childhood affected by and linked to the concept of industrialization and modernization?
4. How did the advent of a multicultural society in western Canada after 1867 affect family life in that region?
5. In the People's Republic of China, how has the stress between traditional Confucian ideas of family and new ideas centred on the one-child family played itself out?
6. With Cuba as a case study, what effects on family life and well-being can macro economic changes bring to the structure of households in a period of economic constraint?

Suggested Readings

Clio Collective (M. Dumont et al.) 1987. *Quebec Women: A history.* Toronto: Women's Press. This book offers an in-depth history of the women who have lived in Quebec during the past four centuries. Its six sections each reflect an important era in Quebec's history.

Harrison, T., and Friesen, J. 2004. *Canadian society in the twenty-first century: A historical sociological approach.* Toronto: Pearson/Prentice Hall. Through a variety of perspectives, this book explores three major relationships responsible for shaping Canada's development.

Mandell, N., and Duffy, A. (Eds.) 2000. *Canadian families: Diversity, conflict and change.* Scarborough: Nelson Thomson. This collection of chapters challenges traditional approaches to family sociology while highlighting a number of family-related concerns that have not been previously addressed in other family books.

Skaine, R. 2004. *The Cuban family: Customs and change in an era of hardship.* NC: McFarland and Company. The author presents a description of historical and contemporary Cuban and Cuban-American families. Based primarily on secondary sources, the book includes a notable bibliography.

Suggested Weblinks

The **Aboriginal Canada** portal offers a variety of Canadian online resources, information, and research; it is the winner of a bronze medal.

www.aboriginalcanada.gc.ca

The **Government of Quebec**'s website provides a historical overview of the province and links to various data sources pertaining to families and households, including the Quebec family, assistance for families, women in Quebec, young people, and senior citizens.

www.gouv.qc.ca/Vision/Societe/PortraitHistorique_en.html

An online ethnographic, historical, and comparative study by David G. Mandelbaum at the **Canadian Plains Research Centre**, University of Regina, presents an in-depth discussion of the Plains Cree, focusing on issues such as kinship, wife exchange, and gender role expectations.

www.schoolnet.ca/aboriginal/Plains_Cree/index-e.html

Ellie Crystal's website has many publications and includes a section on the Iroquois nation that gives a historical overview and tells the traditional creation stories.

www.crystalinks.com/iroquois.html

CHAPTER 3

Contemporary Issues in Family Life

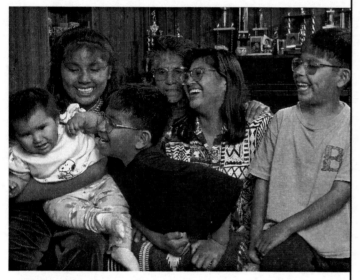

"I think that what affected me the most negatively at that age [6 to 10 age bracket] is that my great-grandmother came to live with us because my family was concerned that she was not getting proper care in her old age home.... She was often in pain and I was terrified because I was so young...my mother was so drained out."

"What made me the happiest at that age was all the sports and activities I was in [11 to 14 age bracket]. My parents were running like crazy trying to meet all of our sports and arts schedules but I had the greatest time. It was exciting, I was never home. (But now my parents admit that they were burdened and were glad when it was over.)"

"The hardest month of my life happened during the winter when I was 13 when I got ganged on by the guys in my hockey team after a game in the locker room because I had scored in our net. They hit me with sticks and one stomped on me with his skate.... I was cut, bruised and had some cracked bones and spent a painful month at home and that was the end of my hockey career. This episode was also painful for my entire family not excluding that my mother had to stay home from her work to put me back together!"

As indicated in the previous chapter, the structure and dynamics of family life have evolved considerably over the centuries, although certain trends, which appear to be recent, were already in evidence in the 19th century and early in the 20th century. Before the anomalous years from 1945 to 1960 that followed the Second World War, fertility had long begun a slow decline in most societies of the western world. Furthermore, single parent families had always been a frequent occurrence as parents' life expectancy was low and children were often orphaned. Remarriage was thus common. Finally, female labour was widespread in previous centuries, although it generally took place within the home economy. Some of these trends, such as lower fertility and later age at marriage, were reversed during the decade following the Second World War—and these few years are the "golden" yardstick by which we tend to compare current families to those of the past.

The reasons these anomalous years have been used as a basis of comparison with whatever happened thereafter are multiple. First, the generation that married during these years retained this period as a benchmark; this cohort and their children are still a powerful influence on our thinking about family life. Second, television was marketed and took hold in households during the anomalous years of the 1950s. The shows that the public watched were family shows and all depicted happily married mothers at home. This family programming in turn influenced some of the baby boomers who, along with their parents, spent their childhood and even adolescence watching these shows. In 20 or 30 years from now, we will be in a better position to see the longer trends in history and will cease to use these decades as a point of reference.

Nevertheless, the fact remains that the years following the 1950s were ones during which key family changes occurred. For instance, as the economy changed, so did the nature of people's employment—including that of women. Furthermore, certain aspects of family structure have since exhibited a dramatic transformation. As we see in subsequent chapters, divorce, cohabitation, births to single mothers, and same-sex-parent families have all increased substantially and have indeed transformed the profile of families. Moreover, even the position and role of children have changed and the cultural context within which families live has been dramatically altered by information technology.

However, one has to remember that families considered traditional in 2005 are quite different from traditional families of the 1950s. Concepts such as "traditional," and "new" or "alternative" forms of families are relatively meaningless because the traditional families of the 1950s were actually an alternative to what had just preceded that decade (Nicholson, 1997). Labelling families simply on the basis of ideological concerns or preferences may prevent us from focusing on the multiple functions that all families fulfill. For instance, cohabiting-parent families are "alternatives"; yet, they fulfill traditional family functions. Similarly, same-sex-parent families are "new" forms; yet, they also fulfill traditional family functions. For example, they all raise their children, love them, and integrate them to the best of their ability within the society in which they live.

Thus, in this chapter, I begin by examining the misleading and much heralded loss of family functions. This discussion will be followed by an examination of what European sociologists refer to as the defamilialization of children. I will then turn to the issue of the impact of certain aspects of the media on family life and child socialization.

HAS THE FAMILY LOST ITS FUNCTIONS?

There is no doubt that the family has lost some of its functions if we compare today's situation with that of the preindustrial period. As Hareven (1994a) puts it, in those days "the family not only reared children but also served as workshop, a school, a church, and a welfare agency. Preindustrial families meshed closely with the community and carried a variety of public responsibilities within the larger society." But society has evolved immensely since. Many of the functions that the family has lost, such as training apprentices, were tied to a specific type of economic and technological tradition that vanished long ago. Thus, these familial functions are no longer necessary for the survival of society and for the integration of family members into society.

However, what is often overlooked—and is the focus of this section—is that the family has acquired other functions. It is also recapturing some traditional ones as the social safety net and social policies fail to care for society's most vulnerable members, particularly children, the elderly, and the mentally, emotionally, as well as physically challenged (Luxton, 1997b). Above all, the family as an institution has become more specialized in certain domains, a phenomenon already noted in 1926 by E. W. Burgess (Bengtson, 2001). These situations are well illustrated in the quotes opening this chapter.

The Reproductive Function

It is often said that the family has lost its reproductive function because, until recently, births generally took place within wedlock. However, wedlock is a marital status rather than a family. As we have seen in Chapter 1, a married couple is not a family until the two spouses have their first child. Similarly, a woman's nonmarital sexual reproduction serves as the foundation to a family form: the mother-headed nuclear family. Understandably, the single-mother form of nuclear family is at times more fragile and at a greater risk of being unable to fulfill its functions as adequately as those headed by two married parents (Ambert, 2002b). But this is another issue discussed separately in Chapter 9. Therefore, while it is true that a large proportion of children are born to single mothers and to cohabiting couples, this does not change anything in terms of families' reproductive function.

The family will lose its reproductive function only when children are conceived, then cut away from their parents, and raised separately in special institutions. Actually, were such a point to be reached, the family as we understand it would disappear because it would lose its intergenerational dimension and all the other functions that flow from it.

Other Traditional Functions That the Family Has Retained

1. The **socialization** or sociocultural reproduction of children still begins within the family. While other institutions soon complement parents or even take over this role, particularly in terms of formal schooling, the entirety of the research literature clearly indicates that, until mid-adolescence, parents are children's most important agents of socialization. Even with adolescents, parents often are able to counterbalance negative peer influences when they exist. As we see in Chapters 12, 14, and 15, there are causal relationships between parenting and child outcomes in terms of mental health, prosocial behaviour, and school achievement (Ambert, 2003d). Similarly, when parenting fails, negative outcomes are more likely to follow. This is not to say, however, that parents *unilaterally* "cause" children's problems—a "causality" model of which I am very critical (Ambert, 2001). As in all societies, our families prepare children for the economic system in which they are embedded (Zack, 1997)—albeit, as we see in Chapters 5 and 7, with different levels of success.

2. The family continues to meet its members' needs for physical security as it did in the past. At the nuclear level, families still provide **shelter**, attend to basic nutritional needs, and insure physical **health** according to their means. But with the drastic cuts in the health care system, families are called upon to expand their functions in these domains (Armstrong and Armstrong, 2003; FSAT, 2004).

3. The family still confers to its members their place within the social stratification or economic system, at least until children are old enough to be on their own. This is referred to as the **status function**. That is, young members of a family belong to their parents' socioeconomic group—or to their grandparents'. Thus, the reproduction of the class system begins within the family, although Canada experiences a great deal of downward and upward social mobility of adult children

compared to their own parents (Corak, 1998). Furthermore, the family contributes to the reproduction of the **religious and ethnic status** of a group, largely through social visibility, socialization practices, and the structure of opportunities available to its members in a racialized society.

4. The family still serves as an agency of psychological stabilization and provides a sense of identity and **belongingness**, particularly for its children. For instance, a French study found that 86 percent of adults mention their family when asked what defines them (Housseaux, 2003). It follows that the family fulfills many **affective needs**. It is within its boundaries that the young child learns to love and be loved, where attachment first develops, where trust is built. The family is one of the prime movers in **personality development** for children and adults alike. However, the family shares this function with a person's genetic background and with other social systems such as schools, work, as well as the peer group. When adults become parents, their personality development continues as they extend themselves into this new role.

New Functions Imposed Upon Families

Not only has the family retained some of its traditional functions, but it also has acquired many new ones, most of which are actually performed in great part by mothers.

1. Parents have become the coordinators of the education and the services that their children receive from various institutions (Coontz, 2000). Thus, the family has acquired the function of **coordination or management**: Parents must make the extra-familial environment (whether schools, child care, or the media) accessible to and safe for their children. They must also interpret these contexts to their children within the perspective of their own values. Furthermore, the various institutions and services available to children, especially schools, make great demands on parents' time, and even more so on mothers. The latter, for instance, have to monitor and help in their children's intellectual development, and this includes homework (Mandell and Sweet, 2004). In turn, because of a longer life span, when their elderly parents become frail, children must manage the care they receive.

2. The family has now been charged with the responsibility of policing what its children and youth access on television and the Internet and what they want to buy. Thus, parents have to filter out noxious influences, whether in terms of consumerism, violence, or exploitative sexual content, which the media unleash upon everyone (Cantor and Nathanson, 2001). This in itself is a very onerous function for which most adults are ill prepared and receive little social support (Ambert, 2003e). While in the past parents had to be vigilant concerning the potentially negative influence of the printed media, contemporary parents have to be vigilant on all fronts of a vastly expanding web of audiovisual media, in addition to the remaining printed media. Thus, the role of **agency of social control** that the family has always fulfilled has vastly expanded in terms of the cultural territory covered.

3. By the same token, the family prevents the fragmentation of its young members' lives that would unavoidably occur in view of the numerous and often conflict-

ing sources of socialization to which children are subjected. As Hays (1996:175) puts it, "the more the larger world becomes impersonal, competitive, and individualistic and the more the logic of that world invades the world of intimate relationships, the more intensive child rearing becomes." The family serves as an **agency of integration** at the personal and social levels. This family function is particularly important in view of the surfeit of choices and alternatives that the consumer market economy and an urbanized society present (Bumpass, 2001). The family serves as a *lone* anchor because, in the past, this function was generally fulfilled with the help of the parish, village, or neighbours.

Additional Responsibilities Taken on by Some Families

1. A significant number of families provide the entire special care needed by their intellectually, emotionally, or physically challenged children and, in some cases, frail elderly parents. The family is again becoming a welfare agency, as was the case in the "old" days (McDaniel, 1996). However, currently, the family is rather isolated in this role while, in the past, it might have received more help from the community. Furthermore, in the past, the frail elderly had a more restricted life span, and most physically challenged children did not survive for long because medicine was too rudimentary to support them. Contemporary advances in nutrition, sanitary conditions, and medicine have increased the longevity and survival rates of the weakest. As a result, families have been forced to be the main caretakers or supervisors of the help that these relatives in precarious health receive—and women do a great proportion of this work (Mitchell, 2004).

2. Many families fulfill additional functions for their members, depending on their means, social class, racial/ethnic membership, religion, as well as citizenship status. (This will become particularly obvious in subsequent chapters.) For instance, some families remain a centre of worship and religious education while others provide at-home schooling. Still others continue to serve as a centre of leisure activities, both for their children and adult members. Amish families are a good example in this respect (Hostetler, 1993). Furthermore, many of the functions performed at the nuclear level (father and/or mother) are being transferred to the extended family, especially to grandparents. One can think here of the increase in the number of grandparents who are completely in charge of raising grandchildren. This situation occurs as a result of problems at the nuclear family level, as well as when both parents are in the military and have to participate in war or peacekeeping duties abroad.

3. Many families, particularly those on farms and owners of small enterprises, still form a unit of production: They train, employ, and pay their members. Finally, immigrant families serve important functions for their members, as many subsidize the immigration of their kin and support their resettlement to Canada. Others send remittances to their relatives in their home country and contribute not only to the sustenance but also to the economic survival of entire societies. Cases in point are the Philippines, Vietnam, and Cuba.

An Overabundance of Family Functions

In short, while Canadian families in general are not always a haven and are far from being a perfect institution, the functions that they fulfill cover an amazing range of personal, social, cultural, and economic needs. And families do so, particularly mothers, with far fewer moral and social resources than was the case in the past, when communities were more cohesive and there was greater value consensus. As imperfect and, at times, limping as it is, *the family still does more and better than any other social institution for its members,* particularly its children and youth. Thus, the fact is not that families have become obsolete or irrelevant. The contrary has actually happened: Families have become burdened with new functions foisted upon them by technology, commercialization, urbanization, and heterogeneity (Castaneda, 2002). While it is quite valid to be concerned about families' functions, it is so only if one is concerned about their burden rather than their obsolescence.

As we have seen, the concern over the "decline" in family functions stems from an inappropriate comparison of today's families with those of centuries past. It also stems from an idealization of the late 1940s and the 1950s when several unusual circumstances coalesced: early age at marriage; higher fertility; low divorce rates; relatively few births to single women, particularly single teens; fathers in the role of breadwinner; and stay-at-home mothers.

Families' Burdens: Society's Failures

Another source of concern over this alleged decline in family functions is probably the result of an analytical and social policy misunderstanding: It results from equating *individual* families' inability or failure to fulfill certain functions to a loss of functions by the family as an **institution** (Stacey, 1996). People correctly observe that more children are delinquent, problematic, unhappy, and in foster care than was the case 20 years ago. But the error begins when this is seen as a failure of *the* family as an institution rather than of individual families—or of society as a whole.

The new social structure based on the market economy, information technology, and the retrenchment of policies aimed at preventing and ameliorating familial problems has bestowed upon the family a new set of responsibilities or functions (Wall, 2004). It is therefore not surprising if more individual families fail at these than in the past: Families are more unstable structurally, are more isolated socially, and are less well supported by other institutions at the cultural, economic, and political levels. Thus, too great a proportion of our families are ill equipped to fulfill their functions, particularly in terms of supervising, guiding, and educating their youth and caring for their elders. Economic deprivation, segregation, social stigmatization and isolation, singlehood, and members' personal deficiencies are among the elements that prevent individual families from fulfilling their functions adequately. Most of these are socially driven problems, not family-produced ones (Connidis, 2001).

Let's expand on the sources of this inability of many nuclear families to care for their members, protect them, and maintain them within a normative life course. One source, at the macrosociological level of analysis, resides in the lack of social and political support that would provide more resources to families and their special-needs members. A second source, also systemic, sees countless families forgotten by society and relegated to segregated enclaves where they are visible only when their members commit crimes. A third cause, at the juncture of the micro and macro levels of analysis, is the absence of an effective community surrounding families. The structural conclusion one arrives at is that the family as an institution certainly requires far more assistance from other institutions to fulfill its numerous functions adequately. Were this assistance forthcoming at the institutional family level, most individual families would benefit and fewer would fail in this respect.

Family life was relatively stable for centuries and then began to change in several aspects following industrialization. After that, the pace of sociocultural change accelerated with technological innovations and the economic restructuring they heralded. By the last decades of the 20th century, unplanned change may well have occurred too rapidly for the good of families as an institution. As a result, while families have been replaced in some of their old functions, such as the schooling of their children, they suddenly inherited a pileup of new functions and responsibilities. Unfortunately, this pileup took place at the same time as drastic changes were occurring in family structure. These changes have actually reduced the number of adults or parents available to children, thus diminishing many families' ability to fulfill their functions adequately, particularly in terms of child socialization. For instance, a single mother who lacks adequate economic and social resources is likely to encounter far more difficulties in keeping her small family running smoothly than a two-parent family with a reasonable income (Pitt, 2002).

A corresponding, major problem has been occurring along with accelerated changes in technology and family structure. It resides in the government having failed to plan or even keep up with change. Political institutions have failed to create social policies favourable to families of all types, as well as policies protecting families, particularly children, against the potentially harmful impacts of technology. We could think here in terms of the structure of the workweek and the workplace, the relative lack of child care centres, and the noxious contents of the media. But we can also think in terms of failure to more adequately assist near-poor and poor families.

Are Family Values Necessarily Under Attack?

As sociologists, we have to consider two other cultural as well as political realities concerning family change. First, in an individualistic, democratic society, everyone is entitled to his or her religious and moral beliefs about family life. Except for abusing one's children or one's partner, or practising polygamy, an individualistic democracy such as Canada ensures individuals' right to live their lives and their relationships according to their personal beliefs (Glendon, 1989). But this democratic right also presumes an obligation: the tolerance of the different ways and values of other families.

This leads us to the second reality: the diversity of family life in the postmodern era (Stacey, 1996). Not only are there more divorces than in 1950 (but less than in the mid-1980s), and more children living in stepfamilies and born to single mothers, but same-sex couples are now raising and even reproducing children. A new wave of immigration has also contributed to further diversity of the familial landscape. Nevertheless, these culturally and structurally diverse families not only fulfill similar functions but share some common concerns, such as the desire to see their children do well, and for many, the hope that they will have a better life than their parents—all cherished Canadian values. While family structures are fluid, family functions remain (Eichler, 1988).

Therefore, if family values are under attack, it is from the roadblocks created by the materialistic forces of society that prevent individual families from fulfilling their functions. What is certainly a concern is that, under individualistic pressures and attacks from various professional interests, many parents themselves have lost their moral authority. Hence, family diversity in itself need not be analyzed within a concern over the loss of traditional *family* values or the "decline of the family." Rather, perhaps, we should be concerned over the loss of traditional forms of *support* for the family—whether structural or cultural—and over the modern *burdens* placed upon families.

Family life viability and family values are far more endangered by other cultural and economic forces than they are by changes in the structure of the family. As we see in a subsequent section and in Chapter 5 on economic context, one can think here of certain television contents promoting infidelity and "sex as leisure"; or of the distorting effect that widely accessible pornography may have on real-life couple relationships (Paul, 2004); and of consumerism, which often controls family time and individual family members' values.

CHILDREN ARE DEFAMILIALIZED AND AGE SEGREGATED

Another two-fold contemporary development in family life pertains to children. The first element finds that children's lives have become more defamilialized. The concept of **defamilialization** was introduced by European sociologists and refers to children being increasingly taken care of by non-family members who earn their living doing so. Children spend less and less time at home interacting with their parents and enter care or educational institutions at an earlier age than was the case before the 1980s. This change began with industrialization, when the family lost its economic function of production, which was one of its foundations of solidarity and of child integration (Martin, 1997). Compared to the 19th century, for instance, when children helped in family productivity, youth now rarely work with their families (Bradbury, 2000; Bullen, 2000). This change accelerated around 1960 or slightly thereafter in Canada and continues to this day.

Childhood is changing from yet another perspective: At the middle-class level, it has become more structured. That is, children's lives are more organized, regimented, less spontaneous and free ranging than in the past (Adler and Adler, 1998). Institutions such as daycare centres, kindergartens, schools, organized extracurricular activities, day and overnight camps, and so on, contribute to child socialization, leisure, and experience (Lareau, 2003). Children's employment of time is rationalized and institutionalized in order to increase their safety and prepare them for the growing rationalization of postmodern life (Ritzer, 2000). Not only do these institutions regiment children's lives into organized time segments, but as the child spends less time

Children's "free time" is now more structured and age-segregated than was the case 50 years ago. This results from a combination of circumstances, including both parents' employment outside the home, concerns for children's safety, and a construction of children as "projects" to be perfected for the future.

within the folds of the family and is increasingly "serviced" by other adults and institutions, he or she becomes defamilialized (Doherty, 2000).

Consequently, children are an important source of economic activities in postindustrial societies because they create childwork. *Childwork* refers to service work done by adults as they care for and educate children as well as organize and control their activities (Oldman, 1994). These adult workers include teachers, as well as child-care personnel, social workers, clinicians, and various other child specialists. Thus, childhood as a structural category creates employment opportunities for adulthood outside of the familial realm. As British sociologist David Oldman (1994) puts it, it is one of the paradoxes of the current economic situation "that parents need non-familial supervision of their own children so they can be paid for providing that non-familial supervision for other children." For instance, parents hire babysitters so that they can become teachers to other adults' children.

Danish sociologist Jens Qvortrup (1995) defines children as useful members of the economy, not only because they create what Oldman calls childwork but because children themselves do work: Their labour consists of schoolwork. Children participate in the societal division of labour by obtaining a solid education. In preindustrial societies, children were useful, like most adults, with their manual labour, but today they are useful through attending school, preparing themselves for their future as voting citizens, adult workers, and taxpayers. As well, by remaining in school longer, children prevent the large-scale unemployment that would inevitably occur were they to enter the labour market prematurely (Côté and Allahar, 1994).

German sociologist Angelika Engelbert (1994) describes children's lives as worlds of differentiation. Not only are children's worlds differentiated because of their class position vis-à-vis other children, but children's worlds are also differentiated from those of adults (Sutherland, 1997). Children are separated from adults in care centres, schools, and other supervisory settings (Coakley and Donnelly, 2004:117). "Children are directly or indirectly excluded from environments that are not specialized to satisfy their needs [such as the world of adult work and entertainment]" (Engelbert, 1994:289). This exclusion serves to protect the standard of efficiency required in the work environment. It also serves to protect children from the physical and moral dangers of, as well as exploitation by, the adult world. Furthermore, children are actually restricted to their special environments. Within this analytical framework, educational institutions are *institutions of exclusion*, even exclusion of children from their parents' world.

In contrast, children living in the villages of Africa and many Asian countries are fully integrated in the life of the community and in their parents' world, including work that is basically familial. Children learn their adult roles by imitating their parents as they help them. They are totally familialized, even though they may attend the village school. Moreover, these children play in mixed-age groups, the 6-year-olds or 10-year-olds watching over the babies collectively.

Thus, in western societies, not only are children segregated into age groups, they are also especially segregated from many of the activities carried out by their parents. As Coontz (2000:290) points out, while youth today are more excluded from productive roles, they are paradoxically much more fully involved in consumer roles. As we soon see, this **age segregation** is promoted by consumerism and is often self-chosen and reinforced by the peer culture that has evolved along age lines. For instance, even when they are at home, children may watch different television programs in their rooms or may be served dinner by their mothers rather than sharing in its preparation. Hence, children themselves contribute to their defamilialization which, in North America, is often referred to as the process of **individuation,** a psychological term referring to children's gaining a sense of identity separately from their connection to their parents. Individualism is largely absent as a notion in many more collectivist societies of the world and even in ethnic groups in Canada that are more oriented toward their families.

THE AUDIOVISUAL MEDIA AND FAMILY LIFE

Perhaps one of the most salient historical developments for society and its families has occurred relatively recently. It resides in the introduction of the audiovisual media, particularly television and the Internet, to the cultural landscape. Major events are now experienced and socially constructed through the prism of the televised media, whether it is the news, sports, talk shows, or sitcoms. At first, in 1951, there were 90,000 television sets in Canadian homes, all receiving American programming. Three months after the advent of the CBC in 1952, there were 224,000 sets (Gorman, 1997). Then, television represented a mode of "family entertainment" that was to prove radically different from anything in the past. It had no historical precedent in terms of its ability to inform, influence, and structure daily life. Between 1951 and 1955, nearly two-thirds of the nation's homes acquired a television set. By 1960, almost 90 percent had at least one set and, at that point, the average person watched television about five hours a day. By the 1960s, television had replaced the piano in family rooms.

Television Restructures Family Life

As people watched television, less time became available for reading and the development of skills, such as musical abilities, creative play, and for family entertainment that might involve all the members. Television changed family leisure patterns. Early studies summarized by Andreasen (1994) indicate that by 1952 in large cities, a great proportion of families reported regularly eating with the television on, which meant less interpersonal exchange during dinner. Families with a television set went to bed later, talked less, and often ate separately while watching different programs at different times. These trends were reinforced in the 1970s and even more so in the 1980s and are still present to this day (Roberts and Foehr, 2004). Television viewing can no longer be considered a form of "family entertainment," as multiple sets were brought into each home. By 1980, 50 percent of families owned at least two sets (Andreasen, 1994). Now children and particularly middle-class adolescents have their own personal entertainment centres in their bedrooms, where they choose what they want to watch or which video game to play (Livingstone and Bovill, 2001). In the U.S., low-income children are even more likely than others to have this equipment in their bedrooms, except for the Internet, and they also read less (Roberts and Foehr, 2004). In contrast, parents with a high level of education tend to restrict television more during mealtimes and to have more rules concerning viewing, especially for small children; their children also read more. Television has become a solitary activity (Larson, 1995). However, family members who view it together find the experience more pleasant than when they watch it alone (Kubey, 1994).

Nearly all college and university students today have grown up with television, video games, and the Internet. Few know what family life is without these audiovisual media. For most, the comparatively low level of time spent talking and sitting in the den or in the backyard just enjoying each other's company seems normal. Nevertheless, one can still find students who feel lonely, at times because of a lack of familial time:

> *"One bone of contention in my family at this stage of my life seeing that I still live at home is that everyone is too busy watching television each in their own room, my father and brother with sports...my mother with soaps and movies, and I am left alone with my school work because I have no one to talk to."*

> *"It really upsets me that my boyfriend is so hooked to sports on TV. I don't know if I can live with that because now with all these channels there is sports every night. We're only in love and he isn't ready to make concessions in this so I wonder how it will be if we get married. I can't live with a TV set on all the time, it just breaks any attempt to have a regular conversation. Maybe that's what he wants after all. So yes I am a little less than happy right now because I may be in for a nasty surprise. So maybe I should split."*

Furthermore, *not a single one* of the writers of the 1,500 or so autobiographies ever mentioned television as a happy salient recollection in his or her past life. In contrast, most placed their parents in this category as well as their friends. In other words, television fills time but it does not create happiness (Roberts and Foehr, 2004). It can, however, create tension and an interpersonal void, as illustrated in the preceding quotes. When taking the place of other activities, it can be harmful to health and contribute to obesity (Gable and Lutz, 2000).

The Family on Television: A Historical Overview

The first television show geared to children, *Howdy Doody*, ran from 1947 to 1960, and with it, the debate about the effect of television on children began and has continued to this day (Wilcox and Kunkel, 1996). The debate has not, however, been accompanied to the same extent by discussions over the impact of television on adults and on family life, although the research done for advertising and marketing firms indicates strong media effects on adults' beliefs and lifestyles as well as on family life. *Howdy Doody* also marked the beginning of the impact of audiovisual advertising on children (Stark, 1997:18).

Situation comedies, or sitcoms, as a lasting form of television entertainment for the entire family began with *I Love Lucy* in 1951. This was also the first show with a woman as its superstar. Except for sports and newscasts, women are the prime TV audience, and the orientation of Lucille Ball's show around themes that concern couples, and particularly wives, contributed to women's devotion to this medium. A little later, *Leave It to Beaver* became the family show par excellence. It ran from 1957 through 1963 and represented the ideal American family: white, middle-class, with a working father, a stay-at-home mother, and two sons. The program was child-centred; that is, it offered a perspective on family life from a child's point of view. Not only did *Leave It to Beaver* become a cultural icon in later decades when the American and Canadian families had changed from the idealized type of the 1950s, but it also set the stage for the nostalgia of what Stephanie Coontz called *The Way We Never Were* (1992).

The public, but particularly women, were used to soap operas, which had long been a staple of radio programming. Therefore, it is not surprising that television adopted this genre early on in the 1950s in Quebec, with programs focusing on family relationships in small communities, as in the very popular turn-of-the-century *Les Belles Histoires des Pays d'En Haut*. In the U.S. in the 1960s, programs such as *As the World Turns* and *Peyton Place* centred more on couples. These melodramas generally ran during the afternoons, which meant that they largely targeted a feminine audience. They included a mixture of largely traditional gender roles and family life on the one hand, with powerful examples of sexually liberated women on the other hand. Other soap operas soon followed: *All My Children, The Young and the Restless, The Bold and the Beautiful, Dallas,* and *General Hospital,* among many others (Walters, 1999).

The plots of the soap or melodrama genre generally revolve around couples or families. The children who are born are not especially nurtured; in fact, they soon disappear to resurface only when they are old enough to be wrapped up in romantic dramas of their own. Children's daily lives are not presented, thereby giving the impression that children inhibit passion and excitement. These shows contain many weddings, love triangles, breakups, and more adopted children than exist in reality (Wegar, 1997). Soaps focus on feelings, melodrama, and talk. Overall, they present a sharp contrast with the daily routine of real-life families, and as such, provide women with an escape from domestic reality.

Sesame Street, which began in 1969, is watched by over half of the nation's children between the ages of three and five. This program emphasizes the acceptance of ethnic differences, as well as values of cooperation and environmentalism. It is devoid of commercialism, violence, and sex. Its goal is to provide skills to help prepare children for school, and research shows that children from varied backgrounds do learn by watching it (Children's Television Workshop, 1991). Accordingly, *Sesame Street* is highly appreciated by parents of all ethnic groups, many of whom grew up with it. It complements parents' role as educators, it does not conflict with family values, and it does not antagonize religious groups. However, the program has surprisingly little to do with family life: For instance, characters such as Big Bird have no parents and neither do the child guests.

Another family-related show that has remained popular, mainly through reruns, is *The Brady Bunch* (1969–1974). Its cast consisted of a widow with three girls who marries a widower with three boys. Like *Leave It to Beaver,* the young actors provided a child's view of the world and child-sized problems. Any child between 6 and 12 years of age could identify with a same-age character, as there were offspring of various ages in this television family. This reconstituted family anticipated the coming wave of real-life stepparenting situations created by divorce, which may explain why reruns of *The Brady Bunch* have remained popular: The show offers a rather pleasant formula for reconstituted families, a safe refuge for those whose families have failed to be so successful.

In the 1970s, *The Mary Tyler Moore Show* represented a turning point in sitcoms—it focused on single adults, particularly in the workplace. Families were not involved, and this in itself was an interesting perspective, especially in view of the fact that the main character, Mary Richards, was a woman. The U.S. Commission on Civil Rights (1977) found that, in the period between 1969 and 1972, almost one-half of the female characters portrayed on television were married, yet less than one-third of the males were. At about the same time, McNeil (1975) revealed that 74 percent of the female interactions on television took place within the context of problems associated with romance and family, compared to only 18 percent of male interactions. Thus, *The Mary Tyler Moore Show* was overcoming many gender stereotypes. For the first time, employment was depicted as a salient aspect in the life of a woman—albeit a single woman, not a married one with children—just as more and more women were entering the labour force. This show paved the way for *Murphy Brown* (and nonmarital parenthood on TV) and *Ally McBeal,* both profiling single, professional women.

The Cosby Show, running from 1984 to 1992, represented another milestone, as it introduced a black family headed by two professional parents. Although the family came closer to approximating a two-paycheque family than any other show had done before, traditional values were emphasized. In the mid-eighties, it was still quite unusual to think of a black family as well-to-do and stable. Thus, the racial context was an important element in its success. It was also probably the first sitcom with which black families could identify, at least in terms of race if not necessarily lifestyle. Then, the *Fresh Prince of Bel Air* followed a similar format, but within an even more affluent and yet more "hip" context.

The last sitcom to be mentioned here is *Roseanne,* which began in 1988: The show introduced a blue-collar family with a hard-working mother, three kids, and loud-mouthed parents, and dealt with issues such as teen sex, among others. Parents and children alike could be unpleasant creatures! *Roseanne* also departed from the usual tendency of representing the feminine body in terms of slimness (Fouts and Burggraf, 1999). All these factors combined to reflect changes in the depiction of family life. In the 1990s and early 2000s, many shows simply dispensed with family life or focused on alternative families or sets of couples. One can think of *Friends, South Park,* or *Party of Five* (Kanner, 2001).

Then, deplorable aspects of family life started to be reflected in the many talk shows that began appearing in the mid- to late-1980s, such as *Donahue*, *The Oprah Winfrey Show*, *Jenny Jones*, *Geraldo*, *Sally Jesse Raphael*, and so on—not to omit more recent arrivals such as the *Maury Show* and the more professional *Dr. Phil*. Many of these programs place the spotlight on the self-disclosure of problems and even deviances, with much sexual infidelity and vulgarity thrown in for good measure (Fox, 1999).

In the spring of 2004, the *Maury Show* seemed to have focused on helping women prove their child's paternity: DNA results were revealed on the show—preceded by much arguing, fighting, yelling, and swearing between the parties, with the audience taking sides. The parties usually involved very young mothers, generally unmarried, and males, also usually, but not always, quite young. One woman had seven prospective fathers tested! Many cried as the males (and even the males' mothers) insulted them and cried even more when the paternity test was negative. When a paternity test was positive, the small child was brought in and put in the arms of the father, and this was the end of that segment of the show. Yet, up to that point, most of these parents had been fighting!

The "therapy" session format is often utilized in these shows, although one wonders what happens to these couples and families after they leave and return home to face the repercussions of the confessions made on stage. The previously mentioned *Maury Show* was particularly problematic in this respect because of the participants' young ages, their lack of maturity, their obvious temperamental fragility, and the high level of conflict occurring between these natural parents. One does not need to be a sociologist to be concerned about the future of the babies that were behind these family revelations and quarrels played out on national television: Who checks up on these small children's well-being after, considering their parents' hostility and volatility?

Effects of Family-Related Programs on Children

One must look at the form and contents of televised programs to understand how they influence family members and particularly children. Weiss and Wilson's (1996) analysis of the emotional contents of family sitcoms applies to soap operas as well: It reveals that negative emotions, such as fear and anger, are more prominent than either positive or neutral emotions. Negative emotions "sell" better. This can lead children to believe that "real" family life (i.e., their family life) should be more dramatic because what they see on television is like that. However, the negative emotions expressed by television family members are largely ignored by the other characters in the play. This may further suggest to "a child viewer that negative feelings are unimportant to other family members" (Weiss and Wilson, 1996:19). Although children can learn that conflict is generally resolved, it is done quickly at the end of the show. Children may then expect fast resolutions in their own lives. On the positive side, they can learn to use humour to solve interpersonal problems.

Dorr et al. (1990) find that children aged 6 to 16 perceive approximately half of the families in the U.S. to be like the families in their favourite television series. For children, the real world should look like the world on television, because children see more about the world, as commercially constructed, on screen than in real life. In one night, a child can "visit" 10 virtual families, but in real life, that child belongs to only one. Not surprisingly, children often want to behave or be like the characters portrayed in the sitcoms (Austin et al., 1990). All in all, children think of these sitcoms as closer to reality; retention of emotional information is higher from family sitcoms than from cartoon or moppet programs (Hayes and Casey, 1992).

Furthermore, family sitcoms emphasize certain types of parent-child relationships (democratic, emotionally expressive, independent) that also impact upon children who are issued of immigrant families (Pyke, 2000). These shows portray nurturing and understanding parents and focus on the successful resolution of minor family squabbles via expressiveness (Skill, 1994). These values may be very different in the parents' countries of origin and may lead these children to devalue their own parents and their parenting messages.

SPECIFIC MEDIA INFLUENCES

The black American activist and politician, Jesse Jackson, has called television "the third parent." Thus, a contemporary and much debated issue is the role that the media play in the development of children's negative attitudes and behaviours. To begin with, it is methodologically more difficult to study specific media as a causal effect in children's attitudes and behaviours today than in the 1970s. Indeed, how can one isolate the effect on children of television contents when children now have simultaneous access to similar contents on the Internet, videos, and video games? And how can one isolate this effect when it pervades the entire culture of our societies? We live in a media-saturated society.

Second, some contend that the media have no effect on behaviours and attitudes. However, it is illogical to deny that violent or sex-suffused media have no effect, while at the same time accepting the fact that the tobacco industry's ads foster smoking among adolescents. Furthermore, why would companies invest so many billions in advertising if it had no effect? Third, there are fears in some quarters that accepting research results pointing to the media in the causality chain of children's problematic behaviours might lead to censorship. Lawyers for the media industry are particularly active in promoting this fear.

The media constitute a very powerful and increasingly interconnected industry and lobby. For instance, many news magazines and newspapers are owned by mega corporations that include television stations, cable networks, and film and record companies. Thus, the media can control the dissemination of research results that could be damaging to their image—and to their bottom line. Two often-heard rationalizations by producers are, first, that the public is given what it wants and, second, that the shows and movies reflect reality.

One could as easily argue that the media fabricate reality. For instance, in the U.S. between 1990 and 1998, the number of murder stories on television news increased by 600 percent while the real murder rate had declined by 20 percent (Glassner, 1999). Over 50 percent of the crimes shown on television are murders, while murders represent only 0.2 percent of the crimes reported by the FBI (Bushman and Huesmann,

2001). As well, between 1950 and 1995, families with children headed by two parents have been underrepresented in television stories in every decade, while those with a single father have been overrepresented (Robinson and Skill, 2001). Observing how children and even some adults dress in imitation of their favourite stars provides a clear indication that the media *create* needs and a reality, while reinforcing stereotypes of ideal feminine body types (Abu-Laban and McDaniel, 2004) and of a tough masculinity (Malszecki and Cavar, 2004).

In the following sections, we focus on the role that the audiovisual media may play in the development of problematic behaviours and attitudes in the domains of aggression, consumerism, and sexuality. However, one question which we cannot address is, What growing-up experiences do children *not* get when they spend so much time watching television, playing video games, and surfing the net (Heath, 1994)?

The Promotion of Violence

The average child has witnessed well over 8,000 murders on television by the end of elementary school (Waters, 1993). In the U.S., the National Television Violence Study (1998) found that over 40 percent of violent acts are perpetrated by "good" characters—thus glamorizing violence—and over 55 percent of victims of violence show little pain or suffering, thus desensitizing people to its true effects (Donnerstein and Linz, 1995). The rate of violent crimes in the U.S. and other western countries rose dramatically after 1965, coinciding with the coming of age of the first generation of children raised with television (Bushman and Huesmann, 2001).

Centerwall found that, between 1945 and 1974, the white homicide rate increased by 93 percent in the U.S., by 92 percent in Canada, but declined by 7 percent among white South Africans where television was banned. There are indications that long-term effects of exposure to violent media occur mainly for children rather than for teenagers and adults. Thus, Centerwall estimated that a 10- to 15-year time lag occurs between the introduction of television and an increase in homicide rates because television exerts its behaviour-modifying effects primarily on children (reviewed in Donnerstein and Linz, 1995).

Using an experimental and longitudinal method, Joy et al. (1986) compared three Canadian towns, one of which did not receive television transmission until 1974 (see Family Research 3.1). Children were tested before the introduction of television and two years after. The children in the town that had received television two years earlier showed a substantial increase in aggressiveness that was not observed among the youngsters in the other town. They also exhibited a sharp increase in sex-role stereotyping (Kimball, 1986).

In the 1980s, researchers began to harvest the results of other longitudinal studies and found that young adults tended to act more aggressively when they had watched more violence as eight-year-olds. The link between adult aggressiveness and childhood viewing of violence on TV was even stronger than it had been at age eight. Boys who had not been aggressive at age eight but had watched more violence had become more aggressive young adults than a similar group of non-aggressive boys who had watched fewer episodes of violence, as reported in Bushman and Huesmann (2001). Studies of

FAMILY RESEARCH 3.1

Experimenting with Real-Life Situations to Determine Causality

In the fall of 1973, Tannis MacBeth (1998) initiated a study on the effect of television on children. She creatively exploited a naturally occurring social situation: At that time, a Canadian town, renamed Notel, was to receive television transmission for the first time. Notel was not isolated but was located in a valley, which prevented transmission. A nearby town, called Unitel, had already been receiving one Canadian channel for seven years, and a third town, called Multitel, had been receiving several U.S. channels in addition to a Canadian one for about 15 years. Notel (no television) became the experimental town; Unitel (one channel) and Multitel (several channels) became the two control towns. In Phase 1, in 1973, students in Grades 4 and 7 from the three towns were tested on a wide range of behaviours and skills. In a longitudinal design, they were retested two years later (Phase 2), in Grades 6 and 9, to measure the effects of television. In order to rule out maturation or growing-up influences, additional students in Grades 4 and 7 were also included in Phase 2.

more recent cohorts have shown that television violence now affects American girls' level of aggressiveness as well (Huesmann et al., 2003).

Such results indicate that it is not only a predilection for aggressiveness that leads children to select television violence but that this violence also leads to aggressiveness. Although exposure to violent television and videos is not the main factor in the etiology of aggressiveness, it is part of the **enabling environment** for problematic behaviours (Garbarino, 1999). Viewing violence may teach children that conflict can be resolved only with verbal or physical aggressiveness. Second, it may be related to the development of a lower threshold for frustration, so that children tolerate irritants less easily and react to them more explosively. Third, exposure to violence may desensitize viewers to the severity of its consequences, so that even killing can appear routine (Cantor and Nathanson, 2001). Lastly, children learn aggressive techniques such as how to punch, kick, and kill via these programs.

In a large study of eighth-graders across the U.S., Muller and Kerbow (1993) found that, during weekdays, African-American parents restricted television less than other groups, including Asian Americans and whites. In the U.S., a disproportionate segment of black families live in poor neighbourhoods with higher rates of criminality. Thus, children in these districts are subjected to real-life violence as well as violence on television and video games (Myers, 2000). This combination represents a potentially dangerous socialization experience.

Killing is often the goal in video games, and a link has also been found between this interactive media and aggressive behaviours (Anderson and Bushman, 2001). However, the research on the effect of video games still has to include longitudinal studies (Sherry, 2001). Furthermore, research would need to separate the effect of violence on television from that on videos, not exactly a small task today (Wartella et al., 2004). As Funk et al. (2000) point out, at the very least, playing violent video games will not improve children's overall behaviour, although it may improve their visual-manual coordination. We must also point out that rates of violent criminality have decreased in Canada and the U.S. in recent years (perhaps because of better policing or cohort changes) at the same time that television and video games were becoming more violent. Thus, at the societal level, it is difficult to establish a causality effect of media violence. But it may well be that this effect took place earlier on in the history of television for children's aggressiveness in general and that other forces in society prevent any further additive effect. In other words, the saturation point in terms of the negative effects of television violence may have already been reached in the early 1990s. Nevertheless, a climate of violence is certainly not an ideal one within which to form relationships and raise children.

The Promotion of Consumerism

The advertising industry spends over $12 billion a year marketing directly to children (Dittman, 2002). Furthermore, pop stars promote lifestyles (clothing, for instance) that preteens and adolescents try to emulate (Quart, 2003). Thus, mass culture creates false needs (Longhurst, 1995). In turn these false needs may contribute to less prosocial attitudes and even behaviours, both among parents and children. The American Psychological Association's Task Force on Advertising and Children points out that "advertising might trigger materialistic attitudes by teaching children to measure personal worth by the products they own" (Dittman, 2002).

Children learn how to dress and to behave according to this clothes-related self-presentation from the media (Quart, 2003). When ads, pop stars, and words on CDs promote premature sexiness in children, for instance, one should study how this inappropriate socialization might affect their sexual behaviour a few years later. One might also want to know if clothing styles promoted by popular entertainers relate to difficult behaviours down the road. In other words, there is no research on how children's consumer behaviours may be linked to the development of problematic or positive behaviours (Côté and Allahar, 1994). As Seiter (1993:193) points out concerning the mass-media targeting of children, "A distinctive, peer-oriented consumer culture now intervenes in the relationship of parents and children, and that intervention begins for many children as early as two years of age."

This situation is often even more acute among some visible minority groups, particularly blacks, because of the omnipresent influence of hip-hop on clothing styles and behaviours. Grewal (2004) reports that a segment of black youths in Toronto are concerned about this influence, while others say that hip-hop reflects their experience. Grewal quotes a student's depiction of an assembly to celebrate Black History Month at her predominantly black high school:

> "There was nothing about the civil rights movement...the diverse black communities here, blacks in politics. It was just one big hip-hop talent show. It was BET (Black Entertainment Television) video, basketball, bling bling and hip-hop, that's what black culture was."

Whenever experts give conferences on issues of media effect, they unavoidably remind the public that parents have to exercise control over what children view, and that they should discuss potentially detrimental programs with children. The entertainment industry follows suit and shamelessly places the entire responsibility on parents' shoulders—*one additional family function*. How this responsibility affects parents and their relationship with their children is not addressed. At least one observational study has shown that, in a supermarket, 65 percent of all parents' refusals to buy food items advertised on television instantly resulted in parent-child conflict or arguments (Atkin, 1978). One can only wonder about the level of conflict that takes place in the privacy of the home when parents attempt to curtail television viewing (Alexander, 1994:52).

The Promotion of Sexuality

One also has to consider the impact of the media's sexual contents (Mitchell et al., 2001). For instance, Lowry and Towles (1989) compared the sexual content in soap operas in 1979 and 1987: There were more episodes depicting sexual behaviours per hour in 1987 than in 1979. The U.S. Kaiser Family Foundation (2003) also found that 64 percent of 1,123 randomly selected programs contained sexual material in the 2001–2002 season: 14 percent included sexual intercourse, up from seven percent only four years earlier. Nearly all soap operas and movies had sexual content, as did a majority of comedies, dramas, and talk shows. Greenberg and Busselle (1996) found that the average number of sexual incidents in soap operas increased from 3.7 per hour in 1983 to five in 1994. There was also an increase in sexual behaviours between unmarried characters. Lowry and Towles (1989) concluded that the 1987 contents gave the following messages:

- Nonmarital sex is the most exciting.
- Spontaneous sex is very romantic, especially between unmarried persons, and carries no consequences.
- All unmarried people engage in sex, often with several partners.
- Indiscriminate sex is not related to unplanned pregnancy and sexually transmitted diseases (STDs).

Sapolsky and Tabarlet (1991) also found that the majority of sexual action and language depicted on television involved unmarried characters. Bryant and Rockwell (1994) have reported that young teens who watch many programs that include nonmarital sex developed a more lenient attitude toward sexual improprieties. They also judged that victims of sexual infidelities and wrongdoings had been less harmed than did two control groups. One control group had watched little television while the other had watched only programs involving marital sex.

In Brazil, the country's famed soap operas broadcast nationally "have pushed the limits of permissiveness" in the 1990s. Reboucas (2002) links this observation to the fact that, by the late 1990s, the age of first sexual intercourse had declined: Of adolescents who had ever had sex, 40 percent had had intercourse before reaching the age of 14. Of these, 64 percent originated from single parent families.

The new genre of "reality" shows in 2003, such as *Temptation Island, The Bachelor, The Bachelorette,* and *EX-treme Dating* promotes sexuality, infidelity, lack of commitment, and superficiality in the selection of partners. Not only do these shows promote values that have been found to relate to low marital quality and high divorce rates, they do not represent reality. One can only wonder how adolescents are affected by such portrayals, whether in terms of expectations, attitudes, and behaviours in their own dating relationships (Orton, 1999:121). As may be the case for the effect of violence, the effect of sexuality on television may already have reached its saturation point, at least among adolescents, because American high schoolers initiate sexual intercourse in 2001 at a later age than in 1991 (U.S. Department of Health and Human Services, 2002a).

Television: An Educational Instrument

Children and adults use media presentations as a source of information (Glassner, 1999). Television has become for many what the critical sociologist Habermas (1987:16) called an insulating expertise that splits children and adults from "the context of everyday practice" and leads to cultural impoverishment. It is true that children are active social actors and participate in the reconstruction of the messages they receive from the media. However, they can make a realistic reconstruction only to the extent that the real world around them, particularly their families, their peers, and schools, offers them this alternative.

Yet, not all children benefit from such healthy alternatives. In fact, perhaps 25 percent of children do not have a home/peer/school environment that can counterbalance the negative effects of the media on their attitudes and behaviours. Furthermore, parents are also subjected to media contents of dubious value and many use talk shows as educational sources. Yet, the contents of these shows often focus on the sensational: conjugal infidelities, incest, child prostitution, mother-daughter rivalry over boyfriends, pregnancies of unknown paternity following intercourse with several sexual partners, and so on. Parents, especially the less educated, show great interest in these shows: What, then, can they teach their children (Austin, 2001)?

Children and Violence in Sports

Another related issue which society faces, often within the context of families, occurs both in the sports fields and especially on television: violence in sports (Coakley and Donnelly, 2004). This issue is salient because about 54 percent of children aged 5 to 14 regularly participate in organized sport activities, including 25 percent who play hockey (Kremarik, 2000b). In Canada, the problem centres on hockey violence—among professional players, among children on competitive teams, often by parents against coaches or other parents, and even in situations where parents encourage their sons to "beat up" opposing team members. At any rate, the constructs of masculinity as related to violence are evident in the culture of sports (Burstyn, 1999; Malszecki and Cavar, 2004). Perhaps one of the reasons some parents get "over-involved" in their children's sports activities is that a substantial proportion are themselves athletes or volunteers (Kremarik, 2000b).

Americans face this challenge as well but, in addition, the off-field behaviour of professional football and basketball celebrities is a concern: Many players have been arrested for criminally aggressive behaviours, including rape and murder. Too many have been implicated in fatal traffic and boating accidents, while others father children in an assembly line fashion! A July 18, 2003 *Toronto Star* article proclaims, "Bad boys of the NBA."

Violence in sports is a problem that plagues the entire society, and there is as yet no solid research on its effect on children's behaviours within the context of the family. When some fathers encourage their sons to behave aggressively in team sports, how do they relate to them at home? What do they allow them to do? And how are these children's mothers affected, both in terms of their relationships with their spouses and sons? When both parents participate in this cycle of sports violence, how does this translate later on in terms of a boy's definition of his masculinity and family dynamics?

THE NEW CULTURAL REVOLUTION: THE INTERNET

By the year 2000, 92 percent of students aged 15 and 16 living in cities with over 100,000 people had a computer at home, compared to 82 percent of rural students. Of these, 69 percent used the Internet at home. However, rural students accessed computers at school or in libraries to a far greater extent (Statistics Canada, 2003d). A survey conducted by Northstar Research Partners, also in 2000, found that 85 percent of teens aged 12 to 17 used the Internet regularly for a total of 9.3 hours a week, including e-mail (McHardie, 2000). Indeed, households with children still living at home are more likely to have the Internet (Statistics Canada, 2004l).

There are indications that the use of the computer displaces television to some extent (McHardie, 2000). However, a U.S. survey of first-year university students revealed that, during their last high-school year, they had spent less time on homework and studies and more on surfing the net (HERI, 2003). Hence, while the Internet displaces television to some extent, it also takes away from time spent on homework and studying. Canadian data clearly indicate that students aged 15 to 24 spend over an hour less studying and over one hour more in leisure activities than in 1986 (Fast et al., 2001). Children aged 9 to 17 report spending 38 percent of their online time on homework—while their parents' perception is that 68 percent of their children's time is so spent (Taylor, 2002)! Children's favourite online activities include downloading music and e-mailing, as well as visiting chat rooms. Internet users also read books and magazines less than nonusers (Williams, 2001a). These facts lead us to pause when we consider that 25 percent of elementary school children and 50 percent of high school students report that they have e-mail accounts of which their parents are unaware (Taylor, 2002).

As is the case with television, the Internet also contains dangers. First, it is far from an unmitigated blessing in terms of providing reliable information, because information is generally mixed with advertising. It is often difficult to assess the origin and accuracy of the material presented on websites (Hansell and Harmon, 1999). Erroneous and misleading information is too frequently accepted by a population that has faith in the power of technology to inform accurately. Second, it is estimated that there are thousands of websites throughout the world with pedophilic and pornographic content. The exploitation of children becomes more widespread because the Internet is not easily policed. A quarter of children aged 9 to 17 say in the survey that they intentionally enter porn sites, while 53 percent have ended up on such a site by accident (Taylor, 2002). This is hardly surprising if one considers that pornography constitutes at least 7 percent of the 3.3 billion web pages indexed by Google in 2003 (Paul, 2004). Furthermore, chat rooms that are preyed upon by pedophiles are a danger to children that parents have to monitor. As well, adult pornographic, racist, and hate websites are so easily accessible to children and adolescents that some schools have had to monitor closely their students' use of the Internet during class time. Finally, advertising and online shopping, which simply promote consumerism, should be mentioned.

What does the Internet do in terms of family life? To begin with, there are indications in the previous and following paragraphs that parents and children's cyber worlds diverge widely (Taylor, 2002). Kraut and colleagues (2002) found generally positive effects on communication, social involvement, and well-being in a small group of individuals studied over time about their home-use habits. But using the Internet gave more benefits to extroverts and to those who already had more social support; it had more negative effects for introverts and for those with less support. Many families took advantage of e-mail to keep in touch with their children in college and other relatives, and teenagers exchanged messages with their classmates after school. As well, some parents use the Internet in order to find information about various aspects of family life, including parenting (Morris et al., 1999). It is too soon, however, to predict the effect of the Internet on adolescents' social relationships. But there are indications that it can break senior citizens' social isolation when they are place-bound (Clark, 2001).

However, large-scale Canadian data analyzed by Williams (2001a) clearly indicate that a good minority of people cut down on visiting or talking with family (14 percent) and friends (13 percent) because of the time they spend on the Internet. Heavy Internet users are even more likely to reduce time interacting with family. Furthermore, after comparing the results of the 1998 and the 2000 General Social Surveys, Williams concluded that Internet users spend about 48 minutes less per day in social contact with others in their households, but spend about 72 minutes more in contact with people outside their households.

Internet use is even more individualistically oriented than television viewing. It follows that extensive Internet exposure by family members, often in their own separate bedrooms/studies, may contribute to lack of interaction and a loss of communication skills. In fact, while a majority of parents say that they talk to their children about the children's Internet activities, only 24 percent of children report the same. Furthermore, 83 percent are alone when they go online (Taylor, 2002). The Internet segments people as well as family members into interest groups and consequently prevents the growth of a sense of membership in a real community constituted of diverse individuals (Calhoun, 1998). But when properly used, the Internet also constitutes both a social (interaction) and a cultural (access to knowledge) resource.

As with other types of resources in a stratified society, access to the Internet is still to some extent reserved to those who can afford it (Clark, 2001). This has contributed to the "digital divide" between those families that are information rich and those that are information poor (Statistics Canada, 2003d). This divide, however, is narrowing; but girls are somewhat less likely to have a computer at home than boys. The largest difference exists in one-parent families, which have only a 50 percent chance of having a computer compared to two-parent families (Willms and Corbett, 2003).

The next few years will indicate the direction the Internet is taking culturally and the type of use family members will make of it. But, as Williams (2001b) points out, when we include all the modes of electronic communication in the possession of all family members and the incessant recourse to them many make (particularly cell phones), we may well be "too connected" in general—but, one might fear, less so with our family in terms of face-to-face interaction.

CONCLUSIONS: FAMILIES HAVE TO BE REEMPOWERED

The research summarized and evaluated in this chapter does not support the pessimistic view of a general family decline and loss of functions. Rather, the research supports pessimism concerning individual families' ability to fulfill their ever-increasing functions adequately, particularly that of the socialization of children. On the one hand, the family as an institution is highly valued and demands are placed on it in terms of its responsibilities in many domains. But, on the other hand, this same sociocultural context generally fails to provide individual families with equivalent moral support and practical help that could allow them to fulfill their functions.

For instance, society is choosing to embrace information technology and market forces as values and as a way of life. Unavoidably, there are high costs to such a choice and families bear a disproportionate burden in this respect, especially those that are marginalized by poverty, segregation, and lack of access to the new types of jobs. As Blank (1997:198) phrases it, given that our society "has chosen a market-oriented economy, it has a responsibility to those who cannot survive in the market on their own." This responsibility should not be displaced onto families. Unfortunately, this is exactly what is happening.

As Hewlett and West (1998:34) point out, too many conservatives fail to recognize the ways in which market values are destroying families and family values. For their part, too many on the liberal side, with their emphasis on rights and freedoms, "fail to understand that we need to rein in untrammeled individualism if we are to recreate the values that nurture family life." The family is the cornerstone of society because it reproduces and socializes its future workers, citizens, taxpayers, and leaders. Thus, a private institution subsidizes an entire society. When families "fail," largely due to income and cultural causes within the same society, such families produce society's future unemployed, welfare recipients, and even criminals. In other words, what happens within the family impacts the entire society just as the economic and cultural agenda of society impacts its families. There is an incessant feedback dynamic between the private and the public spheres of life—between the family and society at large.

Nevertheless, despite this feedback, in most western societies the family is a small and relatively isolated unit in terms of the support it receives while being much affected by its environment (Corsaro, 1997). In recent decades, this cultural and socioeconomic environment has broadened considerably because of globalization and a more pervasive as well as intrusive technology. At the dawn of the new millennium, families experience change at a rapid pace, are contextualized in a larger world, but receive relatively fewer resources in terms of instrumental and effective moral support. Empowering families, no matter their structure, is one of the key social challenges of the 21st century.

Summary

1. Although the family has lost a few traditional functions, it has gained a number of new ones. Its main functions are reproducing, socializing the child, coordinating and managing the external services children receive, stabilizing personalities, meeting affective needs, and providing a sense of belongingness, health care, a place to live, and care of family members who have special needs. There is an overabundance of family functions created by a lack of social support. Thus, too many individual families are unable to fulfill their functions, which should not be taken to mean a loss of functions by the family as an institution.

2. Children spend more time outside of their families and have become defamilialized. Childhood has become more structured in terms of activities than in the past. Children produce "childwork"—that is, work that adults do to educate them and organize their activities. Thus, children are useful to society via their schoolwork and the childwork they produce for the employment of adults. But children in industrialized nations are separated from adults, whereas in non-industrialized societies, they are fully integrated into village life and their parents' work and are totally familialized. This is in contrast to a high level of defamilialization in many western countries.

3. An important historical development took place at the cultural level between 1951 and 1955, as nearly two-thirds of the nation's homes acquired a television set. As people watched television, less time was left for the development of certain skills and family sociability. A historical overview of the trends in television programming pertaining to family life and norms highlights the changes in the content of programs as the decades went by. Family sitcoms are among young children's favourite programs, as children can identify with the child characters. For adolescents particularly, the tone and depiction of sexual content in soap operas has changed and carries messages favouring nonmarital sex.

4. Specific media influences include the promotion of violence, consumerism, and sexuality.

5. The Internet, the latest cultural revolution, contains both positive and negative seeds in terms of child socialization and family relations. It can lead to an increase in social isolation and lack of family participation. The Internet is even more individualistically oriented than television viewing is.

6. Sociologists are generally concerned that certain types of family structure are not sufficiently supported by the economy and the polity. Another concern is the potentially negative impact of the rapid pace of technological change.

Key Concepts and Themes

Analytical Questions

1. Now that you have completed this chapter, re-visit Analytical Question 1 in Chapter 1: What more can you say?
2. Can you think of additional functions that families fulfill in Canada, and especially in other countries?
3. Several European sociologists adopt the position that children should be defamilialized. Can you discuss this perspective?
4. What are some of the changes that have marked the development of television programming since its beginning? Add others you can think of that are not included in the text.
5. Write down a hypothetical time diary that would illustrate your family life on a daily basis this coming week, were you without television, Internet, and cell phones.

Suggested Readings

Bird, G. W., and Sporakowski, M. J. (Eds.) 1994. *Taking sides: Clashing views on controversial issues in family and personal relationships.* Guilford, CT: Dushkin. This collection of articles presents opposite perspectives on various issues pertaining to family life and intimate relationships.

Côté, J. E., and Allahar, A. L. 1994. *Generation on hold: Coming of age in the late twentieth century.* Toronto: Stoddart. This book provides the economic and sociocultural context, including media influences, on the development of the concept of adolescence and on adolescence itself.

Stacey, J. 1996. *In the name of the family: Rethinking family values in the postmodern era.* Boston: Beacon Press. The focus here is on the postmodern family, with change and diversity as key characteristics. The author responds to critiques of family change and recognizes the instability inherent to current structural arrangements. She makes some interesting points concerning gay and lesbian families.

Van Enra, J. 1998. *Television and child development.* Mahwah, NJ: Erlbaum. This book presents a balanced review of the domain as well as some theoretical perspectives.

Zillman, D., Bryant, J., and Huston, A. C. (Eds.) 1994. *Media, children, and the family.* Hillsdale, NJ: Erlbaum. This is a collection of research and review articles on various aspects of family life related to television consumption, including some information on the effect on family interaction. The effect of television contents on children is also examined.

Suggested Weblinks

Canadian Families Project provides some information about the historical approach to the study of families.

http://web.uvic.ca/hrd/cfp

Children Now: The goal of this site is to improve the quality of news and entertainment both for children and about children.

www.childrennow.org

Electronic Policy Network is a collection of member organizations that focus on policy and research concerning the web. Click on *Media*.

http://tap.epn.org/cms

Media Awareness Network provides reports on the use of the Internet by youth, on media portrayal of minorities, and on violence.

www.media.awareness.ca

SafeSurfer: This site provides information on how to make the Internet safer for children and to improve the quality of programming in the media.

www.safesurf.com

PART 2

Social and Cultural Family Contexts

Part 1 has helped us to begin understanding how family formation and dynamics are affected by large sociocultural forces. Gender stratification and the media were analyzed as important contexts impacting on family life. We have also seen how these contexts often create barriers impeding the fulfillment of family functions. Part 2 focuses directly on four additional key environmental influences on family life. This focus allows us to pursue some of the themes that are central to this text—namely, those of social inequalities, family functions, as well as the role of the effective community.

Chapter 4 discusses how families are affected by and adapt to immigration as well as to their ethnic-racial status or diversity.

Chapter 5 describes how the recent changes in the economy have affected both family formation and family members' life course opportunities. A special focus is placed on economic inequalities.

In **Chapter 6,** we turn to the topic of families' neighbourhoods and housing conditions for an in-depth look at how these contexts affect families' lives, particularly child socialization.

Chapter 7 examines the role of two key institutions on family life: education and religion. Both constitute cultural contexts by what they teach; they also constitute a social environment of interactions and potential communities. In this chapter, education is analyzed via child care and schools. In terms of religion, the presentation focuses on religiosity rather than simply religious membership.

CHAPTER 4

Cultural Diversity and Adaptation: Canada's Ethnic and Immigrant Families

Chapter by Catherine Krull, Queen's University

"The most painful part of my life was when I had to leave my grandmother in Jamaica and come here to my mother I had seen only a few times in ten years. I didn't know her and I hated her and I refused to do anything she asked.... Even to this day we aren't close but at least I can feel for her terrible situation." [This student's brother is now in a penitentiary.]

"At that age [10–14] it was total rebellion at home: My parents were first generation immigrants but I was born here and I wanted nothing to do with being different, poor, them having an accent, not being allowed out at night with the others.... Now looking back I realize that it must have been a horrible time for my parents: They only wanted the best for me."

"I am very happy to be in Canada because the country where I come from does not value girls. In Canada I can be anything I want. I just have to study hard. Even my father respects his daughters now." [20-year-old Iranian university student]

"I thought that I had made new friends at school and I would sit with them at lunch every day. About two months after I came to this country, the girls at the lunch table said that they didn't want someone from a 'hick' country sitting at their table. They said that they were sorry and that they knew it was not my fault but it would be better if I ate at a different table." [13-year-old Canadian girl who recently moved from the U.S.]

These students' comments exemplify the number of ways in which ethnic and immigrant status can profoundly affect people's lives and that of their families. This chapter focuses on Canada's more recent immigrant population and its resulting ethnic and family diversity. Following a brief introduction about immigration to clarify important terminology and to highlight Canada's immigration trends and policies, some of Canada's recent immigrant families are presented. Lastly, the impact of globalization on Canadian migration is discussed.

IMMIGRANT FAMILIES

Often one speaks of immigrant families as if they shared common characteristics and experiences, even though there is a great deal of diversity amongst them. For instance, families differ in their reasons for coming to this country, in how they are received, and in their levels of adjustment. Migration is a process rather than a one-time event for, as Ralson (1997:44) points out, it "involves not only leaving a homeland and crossing territorial borders but also continuously crossing social, psychic and symbolic borders which define identity, relations, membership, belonging, meaning systems and worldviews of the realities of everyday life." Hence, for many, migration involves an ongoing process of constructing new identities (Talbani and Hasanali, 2000). Moreover, many immigrants have to negotiate their everyday experiences in the context of prejudice and discrimination.

Ethnic and Minority Groups

The concept of nationality is not the overriding element in understanding the nature of immigrants and their families because most nations in the world are composed of a number of ethnic groups. For instance, British immigrant families can be English, Scottish, Welsh, or Irish. In this context, an **ethnic group** is one that is set apart from others because of its unique cultural patterns (including family structures), history, and language, as well as a sense of distinctiveness. Thus, ethnicity can be assigned based on a country of origin (for example, Germany, Iran, Cuba), a region within a country (as with the Québécois or Irish), a religion (as with people who self-identify as Jewish), or on other classifications (such as race, for example, by individuals who identify themselves as black).

A **minority group** is one that is given inferior status and less power in a society because of its ethnicity, cultural practices, or religion. In Canada, the term typically refers to people who come directly or indirectly from Asia, Latin America, and Africa, and excludes white, Caucasian, and Aboriginal people who comprise the majority of Canada's population (Beaujot and Kerr, 2004). Minority groups are often deprived of resources and opportunities taken for granted by the group or groups that are in the majority or in power. Approximately 80 percent of all recent immigrants to Canada, or 13 percent of the Canadian population, can be classified as belonging to a **visible minority group**. The largest, the Chinese, constitutes 4 percent of the national population; they are followed by South Asians at 3 percent, and blacks at 2.2 percent (Statistics Canada, 2001). Immigrants who belong to visible minority groups are more likely to be economically disadvantaged, despite their having higher educational and occupational status than the more established Canadians of European origins (Kalbach and Kalbach, 1999). For example, 35 percent of recent immigrant women and 38 percent of recent immigrant men have some university education compared to 28 percent of Canadian-born women and 26 percent of Canadian-born men (Statistics Canada, 2001). Despite having more education, recent immigrant women earned $7,500 less, and immigrant men $13,000 less per year, than their respective Canadian-born counterparts (Statistics Canada, 2001).

Immigrants can also be classified by how long their families have been in Canada. In 2001, 22 percent of the population who were 15 years of age and over considered themselves to be **first generation immigrants** (born outside of Canada); 16 percent classified themselves as **second generation immigrants** (born in Canada to parents born outside of Canada); and 61 percent responded that they were **third or subsequent generation immigrants** (they and their parents were born in Canada but their grandparents or even more distant kin were born outside of Canada [Statistics Canada, 2001]). As this chapter will show, intergenerational analysis is important in understanding continuity and change amongst immigrant families (McDaniel, 2000, 2001). This is particularly the case with first- and second-generation immigrants, the latter of whom are often torn between Canadian values and traditional values brought from their parents' homeland.

A Profile of Canada's Immigration Trends

In 2001, 5.5 million immigrants were living in Canada, representing 18 percent of the total population (Statistics Canada, 2001). Since 1990, approximately 220,000 immigrants have arrived in Canada every year, compared to 126,000 per year during the 1980s. However, as Figure 4.1 shows, the number of immigrants entering Canada in any particular year has fluctuated over the past 150 years and the current numbers are not historical highs.

Five distinct phases of immigration can be identified in Figure 4.1: 1860–1896; 1897–1913; 1914–1945; 1946–1989; and 1990 to the present (Beaujot and Kerr, 2004: 97). The first phase (1860–1896), at a time when the Canadian population was still relatively small, was characterized by high numbers of immigrants arriving in Canada but with even larger numbers of people who left Canada for the U.S. where more attractive jobs were plentiful. During the second phase (1897–1913), historically high

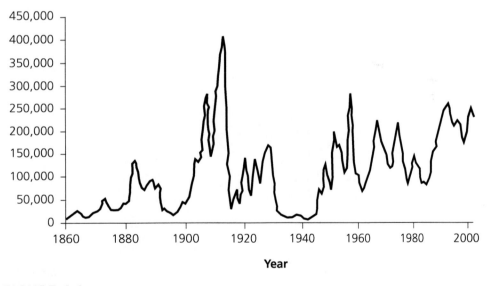

FIGURE 4.1

Number of Immigrants Arriving in Canada per Year, 1860–2002

Source: Statistics Canada. 2002g. "Immigration—Historical Perspective (1860–2002)." *Citizenship and Immigration Canada. Facts and Figures: Immigration Overview.* Catalogue MP43-333/2003E, p. 3.

numbers of immigrants came from the British Isles and, to a lesser extent, central and southern Europe to settle in the Prairies. The third phase (1914–1945) was a period of fluctuation in which immigration collapsed during the First World War, picked up during the 1920s, and then collapsed again during the Depression years and the Second World War. The majority of immigrants in this third phase were British, followed by Germans/Austrians, Scandinavians, and Ukrainians. The fourth phase (1946–1989) was characterized by high peaks, reflecting the high number of immigrants (almost 6 million people) who came to Canada during the post-war years. The fifth and most recent phase (1990 to the present) is characterized by a period of sustained high numbers (above 200,000 immigrants per year with the exception of 1998 and 1999, when the figure drops just below 200,000). Approximately three-quarters of all recent immigrants settled in Toronto, Vancouver, and Montreal; one-fifth of Toronto's and Vancouver's population consists of immigrants who have arrived in Canada since 1981 (Beaujot and Kerr, 2004).

One of the major differences concerning Canada's current phase of migration is that immigrant countries of origin have changed significantly. Figure 4.2 indicates that between 1991 and 2001, approximately 58 percent of all recent immigrants came from

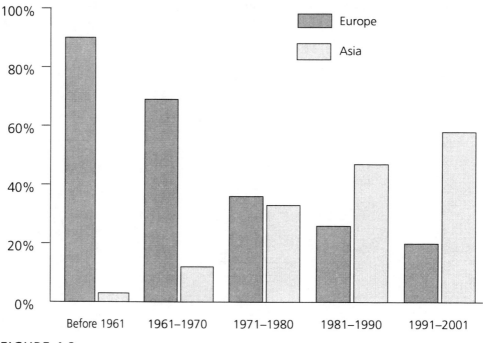

FIGURE 4.2

Proportion of Immigrants Born in Europe and Asia, by Period of Immigration, Canada

Source: Statistics Canada. 2003. *The People: Bring your Families to Canada.* http://142.206.72.67/02/02a_ graph_02a_graph_005_1e.htm#t01, extracted April 13, 2004.

Asian countries but only 20 percent came from European countries, the latter of which have traditionally supplied the majority of immigrants to Canada. Then, as shown in Figure 4.3, the largest percentage of immigrants came from China (15 percent), followed by India (13 percent), Pakistan (6 percent), the Philippines (5 percent), and Iran (3 percent). Moreover, there have been substantial increases in immigrants from Africa, the Caribbean, and South America. As a result of this shift in countries of origin, the cultural and ethnic profile of Canadian families has been and continues to be considerably transformed.

These changes in source countries are reflected in the diversity of languages that are spoken in Canada. Although the majority of the population speaks one or both of Canada's official languages, the top five non-official languages are Chinese, Italian, German, Punjabi, and Spanish (Statistics Canada, 2001). More than half of the immigrants who came to Canada between 1991 and 1996 speak a language other than French or English at home, and about 10 percent of males and 14 percent of females in this group do not know an official language. In contrast, immigrants who have lived longer in Canada tend to use one of the official languages even within the intimacy of their family settings, and fewer do not know an official language (Beaujot and Kerr, 2004).

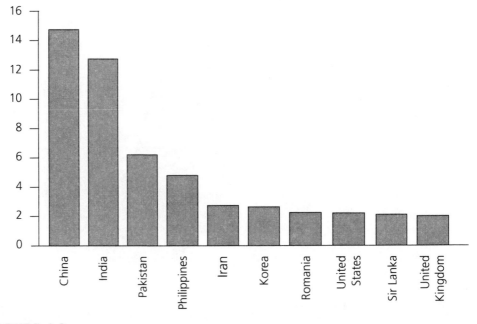

FIGURE 4.3

Percentages of Immigrants by Top Ten Source Countries (Principal Applicants and Dependants), 2002

Source: Statistics Canada. 2002g. "Immigration by Source Country." *Citizenship and Immigration Canada. Facts and Figures: Immigration Overview*. Catalogue MP43-333/2003E, p. 8.

Canada's Immigration Policies and Family Reunification

Canada's immigration policy dates back to the *Free Grants and Homestead Act* of 1868, which was designed to advance population growth, particularly in the Prairies, by promoting massive immigration from countries that the government of the day deemed suitable. Explicitly racist immigration policies restricted several ethnic groups from entering Canada (Harrison and Friesen, 2004). Even when individuals from countries that were discriminated against were given permission to work in Canada, most were prevented from bringing over family members, as was the case for Chinese immigrants. Thus, Canada has a long history of implementing racist policies that not only prevented certain people from immigrating here but also prevented family re-unification. It was not until the 1960s that the federal government removed immigration criteria relating to race or place of origin (Beaujot and Kerr, 2004).

Canada's current immigration policy has three objectives: to reunite families; to foster a strong and viable economy in all regions of the country; and to fulfill Canada's international legal obligations and compassionate and humanitarian traditions respecting refugees. Figure 4.4 shows that the majority of immigrants are admitted into Canada for economic reasons, while the least number are admitted as refugees. Women are more likely than men to immigrate to Canada as family-class immigrants or as the wife of an economic applicant, whereas men are more likely to reach Canada under the economic applicant classification.

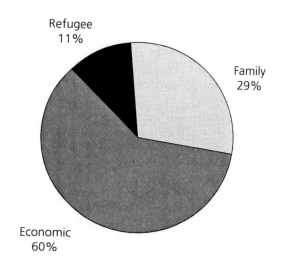

FIGURE 4.4

Percentage of Immigrants Admitted to Canada as Permanent Residents by Category, 2002 (Principal Applicants and Dependants)

Source: Statistics Canada. 2002g. "Immigration by Level." *Citizenship and Immigration Canada. Facts and Figures: Immigration Overview*. Catalogue MP43-333/2003E, p. 5.

CANADA'S FOUNDING FAMILIES

The longest-standing families in Canada are primarily from three groups: First Nations, the Québécois, and the British. These groups differ from one another in history, culture, language, and family structures. Chapter 2 focused on early Aboriginal families and British and French families up to the early 20th century. Modern Canada is still dominated by British ethnicity, with 49 percent of the population claiming British ancestry (Statistics Canada, 2001). The dominance of the English language outside of Quebec, the power of British religious denominations—Anglican, Presbyterian, and even Roman Catholicism—and the residual power of the British parliamentary system at the federal and provincial levels constitute key elements of British-origin supremacy. Given the cultural strength of anglophone Canada—abetted by the American media—British norms, including those relating to the family, dominate. As this chapter is concerned with how minority groups and their family structures have fared in modern Canada, we will look first at contemporary First Nations and Québécois families.

Aboriginal Families

Canada's Aboriginal peoples include First Nations (Native Indians), the Métis, and the Inuit. As we saw in Chapter 2, Aboriginal families—the first and therefore the oldest families in Canada—were complex and diverse social institutions (Deveaus, 2000). Today, 1,365,090 Canadians, or about 5 percent of the Canadian population, claim Aboriginal ancestry, and about 550,000 of these individuals are registered as status Indians (Statistics Canada, 2003l). Approximately 58 percent of status Indians live on one of the 2,284 **reserves** throughout the country. Reserves are lands that have been set aside by the Canadian government explicitly for Aboriginal peoples (Harrison and Friesen, 2004:228). The primary unit of First Nations social structure is the **band**, which originally described small cultural and linguistic groups who either lived together or came together at various times of the year (Harrison and Friesen, 2004). In more recent times, a band refers to an administrative unit that operates under the *Indian Act* of 1876. There are currently 621 bands in Canada, with about 500 members in each (Frideres, 2000).

As discussed in Chapter 2, part of the Canadian government's assimilation program entailed isolating First Nations children from their families by placing them in residential schools. The primary objective was to purge the children of all traditional cultural identifiers. The end result has been a legacy of trauma with which the First Nations people are still trying to cope. For example, because they were isolated from their own families, students of residential schools were deprived of nurturing and of First Nations familial role models (Das Gupta, 2000). Poor parenting skills subsequently prompted Children's Aid Services to remove many First Nations children from their families. A 1979 Canadian report on adoption and welfare found that 20 percent of children in foster care were Aboriginal children, a high figure considering that only 6 percent of the Canadian population was First Nations (Das Gupta, 2000). Until the 1980s, non-Aboriginal families both inside and outside Canada adopted many of these children through foster care programs. Thus, a vicious cycle emerged: Children were removed from their families, placed in residential schools, and made to live in sometimes abhorrent conditions. As a result, many of these children now lack parenting skills with their own children. Rather than dealing with the consequences of its policies, the government acted once again by tearing children away from their families and placing them in a non-Aboriginal environment. Thus, not only were the students affected by the government's residential schools, but subsequent generations and traditional family life have suffered as well.

The effects of the residential schools have also contributed to intergenerational violence. In fact, the prevalence of family violence is much higher in many First Nations communities than in others. In this context, First Nations women and children are the ones most frequently abused; between 75 and 90 percent of women in some northern Aboriginal communities and 80 percent of Aboriginal women in Ontario have experienced some form of family violence (Dumont-Smith and Sioui-Labelle, 1991). It is interesting to note that despite the family and cultural devastation that has been associated with the residential schools, it took the federal government until the 1980s before the last was closed. At that time, the administration of most reserve schools was handed over to Aboriginal school boards (Harrison and Friesen, 2004).

Notwithstanding the damages incurred by the residential school system, massive numbers of Aboriginal children were also taken from their homes and adopted by non-Aboriginal families. "In many cases, children were taken from parents whose only crime was poverty—and being aboriginal" (Fournier and Crey, 1997:85). The impact of forced foster care and adoption had devastating effects on the children involved, on their families, and on Aboriginal communities, as several reserves lost approximately a generation of their children (Johnston, 1983). As one woman recalls: "Our family life was shattered after seven of my eight siblings and I were split apart into separate foster homes. We were never again to reunite as a family" (Fournier and Crey, 1997:85). There were so many Aboriginal children adopted out during the 1960s that Patrick Johnston, a researcher for the Canadian Council on Social Development, referred to this mass exodus of children as the "Sixties Scoop." However, as Fournier and Crey (1997:88) point out, "the wholesale abduction of aboriginal children has persisted long past that decade. By the late 1970s, one in four status Indian children could expect to be separated from his or her parents for all or part of childhood." Today, one-third of legal wards in British Columbia are First Nations children.

Another harmful effect of Canada's assimilation policies has been the deterioration of the Aboriginal languages, especially given the importance that language has in maintaining cultural identity, an important part of which is family life. Of the 50 distinct Aboriginal languages once spoken in Canada, only three are now considered secure: Cree, Inuktitut, and Ojibway. The remaining languages have either disappeared or are spoken by only a few people, which explains why the United Nations Educational, Scientific, and Cultural Organization (UNESCO) has declared Canada's Aboriginal languages among the most endangered in the world (Beaujot and Kerr, 2004).

Poverty is another factor that has had an impact on many First Nations families who tend to have the lowest living standard of any other family group in the country. Using the same index used by the United Nations Development Programme, which consistently ranks Canada as one of the best places to live in the world, Beavon and Cooke

(2003) found that persons designated as "status Indian" and living on reserves would be ranked seventy-ninth. This is only slightly higher than Mexico and Brazil (Beaujot and Kerr, 2004). Canadian Aboriginal peoples suffer from high unemployment rates, substandard housing conditions, and inadequate health care and educational services, which accounts for their having the lowest education, income, and health levels in the country (Frideres, 2000). This has also affected their family life, as they have significantly higher infant mortality rates and substantially lower life expectancies (Harrison and Friesen, 2004). Because of poverty, lack of employment, and generations of family breakdown caused by the residential school system and the forced adoption of Aboriginal children, the suicide rate among Aboriginal peoples is, on average, between two to seven times that of the national population.

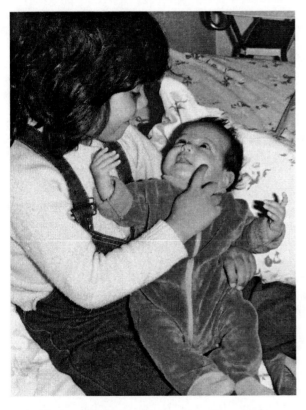

First Nations families are, on average, larger and younger than other families in Canada. In Aboriginal communities, many of the childrearing functions fulfilled by parents in Canadian society at large are shared with relatives, including older children. Sibling influence may be even more important on Aboriginal reserves compared to its importance in society at large—a hypothesis that remains to be tested.

Nonetheless, although many traditional First Nations family structures have ceased to exist, either because of government policies or because of a mass movement from reserves to cities where non-Aboriginals form the majority, "the notion of the caring, effective, extended family, co-extensive with community, continues to be a powerful ideal etched deep in the psyche of Aboriginal people" (Castellano, 2002:16). The importance of the extended family in terms of social identity, economic support, and psychological nurturing cannot be overstated. Fiske and Johnny (2003:182) argue that the "importance of family and kin relations takes precedence over all other emotional and social ties in most, if not all, First Nations communities." Their kin networks are twice as extensive as those of other Canadians, and they are able to identify over 50 different familial relationships to people living with them (Buchignani and Armstrong, 1999). Moreover, Aboriginals are the fastest growing group in Canada. This is primarily due to an increased tendency to identify as Aboriginal, a renewed pride in their unique heritage, and high fertility rates that, although declining over the past four decades, remain one and one-half times higher than the Canadian average of 1.5 children per woman (Statistics Canada, 2003l). The Inuit have the highest fertility rate, with an average of 3.4 children per woman, followed by status Indians with 2.8 children per woman, the Métis with 2.4 children per woman, and non-status Indians with 2.0 children per woman (Beaujot and Kerr, 2004).

FAMILY RESEARCH 4.1

Doing Research on Aboriginal Families

In the 1996 *Report of the Royal Commission on Aboriginal Peoples*, guidelines were established to direct research on issues relating to Canada's Aboriginal peoples. The specific purpose was "to ensure that...appropriate respect is given to the use by Aboriginal peoples to legitimate knowledge." After outlining a series of principles, specific guidelines were placed in the context of the following concepts: understanding Aboriginal knowledge so as "to correct misinformation or to challenge ethnocentric and racist interpretations"; conducting collaborative research with Aboriginal communities; allowing open public access to research results; ensuring research must benefit the Aboriginal community; and monitoring the guidelines.

In terms of the study of families and women, some guidelines were especially important; for instance, that research portraying the multiplicity of viewpoints present within Aboriginal communities be represented fairly, including viewpoints specific to age and gender groups; that informed consent of parents or guardians and, where practical, of children be obtained in research involving children; and that for community-based research, researchers shall give serious and due consideration to the benefit of the community concerned.

In her seminal study of Aboriginal women, Carolyn Kenny (2002) sought to emphasize the importance of Aboriginal women's voices through participatory research: conducting face-to-face interviews, focus groups, and soliciting feedback in eight Aboriginal communities across Canada. The research team worked to ensure liaisons with each community to plan the research, to educate all participants about the research, and to use elders as advisors. In Kenny's view, this project entailed "action research" because it encouraged Aboriginal women to take responsibility for policy by making their own recommendations. One woman's viewpoint encapsulated Kenny's efforts: "When women heal, the family will heal and when the family heals, the community will heal and when the community heals, the nation will heal" (p. 54).

Within an extended family structure, elders tend to be respected and identified as key sources of tradition and wisdom (Buchignani and Armstrong, 1999). Most First Nations elders live with their children or another family member. Elder care is primarily informal, an arrangement which is consistent with traditional values that emphasize familial obligation. Both elder care and visits to elderly family members are most often done by women, especially daughters. However, despite deep-rooted values of elder respect and an informal care system, elderly First Nations people tend to face more hardships than other Canadian elders. For example, First Nations seniors have a total income that is typically below the poverty line. Even more difficult is the fact that many elderly First Nations people support their unemployed children, which means that an entire extended family lives on less income than that required for bare subsistence (McPherson, 1998). Along the same lines, disability rates for First Nations seniors are twice the national average and nursing care facilities on reserves are rare, which forces many elders to live in nursing homes away from their families and friends. In a survey on informal care and older Native Canadians, Buchignani and Armstrong (1999) found that 59 percent of First Nations elders claimed that their income was inadequate for their needs, while 63 percent said that they had no money left at the end of a month. Moreover, they were three times more likely to report their health as "fair" or "less than fair" than other Canadians of comparable age.

Over the past few decades, Aboriginal people have developed strategies to achieve self-determination and self-government. The federal government is currently negotiating various forms of self-government with approximately 90 different indigenous groups across Canada (Frideres, 2000). There have also been strong collective efforts to renew traditional knowledge, values, and customs. Thus, First Nations families have demanded the right to teach their young people and to develop a curriculum that embraces Aboriginal practices and ways of knowing. Given the importance of language in "the transmission and survival of Aboriginal knowledge and culture," the revival of First Nations language is viewed as pivotal to this process (Harrison and Friesen, 2004: 245). The family is fundamental to these efforts to revive the cultures of First Nations people. Changes are now occurring within First Nations families, and the most important of these are an increasing ability to control the education of their young people, a revival of traditional languages, and a determination to take charge of social services and child welfare.

Québécois Families

Since the early 1960s, Quebec society has seen fundamental changes to family life. In 1960, a reformist Liberal government, led by Premier Jean Lesage, took power in Quebec. The Lesage government wanted to modernize the province and strengthen the French language and Québécois culture against anglophone Canada and the U.S., and so undertook wide-ranging reforms that profoundly changed Quebec. This period became known as the "Quiet Revolution" (Behiels, 1986; Comeau, 1989; Thomson, 1984). In this process, the Quebec economy shifted to one based less on agriculture and more on finance and industrialization; Québécois began to replace anglophones in leadership roles, and the French language was used increasingly in the workplace. In social policy, the power of the Roman Catholic Church was curtailed: Its domination of education was replaced by secular government control and its influence over moral issues such as the prohibition on divorce was diminished. As well, the Church's political alliance with the conservative Quebec political elite was broken.

Equally important in terms of family life, women's rights were expanded and entrenched (Clio Collective, 1987). Before the Quiet Revolution, women had few property rights, limited access to education beyond primary school (even then concentrating in the domestic sciences), and few legal rights. The Church and the political elite saw Québécois women principally as mothers and as producers of large numbers of children who would ensure that the province's unique culture and the French language were not overwhelmed by the anglophone majority surrounding them. The Quiet Revolution brought about a sharp decrease in religiosity; access to divorce; access to contraception; significant increases in cohabitation; more nonmarital births; and even voluntary childlessness (Langlois et al., 1992). In this way, Québécois society went from exceptionally high and sustained reproductive levels—spanning more than 300 years—to fertility rates that have now reached historic lows (Krull, 2000).

Nationalism, **pronatalism**, and feminism are powerful elements in understanding contemporary Quebec families. Québécois feminists, a relatively small group in 1960, supported the Lesage reforms. But by the end of the decade, as Quebec feminists became more organized, the province experienced a second wave of feminism. Women's groups developed at an astonishing pace and by 1985, there were more than 300 of these groups involved in political action (Dumont, 1995). Women's roles had changed; therefore, so did family life. Marriage rates have followed an accelerated pattern of decline since the early 1970s, dropping from 8.2 per 1,000 population in 1971 to only 3.3 in 1995, well below the national average of 5.4. Divorce is now over 50 percent higher in Quebec than in the rest of Canada (Chung, 2003). The percentage of never-married individuals at age 50 is almost twice as high in Quebec as in other provinces, and the average age at marriage is about one year later (Krull, 2003). Moreover, by 1991 (and as discussed in Chapters 7 and 8), Quebec had the lowest proportion of married-couple families in all of Canada: 69 percent compared to 80 percent in the other provinces. In fact, 58 percent of Quebec children are now born outside of marriage compared to 33 percent in Ontario (Chung, 2003).

The rapid decline of Quebec's birthrate since 1960 clearly changed family structures in the province, as large nuclear families were replaced by smaller ones and many were led by single or cohabiting parents. This situation has proved problematic in relations between women's groups and Quebec nationalists, including those who want sovereignty for the province. On the one hand, many women's leaders and feminist groups support Quebec nationalism. But nationalists see the decline of Quebec's francophone population relative to the anglophone population of Canada and the U.S. (Henripin and Péron, 1972). In their estimation, for Quebec nationalism and the French language to survive—even if sovereignty is impossible—francophone women must produce more babies (Baker, 1994; Lavigne, 1986). However, Québécois women increasingly control their own lives—cohabiting or marrying as they like; pursuing education and careers; gaining financial independence; and limiting the number of children they will have, by using contraception. As one francophone student from Quebec points out:

> "I find that girls here [Ontario] are less independent than at home especially when it comes to becoming mothers. Here they all say they want children but it was not like that at UQAM, many of us didn't want any or [wanted] only one. I have two older sisters and they both put their babies in childcare and don't have any problem with this. Here I noticed that women are more hung-up about this.... They still feel guilty about it.... Women also breastfeed longer in Montreal than in Toronto.... Anyways...I met this guy but I am worried that his family will find me too liberal for them. So that's my problem right now, figuring out where to go."

To push their agendas in the 1980s and 1990s, both Liberal and Parti Québécois provincial governments supported pronatal policies (Ansen, 2000; Krull and Pierce, 1997). Financial rewards were available for women who had multi-child families: $500 for a first birth, $1,000 for the second, and $8,000 for the third and for each subsequent birth. Incentives also included a family allowance for all children under 18 years and an additional allowance for children under age six (Baril et al., 2000). Québécois feminists argued that by advancing pronatal policies, the Quebec government was supporting a "traditional" family structure in which women are valued primarily for their domestic role. In fact, some feminists argued that the so-called fertility crisis was fabricated by nationalists (Baker, 1994; Maroney, 1992; Hamilton, 1995). Accordingly, the birthrate did not increase and Quebec abandoned its pronatal policies in favour of pro-family policies. As renowned Quebec demographer Lapierre-Adamcyk stated about Quebec's current policies, "the intention is not so clearly directly pronatalist as it is a way to recognize that people who have children are doing something for society" (in Chung, 2003). In 2000, for instance, Quebec introduced a progressive, government-subsidized daycare program for working families, which operated twenty-four hours a day, seven days a week at a cost of only $5 per day per child (Dougherty and Jelow-icki, 2000). With the cost now at $7 per day, the program has a waiting list of up to three years. Yet, because every subsidized daycare in Quebec follows a formal, age-appropriate curriculum that emphasizes school readiness and basic skills such as language and socialization, the Canadian Policy Research Network points out that "Quebec is the only province in Canada that has made a commitment to early-childhood education, and not just daycare" (Anderssen and McIlroy, 2004). In addition, the provincial government is proposing to expand its provision for parental leave. Overall, Quebec families receive nearly $4 billion annually in direct and income-tax assistance from the provincial and federal governments.

Despite Quebec's smaller families, Québécois culture and the French language remain as strong and durable as ever. Although the nexus of nationalism, feminism, and pronatalism still exists in Quebec and the debate has yet to be resolved, there is no doubt that families in Quebec have altered significantly over the past 40 years.

OLDER IMMIGRANT FAMILIES: ITALIAN-CANADIAN FAMILIES

By coming to this country to pursue new lives and find new opportunities, immigrant groups other than the French and British have transformed the Canadian social and cultural mosaic. Italian Canadians provide a telling example of an older immigrant group with unique cultural traditions and family structure that, over time, has melded into Canadian society while retaining many of its traditions and adhering to the importance of family. Italians began to arrive in significant numbers in the late 19th century. Between 1870 and 1900, Italian immigration to Canada was steady if unspectacular; by 1901, there were 10,834 Italian Canadians here (Vangelisti, 1956). Between 1900 and 1914, however, immigration exploded: By 1911, Italian immigrants to Canada numbered 45,963. Although the First World War reduced immigration, once peace returned, Italian immigration resumed: The prosperous 1920s saw 26,183 new arrivals (Ramirez, 1989:7). In the 1930s, as immigration was restricted to protect Canadian workers during the Great Depression, only 3,898 Italians arrived. Then in 1940, Italy's fascist dictator, Benito Mussolini, aligned Italy with Nazi Germany, and Canada, as an ally of Great Britain, went to war against Germany and Italy. The immigration of Italians came to a halt.

After the Second World War, Italian immigration to Canada resumed, and by 1981, over 500,000 Italians had come to this country—an immigrant group second in size only to that from the British Isles (Sturino, 1984). Since then, Italy's economic situation has improved markedly via the European Economic Community. Consequently, Italian immigration to Canada and the U.S. has declined. Still, despite lower immigration rates, Italian Canadians retain a significant presence in Canada, numbering over one million. Indeed, after the United Kingdom and China, Italy is the third most common birthplace of immigrants to Canada (Statistics Canada, 2001).

Italians have traditionally placed great importance on family life and especially on family solidarity between all blood relatives, in-law relations, and godparents. "One's personal identity was derived from his family, and family membership was essential in terms of defining one's place in society.... The strength of the norm of solidarity meant that the disgrace of one member of the family affected everyone—a disobedient child was the concern not only of the parents but of the extended kin as well" (Quadagno, 1982:62, 63). The extended family was headed by a male *capo di famiglia*—usually the oldest married male member—who made the decisions about all family matters, including children's education, dowries, and funeral expenses. Although the Italian family was patriarchal, women were not without power. Even in Italy, a woman could own property and contribute economically to her family by working part-time in the fields. She also retained her dowry after marriage, which gave her economic leverage and went to her children, not her husband, upon her death (Quadagno, 1982).

Many aspects of traditional Italian culture and family life were transplanted to Canada. Primarily from poor and agrarian southern Italy, early Italian immigrants came largely as families (Sturino, 1990). Unmarried Italian men who decided to stay in Canada soon contacted their families in Italy in order to find wives (Davies, 2002). As Ramirez (1989:12) notes, early Italian immigrants brought with them "a notion of the family that rested on strict norms of authority, mutual responsibilities and honour. The family was viewed essentially as a cooperative enterprise whose material and emotional well-being was dependent on the specific roles that the various members were expected to perform."

Men's responsibilities centred on providing for their families. Although the first waves of immigrants who reached Canada were largely peasants and farm labourers—and some Italian farming communities were founded in places like Naples, Alberta—the majority of men worked in industrial jobs: mining, logging, and building and maintaining the railway. Women, on the other hand, were relegated to the domestic realm and were responsible for producing homemade articles (both for their families and to exchange for other goods and services); processing and preserving food; raising domestic animals; and tending their gardens (Ramirez, 1989). As in Italy, women also continued to be responsible for maintaining kinship ties, particularly with female relatives, and for nurturing their children. "In a world where the family status was judged not by the occupation of the father but by the signs of family well-being which emanated from the household, the mother played an important role in securing that status" (Quadagno, 1982:63). The extended family was still evident in many Italian-Canadian homes after the Second World War. Although these first-generation immigrant Italian women were discouraged from entering the wage-labour force, it was not unusual for them to take in boarders and thus contribute to the family earnings (Ramirez, 1989).

At first, new immigrants brought with them Old World notions such as "pride in one's village or regional origin"; identity as Canadians remained elusive (Ramirez, 1989: 16). However, as they began to see Canada as a land of opportunity, many second- and third-generation Italians conformed to the social norms of the English-speaking majority, pursued an education, and began moving into the middle classes as restaurateurs, small business owners, and professionals (Bagnell, 1989). Migrating to cities—primarily Toronto and Montreal—they tended first to settle in areas with low real estate prices (Carbone, 1998). Consequently, there emerged in every major city a "Little Italy" with Italian shops, restaurants, and a strong social life built around the Roman Catholic Church and social and cultural organizations.

Post-1945 immigration also says much about the cohesive nature of Italian-Canadian society built around family, kinship, and friends. By 1950, the federal government's more liberal immigration policies allowed Canadian citizens to sponsor family members, including cousins, as new immigrants. In this way, and wanting to reunite their families, members of the established Italian-Canadian community brought family members from war-torn Italy to Canada, where housing and employment awaited them (Harney, 1998). In the post-war economic boom in Canada, labourers were needed in construction and in the burgeoning industries in southern Ontario. Thus, if an Italian bricklayer brought his brother or a cousin to Canada, his brother or cousin would also work as a bricklayer. As these new Canadians became established, they in turn sponsored other immigrants to Canada. In his study on Italian immigrants in Alberta, Aliaga (1994) found that family was a key factor in the decision to immigrate to Canada and to adjust to the new environment once they were here. More than 90 percent of all Italian immigrants who came to Canada between 1946 and 1967 were sponsored by a family member who was already residing here (Ramirez, 1989). This enhanced the already existing notion that, despite social divisions in the working-, middle-, and even upper-classes, Italian Canadians constituted a distinct ethnic community in which family was central (D'Alfonso, 2000). Admittedly, the majority of new Italian Canadians settled in Toronto and its hinterland; but because of overall increased immigration, other Italian communities across the entire country expanded proportionately (Wood, 2002).

Italian immigrant husbands tended to be more educated than their wives, but both were less educated than the general Canadian population. This situation is indicative of the low levels of education that Italians had when they immigrated to this country. As late as the 1980s, 50 percent of Italian-Canadian husbands had less than a Grade 9 education, compared to 22 percent of Canadian husbands. Likewise, 56 percent of Italian immigrant wives had less than Grade 9 education, compared to 21 percent of Canadian wives (Jansen, 1987:75). However, only 8 and 10 percent of younger Italian males and females, respectively, had less than a Grade 9 education, indicating that significant improvements were being made in levels of education (Jansen, 1987:37).

Howell et al. (2001) reported from their study on ethnic groups in Toronto and Montreal that the majority of Italian men who immigrated to Canada after the Second World War were employed in non-professional occupations that required long hours and backbreaking toil. Despite these hardships and their lower educational levels, the majority of families were economically successful (Sturino, 1984). Italian Canadians placed great importance on owning their own home and, although they tended to be employed in lower status occupations and earned less than the general population, they were more likely than other Canadians to own their own home, even an expensive one

(Jansen, 1987). As Ramirez (1989:14) notes: "This ancestral desire for a measure of economic and psychic security to be concretized in the possession of a house became part of Italian migration folklore: during the post–World War Two era, one of the most popular songs in Italy spoke of 'a little house in Canada which had a pool with fish inside, was surrounded by lots of lily flowers, and was admired by passers-by.'"

The economic success of Italian immigrant families has been due in part to women's economic contributions. Given that Italian immigrant men earned considerably less on average than Canadian men, women's salaries in the post-1945 era were crucial to a family's economic well-being (Ramirez, 1989). After the Second World War, large numbers of young Italian immigrant women entered the paid labour force, indicating greater gender equality among second and subsequent generations of Italian immigrants. Because of their lower educational levels, most Italian immigrant women gained employment in the clothing, food, and light–manufacturing industries, and in service jobs such as cleaning. Whereas 52 percent of Canadian-educated females were in the labour force, 63 percent of Canadian-educated Italian females were employed (Jansen, 1987:39). In one instance, Aliaga (1994) found that 84.7 percent of married Italian women in Calgary were either employed or had been in the workforce. Many employed Italian mothers relied on family members, friends, and neighbours to help with the children in their absence.

Increased participation by females in the labour force is not the only change that has taken place amongst Italian Canadians. Research indicates that, as early as the 1950s, second and subsequent generations of Italian immigrants increasingly detached themselves from traditional Italian cultural values and family structures and assimilated into the Canadian population (see, for example, Handlin, 1951). There has been a steady increase in the number of Italians who speak English rather than Italian in their homes, and more Italian Canadians have married non-Italians (Trovato, 1985). Where first-generation families tended to be large, families of second and third generations have become smaller; though still strongly attached to the Church, younger women do not want the same kinds of domestic burdens that affected their mothers and grandmothers (Del Negro, 2003). Canadian-educated Italians, who are typically second- and subsequent-generation Italians, are more likely to be single (never married) and to have lower fertility rates than foreign-educated Italians, who tend to be first-generation immigrants (Jansen, 1987).

Evidence now suggests that as immigration has slowed and Italian Canadians have rejected large families, the Italian-Canadian community has begun shrinking relative to the rest of Canada's population (Trovato, 1985). **Ethnic exogamy** (marrying a spouse of a different ethnic origin) amongst Italian Canadians is also contributing to assimilation. Ethnic exogamy amongst Italian-Canadian men has increased from 19 percent in 1921 to 33 percent in the 1990s (Kalbach and Kalbach, 1999:115). However, the percentage of ethnic exogamy amongst second and subsequent generations of Italian immigrants is even more telling—approximately 70 percent of Canadian-born Italians are married to a non-Italian spouse, compared to 20 percent for foreign-born Italian Canadians (Kalbach and Kalbach, 1999). Often, these changes have created intergenerational conflict, as many first-generation Italian immigrants do not understand how their children and grandchildren can abandon the most cherished values of their culture (Aliaga, 1994). When first-generation immigrants were asked what they were most troubled about, they tended to speak "of their worries about their children's (and grand-children's) marital prospects and adherence to Italian religion, language and culture" (Howell et al., 2001:128). For the most part, Italian parents hoped that their children would marry other Italians from good families or, at the very least, marry Catholics from good families. As two students explain it,

> "My brother made my parents very happy because he married a 'good' Italian girl whereas my sister myself and my younger brother have been disappointments here.... Mind you we are all engaged or going out with persons of a better social class than us and this would make other parents happy but not mine.... My parents don't even notice that my brother's marriage is rather shaky...."

> "My parents are second-generation Canadian and it was impossible for them to marry a person that was not Italian and my mother therefore did not marry the man she loved. But us three kids will marry as we wish even though I am fortunate enough to have met a nice and kind Italian fellow who on top of it all is a real hunk and my parents are happy with whoever we bring home provided they come from good families. But there are limits and even though I didn't mind, when my brother brought a girl from Jamaica home, this didn't go over well...."

Despite the many ways that Italian immigrants have assimilated into Canadian culture, they have also preserved important aspects of Italian culture and the primacy of family. The daily activities of churches and community centres within Italian communities have been pivotal in keeping individuals of Italian descent connected and in sustaining various cultural practices. Large Italian weddings also provide a means of ethnic solidarity. "Guest lists of four hundred to six hundred people, generous gifts to the bridal couple, elaborate meals and drinks, and entertainment at the reception have all become cultural expressions of Italian spirit in Canada" (Howell et al., 2001:138). The Italian-Canadian community remains a vibrant and cohesive ethnic group built around the family and a strong sense of their unique culture and heritage.

RECENT IMMIGRANT FAMILIES

As pointed out, in the past few decades there has been a marked change in immigrants' country of origin. More than half of Canada's recent immigrants now originate from Asia, a high figure compared to before 1960, when only 2.4 percent of immigrants came from this region. Indeed, between 1996 and 2001, approximately one-quarter of all immigrants to Canada were either of Chinese or South Asian origin (Statistics Canada, 2001). The three largest ethnic groups to recently immigrate to this country—and the ones focused on in this section—are Chinese (just over 1 million, or 4 percent of Canada's population); South Asians (900,000, or 3 percent of the population); and blacks (660,000 or 2.2 percent of the population). Each of these diverse groups has uniquely contributed to the cultural diversity of Canada. Yet as visible minorities, each has experienced and continues to experience many barriers, especially racial discrimination in housing, employment, and other spheres of life (Owusu, 2000). Moreover, government policies and services are often modelled on the ideal of the nuclear family, which does not always fit the diverse circumstances of many immigrant families. And given the changing international environment marked by the end of the Cold War and the advent of economic globalization, both of which have affected immigration to Canada, this section concludes with a discussion of globalization and transnational families.

Chinese-Canadian Families

Having long resided in this country, Chinese Canadians currently represent Canada's largest visible minority group: Almost 4 million Canadians or 13 percent of the population come from or trace their descent to China (Statistics Canada, 2001). However, as discussed in Chapter 2, it was only after the *Immigration Act* of 1967 that Chinese immigrants were able to begin reunifying their families in Canada. Thus, despite a long history in Canada, family formation by Chinese immigrants has only taken place over the past four decades. Early Chinese Canadians settled chiefly in urban centres, a function of laws that restricted their ownership of land. Although Chinese-Canadian communities existed in every province and region of the country, the majority of Chinese immigrants settled in British Columbia and tended to reside with other Chinese Canadians in the same areas. This produced a series of "Chinatowns" in most urban areas, with Chinese shops, restaurants, and other cultural and social elements of life (Anderson, 1991). Today, approximately 72 percent of the Chinese people in Canada live in Vancouver or Toronto, and compared to many other ethnic groups, they tend to live in concentrated areas of a city (Balakrishnan, 2001). Moreover, having come to Canada under the family reunification clause, many live with family members already residing here. Interestingly, there are now more Chinese women immigrating to Canada from Hong Kong than there are Chinese men doing so (Man, 2001).

It follows that, as the Chinese-Canadian population grew, it transplanted a number of traditions from China into its Canadian communities, including the dominance of patriarchy, arranged marriages, extended families, and social stratification based on wealth and social position (Burney, 1995; Tian, 1991). However, although it is not unusual for three generations to reside together, this is no longer the dominant Chinese-Canadian family structure, though couples who live in a nuclear family tend to have extended family members in close proximity. In either case, there is a strong family support network, particularly in child care and assistance in housework (Man, 2001). Two Chinese-Canadian students describe how these social networks maintain cultural identity and help parents reinforce traditional values in their children:

> *"I live in a big house in Toronto with my parents and my grandparents live in a nearby condo and I have all in all six uncles and aunts who live around and in Markham. So it's easy for us to remain Chinese and my grandparents never have to speak English. They might as well be in Hong Kong for all I know.... Sometimes though it's hard because I'd like to be more Canadian but there is so much pressure to be and marry within our group, I feel like I am being choked and I'd like to move to Vancouver later but then who would babysit for me?"*

> *"My peers' values have always been similar to those of my family's because I have always hung around with other Asians. Living in Chinatown has made my life easier.... We are different but I do not think that we ever cared much because there always were so many of us."*

As pointed out by the first student, without their extended families, women in particular may encounter problems with child care and household maintenance. This situation is exacerbated by the fact that child care and housework is considered the wives' responsibility. Man (2001:434) reports from her study on Hong Kong female immigrants to Canada that "the physical spread of Canadian cities, and the lack of transportation systems in suburbia—where most of the Hong Kong immigrants reside—heighten children's dependency on their mothers, intensifying women's workloads. Consequently, some of them experience an intensification of traditional roles, unequal distribution of household labour, and gender and sexual oppression in the home." Moreover, she found that most Chinese women linked power to the ability to manage and control every aspect of family life, and thus, to relinquish control is to relinquish power or to lose face. Thus, Chinese women are reluctant to ask their husbands for help, even though Chinese women are less traditional than Chinese men with respect to beliefs about gender roles and family hierarchy (Tang and Dion, 1999).

Following the dictates of Confucianism—which have dominated Chinese culture and family life for more than two millennia—Chinese-Canadian family relationships are, for the most part, based on the notion of filial piety: respect, obligation, and obedience to one's parents, and reverence for the elders in their communities. In Lam's (1982) study of Chinese-Canadian families in Toronto, 90 percent of respondents reported that they visited their parents rather than their parents visiting them, while approximately 65 percent of respondents reported that they visited their parents more than once a week. All respondents in his study mentioned that they helped their parents—because of affection, duty, or obligation—by doing repairs, taking them to medical appointments, buying them things, and running errands for them. However, Ishii-Kuntz (1997) found that financial resources, distance, and parents' needs are important factors in determining how much financial support Chinese children provide to their elderly parents. This means that despite a strong belief in filial piety, poorer Chinese immigrants are less able to help their elderly parents. Other studies have also determined that this helping behaviour is reciprocal, as parents often assist their adult children with financial matters and child care (Lam, 1982).

Chinese parents tend to be lenient and indulgent until their children reach school age. At that point, children fall under stricter control (Buriel and De Ment, 1997). Approximately 25 percent of Chinese adolescents state that their parents want to choose careers for them, compared to about 8 percent of other Canadian adolescents. Moreover, 89 percent of Chinese parents expect their children to go to university, whereas just 45 percent of other Canadian parents have such expectations (Helm and Warren, 1998). Tang and Dion (1999:26–27) learned that the majority of Chinese young people are torn between two cultures in which the family has a central place: "They live in the heritage culture of their parents at home, while constantly being exposed to the very different social environment of the host culture. Their world is not essentially 'traditional' or 'modern,' but rather both." When one or both parents are not proficient in English, young Chinese immigrants are often faced with having to link the two cultures by taking on the role of **cultural brokers** (Buriel and De Ment, 1997). This role entails serving as translators for their parents, which often requires accompanying them as they take care of their daily needs, such as shopping and paying bills.

In this way, while retaining strong family, kinship, and community ties amongst themselves, Chinese Canadians have increasingly involved themselves in mainstream Canada, sustaining established and new cultural organizations, expanding into business and the professions, and participating in the political process. This involvement has always had two principal aims: preserving ethnic identity and traditions, and contributing to the development of their new homeland (Ng, 1999). The process has not always been easy, as established Chinese-Canadian families and new immigrants have abandoned Chinatowns for homes in other parts of urban areas (Balakrishnan, 2001). Patriarchal traditions have been weakened and Chinese-Canadian youth have tended to seek greater integration in the Canadian mainstream, including a still modest degree of intermarriage. The economic demands of life in Canada have also affected gender roles, as more Chinese-Canadian women work outside the home (Spitzer et al., 2003). Yet, the fact remains that Chinese and other immigrant families have come to Canada because this country offers parents and children greater opportunities to advance in life. They realize that change in their lives, including family change, has to occur. Parenting courses for immigrants are now available in most Canadian communities. As one Chinese parent has remarked,

> *"It is very important that children learn their heritage language, but it is an absolute necessity that we, their parents, learn a Canadian language—the language our children are most comfortable with. We need to keep our minds open to the new culture our children are exposed to so that we can understand what they are going through. If we prejudge this culture we may slam shut the door of communication with our children."* (Helm and Warren, 1998)

Overall, Chinese-Canadian parents have so far been quite successful at helping their children retain traditional values. For instance, Chinese youths are generally more conservative sexually (Meston et al., 1998). In the U.S., Feldman and Rosenthal (1990) suggest that adolescents of Chinese origin are slow to shift their expectations toward the North American model of early autonomy because of the effectiveness of the family in transmitting its values. No matter how it is developing and what paths it might take, the Chinese-Canadian community will continue to find ways to preserve the family as the core of its ethnic identity while it contributes to the economic, social, and political well-being of the country.

South Asian-Canadian Families

The term "South Asian" refers to distinct ethnocultural groups who have come to Canada either directly from the Indian subcontinent (India, Pakistan, Sri Lanka, and Bangladesh), or indirectly, through East Africa, the Caribbean, or Fiji through their ancestors (Ralson, 1997). Until 1947, South Asians were all but banned from immigrating to Canada (Das Gupta, 2000; Jamal, 1998). Restrictions were even more severe for women, who were banned altogether from entering Canada until 1919, and then only as wives (Das Gupta, 2000).

Once the racial barriers in Canada's immigration policies were lifted in the 1960s, many South Asians immigrated to this country. Between 1971 and 1981, South Asian

First- and second-generation Indian families have assimilated into the Canadian economy while at the same time retaining many elements of their culture. This is particularly evident at weddings where couples begin life within the rituals of their traditional culture.

immigration more than quadrupled (Buchignani, 1987). But despite liberal changes to our immigration policies, it continues to be difficult for Asians and other minority immigrant groups to participate in family life (Das Gupta, 2000; Dua, 1999). For example, it takes an average of 10 years to sponsor a spouse and children from India, and South Asian migrants are more likely to experience difficulties and delays in sponsorship than European or American migrants (Dua, 1999). Canada's current immigration policies tend to reinforce the nuclear family, making it difficult for some South Asians to live in extended families, a structure that most lived in prior to coming to this country. For example, although there are many exceptions, immigrants can generally sponsor their spouse and dependent children, but no other family members, such as grandparents, who lived in their household in their country of origin.

The roles and status of family members are well defined and understood within the extended South-Asian family structure. However, roles and status are challenged when families move to Canada and must live as nuclear families—although many still live in three-generational households. For example, in the traditional extended family, men contribute economically to the family whereas women contribute their domestic work. Living in a nuclear family means that there are no longer several males to contribute to the family's economic base, so that for many South Asian immigrant families, economic survival depends on the wife taking on paid employment. This process not only challenges traditional South Asian gender roles, it accounts for increased conflict between many husbands and wives (Buchignani, 1987:118). However, many South Asian wives are happy and feel free because they no longer fall under the control of their husband's mother. When asked about her current happiness, an Indian student recently conveyed anguish over her mother's situation:

> *"At this stage of my life I am not the happiest. I would like to leave my parents' home because it is really not their home, it's my grandparents and it is too painful for me to see how badly my grandmother treats my mother as [if] she is her slave and my father lets her do it.... She even treats my father badly [she prefers the student's uncle who still lives in India]. I don't understand that my father accepts this because he owns his home and he paid for his parents to come here and my mother worked hard helping him do this. It hurts me so much that I want to run away and take my mother with me."*

The parent-child role has also undergone major changes, notably the loss of authority in choosing a child's marriage partner. According to Talbani and Hasanali (2000:625), gender roles are "expressed, validated and perpetuated through rites and symbols related to marriage [and] are pivotal in the search for stability in a new cultural milieu. Therefore, families and communities will try hard to keep the institution of marriage intact." Thus, first-generation South Asian immigrants have strong expectations that their children will uphold the tradition of arranged marriages and all the values that such marriages evoke. Although these wishes are often challenged by children who are raised in a culture that devalues such marriages, many other young adults feel comfortable within this cultural perspective, as described in Chapter 2 (Porter, 2003).

Several studies have looked at the intergenerational attitudes and values of South Asian immigrants (Aycan and Kanungo, 1998; Kurian, 1991; Ralson, 1997). Zaidi and Shuraydi (2002:512) found a definite "cultural" generation gap between the family values of second-generation Muslim Pakistani immigrant women and their parents, who typically favour arranged marriages. "This non-conformity to arranged marriages creates a mood of uncertainty for many females as they feel confused, uncertain, and torn between their own thoughts and their parents' belief system." Still, South Asian women have been seeking to adapt to modern Canadian society. Although they have made advances such as being able to pursue post-secondary education and seek a career, it has not always been easy. For instance, Talbani and Hasanali (2000:625–626) found that second-generation South Asians tend to adapt to Canadian culture "in dress code, language and the acceptance of other social norms," but they "find it difficult to negotiate between cultural control and individual freedom." This may account for why "many adolescent girls in South Asian communities face mental problems."

Intergenerational conflict often results from the diverse expectations of parents and their children. However, it is through this process of negotiation that second generation South Asians, particularly females, ultimately integrate South Asian and Canadian identities into their everyday life. Just as traditional Chinese-Canadian families continued to adapt to Canadian society, so too do South Asian ones. And the result will probably be the same—finding a balance whereby the family as the core of South Asian ethnic identity will change but not be destroyed.

Black-Canadian Families

Family researchers have to exercise caution when placing individuals into one group based only on their being black (Grant and Danso, 2000). There are important cultural differences in this group: Coming from the Caribbean, the Americas, or Africa, they differ in their history, language, geography, social experiences, family structures, and in their reasons for emigrating (Galloway, 2004). However, there are common experiences shared by black families. Perhaps more than any other ethnic group in Canada, the presence of black communities brings into stark relief the issues of race, class, and gender. In this respect, an understanding of black families is important, but studies on Canadian black families have for the most part been ignored in social science research (Calliste, 2003; Christensen and Weinfeld, 1993). The fact that little research has been done on black families in Canada—particularly given their longstanding presence in this country, as indicated in Chapter 2—illustrates their marginality. However, scholars are beginning to produce insightful studies on black families, many of which throw light on their evolution and how they function in a society and economy dominated by whites.

The number of black families in Canada dramatically increased after racial barriers were removed from Canada's immigration laws in the 1960s. During the 1970s and 1980s, the majority of blacks came from the Caribbean, South America, and Central America; since 1990, they have come primarily from Africa to escape political unrest (Owasu, 1999). Blacks, who represent 2.2 percent of the Canadian population, constitute the third largest *visible* minority group (Statistics Canada, 2001). Cultural factors retained by black immigrants when they come to this country, as well as racism and structural inequalities, have played some part in the evolution of black family patterns. For example, the "role of women in contemporary black families must be viewed in light of harsh and unique social environments in which they must function, and resulting coping strategies" (Christensen and Weinfeld, 1993:7).

Despite their growing numbers, black families continue to be disadvantaged (Galloway, 2004). Blacks—particularly black women—experience unemployment and income inequality more than any other minority group (Calliste, 2003), despite having the same education level as the Canadian population (Galloway, 2004). Statistics Canada (2004h) recently pointed out that Canadian-born blacks between the ages of 24 and 54 were paid on average $7,500 less per year than other Canadians with the same education. Low socioeconomic status, high unemployment rates, and few employment opportunities have contributed to family breakdown amongst black Canadians. Black spouses, especially in working-class families, are more likely to be separated or divorced and less likely to be formally married, a situation also found in the U.S. and throughout the Caribbean region (Christensen and Weinfeld, 1993). As a result of economic circumstances—unemployment among black males along with low wages—blacks place less importance on marriage as a context for childbearing (see Chapter 9). However, upper-income blacks are more likely to marry before having children, and this is also true for the Caribbean (Barrow, 1996). The high divorce rate and the higher tendency for black women to have nonmarital births have made it quite common for many black families to be headed by a woman. Black children are approximately three times more likely than other Canadian children to be living in a low-income, single-parent family (Christensen and Weinfeld, 1993). Unstable employment and discriminatory immigration laws, particularly in the past, have also made it difficult for black people to sponsor family members still living outside of Canada, which makes family reunification difficult. Also contributing to low marriage rates is an unbalanced gender ratio. There are more black women of marriageable age in Canada than black men, primarily the result of earlier policies that admitted massive numbers of black women to Canada as domestics. As well, there is a tendency amongst black men to enter into interracial marriages (Calliste, 2003).

In comparison to white children, black children are less likely to live in single-home dwellings. Moreover, there is a high concentration of people in poor black neighbourhoods. This means that black children living in these neighbourhoods reside in close proximity to siblings, cousins, young aunts and uncles, same-floor neighbours, and street peers, all of whom contribute to their socialization. Most black-Canadian parents believe that the community is important and tend to "share the African proverbial saying that it takes the whole community to educate a child. While parents believe that individual rights are important, they also think they should be matched with a strong sense of social responsibility" (Dei, 1993:17). A black student recalls her relationship with her parents when she was 10 to 14 years of age:

> "We all had a hard time together mainly because our parents couldn't cope with us three children. We weren't bad or anything of the sort but we lived in a cramped apartment near a subsidized project and there were kids, kids, kids everywhere. We were always with kids and I think that after a while our parents couldn't tell us apart (smile!). We had a lot of fun some days but my parents didn't. They were trying to raise us well but the other kids we were always hanging around with would have none of it and their parents weren't always the best either, they'd let them stay out late at night, go wherever, invade and control the hallways, parking lots, you name it. They were up to no good but my sister, brother and myself couldn't appreciate that our parents were trying to protect us from this mayhem. I resented my parents but at the same time I loved them and we had the only father on the block and that made us special also."

An important point stressed in recent research is that many government policies have contributed to black women experiencing the family differently from other women. In favouring unskilled immigrant black women over black men to fill undesirable vacant positions such as domestic workers, recent immigration policies have adversely affected black families by contributing to a sex ratio imbalance. Moreover, black female domestics were also denied reproductive freedom in that they were not allowed to marry or have children without facing deportation, a restriction that did not apply to white immigrant women (Calliste, 2003). Dua (1999) argues that many policies are grounded in nationalist ideologies that date back to the beginning of this country; namely an ideology that revered white women as ideal mothers whose participation in the nuclear family was crucial if they were to populate the nation. On the other hand, women of colour were cast as posing a triple threat to the nation: They could not reproduce a white population; they allowed for the possibility of interracial sexuality; and they challenged the very racialized moral order that the nuclear family was meant to protect. Calliste (2003) similarly argues that until the mid-1960s, blacks were portrayed as promiscuous, undesirable immigrants who were less deserving of parenthood, an image which further rationalized and reinforced their subordination in Canada. Thus, feminist scholars have argued that the nuclear family has not only been used by the state as an instrument to reinforce gender relations, but also to reinforce race relations (Das Gupta, 2000). The experiences of many black families point to how racism has been a powerful force in shaping family structures and relations.

Transnational Families

Globalization has had a tremendous impact on migration and family structures. With more international trade and exchange, international boundaries have become blurred. Many men and women now cross nation-state boundaries to live and work as easily as they once travelled to different cities in the same country. As a result, transnational families (also referred to as "astronaut families") have become more commonplace in recent times. Transnational families are "families that live some or most of the time separated from each other, yet hold together and create something that can be seen as a feeling of collective welfare and unity, namely 'familyhood,' even across national borders" (Bryceson and Vuorela, 2002:3). Transnational families have often been distinguished from other migrant families in that they tend to have higher socioeconomic status and educational levels than conventional migrants and, as such, they have been viewed more auspiciously by countries that receive immigrants. But as Beaujot and Kerr (2004:98) point out, "there are winners and losers in globalization, and the glaring disparities in standards of living around the world are themselves a leading cause of migration." Consequently, the experiences of transnational families vary by ethnicity, gender, country of origin, and occupational class.

As part of a larger project on immigrant families, Waters (2002) interviewed transnational families in Vancouver. She was particularly interested in the experiences of Taiwanese and Hong Kong astronaut wives, immigrant women whose husbands, within a few months after their arrival, had returned to their country of origin to work. For the most part, Chinese and Taiwanese astronaut families in Vancouver—and also in Toronto—are of higher social class. According to Waters (2002:118), astronaut families exemplify "the ways in which social relationships can operate over significant distance, spanning national borders, and reducing the importance of face-to-face context in personal interaction." However, she found that family members differentially experienced transnationalism. Migration tended to be empowering for men, but women tended to view migration as a necessary sacrifice for their children rather than as a way to improve their own life chances. For the most part, migration for these women was more about losses than gains; they surrendered their jobs and thus economic independence, they left behind their support system with extended family and friends, and they lost the daily companionship of their husbands. However, Waters found that women's sense of oppression dissipated over time, especially once they learned English, developed new support networks, and felt more connected with their community. She also points out that there was often conflict between spouses when husbands returned to Canada because most husbands were unable to deal with their wives' newly found independence and preferred the patriarchal dominance that defined their relationships prior to the husband's leaving.

Current trends in transnational families find children increasingly separated from one of their parents. Traditionally, the father is away and the mother raises the children alone. However, a global market economy has also resulted in an increase in female-headed transnational families where the mother works in a country different from where some or all of her children reside. Female-headed transnational families are becoming more common as developed countries continue to demand low-wage female domestic and service labour from developing countries. This trend in transnational mothering has disrupted the notion of family in one place: "transnational mothers are improvising new mothering arrangements that are borne out of women's financial struggles, played out in a new global arena, to provide the best future for themselves and their children" (Hondagneu-Sotelo and Avila, 1997:567). However, what is often overlooked are the detrimental effects of transnational mothering (mothering one's children from a distance), a situation often forced on migrant **domestic workers** with children. "The pain of family separation creates various feelings, including helplessness, regret, and guilt for mothers and loneliness, vulnerability and insecurity for children.... [Mothers] may long to reunite with their children but cannot, because they need their earnings to sustain their families" (Salazar Parreñas, 2001: 368, 371). In the absence of their mothers, children of transnational women are generally raised by their grandmothers. When these children are reunited with their mothers, they often resent her authority, not wanting to obey a mother they have never met or have rarely seen. A student who was reunited with her transnational mother explains:

> "What was the hardest at that age [10–14] was leaving my grandmother behind in Jamaica. I had been so excited about living with my mother.... I had seen her only three times since she left when I was 4.... She really was like a stranger and she was so busy.... I thought she had money but we had to live in a poor place, real tough kids that I can see now were bad but for me they were exciting because life with my mother and her boyfriend was no fun. I paid no heed to her and him and I skipped school.... I missed my grandmother and I wanted her here but she had to help with my other cousins over there."

Many transnational mothers are forced to hire domestic help to care for their own families in their absence. This causes many women to feel guilty, a feeling that is only intensified by traditional cultural norms that value women primarily for their roles as mothers. Globalization may have increased flexibility in the labour markets and, in eroding the material conditions for the male breadwinner system, produced greater equality between professional men and women—but it has also created new forms of marginality (Young, 2001). As Salazar Parreñas (2001) so poignantly points out, migrant women may be diminishing the reproductive labour of employed women in postindustrial nations, but the result of this has been the formation of an international division of reproductive labour. Women's reproductive work, whether paid or unpaid, remains undervalued.

CONCLUSIONS: CULTURAL HERITAGE AND CANADIAN IDENTITIES

In both historical and contemporary terms, Canada is a country composed of ethnic and immigrant groups. This does not mean that there is no such thing as a "Canadian." However, the notion of what being "Canadian" means precisely has changed over time. From the early French colonials who saw themselves as *canadiens*, to the modern, multicultural Canada peopled by "hyphenated" Canadians—Italian-Canadians, Chinese-Canadians, Indo-Canadians—Canadian identity has developed in unique ways among the various ethnic and immigrant groups in this country. In general terms, this identity has been defined by the cultural heritage that these groups have either developed in Canada or have brought with them to this country. "Family" is a crucial element of Canadian cultural heritage, but it is also as unique an institution as the various ethnic and immigrant groups who comprise this society. Therefore, being a member of a First Nations family has a different meaning—a different identity—than that of being a member of an Indo-Canadian family. And to live in a Québécois family means something completely different from living either First Nations or Indo-Canadian experiences, or the experiences of other ethnic and immigrant groups.

The production of identity is both subjective and objective. It is subjective in terms of the meaning a person attaches to being part of a group, and objective because it is shaped by state policies. Throughout this chapter, we have looked at several case studies in which immigrants not only engaged in a struggle to construct a new identity (Talbani and Hasanali, 2000), but did so in the context of prejudice and discrimination. This is particularly the case for visible minority immigrants. In the context of this struggle, family has been fundamentally important to all Canadians. But as the identity of First Nations, Québécois, the British, and other immigrant groups has changed because of time and circumstance, so too has the family. In this sense, as much as it is a country composed of diverse ethnic and immigrant groups, Canada is also a country defined by the diverse nature of its immigrant and ethnic families. There is no such thing as a homogeneous Canadian family.

Summary

1. There is a great deal of diversity amongst Canadian families based on their ethnicity and their origins. As well, immigrant families differ in how they are received and in their level of adjustment to Canadian society; immigration should be viewed as a process rather than a one-time event.

2. Nationality is not the overriding element in understanding the nature of Canadian families because most nations in the world are composed of a number of ethnic groups. Ethnic groups and minority groups are defined. Immigrants can be classified by how long their families have been in Canada: first-generation immigrants (born outside of Canada); second-generation immigrants (born in Canada but whose parents are born outside of Canada); and third- or subsequent-generation immigrants.

3. Since Confederation, Canada has experienced five distinct phases of immigration: 1860–1896; 1897–1913; 1914–1945; 1946–1989; and 1990 to the present. In the first four phases, immigrants came mainly from the British Isles and Europe. Beginning in the fourth phase, immi-

grants increasingly came from Asia, Africa, Latin America, and the Caribbean. In the fifth and most recent phase, immigrants have come mainly from Third World countries. Immigrant families in Canada are also marked by generational differences, and they reflect the different cultures and structures of Canada's older and recent immigrant arrivals.

4. First Nations families are the oldest families in Canada and they encompass distinct nations with dissimilar identities, ancestries, cultures, and social structures. They are based on kinship, communal sharing, and defined familial responsibilities for all members. Despite a range of social, economic, and other problems affecting their society, First Nations are the fastest growing ethnic group in Canada, and the traditional extended family remains an important emotional and social foundation for them.

5. In the 1960s, Quebec society began to experience significant change. As a result of the many processes of the Quiet Revolution, Quebec's family structure was transformed and women's rights were expanded. Smaller families have

replaced patriarchal families and many are led by single or cohabiting parents. Worried about preserving French culture, the Québécois government has encouraged larger families and has worked to strengthen family life by introducing innovative policies such as universal daycare.

6. Italians comprise one of the oldest ethnic groups in Canada, having arrived in significant numbers in the late 19th century. Traditionally, Italians had extended patriarchal families, and these families immigrated together to Canada. But traditional Italian-Canadian family structures have changed over time through the increased labour force participation of women, improved education, and ethnic exogamy for both sexes. Nonetheless, the Church, community centres, and organized social gatherings play a pivotal role in Italian families by keeping them connected and providing a means for ethnic solidarity.

7. It was not until 1967 that the Chinese, Canada's largest visible minority group, received the same rights as other groups, and Chinese family formation and reunification was allowed to take place. Now, through marriage and immigration, extended Chinese families have been transferred to Canada. But traditional family structures have been modified through intergenerational divisions. Patriarchal traditions have been weakened and the economic demands of life in Canada have affected gender roles.

8. Because of racist immigration policies, South Asians only began to immigrate to Canada in significant numbers after the 1960s. However, the high cost of family sponsorship and its restrictions have made it difficult for South Asians to participate in the extended family life that is culturally their own. And intergenerational conflicts with regard to traditions like arranged marriages are especially important amongst South Asian families. Nevertheless, these families seem to be finding a balance whereby the family as the core of their ethnic identity will change but not be destroyed.

9. Blacks represent the third largest visible minority group in Canada, and they continue to experience higher unemployment and income inequality than any other minority group. These disadvantages are related to blacks' higher conjugal dissolution rates and single motherhood. In addition, migration policy and family sponsorship have made black family reunification difficult, and government policies that favour unskilled black women over black men may contribute to the unbalanced gender ratio, resulting in lowered marriage rates.

10. Largely as a result of globalization, transnational families vary by ethnicity, gender, country of origin, and occupational class. With generally higher education and incomes than other migrant families, they are examples of family networks that transcend national boundaries. Female-headed transnational families are becoming more common as developed countries continue to demand low-wage, female domestic and service labour from developing countries.

11. Canadian identity is fluid and has changed over time, largely as a result of its composition of different ethnic and immigrant groups. To understand Canada's cultural diversity is to understand the processes by which its ethnic and immigrant families have adapted to produce modern Canadian society.

Key Concepts and Themes

Analytical Questions

1. Why is an intergenerational analysis important when analyzing immigrant families?
2. What stresses might the child of a traditional Chinese-Canadian family experience?
3. What are the benefits and costs associated with the increase in the number of transnational families? Are these benefits/costs different for women than for men?
4. How has racism historically impacted family policy in Canada?
5. Why do families continue to immigrate to Canada, given the hardships associated with belonging to a visible minority group?

Suggested Readings

Fournier, S., and Crey, E. 1997. *Stolen from our embrace: The abduction of First Nations children and the restoration of Aboriginal communities*. Vancouver/ Toronto: Douglas and McIntyre. A compelling account of how Aboriginal family life was decimated by government policies. The book concludes with a discussion of how Aboriginal people have begun to empower themselves and help their families.

Kalbach, M. A., and Kalbach, W. W. (Eds.) 2000. *Perspectives on ethnicity in Canada*. Toronto: Harcourt. This compilation of research articles focuses on theoretical perspectives on race and ethnicity, Canada's changing cultural mosaic, ethnic persistence and integration, power and inequality, prejudice and discrimination.

Lynn, M. (Ed.) 2003. *Voices: Essays on Canadian families*. 2nd Ed. Scarborough: Thomson Nelson. This book offers a rich and diverse collection of cross-cultural perspectives on family life in Canada.

McDaniel, S. A. 1997. Intergenerational transfers, social solidarity, and social policy: Unanswered questions and policy challenges. *Canadian Public Policy/Canadian Journal on Aging* (joint issue), 1–21. The author provides an insightful analysis of issues pertaining to intergenerational transfers. Policy implications are also discussed.

Suggested Weblinks

Health Canada dedicates a section of its site to immigrant and refugee health. Lists of research publications are given on various topics including family violence, immigrant women, and isolation of older immigrants.

www.hc-sc.gc.ca/english/for_you/immigrants.html

The **Japanese information network**, known as Web Japan, includes a comparison of international cohabitation rates, shown in the proceedings of the International Population Conference in Beijing, 1997. Subjects and sources are listed.

www.jinjapan.org/stat/stats/02VIT34.html

A family index produced by **Dr. Michael Kearl** at the **University of Trinity** focuses on the spectrum of family relations across cultures and time.

www.trinity.edu/~mkearl/family.html

Canadian Heritage is responsible for national policies and programs that promote Canadian content, foster cultural participation, and strengthen connections among Canadians. Their website includes a variety of links on diversity and multiculturalism, including recent articles that have appeared in the media.

www.pch.gc.ca/index_e.cfm

and

www.culturescanada.ca

CHAPTER 5

Effects on Families of Economic Changes and Inequalities

"In 10 years from now I will be either a lawyer or a doctor. I want to make money, lots of it. That's my primary goal."

"In 10 years I hope to be out of this noisy apartment building and live in a modest house in the countryside. I hope to have travelled a bit and especially help my mother and sister out of here. I would want my mother to stay home and not to have to worry about money for the first time in her life."

"Right now my big problem is lack of money, nothing new here but now that I am getting close to becoming a teacher and having a bit for myself for the first time in my life, I can't stand it any longer!"

"This autobiography is going to be rather boring. I have lived the typical 'American dream' or should I say 'Canadian'? Born to poverty, hard working parents, moves to better neighbourhoods and now our dream come true: a big house on a street with other big houses."

"My father is a lawyer and when I turned 10 my mother became a stock broker.... We've always lived in the same lovely neighbourhood in a fairly large home with lots of trees and flowers, in two homes actually because my parents at some point decided to have a house with a two-level foyer with French doors and matching staircase."

"At that age [10 to 14] all I can remember is being hungry most of the time but especially by the end of each month and never having something special or nice that belonged to me. I don't have one pleasant memory."

In the preceding quotes, we hear from students who want to become doctors or lawyers because their dreams include a lot of money, students who simply want to have just enough for a decent life, students who suffered from the deprivations and fears of poverty, and students who lived in affluence. As these quotes begin to illustrate, economic circumstances and the economic system in which people live affect all facets of their lives as well as their families' lives. The decades of the 1970s through the 2000s are characterized by an economy that has been radically transformed by information technology. These sweeping changes have contributed to the contemporary profile of families and to what some see as upheavals in the social fabric. Without some understanding of the economy, we cannot fully grasp the sources of the recent family transformations that are discussed in this book. Thus, there is a historical parallel between the Industrial Revolution which came to Canada in the 19th century, as discussed in Chapter 2, and the ongoing technological revolution: Both have impacted families' lives and roles (Bradbury, 1996; Mandell and Momirov, 2000).

OVERVIEW OF ECONOMIC CHANGES

We now live in what is called the postindustrial economy. It is characterized by **information technology,** high finances, including "paper" speculation, and the predominance of the service sector. The economy is no longer organized along regional or even national lines; rather, it is international or global. This phenomenon is referred to as the **globalization of the economy** and is driven by multinational corporations operating throughout the world (Menzies, 1996). In order to increase their profits, these corporations—whether Ford, Microsoft, or Sony—move production plants and call centres around the globe, depending on the availability of cheap labour (Thurow, 1999). Hence, national economies are at the mercy of worldwide financial fluctuations more than ever before (Rinehart, 1996). It is now difficult for governments to control their country's labour markets and financial sectors because multinational corporations' hunger for profit dictates trade and commercial laws as well as who will work, where, at what wage, and under what conditions (Rhodes, 1996). Therefore, globalization and various free trade agreements have important consequences for families (Bakker, 1996): It is more difficult than before for governments to step in to improve the economic opportunities of a disadvantaged neighbourhood or of an area that is threatened by plant closure, for instance.

Until the 1970s, some of the largest Canadian employers were industries producing materials and goods such as steel and cars. In 1951, 27 percent of jobs were in manufacturing, but this number had plummeted to 15 percent by 1995 (Glenday, 1997). Manufacturers provided well-paying entry-level jobs, employment security, and, later on, benefit packages to young workers fresh out of high school. These industries hired large numbers of youths, often immigrants; with such jobs, youths, especially males, could marry and support a family. After the 1970s, as technology progressed, fewer low-skilled workers were needed. Plant closures, downsizing, relocation, and imports from abroad, particularly Asia, followed and the proportion of males working in manufacturing declined. All of these and other factors began to restrict working-class individuals' ability to earn decent wages and, during certain periods such as the early 1990s and the early 2000s, to secure a job. In the 1990s, even traditionally feminine domains of employment were affected by job losses, whether clerical or in the clothing industry (Phillips and Phillips, 2000).

While this phenomenon was occurring, another also arose that changed the entire employment profile: The **service sector** expanded, a large segment of which offered only low-paying and part-time jobs—for example in the restaurant, hotel, and retail industries (Sassen, 1994). These jobs constituted only 18 percent of the labour market in 1951 but employed 37 percent by 1995 (Glenday, 1997). Furthermore, in the face of a more competitive and high-tech economy and the requirements of corporations, many jobs have been downsized into **part-time positions** and contracts; these jobs are less secure, less well paid, and do not provide any health or pension benefits—and ultimately contribute to poverty. In 2000, 19 percent of all Canadian workers were employed part-time: 28 percent of employed women and 11 percent of employed men. Although women turn to part-time work in order to combine employment with maternal duties, 30 percent would prefer full-time jobs.

Thus, the traditional gender division of labour and of income, with women earning less, is continued in the new economy (Duffy, 1997). This detrimental feminine wage and labour situation contributes to poverty in single-mother families and in low-income families in which two salaries are necessary. However, at the two-parent family level, the losses incurred by males on the labour market were accompanied by feminine gains. The former affected couple formation while the latter affected fertility. Despite this increase in two-earner couples, families are not much better off financially than they were in the 1960s (FSAT, 2004; Statistics Canada, 2002f, j).

Another consequence of the emerging postindustrial economy has been an **inflation in educational requirements**. About two-thirds of all new positions created—even some low-paying ones—require at least 13 years of formal education, and 45 percent require more than 16 years. In turn, the need for a longer education forces youth to seek part-time and summer jobs to defray the increasing costs of their education (Beaujot, 2004). In this type of economy, school dropouts and youths with only high school diplomas face a life of part-time or low-wage jobs. Indeed, Canadians with only a high school diploma are more likely to earn low wages and to be unemployed than better educated Canadians (Sauvé, 2002a). In part, this stems from the fact that employers require more education, even if, in reality, on-the-job training would suffice. This leads to a new and more intractable type of poverty (Cheal, 1996). Furthermore, the gap between the rich and the poor in terms of wealth (assets such as real estate, stocks, and savings accounts) has also increased—and this gap favours the more educated.

EFFECTS OF ECONOMIC CHANGES ON FAMILIES

Overall, the new economy presents a less secure employment and financial environment for families than was the case in the 1950s and 1960s. It is a more demanding environment, which has many consequences for family structure, lifestyle, and dynamics. Among these consequences are the increase in maternal employment and two-income families, as well as the "time crunch," the rise of a consumerist culture, and the lengthening of youths' dependence on parents. Other consequences such as delayed couple formation and fertility are further discussed in Part 3.

The Rise of Feminine Employment and the Dual-Income Family

The first effect of the new economic situation on families over the recent decades resides in an **increase in feminine employment** and consequently in **two-income families**. In 2000, 79 percent of Canadian families headed by a non-retired couple had two or more earners (Sauvé, 2002b). In the U.S., Gardner and Herz (1992) estimated that, without the earning of the second worker, the number of families living in poverty would more than double, a reality that is even more evident today, both in Canada and the U.S. Indeed, in two-parent families, mothers' wages have become increasingly important. For instance, in Canada in 2000, among married couples with children, when both husbands and wives were employed, the average income was over $61,000 (after transfers and income taxes) compared to $43,000 when the wife was not employed. Generally, a second earner adds about $15,000 to family income after taxes (Sauvé, 2002b).

Recourse to women's labour for family survival is a recurrent theme in history (Bradbury, 2000; Parr, 2000). Not only did women (and children) fully participate in the family economy in past centuries, but in the 19th century, many low-income families already had (needed) two or more incomes (Bradbury, 1996; Parr, 1980). What is unprecedented is that the majority of women of all classes now work for wages while children no longer do; also unprecedented is the combination of economic and cultural forces driving feminine employment (Chafez, 1995).

Thus, in many two-parent families, two wages have become a necessity because of a rise in economic instability and consumer expectations (Edwards, 2001). Furthermore, higher divorce and single parenting rates make it necessary for divorced and unmarried mothers to be employed. But feminine employment would have nevertheless grown despite these economic necessities, although perhaps to a lesser extent. Indeed, the 1970s wave of the Women's Movement has led to the liberalization of attitudes concerning women's roles in society. This cultural change has allowed women to enter the labour force in greater numbers and to penetrate occupational fields that had been traditionally masculine, such as law, medicine, and the physical sciences.

Below, we note the sharp increase in the percentages of *married* women in the labour force from decade to decade (Statistics Canada, 2003b):

1931	3.5%
1951	11
1961	22
1971	37
1981	52
1991	63
1998	78
2003	80

In the past, women generally left the workforce after marriage to await the birth of their first child. Recent studies have found that women who delay motherhood by at least one year past the average age at first birth for their cohort earn higher salaries—up to 17 percent higher. Postponing a first birth is even more important among younger cohorts of women, in part because of the types of careers now open to them. As Drolet (2003:21) points out, "wage growth and promotion opportunities are substantial early in one's career." Women who delay childbirth are more flexible for career moves, additional training, and may also be inherently more career oriented than women who begin childbearing earlier.

These observations are important in view of the fact that women's wages still lag behind men's, even among younger cohorts: This is a fairly universal phenomenon, even among the very educated (Brouillet, 2004; Djider, 2002). This gap in part stems from women occupying positions that are less well remunerated in the service sector (such as retail salespersons, cashiers, and babysitters) and also because a larger proportion work part-time. Thus, women experience only 78.7 percent of the time men actually spend employed (Drolet, 2001). Nevertheless, even women in the 24 to 34 age bracket who are employed full-time earned only 78 percent of same-age men in 1997 (Statistics Canada, 2000). Therefore, there is a gender gap in terms of earnings in two-paycheque families whereby husbands are generally the main wage–earner, even though at least 20 percent of women earn as much or more than their husbands do. The unequal division of labour in the home contributes to the wage gap between husbands and wives (Noonan, 2001).

Indeed, as women try to link their paid work life with their home life (production and reproduction), they often have to choose economic sectors that have more flexible hours but pay much less; or they have recourse to part-time employment while yet others interrupt their work cycle for a substantial period of time, thus delaying promotions and salary increases. As Duffy et al. (1989) put it, women have few choices. One should, however, consider that a proportion of women still choose and enjoy being homemakers and full-time parents and have minimal aspirations as far as paid employment is concerned. There is a lack of attention in feminist theories to this aspect of many women's condition, as we have tended to focus on paid employment (Marks, 2004). One could as easily see that many men might also want to become full-time fathers were they socialized within this perspective.

Another aspect of labour force requirements that needs far more research in terms of its consequences on family and couple life is the shift work done by 30 percent of men and 28 percent of women. In fact, shift workers report higher levels of work-related stress, even more so for women than men. As well, both men and women on evening shifts report more relationship problems with their spouses than those with daytime employment (Presser, 2000; Shields, 2003).

Domestic Division of Labour along Gender Lines

Today, a majority of mothers, even those with very young children, are gainfully employed (Schellenberg and Ross, 1997). Paradoxically, this shift toward maternal employment has occurred at a time when the care of small children has become more labour intensive and the pressure on women as mothers has mounted (Hays, 1996). The net result is what sociologist Arlie Hochschild has called *The Second Shift* (1989). That is, although society has become more liberal concerning women's status and role in the workplace, this development has not been accompanied by a similarly liberating one on the domestic front. In the "second shift," women come home from work to work even more. After picking up children at the daycare centre or at the sitter's, they cook and serve dinner, prepare lunches for the next day, perhaps do laundry, and help the children with their homework and bedtime (Hessing, 1993; Hochschild, 1997). True, fathers participate somewhat more than in the past, particularly when mothers are employed, but their participation is still unequal. The end result is that women who are employed full-time toil more hours per week than men when housework and paid work hours are combined, a topic that is discussed at greater length in Chapter 11 (Frederick, 1995; Lee and Duxbury, 1998).

As indicated in Figure 5.1, which considers the workforce status of both spouses, wives with children do more housework per week than husbands—and these results have remained largely unchanged since 1996. Not shown is the fact that there is a similar pattern for child care. Furthermore, wives who are not in the labour force do more than other wives, and wives employed part-time do more than wives employed full-time. The scenario that comes closest to equality in terms of housework is when the husband is not in the labour force but his wife is employed full-time (top set of bars in Figure 5.1). Not shown in Figure 5.1 is that, when both spouses are employed full-time, wives still do more child care and housework than husbands (Lupri, 1991). As a result, married fathers have more leisure time per day than married and single mothers also employed full-time (Daly, 2000). One consequence of this situation is that women take more time off work for family reasons other than maternity. In fact, married women with children took 12 days off versus one day for husbands with children and four for single-parent women in the year 2000 (Sauvé, 2002b).

An important gap in the literature is the lack of widespread research on children's contributions to household tasks and child care—including self-care. Not only do we need to know how much work children do and what they do, but, as well, how easy or difficult it is for parents to obtain their cooperation in this respect. Furthermore, Statistics Canada (2003g) informs us that 10 percent of husband-wife households em-

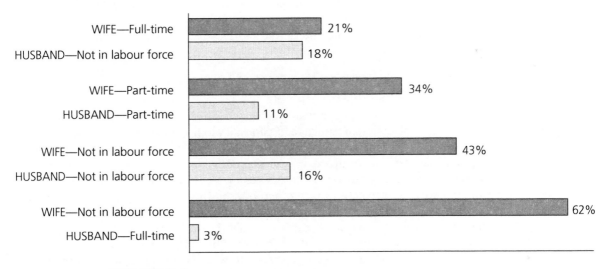

FIGURE 5.1

Percentage of Spouses with Children Who Do 30 or More Hours of Unpaid Housework per Week by Labour Force Status, 1996

Source: People Patterns Consulting, based on Statistics Canada Census–Sauvé, 2002b.

ploy some domestic help. Among couples (and professional singles), domestics, who are usually immigrant women, contribute to alleviating better-off women's own domestic burdens and time squeeze, thus participating in the gendered division of household labour. They are more likely to be hired when wives' incomes constitute a greater share of the joint income and house size is larger (Palameta, 2003).

Employed mothers (and fathers) are healthier mentally and physically than stay-at-home mothers, perhaps as a result of the benefits of occupying multiple roles (Barnett and Hyde, 2001). Nevertheless, they encounter problems specific to their combined triple role of worker, mother, and housekeeper (Glass and Fujimoto, 1994). In turn, these problems, which are actually the result of lack of social support, differ markedly across the social classes, between what is called the *two-wage-earner families* versus the *two-career families*. The latter families are in a far better financial situation to buy services, mainly quality child care and prepared meals, that can alleviate maternal role strain (Lennon and Rosenfield, 1994).

Still, employed mothers, whether married or single, on average have little time for themselves, are overworked and stressed, frequently worry about their children, and often feel guilty, even more so when child care arrangements are not optimal or when their children are alone at home after school or in the company of problematic peers. Overall, there are both negative and positive work/family spillovers (Grzywacz et al., 2002), but these differ depending on each family's work/family context. A national survey reveals that fathers and mothers in two-parent families are happier at home than at work, but divorce often reverses this trend (Kiecolt, 2003). However, for women who shoulder most of the burden at home, paid work outside is often less stressful than housework and childrearing (Larson and Richards, 1994). It is, nevertheless, quite possible that the ideological devaluation of housework in recent decades has contributed to the fact that it is now generally viewed as stressful and as something that everyone prefers to avoid (Zimmerman, 2003).

The Discussion Concerning the Effect of Maternal Employment on Children

The research literature, public policy debates, talk shows, and magazines still focus on the effects of *maternal* rather than paternal employment. (For an exception, see Harvey, 1999.) Why is so much attention devoted to maternal employment and its presumed negative consequences on children? Why not consider fathers' employment in these respects? The answer to this question resides in the overall gender stratification and social constructions of motherhood and fatherhood, further discussed in Chapter 10. Under the existing gender-based division of responsibilities, mothers are still viewed as children's primary caregivers. But the notion that mothers are children's best caregivers is unscientific. If mothers were "by nature" the best caregivers, why would an army of social workers be needed to watch over the thousands of children abused or neglected by their biological mothers and fathers? Being a competent child-care giver is more a matter of training, personality, and social encouragement than femininity versus masculinity.

Evolutionists may point out that mothers' nursing and caregiving were essential to children's survival at the beginning of humanity and thus have come to constitute part of human nature. However, as seen in preceding chapters, both historically and cross-culturally, the fact remains that *shared* child care is the norm rather than the exception (Scarr, 1998). Throughout the world, mothers share the care of their young ones with female relatives, older children, co-villagers, and even elderly men. The same situation probably prevailed during evolution. Shared care ("other mothers") is often encountered among African Canadians and people from the Caribbean region, perhaps a remnant of traditions that continue to exist in contemporary African villages (Barrow, 1996; Collins, 1992).

This concern about the effect of maternal employment arose at a time when mothers were encouraged to leave work after their Second World War effort in order to give back jobs that "naturally" belonged to returning male veterans. Not only were women "sent home" but child care centres built during the war were dismantled, thus making it difficult for mothers to continue their employment activities. However, very little in the way of negative impact of maternal employment was ever found in the research (Harvey, 1999; Menaghan and Parcel, 1991). Possible exceptions may exist for very small children (Han et al., 2001), especially when their mothers work more than 30 hours a week (Brooks-Gunn et al., 2002), or children of mothers whose employment is substandard (Raver, 2003). Thus, in more recent studies, when the impact of maternal employment on children is examined, mothers' work circumstances and the quality of care children received are considered, especially within the first year of a child's life (Waldfogel et al., 2002). For instance, maternal employment carries more risks among poor than non-poor children because there often is no quality substitute care, mothers earn too little to make ends meet, their jobs are boring, and they are too exhausted to be enthusiastic parents when they return home (Ali and Avison, 1997:358). These difficulties may increase when families live in an unsafe neighbourhood (Sampson and Laub, 1994).

So what can we conclude? *All things being equal,* children whose mothers are employed do not have more negative outcomes than children of stay-at-home mothers. Maternal employment may even be advantageous to some children, particularly girls, in terms of school achievement and self-esteem. This is especially so when mothers' occupations are highly skilled and complex (Cooksey et al., 1997). Even for disadvantaged children, a mother's salary may raise the family's standard of living and thus provide compensation against risks for children (Harvey, 1999).

Parental Employment in General and Children

It is important to reframe the question of maternal employment within the context of parental employment. Analyzed within an interactional and transactional perspective, the effect of the employment of one parent cannot be separated from the effect of the employment of the other parent. To begin with, no matter what their social class, when *both* parents work *long* hours and there are no adult substitutes at home, children and adolescents may not have sufficient interaction with caring authority figures. A study looking at the effect of both parents' employment found that, when mothers' hours at work increased, fathers became more aware of their 8- to 10-year-old children's activities, as a compensating mechanism (Crouter et al., 1999). But the researchers also found that children were less well monitored when both parents had demanding jobs (Bumpus et al., 1999).

According to James Coleman's (1990a) rational theory, in situations where parents are overworked, children are deprived of social resources or social capital. Possibly, children go unsupervised, which is a risky matter in this society where opportunities for problematic and even delinquent behaviours abound. Depending on their personalities, some adolescents may take advantage of negative opportunities and use drugs, become sexually active prematurely, or even engage in delinquent acts. Actually, there is a direct correspondence between delinquency and lack of supervision by *adults* in general, including parents (Mekos et al., 1996). In other words, the better supervised adolescents are, the less likely they are to commit delinquent acts. When no adults are in charge, children may fail to learn certain coping skills, others may not do their homework, and still others may not learn how to communicate effectively. In other words, even when their parents are relatively affluent, many of these children may not develop sufficient human capital and may be undersocialized. That is, they may not learn what they are required to know at a given age in order to function effectively and ethically in this society.

Another potential problem related to parental employment resides in the combination of materialistic values with a *preoccupation for upward mobility*, or "moving up socially." These parents (who also have a high divorce rate—see Clydesdale, 1997) spend many hours at the office or on business trips and, when at home, often pursue their career-related activities rather than engage in family interactions. They are now encouraged in this direction by the omnipresent cell phone and laptop computer. Such parents do not have the time to relate to their children authoritatively or to teach them appropriate values. Also, the lives of working parents' children are sometimes hectically packed with activities and their days are lived at a frenetic pace. Let's look at the example of a young, affluent family from my 1998 home interviews of two-career couples.

This suburban family consists of two parents aged 35 (husband) and 33 (wife), both professionals in large brokerage firms, and two boys of 3 and 6 years of age. The family rises at 6:00 a.m. The parents alternate taking the boys to the day care centre where they arrive at 7:00 a.m. From there, Glenn, the oldest, is picked up by minivan at 8:45 and brought to a nearby school, where he is in grade 1. The parents take turns fetching the children at 6:00 p.m. at the day care, where Glenn has been since 3:15 after another ride in the minivan. Once a week, a taxi drives him to music classes after school and returns him to the centre. One parent takes the hungry children home and promptly serves them supper; the other parent arrives at 7:00 p.m., equally hungry and tired. The children are in bed at 8:00, quite exhausted by then.

Saturday morning, the father takes the boys for swimming lessons; the mother takes them for skating lessons in the afternoon. Sunday is spent going to church, shopping, and visiting with friends and relatives. Both parents are intelligent, attractive, and sociable. The boys get along well and play together in the few hours of unstructured time they have. They are apparently intelligent. However, Glenn's report card indicates that his verbal skills are below grade level. His visiting grandmother explains that this is due to the fact that the children are always in the company of other children and are rarely alone with adults who, at any rate, are obviously of no interest to the child-oriented boys. The boys basically spend only two hours daily with their parents who are all the while busily engaged in housework activities. Little conversation takes place. Life is fast paced.

Economic Realities and Changing Family Time

When both parents, and especially mothers, have demanding hours, less time is available for personal needs, as well as family and couple interaction (Clark, 2002). However, when adults feel that their work environment provides flexibility, they benefit from a more favourable work-family balance (Hill et al., 2001). As well, when children's activities outside school are regimented into a variety of lessons and sports, they have less time for spontaneous play—even though these structured activities may be favourably related to cognitive development (Hofferth and Sandberg, 2001). Furthermore, information technology has spawned "gadgets" such as cell phones, to which one could say adults and children are tethered, and which occupy a great deal of their time in interaction with other persons, often to the detriment of interactions with family members. The sociology of the family has yet to research the impact of these types of technology on parent-child interaction and on family dynamics in general.

Thus, another effect of economic changes on families consists of what is called the **time crunch:** Too many activities are crammed into too few hours, as seen in the example above. Spouses have less time for each other, especially if they work different shifts, and parents can devote far fewer hours to their children (Hofferth et al., 1998). The use of the Statistics Canada Time Crunch Instrument has revealed that 23 percent of parents of children under the age of six are "highly time-stressed"; 68 percent feel that they do not spend enough quality time with their children (Invest in Kids, 2002). The U.S. Bureau of the Census has estimated that, between 1960 and 1986, parental time available to children has diminished by 10 hours per week for whites and 12 for blacks (Fuchs, 1990). The phenomenon of "latchkey" children comes to mind here, as well as of older siblings taking care of a younger one after school (Riley and Steinberg, 2004). However, when comparing 1981 and 1997, Sandberg and Hofferth (2001) concluded that children did not spend less time with their parents. The major shift in children's loss of time spent with parents seems to have occurred between 1960 and 1980.

But there is far from unanimity in the studies: Other researchers have found that adolescents now spend an average of three hours a day alone at home (Schneider et al., 2000). As well, another study found that, "In low and high income households, parents report spending under 5 minutes a day reading or talking with their children and less than 20 minutes a day playing with them" (Williams, 2002:10). However, while total parental time has diminished in two-parent families, time per child may have increased—because there are fewer children (Wolff, 2001). Overall, mothers have been able to maintain their hours with children by doing less housework, for instance (Schor, 2001). Nevertheless, both mothers and fathers would prefer to have more family time, and half of them wish that their partner would spend more time with the children (Bond et al., 1998). It is difficult, however, to know if the children themselves feel deprived of "family time" as, in great part, family time is a social construct of our decades (Daly, 2001).

High-income families may be even more affected than low-income families in patterns of time consumption. Parents with a higher income work at least six hours more per week than those on a low income (Williams, 2002). For instance, the General Social Survey of 1998 revealed that high earners between the ages of 25 and 54 spend on average 4.6 hours a day on leisure activities compared to 5.3 hours among low-earners (Williams, 2002). This is less leisure time than available in 1971 (Harvey and Elliott, 1983). As an illustration of this time squeeze, let's hear what another young professional couple, with both spouses employed full-time, said when interviewed in 1998:

> The spouses in their early thirties both complained during their separate interviews that they had "no time for each other; it's even difficult to put some sex in our lives because we are always on the run" [wife]. For his part, the husband felt that his wife "could work fewer hours; that way, it would be easier to arrange our schedules so that we can take some time out for our relationship." He did not mention that he could also work fewer hours, a realistic possibility, given that he stayed at the office daily until 8 p.m. This was a very affluent couple with extremely high material expectations—costly expectations. In contrast to the other couples interviewed, this couple was not concerned about having practically no time for their 4-year-old son. Fortunately, the little boy appeared to be good-natured and easily contented. He made no demands during the two hours I spent at his home and he occupied himself peacefully.

The Rise of Consumerism in Family Life

One reason families now need larger incomes resides in the rise of consumerism fuelled by advertising and television programming, which all contribute to a sense of relative deprivation (Easterbrook, 2003). For instance, when families watch certain shows focusing on the well-to-do, they may feel deprived in comparison (Friedman, 1999). New "needs" are created by advertisers, whether for clothes, cell phones, computers, entertainment units (DVD players, large-screen TVs), or more cars per family. This may affect young persons even more because they do not have a past that would allow them to see that life can go on without these "necessities." As well, the size of houses has increased substantially as has their cost, and these large spaces have to be furnished. Furthermore, children are exposed to a great deal of peer pressure to conform to the latest fashions in toys, clothes, and accessories—often imitating those worn by pop stars such as Britney Spears or marketed by the Olsen twins—all American exports.

Therefore, many activities coordinated by parents and carried out by all members of the family, whether individually or communally, are related to consumerism. Family members dream of objects, shop for them, buy them or fail to do so, agree or disagree on their necessity, their costs, their appropriateness, and develop a sense of identity in part related to their possessions (Côté, 2000; McCracken, 1988). Furthermore, consumerism—looking at catalogues and online displays, going to malls, searching for items in mega stores—takes time (Pupo, 1997). This time could be used for other family activities; thus, consumerist activities may compound the time crunch felt by parents (Cross, 1993).

Long ago, the sociologist Thorsten Veblen (1899) developed the concept of *conspicuous consumption* as related to the class situation in which families are embedded or expect to reach. In other words, families acquire possessions that are visible (conspicuous) and give them a certain status. However, technology and fashion change so rapidly in this century that families have to keep upgrading their possessions to reflect their affluence (Frank, 1999). As well, in past centuries, families were both sites of production and consumption, whereas they have now largely become sites of consumption. In fact, much consumption takes place at the individual level, outside the family realm. In view of these observations, it is somewhat surprising that contemporary sociologists of the family have paid little attention to these processes and dynamics of market forces. As Daly (2003:778) points out, we have given little "attention to understanding how spending behaviors and consumer goods are the basis for the construction of meaning in the everyday experience of family life." The culture of consumerism within the family should be an important topic of research, as it permeates the self-construction of family members, young and old (Katz and Marshall, 2003).

Consumerism has other forms, such as the consumption of "Mac" foods and other foods rich in fat and carbohydrates—and in ever-larger quantities. The end result has been an explosion in body weight and obesity, which in turn is affecting the current and future health of family members. While this is occurring, the market forces churn out diet books, and people's anxieties about their body mass increases. Magazines and television also present body models of slim women and muscled and fit men. A small study in Winnipeg has indeed shown that men and women who read such magazines tend to accept these standards and, for many, their concerns about their appearance are related to eating disorders (Morry and Staska, 2001). It is important to do more research on how these simultaneous but conflicting marketing trends affect family dynamics.

Young People Remain Home Longer

Another effect of economic changes on family life, which is further discussed in Chapter 12, rests on the fact that young adults remain at home with their parents longer and delay marriage (Statistics Canada, 2002a). Remaining at home enables youths to pursue their education without paying residence fees. Furthermore, once employed, free parental room and board allows those who earn low salaries to afford the luxuries of life that are now defined as necessities, such as cars, electronic equipment, regular changes in clothing styles, and even travelling. In disadvantaged families, particularly among immigrants who sponsor the arrival of other members of their kin group, young workers may stay home to pool their resources with those of their parents or, at the very least, to help pay for household expenses. Other youths remain or return home because of unemployment (Mitchell, 1998). As well, a large proportion of teen, single mothers stay home for a few years, often with their mothers, either to complete their education, to work, or simply because they are too poor and inexperienced to live on their own.

FAMILY POVERTY

Canada is a very advanced society technologically; yet, poverty, even if diminished, has persisted, particularly among the working poor. The **working poor** are those whose wages are too low to raise their family above the poverty line or to the income-to-needs ratio determined by the government. When wages are minimal, many families become or remain poor, despite the fact that both parents are employed. Part-time work and minimum-wage jobs are largely responsible for this situation. Statistics Canada calculates a "Market Basket Measure" based on a formula that includes the costs of food, clothes, shelter, and transportation for each region. This formula tells us how much, in theory, a family needs to earn in order to meet its basic needs: Families who earn less are considered disadvantaged, thus the concept of "living below the poverty line," or LICOs, which stands for low-income cut-offs. In 2003, the following poverty lines were established for Canada's major cities for a family of *four*, from most to least expensive cities to live in:

City	Amount	City	Amount
Vancouver	$27,791	Fredericton	23,940
Toronto	27,343	Hamilton	23,745
Ottawa	26,503	Edmonton	23,571
Charlottetown	25,434	Winnipeg	22,750
Halifax	24,607	Regina	22,442
Calgary	24,180	Montreal	22,441
St. John's	24,096		

Rural areas have a different component: a car allowance for the equivalent of a five-year-old Chevy Cavalier, and related expenses, as a means of transportation. Hence, the rural Ontario poverty line is $25,117 (because of lower housing costs than Toronto), while rural British Columbia is the most expensive place for disadvantaged families to live in, at $28,376 a year.

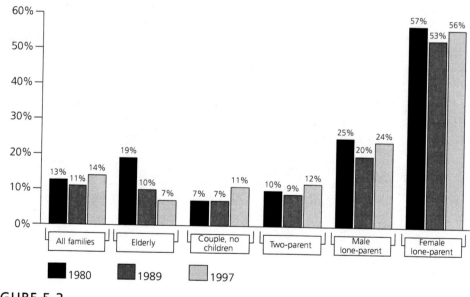

FIGURE 5.2

Poverty Rates Among Canadian Families

Notes: Poverty rates based on Statistics Canada's Low Income Cut-offs (1992 base). Elderly families are those with head 65 years of age or older. Couples without children, two-parent families are non-elderly. Two-parent and lone-parent families restricted to those with at least one child under 18 living at home. (Vanier Institute of the Family, 2000:117.)

Figure 5.2 gives poverty rates from 1980 to 1997 for different types of families, and the 2004 profile is similar to that of 1997. In Toronto, fully 70 percent of lone-parent families are poor (FSAT, 2004). To these statistics, one must add at least another 10 to 15 percent of families and children who hover precariously above the threshold. These vulnerable families constitute the near poor, or the economically marginal (Morissette, 2002a, b). Any crisis can send them tumbling below the poverty level—crises such as a dental emergency, the need for prescription medicine, the birth of an additional child, or the loss of even one of the many part-time jobs these families may hold.

The average wealth (assets minus debts) for all families rose by 37 percent between 1984 and 1999. Yet, *young* families experienced a decrease in both their median and average wealth of 30 and 20 percent, respectively (Morissette, 2002a,b). In fact, the percentage of families with no assets or with only debts rose to 16 percent. In the year 2000, the poorest 20 percent of families had an average income of $19,844 while the richest 20 percent had an income over $106,000 (Sauvé, 2002b).

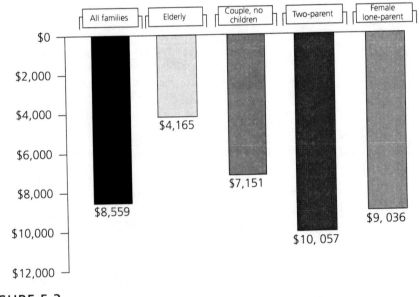

FIGURE 5.3

Depth of Poverty Shown as $ Below "Poverty Line" by Family Type (1997)

Notes: Poverty gap based on Statistics Canada's Low Income Cut-offs (1992 base). Elderly families are those with head 65 years of age or older. Couples without children, two-parent and lone-parent families are non-elderly. Two-parent and lone-parent families restricted to those with at least one child under 18 living at home.

Source: Statistics Canada. Low Income Persons, 1980 to 1997, 1980 to 1997. Catalogue no. 13-569-XIB. Vanier Institute of the Family, 2000:123.

Another aspect of poverty is its **depth**—that is, disadvantaged families often earn far less than the poverty line. For instance, in 1999, half of all one-parent families with one child who were poor had incomes of $10,000 or less—this is called deep poverty (United Way, 2001). This is well illustrated in Figure 5.3 for the year 1997. The profile is similar for recent years. In Toronto, more than $15,000 would be needed on average to lift poor families with children out of poverty (FSAT, 2004). Thus, most disadvantaged families cannot afford some of the basics of life. For instance, in 2002, households with an income below $23,000 spent $3,500 on food, while households with an income between $40,000 and $60,000 spent $5,060. In fact, the average household expenditures for food stood at $6,680 (Statistics Canada, 2003k). Even when they deprive themselves, disadvantaged households spend over 51 percent of their budget on food, shelter, and clothes, compared to only 28 percent among those who earn the most. Thus, the rich have more money to spend on luxuries and with which to accumulate assets.

SOURCES OF FAMILY POVERTY

Why are there so many disadvantaged families amidst the affluence in Canada? What are the causes of families' poverty? At the risk of oversimplifying what is a highly complex issue, the sources of poverty fall into two categories: the **systemic,** or structural, sources at the social level, and the **personal** ones. *Structural* and *systemic* refer to overall social conditions, whereas *personal* refers to attributes and behaviours of the poor. The personal sources are generally preceded by the large-scale socioeconomic or structural causes that generate both poverty and the personal sources of poverty (Haveman and Wolfe, 1994). If the economic and social causes of poverty were eliminated, the personal sources, while not vanishing entirely, would be radically reduced.

Structural Sources of Poverty

In Canada and the U.S., poverty is the result of an unequal distribution of resources among families rather than an overall lack of riches (Ambert, 1998; Orton, 1999). Indeed, the gap between rich and poor families has widened in the past two decades, both in Canada and the U.S. (Schor and Menaghan, 1995; Sauvé, 2002b). At this time, the following structural aspects of the organization of our society probably constitute the major causes of family poverty:

- the loss of employment due to the restructuring of the labour market, such as companies relocating jobs "offshore"—that is, to other countries where salaries are extremely low
- unemployment related to low educational qualifications in some segments of the population, particularly First Nations individuals
- low-paying and part-time jobs, especially among women and minority groups, and the lack of a subsidy for minimum wages
- the decline of well-paid, unionized entry-level positions in manufacturing
- pay inequity by gender (women are paid less than men for comparable job qualifications) and overall inequality

- "corporate welfare," which consists in subventions paid by various levels of government to corporations, or very low taxes paid by corporations (corporate welfare represents monies that governments cannot spend on child care, family subsidies, and health care)
- discrimination and segregation, which prevent various population groups, particularly First Nations families, from accessing good schools and job opportunities
- insufficient social benefits for families

The Issue of Deficient Social Policies

Two deficient social policies are examined that contribute to creating poverty or maintaining it. First, a study by the AFL-CIO has shown that, on average, women would earn over $4,000 more each year if they were paid as much as men who hold comparable job qualifications (Lewin, 1999). This is referred to as **pay inequity.** As an example, a social worker (now a largely feminine occupation) earns $35,000, compared to a probation officer who is paid $50,000. The educational requirements are equivalent and the work demands are quite similar. If women were paid equitably, the poverty rate in families where mothers are employed could be cut by half. Pay equity legislation has been passed in Canada for federal employees. Nevertheless, there are many loopholes in other employment

The working poor include families in which both parents are employed in low-paying jobs. One parent may even hold two jobs. These families are hovering precariously, just one slippery step above the poverty level. This situation is even worse in the U.S., where these families rarely have health insurance.

sectors. Canadian women earn 80 cents for every dollar earned by men. In Toronto, the wage gap is smaller: 86 cents for women, which still results in a gap of $2.25 per hour (FSAT, 2004).

Second, when families are already poor and receive minimal welfare benefits, and for only a restricted period of time, as is the case currently, these meagre social assistance payments contribute to keeping them at or below the poverty level (Edin and Lein, 1997b). In Ontario, for instance, social assistance has been so eroded that it provides families with about half of a poverty-line income (FSAT, 2004). If benefits were more generous and if they were maintained once a parent has found a low-paying job, poverty would diminish. Thus, from this perspective, it can be said that the welfare system contributes to familial poverty. Furthermore, not only do most disadvantaged people work at least some months during the year, only a minority receive welfare benefits at any point in time (Wertheimer, 2001). Therefore, a more appropriate social policy would guarantee a living wage to all Canadians.

With the recent cuts in social assistance, the number of individuals forced to have recourse to food banks has grown—up by 5.5 percent in 2002 alone—for a total of over 778,000 Canadians who turned to food banks in a one-month period, a number which exceeds the population of New Brunswick. For instance, while a month's worth of groceries for a family of four is estimated at $629, Ontario welfare provides only $203, or a mere one-third of what is needed to survive (Lawton, 2003). Furthermore, even though the population has increased since 1994, the number of persons who receive social assistance has come down drastically from over 3 million to 1.7 million in 2003. This reduction is partly driven by Alberta and Ontario where the numbers were more than halved (NCW, 2004). Although families leaving welfare generally experience an increase in income, still 30 percent experience a deepening of their poverty (Statistics Canada, 2003c).

The Sociopersonal Sources of Poverty

The personal sources of family poverty are generally the ones favoured for discussion by the public, the media, and policy-makers. These personal sources imply that individuals who bear certain demographic characteristics, such as single motherhood, are responsible for their poverty and for all the consequences flowing from it, including a child's delinquency, for instance (Caragata, 1999). An emphasis on the personal sources of poverty leads to the reasoning that, were these persons to change their attitudes and behaviours, poverty would be eradicated. While this may be true in some cases, this emphasis nevertheless precludes a consideration of the larger socioeconomic causes of poverty and conveniently precludes political change to remedy the situation. This is why, in decades of budgetary restraint, welfare programs for mothers with dependent children are popular targets of suspicion and cuts: Welfare policies are gendered (Vosko, 2002).

Divorce as a Source of Poverty

Divorce is a direct source of poverty for women and children, although a sizeable proportion of divorces are themselves caused by economic hardship (Smock et al., 1999). Indeed, families under economic pressure are more likely to experience negative interactions, spousal conflict, domestic violence, and child abuse. Any of these problems can lead to divorce; thus, disadvantaged families are more likely to break apart (Aseltine and Kessler, 1993). Once separation takes place, the mother and child unit becomes even poorer (Statistics Canada, 1999). Studies carried out by Galarneau and Sturrock (1997) as well as Bianchi et al. (1999) indicate that, in the year after divorce, and adjusting for family size, women's household income falls by about 20 to 40 percent, whereas men's income increases slightly. Hao (1996) has documented that divorced fathers accumulate about $23,000 in wealth, compared to $600 for divorced mothers.

When divorced mothers become poor, however, they remain so or stay on welfare for a shorter time than never-married mothers (London, 1996). This is in part a matter of age and education as well as previous work experience. For those women who were comfortably middle class before divorce and who fall into poverty after, this situation usually is transitory; after several months to a few years, they are generally able to lift themselves out of poverty through employment, their parents' help, fathers' child support, and especially remarriage and cohabitation.

Single-Mother Families as a Source of Poverty

Never-married parenting more often than not stems from poverty and leads to poverty (Singh et al., 2001). As we descend the socioeconomic ladder, the number of births to unmarried women increases noticeably (Morris et al., 1996). Nevertheless, poverty is not the only source of nonmarital birth because most single women who are poor do not have children. Following Wilson's (1987) example, American demographers, such as South (1996), have studied the impact of men's and women's wages on marriage formation for all races. They found that both men's and women's marriage rates rise with each additional thousand dollars that men earn. Overall, in Canada, the U.S., and Caribbean nations, black women's lower marriage rates are to some extent a matter of economics, as well as a more permissive attitude about single motherhood (Sassler and Schoen, 1999; see also Butler, 2002). But even black women with a higher educational level are less likely to bear children alone than other black women (Musick, 2002). Disadvantaged adolescents who hold low educational and vocational expectations may feel that they have little to lose by engaging in unprotected sex that might lead to pregnancy (Furstenberg, 1992). This attitude is well expressed by a student:

> "I am 28 and had my son at 16. At the time I was fed up with school and my mother and I didn't care to work and I thought the baby would be fun to have. I didn't go out of my way to have one but I certainly took no precautions.... It didn't end up being the rose garden I had wanted.... I was on welfare for many years...and bored. I went back to school at 23 and it has been a struggle."

In contrast, whether they are poor or not, youths who are pursuing their education and who maintain reasonable expectations of finding a decent job after college or postsecondary training, or who already have achieved these goals, are generally motivated to avoid unmarried pregnancy and early pregnancy in general. As Devine and Wright (1993:139) state, "For the average middle-class girl...having a baby is a quick path to downward mobility." In the short term, nonmarital motherhood makes relatively little economic difference in the life of an already impoverished teenager or young woman. In the long run, however, too many of the women who were already poor remain locked in poverty (Laroche, 1998). Those who work at low wages have more expenditures (child care, health care, transportation) and often experience more hardships than those who remain on welfare—and welfare itself is difficult enough (Edin and Lein, 1997a). Once an already disadvantaged young woman has a child, her maternity merely entrenches her poverty or makes it last longer, and her chances of marrying decrease (Bennett et al., 1995; Turcotte and Bélanger, 1997a). Her motherhood also creates poverty for her child.

When a single mother is employed, not only is she the sole wage earner for herself and her child, she is also far more likely than a male worker to earn a low salary (Edin and Lein, 1997b—see Family Research 5.1) and to fall behind in her loan and housing payments (Pyper, 2002). She generally earns less than an employed divorced mother, even though the latter does not earn as much, on average, as a male breadwinner. Therefore, the economic disadvantage of *women in general* is especially detrimental to single mothers' families, both divorced and never married, but particularly the latter.

Surprisingly perhaps, in the past, a majority of these mothers have eventually left poverty while still young, although most remain near the poverty level. One has to be

Interviewing Is Easier Said Than Done

Kathryn Edin and Laura Lein (1997b) wanted to resolve the discrepancy reported in large surveys that single mothers' expenditures are higher than their incomes. They interviewed 214 welfare-reliant and 165 wage-reliant, low-income mothers several times in order to track their unaccounted sources of income as well as types of expenditures. During the first meeting, the researchers asked mothers to detail all their monthly expenses. Edin and Lein point out that it was crucial to ask about expenses first and sources of income later. In their very first trial interviews, respondents who had talked about their incomes first had then adjusted their expenses downward to fit the reported income. Once the mothers had claimed that they spent nothing on clothes, for instance, it was impossible to make them

retract, even if the interviewer saw the clothes on them! Thus, the order in which the questions are presented is extremely important in surveys.

Edin and Lein also emphasized that interviewers must listen carefully to the meanings that respondents attach to questions and words. For instance, the researchers learned that, when responding to large multiple-choice survey questions, most of the single mothers acknowledged receiving "child support" only when it was collected by the state. As a result, Edin and Lein found that the total value of money or gifts the women actually received from their children's fathers far exceeded what they reported in official surveys under the rubric of child support.

careful here because economic conditions have changed drastically since this research was carried out in the 1980s. Indeed, a more recent study found that, once in poverty, a mother who remains single can expect to spend 5.1 to 6.9 years in that state (Laroche, 1998). Morissette and Zhang (2001) report that lone parents have a 16 percent probability of being poor for at least four years, compared to 3.5 percent for couples with children.

In the future, it may become more difficult for such young women and their children to exit poverty, both because of the educational requirements of the new economy and lower social assistance payments (Hofferth et al., 2001). Furthermore, there are indications that mothers of teen mothers in dangerous neighbourhoods are frustrated by the uncooperative and menacing peer culture that often engulfs their daughters and are consequently not as supportive as previous generations had been (McDonald and Armstrong, 2001). This said, while admittedly relatively few young mothers become affluent, a good proportion never need to resort to welfare or return to it. For their part, Menaghan and Parcel (1995) find that single mothers who are employed in well-paid occupations provide their children with a home environment equivalent to that available in similar two-parent families. Unfortunately, among the never-married, these mothers are the exception, unless they had their first child later in life and were able to accumulate both social and financial resources. For many impoverished young women, having a baby out of wedlock may be the only form of social status they can look forward to (Fernandez-Kelly, 1995). Motherhood provides an important source of satisfaction and esteem (Cohler and Musick, 1996) when economic opportunities do not exist (Caragata, 1999). From the individual point of view of the young mother, it makes short-term sense to have a child because there are relatively few males who could marry her and help support her child, particularly if she is black (Coley and Chase-Lansdale, 1998).

On the other side of the coin, it makes no economic sense *for the child* who is born in poverty or who becomes at higher risk of poverty (Smith et al., 1997). Even when his or her mother exits poverty two to four years later, these few years represent a sizeable proportion of a young child's life (Phipps, 1999; Morissette and Zhang, 2001)—and early poverty is most detrimental to a child's educational and occupational outcomes (Duncan et al., 1998). Indeed, whether children in single-mother families have divorced or never-married parents, two salient facts emerge. First, these children are much more likely to be poor than those who live with both parents. In 1997, as seen in Figure 5.2 earlier on, 56 percent of mother-headed families were below the poverty level, compared to 29 percent for single-father families, and 12 percent for two-parent families. Second, having a single mother who is a member of an ethnic minority places children at an extraordinary risk for poverty because of discrimination (see also Kaufman, 1999). Single mothers, even when not poor, are less likely to accumulate net assets (Morissette, 2002a). Thus, one can be concerned that the near future will result in a larger proportion of poor elderly women who have been single mothers most of their lives.

CONSEQUENCES OF FAMILY POVERTY

Overall, poverty contributes to isolating people socially; for instance, low-income Canadians are much less likely to say that they trust other people or to participate in community activities than are other Canadians (Statistics Canada, 2004n). Put differently, poverty deprives families of social capital. But it affects mothers, fathers, and children differently, in part because of gender roles (mothers versus fathers) and in part because of life stage: Children are affected early in their life course, whereas fathers and mothers are impacted as adults. However, in the case of teen mothers, the effect can be a recurrent one, as they generally were poor as children and are poor again as young mothers. This section is linked to Chapter 9 and is complemented by material in Chapters 4, 6, and 7, where we have seen and will see that the consequences of poverty at the family level are compounded or alleviated by race and ethnicity as well as neighbourhood factors and educational opportunities.

For Mothers

Impoverished mothers who live in neighbourhoods with a high concentration of poverty, especially when criminality is added, are particularly vulnerable to failure as mothers because the circumstances under which they raise their children are simply unfair (see Kotlowitz, 1991). Their ability to supervise their children is often impaired by the conditions imposed by poverty (Sampson and Laub, 1994). In view of this situation, it is not the elevated rates of negative child outcomes that are surprising, but the fact that they are not higher. That so many of these mothers' children grow up to be decent citizens is a tribute both to the resilience of some children and to their mothers' extraordinary diligence and devotion.

These mothers, who are both poor and live in low-income areas, are deprived of the resources that a middle-class woman takes for granted in raising her children (Edin and Lein, 1997a). In addition, they often lack credibility in their children's eyes, due to their poverty and, in some cases, due to their never-married status, as described recently by the following student:

> "What made me the most unhappy between ages 10 and 14 is the conscious struggle I went through because of my mom [who had her first child nonmaritally at age 18]. I loved her but didn't pay her any respect and obedience and my brother didn't [either]. We had big mouths and we knew that we could get away with murder because what could she do all alone with us?...I got pregnant twice and had two abortions before I turned 17. I felt guilty about my mom but I wanted to have fun.... My brother had babies...and did time.... At 18 I finally got my act together probably because my mom was a good woman, she worked so hard and she wanted me to get an education. I wanted the respect she never got and I am no unwed mother, I tell you."

As Cook and Fine (1995:132) note, low-income mothers have few childrearing options and cannot afford to make errors. In many neighbourhoods, they have to be more strict and vigilant because "errors" lead to delinquency, drug addiction, early pregnancy, and even death. Therefore, success in socialization goals is seen in terms of "sheltering their children from the pitfalls of self-destruction, such as drugs, crime and cyclical government dependency" (Arnold, 1995:145). Loftier goals, such as the development of children's verbal and reading skills, are a luxury in such environments. The basic tasks of feeding, housing, and shielding their children, and especially their adolescents, from danger are at the forefront of these mothers' thoughts and energy. When Alisha, a student, was small, her mother emigrated from Jamaica to Baltimore, where Alisha and her two younger brothers joined her. Alisha was then 10 years old and was 13 when the family relocated to Toronto. In both cities, they lived in a poor neighbourhood. She recalls her life in the Baltimore "ghetto":

> "In the morning, we were often late for school and I had to get my brothers ready because my mother had left a long time ago; she had to commute to her job.... After school, we'd go back home minding our own business and careful to stay away from the older boys as my mother had told us to do. We'd get something to eat and then watch TV and my mother would come home around 8:00. When it was dark in the winter months we used to be real afraid alone and sometimes Jamal would disobey and leave the apartment and get into trouble with the boys down the hall. I was so scared that my mother would blame me.... During weekends my mother would take us grocery shopping and then we'd stay home. We didn't have friends because my mother was afraid that we'd run with the wrong crowd.... We were not doing well at school and when we got to Toronto we were put back two years. I was so lonely in Baltimore...my mother was no fun to be with because she was real strict with us because she was afraid we'd go wrong or we'd get killed."

As they become single parents, many women and their coprogenitors perpetuate and even create poverty. But this occurs mainly in countries that have very limited pro-familial and prochild social policies. For example, in countries such as Sweden, single mothers' poverty rates are not much higher than that of married mothers. Why? First, Sweden and other European governments provide adequate subsidies and child care arrangements that allow mothers to be employed, whatever their marital status. A second reason why the poverty rate in single-mother families is not much higher in some countries is that most first-time single mothers are older: Rates of single teen childbearing are very low, thus further reducing the potential for poverty.

For Fathers

The effects of poverty on men as fathers have been less extensively studied than those on mothers, in great part because fathers are often absent in indigent families. Fathers are affected by poverty differently, depending on the place they occupy in their families of procreation. In this respect, at least four categories of economically disadvantaged fathers exist:

1. fathers who are part of two-parent families and are gainfully employed (their salaries are low and they may have to combine two jobs, or their work is seasonal)
2. unemployed fathers in two-parent families
3. separated or divorced fathers with minimal income or who are unemployed
4. men who have fathered children out of wedlock, do not reside with them, and are either unemployed or earn inadequate wages

The first two categories of fathers are the most negatively affected by poverty, particularly when they are unemployed. They experience a great deal of pressure, even if only from within themselves, to support their family more adequately. In addition, they may be working two jobs, in itself a source of stress and a potential for ill health. Society defines fathers as the chief breadwinners and this assigned role can be a heavy psychological burden on the shoulders of a disadvantaged man. His self-esteem may be badly bruised; he may feel that he has little control over his life or that he is failing his children and wife (Rubin, 1994). In stark contrast, a man who earns a decent income is proud of his ability to support his family.

For a man who has a family to support, unemployment becomes a source of friction, general tension, and irritability between husbands and wives (Elder et al., 1992). Men feel diminished, experience psychological duress due to their unacceptable status and their humiliating and fruitless job searches, and may react more abrasively and withdraw emotionally from their wives. These behaviours may undermine the spousal relationship and contribute to marital instability. Wives may become resentful of their lack of financial resources and, when employed, may complain that they are shouldering the entire family's economic burden.

For their part, divorced or separated fathers who are too poor to contribute child support may distance themselves from their children. Their ex-wives may also prevent these men from seeing their children, either because they fail to support them, they are a "bad example" or a "bad influence," or were abusive before. As for those men who have fathered children nonmaritally, do not live with them, and are too poor to support them (which may well be a majority of adolescent mothers' boyfriends), very little is known as to how poverty affects them *as fathers*. How poverty affects single fathers and their relationship with their offspring as well as the mother(s) constitutes a very interesting field of research that is largely unexplored (Tamis-LeMonda and Cabrera, 1999).

For Children

Child poverty denies human beings the chance to develop adequately and securely from the very beginning of their lives. However, not all children are affected in the same way by poverty and, in fact, despite the high risk factor that it creates, most poor families are resilient. Thus, how children are affected is contingent upon a *combination of factors*, including:

- the age of the child (the younger the child, the higher the risks)
- the extent and length of the poverty episode
- family structure and functioning (home environment)
- race/ethnicity (segregation and discrimination)
- neighbourhood quality
- parental education, mental health, and warmth
- parental monitoring of child's activities, particularly during adolescence
- presence of antisocial peers
- the child's personal characteristics and resources

At their negative level (e.g., low maternal education and lack of parental supervision), all of these variables represent risk factors: The greater the number of risk factors accompanying poverty, the more negative the effect (Sameroff and Seifer, 1995). At their positive level (e.g., maternal warmth, stimulating activities), these variables offer resilience against the potential negative effects of poverty (Kim-Cohen et al., 2004). Mounting evidence shows that, in terms of IQ development and school achievement, the most devastating impact occurs when children begin life in poverty (Pagani et al., 1997). Thus, **early** child poverty is the most detrimental in terms of a child's future adult status in society (Caspi et al., 1998; Duncan et al., 1998), in great part because homes that are disadvantaged are more likely to be less stimulating cognitively (Eamon, 2002).

Any problematic child characteristic, such as low birth weight or deficient cognitive abilities, can combine with poverty to produce additional negative effects for the child, both currently and in the future, while a similarly frail child raised in an economically secure family generally has a more positive life course (McLoyd, 1998). In contrast, children with qualities such as a more outgoing temperament are less affected by deprivation (Kim-Cohen et al., 2004). Young children who live in persistent economic hardship develop more problems, particularly at the cognitive level, than those whose poverty is temporary (Ross et al., 1996). In turn, the latter have more problems than children who have never experienced disadvantage (Duncan and Brooks-Gunn, 1997). The **depth of poverty** also exerts a dramatic effect on children's abilities and performance: Children in families with an income that is 50 percent below the poverty level are at a great disadvantage.

Children born into indigence or who are poor for many of their formative years are denied the opportunity to actualize their abilities, to receive a good education, often to live in a safe neighbourhood, and even to be fed adequately (McIntyre et al.,

---

National Longitudinal Survey of Children and Youth (NLSCY)

This ongoing large-scale research program should shortly begin to give us a deeper knowledge of the role that poverty plays in a child's developing life. The NLSCY has been conducted by Statistics Canada and Human Resources Development Canada every two years since 1994/95. It follows a representative sample of children aged newborn to 11, in all provinces and territories, into adulthood. The sample originally included 22,831 children from 13,439 households. In each family, the person considered most knowledgeable about the child answers a set of questions designed to provide socio-economic and general health information about himself or herself, the spouse or partners, and the child, including the child's health, general development, and social environment. Were the data for all these family members analyzed jointly, much information could be gathered on families rather than just on individuals.

However, as Moss (2004) points out, there are several limitations to this study, one of which is that there is only one informant about the child (generally the mother), and that informant may not always be aware of what the child experiences at school and how the child behaves in other contexts. For instance, in terms of violence, the informant is asked, "How often does the child see adults or teenagers in the home physically fighting, hitting or otherwise trying to hurt each other?" This question can address only the violence the mother witnesses with the child and does not address other violence the child witnesses alone, nor does it address emotional or verbal violence and the severity of such.

2002). In turn, these cumulative disadvantages can later produce deficits in employment and health that persist into adulthood. For instance, malnutrition and stress caused by poverty imperil health and well-being in midlife and old age, and ultimately reduce life expectancy. Children who experience poverty *at any point* are three times more likely to be poor in adulthood than children who have never been disadvantaged, and are also more likely to earn less—even when the economy is flourishing (Corcoran, 1995). In other words, the consequences of child poverty and its accompanying misfortunes may far outlast the initial period of poverty itself and may be lifelong.

The most visible and consistent deficit related to poverty is that disadvantaged children, on average, have lower IQs, academic skills, and school achievement, and have more behavioural problems than non-poor children (Willms, 2002c). On average, therefore, poor children repeat grades, drop out of school, and become unemployed or enter dead-end jobs more often than children who have never been poor. Studies also agree that poverty during the preschool years is more pernicious than later poverty in terms of these consequences (McLoyd, 1998). Unfortunately, small children have higher rates of poverty than older ones because the latter have older parents who earn more. Thus, one can see why it is so important to prevent infant and preschool poverty, both for the short and long term.

Disadvantaged children have more frequent accidents than other children because their surroundings are less safe and they are less well supervised; they are also less healthy (Chase-Lansdale and Brooks-Gunn, 1995) and witness violence at home more often (Moss, 2004—see Family Research 5.2). As well, their level of mental health problems far outstrips that of other children (Carey, 2001). Moreover, disadvantaged children are more often identified by teachers than other children for behavioural problems. Even if one reduces this figure by half to account for possible teachers' prejudice against disadvantaged children or their parents (or against minority children or children in single-parent families), the difference remains substantial and is confirmed *across the world.*

As illustrated in the following student quote, disadvantaged children often stand out from others in a multitude of ways that are psychologically painful. For instance, some live in a housing project and may be ashamed of it. They may not want to let their peers know about their predicament and may not invite them home. Furthermore, poor children are unlikely to have the pocket money received by their schoolmates. They may be unable to participate in extracurricular activities with their peers, which can lead them to be ostracized. In fact, low-income children in economically mixed schools are less popular than more affluent children (Pettit et al., 1996). Their parents may be less well dressed, may not have a car or may have an old and rusty one, and may be unemployed. These children may receive free meals at school. All or any of these visible social stigmas are humiliating and painful to bear, although they may be less so in a school where a great proportion of the children are equally disadvantaged.

> *"What I recall as having been the most painful between the ages of 10 and 14 is that we were poor. At least that's when I realized that we were poor, until then I guess I had not noticed and I had had other problems on my mind [her father's drinking and violent outbursts]. At that age kids can be cruel and they found out that I lived in a dump and even the other little scums as poor as me would pick on me to make themselves look superior. My mother was trying very hard to raise us well and always sent us to schools in the other neighbourhood. That's probably why nobody found out or made me notice [that she was poor] until that age.... There were so many days when we were hungry, what can I say, my father drank every bit of money we could get.... I am ashamed now to think that I dreaded it when parents had to meet the teachers because my mom looked so tired, so old, her clothes were so out of style. She was so so tired and so so sad and often so ill but she hung on for us.... What I recall as having been the happiest time since 15? It's when my mom and older brother told my father to leave and dumped all his stuff outside and she got a better job and my brother got off school for a year to help her. We moved to a better place, I mean not rich but better and things started picking up from there. We were still poor but we were on our way and didn't have to tiptoe around my father." [When this autobiography was written, the siblings were in university and doing well.]*

CONCLUSIONS: THE COSTS OF FAMILY POVERTY

When all the consequences (both short term and long term) of family poverty are taken into account, it becomes obvious that it is much more economically advantageous for a society to invest in families and children to *prevent* child poverty—a topic to which we return in the last chapter of this book. Otherwise, society has to keep paying throughout the decades for poverty's multiple, recurring consequences. This means that subsequent generations will pay for the current societal neglect of poor children in terms of remedial schooling, illness, mental hospitals, juvenile courts, prisons, drug rehabilitation programs, and, later on, unemployment and medical care in old age—to name only a few of the long-term economic costs on society of child poverty.

Today, people live in a society and in an era in which the economy, broadly defined, is probably one of the most determining features of family life, along with gender, although people are rarely conscious of this effect as they go about their daily activities at home. The economy and its accompanying technology determine job and income availability, which, in turn, impact on family life and even family formation and structure. These same larger, structural forces contribute to poverty, which then creates a fertile ground upon which personal sources of poverty (such as divorce and single parenting) can grow. In turn, the personal sources of poverty reinforce the effect of the larger economic forces that cruelly bear down upon the poor. When detrimental neighbourhoods are added to this cauldron of forces, there is, on the one hand, a potent recipe for an enormous range of familial problems, and, on the other hand, an even wider range of familial resilience, survival, and success against all odds.

Summary

1. Economic and technological developments have contributed to the current profile of families. Manufacturing has become a less important source of good entry-level jobs for youths with only a high school education. The service sector has expanded to provide jobs that require high educational credentials, and yet others that pay little and are often part-time. The latter are disproportionately held by women, particularly minority women. As a result of the changes in the economy, the gap between poor and rich families has widened.

2. Economic changes have had the following effects on families: They have resulted in an increase in feminine employment and in two-income families, a continued domestic division of labour along gender lines, a reduction of familial as well as individual time, the rise of consumerism in family life, and the fact that young adults remain at home with their parents longer and delay marriage.

3. There has also resulted an increase in poverty among the employed (i.e., the working poor), although poverty in general has slightly decreased.

4. The dual-income family creates a second work shift for mothers. The main question asked concerning the effect of parental employment is this: Is maternal employment detrimental to children? Recent studies have found no important detrimental effect of maternal employment on children. However, the possibility remains that when both parents work extremely long hours, children are deprived of adult attention and may not be adequately socialized.

5. The structural sources of family poverty are reviewed. One issue is that of deficient social policies related to pay equity and insufficient social assistance. Among others, the two main sociopersonal sources of family poverty discussed in this chapter are divorce and the formation of families by single women.

6. After divorce, many women's income plummets, and a good proportion become poor, as they have to support their children on a reduced budget. Families formed by single mothers are both a result and a source of poverty: A majority of the mothers are from poor families. However, a substantial proportion escape from poverty, particularly if they do not have any

other nonmarital births, complete their education, secure a reasonably paying job, and/or remarry.

7. The consequences of poverty for mothers reside in the difficulties inherent to raising children within a very negative environment, particularly for those who live in high-risk neighbourhoods. Men have not been studied in terms of how poverty affects them as fathers. We know that their unemployment becomes a recurrent source of friction within the family and that divorced fathers who cannot afford to pay for child support often become alienated from their children.

8. The consequences of poverty for children are more numerous and more severe when they are poor during their early childhood, when they are poor for a long period, and when they live in an unsafe neighbourhood with a high ratio of delinquent peers. Poor children are particularly affected in the domain of cognitive development, school progress, and conduct problems.

9. It would be economically advantageous for society to eliminate child poverty. Poverty is related to familial problems, but it also highlights familial survival and success against all odds.

Key Concepts and Themes

Conspicuous consumption, p. 128
Consumerism, pp. 128–129
Deficient social assistance benefits, pp. 133–134
Depth of poverty, p. 134
Divorce, p. 134
Downsizing, p. 119
Dual-income families, pp. 120–124
Globalization of the economy, p. 119
Feminine employment, pp. 120–122
Gendered labour, pp. 120, 122–124
Inflation of educational requirements, p. 120
Information technology, p. 119

Low-paying jobs,   p. 132
Maternal employment, pp. 124–125
Parental employment, pp. 125–126
Part-time jobs, pp. 119–120
Pay inequity, p. 122
Preoccupation with upward mobility, p. 126
Shared child care, p. 125
Single-parent families, pp. 135–137
Systemic causes of poverty, p. 132
Time crunch, p. 120
Working poor, pp. 129, 130

Analytical Questions

1. Given the structural economic forces discussed at the beginning of the chapter, what could the government do for the future of our country in these domains so that families are not further burdened?

2. Analyze the two-way relationship between poverty and the formation of families by single mothers.

3. Above all, what role do men play in this economic causality path?

4. Within the family itself, how can parents alleviate the negative effects of poverty on their children?

5. What other social policies would prevent family and child poverty?

Suggested Readings

Ambert, A.-M. 1998. *The web of poverty: Psychosocial perspectives*. New York: Haworth. This book focuses on the consequences of poverty for neighbourhoods, schools, families, mothers, and child-rearing, as well as child and adolescent outcomes.

Bradbury, B. (Ed.) 2000. *Canadian family history*. Toronto: Irwin Publishing. Sections of this book contain several articles on feminine employment and the gendered division of labour in the late 19th and 20th centuries, especially the chapters by Bradbury, Bullen, Parr, Rosenfeld, Iaconetta, and Luxton.

Duncan, G. J., and Brooks-Gunn, J. (Eds.) 1997. *Consequences of growing up poor*. New York: Russell Sage Foundation. The various articles are quite readable. The contents present state-of-the-art information on the consequences of child poverty.

Hochschild, A. 1989. *The second shift*. New York: Avon. The author documents the disproportionate amount of work that employed mothers do, their exhaustion, and, often, the strain that the father's not sharing in housework brings to the dual-income marriage.

Suggested Weblinks

Canadian Council on Social Development provides information on policy aspects related to various issues, including the economy.

www.ccsd.ca

National Council on Welfare is an advisory group to the government. Its site includes data, such as social assistance statistics.

www.ncwcnbes.net

Raising the Roof is an action website on homelessness.

www.raisingtheroof.org

Statistics Canada's website, particularly through *The Daily*, regularly provides information on the economy and families.

www.statcan.ca

In the U.S., **The Urban Institute's** website offers special sections related to the economy.

www.urban.org

CHAPTER 6

Impacts of Neighbourhoods and Environments on Family Life

"We lived in three different places since my birth moving each time to a bigger better house. The first was a rented semi-detached that I lived in until I was 5, then we moved to a semi-detached we owned on a better street also downtown and then we moved to where we are now when I was 12 in our own house with three bathrooms and a big yard."

"My parents bought a three story semi-detached house downtown one year before I was born and we still live in the same house today. My family occupied only two rooms, a kitchen and a washroom. Every other room in the house was rented [to pay for the mortgage]. In four years, we started taking up more rooms for ourselves."

"I grew up on a farm that we still own. We could see the neighbours' farmhouses but we could not see the neighbours themselves. Except for the road turning into a near highway with more traffic coming through, nothing has changed much. Some neighbours have died and some farms have been sold but we know everyone even though we do not see them often. I like the feeling of community and I miss it here where I live during the school year. Everyone is in a rush and no one knows who lives where."

"My family has always lived in a two-bedroom apartment except that we have not lived in the same one all the time. I think we have lived in eight different ones. According to my mother we have moved because we were evicted once, we couldn't afford the rent. Then the other times we moved because the neighbours were either too noisy or too rough or too criminal. Now that we are older we are thinking of buying a townhouse just north of here [beginning of an inexpensive suburb]."

Housing and neighbourhoods constitute a family's first immediate context. As the students' quotes well illustrate, families' economic conditions and lifestyles are expressed through their dwellings and surroundings. Additional quotes later on in the text show how families' daily lives—and, in turn, their children's opportunities, health, and behaviour—are affected by these surroundings. Although rarely encountered in family textbooks, the study of neighbourhood effects on families is a domain of sociological inquiry with a long tradition. This tradition has recently been renewed and has become particularly visible in reports by Statistics Canada and in sociologically oriented sections of child development publications. It is a field inspired by the Chicago School of Sociology (Park and Burgess, 1925) and by current concerns about the difficulties families encounter in American inner cities—problems which are replicated to some extent in many Canadian cities (Kohen et al., 2002a). In this chapter, the discussion is extended to an entire spectrum of families' housing conditions.

TYPES OF URBAN AND SUBURBAN AREAS AND FAMILY LIFE

Most of the currently available research focuses on urban families. In recent decades, there has been little research on family life in smaller cities, and affluent neighbourhoods have not been studied. Rather, the focus has been on large urban aggregations and particularly Americans' often troubled inner-city neighbourhoods. During the past two decades, the largest urban areas in Canada have experienced two phenomena. First, a greater proportion of the population now lives beyond the boundaries of cities in successive rings of suburbs that combine to form metropolitan areas. Second, suburbs have evolved and many have become cities themselves; thus, many suburbs have diversified and are no longer strictly residential.

The types of families residing in these various areas differ by social class, household composition, and now more often than in the past, ethnicity. For instance, singles and empty-nesters who have sold their houses are rarely encountered in the residential parts of suburbs, preferring the more diverse lifestyle of the city or of suburbs that have become satellite cities unto themselves, such as Mississauga or Thornhill in the Toronto area. In contrast, families with small children tend to gravitate toward residential suburbs. But even some of these suburbs are fast changing, as many include industrial zones, office and commercial areas, high rises, and malls complete with hotels, restaurants, and entertainment centres.

Although most Canadians, especially the affluent, find their neighbourhoods safe, the issue of security is nevertheless present (Peters, 2002). Security essentially means being away from property crime, violence, and drugs. As a result, many families, especially in middle-class and affluent areas, now opt to enrol their children in supervised activities after school, rather than allow them free play time on the streets of their neighbourhood (Adler and Adler, 1998; Hofferth et al., 1998). In the past, children had the potential of turning a set of streets into a community because they played outside and established links between families, as described by this student who grew up in the 1970s:

> *"I also remember how much fun I used to have playing on our street. When my family moved into our house, the housing area was new and just starting to develop and many young families also moved into the area. The street was full of kids in the same age group, and we would get together and play games such as hide-and-seek, and almost everyone would play. There used to be something to do almost every night, especially in the summer. If it wasn't baseball, it was football or road hockey. As I now realize today, it was the kids of this age group which linked our street together, and as we got older we spent less and less time with each other."*

Therefore, children's role as informal community organizers and links between families may have eroded. As well, in some large cities, the advent of video games and the Internet, along with television, has changed children's patterns of play and social interactions (Chapter 3). Despite this increased isolation, when neighbourhoods are reasonably stable and have no social problems, adolescents can find support in times of familial difficulties or personal transitions (Rodgers and Rose, 2002).

It is difficult to know to what extent there is less "neighbourliness" than in the past. But, generally, couples with children have more contact than others with their neighbours, and level of contact is higher in areas that have detached homes. Provincially, families living in the Maritimes and Saskatchewan have the most interaction with neighbours, and Québécois have by far the least (Kremarik, 2000a). While perhaps contact can be explained by having lived in the same area for several years, as may be the case in the Maritimes, it is difficult to explain the Quebec difference in this respect. However, Québécois are also less likely than other Canadians to engage in community activities (Jones, 2000) and to express trust in other individuals (Statistics Canada, 2004n).

AFFLUENT NEIGHBOURHOODS

In Chapter 5, we indicated that the effects of the culture of consumerism on family life have not been researched (Daly, 2003). Similarly, while there are many studies comparing families in low-income neighbourhoods with those in average or middle-class areas, very little information exists on family life in affluent or upscale neighbourhoods. As Marks (2000:613) points out, affluent families are part of *family diversity*, yet they are rarely studied and tend to be positively stereotyped in view of their economic and social capital advantages.

In well-to-do areas, a majority of the households have incomes well over the $125,000 level. Above all, these families have a great deal of assets in the form of real estate, stocks, bonds, and financial enterprises. They own or manage a majority of the means of production in society. Their heads are heirs, investors, and top executives of large corporations (at the upper-upper class level), while others are bankers, successful stock brokers, highly educated persons in the top echelons of the civil service, as well as owners of smaller private corporations (at the lower-upper class level). The neighbourhoods of the affluent are also home to scholars, physicians, lawyers, and entertainers at the upper-middle-class level. These families together account for about 15 percent of the population.

A large segment of parents are achievers but do not necessarily worship material possessions and do not particularly value such extrinsic rewards as fame and wealth over interpersonal relations and community service (Csikszentmihalyi, 1999). The parents will not sacrifice time with their children for their fortune and will manage their social schedule so as not to compromise familial duties. The values they pass on to their children do not centre on the acquisition of material possessions and they may, in fact, be concerned about giving too much to their children at the material level. These parents provide their children with as many educational and developmental opportunities as possible but do not push them to be competitive.

At the other extreme in this group of affluent families are parents who, above all, value social and material success; the pressure to work, acquire, and consume depletes their personal energies to the detriment of interpersonal relationships (Schor, 1999). As a result, these parents have very little time for their children and are minimally involved in their upbringing, so that the children feel isolated (Luthar and Becker, 2002). Furthermore, the parents are teaching values that are materialistic and competitive: Often, as Myers (2000a) points out, material acquisition leads to a need for further acquisitions rather than satisfaction. Frustration may result. Children are put on a "treadmill" of acquisitiveness and they measure their sense of self by what they have. Because these well-to-do areas are more "private" and there is a greater distance between houses, children and parents are also less likely to exchange services with friends or to feel connected to a social community in their neighbourhood (Myers, 2000b).

One can therefore hypothesize that the first group of adolescents whose parents are not disproportionately invested in materialistic and status-related rewards should have a higher level of social conformity, lower anxiety, and feel more connected to family and community than the other group of adolescents (Kasser, 2002). At the adult level, studies of physical and mental health show a positive correlation between neighbourhood income and well-being (Diener and Biswas-Diener, 2002). Nevertheless, one has to emphasize the fact that the rich are a heterogeneous group of families and that their family dynamics will be related to the lifestyle they adopt and the degree to which they emphasize values that are, or are not, purely materialistic and competitive. These remarks apply to any cultural group as well as to any income group (Ryan et al., 1999).

The few studies that have appeared on children who live in affluent neighbourhoods are American and focused on young adolescents living in suburbs. As Luthar (2003) points out, we do not know if these results apply in all regions and to adolescents who live in affluent neighbourhoods within cities. Luthar and D'Avanzo (1999) as well as Luthar and Becker (2002) have found that a higher proportion of these affluent suburban teens suffer from anxiety and depression, and use alcohol, marijuana, and other illicit drugs more than disadvantaged inner-city students do. They are also less supervised in their home, as young as age 10 to 12, perhaps because parents rely on the relative safety of their neighbourhoods (Luthar, 2003). Thus, obviously, family studies would benefit from an injection of research on affluent families, both in rural and urban Canadian neighbourhoods.

LOW-INCOME NEIGHBOURHOODS

The study of families in low-income neighbourhoods is important because, although most are stable, well adapted, and resourceful, the risk factors of poverty and of the concentration of poverty in a given area negatively impact on too many families. Even resilient families find it more difficult to cope in such environments.

The spacious houses and affluent lifestyle described above contrasts with the world of neighbourhoods marked by a high concentration of low-income families. An area is defined as low-income when at least one of every five households, or 20 percent, fall under the poverty level (Statistics Canada, 2004a). For instance, in 1999 in Toronto, the 12 lowest-income neighbourhoods had poverty rates of 29 percent or higher—thus very high poverty (United Way, 2001). Overall, low-income areas have a detrimental effect on family life and on individuals, even when families are well functioning. Their residents' health is poorer on average, and life expectancy is five years lower for men and 1.6 years lower for women than in the highest-income areas (Wilkins et al., 2002). This deficit in life expectancy is especially salient among Aboriginals (Maxim et al., 2003). In Montreal, Toronto, and Vancouver, low-income families *moving into* a low-income neighbourhood tend to remain locked in for an average of five years (Statistics Canada, 2004a). Other families are started in these disadvantaged areas and may remain in them even longer.

When Social Problems Are Added

Often, but not always, low-income neighbourhoods suffer from visible cues indicating the breakdown of social order (Ross et al., 2000). As indicated in Family Research 6.1, residents can perceive this situation. Generally, many of these neighbourhoods experience a quadruple concentration of disadvantages, each feeding on the other: poverty, deteriorated housing, criminality, and single-parent households. Sociologist Robert Sampson (1993) suggests that social disorganization follows when a community is no longer able to maintain **social control** or to supervise youth peer groups. The concentration of female-headed households not only means that children may be less well monitored when their sole parent is employed, but also that large numbers of unattached young males roam the district with few responsibilities and too much free time on their hands (Land et al., 1990). A heavy concentration of out-of-school and unemployed young males generally precludes effective social control of their activities and those of male children who grow up imitating them.

FAMILY RESEARCH 6.1

Measuring Respondents' Perception of Problems in Their Neighbourhood

Ross and Mirowsky (1999b) designed a 15-item scale to measure respondents' perception of neighbourhood problems. Respondents are given statements and indicate the extent to which they agree with them. Examples are:

- Vandalism is common in my neighbourhood.
- There is too much drug use in my neighbourhood.
- There is a lot of crime in my neighbourhood.
- In my neighbourhood, people watch out for each other.
- People in my neighbourhood take good care of their houses and apartments.

For each question on this and similar surveys, respondents are given choices ranging from "totally agree" to "totally disagree."

Each response is scored so that computers can make calculations, just as in multiple-choice questions in a test. For instance, totally agree = 5, and totally disagree = 1, if the scale is a 5-point scale. Some scales range from 1 to 7 while others have choices from only 1 to 3. A larger range allows respondents to give answers that are closer to their feelings. With only three choices, respondents are very restricted in the choice of answers, and this may introduce a bias in the results. (The results may not be as valid.)

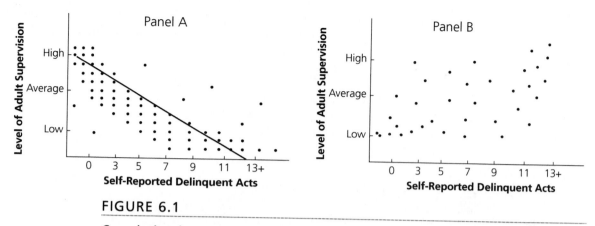

FIGURE 6.1

Correlation between Adult Supervision and Number of Delinquent Acts

Each dot represents an adolescent who is placed on the diagram depending on how many delinquent acts he or she reports and how well supervised he or she is by adults (parents, teachers, neighbours, etc.). When the dots fall in a well-ordered pattern, as in Panel A, this is an indication that a good correlation exists. The straighter the line, the higher the correlation, as illustrated in Panel A. However, in Panel B, there is no correlation because there is no pattern: The dots are scattered, which means that there is no relationship between level of adult supervision and self-reported delinquent acts. Panel A describes reality (more or less), while Panel B is presented only to illustrate what a lack of correlation looks like.

These young males, neither responsive to their mothers' demands nor to their children's needs, are the most important element of community disorganization (see Luster and Oh, 2001). Furthermore, the absence of responsible adult males in households often leads to the perception of women and children as more accessible targets for theft and sexual assault. Many adolescents become easier recruits for delinquency, as they are less supervised. As mentioned in Chapter 5, there is a correlation between low supervision and delinquency. This is illustrated in Figure 6.1 above. (The purpose of Figure 6.1 is to allow the reader to visualize what correlations look like; a further definition appears in the Glossary.) In some areas of Toronto, for instance, youth gangs kill a shocking number of other males of their own race—assured that the numerous eyewitnesses to their crimes will not report them to the police out of fear of retaliation: This is a reversed form of social control.

Risk Factors for Children of Low-Income Areas

The wording of this subtitle is important: "Risk factors" mean that there is a *higher probability* that problems will arise for families in low-income areas than in other areas. But it certainly does not imply that the majority of families are malfunctioning or yet "pathological." Nevertheless, parents in these areas are aware of these risks, for only 35 percent of Canadians with low income agree that their neighbourhood is an excellent place in which to raise their children. In contrast, a majority of middle-class and affluent families have a positive image of their neighbourhood in this respect (Peters, 2002).

The Risk of Inadequate Mainstream Socialization

Children in neighbourhoods that are both poor and beset by social problems, especially when their parents are also poor, may be less adequately socialized; that is, many may not be taught the social skills needed in the workplace or in their personal lives, or general habits expected in mainstream society (Wilson, 1996). For instance, even when their families' SES is taken into account, children as young as four and five years of age who live in poor neighbourhoods have lower verbal skills and more behavioural problems than children whose neighbours are more comfortable financially (Kohen et al., 2002a). A student from a very deprived family and neighbourhood describes the difficulties she encountered in Grade 1 when she went to a religious school out of her area. This quote well illustrates a child's resilience and strategies to overcome disadvantage:

> "Going to school for the first time was supposed to be a wonderful experience and I had so much looked forward to it: at last I was going to have something special that my four younger brothers and sisters didn't have. But things turned out differently than expected.... I was always late in the morning because my parents never got us up on time and we were too tired because we had watched TV late, even the babies. Then I would often fall asleep at my desk so that I missed out on a lot of things and most of the children seemed to know what to do and I didn't and I didn't know what to ask my parents to buy for me and they had other things on their minds anyways; for them my being at school was just one fewer child in the house but as far as the rest was concerned they were hopeless. Then I dressed differently than the other children or my clothes were dirty because we didn't have a washing machine in the apartment and my mother had to go to the laundromat.... I tried to fit in by copying the other children's behaviours and even watching what their parents did for them when they picked them up. Slowly by the end of grade 1 I had learned my way around school in terms of expected behaviour and I've wanted to be a teacher ever since."

Where large housing developments are located, and fear and mistrust reign (Ross et al., 2001), parents cannot establish links among themselves and collectively monitor the whereabouts and activities of each other's children (Sampson et al., 1999). Thus, parents in such areas are deprived of adequate power of supervision over their children and even good parenting practices may not prevent child antisocial behaviours (Simons et al., 2002). Indeed, studies have shown that community adversity affects adolescents' mental health; in some cases, a favourable family environment cannot even compensate for the negative impact of the neighbourhood (Wickrama and Bryant, 2003). Indeed, Steinberg and colleagues (1995) point out that parenting is "more than the individualistic process that contemporary society makes it out to be." It is a group phenomenon. **Collective efficacy** refers to those social ties within the community that facilitate the collective supervision and socialization of children concerning shared norms and behaviours (Sampson et al., 1999). This also overlaps with the concept of the **effective** or **caring community** (Bould, 2004). In such a community, parents are involved in school activities, supervise their children's behaviour and associations, and get acquainted with other children's parents (Coleman and Hoffer, 1987:7).

Kupersmidt and colleagues (1995) compared children with familial vulnerabilities living in relatively low SES areas to similar children living in somewhat more affluent neighbourhoods. They found that the latter neighbourhoods served as a protective shield against the development of aggression in high-risk children. These areas do not tolerate street and school aggressiveness. Therefore, children are less likely to associate with difficult peers; consequently, inadequate parental supervision is not as detrimental as it would be in a low-income area. In an American social program designed to improve families' living conditions, inner-city families were relocated, some to the suburbs, others to another area of the inner city (Briggs, 1998). These households were followed up by researchers over time. The children who had moved to suburban apartments were more likely to go on to college and, once adults, to earn higher salaries than children who had moved to apartments in the inner city (Rosenbaum, 1991). Thus, it seems that a certain percentage (a **critical mass**) of low-income neighbours increases the risk for behavioural problems and subsequent school difficulties. In contrast, a critical mass of affluent neighbours raises a child's chances of completing high school (Brooks-Gunn et al., 1993). More recent research indicates that low-income neighbourhoods begin producing a negative effect on the development of a child's IQ by age three, above and beyond the family environment (Klebanov et al., 1998). Moves to higher-income areas seem to result in a lower crime incidence and improvements in health (Katz et al., 2001; Ludwig et al., 2001).

However, as pointed out in a previous section, in some affluent neighbourhoods, no collective socialization by adults takes place and there is no effective community in evidence. Parents are largely absent, permissive, and even uninvolved. Such parents tend to be materialistic and overinvolved in high-paying jobs. Thus, a segment of relatively affluent adolescents spend their time in cars, at various "hot spots," or partying with drugs in otherwise empty homes, and even engage in gang activities leading to break-ins and thefts. Hence, one should not err in the direction of attaching an aura of superiority to a district simply on the basis of material affluence and lack of visible street criminality. An affluent neighbourhood is not automatically a "good" one in which to raise children.

The Risk of Inadequate Supervision and Protection

It is apparent, then, that many poor children in unsafe areas are at risk of not being as adequately supervised as children in other neighbourhoods. They may have peers who belong to gangs that largely escape the supervision of responsible adults. Moreover, these neighbourhoods are also disproportionately populated by single-parent families. On average, children from such families are less well monitored (Fischer, 1993), particularly when mothers' educational level is low (Quane and Rankin, 1998). Single mothers are frequently beset by problems that worry them and that take away attention and time that could be devoted to their children. When single mothers are employed, their children may return to an empty home after school, to the homes of equally unsupervised peers, or they may "hang out" in places where risks abound. Supervision is one of the elements that is generally lacking in cases of juvenile pregnancy, drug use, and delinquency. However, as emphasized earlier, supervision by parents in individual families may no longer be a sufficient element (Baumer and South, 2001). Rather, it is a collective level of supervision that is necessary (Sampson, 1997).

Finally, children and adolescents who live in areas of poverty are more at risk of being inadequately protected; many mothers feel powerless in controlling teen daughters whose deviant peers are at the centre of their lives (McDonald and Armstrong, 2001). Lack of collective supervision leaves children free to roam buildings and streets that are unsafe. It also allows them to be prey to temptations that may be too difficult to resist, particularly because they are exposed to peers who may not resist the lure of deviant activities. These children are not sufficiently protected from bullying, sexual abuse, substance abuse, delinquency, and early pregnancy. Adolescents in low-income areas perceive their neighbourhoods as more threatening and hazardous (Aneshensel and Sucoff, 1996). In the following excerpt, a visible-minority student describes her childhood neighbourhood in Toronto:

> *"My area had developed a reputation of being full of poor non-white crime-related people.... I lived in a large dirty very unsafe apartment with thirteen floors that had no security or superintendent. Each apartment had a small balcony that was shared by two homes, and every home had two storeys.... I specifically remember one night when our family was home and we heard people yelling and scuffling at the front door and in the hallway, it was intense and loud.... I peeked out of the mail slot and saw two guys fighting, they looked about 18 but I knew they were much younger than that. As I continued to look I saw more guys were fighting, it had turned out to be a huge gang fight.... In the morning as I left to go to school...there was blood all over the walls and on the doors, pieces of clothing and knives were all over the floor. I wasn't as much horrified by the blood, it was the violence of such young people that had got to me. It was a sight and a feeling that I would never forget."*

This student later reminisces on the contrast between her old and new neighbourhoods:

> *"Well at this age the happiest moment I remember was when we moved away from the apartment and into our new house.... I remember finally being able to feel the freedom to play out in the streets whenever I wanted. In the summer we would stay outside until eleven o'clock and I wouldn't be scared.... That was something we wouldn't even think of doing at the apartment, so it was nice to know I could be safe."*

Well-Functioning Families in Low-Income Areas

The focus of research and social policies is on poor families and their problems; consequently, very little is known about the majority of families that succeed despite all the risks surrounding their lives. Poor neighbourhoods still contain a majority of families that are not poor but may be forced to remain where they are because they do not have the means to move, because of discrimination or because they feel more at ease with people of their ethnic background. Therefore, poor areas contain both poor and non-poor families that function well.

High levels of parental monitoring are particularly protective for children in poor neighbourhoods that are beset by social problems (Pettit et al., 1999). These families try to protect their children from the negative influences that pervade their area. Their tasks are numerous—they have to keep their adolescents in school and ensure that they make good grades. This is difficult to achieve in neighbourhoods with a high dropout rate and the presence of gangs whose lifestyle may appear exciting to a teenager from a good family, "where nothing ever happens." Parents also have to delay or prevent early sexual activity that could lead to premature parenting (Moore and Chase-Lansdale, 2001). Then, they have to shelter their adolescents from the attraction of drugs and criminal activities. They also have to orient their youths toward the job market, a difficult task when many neighbours are unemployed.

How do parents manage? Many succeed only by using drastic measures such as controlling their children's activities outside the home. They may take them to public libraries, to swimming pools and parks, or to lessons at church. Many children (and even adolescents) are kept at home after school hours and during weekends. Overprotection is necessary to weed out negative influences and physical dangers. In other families, mothers sacrifice their own needs for companionship (see Burton and Jarrett, 2000). A student describes his reaction to his parents' efforts to keep him safe in a high-risk area:

> "At the time I didn't appreciate having to be home early and not going in the schoolyard to play ball with the other guys. My parents were afraid that I would get into drugs, that I would get a girl pregnant and whatever. I don't know if any of this would have happened but I know that it did happen to most of my old buddies so now I can appreciate their devotion and the fact that they put up with the fuss I stirred up."

Some of these parents help organize support groups, crime prevention patrols, and other constructive activities in their immediate neighbourhood. Furstenberg and colleagues (1994:243) appropriately write of the "supermotivation" that such parents, often single mothers, need in order to protect their children and to create opportunities for them.

ETHNICITY AND RACE IN NEIGHBOURHOODS

Often, immigrant families settle in areas where they feel comfortable at first, which may mean neighbourhoods that "contain a relatively large number of people from the same ethnic background" (Murdie and Teixeira, 2003:137). According to Statistics Canada, the number of neighbourhoods that can be considered populated by visible-minority groups has increased from a mere six in 1981 to 254 in 2001. A "visible-minority neighbourhood" is so defined by Statistics Canada when more than 30 percent of the population is from a particular group other than white or Aboriginal (Hou and Picot, 2004).

More than 60 percent of these neighbourhoods are Chinese, primarily in Toronto and Vancouver. Nearly a third are South Asian, and only 13 percent are primarily black. Thus, only five percent of all blacks live in predominantly black neighbourhoods.

Hence, blacks are often less segregated from whites than Chinese are—which is a reversal of what takes place in the U.S. (Fong, 1996; Myles and Hou, 2004). Perhaps one reason why black families are less concentrated geographically is that the black population is more fragmented than are other visible-minority groups: It is fragmented by language, culture, and geographic origins (Owasu, 1999). For their part, Aboriginal families are found in higher concentration in Winnipeg, Regina, and Saskatoon, where they tend to live in low-income neighbourhoods (Binda, 2001).

In Vancouver, Toronto, and Montreal (which contain a majority of recent immigrants), black families have also been more likely to live in neighbourhoods with a low SES. Hou and Milan (2003) have actually found that neighbourhoods that have larger proportions of blacks are characterized by lower SES, and this association has increased since 1986. This phenomenon has also been observed for Southeast Asians in Toronto and Vancouver. However, when black families' income rises and, especially when they buy a home, they generally exit minority neighbourhoods and have more white neighbours (Myles and Hou, 2004). In contrast, among the Chinese, home ownership leads to the formation of ethnic enclaves, as has been the case for Italians. This situation was predicted by Logan et al. (2002) who foresaw that segregation by choice would become more prevalent among ethnic groups with high levels of capital. These enclaves are often in suburbs, especially around Vancouver and Toronto. However, these tendencies do not (yet) result in racial segregation as it exists in the U.S., for instance; rather, what we have is segregation by income first (Balakrishnan and Hou, 1999; Ley and Smith, 2000). The lower incidence of residential segregation of blacks than that of the Chinese may be one of the reasons why blacks have high rates of interracial unions (43 percent) while only 16 percent of Chinese are in mixed unions (Milan and Hamm, 2004).

HOMELESS FAMILIES

The number of homeless people, particularly families, has increased greatly, especially in the late 1990s following welfare cuts and increases in rents. For instance, in Toronto alone in 1999, nearly 30,000 people used emergency shelters, up from 22,000 persons one year before. But, especially within the same time, 6,200 children stayed in the city's shelters, an increase of 130 percent in one year (Lakey, 2001).

The Sources of Homelessness

The homeless are the most destitute among the poor, even though theirs may be a transitory condition, particularly in the case of two-parent families. A majority of the homeless have either been poor all their lives or poised at the margin of poverty. Many have never been on welfare. Families are homeless because of a lack of affordable housing. They can no longer pay rent and are evicted. Others have left their homes because of domestic violence or family breakdown (Shinn et al., 1991). Among adolescents, running away is a contributing factor to homelessness. Runaways generally have a conflictual relationship with their parents, although this does not unavoidably involve bad parenting (Shane, 1996:5). Many youths from foster care also run away. Other adolescents are forced to leave their homes after disclosing that they are gay or lesbian (Mallon, 1997). Whatever the causality, homeless youths' mental health is more precarious (Taylor et al., 2004) and they experience more problems with their parents (Wolfe et al., 1999). But compared to the other homeless, youths do not uniformly originate from the disadvantaged class, although a majority do. A student from a well-to-do and educated family describes her former street life after she was "kicked out" by parents who had, until then, tolerated all her drug and sex-related activities:

> "I went and stayed at various friends' houses. I continued this for some weeks, but I soon ran out of friends. When one lives nowhere, on the street, one loses common ground with one's old companions. They want to talk about things they've done or seen. You're more concerned with basics. A shower for the first time in days. Some socks. Perhaps eating or actually washing your clothes. Frankly, you turn into a bum. 'Hey, what's happening man? Like, can I have your clothes, shoes, underwear, food, money, cigarettes? Cool! Blankets! Like, I've been sleeping in this stairwell, you know. It's not so bad, ya don't get caught or nothin, ya just gotta get out before the mall opens in the morning. Ya got a smoke?'...I spent nine months as a street kid. My experiences were, for the most part, fun. I think this is partly because I knew that I could always go home. I still don't know why I kept it up for so long.... It's a complete sub-culture and many kids simply don't want to leave even if they do have somewhere to go."

In addition to poverty, disabilities and addictions contribute to continuing homelessness once it has begun. Over 50 percent of homeless adults have never married; most others are either separated or divorced (Rossi and Wright, 1993). Most have no relatives or even friends who can take them in during hard times, possibly because their own families are equally poor or because they have lost touch with them. The magnitude of the personal problems many suffer from may have worn out their welcome with their families or depleted the support the homeless person could receive from them. It is also possible that many of their families are equally maladapted. At the very least, the personal problems of many of the homeless certainly prevent their reintegration into society at large.

Psychiatric problems as well as various addictions are endemic and contribute to social isolation (Shane, 1996). Moreover, the decades-old trend to deinstitutionalize the mentally ill, without the safety net of community care that had been promised by politicians, has exacerbated the problem: Too many families are unable to shelter and care for their mentally ill relatives. For many former mental patients, the streets become the only place they have to go. Domestic violence, rather than psychiatric or substance abuse, is often a cause of homelessness for women and their children, and may serve to isolate them from at least a part of their family. In fact, homeless mothers often have a long history of victimization (Bassuk et al., 1996). Once homeless, a mother's mental health easily deteriorates (McChesney, 1995). In other words, homelessness is a risk factor for emotional disorder and general ill health (Carey, 2004; Rochère, 2003). Nevertheless, many mothers develop coping mechanisms in order to keep their young families together and reduce the effect of the daily stressors they encounter.

The Effects of Homelessness on Mothers and Children

According to Rafferty and Shinn (1991:1175), "Homeless parents often encounter difficulties balancing their own physical, social and personal needs and those of their children. The loss of control over their environment and their lives places them at increased risk for learned helplessness and depression." In fact, a large proportion of homeless mothers suffer from mental disorders (Zima et al., 1996). Several researchers have documented the difficulties that mothers encounter in fulfilling their parental role in shelters. They no longer have control over the daily routine of their family life, whether it is bedtime or other rituals. They are not able to be effective parents because of interference from other residents or staff—even though the children themselves may enjoy all this attention. Despite these difficulties, as described below by a woman student on welfare, mothers often report a sense of becoming closer to their children while in the shelter (Lindsey, 1998):

> *"The most painful event in my life occurred two years ago after my husband left me with my two preschoolers. I became very depressed, didn't do much of anything and ended up evicted. I had no family here and we ended up in a shelter. I got even more depressed, was briefly hospitalized, my children were in foster care, and back into the shelter where I finally bounced back or else I was going to lose the children. A social worker helped me find a job and day care and then a small apartment. But it had been a nightmare: we couldn't sleep, the children were totally out of it and went berserk, it was awful."*

In their study of homeless families in New York City hostels, Rafferty and Rollins (1989) found that 60 percent had been in at least two different shelters, 29 percent in at least four, and 10 percent in seven or more.

In order to separate the effects of homelessness from those of poverty, studies have compared homeless children in shelters to disadvantaged children who live in their own home (e.g., Schteingart et al., 1995). The two consistent disadvantages of homelessness reside in health and education. In terms of **health**, homeless children are ill more often than other poor children. Their incidence of respiratory infections is especially elevated as a result of crowded conditions and the sharing of inadequate sanitary facilities. One can also presume that noise, overcrowding, and parents' distress depress children's immune system so that they easily catch viruses. This health crisis is exacerbated by a lack of follow up in terms of medical care among homeless children compared to other poor children.

The second domain in which homeless children are at a particular disadvantage is **schooling**. For one thing, their rate of absenteeism is higher. They are also more likely to repeat grades (Rafferty and Shinn, 1991). We know from the previous chapter that poor children do not, on average, achieve as well in school, and homeless children are even more adversely affected in this respect. This may lead to increased dropout rates in the future, especially among those who have repeated one or more grades.

Homeless children's disadvantage in school stems from a variety of interlocking causes: They change schools and are sick more frequently than other children. The crowded conditions in which they live are not conducive to homework, and may even deprive them of sufficient sleep. Their nutrition is inadequate; many go hungry and are not able to focus in class. Their parents may be too distressed or emotionally unbalanced to help and guide them. Older children may not want to go to school because they fear the ridicule of peers who, even though poor themselves, at least can claim a permanent address. Frequent school changes isolate homeless children socially, lead to disengagement from school, and even to falling in with a crowd of antisocial peers. Moreover, schools are unprepared to address these children's multiple problems.

RURAL AREAS AND FAMILY LIFE

The lives of rural families have undergone substantial change in recent decades because of increased proximity to urban areas, technological development, and economic uncertainty. In some regions, particularly when rural life involves the fishing industry, young people migrate to larger cities, thus leaving many rural communities populated by seniors and middle-aged householders (Vanier Institute of the Family, 2002). This phenomenon is especially relevant to Newfoundland and Labrador. In some cases, rural areas become populated by young families who have recently moved to a new housing subdivision. In others, fathers and mothers commute to work in the nearest city or even metropolitan area, sometimes an hour or more each way. Rural couples are generally willing to tolerate long commutes to remain in their towns where housing and land prices are lower and where they feel that it is easier to raise a family away from the dangers of the big cities. Rural areas offer families a better chance of being members of a true community, as well as the benefits of a more egalitarian lifestyle that narrows socioeconomic differences. Greater social cohesion may offer family members advantages from which urbanites do not benefit (Hayward et al., 1997).

Of course, many rural residents make their living without relying on nearby cities. However, when rural family members lose their jobs, it is more difficult for them than for urbanites to find another occupation at reasonably close proximity. This stems in part from the fact that rural areas are less diversified at the economic level: They contain a higher proportion of blue-collar workers than do urban zones (Anisef et al., 2000; Swaim, 1995). White-collar workers with more education tend to move out of rural areas so that this selective out-migration reduces the diversity of human resources available to all rural families (Lichter et al., 1995).

There are several types of rural lifestyles, depending on the occupation of the family heads. The main ones consist of farming and ranching or fishing; vacationing is another key aspect of rural life, but for city residents. There is, once again, very little research on any of these types of familial lifestyles for Canada as a whole, although a few studies on farm families have been carried out in the U.S.

Farm Families

Farm families constitute a tiny minority of the total population, even though they feed the entire country and many other parts of the world as well. Farm productivity increased tremendously in the 20th century: In 1946, about 1.2 million Canadians

Children growing up on farms are not only more involved in the family's economy, but when small, they also benefit from the lessons of the natural environment and helpful relationships with neighbouring families.

worked on farms as a main job while only 313,000 did so in 2001, even though the farmed acreage has increased (Bowlby, 2002). Farmers are far from being a homogeneous category as they vary in terms of their economic circumstances: Some are tenants, and others are migrant workers; some own small acreage and are struggling financially, and others are involved in large-scale agribusiness and ranching. Moreover, there are differences in the farming lifestyle, depending on the crops produced—from grain to cattle in the Prairies and the west, to fruit, vegetables, and wine-grapes in southern Ontario, to dairy products in Quebec.

The level of technology utilized also determines the daily activities of farm families, from the Amish and Mennonites who generally do not have recourse to fuel- or electricity-propelled machinery, to farms where computers dictate levels of feed, fertilizers, and pesticides. Farm families also vary with respect to their degree of isolation. Many farms cluster along well-travelled rural roads, yet others are more remote and connect with neighbours in their area only via long drives, a ferry, the telephone, and for a few, the Internet.

Kinship and Gender Roles

Farm families tend to be patrilineally oriented because property is generally acquired via the son's inheritance. In fact, his parents frequently live nearby. Consequently, although grandparents play a more salient role in rural families than in urban ones, paternal grandparents are particularly important (King et al., 2004). This is in contrast to the usual urban situation where maternal grandparents play a larger role. The pattern of inheritance is a long one across the two generations and involves decades of shared familial work, which leads both to family cohesiveness and stress (Wilson et al., 1991). The intergenerational situation can become problematic when middle-aged parents begin to think about their wills (Zimmerman and Fetsch, 1994). If they decide the inheritance should favour the son who is interested in farming, then the bulk or even the entirety of the estate has to go to him if he is to survive at all economically. Perhaps very little can be passed on to the other children—a situation that may create sibling conflict later on in life (Taylor and Norris, 2000).

Despite the hazards of farming, Swisher and colleagues (1998) found that marital and familial conflict was less frequently reported by farm men than non-farm men in Iowa. However, when conflict exists, it is particularly detrimental because farm families are among the last remnants of families as units of production. Thus, conflict threatens the normal pattern of interdependence of kin. Non-farmers, in contrast, establish more obligations based on friendship and can escape, to some extent, from the potentially negative impact of family conflict. The potential for conflict and the experience of stress is especially great for a daughter-in-law in two-generation farm families, particularly if she feels left out of the decision-making process and perceives her relationship with either of her in-laws as deficient (Martoz-Baden and Mattheis, 1994).

Farm machinery does not require as much physical strength to operate as before, thus many wives work in the fields and even prefer this lifestyle to staying home. Children raised on farms are used to large machinery and are initiated in its use early in life. It is not uncommon for 12- to 15-year-old boys to drive combines alongside their fathers in the fields. Sonya Salamon (1992:52) reports the amusing anecdote of a farmer watching a combine no one was driving come toward him:

> *"When the machine stopped, his three boys, ages three, four, and five jumped out. They were all driving—one at the wheel, one at the gas pedal, and the third working the clutch."*

The 1996 census enumerated nearly 67,000 farms that were operated jointly by a husband and a wife—or 24 percent of all farms in Canada (Silver, 2001). On most farms, however, one or both spouses engage in some type of paid work elsewhere in order to make ends meet, whether part-time or full-time for one or both. In fact, more and more farmers have a job other than farming as their primary employment (Bowlby, 2002). These non-traditional farming couples have, on average, a higher income than couples whose sole source of revenue is the farm. Farm couples devote more time to their livelihood than do other Canadians—as much as 108 hours a week on large dairy farms. On traditional farms, couples share their long hours, but husbands put far more time on farm work while wives do a much larger share of the housework. This division of labour, however, is more egalitarian on small than on large farms. As well, when young children are present, wives do somewhat fewer hours of farm work but much more housework than their husbands, or than wives without young children (Silver, 2001).

Farm Families' Adaptation to Economic Crises

A few researchers have studied farm families' stress, survival, adaptation, and defeats in the face of mounting economic pressure. They have found that mothers who have to seek off-farm employment benefit their families financially and gain personal and occupational skills as well as social contacts. However, most miss their previous lifestyle and long to return to work alongside their husbands (Elder et al., 1994c). This finding is duplicated in other studies describing how a wife's satisfaction with life decreases when she is employed off-farm, in part because she has too many tasks left to do at home when she returns from her job (Bokemeier and Maurer, 1987). In some families, even adolescents increase their off-farm employment hours or leave school and take a job in order to help the family financially or to be self-supporting, thus minimizing family expenditures. In other families, both boys and girls increase their on-farm economic activities or work for relatives (Elder et al., 1994b). Thus, children and adolescents living on farms are far more familialized than urban children. A student explains how her contribution to her family's economic survival as an adolescent had shaped her sense of self:

> "Between the ages of 10 to 14 I recall being very happy because I really felt that I was important in my family. I helped my mother with cow milking before I went to school and we enjoyed each other's company. After school, I helped my father feeding the same cows and cleaning up. It was dirty work but it was meaningful because we all had to pitch in as we were afraid to lose the farm."

Economic pressure leads parents to become more preoccupied with survival and less involved in parenting. When adolescents transgress, these parents are more likely to react harshly and with hostility. This situation occurs less frequently when the parents' relationship has remained warm and supportive (Simons et al., 1994b). In families that experience serious economic pressures, husbands often become more hostile toward their wives, and wives become more depressed. The quality of the marriages decline, both because of the wives' depressed moods and the husbands' increased hostility. Husbands are also particularly upset when their wives are irritable toward them: "This difference may be the result of social norms that are more accepting of male than female aggressiveness" (Conger et al., 1994:202). Overall, these family dynamics in the face of economic hardship are similar to those of many poor urban families.

Vacation Areas

Some rural areas not only serve as residences to rural families but also function as vacation spots for urbanites who can afford a second property: a cottage, a condo, a hobby farm, or other form of rural property where the family can choose its lifestyle and replenish its relationships, as described by a student:

> "I was especially happy there [at the cottage] because my family was always around, and there was a certain air of freedom that we could not find anywhere else. This is probably due to the fact that the cabin had no electricity or hot or cold running water. So essentially we were roughing it. We received water from a manual pump in the kitchen, and we got light from oil lamps and warmth from blankets and each other. We never knew or cared what time it was or what anyone else was doing, just as long as our little world was happy, and we only had guests on the rare occasion. It seemed like a different world because we were the only ones [in the area] with no means of communication, such as telephone, radio, television, or close neighbours to rely on.... For instance, we counted on catching fish at least three dinners of the week, so it became a matter of survival."

This quote is interesting from yet another perspective: It illustrates the lifestyle contrasts that may exist between urban families on vacations and the neighbouring rural families. The former at times embrace a temporary frugal lifestyle, whereas the latter often have to struggle to avoid it. In many areas, rural families make a living by offering goods and services to these tourists and cottagers.

Ownership of a second residence in the countryside used to be a privilege reserved for the wealthy, but spread to the middle class after the Second World War and even to a segment of the working class. Nevertheless, a higher income and level of wealth tends to accompany ownership of a vacation residence. About seven percent of Canadian households own a vacation home. Of these, only 26 percent are owned by married families with children. However, many other children have free access to such homes via their grandparents or other relatives (Kremarik, 2002). It would be interesting to study the organization of family time and dynamics as families shift from urban residence to vacation home. This is yet another element of family life on which no research exists.

FAMILIES' HOUSING CONDITIONS

Much has already been said in this chapter about families' housing conditions. But the focus so far has been on the external conditions. In this section, we look at the quality of the interiors in which families live. Not only are families affected by their neighbourhood surroundings, but their functioning is also impacted by the size of the lodging, the state of its maintenance, the personal space it allows, and the level of noise.

The state of maintenance or deterioration of a dwelling can have an impact on family atmosphere as well as on health. Old houses often contain asbestos or paint laced with lead—hazards for young children that have been related to intellectual and behavioural deficits (Boivin and Giordani, 1995). The houses and apartments in which low-income families live may be poorly ventilated in the summer and inadequately heated in the winter, and the plumbing may have so deteriorated that leaks frequently occur. Such situations occur mainly in rental housing and in poor neighbourhoods, thus further adding to the diminished state of well-being of disadvantaged families (*Toronto Star*, November 1, 2003).

Overall, the burden of housing costs has increased since the 1970s. This burden has become particularly difficult for renters, compared to homeowners: In 2001, 19 percent spent over one half of their income on rent compared to six percent of owners who spent that much on their mortgages and condo fees (Statistics Canada, 2004c). This burden is particularly heavy for single-mother and minority families with three or more children (Chi and Laquatra, 1998). Two-thirds of Canadians own their home; ownership is most common in the Atlantic and Prairie regions (about 75 percent), while Quebec has the lowest rate at 58 percent (Lefebvre, 2003). Before the Second World War, ownership hovered around 45 percent. The Canadian rate of ownership is similar to that of the U.S., lower than that of Ireland and Spain, and higher than that of France and Germany.

Home ownership tends to be the rule among top-earning families, but what is of particular significance among the more affluent is that ownership occurs early on in family formation and remains stable thereafter. Young couples coming from high-income families are often helped by their parents. (This is referred to as the inter-generational transmission of wealth.) In contrast, home ownership occurs later in the family life cycle among other social groups, including the middle class (Clark and Dieleman, 1996). Thus, at the higher-income levels, children grow up in homes that are owned by their parents, whereas children in other families reach this goal at a later age or never.

The "Mansionization" of Housing

In addition, the size of the family home has been increasing steadily at a time when the number of persons living in the average household has decreased from 3.7 persons in 1971 to 3 in 2000 (Statistics Canada, 2002e). Between 1951 and 1996, homes passed from having 5.3 rooms to 6.1 rooms and even the most modest new homes now have two and even three bathrooms. Currently, among the well-to-do, particularly the new rich, the tendency is to build homes with over 5,000 square feet. This phenomenon is often referred to as the "mansionization" of housing; others call them "monster" homes.

This tendency toward extremely large homes would make an interesting study: The space per capita is vast and family members may be scattered throughout the house with only minimal contact with each other. There is less sharing of familial space (Clark, 2002), a factor that may contribute to feelings of loneliness (Pappano, 2001). Researchers might focus on how families who live in large dwellings (where each member has his or her own separate suite, often on different floors) develop mechanisms that contribute to family cohesiveness and interaction as opposed to isolation and interpersonal distance. Such families may have more clearly delineated boundaries within their system than others: the parents on one side and each child separately on the other side. Currently, very little is known about how family space contributes to increasing or eroding intimacy as well as parents' ability to socialize their children.

Mobile Homes

At the other extreme of housing conditions are mobile homes, which, in 1996, represented about one percent of private dwellings. Although 57 percent are located in rural areas, others can be found in small cities and towns (Kremarik and Williams, 2001). Mobile homes are more likely than other dwellings to house smaller families and single people. Families living in such homes have on average a lower income and over half of the adults have not completed high school. In fact, mobile homes are convenient for lower-income families because they are less expensive to acquire and to afford in terms of shelter costs. However, as they are built less solidly, they require more repairs and maintenance than other dwellings. As a result, a larger proportion of mobile homes are in poorer condition than other types of residence. Although well over 300,000 Canadians live in mobile homes, there is no research on family life and community dynamics in this alternative type of residence.

Family Privacy

Family privacy is both a characteristic within the family itself and a situation of the family toward the rest of the world (Coontz, 2000:284). Family life is much less public than it used to be when homes were designed with front porches, for instance. Now, the family has retreated inside or to the backyard (Bird and Melville, 1994). Families have become more individuated, as individualism is closely related to the concept of privacy. Nock (1998b) emphasizes that technological change—such as air conditioning (the windows of the house are closed); few, if any, trips to the laundromat (most homes have washers and dryers); and even a reduction in neighbourhood grocery shopping (as online shopping increases in popularity and as many families shop in larger malls or superstores where they go by car)—has also enhanced privacy. Functionally, families have become more self-reliant and isolated; this may be more so in suburbs than in cities.

In modern societies, the social construction of what proper family life should be dictates that parents need some privacy and children need a place where they can do homework, play games, talk on the phone, and interact among themselves. In fact, so well accepted is this ideology that many researchers believe that children need space that is their own and that they can control and where they can "individuate"—in psychological terms.

The separate space occupied by each family fulfills certain functions, but it can also be problematic. As reviewed by Berardo (1998), family privacy allows couples to resolve their problems without external pressure. It serves to protect family members against the pressures of the external world. In this sense, privacy functions as a buffer as well as a protection. In fact, public exposure is probably one of the elements that contributes to the rapid and successive divorces often occurring among film and entertainment personalities. On the other side of the coin, as each couple and each family leads its life separately, they have few points of comparison that would allow them to improve their family functioning or even appreciate how good it is compared to that of others. Privacy also means that abuse and neglect can go on for extended periods of time without external detection and/or intervention.

Overcrowding

Overcrowding is often a result of poverty (Rizk, 2003). Consequently, it is not generally a valued state, so that Canadian-born or raised families do not accept it as a fact of life and may find it highly stressful. Therefore, when too many family members congregate in too little space, the following is likely to happen.

First, parents may not be able to spend time alone, thus their level and quality of communication and intimacy may suffer. Second, personal hygiene may become problematic when the facilities have to accommodate too many persons. Third, contagious illnesses, such as colds and flu, may spread more easily in families living in cramped quarters, so that work or school days are frequently missed. Moreover, neither children nor adults may get enough sleep; as a result, their physical and mental health may suffer. Fourth, the noise level may distract children and prevent them from doing schoolwork, particularly when the television is on at all times in the small dwelling. (Here, one can see that technology exacerbates the effect of our ideological preference for private space.) Children with an attention deficit disorder may be particularly affected in this context. Fifth, family members unwittingly compete for scarce space so that conflict may arise; in some families, siblings may quarrel more, parents may yell at them and tell them to "shut up," and the atmosphere is one of exasperation.

Nevertheless, some families do cope well in cramped quarters. These are often immigrants who were used to very little space in their home country because of weather, culture, or poverty. In fact, their crowded situation in Canada may be an improvement over what they had at home. Others came from high-density areas—such as Hong Kong, where small apartments are the norm, or Moscow, where several families may share a few rooms. Again, these new Canadians may adapt well to their new situation as it compares favourably with what they left behind and, at any rate, they expect to do better in the near future. Tolerance of overcrowding therefore depends on cultural norms and the family's stage in the life course.

RESIDENTIAL MOBILITY

Between 1996 and 2001, 42 percent of the total population aged five and over had moved. Half of these moves took place within the same municipality (Statistics Canada, 2004k). Kremarik (1999) has estimated that, when Canadian adults move, 60 percent improve the quality of their lives, whether they move to a larger home or a better area, or relocate for a better job. However, although one-parent families are more likely to move, less than half are better off as a result. In general, low-income people have similar rates of residential mobility as do others, and do gain from moving—but much less so than persons with more education who move.

Moving from one home to another and, particularly for children who are already in school, from one neighbourhood to another, is an important transition in a family's life. Not only does it require adjustment to a new interior spatial configuration and functioning, but all the members have to become acquainted with a new neighbourhood, town, and even province.

A family move does not benefit its members equally (Audas and McDonald, 2004). Several studies have documented that the number of moves experienced by children and adolescents correlates with lower school achievement and rates of high school completion, and even to behavioural problems (Wood et al., 1993). This may be related to the fact that school-age children who move the most come from single-parent families (Astone and McLanahan, 1994)—thus children already at risk of poor school performance (Pribesh and Downey, 1999). When divorced families relocate, they tend to go from being owners to renters because their economic situation has deteriorated. Their mobility is particularly elevated in the first two years after separation (Clark and Dieleman, 1996). Consequently, the adjustment that children and adolescents have to make may be too demanding, for they incur three losses simultaneously: their old family structure, their former peer group, and their house (Maccoby et al., 1993).

Adjustment may be particularly difficult when a move leads to an unstable neighbourhood where the social control of youths is largely nonexistent. In such contexts, an adolescent from a family that has just suffered a breakup may be particularly susceptible to opportunities for delinquency (Sampson, 1997). School performance suffers with mobility, but this impact applies more to one- than to two-parent families. Children in one- or stepparent-families seem to suffer from any mobility (Tucker et al., 1998). The reason is that such families have less social capital or time that can be devoted to children to counterbalance the potentially negative impact of moving. In general, however, school-age children move less than preschoolers, because parents are aware of the adaptational difficulties inherent to a school change (Hensen, 1993).

When a family relocates in order to enhance a father's position on the job market, the mother may not benefit; she may actually have to abandon her own job, and if the move takes the family to another province or even to the U.S., she may lose her social support network (McCollum, 1990). Nevertheless, spouses who move because of the relocation of the chief breadwinner also experience wage growth (Audas and McDonald, 2004). But children have to adjust to new schools, new peer groups, and new neighbourhoods. A male student describes part of this dilemma:

> "The most painful thing that happened to me was when I had to move. I lost all my friends and had to leave my school but the worst part wasn't even leaving. The worst part was coming to a new school with new kids. They aren't very nice in Grade 6 if you don't wear the same clothes as them or have as much money, etc. This was truly one of the hardest periods of my life. I remember going into the cafeteria at lunch and having to sit by myself or with some other losers who were in the same position as me. I was bothered and picked on by a lot of people because I was small and it took me a long time to adjust to my situation. Of course I eventually made friends but I never quite made it with the people who I most wanted to be friends with."

(As an aside, it is interesting to note that the student labelled other children in the same situation as "losers." This evaluation reflects cultural norms of what is entailed in being successful in one's peer group [Adler and Adler, 1998]).

Elder's (1995) developmental or *life course theory* offers a new perspective on this situation. What is an advantage for the father becomes a dislocation in the children's lives: The two generational stages in the life course of a family do not mesh and the goals of one are incompatible with the needs of the other. However, this disparity in the life-course timing of the family members can be mitigated in several ways. Husbands can compensate to some extent for their wives' loss of social support, and may even accept a promotion requiring relocation only after their wives have also found a new job.

As far as children are concerned, a harmonious home (Stoneman et al., 1999) as well as the continued or even increased involvement of both parents in their lives is an important stabilizing element. Mothers' involvement helps, but the *combined* paternal and maternal involvement mitigates the disruptive effects of mobility on children more effectively (Hagan et al., 1996). When only one parent is involved, the social capital from which children can draw on may not be sufficient during a transition period. When neither parent is involved, because of financial or career pressures or because of personal problems, children are at high risk of failing to integrate themselves in a positive way in their new neighbourhood and school.

CONCLUSIONS: THE MEANING OF NEIGHBOURHOOD AS CONTEXT

Children and unemployed youths are often the most visible persons in a neighbourhood, the ones who are the most affected by its social climate, and the ones who impact it most heavily. For many children and youths, the streets are a nexus of same-age sociability and of links between families. In other neighbourhoods, the homes and the backyards fulfill this purpose; close acquaintances and friends often come from other areas to visit. Thus, a family's social life may be located within its spatial framework or neighbourhood or may extend to other areas and may even include several residential spaces.

Neighbourhood structure and housing conditions not only have an impact on people's lives but also reflect a society's values concerning social diversity. This chapter reinforces and extends the findings presented in Chapters 4 and 5 on ethnic and economic inequalities. It also serves as a link between these chapters and the next one, on education and religion, two institutions that constitute additional contexts influencing family life—in some cases, limiting family members' opportunities and, in other cases, enhancing them.

Summary

1. Neighbourhoods constitute families' first immediate, external context. Urban areas vary widely, ranging from metropolises to small towns, and include a great variety of suburbs. The types of families residing in these various areas differ by social class, race, and household composition.

2. Affluent neighbourhoods are described with an emphasis on the fact that little research exists on families who are well-to-do. Neighbourhoods that are poor and to which social problems are added present several risk factors for children. First, they may receive inadequate mainstream socialization: There is no effective community helping children develop the social and academic skills needed for the current labour market. Instead, there is a critical mass of low-income neighbours, a factor that is related to behavioural problems and low school achievement. Parents' conscientious childrearing is often defeated by the negative peer context and adult example. Second, children may not be adequately supervised, and third, may therefore not be protected from the dangers of their areas.

3. Disadvantaged areas nevertheless contain a high proportion of families that function well and are resilient. But the task facing parents of successful children are enormous, as they have to be far more vigilant than similar parents in middle-class areas. These parents have to ensure their children's physical safety, moral development, school success, and conformity to norms amidst a social climate that provides opposite models and opportunities.

4. Canadian minority groups are not as segregated as they are in the U.S., particularly blacks. However, Chinese families are becoming more segregated by choice.

5. Entire families have joined the ranks of the homeless and are generally found in shelters. Poverty, lack of subsidized housing, domestic violence, mental illness, and addiction are some of the key forces leading to homelessness. Family life is severely disrupted in shelters, and mothers encounter many difficulties in the fulfillment of their parental duties. Homeless mothers are often depressed as a result, and the general health of both mothers and children suffers. Compared to poor children living at

home, homeless children also have more health- and school-related problems.

6. Rural areas vary in their settings and in the employment opportunities they offer to families. Farm families are now in the minority and many are severely stressed economically. Today, most farm couples combine off-farm work with farming to make ends meet. In most farm families, adolescents contribute to the family economy. Patterns of farm inheritance lead both to family cohesiveness and stress. Rural areas also contain vacation neighbourhoods for city families, another topic on which little research exists.

7. The state of maintenance of a dwelling can have an impact on family atmosphere and health. Two types of housing trends are discussed: mansionization and mobile homes. Family space connotes privacy and the trend is toward larger space (square footage) at a time when family size is relatively small. There are problems related to overcrowding but one has to consider that certain cultures tolerate tight living space better than others.

8. A family's residential mobility does not benefit its members equally. Children and adolescents who experience many moves are more likely to suffer from school difficulties and disruptions in their social networks. Particularly affected are children in one-parent families.

9. Neighbourhood structure and housing conditions affect families' lives and reflect society's values concerning social diversity.

Key Concepts and Themes

Collective socialization, pp. 154–155
Correlations, p. 151
Critical mass, p. 154
Effective community, p. 153
Homelessness, pp. 157–159
Inadequate mainstream socialization, p. 153
Inadequate protection, pp. 154–155
Inadequate supervision, pp. 154–155
Mansionization, p. 165

Minority groups, pp. 156–157
Residential mobility, pp. 167–168
Social class, pp. 149–150
Social control, p. 152
Social disorganization, p. 151
Social problems, p. 151
Victimization, p. 155
Well-functioning families, pp. 155–156

Analytical Questions

1. Reread Family Research 6.1. What is yet another step that researchers using such coding (numbers attached to the responses) have to take before computers begin totalling all the responses?

2. How can the theme of the effective community help determine social policies that could improve the lives of children and parents living in high-poverty areas where social problems may exist?

3. How different are well-functioning families living in high-risk areas compared to those living in middle-class neighbourhoods?

4. Given what you have read in this chapter, is the building of "social" housing developments in certain areas of town a good social policy? (Support your answer with the help of research results.) If your answer is no, what might be a better solution?

5. Suggest at least three research questions that are lacking concerning rural families and housing conditions in general.

Suggested Readings

Conger, R. D., et al. (Eds.) 1994. *Families in troubled times: Adapting to change in rural America*. New York: Aldine de Gruyter. This book reports the results of the Iowa Youth and Family Project on various aspects of family life on farms.

Jencks, C. 1994. *The homeless*. Cambridge, MA: Harvard University Press. This book studies the socioeconomic causes behind the more recent waves of homelessness and offers potential solutions. Although there is some material on the family as background, the focus is on homeless individuals.

Kazemipur, A., and Halli, S. S. 2000. *The new poverty in Canada: Ethnic groups and ghetto neighbourhoods*. Toronto: Thompson. This book focuses on the links between poverty and ethnicity. It also offers comparative material from the U.S. and European countries.

Wilson, W. J. 1987. *The truly disadvantaged*. Chicago: University of Chicago Press. This book is a historically grounded classic that is still very relevant and influential in the U.S. It presents an interesting perspective for Canadian students.

Suggested Weblinks

Statistics Canada regularly presents statistics on neighbourhoods, home ownership, the rental market, and housing conditions.

www.statcan.ca

In the U.S., **The Urban Institute** is an economic and social research organization focusing on problems confronting the nation and the search for appropriate social policies. One concern is poverty, both rural and urban; another is neighbourhoods.

www.urban.org

CHAPTER 7

Roles of Education and Religious Participation in Family Life

"Between the ages of 14 to 18 the hardest part was school, school, school. I was not a good student, not motivated and a shit disturber, it seems I did my best to be the worse [sic].... I ended up suffering for this and dropped out and [moved] back in at my parents' pleadings so that I was still in high school at age 20.... It wasn't all my fault because the school was the pits, the teachers didn't care, they just gossiped about their divorces and whatever and the students were more or less like me so we all deserved each other except that our parents didn't deserve this and it took them four years after that to convince me to go to a community college from where I enrolled here."

"High school was my best experience, better than my friends because my teachers were supportive and I got involved in about 10 clubs and participated in various contests and won and my parents were proud of me. It was an exciting time for all of us because both my parents volunteered, my father as a coach, and my mother helped organize many school functions. They were well liked by all the teachers and even the students and it was just great, I felt at home everywhere I went."

"For sure the cornerstone of all my values and of my life for that matter is my faith in God. We're very religious by today's standards in the younger generation and at times I used to be teased by kids in high school about it so I like the freedom of university life in this respect. The only problem is that university life says nothing about religion. I haven't had a single prof in sociology who even went so far as to say a single word about it."

"I get along reasonably well with my parents now that they accept my lack of interest in religion and a few other deviances on my part. But I've never been religiously inclined and I don't feel I miss out on anything."

Education and religion are key cultural and social institutions that have a great impact on family life. In view of the salient role that education plays in children's outcomes, it will not surprise the reader to learn that my students' autobiographies contained a great deal more material about their experience with child care and school systems than about religion. In fact, schools are the second most frequently mentioned source of past misery, after peers. However, schools are not often referred to as a key source of happiness. For its part, religion plays a dominant role in the lives of only a minority of students. For the majority, it is a matter of membership and general beliefs rather than active participation. However, in recent years, more and more of my students have come from Asian and Muslim countries; these students mention religion as a central theme in their lives more often than most other students. In this chapter, the focus is on religiosity rather than religion per se, in order to link with the lived experience of families.

THE EDUCATIONAL SYSTEM: AN OVERVIEW

Although schools existed over 2,000 years ago in ancient Greece and Rome and later in China and Japan, they were the prerogative of a select group of students. The remainder of the child population worked alongside adults. In western Europe, North America, and Australia, primary school attendance became compulsory between 1840 and 1890. Middle-class children were the first to benefit, whereas working-class and rural parents had some difficulty adjusting their economic circumstances to the loss of their children's labour and wages. Therefore, several decades elapsed, well into the first part of the 20th century, before mass schooling spread to all social classes equally. The first infant school and the first daycare opened in Montreal in 1828 and 1858 respectively; all were charitable organizations for poor children. In English Canada, the first child care facility opened in Toronto in 1857 (Prochner, 2000). But these developments spread very slowly, in part because industrialization was less advanced than it was in the U.S.; thus, there was not a sufficient number of poor wage-earning mothers serving as a base for charitable early childhood education centres. From the 1920s to the 1950s, the focus of early education was on children's emotional and social development, while from the 1960s until now, the focus shifted to intellectual development (Varga, 1997). Hence the emphasis of early education on preparing children from disadvantaged families for a schooling system that is becoming more and more oriented toward a global, technological labour market (Pitt, 2002).

In Canada, the majority of children begin school earlier today than they did 30 years ago. Currently, most attend kindergarten, and a substantial proportion participates in preschool programs. Moreover, about a third of preschool children whose parents are employed are in daycare centres, some as young as six weeks old. Therefore, the educational function traditionally assigned to families has been taken over by institutions at younger ages. However, as the contents and structure of the schooling experience change because of funding cutbacks and technological as well as economic demands, parents now have to be more involved in their children's grade-school and high-school education than they might like to be or can afford to be, because of other time constraints in their own lives. Parents have to do far more planning than was the case in the 1960s, for instance (Sweet and Anisef, 2005). After parents, schools have traditionally been considered the main agent of socialization. In essence, the educational system pursues family goals of gender-role differentiation and of the social integration of children in society and its economy (Reynolds, 2004). In other societies, particularly Muslim ones, schools emphasize religious observance and children's integration into the faith of the country.

This chapter focuses on child care, as well as on primary and secondary schooling as contexts for families, parenting, and children's outcomes. Post-secondary education is becoming a more important context for family life than in the recent past, as more students attend university while living at home and need more parental assistance than was the case just a few decades earlier (Bouchard and Zhao, 2000). However, research is lacking in these respects concerning family context and dynamics. We begin with child care in order to follow the chronological order of a child's life.

CHILD CARE: QUALITY AND CHILD OUTCOMES

Child care generally refers to the care given to a child by a person other than his or her primary caregiver—and the primary caregiver is usually defined as the mother (see Chapter 10). As women are generally employed, the necessity for early child care arises in a majority of families, although increased parental leave now allows infants to be cared for at home. But, overall, Canada suffers from a lack of government-funded child care facilities, and waiting lists are very long, especially for subsidized care (Friendly, 2000). Furthermore, Canada does not have a national strategy for early childhood education and care (Friendly et al., 2002). In Quebec, inexpensive daycare is provided but there are not enough places to meet the demand. Parents have recourse to a variety of other child care arrangements, from alternating shifts between mothers and fathers to care in another individual's home or care by relatives, especially grandmothers, or a nanny or at-home sitter (Baker, 1995). Compared to the 1960s, proportionally more children are in centres than with female relatives, because the latter tend to be employed. Furthermore, affluent families are the least likely to choose care by relatives.

Child care of high quality includes a low child-to-caregiver ratio that allows for more adult-child interaction (Volling and Feagans, 1995). The qualifications of the caregivers, the availability of activities, toys, and educational materials, as well as the amount of space, are other indicators of quality. Nutritious food and an age-appropriate structuring of daily activities, including naps, are other important elements of quality. More and more, an integrated educational component is a requisite of a good child care system (Brauner et al., 2004). We should also consider staff's low salaries as an indicator of quality: Low salaries lead to high turnover rates, thus instability in children's lives (Mill and White, 1999). In Canada and the U.S., caregivers' salaries are much lower than those in Europe, and their turnover rate consequently is around 40 percent per year (Corsaro, 1997). In Canada, non-profit centres generally provide better quality child care, and have better trained staff and lower turnover (Friendly, 2000; Mill et al., 1995). Caretakers who are more adequately trained and are satisfied with their working conditions provide a more optimum environment for children (White and Mill, 2000).

The Effects of Child Care on Children

Poor-quality care has been related to child disadvantages in the domains of cognition and language, as well as social and emotional adjustment (Lamb, 1998). Some of these results are found in follow-up studies of children after they have begun school. Unfortunately, research on the effect of nonfamilial care on children has until now largely failed to take family characteristics into consideration. It is entirely possible that some of what are believed to be negative consequences of daycare centres are actually results of other activities the children are involved in (NICHD, 2004) or of certain family characteristics, such as a mother's low educational level or a detrimental housing situation (Scarr, 1998). Naturally, to some extent, parents choose or are forced to accept a quality of care corresponding to some of their own characteristics (Kohen et al., 2002b), such as income (Singer et al., 1998)—although this may be less the case in Quebec than in other provinces. In studies that have controlled for family variables, the quality of daycare centres still produces a small but evident difference in terms of language, cognitive development (Wasik et al., 1990), and overall adjustment (McCartney et al., 1997).

A review of large-scale studies of hundreds of centres that was carried out in the U.S., Bermuda, Sweden, and Holland concludes that the differences found in children raised at home versus in daycare do not have *persistent* consequences. Furthermore, daycare centres have no major impact on children's development when the children come from average homes. "These results may differ for the children from disadvantaged homes, for whom quality child-care programs may supply missing elements in their lives" (Scarr, 1998:105). These children benefit from quality daycare, particularly in terms of school achievement later on (Votruba-Drzal et al., 2004). But children from high-SES families probably derive the same benefits they would obtain at home, at least at the educational level. However, as seen in the case study on p. 126, even children from well-to-do families could benefit when their parents do not read to them or do not have enough time to talk with them—as indicated in a recent Toronto study (Rushowy, 2004).

Several studies find that children in daycare centres are more self-confident, outgoing, assertive, verbally expressive, and helpful, as well as less timid in new situations than children in other types of care (Clarke-Stewart, 1992). But other studies also report that many of the children in nonmaternal care are less polite, agreeable, and compliant with mothers' or teachers' requests, and more irritable, aggressive, and boisterous (NICHD, 2003). These results are particularly evident for children who have been placed in care when very small. However, a restructuring of daycare educational ideologies that would foster cooperation and responsibility, as is the case in the Japanese educational system, might be beneficial (Maccoby and Lewis, 2003).

Children who have too much peer contact and too little adult attention early in their lives may be at a deficit in terms of social adjustment, especially when they are more socially fearful by nature (Watamura et al., 2003). We already know from other studies on large family size that such children are at a disadvantage in terms of language skills and intellectual development (Downey, 1995). There is nevertheless one important question that is still being debated: Are children who are in daycare from an early age for over 30 hours a week less influenced by parents' teachings and other family characteristics than children who are in care fewer hours (NICHD, 1998)?

In comparison to the numerous studies of children in child care centres, not enough research has been carried out on at-home child care in terms of its impact on children. The following student quotes reflect the wide variety of conditions that small children can encounter:

> *"At first I didn't like being separated from my mother but the lady was so nice. She took in two other children who were more or less my age and she gave us such a great time. She really loved children and looking back on that I wonder*

Good child care centres are a society's investment in the stability of young families and in the future of their children. Child care that is affordable contributes to parents' and children's well-being. It also contributes to job creation and satisfaction. Quality child care centres are thus functional for families, children, and the economy.

where she got all her ideas because she had dropped out of school after Grade 9. She used to take us on long walks and we went to the park where we collected 'treasures' such as pine cones, leaves, bugs and she taught us things and then she had all these story books from the library, always different ones. It was never boring and we all learned to read with her and count, and when we got to school I was placed in Grade 2." [woman student]

"What I hated the most [during ages 4 to 5] was this old woman who came home to babysit us each morning. She was like an old witch, nice with my parents but a real sulk as soon as they were out. She had nothing to do with us for the entire day except to feed us and stuff her own face. She knitted and watched TV and ate some more.... My parents noticed that we were becoming withdrawn and shy and my mother became concerned. We were too small to tell her much...but my mother probably guessed that something was wrong and found another woman." [male student]

The Effects of Child Care on Parents

Child care should also be studied in terms of its effects on parents, particularly on their well-being. Care that is too expensive reduces parents' well-being as well as that of the entire family. If too great a proportion of the domestic budget goes into child care, it depletes resources that could be utilized for other aspects of family life, such as better housing, nutrition, and leisure activities. Furthermore, expensive daycare may prevent some parents from having a second child, or, when a second baby arrives, one of the two parents (generally the mother) may be forced to leave her employment. Thus, indirectly, via the expenses required, child care may reduce parental well-being—hence the importance of inexpensive child care in Quebec.

There is a second path via which child care can lessen parental well-being: Low-quality care not only impacts negatively on children's development, but parents are worried about their child as they attend to their job during the day (Erdwins et al., 2001). Mothers especially may feel insecure and guilty. In other instances, the child is well cared for, but by relatives or sitters who exact a psychological price from parents, particularly mothers, by being intrusive or quarrelsome. Also, parents may feel that their child needs more attention, but they may be afraid of antagonizing relatives by making additional requests.

Thus, child care availability, affordability, and quality are key ingredients in contemporary children's development (Friendly, 2000), but they are also key ingredients in parents' well-being. From a societal perspective, quality and affordable child care increases productivity, lowers employee stress and absenteeism, and offers a wider pool of potential workers. It also contributes to a healthier family situation. Hence, child care availability should be a prime target of social policies directed at improving family life.

Early Childhood Education for Children in Low-Income Families

Children from low-income families living in disadvantaged areas are often unprepared when they enter Grade 1 and consequently fall behind at each subsequent level. Many such children repeat grades and then drop out of school to join the ranks of the unemployed and underpaid. Programs such as Head Start, which was created in the U.S. in 1965, raise the level of disadvantaged children's school readiness. Much of the research on this topic is thus American, but its results apply to the Canadian situation, as there is discussion to expand early childhood education for the purpose of helping disadvantaged children. Furthermore, an Aboriginal Head Start program was initiated in 1995 for northern and urban communities and was expanded to include reserves in 1998 (Goulet et al., 2001; Mayfield, 2001). By 2002, 16 percent of six-year-old Aboriginal children had attended a preschool program designed for their culture (Statistics Canada, 2004m). Each program is locally developed to meet the culture and the needs of the community (RCAP, 1996). The following conclusions about children who have participated in Head Start are distilled from the research of Barnett (1998), Brooks-Gunn (2003), Gamble and Zigler (1989), and Raver and Zigler (1997):

1. Children experience a short-term boost in IQ scores that may last for a few years.
2. Once they are in Grade 1, these students do better than comparable students not previously enrolled in Head Start.
3. Only a small group is eventually placed in "special education."
4. Only about one-fifth are eventually retained in a grade, compared to one-third of a control group that did not attend Head Start.
5. More Head Start children graduate from high school.
6. More of these children are eventually employed than those children in the control group.
7. Children show an improvement in family interaction, health and nutritional status, as well as socioemotional adjustment.

Mothers are also more satisfied with the children's school performance and develop higher occupational aspirations for them later on. Quality Head Start programs generally provide a great deal of positive parent-teacher contact that encourages mothers to help their children remain highly motivated. Moreover, some of these programs have reduced abuse and neglect over the children's life span to age 17 (Reynolds and Robertson, 2003). When children arrive in Grade 1 free of behavioural problems, not only are they more attentive in class and better able to learn but they also impress their teachers and peers more favourably (Ladd et al., 1999). Teachers, in turn, expect more of them, which then carries through the rest of their school years, even though their initial IQ gain eventually disappears. As Entwisle and colleagues (1997:18) remind us, "It is key to realize that only modestly better achievement in the first couple of grades might be enough for children to avoid retention or Special Education."

Full-day programs carry longer benefits than half-day ones. In fact, the longer children stay in school daily and the less they miss school, the better they do on aptitude tests (Ceci, 1991). Similarly, a longer school day seems to raise reading and math scores (Frazier and Morrison, 1998). Most child development experts now agree that disadvantaged children who are segregated in poor neighbourhoods would do far better if they were to start preschool as early as possible, even at age two (Kagan and Neuman, 1998). They also agree that such an early intervention should extend through grade school to build on the initial progress and to involve other aspects of these families' lives (Reynolds and Temple, 1998). Such an extension would prevent the loss of early gains, a situation that currently occurs as a result of the low-quality school environments in which disadvantaged children find themselves after Head Start.

Head Start programs for low-income families are thus an excellent investment for a society with a large pool of disadvantaged families (Rushowy, 2004). It is an investment in education, in children's present and future, and in families, including these children's future families. Inasmuch as such programs are both remedial and preventive, they are cost effective and save taxpayers enormous burdens in the long run, in terms of lower rates of delinquency, unemployment, ill health, and even adult criminality.

SCHOOLS AND FAMILIES

Schools and families are intersecting environments in the unfolding lives of children (Crosnoe, 2004). For one, schools constitute a key context for child development and family relations. In turn, family characteristics, such as their SES, dictate to some extent the type of school children attend. From the perspective of rational theory, schools that serve as an effective community can add resilience to a child whose family is experiencing a stressful situation, such as divorce (Leon, 2003). Ma and Zhang (2002) found that schools that create a prosocial environment, as perceived by children, contribute to their health and behavioural outcomes. Other key school variables are fair and consistent discipline, safety, extracurricular programs to encourage physical activity, school commitment, and parental involvement.

Teachers may also play an important role in children's lives and may counterbalance or exacerbate negative familial environments (Forehand et al., 2002). In terms of motivation and behaviours at school, good and supportive teachers can be even more influential than parents (Wentzel, 2002). In normal situations, the more schooling children receive, the larger their cognitive growth (Huttenlocher et al., 1998). Years of schooling tend to increase IQ levels, and absence from a good school for a prolonged period results in lower scores (Neisser et al., 1996). Furthermore—and to pursue a theme just discussed—in terms of social capital, when the number of pupils is too high and/or the teachers are indifferent, children from homes with less capital become particularly at risk developmentally (Parcel and Dufour, 2001). This may be especially so for immigrant adolescents whose command of English or French is not yet fully developed (Anisef and Kilbride, 2003).

Vulnerable children who attend schools with relatively few difficult students are less likely to associate with peers who reinforce their own negative tendencies, thus lowering their opportunities for negative behaviours (Cleveland and Wiebe, 2003). Female teens who attend schools with a large percentage of disadvantaged students are more likely to become pregnant than if they attended a school with a different SES profile (Manlove et al., 2000). Along the same lines, when a school is predominantly populated by students from single-parent families, the children's test scores are significantly reduced, in great part a function of poverty (Bankston and Caldas, 1998). For their part, children from female-headed families who attend a school where most peers have two parents, and therefore more resources, are positively affected in their test scores. In contrast, children from two-parent families who attend a school where most families are headed by lone mothers do less well in terms of test scores (Pong, 1998).

The presentation in this chapter is limited by the type of research that exists on the link between families and schools. The bias is toward school success or lack thereof. Therefore, in this section, we investigate family variables that promote or impede school success. Four interrelated variables are discussed: parental involvement, social class, family-school compatibility, and minority-group status.

Parental Involvement

Parental involvement in education is related to children's achievement and is consequently a key concern of teachers who expect parents to support them and to prepare children for school. In Aboriginal communities, it is recommended that schools involve Elders and other members as well as parents to insure cultural continuity (Goulet et al., 2001). Education manuals emphasize the "partnership" that exists between teachers and parents. Yet, the word *partnership* implies equality, and this is generally not what teachers seek. Teachers approve of meetings with parents but only when they, and not parents, initiate them (Steinberg et al., 1996:129). Moreover, as Kerbow and Bernhardt (1993) point out, the traditional concept of parental involvement implies that it rests solely on parents' motivation. In practice, there are several elements that either encourage or discourage parents from being involved, such as teachers' attitudes and mothers' work load (Pena, 2000).

Parents can involve themselves directly in school activities—for instance, by volunteering—or they can closely follow their children's education from home by showing interest, maintaining high expectations, and supervising homework (Mandell and Sweet, 2004). Parental participation and empowerment is related to children's school performance (Griffith, 1996) and interpersonal relationships (Ma and Zhang, 2002—

How to Study Parental Involvement

Xin Ma and Yanlong Zhang (2002) used the 1998 data from the Canadian Cross-National Survey on Health Behaviours in School-Aged Children (HBSC) to examine the effects of some aspects of school experience on health and behaviours of students enrolled in Grades 6 to 10. About 10,000 students participated in the survey during school time. Health behaviours were measured with questions pertaining to the use of drugs, recent medical treatments and injuries, exercise habits, hygiene, and eating patterns. Other questions addressed interpersonal relationships, such self-esteem and the ability to make new friends.

Parental involvement was measured by the following statements:

- If I have problems at school, my parent(s) are ready to help me.
- My parents are willing to come to school to talk to teachers.
- My parents encourage me to do well at school.

Other statements pertained to the quality of the child-parent relationship:

- My parents understand me.
- My parents expect too much of me.
- I have a lot of arguments with my parents.
- What my parents think of me is important.

see Family Research 7.1). All in all, a great deal of research indicates that parents can have a positive effect on raising their children's school achievement, as well as educational expectations and personal aspirations (Carey and Farris, 1996; Trusty, 1998).

Parents' Higher Social Class and Involvement

Building on Coleman's (1988) **theory of resources,** Lareau (2003) demonstrates how parents' social class position equips them with an unequal set of resources that can differentially impact their ability to be involved in their children's education. In her sample including both black and white families, upper-middle-class executive or professional parents have the competence to help when their children encounter difficulties with the curriculum. These parents feel self-confident with teachers and do not hesitate to request changes that could benefit their children or to question teachers' decisions. At the negative level, it is not uncommon for such parents to flatly reject teachers' suggestions concerning behavioural difficulties children are encountering. This situation is described by a student teacher who is doing her practicum in a new upper-middle-class neighbourhood where parents are upwardly mobile and are extremely busy with their careers:

> *"Right now I can't wait to get out of that school because some of these parents aren't used to money and what comes with it and they treat you as if you were their maids. Most kids are fine but we have a few bad apples and the parents are high on denial, perhaps because they are never home to see what's wrong with their precious children. There's nothing that their Danny Boy or whoever can do wrong, yet the boy is a regular delinquent. Oh no, he doesn't steal, how dare we complain, accuse him of this! More or less they tell us to learn manners, which they don't even have themselves. It ruins your life as a teacher."*

In their own social networks, upper-middle-class parents often have access to professionals, such as psychologists and other teachers whom they can consult on school matters. These parents are also better equipped to meet teachers' requests, because they have more material resources at their disposal (Zill and Nord, 1994). They can provide their children with educational supplies, computers, tutors, art or music lessons, and perhaps summer camps (Ertl, 2000). Lareau (2003) also mentions that these parents often bring work home from the office. The visibility of their work expands children's educational horizons, gives them at least some preparation for the adult world of employment, and may serve as an incentive for homework. Educated parents are also more likely to read to their children and spend time with them, although this frequency is much lower when mothers are employed full-time and as children get older (Cook and Willms, 2002).

Above all, middle-class parents engage in a process of **concerted cultivation** (Lareau, 2003). That is, they deliberately stimulate the development of their children's cognitive and social skills by fostering larger vocabularies, familiarity with abstract concepts, and negotiating abilities. They enrol their children in an array of organized activities. (Indeed, both Aboriginal and other Canadian children who participate in extracurricular activities do better in school and in relations with their friends—Statistics Canada, 2004m). All of this gives children an advantage with institutional representatives, raises their sense of entitlement, and transmits habits that will be useful for higher education and on the individualistic labour market later on (Knighton and Mirza, 2002). In contrast, in working class and disadvantaged families, children experience a socialization pattern that includes more free time, clear boundaries between parents and children, parental directives, a more simple speech pattern, and lower expectations of personal entitlement.

This concerted education, although western in origins, can be observed in educated families of most ethnic groups. However, because a smaller proportion of blacks and Aboriginals are middle class, as is the case for other Aboriginal groups elsewhere, this parenting style is less frequently encountered among them, which often places children at a disadvantage in schools—but not necessarily in their personal relationships. For instance, Baker (2001b:45) points out that Samoan children in New Zealand are disadvantaged by the school system because they are taught at home not to question their elders, and their learning style is of the "passive" type. This process of concerted education stems from the individualistic and competitive nature of middle-class western education and places additional demands on mothers (Pitt, 2002; Wall, 2004). It is in itself an ideology supported by the technological and capitalist infrastructure of society.

Barriers to Low-Income Parents' Involvement

Although disadvantaged parents generally value education as much as their wealthier counterparts do, they often have low achievement expectations for their own children because several problems stand in their and their children's way that prevent the actualization of their values, and consequently lower their aspirations. This is unfortunate because studies indicate that parental expectations are key predictors of school achievement, starting in Grade 1. Entwisle et al. (1997:93) point out that raising parents' expectations could affect performance indirectly for several years after Grade 1.

As we have seen, programs such as Head Start often lift parents' expectations, which in turn contributes to their children's success.

Disadvantaged parents encounter several problems that prevent them from actualizing their high value for education. First, they often lack the skills to help their children when they have school problems (Kralovec and Buehl, 2001). This was well illustrated by a student describing her Grade 1 experience in the previous chapter (p. 153). Second, they often feel intimidated or stigmatized by teachers, as discussed by a mature and already well-educated student on welfare:

> *"Currently, one of my worries is my daughter's school, rather, her teachers. They know that I am a single mother on welfare and it does not matter to them consequently that I have as much and even more education than they have. I can't talk to them, any of them, because they have subtle ways of putting me down, of making me feel that I am not a competent parent and person because I am poor. I wanted to get them involved in making sure that the children spell correctly...well, what a mistake because they can't spell themselves! But, of course, I am the problem: I am poor. Who am I? How can I have an opinion about my daughter's education, least of all spelling?"*

Third, teachers make more frequent requests for involvement from disadvantaged parents, but these requests are often negative, in part because poor children have more learning or behavioural problems (Sui-Chu and Willms, 1996). In fact, when children's grades are low, parents have more contact with the school (Muller and Kerbow, 1993). Otherwise, low-income parents attend parent-teacher conferences far less frequently. Often, lack of child care prevents them from doing so. Others may not have a flexible work schedule that would allow them to participate in school activities such as volunteering, which would give them the opportunity to become informally acquainted with teachers and other parents. Such activities would, in turn, give their children an advantage within the system—an "inside track." First Nations parents too often feel out of place and do not feel welcome by teachers (Poonwassie, 2001).

A fourth aspect of a family's low position in the class system that affects parents' expectations and children's education resides in the fact that, when these parents want to help their children with school work, they often meet resistance because the youngsters lack confidence in their competence. A student, reminiscing on her own experience growing up in a disadvantaged family, makes this point:

> *"When I look back on that period what I regret the most is the way I treated my mother; just because we were poor I felt that she was not as good as other mothers and whenever she'd try to help me with homework, I'd turn to her and give her my most despising look. Not only [did] I hurt her a lot and made her feel useless as a mother but I made her feel worthless as a person because even then she was more educated than I am now especially when it comes down to writing proper sentences."*

Nevertheless, among school students, Mandell and Sweet (2004) have not found any difference by social class in the level of mothers' involvement in their children's homework. However, the gendered division of labour and child care which focuses on mothers presents a serious roadblock in parental involvement. The intensive mothering that society and schools now expect of mothers (Hays, 1996) cannot easily be fulfilled by women on low income who may be struggling to simply feed their children. The child as a project is often out of reach of these mothers, their best intentions notwithstanding (Wall, 2004).

Families' Social Class and Children's Achievement

As indicated in Figure 7.1, children from families of higher socioeconomic status (SES) do better in reading, writing, and mathematics (Lipps and Frank, 1997). This observation holds internationally (Willms, 2002c). As well, university attendance is still related to social class (Knighton and Mirza, 2002), and inequalities in achievement continue over the life course (Anisef et al., 2000; Pallas, 2002). Furthermore, children who attend schools with a greater percentage of students from higher SES backgrounds do better academically (Frempong and Willms, 2002).

Pong (1998) found that, at the group level, high parental participation in educational activities to some extent alleviated the economic deficit by providing a positive community effect on the school and its students. Thus, students did better when parents' participation was high, in general, even though their own individual parents may not have been involved. The same findings applied for the extent to which parents were acquainted with each other. When parents knew many other parents, they served as sources of information and reinforcement for each other. This, in turn, helped them create a pro-educational climate within the school for the benefit of all students. These results support Coleman's (1988) theory of **social capital** and the positive effect of an **effective community** above and beyond a family's social class and structure. However, Crosnoe (2004) found that there is overlap between social capital available in families and schools so that students who receive more emotional support from their parents then benefit more from the socioemotional resources of school. Thus, families and schools together can contribute to reproduce inequality.

Family-School Compatibility

Although Canada is a multicultural society, the structure of its economy is middle class. However, a larger dose of cultural diversity in the contents of the curriculum and in the school climate would contribute to the academic success of minority-group children (Manning and Baruth, 2000). Nevertheless, children are more successful at school and better adjusted to its requirements when family life is similar to the middle-class climate of school organization. Children in families that have a **schedule—** where they eat breakfast, where rules are followed, and where educational activities are encouraged—are more easily integrated into the school system (Rumberger et al., 1990). Households with no employed adults are less likely to provide such a structure. In homes where everyone gets up whenever he or she wants, does not dress until later or not at all, eats meals whenever hungry, watches unlimited hours of television, and where reading material is absent, daily life is a world apart from school routine and even goals. As a result, children from these families may experience more difficulty fitting in at school, as well as have more trouble learning, because the two lifestyles actually clash.

FIGURE 7.1

Percentages of Children Ranked Near the Top of their Class by Their Teachers (by SES)

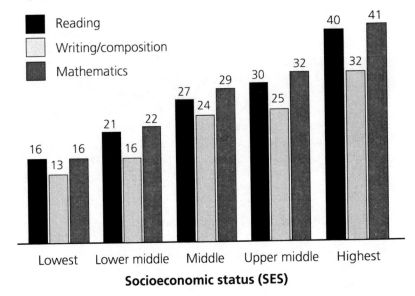

Percentages of Children Who Scored in the Top 20 Percent on Math Test by SES

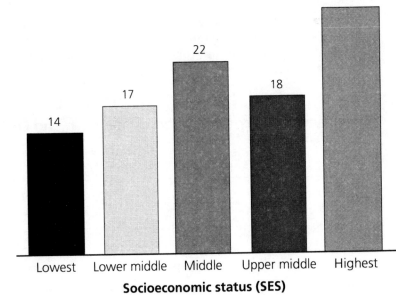

Source: Human Resources Development Canada and Statistics Canada, National Longitudinal Survey of Children and Youth, 1994–95; Lipps and Frank, 1997.

Several researchers have emphasized the differences that exist between children of diverse social classes in terms of summer activities. Middle-class children benefit from summer activities that are compatible with school routine. For instance, many attend special camps. In contrast, disadvantaged children often spend their vacations in pursuits that increase their distance from what is required for school performance (Heyns, 1988). A knowledge vacuum is created and they have more difficulty in readapting themselves to school work once classes resume. Not surprisingly, these children lose a few points on the IQ scale as well as on tests of mathematical ability during vacations.

Entwisle and colleagues (1997) tested children and examined their school grades at the beginning, middle, and end of the school year. They found that, although disadvantaged children begin the school year with lower scores and less knowledge than those from more affluent families, they gain as much proportionately. In other words, some of the yearly difference in test scores between poor children and children of higher SES is caused by summer loss for the former.

Minority-Group Children

Family and school compatibility may be particularly challenging for minority-group children. For instance, as indicated in Table 7.1, a study of 15-year-olds' reading achievement in five provinces shows that those who attend the French school system in English provinces have much lower scores than those who attend the English school system (majority language). In provinces that are predominantly English speaking or mixed (such as New Brunswick), French-speaking children often attend schools that are of lower quality than their English counterparts; moreover, many of these francophone children live in a family that may no longer be technically fluent in their French language (Statistics Canada, 2004e).

Immigrant adolescents who arrive without sufficient Canadian language skills often acquire them more rapidly than do their parents and then may have to act as cultural brokers or translators for them (Anisef and Kilbride, 2003). One of the consequences of this situation is that, while these parents generally hold high educa-

TABLE 7.1	Reading Averages of Students in French and English School Systems by Province		
	English School Systems	French School Systems	Provincial Average
Nova Scotia	522	474	521
New Brunswick	512	478	501
Quebec	543	535	536
Ontario	535	474	533
Manitoba	530	486	529

Source: Statistics Canada, *The Daily*, March 22, 2004e.

tional aspirations for their children (James, 1999), they are not in a position to become involved with the school system or to help their adolescents with homework, even though they may be highly educated themselves. Furthermore, the Anisef and Kilbride study group also encountered immigrant youths who resisted conformity to "the culture, values, and established norms of the mainstream society" as coping mechanisms (p. 245). The end result is often conflict with parents and failure at school. This may be compounded by the fact that parents are struggling to make ends meet and are unable to be as supportive as they might have been in their country of origin.

In terms of Aboriginal families, village- or band-controlled schools value their children's culture more and understand their family dynamics better. For instance, Wall and Madak (1991) have found that high-schoolers who attended tribal schools reported that their teachers and parents held higher educational aspirations for them than did Natives who attended regular public schools. In the latter case, cultural heritage may be substantially diluted and staff may lack an understanding of Natives' family processes. These two factors combine to place children at a disadvantage in terms of school achievement. However, the fact that Aboriginal languages are still being lost in these schools remains a major problem in the cultural continuity of these families (Nicholas, 2001). As well, a reverse problem exists when a Native language is taught at school but parents no longer speak it (Paupanekis and Westfall, 2001). These issues are being studied at the educational level, but there is little research in terms of effects on families and their dynamics, as well as stability.

Furthermore, family characteristics (parents' education, employment, and marital status) do not necessarily have the same impact on school success on reserves as they do off reserves and in the population at large (Ward, 1998). Reserve Native parenting style is less supervisory than is the case in the rest of society, because it is their custom to rely on assistance from their extended kin or community for child supervision. For these parents, then, how well their children do in school may depend more on the social capital the community makes available to children than their own socialization practices. However, many Native parents have actually been alienated from the education of their children because of historical factors, and their reintegration into the educational system is needed (Poonwassie, 2001). This reintegration is particularly important for Natives who live off reserves, especially in cities such as Winnipeg where they are concentrated in disadvantaged areas and may no longer benefit from the support of their original community.

When an Aboriginal village controls the school, parents and other community members can voice their concerns and have a greater impact on the curriculum (Ward, 1998). When a school has a very high proportion of Native students, the students are more likely to participate in extracurricular activities and to develop an attachment to their school. Both variables, in turn, prevent drop out, which is an enormous problem among Aboriginals (Mackay and Miles, 1995). However, in some cities such as Winnipeg where certain schools have a high percentage of alienated Aboriginal youth, students are often placed in classes for "special needs" children, which in effect pathologizes their history of discrimination (Binda, 2001). This situation prevents Native families from accumulating human capital that could be passed on to the next generation and allow them to become integrated at the economic level.

PRIVATE EDUCATION

We look at two different alternatives to children's education: private schools and home schooling.

Private Schools

Private institutions include public schools that are religious in nature, such as the public Catholic school system in many provinces. There are also schools that are sponsored by religious groups—whether Jewish, Mennonite, or Muslim—that do not receive taxpayers' subsidies (Seljak, 2005). Next are private schools that focus on academic excellence and are a means for rich families to raise their children within an exclusive environment. Boarding schools, or residential education, are included in this category; for example, Upper Canada College for boys and Havergal for girls in Toronto, among others. Students who attend these schools tend to have higher occupational and social class outcomes later on than students in public schools (Persell et al., 1992). This result remains even after family selection factors are controlled (Brewer et al., 1999). A third type of school, often called the alternative school, serves children whose parents are ideologically opposed to certain tenets of mass schooling (i.e., sexism, competitiveness, individualism) or children who have not adapted to regular schools because of behavioural, emotional, or intellectual challenges. Some of these alternative schools are publicly funded to meet certain students' needs while others are entirely private.

Parents expect that private schools will pass on their values as well as their lifestyles to their children, whether religion- or class-inspired. From this perspective, such schools serve as an **extension of the family** far more than public schools can:

> "I had a wonderful adolescence! My parents put me in this wonderful private school in Grade 7 and I just bloomed. It was like one very large family that sheltered us from the bullies we had had at the public school. I was a nerd and there certainly was no problem with this at this school. I was actually encouraged to read, explore new fields, ask questions, and tag-along [with] the teachers. We were all nerdy and it was just great. Both boys and girls were like that so that even dating was not a problem even though the teachers and our parents all made us understand that this was a stage of life that could wait. So we waited. We did not have to conform to the 'peer culture' (some Culture!) at other schools. We never envied them and all of us grew up to be very well rounded, sociable, and athletic nerds. If we had gone on to public high schools, we would have grown up screwed up or most of us would have given up being intelligent just to fit in." [male student]

The staff of a private school are hired on the basis of how well they conform to the school's ideology, which in turn reflects parental ideology. The compatibility between the two is particularly evident in the preceding student quote. Parents and teachers encouraged their adolescents along similar lines of intellectual and social development.

Home Schooling

Home schooling is where the worlds of children and parents are most intertwined. It is the most clear-cut example of parental resistance to the defamilialization and institutionalization of children, discussed in Chapter 3. Home schooling is currently considered somewhat unusual. Yet, when one examines human history, home education has always prevailed until recently. Parents who resort to home schooling are reacting against the philosophy, structure, and functioning of the formal educational system. Others home-school for religious and moral reasons, while many are responding against what they perceive to be dangerous peer influences (Smith, 1993).

Both in Canada and the U.S., home schooling has been growing substantially each year (Luffman, 1998). The timing of this growth is somewhat paradoxical: It occurs while most married families have two wage earners. Yet, most home teachers are mothers, which means that they, in effect, have to forgo paid employment. In 2000–2001, there were between 60,000 and 95,000 registered home-schoolers in Canada (Ray, 2001). Over 60 percent are elementary-school students. In Ontario, only 8 percent are high-schoolers compared to 45 percent in Alberta and Saskatchewan (Luffman, 1998). In the U.S., there are approximately one million home-schooled children. Home-schooling parents do not generally function in a vacuum (Brabant et al., 2004). To begin with, every province supervises home-schoolers for compliance with the *Education Act*—although some parents fail to register their children with their local school board. In some provinces, these students can use public school libraries and other resources. Both in Canada and the U.S., several national, state, and provincial organizations exist for the purpose of offering instrumental and moral support to the families involved in home-schooling. Similarly, several relevant magazines are published; jointly, they probably reach most of home-schooling parents (Mayberry et al., 1995).

Objections to home schooling, especially by the educational establishment, largely fall into three broad categories: (1) worries that the education provided by parents may not meet national standards, (2) concerns that "zealot" parents may brainwash their children ideologically and religiously, and (3) criticisms to the effect that these children will lack peer contact, will not develop appropriate social skills, and may become socially isolated.

In order to examine the validity of the first objection, Brabant et al. (2004) and Mayberry et al. (1995) have summarized the social profile of the parents of home-schooled Quebec and American children respectively. The majority are white, and tend to engage in occupations at the professional and technical level more than is the case nationally. The educational level is quite high, especially in Quebec. On average, the familial income is higher, situating them at the middle- to upper-middle-class level. There are two types of parents involved in home schooling. Those with a religious motivation and who are devout Christians, primarily fundamentalists, are found mainly in the U.S. The others consist of parents motivated by lifestyle, pedagogic concerns, or a desire to strengthen their bond with their children (Van Galen, 1991).

Overall, these parents are educationally qualified, even though they have not generally been trained as teachers. At any rate, research fails to find any significant relationship between fathers' educational level and home-schooled children's achievement scores (Ray and Wartes, 1991). In other words, the children of parents with a high school education are doing as well as those with parents who graduated from university, which is the opposite of what occurs in regular schools. What probably counts for children's achievement in home schooling is parents' unusually high involvement. The children perform at the national average and frequently exceed it on standard tests. Many actually accelerate while being home schooled and enter higher education at a younger age.

As to whether parents brainwash their offspring and offer them an education that is, for instance, so religiously oriented that it closes the door to children's options in the future, there is no direct research that could answer this critique scientifically. However, it would seem that "brainwashed" children would not do very well on the standard tests they have to take to enter college or that researchers have given them. Yet, we have seen that the contrary happens, although there are certainly exceptions to that rule. Furthermore, parents themselves have an answer to this particular objection. They point out that secular humanism taught in public schools does brainwash children into values and beliefs that go against their principles.

In terms of growing up socially inept and isolated, as well as emotionally maladjusted, the tests that have been carried out indicate normal development. But the samples employed may not have been representative, so no generalizations can be made. However, it can be argued on the basis of other material presented in this chapter that the potential for maladjustment exists for too many children who attend regular schools. As we will see in Chapter 15, studies unanimously indicate that children are often bullied and victimized by peers. These statistics and experiences actually lead many parents to begin home schooling.

Furthermore, children who are home schooled generally have at least one sibling. They also meet others who are in similar circumstances; they know their peers in the neighbourhood and many participate in extracurricular activities, such as sports teams and Scouting, which put them in frequent contact with regularly schooled peers. At the high school level, many home-schooled teens have jobs like other youths. Overall, although home schooling is unusual, it does not appear to produce negative effects for families and children, and perhaps quite the opposite occurs (Rothermel, 2000).

RELIGIOUS PARTICIPATION AND FAMILY LIFE

Religion constitutes one of the most important cultural domains in most societies. In Canada, it still plays an important role in the lives of a substantial proportion of families, even though its institutional role and moral authority have declined, as is the case for most western societies (Bibby, 2002). Its impact on family life is therefore likely to be more obvious among the observants, hence the focus on religiosity. Nevertheless, new arrivals to Canada are often very religious (Biles and Ibrahim, 2005) and family studies do not adequately reflect this reality.

The Factor of Religiosity

How is the importance of religion to a family or to some of its members measured? A great deal of controversy revolves around this matter, as one can well imagine, because religiosity is difficult to define and measure. The most obvious and commonly used *indicator* of or way of measuring religiosity is attendance at religious services (see Family Research 7.2). Generally, phone or door-to-door surveys ask questions such as: "Did you, yourself, happen to attend church, mosque or synagogue in the last seven days?" This is actually a Gallup survey question (Smith, 1998). (However, Canadian Social Surveys now include the word "meetings"—Statistics Canada, 2004n). The first problem with these and similar questions resides in the increasing religious diversity in Canada. For instance, among Hindus, religious ritual is often focused on the home and in a variety of practices; thus the question asked will fail to tap their level of religiosity, even though they do have *gurudwaras* or multi-use temples (Banerjee and Coward, 2005). Furthermore, for many, attendance at temple functions may be more a matter of maintaining their culture and socializing within their ethnic group than being religiously observant. Tapping into Chinese religiosity is even more complex because it focuses on home altars, temples, festivals, and Chinatowns. As Lai et al. (2005:100) point out, "since Chinese religion is so completely intertwined with daily life, culture, and family, one could argue that the many Chinatowns are themselves the most accessible public expression of Chinese religion in Canada."

FAMILY RESEARCH 7.2

What Can Be Done with a Question on Religiosity?

Statistics Canada conducts an annual General Social Survey from a sample of 10,000 Canadians. Since 1985, two questions about religion have been included. One question concerns religious affiliation and the other pertains to religiosity: It inquires about the frequency of attendance at religious services or meetings. Clark (1998) first controlled for or took into account income, family structure, education, age, sex, and employment because it is well known that these variables are related to various aspects of well-being. Then, with these controls in the background, the researchers still found that persons who attend religious services or meetings weekly are half less likely to feel stressed and 1.5 times more likely to have a very happy marital relationship than those who do not attend religious services at all. Weekly attendees' marriages are also far more likely to last, regardless of which decade the individuals were married in. Overall, weekly attendees hold more traditional family values and adopt better health practices. For instance, in the 1996 survey, only 18 percent of weekly attendees aged 15 to 35 smoked, compared to 38 percent among those who never attended.

Obviously, there is far more research that could be done on religiosity. It would be interesting to break down the results by religious affiliation, given the fact that Canada is such a diverse society: Would these results apply equally well for Chinese religion, Hindus, Sikhs, Buddhists, or Muslims?

Another complication arises in the double matter of truthfulness and of errors of recall. People forget that they did or did not go to church or synagogue in the past week; others may do some "forward telescoping"—that is, remembering having gone recently while in reality they went several weeks ago. Furthermore, people may feel put "on the spot," so to speak, by the question. This refers to what is called the *social desirability bias*. It means that people want to look good or proper in the eyes of the interviewer. Individuals may then exaggerate their behaviour or that of their family toward the positive. (For the same reason of social acceptance, people might say that they drink two beers a day when they actually have five.) Therefore, there is quite a debate going on among sociologists concerning the impact of social desirability and memory or accurate recall on measures of religiosity (Hout and Greely, 1998; Woodberry, 1998). Nevertheless, it is possible that such issues are more relevant to the U.S. than to Canada because religiosity is less salient here, particularly in political life.

In 2001, about 20 percent of the adult Canadian population attended religious services on a weekly basis, down from about 67 percent in 1946. All in all, 31 percent attended at least once a month (Clark, 2003). The monthly rate in the U.S. is 45 percent, thus much higher. In Canada, there are regional as well as immigration-related differences. Monthly attendance ranges from 53 percent in Prince Edward Island, 36 percent in Ontario, and 25 percent in Quebec and British Columbia. Table 7.2 illustrates the fact that attendance has declined among the Canadian-born but has increased among immigrants, except in Quebec—probably as a result of the strong secular effect of that province. The increase of religious attendance among immigrants may stem from a change in the countries of origin of immigrants (Chapter 4). More Filipinos now attend Catholic churches; in addition, mosques and Hindu temples have been erected during the past decade (McDonough and Hoodfar, 2005).

TABLE 7.2 | **Change in Religious Attendance by Place of Birth in the Three Largest CMAs: Percentages of Those Who Attend at Least Once a Month***

	1989–1993	1999–2001	Difference
Montreal			
Canadian-born	26 %	17 %	– 9
Born outside Canada	44	40	– 4
Toronto			
Canadian-born	31	28	– 3
Born outside Canada	44	50	+ 6
Vancouver			
Canadian-born	19	21	+ 2
Born outside Canada	35	39	+ 4

Source: Statistics Canada, General Social Survey; Clark, 2003.
* For the population aged 15 and over.

Considering all the religious indicators together, but particularly attendance at services, women are more religious than men, the older more than the younger, "conservative" Protestants more than "liberal" Protestants, and the married more than the single and divorced (Presser and Stinson, 1998). However, we yet have to obtain similar information for other religious groups in Canada that are becoming more numerous, whether Chinese, Hindu, Sikh, Buddhist, or Muslim. Among two-parent families, those in which the wife is a homemaker or is employed only part-time tend to attend religious services more frequently than families where the mother is employed full-time (Hertel, 1995). It is not known whether this is a matter of beliefs or perhaps because housework needs to be done on weekends and thus competes with religious attendance in terms of time availability. In the U.S., black families attend religious services and participate in other religious activities far more frequently than do non-Latino white families (Aldous and Ganey, 1999). Overall, there is a greater mixture of secular and religious functions in the black community (Lincoln and Mamiya, 1990).

Parents' and Children's Religiosity: The Socialization Aspect

Parents transmit their beliefs to their children by their teachings and their example (Myers, 1996). Parents' attendance at church, synagogue, temple, or mosque is itself a powerful socialization situation, and the example set by mothers who are warmly accepting of their children is particularly powerful in the transmission of religious beliefs (Bao et al., 1999).

Secular Society, Religious Parents

Using a cross-cultural perspective, Kelley and De Graaf (1997) examined the dual effect of parents' religiosity and a society's level of religiosity on adult children's own religious practice. For this purpose, they have classified 15 western societies on the basis of the overall level of their citizens' religious beliefs and attendance. They ranked societies from most secular (East Germany and Norway) to most religious (Northern Ireland, Poland, and Ireland). The U.S. and Italy were just somewhat less religious than the last category. (Canada did not participate in the study.) The researchers then examined the level of church attendance and religiosity of parents compared to that of their adult children. They found that, in religious societies, people tend to report themselves to be religious even when their parents are not, thus showing the influence of the general cultural climate on socialization. However, even in these religious societies, adults were more religious when their parents also were (score of 85 out of a possible 100 in Figure 7.2) than when their parents were secular (score of 60). In a secular society, people report themselves to be less religious; nevertheless, adult children with devout parents were far more likely to be devout themselves (score of 73) than those whose parents were secular (score of 16).

In religious societies, religious parents' beliefs are simply reinforced by the general cultural climate. In a secular society, the familial climate is also quite successful at transmitting religious beliefs to children. However, religious parents have to be far more vigilant and invest far more effort in their example and their teachings than similar parents who live in a religious or fairly religious society. In secular societies, religious parents

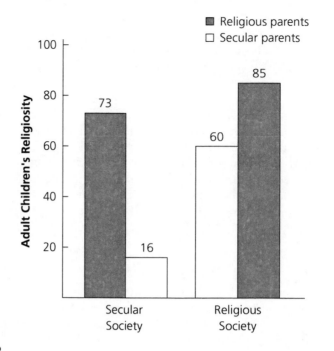

FIGURE 7.2

Adult Children's Religiosity by Society's and Parents' Religiosity

Source: Based on Kelley and De Graaf, 1997.

have to find means to insulate their children against the general secular climate; they are not always successful in this endeavour because there are too many social pressures against them.

In a religious society, secular parents probably do not see any harm in their children's religious participation and therefore do not discourage them from following cultural norms. But when both society and parents are secular, most children end up secular themselves (low score of 16 in Figure 7.2). Thus, in a society such as the U.S., which is considered to be quite religious, devout parents do not have to fight against a climate of secularism that is as strong as that of other societies. However, because religion and state are separate, and because the media themselves are secular and materialistic, Canadian and American parents who are religious still have to be fairly vigilant.

Factors in the Successful Transmission of Religiosity

Myers (1996) tried to see what characterized religious parents who were the most successful at transmitting their beliefs to their children. Parental religiosity was measured in 1980, when the offspring were still living at home and thus under direct parental influence. In 1992, the offspring, who by then had reached adulthood, were interviewed. Myers's results showed that highly devout parents had children who, on average, were less similar to them than were the offspring of parents who were either moderately religious or not religious. In other words, the religious standards of many devout parents may have been too high to emulate; hence their children became only moderately religious later on—or rebelled against religious practice—thus becoming less similar to their parents in this dimension. A student describes a pertinent experience:

> *"One constant source of unhappiness throughout childhood and adolescence was religious observance. My parents are extremely religious.... I hated having to go to church weekly and say family prayers and having to go to religious school...even the teachers thought that my parents were overdoing it. My parents and I fought constantly over religious issues and even theological matters. The end result is that I am religiously atheist."*

Myers (1996) also found that parents who both agreed on religious or secular beliefs had been more successful at transmitting them, which makes sense because children learn better in a consistent environment. In families characterized by high marital happiness, offspring were more likely to resemble their parents in religious beliefs—whether these beliefs were orthodox, moderate, or lukewarm. This is related to other findings described in Chapter 12, indicating that a harmonious parental relationship constitutes a positive child socialization context.

THE ROLE PLAYED BY RELIGIOSITY IN FAMILY LIFE

Does religious participation fulfill any role in family life and for the individuals concerned besides the transmission of beliefs and related behaviours? What does religiosity do *for* the family and its members? Religious beliefs can be analyzed as a form of capital—**religious capital** as Iannaccone (1990) calls it—from which families can, in theory, draw cohesion as well as strength. Religious activities that include participation within a congregation may constitute a form of **social capital** in the guise of informal networks of social support (Ellison, 1994). The following discussion is based on studies of Christians and to some extent Jews, as research is lacking concerning other religions, whether Chinese, Hindu, Sikh, Buddhist, or Muslim. However, I would hypothesize that the research described below applies equally well to them, with differences pertaining to matters related to gender roles and marital quality (see Bramadat and Seljak, 2005).

Religiosity Correlates with Well-Being

A substantial body of literature indicates that religious involvement and strength of beliefs are related to general feelings of well-being (Clark, 1998; Levin, 1994) as well as psychological and physical health, including lower adult mortality (Hummer et al., 1999). This benefit may even be manifest as early as adolescence (Crosnoe and Elder, 2002). Religiosity provides internal coherence; it serves as an explanatory platform that enables individuals to make sense of everyday life and its adversities. It may help individuals by giving them guiding principles of action, and make them less individualistic and more duty bound.

Religiosity serves as an internal and external **agent of social control** (Durkheim, 1951); hence, religious commitment lowers health risks such as alcoholism, drug addiction, and precocious sexual activity, and may serve to prevent depression. In fact, there are indications that religiosity may deter drug use and delinquent behaviour among adolescents, in part because religious adolescents are less likely to associate with peers who use drugs (Bahr et al., 1998; Johnson et al., 2001). Church attendance itself, because of its social nature and the level of commitment that it requires, facilitates adjustment and also leads to positive evaluations of one's health (Broyles and Drenovsky, 1992). Other studies show that private religious practice among adolescents, or the degree to which their religion is internalized, is related to fewer behavioural problems in environments in which violence is often witnessed and victimization occurs (Pearce et al., 2003).

Religious participation contributes to extend a family's social network and sources of social support (Ellison and George, 1994). Frequent churchgoers have somewhat larger social networks than others and enjoy more frequent person-to-person contacts. They are also more likely to be involved in their community (Jones, 2000). Furthermore, frequent churchgoers receive more help and report feeling cared for and valued (Ferraro and Koch, 1994). Therefore, religious participation becomes an important social resource or social capital for families (Bramadat and Seljak, 2005):

> *"My mother is a concern to me at this stage because she is 65 and widowed and unemployed [but not poor]. But I think that her church activities and all the friendships she's made there help her a lot and will sustain her for some years to come. Sometimes I even go with her because I like meeting all these people of all ages. Anyway, my mother says that religion keeps her in good health and she is far from being a zealot."*

Religiosity Relates to Marital Quality and Stability

Adults who declare a religious affiliation are more likely to see marriage as a lifetime commitment than adults who profess no religious affiliation (Stanley et al., 2004). They are also less likely to engage in extramarital sex (Treas and Giesen, 2000). Those who hold beliefs that are more religious experience higher conjugal satisfaction (Tremblay et al., 2002). Call and Heaton (1997) and Clark (1998) find that couples who regularly attend church together have a lower rate of divorce than those who attend infrequently or not at all. However, couples in which only one spouse attends are even more likely to divorce than couples who never attend. The latter finding can probably be explained in terms of religious similarity, or homogamy, described in Chapter 8. Couples who differ in religious matters have one potentially large source of conflict. In contrast, couples who attend church together benefit from the sharing of a social and spiritual activity that reinforces their solidarity. They may also benefit from exposure to more *altruistic values* than non-churchgoers, and this would in turn contribute to a less individualistic pattern of marital interaction (Pearce and Axinn, 1998). A student expresses this sociological observation within the context of his intimate relationship:

> *"My problem right now is that my girlfriend is not religious and this worries me a lot because I know from my parents' experience that sharing beliefs and especially [going to church]...give a couple a lot in common. Above all I am concerned*

that my girlfriend may miss out on the importance of values that help keep a marriage together, like learning how to be committed and think in terms of the good of the relationship and not just about your own personal desires."

Similarly, mutually shared religious beliefs strengthen marital stability as religions tend to be pro-marriage rather than pro-divorce.

Amato and Rogers (1997) report that frequent church attendance may reduce the likelihood of divorce through a reduction in marital problems. Why would couples who attend church frequently experience fewer marital problems? Their explanation is congruent with the ones just presented. They reason that church attendance allows for the internalization and thus acceptance of norms of behaviour that encourage couples to get along. They also refer to the social aspect of church attendance: It serves as a **support group** as well as a control group or an effective community. The sum of these studies therefore indicates a salutary effect of religiosity on the quality of the marital relationship as well as on the stability of the family unit. However, in the U.S., there is a curious paradox. Religiosity reduces the risk of divorcing for individual couples, but when aggregate data are used, some states that are both conservative and religious have the highest divorce rates—such as Oklahoma and Arkansas (Hawkins et al., 2002). In other words, there is a discrepancy between the individual and the aggregate levels of analysis that has yet to be explained by research. It is possible that, in these states, the non-religious as a group have particularly high rates of divorce and perhaps other problems as they may be deprived of the major sources of social support in their relatively religious communities.

Religiosity Supports the Parental Role

Religious beliefs strengthen parents' involvement with their children, even when the latter become particularly difficult and stressful. Pearce and Axinn (1998:824) surmise that "exposure to religious themes such as tolerance, patience, and unconditional love" through religious activities constitutes a resource that helps parents and children maintain a good relationship. Mother-child similarity in religiosity strengthens the bond between the two. Some studies indicate that, especially among African Americans who are disadvantaged, religious parents use fewer coercive methods with their children than non-religious parents (Wiley et al., 2002). Overall, research shows that religious mothers experience a higher quality of relationship with their children (Pearce and Axinn, 1998), that religious fathers, whether married or divorced, are more involved in their role (King, 2003b), and that religiosity brings a closer grandparent-grandchild relationship (King and Elder, 1999).

Following a *family developmental perspective*, Stolzenberg et al. (1995) demonstrate that people often become more religious as they age. But the addition of children to the family unit further enhances this increase in religious participation (Nock, 1998c). In contrast, as childless married adults age, their religious participation does not increase to any great extent. One explanation for this finding may be that adults with children seek religious membership and participation in order to become better anchored in the community and as a means of social support in their parenting role. Along this line of reasoning, a student projects a greater role for religion later in her life:

Worshipping together constitutes a form of social capital. Religious participation can also be the basis of an effective community, which contributes to child and adolescent socialization, and buttresses the parental role.

"*Right now I don't go to church often but I intend to become active again as soon as I have children, just as my parents did. I think that a bit of religion is very helpful to children: it teaches them values other than what they see on TV. The few times I go to church I am always struck by how civilized people behave and it gives you a warm feeling of humanity.*"

One could perhaps speculate that many parents *need* religion nowadays in order to feel more secure in their role in a very demanding and confusing world. Chaves (1991) points out that conventional families form the mainstay of organized religion. This would mean that parents may get gratification for their role within the context of religion, which would serve as a compensatory mechanism for the blaming and disempowerment they receive from so many quarters. Wilcox (2002:791) concludes: "The irony is that religious institutions, generally taken to be carriers of more traditional mores, seem to be showing some success" in fostering paternal involvement in times of change. Parents may also use religion as an agent of socialization and as a source of support for their children.

Limitations of Religion for Nontraditional Families

Organized religions, which have been culturally developed by men over several millennia or centuries, support gender stratification (Sered, 1999). It follows that families headed by women and men who have a heightened sense of inequalities based on gender may not find spiritual sustenance and stability in religion as much as do other families. Furthermore, most religions frown on nonmarital forms of sexuality, and individuals who regularly attend religious services are less favourable toward nonmarital sex (Thornton et al., 1992). Depending on the religion, churchgoers may also strongly disapprove of homosexuality.

Therefore, while faith and religiosity are very positive for the faithful's well-being on many levels, they are less so for the well-being of those who engage in nontraditional forms of family life, such as families headed by same-sex couples. Religious communities by and large exclude these couples so that these families are deprived of a powerful instrument of child socialization and a powerful source of family stability. There are indications that many gays and lesbians are deeply religious but fear rejection, as explained in a student autobiography:

> "My lover and I both come from religious families and this has probably contributed to our mutual attraction. We're basically both moderately religious but we can't go to church. I suppose we could go separately and I could even join the choir...and he might volunteer in the child care. But we can't do this because we'd stick out like sore thumbs and we might even be discouraged from participating. We could go with my parents but what if they were ostracized as a result? I'm sure that there must be other gays out there who are religious but Bob and I don't mix much with the gay community because we're a monogamous couple."

(It is probably not a coincidence that this couple is planning to adopt children; their general values are mainstream.) In many areas, various congregations are opening their community to homosexuals and have been at the forefront of gay rights issues. But overall, one can conclude that religious establishments do not serve the entire spectrum of families equally well, although some congregations are far more proactive than others in this respect.

CONCLUSIONS: THE BALANCING ACT OF FAMILY FUNCTIONS

Children and adolescents served by educational facilities and child care centres come to school from their families and return to their families when the school day is over. Children serve as a link between the educational and familial systems. Their parents must manage this link and remain vigilant so that the best interest of their child is well served. This is an especially difficult role for families because school systems serve the economies in which they are nestled and economies are currently largely driven by a relentless technological and globalized marketplace. Many families are unable to compete and even survive within the harsh realities of this context.

In particularly deficient schools, parents have to supplement their children's education. As well, when schools harbour a critical mass of antisocial and aggressive children, parents have to step in, if they can, to protect and even shelter their children. Thus, although schools have taken over some of the functions previously fulfilled by families, schools have also forced an extension of family functions into the public domain. Furthermore, depending on family structure and place within the social class system, schools create a host of demands on parents.

Thus, to return to the discussions in Chapter 3, the educational system often expands family functions and may even burden the family system and, more specifically, mothers. For families that are religiously oriented, however, religion seems to offer them support in their socialization role—support for the parental role and support for adolescents and youths who wish to lead a life devoid of lifestyle risks. Therefore, at least for religious families, the practice of their faith generally strengthens their ability to fulfill their functions in a society that often provides pressures against this goal.

Summary

1. After parents, schools are a main agent of child socialization. Children today begin school earlier, and for many, this experience includes child care other than parental. Among the several types of non-parental child care available are centres or minischools, women who take one or several children into their homes, care by relatives, and care by a nanny. Poor-quality care has been related to disadvantages in cognition, language development, as well as social and emotional adjustment. Questions still remain concerning potentially negative effects of very long hours, too much peer contact, and too little interaction with adults. Child care availability, affordability, and quality are key ingredients in contemporary children's development and in their parents' well-being. Head Start programs benefit poor children living in disadvantaged areas, as they prepare these children for school, both cognitively and behaviourally. Some Aboriginal groups have initiated Head Start programs.

2. Parental involvement in their children's education contributes to school success. However, parents' social class largely determines the extent as well as the effectiveness of their involvement. Parental social capital benefits children's access to social as well as material resources that help them increase their adaptation to school. Overall, children from higher SES families do better academically, as do children who attend schools with greater percentages of students from higher SES backgrounds (a critical mass). Middle-class parents engage in the process of concentrated cultivation. Disadvantaged parents value education as much as others but practical problems often prevent this valuation from translating into higher aspirations and then achievement for their children. Incompatibility between family life and school routines often prevents children from adapting successfully at school. The summer activities of low-income children are often incompatible with learning, and they usually return to school even farther behind higher-income students. Family and school compatibility is especially important for Native children in the guise of tribally controlled schools. Immigrant adolescents, in particular, face challenges in this respect.

3. Private schools are selected by parents who can afford them and who expect that their own values will be reinforced. Private schools, particularly religious ones, constitute an effective community that enhances children's academic abilities. Home schooling is another system that parents turn to in order to ensure the passage of their values to their children as well as their educational success. It is a growing phenomenon, and concerns for the home-schooled children's well-being and academic success do not seem to be warranted.

4. Religion plays an important role in the lives of many Canadian families. The most commonly used indicator of religiosity is church or temple attendance. Each week, about 20 percent of Canadians attend religious services. Americans' church attendance is higher.

5. Parents transmit their religious beliefs to their children by their teachings and example, but the overall religious climate in a society also contributes to child socialization in this respect. Parents are more successful at passing on their beliefs within the context of a sup-

portive religious climate. Parents' marital happiness may also be a factor contributing to the transmission of their religious values to their children. Overall, religious involvement seems functional in terms of health, psychological well-being, marital stability and happiness, as well as child socialization. Religiosity supports the parental role. However, some religions are less supportive of nontraditional families.

6. While the educational system often increases the functions that families have to fulfill, the religious system may offer a supportive framework for the fulfillment of family functions.

Key Concepts and Themes

Agent of social control, p. 196
Consequences of child care, pp. 175–178
Critical mass, p. 199
Cultural and language factors, pp. 186–187
Effective community, pp. 179, 184
Extension of the family, p. 188
Family developmental perspective, p. 197
Family functions, p. 199
Family and school compatibility, pp. 184, 186
Head Start programs, pp. 178–179
Home schooling, pp. 189–190
Indicator, p. 191

Marital stability, pp. 196–197
Marital status, p. 180
Nontraditional families, pp. 198–199
Parental involvement, pp. 180-184
Quality of child care, p. 175
Religiosity, pp. 191–198
Religious capital, p. 195
Resources theory, p. 181
Social capital, pp. 180, 184, 195
Social class, pp. 182–185
Social desirability bias, p. 192

Analytical Questions

1. What would be some methodological difficulties involved in the study of the effect of child care on child development?

2. Why do you think that school officials and even some researchers are worried about home schooling? (Note: The question is *why* they are worried, *not what* they are worried about.)

3. How could the school system be reformed to meet the needs of families of immigrants as well as low-income families?

4. Religion and especially religiosity are rarely discussed in family textbooks. Why do you think that this is so?

5. What role does religiosity play in families that are not Christian or Jewish? (You will need to use other sources or your own personal experience/observations to address this question.)

Suggested Readings

Bramadat, P., and Seljak, D. (Eds.) 2005. *Religion and ethnicity*. Toronto: Pearson Education. This collection of original articles presents an overview of more recent ethnic groups in Canada and their religious organizations.

Castellano, M. B., Davis, L., and Lahache, L. (Eds.) 2000. *Aboriginal education: Fulfilling the promise*. Vancouver: University of British Columbia Press. This book contains a series of research articles, some of which originally served as a basis for the 1996 report of the Royal Commission on Aboriginal People. The articles, however, were not intended to have a focus on families.

Entwisle, D. R., Alexander, K. L., and Olson, L. S. 1997. *Children, schools, and inequality.* Boulder, CO: Westview. The researchers marshal an impressive array of data to study the effect of schooling on children as well as the effect of social inequalities (parents' social class, for instance) on children's progress and test scores.

Houseknecht, S. K., and Parkhurst, J. G. (Eds.) 2000. *Family, religion and social change in diverse societies.* New York: Oxford University Press. This collection of articles focuses on religion and the family in various cultural contexts of social change. It includes sections on gender as well as on economic factors.

Suggested Weblinks

Canadian Child Care Federation provides news, information, and links to other sources regarding child care practice and issues.

www.cccf-fscge.ca

Various associations for home schooling include the **Ontario Federation of Teaching Parents** at

www.ontariohomeschool.org

Others are **Home School Legal Defence Association,** and the **Canadian Association of Home Schoolers.**

Patterns of Partnering and Family Formation

Part 3 focuses on the beginnings of couple relationships and on family formation, as well as development of life course.

Chapter 8 studies couple formation and sexual relations. It begins with dating and includes marriage and cohabitation, both from a heterosexual and homosexual situation. Social exchange theory is a particularly helpful perspective in the context of couple formation and is related to gender differences. Singlehood is also included as an alternative to coupling.

Chapter 9 examines the various modes or patterns of family formation. This textbook defines family as an intergenerational entity, and this chapter discusses family formation via marriage, cohabitation, and single parenting. By the same token, same-sex parenting is included. Family planning and fertility are important components of family formation. Reproductive technologies and adoption are discussed as alternative modes of family beginnings.

Chapter 10, for its part, complements Chapter 9 in that it follows the development of families' life course, from the pre-birth stage to the death of elderly parents. Thus, various stages of families' life course are examined, including the years during which children are living at home and the many facets of the grandparenting stage. This chapter opens with a discussion of the gendered social construction of motherhood and fatherhood.

CHAPTER 8

Couple Formation and Sexual Relations

"The most painful aspect of my life at this age [about 21] is that I don't have a steady boyfriend. I haven't had one in two years and I am worried that life is passing me by."

"I rate myself as very happy.... Before I broke up with my boyfriend of two years I had no life. I was entirely wrapped up in a relationship that denied my identity.... It's freedom now and time for me to use it to mature."

"I live with my boyfriend and I really like it for now but I worry about the future. I am 23 and want to get married one day but the way I see it, he likes it just fine the way it is and won't want to commit himself to something more serious."

"In 10 years from now I realistically see myself living with a partner but it will not be the one I am with now as you can guess [this lesbian student is currently living with a woman at least 15 years her senior who supports her financially but is also very controlling and possessive]. This relationship has left me with some 'emotional' baggage I have to get rid of before I can contemplate another relationship and I plan on living on my own for some years after school is over."

"What has made me the most unhappy in the past years has been the gay social scene. I really hated every minute of it.... What has made me the most happy in the past year has been getting out of the gay social scene and finding my lover who just feels the way I do. [This student lives with his parents.]

"I am still a virgin and it has its inconvenience socially [popularity].... I am proud of myself because I have stuck to my principles and my parents' and one day the full discovery of sex will be a very exciting experience to share with my husband. It will add something to our marriage and he will know that I have waited for him."

The preceding students reveal how they feel about dating, cohabitation, being partnered, and sexuality—all main topics of this chapter. These quotes were chosen to reflect the variety of personal experiences and expectations in student populations. This chapter starts with the chronological beginning of life as a couple: Individuals select partners, become couples, and initiate sexual relations, while others remain single, if not necessarily celibate.

DATING

Dating is an American institution that emerged after the First World War. To this day, nowhere is dating as ritualized among adolescents and students as it is in the U.S. and only to a slightly lesser extent in Canada. In addition, nowhere else does it exist at the preadolescent level (Adler and Adler, 1998; Merten, 1996). Even U.S. researchers seem to accept the ages of 13 and 14 as "developmentally appropriate" for the onset of dating (Longmore et al., 2001). When it began, dating was revolutionary because it replaced the traditional *courtship* system as a prelude to marriage. Thus, dating represented a shift in terms of control over couple formation—from parents to the youths involved. But this social invention has also evolved over time: As the period of adolescence lengthened and age at marriage was delayed, dating was separated from marriage as a goal; its purpose became recreational and sexualized. Furthermore, today many youths are simply more interested in "hanging out" with their "crowd" of male and female friends than in traditional dating.

Heterosexual Dating

Children as young as age seven are occasionally asked if they have a girlfriend or boyfriend yet; they soon learn that a couple culture pervades North American social life, which later makes it difficult for unattached individuals to feel that they "belong" if they do not have a steady date or partner. Thus, steady dates represent a measure of social and personal predictability and security in a youth's social life. However, when concerns about being a couple occur early in a child's life, they may supplant other experiences and sources of self-definition and prematurely bring adult preoccupations to the fore. Not surprisingly, research indicates that young adolescent females who are romantically involved are more vulnerable in the emotional and academic realms than are older adolescents (Brendgen et al., 2002; Joyner and Udry, 2000). Dating often becomes a form of social pressure and a key source of popularity. It also serves the function of socializing youths, both positively and negatively, for the role that they will play when they cohabit or marry. For many, it is a prelude to marriage, and for others, dating takes place while cohabiting.

Young women tend to invest more in their dating relationship than do young men (Sacher and Fine, 1996). This pattern of **gender roles** in the emotional domain is pursued at all levels of romantic relationships (Kirkpatrick and Davis, 1994). The greater female investment stems in part from their socialization, which has taught them to be nurturing and understanding of others (Onyskiw and Hayduk, 2001:382). It also stems from females being socialized to depend on males and to perceive that they have access to fewer desirable alternatives outside their relationship than do males (Floyd and Wasner, 1994). Students' autobiographies indicate that this situation cuts across ethnicity and class:

> *"The most painful experience at this stage has occurred three months ago when I broke up with my boyfriend of three years.... I should have broken up with him two years ago...but I was afraid to be left alone, that I wouldn't be able to go out without a boyfriend, that I couldn't find another one, but now I realize that I have wasted two years of my life, and that's terrifying."*

This perception of a lack of alternatives contributes to reinforcing young women's tendency to work harder at relationship maintenance. However, in terms of **social exchange theory**, females with the most desirable resources (generally defined by males as attractiveness, social status, personality) can "afford" doing less maintenance work, as their alternatives may be more numerous and desirable than those of their date. Several studies confirm that dating interactions are nonegalitarian, at least at the beginning (Laner and Ventrone, 1998). This pattern is pursued into pre-wedding relationships (Humble, 2003) and spousal relationships, as discussed in Chapter 11.

Same-Sex Dating

It is not yet possible to provide solid information on same-sex dating because little research exists on this topic. To begin with, gay youths are not readily accessible for research purposes (Anderson, 1998). Not only do many shun publicity so as to avoid stigmatization but they also constitute a small minority. Furthermore, there is not always a clear-cut demarcation between homosexual and heterosexual self-identity so that, at some point in their life course, but not necessarily throughout their entire adult years, a number of persons identify as homosexuals. Many may have had a heterosexual past: Based on three large American data sets, Black et al. (2000) estimate that possibly as many as 30 percent of gay men and 46 percent of lesbian women have been or are married heterosexually. In fact, until now, a good proportion of lesbians, especially those older than 30, have discovered their identity later in life (Morris et al., 2001). Some may identify as bisexual and many do not engage in genital sex (Rothblum, 2002).

The carefully designed studies carried out by Laumann et al. (1994) indicate that 2.8 percent of men identify as gay and 1.4 percent of women identify as lesbian. These figures are similar to the rates for men and women who have *exclusively* same-sex relationships: 3 percent for men and 1.6 percent for women. In the Black et al. (2000) analyses, 4.7 percent of men and 3.5 percent of women had had at least one same-sex experience since age 18. But only 2.5 percent of men and 1.4 percent of women had engaged in *exclusively* same-sex activities over the year preceding the survey. Overall, it is estimated that 2 to 5 percent of men and 1 to 3.5 percent of women are homosexual.

These estimates contrast with the much-publicized 10 percent figure that originated from the hastily interpreted results of the poorly designed 1948 Kinsey Report: Their sample was not representative and was largely self-selected. But even Kinsey and his colleagues estimated that only four percent of males were exclusively homosexual (Kinsey et al., 1948). Yet, this figure was overlooked and it is the figure of 10 percent that caught the media's attention, became entrenched in the public's perception, and was accepted by gays themselves.

Lesbians and gays appear to be more numerous than they are because they live disproportionately in large metropolitan areas such as Vancouver, Toronto, and Montreal, or in smaller cities that contain a major university: This concentration gives them higher social visibility (Black et al., 2000), allows them to advocate for equality, and gives them media exposure. Furthermore, there is a tendency among homophobic persons to exaggerate the size of the homosexual population in order to sustain their "worst-fear" scenarios and prejudices. And, among some homosexuals, there is a tendency to inflate the numbers for political and social purposes. Hence, many misleading "facts" abound.

This being said, one can presume that "dating" may fulfill emotional functions for homosexuals similar to those among heterosexuals. Same-sex dating may, however, be difficult in terms of high school popularity as well as social acceptance in colleges and universities located outside key metropolitan areas (Bell and Valentine, 1995). The high school environment is often anti-gay, as it is at some universities. As a result, gay youths may be harassed, which in turn can lead to mental health problems (Waldo et al., 1998).

Gay adolescents and young adults, then, might not be able to date as do their heterosexual peers for fear of being socially stigmatized. Or, they may not yet know how to recognize a potential partner, while others may rely on sexual minority youth groups to find partners (Elze, 2002). Furthermore, for many, "coming out" (revealing their sexual identities) may occur only when they reach adulthood. Yet, the much publicized case of Marc Hall in Oshawa, Ontario, who, in June 2002, won the right to bring his boyfriend to his Catholic high school prom indicates that, at least in some districts, gay youths follow a dating pattern similar to that of other youths.

DATE AND PARTNER SELECTION

Dates are largely selected from schools, neighbourhoods, part-time work sites, and social clubs to which adolescents or their parents belong. Parents, siblings, and their friends may also constitute a source of dates, particularly in some religions or ethnicities among whom marriage within the group is preferred. Overall, **propinquity,** or physical proximity, is the first rule that explains how adolescents choose dates and, later on, partners. In young adulthood, proximal availability continues to be an important factor, but its scope broadens to include the worlds of higher education and employment. Thus, the new phenomenon of Internet dating defies the first rule of mate selection (Merkle and Richardson, 2000).

As they age, young adults generally become more selective and the pool of eligible dates narrows because each individual then tries to select only certain types of persons. This is called **assortative mating,** a term which refers to choosing a date on the basis of certain characteristics. When two persons choose each other on the basis of some elements of similarity, this is called **homogamy.** When homogamy is analyzed at the level of the demographic characteristics or resources that are important in a society's stratification system, the term used is **endogamy.** That is, people date, cohabit, and marry within their own status group or with persons who are similar to them in terms of basic social characteristics (Kalmijn, 1998). Assortative partnering of the homogamous type leads to compatibility of interests, values, and lifestyle (Surra, 1990). It facilitates an equitable exchange of resources, both personal and social. Cohabiting couples are only somewhat less endogamous than marrying couples (Forste and Tanfer, 1996). Overall, the qualities that men and women seek in a partner have been converging in recent decades, although males still value physical attractiveness more than women (Buss et al., 2001).

Elements in Heterosexual Partner Selection

Race and even **ethnicity** are usually the first two elements that are considered in partner selection. Although intermarriage or *exogamy* has become much more acceptable at the attitudinal level in Canada (Bibby, 1995), and there has been an increase in mixed unions between whites and visible minority groups, only three percent of married couples and four percent of cohabiting couples are racially mixed (Milan and Hamm, 2004). As the number of Canadians who belong to visible minority groups increases, interracial marriages will also increase over the years. Indeed, Kalbach (2000) has found that, at least for *ethnicity*, the Canadian-born have higher exogamy rates than the foreign-born. Furthermore, interethnic marriages are the norm rather than the exception among Canadian-born groups from (white) northern and western Europe. As well, 57 percent of Canadian couples involving blacks are composed of two black partners, while 43 percent comprise one black person, and generally, a white female (Milan and Tran, 2004). This creates a serious imbalance for black women—what has been called the "new marriage squeeze" (Crowder and Tolnay, 2000). Intermarriages, however, can involve partners who, except for race or ethnicity, are very similar in terms of religion, education, lifestyle, and values (Yancey, 2002).

Social class, or socioeconomic status (SES), as well as educational endogamy, is widespread. As Nelson and Robinson (2002:314) put it, "Mates come from generally similar backgrounds with only slight, but often important, differences in the status characteristics that each possess." This is partly explained by the fact that the proximity factor is driven by parents' social class, which dictates where their children live and which schools they attend. Even at work, people are attracted to one another because of common interests and shared topics of conversation that are partly related to their class-linked resources, including education, and their leisure activities. When the partners are discrepant, the more common scenario involves a woman in a relationship with a man of slightly higher SES.

Religious endogamy is more important in some groups, including the Jewish and other non-Christian faiths such as Hindu and Muslim, than among Protestant groups. When couples are interreligious, Catholics, Jews, and Muslims are more likely than others to encourage their partners to convert, generally before marriage (Shatzmiller, 1996). Nevertheless, it is estimated that Canadian Jews marry outside their faith in about 30 percent of the cases (Weinfeld, 2001). However, substantial proportions of these marriages are remarriages.

In 58 percent of couples, the spouses are no more than three years apart in age while 24 percent have a spouse who is four to six years older, thus reflecting a preference for **age** homogamy. However, when there is an age difference, norms favour an "older man–younger woman" coupling: While 36 percent of Canadian couples have a male who is older by three years, only six percent of couples include a woman who is more than three years older than the man (Boyd and Li, 2003). When men marry at an older age, or remarry, they usually do so to women considerably younger than they (Wu et al., 2000). The age gap increases with subsequent remarriages. Because there is a double standard of aging, men are generally less receptive than women to the idea of marrying someone older than they (Buss et al., 2001), and they value good looks in women when seeking a partner (Abu-Laban and McDaniel, 2004). Overall, large age differences tend to be found more often among the foreign-born, visible minorities, cohabitations rather than marriages, and lower-income groups (Boyd and Li, 2003).

Both from a functional perspective and exchange theory, endogamy and homogamy make sense; this is reflected in the observation that interreligious, interracial, and interclass marriages have higher divorce rates than endogamous ones (Lehrer and Chiswick, 1993). A study in Hawaii found that, within each religious group, women who had married interracially were experiencing a lower level of marital happiness; husbands, however, were not affected (Fu et al., 2001). Similarity of lifestyle, values, and interests means that couples have a larger pool of experiences they can share and activities they can engage in together. It strengthens mutual feelings, "we-ness," and companionship—key elements in modern relationships.

Same-Sex Partner Selection

Overall, there are indications that the principle of homogamy or assortative matching is somewhat less important among same-sex couples (Jepsen and Jepsen, 2002). Homosexuals are nonconformists in at least one area of their lives—their sexuality (Bell and Weinberg, 1978). This may well lead them to be nontraditional in other domains as well, including the criteria that dictate choice of partners. Furthermore, as a minority, they may have to cast a wider net than do heterosexuals because suitable mates may not be readily available nearby. Thus, because of necessity or rejection from their ethnic group, gays and lesbians who belong to minority groups have high rates of interethnic and interracial partnering (Jackson and Sullivan, 1999; Peplau et al., 1997).

As pointed out earlier, males are less willing than women to select dates who are not good looking (Buss et al., 2001). Hence, partner selection among gay men may be more influenced by physical appearance than is the case among lesbian women. There is, in fact, a certain obsession about "partner-shopping...for Mr. Right only if he is also Mr. Buff—muscled and perfectly toned" (DeAngelis, 2002), a theme developed by the gay student quoted at the outset of this chapter:

> "What was so hard for me is that I am not Mr. America, I am small framed and at the same time I look a bit older so that I don't appeal to males who are looking for a well built body and especially an adolescent type. I am not particularly sexy. I am just a plain guy with plain habits and the bar and club scene was very hard on me. Another problem is that I am not the promiscuous type and there is no way, but no way, that a gay guy is able to find a partner if he is not willing to do a lot of compromising in this respect. Maybe things will be better when guys like me can meet partners in a more normal environment like at school or whatever. Maybe then the gay scene will evolve from muscles and flesh (the meat market) to personalities and feelings."

In contrast, many lesbians are less concerned about femininity and general appearance (Krakauer and Rose, 2002). In fact, Cochran et al. (2001) found that American lesbians who were overweight or obese were less likely than other women to so define themselves. Therefore, the principles guiding partner selection may differ somewhat for male and female homosexuals.

COHABITATION

Cohabitation is referred to as a common-law union in Canada, and after one to three years of coresidence, the partners are legally protected as are married couples in terms of health care plans, insurance, support, and even residence ownership. As indicated in Table 8.1, the proportion of all couples living common-law has been increasing rapidly in Quebec but much more slowly in the rest of Canada. But even within Quebec, cohabitation is a francophone phenomenon. It generally is a relatively short stage in the life cycle of most couples, who soon marry or break up (Bumpass and Lu, 2000). However, a substantial proportion of Canadians now choose common-law rather than marriage as a *first* union (Le Bourdais et al., 2000). Turcotte (2002) contrasted two age groups of women: those aged 50 to 59 years, who are expected to be more traditional in this respect, and those aged 30 to 39 years, who have had the time to be influenced by more recent trends. He found that 70 percent of the younger Quebec cohort of women have chosen or are estimated to choose cohabitation as their first union. In comparison, same-age women in other provinces are half as likely to opt for cohabitation as a first union and are more likely to choose marriage. Among the older cohort, marriage still predominates, even in Quebec.

Furthermore, when studying Canadians' willingness (attitudes) to live common-law, the 2001 General Social Survey found that those most willing are young people aged 15 to 25, francophones, the non-religious, and those born in Canada (Milan, 2003). Within each of these categories, there is a substantial **gender difference**: As reflected in Figure 8.1, women are much less willing than men. In Latin American countries, where consensual unions have a long history, educated women are less often found in such unions than in marriage (Martin, 2002). Cohabitations are more likely to result in marriage when the male partner has economic resources (Smock and Manning, 1997), and when educated women have children, they are more likely to be married (Statistics Canada, 1997). This phenomenon is also observed in Latin American countries (Martin, 2002).

Some individuals choose cohabitation because it requires, in their opinion, less sexual faithfulness than marriage (Bumpass et al., 1991). Furthermore, fewer cohabitants than married persons feel that it is very important to have a lasting relationship to achieve a happy life (Milan and Peters, 2003). Overall, as we see in the following sections, the "role demands of cohabitation are less than those for marriage" (Thorn-

TABLE 8.1	Proportion of All Couples Who Are Cohabiting in Quebec Compared to Other Provinces/Territories of Canada, 1981–2001	
	Quebec	Other provinces
1981	8%	6%
1991	19	9
2001	30	12

Sources: Belliveau et al., 1994; Statistics Canada, October 22, 2002e.

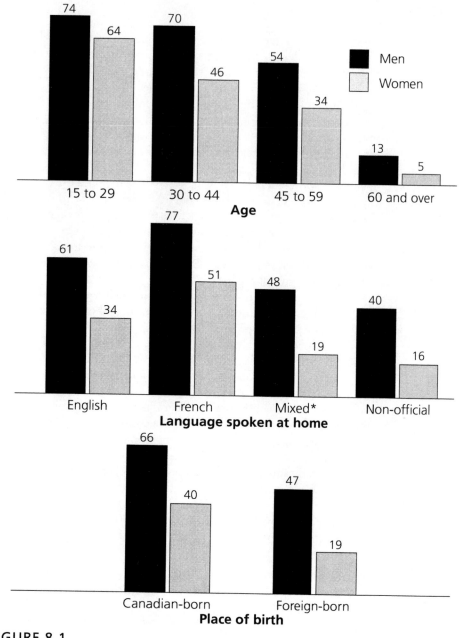

FIGURE 8.1

Percentages of Canadians Who Are Willing to Live Common-Law by Age, Language, and Place of Birth

Source: Statistics Canada, General Social Survey, 2001; Milan, 2003.
*Mixed refers to any combination of English/French and/or unofficial language.

ton et al., 1995:72). In other words, it is easier to enter into a cohabitational than a marital relationship because it is *less institutionalized.* For the same reason, it is easier to dissolve because there are fewer barriers against dissolution—whether legal, economic, or social—than is the case for marriage (Johnson's notion of structural commitment, 1999).

Relationship Stability and Types of Cohabitation

More than 50 percent of all cohabitations end in dissolution within five years (Milan, 2000), a phenomenon that is also noted in Latin American countries. In North America, instability has even increased in recent years, in great part because fewer such unions result in marriage than in the past (Bumpass and Lu, 2000). Thus, cohabitations are not as stable as marriages—and this is true in all western societies (Wu, 2000). Furthermore, they tend to dissolve more rapidly and cohabitants attempt reconciliation more rarely than married couples do (Binstock and Thornton, 2003). The reasons for the relative instability are detailed later. However, in a society such as Sweden where cohabitations are more institutionalized, such unions are of longer duration (Duvander, 1999). This is also the case for Quebec compared to the rest of Canada (Le Bourdais and Juby, 2002). It is estimated that 55 percent of Quebec women aged 30 to 39 who opted for a cohabitation as a first union go through a separation, compared to 66 percent among women in the other provinces (Turcotte, 2002). Nevertheless, no matter how one looks at these numbers, they are far higher than the 30 percent divorce rate after five years of marriage that occurs in Canada.

However, cohabitations are not a homogeneous category, so that stability depends in part on the reasons why a couple cohabits and how quickly the relationship is transformed into a marriage (Brown, 2004a). The term "stability" includes cohabitations that last and others that are transformed into a lasting marriage. The latter are forming a smaller proportion of all cohabitations than before. For instance, in the 1970s, about 50 percent of cohabitants went on to marry their partner within five years of the onset of living together. This compares to only about 30 percent in the early 1990s (Turcotte and Bélanger, 1997b). Thus, **"trial" marriages** are probably more rare than believed or than was the case just 20 years ago (Dumas and Bélanger, 1997). This cohort difference stems from the greater acceptability of cohabitation: In the past, couples who moved in together were often planning on getting married. This goal made their cohabitation socially acceptable. Today, couples do not need this "excuse" to cohabit and do not need to be concerned about marriage as the "next step" (Seltzer, 2000).

A large proportion of young couples who cohabit now begin living together rather quickly after the onset of dating, with little thought of permanency and least of all of marriage (Sassler, 2004; Wu, 2000). One would expect very high rates of eventual dissolution, as a short acquaintance is a precursor to divorce among the married. It may well be that instability is in the very nature of casual and/or rapid-onset cohabitations. Such casual cohabitations are more akin to "glorified" dating than to other types of cohabitations. Unfortunately, they may also be more painful and complicated to end than dating is (Wu and Hart, 2002). More research is needed to define the various characteristics and trajectories of types of cohabitations, including those that are entered into as a precursor to marriage (Bianchi and Casper, 2000), as described by a student:

"We're getting married this summer and we're both looking forward to it. We've lived together for one year because we could not afford the wedding and we felt that paying for one apartment as opposed to two would help us financially for when we get married. I would not however have lived with him had we not been engaged. That's a good way to get burned."

Benefits/Disadvantages of Cohabitation for Adults

Interestingly, despite an increasing acceptance of cohabitation in society as a whole and particularly among sociologists, there is no body of research documenting its benefits. Similarly, there is little research examining its disadvantages. But disadvantages frequently emerge in research comparing cohabitants to daters and to married persons.

Convenience and Sexual Availability

Cohabitants find it easier to be with each other sexually than when living separately (Sassler, 2004). Thus, sexual availability motivates many persons to cohabit rather than to continue dating, as a woman student expressed it in her autobiography:

"Right now I'd rate myself as being fairly unhappy and it's because I have found out that my boyfriend I live with lives with me just so that he can have sex that he knows is safe.... That means that I have wasted the past 18 months of my life that I could have better spent looking for a better guy and also one that would have accepted me as a whole person and not just as a sex machine.... Now I have to think about ending this relationship but it's hard you know because I am really attached to him."

It is remarkable that, in the many autobiographies of cohabiting women students, I have been unable to find material that was unequivocally favourable to this lifestyle, except among women who were engaged. This reflects Canadian women's lesser willingness than men to cohabit, which was mentioned earlier (Milan, 2003).

Living together also results when one or the other dater is looking for an apartment (Sassler, 2004). Cohabiting is then a form of savings: Sharing an apartment is less expensive than maintaining two separate ones (Wu, 2000). Couples who move together for such reasons generally do not think long term, and this arrangement is currently pleasant, economically advantageous, and less complicated. Some even move in together to escape from their families. Adults who divorce may also find similar economic advantages in cohabitation, especially in view of the fact that many divorced men have to support a child who lives elsewhere. It is a matter of convenience and **economies of scale,** even though cohabitants are more likely than married couples to keep money separately, especially when one or the other has previously divorced (Heimdal and Houseknecht, 2003). Young couples who are engaged often find cohabitation similarly convenient for financial reasons.

Relationship Aspects

As we see later, cohabitants have more frequent sexual intercourse than married couples (Laumann et al., 1994). In part, this is because cohabitations are of shorter duration and the frequency of sex is generally higher earlier on in unions of any type. This result may also stem from the nature of cohabitation itself: These relationships are more individualistic and may be more invested in sexuality, while marriages may be more characterized by a greater general commitment (Clarkberg et al., 1996). Although married spouses are usually happier with their relationships than are cohabitants (Nock, 1998a), when cohabitants plan to marry, the quality of their relationship is not much different from that of a married couple that has been together for the same duration (Brown and Booth, 1996).

Another potential benefit of cohabitation is that, because it is less institutionalized, couples may feel freer to invent their relationships outside the mould of traditional expectations and gender roles. Yet, recent studies are not unanimous: Some do not find a more equal division of labour within cohabitation than within marriage while others do (Wu, 2000). Generally, young cohabiting women do less housework than married ones (Smock and Gupta, 2002). Women who cohabit feel less secure in their relationship; consequently, they are less willing to sacrifice their employment opportunities and to invest as much in housework as do married women (Seltzer, 2000). Matters may be different in countries such as Sweden that have higher gender equality (Batalova and Cohen, 2002).

In a study carried out by Aquilino (1997), parents felt closer to their married children than to their cohabiting ones, even though they were involved in social activities with both. Parents may invest less emotion in their adult children's cohabitations as they perceive or worry that these relationships are less stable. In contrast, in-laws loom larger in a marriage because it is a more family oriented institution.

The Issues of Commitment and Fidelity

Some of the benefits of cohabitation have a negative facet. For instance, as we see later, cohabitants are **less faithful** to their partners sexually than married persons, even after controlling for personal values regarding extramarital sex (Treas and Giesen, 2000). For their part, Forste and Tanfer (1996) report that cohabiting women are more likely than married women to have had another sexual encounter since the beginning of their relationship. In fact, they are slightly less faithful than dating women. The above authors agree that their data support the view that, in many cases, cohabitation is selective of less committed individuals (Clarkberg et al., 1996): Cohabiting men especially are often **less committed** to their relationship and partner than are married men (Stanley et al., 2004). This sentiment is expressed by a divorced man during an interview, and then by a student in her autobiography:

> "No, I don't know if I'll get married [to the woman he lives with].... Right now I am not even sure that she's the right woman for me so that I prefer to take it easy; I have a wait-and-see attitude at this point." [At the follow-up interview two years later, this couple had separated. He was casual about it, but the woman was very upset.]

> "I have lived with two different guys and that's it! No more! It's always the same thing: we just play at being married because they don't want to do anything except play. They couldn't get married because...the usual line is 'I'm not ready for such a commitment.'"

What these quotes, as well as one of the chapter's openers (with the recurring themes of "play" and lack of commitment), well illustrate is another advantage that cohabitation has over marriage for *one* of the partners: It can serve to delay commitment and give a longer time lead during which to find a better alternative. Naturally, the more committed partner is at a disadvantage. Many cohabitants, perhaps more male than female, remain in a **permanent state of availability.** In other words, they are still "playing the field." In terms of exchange theory, the committed partner has less power because the relationship is more important to him or her than it is to the partner who has less invested. As a result, the partner with more invested is unhappy, may feel depressed, harbour regrets, and feel more insecure and less in control of his or her life (Brown, 2002). Furthermore, in view of the fact that marriage is still the most valued conjugal state in our society, one partner often wishes to transform the cohabitation into a marriage. Therefore, cohabitations may be problematic for many young and middle-age adults, particularly women. There is also evidence that entry into cohabitation does not provide the same protective benefits against depression as does entry into a marriage (Lamb et al., 2003)—and entry into cohabitation heightens a woman's risk of physical abuse (GSS, 2000; Sev'er, 2002). However, overall, Wu et al. (2004) did not find significant health disadvantages related to cohabitation.

For Older Adults

For older adults who have already been married, cohabitation may carry far fewer risks than it does for younger adults. For those who are widowed or divorced, an eventual marriage may not be important at all because they have already reached this goal once (Wu, 2000). Cohabitation becomes a substitute to marriage, a relationship in its own right with a similar level of commitment. In fact, in later life (after age 60 perhaps) the double standard of commitment that often exists among young and middle-aged cohabitants may disappear entirely because, in terms of exchange theory, males may need a partner as much as or even more than females. Hence, older males are likely to be more committed than younger males. We know, for instance, that after widowhood, older men do not adapt easily to the loss of their wives and are more bereft than are widowed women (Lee et al., 1998).

Men generally benefit highly from living with a partner (Cooney and Dunne, 2001). In comparison, widowed and divorced women in later life are often hesitant to give up their newly acquired independence or to replace a late spouse whom they loved. They may also be afraid that a marriage will soon return them to the role of nurse for an ailing husband. Such women may indeed welcome a new form of partnership and may find cohabitation functional. Others may actually look for an emotional and sexual relationship that does not involve the sharing of a dwelling—thus maintaining their independence. The economic benefits of cohabitation may be even more important among the older generation (Chevan, 1996). Cohabitation offers the advantage of economies of scale while, at the same time, it may allow the partners to maintain their respective children's inheritances intact.

ROMANTIC LOVE

In Canada as well as in western countries in general, couples "fall in love," or, at the very least, one of the two does. Being "in love" has been the main overt reason to marry for over a century (see Shumway, 2003). Failing to keep this love alive has led to many divorces and separation. The "fact" that people need to be romantically linked to marry represents a specific social construction of the marital relationship that does not exist universally (Noller, 1996). Marriage itself has become individualized and isolated from the context of the extended family system that predominates in so many other societies that are more collectivist culturally (Dion and Dion, 1993).

Romantic love is not new historically. Indeed, since time immemorial, couples have married with emotions as exalted toward each other as they now do. It is impossible to know what proportion of couples they represented—probably a minority, even among the ruling class. Furthermore, romantic love, called **courtly love** during the Middle Ages, often involved relationships that did not include physical sexuality. The noble lady who was the object of a knight's courtly dreams was usually married and his attention, which was fashionable at the times, did not constitute a risk to her marriage. In turn, courtly love had itself been influenced by Greek and Roman concepts found in the philosophies of Ovid and Plato. Hence, the term "platonic" love. There was also the phenomenon that can be called **passionate friendship**, a totally platonic but intense relationship between a man and a woman who were often married to others (Harris, 2002). The term reserved for this relationship in French is *amitié amoureuse*.

In other words, there have been many types of romantic love throughout the centuries and not all were related to marriage or sex. Romantic love tends to be associated with the development of individualism in western societies, which was particularly anchored in Great Britain and the U.S. Since the last half of the 20th century, romantic love has become the necessary ingredient in the decision to marry and in the definition of what constitutes marital happiness (Grunebaum, 1997). As marriages develop and children arrive, romantic love is often replaced by more practical forms of love or companionship. The reverse may happen in arranged marriages in which love may grow and romance may flourish (Nanda, 1991), as discussed in an earlier chapter.

HETEROSEXUAL MARRIAGE

As indicated in Figure 8.2, the yearly rate of marriage per 1,000 population has diminished substantially since 1941, its peak year, in part because of the low marriage rates in Quebec where cohabitation is so frequent; in part because a proportion of persons cohabit and will never marry; and also because the aging of the population means that fewer people of marriageable age are present. Currently, marriage is still a more secure and committed institution than cohabitation and provides more socially visible links between two families; it has a greater potential to increase social support. At the emotional level, spouses act as confidantes to each other and men confide to their wives more than they do to other persons. Sexuality is a powerful ingredient in marriage, both physically and emotionally. As mentioned earlier, cohabitants engage in sex more often than married couples. Logically, this should make them happier. Yet, Laumann and colleagues (1994) show that men and women are by far happiest when they have had only one sexual partner in the past 12 months and when they are married to that partner. On the basis of all the statistics they gathered, the authors conclude that "a monogamous sexual partnership embedded in a formal marriage evidently produces the greatest satisfaction and pleasure" (p. 364). Moreover, STDs are far less likely to occur within a monogamous marital relationship than under any other circumstances.

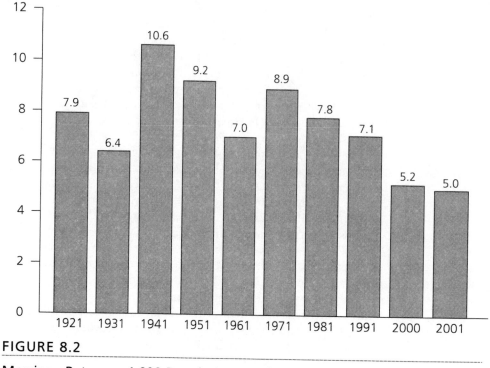

FIGURE 8.2

Marriage Rates per 1,000 Population, 1921–2001

Source: Statistics Canada, Selected Marriage Statistics 1921–1990. Cat. 82-552. *Canadian Social Trends,* 68, 2003, p. 27; Vanier Institute of the Family, 2000.

Research shows that both married men and women, compared to men and women in any of the other marital status categories, do better in the domains of physical and psychological well-being and even in terms of longevity (Waite and Gallagher, 2000). They have lower rates of emotional problems, are healthier physically, and live longer (Coombs, 1991)—although the latter result may be equally a consequence of married people generally having higher incomes, which in turn is related to better health and lower mortality. However, in a study of 17 western countries and Japan, Stack and Eshleman (1998) have found that being married is 3.4 times more closely tied to happiness than is cohabitation. Their results indicate that marriage, rather than cohabitation, increases both financial and health satisfaction, which in turn increase happiness. Naturally, the question that arises here is: Does marriage contribute to well-being (social causation) or does it simply capture people who are healthier, better balanced, and more attractive partners to begin with (social selection)?

Social Selection or Social Causation?

Let's first examine the evidence favouring the **social selection** hypothesis, which suggests that there is a selection into marriage of the healthiest individuals. Studies indicate that persons who suffer from serious mental illnesses, such as schizophrenia, are

Marriage formation, happiness, and stability are important elements in the social organization of western societies: They contribute to couples' well-being and productivity as well as to their children's positive outcomes, both currently and in the long term.

less likely to marry, particularly men (Link et al., 1987). Highly dysfunctional persons either do not marry or, when they do so, their marriages do not last, after which it becomes difficult to re-marry (Forthofer et al., 1996). Very ill persons as well as persons who are intellectually incompe-tent do not get selected into marriage as fre-quently as others. Therefore, a selection process takes place, particularly among men. Once people are married, another selection process is activated: The marriages of disturbed, incompe-tent, or antisocial persons are less likely to last, as these individuals become very difficult spouses with whom to live. Psychological balance cer-tainly contributes to marital stability (Aseltine and Kessler, 1993).

Nevertheless, most people still marry at least once, whether they are well balanced or not, and a certain number of well-balanced persons choose not to marry. This means that the positive effects of marriage are probably more important than the selectivity effects in explaining the differences in well-being by marital status (Daniel, 1996). In other words, **social causation** often explains far better the differences in well-being between the married and the non-married (Wu et al., 2004). Indeed, marriage helps adults stabilize their per-sonalities, gain self-esteem and personal security, and develop competencies and a sense of responsibility that were not necessary as single persons, particularly among men (Nock, 1998a). Warm and supportive relationships enhance happiness, psychological well-being, physical health, and consequently longevity (Gove et al., 1990; Hu and Goldman, 1990; Lillard and Waite, 1995).

Interestingly enough, there are indications in a rather old but still relevant study of homosexuality that gay men and lesbians who belong to a stable and monogamous cohabitation enjoy better mental health than nonexclusive homosexuals (Bell and Wein-berg, 1978). Except in seven provinces and territories, at this time (2004) homosexual couples cannot yet legally marry; monogamous cohabitation is as close to marriage as they can get, and its benefits may approximate those of marriage among them.

Married men are more often regularly employed than other men, which provides them with greater personal stability (Daniel, 1996). When they change jobs, it is more to increase their economic gains than is the case among single and divorced men (Gor-man, 1999). Furthermore, when his wife is employed, which has become the norm, a husband is now far better off financially than a single man. Married couples with an employed wife have an income advantage of at least $15,000, on average, over mar-ried couples with a wife who is not gainfully employed (Sauvé, 2002a). Therefore, men are generally far more secure with a wife than without because married couples are more likely to pool their resources than are cohabiting couples. Waite (1995) calls marriage an "insurance policy." Of course, the same applies to women financially. As Lerman (2002:6) puts it, "The presence of more than one potential earner helps diversify the risks arising from unemployment, lost wages, or shifts in demand for various occupations."

Moreover, married adults are more likely to maintain a healthy lifestyle and diet than nonmarried adults. The former eat at home more, stay out late less, use alcohol and illegal drugs less, and are better organized to take care of their basic needs (Bachman et al., 1997). A cohesive marriage is an important social resource and brings an *informal element of social control* into the life of individuals. This may be the reason why married people drink less than cohabitants (Horwitz and Raskin White, 1998). Furthermore, Horney et al. (1995) as well as Laub and colleagues (1998) have found that when a person who engages in illegal activities enters into a good marriage with a prosocial partner, the marriage eventually contributes to the cessation of illegal activities by the criminal.

Are Marriage Benefits Gendered?

Some literature indicates that marriage may be more advantageous to men than to women—even though women want it more than men (England, 2000; Marks, 1996). Indeed, there is a larger difference between the scores of well-being of married men compared to divorced and single men than there is among women of various marital statuses. Why would marriage benefit women less? To begin with, once children arrive, women have more responsibilities than men, particularly when both spouses are employed (McLanahan and Casper, 1995), and they suffer from more work interruptions than men (Cook and Beaujot, 1996). Therefore, for many women, marriage becomes a mixed blessing, thus explaining in part why the scores of well-being of single women are not all that different from those of their married counterparts. These scores have actually become more similar in recent decades and, in some instances, by mid-life the scores of single women are more positive than those of married women on some dimensions (Marks, 1996). Unfortunately, these studies do not inform us of the *past* marital status of single women or of their ethnic and cultural affiliation.

However, it should be noted that no study has yet compared married men and women with cohabiting ones in terms of the diverse facets of well-being. Neither do studies exist on the relative responsibilities of cohabitants who have children. The quotes presented earlier highlight problems of emotional security, powerlessness, and unhappiness among young cohabiting women who were not engaged to their partner. There were clear indications in these quotes that the benefits of cohabitation are gender specific among the young: They may favour males even more than marriage does and this may well be more so when children are present. However, the following hypotheses deserve to be tested: Women may be as advantaged by cohabitation as men in cultures where the phenomenon is more widespread, such as Quebec and Sweden. As well, both genders may be equally advantaged when they cohabit later in life after a divorce or widowhood and after children from previous unions have become independent. Such advantages are not likely to exist, however, among groups for whom cohabitation is not sanctioned, such as people of Hindu or Muslim faith.

Within marriage, the quality of the relationship is an important determinant of well-being (Ren, 1997). All in all, marriage is beneficial to adults, but a troublesome marriage negates some or all of these benefits, particularly for women. Second, the benefits accrued in marriage may differ for men and women depending on the domains studied—emotional well-being, physical health, happiness, or security. These gendered benefits may also differ depending on ethnicity and the stage of the life course or age of the person. For instance, it is not clear whether marriage is more or less beneficial among young than middle-age persons (Marks and Lambert, 1998). Finally, the benefits of marriage depend on the time or cohort period that serves as a context for marriage (Glenn and Weaver, 1988). For example, more recent cohorts of women seem to benefit from marriage less than preceding cohorts, and this would be especially so for career women. But, here again, one has to consider the dimensions of personality and life that are measured in these studies because it is possible that more recent cohorts of researchers favour some aspects of life (i.e., independence) over others.

Thus, it is also possible that research may not have focused on all the benefits of marriage for women. Marriage has advantages for women, especially over their life span, in terms of wealth accumulation (Wilmoth and Koso, 2002), and this effect is particularly evident when women reach retirement age. In this respect, marriage is also functional for men and should continue to be so as married men tend to earn more than single men (Beaujot, 2000) and as most wives are employed and many earn more than their husbands. Thus, financially, marriage is advantageous to both genders, so long as it lasts. Overall, the fact that on some issues (particularly the division of household labour) women are generally at a disadvantage compared to men does not mean that marriage is no longer functional for a majority of them. What it means is that marriage could become more functional for women than it now is, with the help of changes in our values in terms of gender roles and with increased governmental investment in child care centres, for instance (Beaujot, 2000).

SAME-SEX MARRIAGE: FACTS AND ISSUES

In 2000, Parliament enacted the *Modernization of Benefits and Obligations Act* which extended benefits and obligations to common-law couples, be they of opposite sex or the same sex. Furthermore, the definition of "spouse" was changed to include any two persons who have lived together in a "marriage-like" relationship for at least two years. In 2001, the Netherlands became the first country to legalize same-sex marriage and was followed by Belgium in 2003. The provinces of British Columbia and Ontario did so in 2003, and five other provinces and territories followed suit in 2004. But neither Canada nor the U.S. have yet to follow suit as countries. However, while the U.S. government is officially opposed to same-sex marriage, the Canadian government is willing to allow it.

The question generally asked is, Would same-sex marriage devalue the institution of marriage? This question has both legal and moral substance. The answer hinges on the definition of marriage and on the type of marriage that lesbians and gays are seeking. The answer also hinges on the distinction between marriage and cohabitation (Ambert, 2003a).

Marriage versus Cohabitation in General

As seen in Chapter 1, marriage is an institution that has so far been legally and socially defined as a union between a man and a woman—thus a heterosexual covenant. More importantly perhaps, marriage is defined as a sexual, economic, social, and emotional partnership involving **obligations** as well as rights. Furthermore, **commitment** is a key aspect of the institution and so is **fidelity**. When children are involved, marriage (and cohabitation) also entails a parental relationship and the rights and obligations assumed jointly by parents to provide and care for their children.

As described earlier, cohabitation is seen as entailing fewer responsibilities at the legal, emotional, and economic levels, and is thus perceived to be a **freer lifestyle** (Ambert, 2003b). Yet, in recent years, by virtue of the legal recognition of the rights and obligations of cohabiting partners, many couples who have chosen to cohabit have found themselves subject to various legal obligations, even though they had not sought the rights previously given to married persons only. Accordingly, many now ask whether cohabitation still constitutes an *alternative* to marriage (Willetts, 2003).

For Same-Sex Couples: Cohabitation or Marriage?

In the 1970s and 1980s, the gay and lesbian cultures were most often characterized as **countercultures** and still are to a great extent. Lesbians rejected motherhood and traditional family values. Some of their banners read "Smash the Family" and "Smash Monogamy" (Stacey, 1998:17). In the midst of this rejection, a movement toward integration within the mainstream family culture emerged, with a focus on stable couple formation and family life—although many homosexuals are still against marriage, which they see as a heterosexist institution (Eleanor Brown, *Globe and Mail*, Aug. 8, 2002, p. A17). The movement among gays and lesbians to form families and be recognized legally by both civil and religious authorities as married couples invites consideration of a number of **ideological contradictions**. Two are mentioned here (Ambert, 2003a).

1. The first contradiction stems from the fact that, although many gays and particularly lesbians are becoming more pro-family and pro-marriage—values that average citizens cherish—this cultural conversion has been largely dismissed by the rest of society. Same-sex-parent families are often stigmatized and parents are denied the right to marry, ironically, at a time when concerns are raised about the decline of marriage itself as a binding force and fundamental institution. One could argue here that allowing those homosexuals who intend to enter into a stable, committed, and sexually exclusive relationship to marry would reinforce the value of the institution of marriage itself (see Woodill in Mandell, 2004:200). Furthermore, the children of same-sex parents would benefit if their parents had social and legal incentives that would stabilize their relationship (Schwartz and Rutter, 1998).

2. The second ideological contradiction leads us back to the initial question about what is essential and crucial to the definition of marriage. It arises when some homosexuals wish to pursue an "open contract"—that is, a relationship that includes extramarital outlets (Sullivan, 1995). This is a contradiction in terms because marriage is meant to be a committed and exclusive relationship. It could be argued

that gay men who espouse this definition of marriage should cohabit because their marrying would weaken the elements of commitment and fidelity in the institution of marriage. Of course, this does not mean that some degree of infidelity may not occur as it does among some heterosexual marriages.

However, same-sex partners who wish to form an exclusive relationship based on love and cooperation do not present this contradiction. In fact, one could expect that, generally, "lesbigay" partners who seek marriage will be a select group who have been together for many years and wish to legalize their commitment to each other and those who are "engaged" and also wish to pursue an exclusive and committed relationship. Indeed, the couples whose marriages were celebrated at City Hall in Toronto in 2003 and 2004 generally fit these profiles. (Between June and December 2003, about 2,000 same-sex couples, including 600 American ones, have married in Ontario and British Columbia. By July 2004, one couple had petitioned for divorce.)

Thus, it could be argued that homosexuals who intend to marry share a commitment to monogamy and fidelity. It would also be important that a similar cultural consensus concerning the unacceptability of same-sex extramarital infidelities emerge in the public at large. Otherwise there would be a **double standard**: one for heterosexual marriage and one for gay marriage. This would mean that homosexual marriages are "second best" (Woodill in Mandell, 2004:200).

SINGLEHOOD

The single status includes never-married, divorced, and widowed persons who do not live in a union. People who cohabit are not herein considered single. The 2001 census reveals that fewer young people between the ages of 20 to 29 are living in couples than before (Statistics Canada, 2002e). However, at this time, it is premature to state that a greater proportion of people than before are choosing to remain single. More live alone or with their parents, but most of these individuals are simply delaying cohabitation, marriage, or even remarriage. At the very least, a prolonged period of singlehood before a first marital transition is becoming the norm and is a choice for many. For other persons, including a proportion of young women who give birth nonmaritally, as well as minority women who are poor, singlehood may be imposed by demographic circumstances, such as a scarcity of eligible partners within one's age group, social class, or race. Others are older widowed or divorced individuals, particularly women who, because of better health and the unavailability of potential mates, live alone.

Urbanization has contributed to making the single life a more viable option; singles were both more isolated and visible socially when society was largely rural. (In the 17th and 18th centuries, single persons were discouraged from living alone.) In a city, in contrast, singles are less visible because they are far more numerous, and this lowers the potential for isolation. They have access to a larger and more varied social network. The availability of a range of food- and household-related commercial services has also facilitated single life.

Economic independence for a segment of women, especially the well educated and the professional, is another structural/historical factor making singlehood a more accessible alternative than in the past. As well, the postponement of marriage and the high divorce rates contribute to making the single status a more fluid and less socially visible one than used to be the case. The greater acceptance of sexuality outside of marriage is also a factor that facilitates remaining single, or, at the very least, postponing union formation. The acceptability of giving birth nonmaritally or the possibility of adopting a child as a single person are also facilitating factors. Finally, it should be added that the growing trend among young adults to remain in their parents' home fosters single life.

Types of Singles

A long while ago, Stein (1981) proposed four types of singles—a typology that is still relevant today, with some minor corrections. Stein's first two categories of singles are **voluntary**. Voluntary, *temporary* singles are simply delaying marriage, whereas voluntary, *stable* singles have chosen to remain single. The latter would include nuns and priests who accept celibacy. Stein, however, includes cohabitants in the category of voluntary singles. Cohabitation was relatively rare when he developed his classification and was not then as socially acceptable. Today, cohabitants are considered partnered rather than single in Canada. I suggest instead that voluntary, stable singles are individuals who choose not to be in a union that could become long-term. Under this definition, the voluntary, stable single category includes divorced and widowed persons, as well as persons who have cohabited, but who do not wish to marry or cohabit in the future. This definition may or may not include individuals in "living apart together" unions: One would have to defer to their own perception in this matter.

Stein's two other types of singles are **involuntary**: Involuntary, *temporary* singles are still seeking a mate and would like to be part of a couple. They become involuntary, *stable* singles later if they have not been able to achieve the goal of marriage or cohabitation. Included here are some widowed and divorced persons who would like to remarry but will not find a mate. Stein's (1981) typology applies both to heterosexuals and to homosexuals. Gays and lesbians basically can choose to remain single or to cohabit or even marry in some provinces. Similarly, they may either be voluntary, temporary singles or involuntary, stable singles.

Among singles are those who have been so all their lives—even if they have children (Siegel, 1995). Davies (2003:347) has utilized the life course perspective to study how and when a transition occurs in these persons' lives, at which point a shift occurs when they realize that they will remain single, very likely for the remainder of their lives. "...With age, singlehood is increasingly experienced as less temporary and therefore more stable. It becomes a more comfortable status [in a couple-oriented society], a status with advantages...the change is gradual" and is associated with age and gender. A birthday or the breaking of a long-term relationship or, for women, the purchase of a home, may be a marker event. Others who never had an interest in marriage or even living together may not experience a transition.

Advantages and Disadvantages of Single Life

For both sexes, remaining single is synonymous with various forms of independence. This involves flexible schedules, the possibility to change career or relocate, the ability to engage in leisure activities spontaneously, being responsible only for oneself, and financial independence. For mature women, "going solo" may contribute to personal autonomy and growth (Gordon, 1994). In many instances, however, it is actually financial instability that leads to remaining single, particularly among men (Nakosteen and Zimmer, 1997). For others, being single means a "revolving door" policy in terms of dating and sexual relationships, with no strings attached. The main disadvantage of remaining single resides in the couple orientation and structure of society (Davies, 2003). Thus, single people lack a "built-in" partner for social activities. Other drawbacks are loneliness for some and a low income for others. Singlehood is most disadvantageous in old age, in terms of social support, help, and finances—although women are more disadvantaged than men on the latter point (Hirschl et al., 2003). Hence, the disadvantages and advantages of remaining single are, to some extent, **gender** and **personality specific**. In general, single women maintain higher scores of mental and physical well-being than single men (Marks, 1996). They have more confidantes than single men (Davies, 1995). In fact, single women are not all that different from married women in terms of happiness, although surveys have not taken into consideration the element of choice in singlehood. Furthermore, single women who choose not to have children may not be as disadvantaged as in the past, compared to their married counterparts with children, because children no longer constitute an unmitigated blessing in a woman's life (Ambert, 2001). There is, however, a difference between single and married men on all indicators of health and well-being in favour of the married. Thus, it would appear that being single carries fewer disadvantages for women than men—except, as pointed out, in old age where women outnumber men. But older single persons, although not lonely, have fewer sources of friendship and familial interaction than their married or previously married age-mates (Barrett, 1999), a result of the couple orientation of our society. They also rely more on paid help for assistance in daily activities, a difference that may reflect a long-term pattern of maintaining independence (Connidis and McMullin, 1994).

SEXUAL RELATIONS

The focus of studies on sex has been on measuring attitudes toward premarital and extramarital sexual intercourse and frequency of intercourse. Traditionally, "premarital" has referred to sex that occurs before a person marries, an emphasis which is changing. Extramarital intercourse refers to infidelity on the part of one or both spouses. In this textbook, I will use the term "extracouple" sexual relations in order to consider instances of infidelity in cohabitation, whether heterosexual or homosexual.

Sexuality: Social Constructs and Attitudes

Measuring the frequency of sexual intercourse alone may represent a **masculine bias** in the research and may also misrepresent the level of sexuality among heterosexual and lesbian couples (Patterson, 2000; Rothblum, 2002). There is more to sexuality than penetration: Mutual masturbation, kissing, and caressing are important elements of sexuality (and affectivity) among couples. Thus, the incidence of sexuality in general is likely to be far higher among some groups than depicted in the statistics on intercourse. Furthermore, the focus on intercourse reflects an orientation toward performance, as in "scoring," as opposed to self- and partner-fulfillment.

It follows that our approach to the study of sexuality is influenced by our social constructions. To begin with, sexuality is a prime concern in western countries, as illustrated by the contents of television programming, advertisements, literature, as well as magazines and newspapers. People from non-western cultures and especially previous centuries might well view our concern as an obsession. Sex, especially in the form of intercourse, has come to be defined as a primary need. While it is indeed a basic human "instinct," its absence in a person's life cannot be equated with the consequences of being deprived of air, food, or light. The psychological consequences of abstaining from sex much depend on how we construct its meaning and importance.

Attitudes about nonmarital sex have become more permissive. By 1995, only about 20 percent of Canadians disapproved of nonmarital sex. Quebecers and younger generations have become the most accepting, while Canadians living in the Prairie and Atlantic provinces are less so (Bibby, 1995). Furthermore, Hobart (1996) found that more Canadians, particularly men and francophones, were adopting the "fun" or recreational standard, although a majority still define sexual relations as appropriate only when the partners love each other. Multiple partners still remain more acceptable among men than women, another gulf separating the **genders** in terms of relationships (Hensley, 1996). Bibby and Posterski (2000) also found a gender difference both among adults and adolescents concerning the propriety of having sex before marriage. While the majority of adolescents (82 percent) agree that sex before marriage is acceptable when people love each other, this acceptance declines to 48 percent among females but remains fairly high at 68 percent among males when "people like each other" (Bibby, 2001). Only five percent of females but 20 percent of males approve of sex on a first date. This gender divide means that many young women actually have sex at a time when they are not emotionally ready for it, as explained by a woman student:

> "I got conned into having sex when I look back on my first experience [age 16]....
> [H]e told me all the things he knew I wanted to hear, but none were true...and I
> felt really cheap after...plus it was very, very painful, you know, I cried out and it
> was humiliating.... I lied and told my friends it had been great but I stayed away
> from guys for a year after that."

Early Sexuality

Early sexuality is herein defined within the *current* cultural context of Canadian society; what is early here may be "on time" in other societies where reproduction begins sooner because of high child mortality, lower life expectancy, and a lesser need for secondary education (Kaufman, 1999:26).

We do not have precise information as to the average age when young Canadians begin having sexual intercourse. The only national study including high schoolers was analyzed by Bibby and Posterski: 62 percent of males and 49 percent of females reported having had sexual intercourse, presumably by age 18. In the U.S., fewer adolescents in Grade 12 reported ever having had intercourse in 2001 than in 1991 (61 versus 67 percent). This decline held for both genders and was particularly pronounced among black teens (from 81 to 61 percent), and corresponds to a decline in teenage pregnancy (U.S. Department of Health and Human Services, 2002b). The 2001 survey by Bibby of 15- to 19-year-old students found that 51 percent never engaged in sex. Unfortunately, no age breakdown is presented.

Besides gender, the following variables contribute to a *later* sexual initiation: higher parental social class, two-parent family, school achievement, and religiosity (Beeghley, 1996). Among girls, engagement in sports is also related to postponement of sexual activities (Manlove et al., 2002). As well, both high-quality parent-child relations and less permissive parental attitude toward early sexuality delay initiation (Davis and Friel, 2001). In contrast, teens who engage in risky behaviours such as alcohol and drug use, who have been sexually abused, and who mature early physically are more likely to begin sexual intercourse at a younger age than other teens (Kowaleski-Jones and Mott, 1998). Young teen girls who have a boyfriend who is six years older or more than they are have a higher chance of beginning intercourse than other girls with a same-age boyfriend (Kaestle et al., 2002).

In 1960, only 23 percent of American women age 18 had had sexual intercourse; this proportion grew to 46 percent in 1975 and 67 percent in 1990 (Beeghley, 1996:23). Rubin (1990) points out that, just three decades ago, a teenage girl who was sexually active had to pretend that she was a naive innocent. Today, it is the uninitiated who must play the role of the sexual sophisticate. However, among recent immigrant groups from Asia or the Middle East, for instance, premarital sexuality is particularly discouraged, especially among girls. Overall, were it not for general **peer pressure** and, in many instances, rape or psychological coercion, perhaps a majority of young women would initiate sexual intercourse later than they currently do (Abma et al., 1998). Even some males obviously feel pressured as well as "left out":

> *"I always felt left out in high school just because I didn't get laid. I was the only guy still a virgin at graduation. [Note that this was probably his perception based on peer boasting rather than a fact.] The counsellor told me there was nothing to worry about and he was right but to a 16-year-old that's not what you want to hear."*

Thus, simply mentioning when first sexual intercourse takes place camouflages an important reality: the degree of **voluntariness** and desire for the experience (Orton, 1999). There is also a great deal of difference by gender in the quality of the experience at first intercourse among adolescents. In part, this may stem from the fact that sexuality is more goal oriented toward intercourse—and rather quickly—which may be more a male than a female vision of sexuality, as mentioned earlier (Schwartz and Rutter, 1998:94). For their part, males describe their first intercourse as exciting and satisfying, whereas more females report fear, anxiety, embarrassment, and even guilt. Two women students' recent memories are presented:

> *"The first time I had sex was both most exciting and most painful."*

> *"I did not enjoy my first sexual experience at all because I was not ready for it and that's why I mention it here because it became something I regretted for a long time after and made me feel dirty. It took me three years after that, until with my boyfriend, to consider it again and the experience was so different because I felt loved."*

The element of control is important for women and may be lacking in many cases due to peer pressure and lower self-esteem, compared to what is the case among males. Kowaleski-Jones and Mott (1998) report that, often, male teens who are sexually active feel more in control of their environment and express lower levels of depression than male teens who are not sexually active. The contrary is reported by many young females.

One problem concerning sex among adolescents is the high rate of sexually transmitted diseases (Orton, 1999). Let's just take one instance, chlamydia, an infection that does not have overt symptoms and generally goes undetected but can lead to infertility or tubal pregnancy. Although its incidence has decreased over the years, young women aged 15 to 19 are far more likely to contract this disease than their older counterparts (Health Canada, 2000). Adolescents who have *multiple* partners and do not practise safe sex tend to have other problems as well, such as more frequent alcohol consumption, lower school achievement, and a more difficult parent-child relationship (Perkins et al., 1998). They are also less likely to receive a great deal of supervision; permissive maternal attitudes about sexuality are equally related to having multiple partners (Miller et al., 1999). Family Research 8.1 further discusses this particular study.

Marital and Cohabitational Sexual Relations

Interestingly enough, conjugal sex is not as popular a topic of research as is sex outside of marriage! In the Psychlit database, for instance, one can find hundreds of articles on human sexuality published in scholarly journals, but very few on marital sex. In the sociologically oriented literature, the few studies on marital sexuality tend to focus on the following questions: How often do couples have sex? What factors differentiate those with a high frequency compared to those with a low frequency?

FAMILY RESEARCH 8.1

Interviewers Have to Be Trained: A Study of Adolescent Sexual Behaviour

The goal of the research conducted by Miller, Forehand, and Kotchick (1999) was to study adolescent sexual behaviour in relation to family variables among black and Latino youths, including a sample in Puerto Rico. The adolescents were aged 14 to 16 and still enrolled in high schools from where they were recruited: 982 mother-adolescent dyads were contacted. Mothers and sons were interviewed separately at school or at a research office. Interviewers were matched to the respondents by sex, language, and ethnicity. Older women interviewed mothers, and younger persons worked with the adolescents.

The interviewers' training took place over several days for about 25 hours. The project and its goals were explained and interviewing techniques were reviewed. The interviewers familiarized themselves with the separate questionnaires they were to use with mothers and sons, and they practised among themselves. Each one had to conduct an interview while being observed, and received feedback on his or her performance. Training also included crisis management and "addressed the interviewer's legal responsibility to report any abuse of a minor revealed during an interview."

Frequency of Sexual Intercourse and Aging

There is agreement that the frequency of sexual intercourse in marriage diminishes with age (Call et al., 1995; Laumann et al., 1994). This downward trend is illustrated in Table 8.2. But these authors caution the reader that averages are not the best measure of couples' sexual activity after age 50 because couples who stop having sex depress the overall average. For instance, for respondents older than age 75, the average stands at about once a month, but when only those who have sexual intercourse are considered, the average rises to three times a month.

The question to address here, however, is how to untangle the effect of age from that of marital duration. In other words, as couples age, so does their marriage and habituation could be a factor. Call et al. (1995) have done the calculations to answer this question. First, they found that age *is* the main variable. Second, if habituation has any effect at all, it occurs early in the marriage. That is, couples' frequency of sex was highest during the first two years of marriage, regardless of age. After two years, or what is called the **honeymoon period,** the frequency of sex declined sharply. The researchers explained that, if habituation kept producing an effect, sex would then keep diminishing in frequency as the marriage continued, which is not the case.

The same phenomenon is observed in remarriages. The frequency of sexual intercourse is high at the beginning of the relationship, no matter the age, and drops after the initial period. After that, it becomes a matter of age rather than length of marriage. Generally, couples who are younger at marriage or remarriage have a higher frequency of sexual intercourse than couples who are older. It is possible that, in a few years, this section will be rewritten to include references to the effect of sexual enhancement pills such as Viagra on older couples' sexual lives. We are beginning to hear anecdotes to the effect that lawyers are seeing more divorces stemming from older men who have discovered "the fountain of youth," "trespassed into younger pastures," and discarded less attractive wives.

Frequency of Sexual Intercourse and Cohabitation

Laumann and colleagues (1994) as well as Call et al. (1995) find that cohabiting couples have sexual intercourse much more often than married couples. For instance, Laumann and colleagues report that only about seven percent of married men mentioned

TABLE 8.2	Average Frequency of Sexual Intercourse among Married Couples by Age	
	Age Bracket	**Monthly Frequency**
	19 to 24	11.7
	30 to 34	8.5
	50 to 54	5.5
	65 to 69	2.4

Source: Data from Call, Sprecher, and Schwartz, 1995.

having sex four or more times a week compared to nearly 19 percent of cohabiting men. The women's reports were similar. The reader may then perhaps conclude that, at least as far as sex is concerned, cohabitation is more enjoyable. Is it?

Unfortunately, most long-term cohabiting unions tend to last, at best, for the same duration of time as the honeymoon period in marriage (Milan, 2000). Therefore, it is entirely possible that a higher frequency of sex among cohabitants simply reflects the fact that they are mainly honeymooners. When the couple remains happy together, most then go on to marriage and, at least at the beginning, may maintain a higher frequency of sex. So far, there have not been sufficient numbers of cohabiting couples at older ages whose relationships have remained intact for 10 to 25 years to compare with married couples of the same age. However, one cannot eliminate the possibility that sex plays a more important role in cohabitation than it does in marriage and constitutes a larger part of the mutual attraction. Nevertheless, the frequency of sexual intercourse must also diminish with age among cohabitants who remain together. Longitudinal research is needed in this domain, comparing couples consisting of two men, two women, or heterosexual partners (Patterson, 2000).

Frequency of Sexual Intercourse and Relationship Quality

Couples with a higher frequency of sexuality experience a happier relationship. The more vital couples are, the more likely they are to remain interested in each other, and this interest generalizes into the sexual aspect of their relationship. Couples who get along better and share a higher level of companionship are inclined to be more physically affectionate, which leads to a desire and opportunity for sexual activities. Another complementary process is also at play: Having intercourse leads to a greater satisfaction with the marriage and the partner. Sex is a valued activity, and when it is satisfying, it increases a person's sense of well-being and appreciation. The partner feels rewarded. In contrast, when frequency diminishes too much or sex becomes less pleasant, the overall relationship may be negatively affected. Furthermore, when a couple quarrels a great deal or is more distant, this in turn depresses marital satisfaction and contributes to a decrease in sexual activity (Call et al., 1995). One actually encounters both processes when studying how divorced couples' marriages deteriorated. One woman put it this way about her ex-husband in my study on divorce/remarriage:

> "He always wanted sex more than I did and he was always mortally offended that I didn't. But he was always so mean to me otherwise that I had developed a sense of physical, you know, I felt repulsed at the thought of even touching him. I mean, you can't just separate the two. He used to call me a cold bitch, frigid, and that explained it all [her lack of interest in sex] in his mind. But, you know, my husband [remarriage] will tell you that I am a very physical woman [laughs]. If someone, your husband, is wonderful to you, it goes without saying that sex comes easily."

The next respondent, also remarried, is explaining why he stayed so long with his ex-wife even though he did not like her much:

> "Don't take me wrong here, I am not a pervert [we both laugh] but sex is the answer. We didn't get along well at all and didn't share much, but our sex life was great. It's difficult to explain but it was a nice release at the end of a hard day at work and even at home. That's why I stayed: I had a lot to lose here."

Extracouple Sexual Relations

Generally, no matter the type of union they are in, males engage in extracouple sex more than women, as indicated in the percentages provided by Blumstein and Schwartz (1990). The respondents were men and women who reported at least one instance of extrapartner sexuality:

Husbands	11 percent
Wives	9 percent
Male cohabitants	25 percent
Female cohabitants	22 percent
Gay unions	79 percent
Lesbian unions	19 percent

In the 1994 study by Laumann and colleagues, the results were essentially similar. Whatever their marital status, most men and women reported having had only one sexual partner in the past year (67 and 75 percent, respectively). Of those who were married, 94 percent had been monogamous compared to 75 percent of the cohabitants. These authors also report that people whose first union was cohabitational have had more sexual partners than those whose first union was marital. Furthermore, Liu (2000) found that, while women's extramarital sex decreased with the number of years of marriage, men's also decreased but then increased after 20 years of marriage.

Hence, there is general agreement in the various sources of statistics on this topic, and several salient conclusions emerge. First, heterosexual men and women are more faithful than are homosexual men. Second, among gay unions, men are less monogamous whereas lesbian women are more. And third, married spouses have the lowest rate of infidelities. Cohabiting couples are far less monogamous, but there is little difference between men and women (Treas and Giesen, 2000). The least that can be said is that married couples are more sexually faithful than portrayed in the media. In fact, in the U.S., attitudes toward extramarital affairs have become less accepting in recent decades (Thornton and Young-DeMarco, 2001). There is actually a great deal of consensus among western countries that extramarital infidelities are unacceptable. For instance, Swedes who are very liberal in other domains of sexuality nearly unanimously disapprove of conjugal infidelities: 96 percent compared to 94 percent among Americans (Widmer et al., 1998).

CONCLUSIONS: THE CHANGING PROFILE OF COUPLES

The past three decades have brought about changes in cultural attitudes concerning sexuality and couple formation. This was followed and accompanied by a greater acceptance of nonmarital sexuality. At the same time, many couples included sex in casual dating, while cohabiting became more prevalent and the age at first marriage crept up substantially. Homosexual coupling is now a more public phenomenon and Canada is one of the first four nations to have legalized same-sex marriage in several of its provinces. Despite all these changes, marriage is still the preferred type of union, especially among heterosexual women, and gays' recourse to this institution in itself confirms its desirability.

However, changing trends are not equally shared by all ethnic or religious groups in Canada, especially among recent arrivals whose cultures still emphasize marriage and restrict sexuality within its boundaries, particularly for women. Thus, the new lifestyle alternatives, so prized among some scholars (whether for ideological reasons or because of a pleasant life experience) and practised by so many Canadian-born citizens, constitute a difficult environment for immigrants from different cultural backgrounds, and especially for their children. Textbooks that emphasize the changing aspects of family life in Canada may inadvertently misrepresent reality—when "changing" refers to liberalization, especially in the domain of sexuality, rather than cultural diversity (values, religion) under our large Canadian roof.

Summary

1. Dating as an institution originated in the U.S. and replaced traditional courtship. Young women tend to invest more in their dating relationship than do young men. A discussion of statistics on homosexuals is presented. More research is needed on gay and lesbian dating.

2. The choice of heterosexual dates (and later, partners) first follows rules of propinquity. Assortative mating becomes more prominent later on, and the term homogamy is used to refer to couples who are similar to each other in some characteristics. Homogamy becomes endogamy when couples partner themselves within their own group. Endogamy takes place largely along lines of race, social class, religion, and age. Research is needed on partner selection among homosexuals.

3. Cohabitation has increased in Canada from six percent of all couples in 1981 to 11.7 percent in 2001; however, the largest increase took place in Quebec, where 30 percent of all couples cohabit, a rate similar to that of Sweden. Women are less favourable than men to cohabitation. This type of union is less stable than marriage. Its benefits and disadvantages are discussed in terms of its convenience, the availability of sex, its relationship aspects, issues of commitment and fidelity, and its ramifications for older adults.

4. Romantic love is examined historically and within the context of the western world.

5. Marriage is discussed as an institution that provides advantages to the partners in terms of well-being. A certain degree of social selection in marriage explains some of this well-being; but social causation is a more important explanation. Marriage is more of a mixed blessing for women than for men.

6. Same-sex marriages are discussed within the context of cohabitation with fidelity, which is somewhat controversial among some homosexuals. This discussion posits that only one standard for marriage should exist.

7. Singlehood is examined within its four subcategories: voluntary-temporary versus voluntary-stable singles, and involuntary-temporary versus involuntary-stable singles. The advantages of single life largely rest on independence and flexibility, whereas the disadvantages are age- and gender-specific.

8. Issues of gender are first introduced regarding sexuality. The study of early sexual relations largely centres on factors related to delayed initiation into sexual intercourse. Variables that contribute to later sexual initiation are high parental social class, a two-parent family, school achievement, and religiosity. Young women's first sexual intercourse is not, on average, as pleasant as that of young men, and there are degrees of voluntariness and desire in the experience.

9. Within a marriage or a remarriage, couples' frequency of sex usually peaks during the first

two years. It then diminishes drastically but remains stable in subsequent years, only to be gradually affected by age. Cohabiting couples experience higher rates of sexual intercourse, but there are no studies on long-term cohabiting couples. Frequency of sexual activity is related to marital happiness. Contrary to myths, a majority of married couples are sexually faithful. Cohabitants are less faithful. Least monogamous of all are same-sex male cohabitants. Lesbian cohabitants are less monogamous than wives but slightly more than cohabiting women.

10. The new changes in couple formation are not shared equally by all ethnic or religious groups in Canada, especially among recent arrivals.

Key Concepts and Themes

Age homogamy, p. 209
Assortative mating, p. 208
Cohabitational sexuality, pp. 228 ff.
Cohabitation is less institutionalized, p. 215
Coerced sex, p. 227
Courtship, p. 206
Dating, pp. 206–208
Early sexuality, pp. 226–228
Economic homogamy, p. 209
Endogamy, p. 208
Exchange theory, p. 207
Exogamy, p. 209
Extracouple sexuality, p. 231
Gender differences, pp. 211, 220
Gender roles, pp. 206, 226
Homogamy, pp. 208, 210

Homosexuality, p. 207
Intermarriage, p. 209
Marital sexuality, pp. 228 ff.
Masculine bias, p. 225
Peer pressure, p. 227
Personality specific, p. 225
Propinquity, p. 208
Race homogamy, p. 209
Religious homogamy, p. 209
Same-sex marriage, pp. 221–223
Same-sex partnering, pp. 207–208
Sexual intercourse and aging, p. 229
Sexual relations, pp. 225 ff.
Singlehood, pp. 223–224
Social class homogamy, p. 209

Analytical Questions

1. What makes dating an American institution?

2. Cohabitation has increased in Canada. Yet, as we see in Figure 8.1, there is a large difference by gender in terms of willingness to live common-law. What are the implications of these two seemingly contradictory trends?

3. If you were entirely free to choose your own union type, which would you prefer: cohabitation or marriage? Examine the reasons behind your choice.

4. Does same-sex marriage endanger the institution of marriage?

5. Discuss the notion that sexuality is a largely male construct in our society.

6. If this chapter were written in a Hindu or Muslim country, how different would it be?

Suggested Readings

Anderson, C. M., Stewart, S., and Dimidjian, S. 1994. *Flying solo: Single women in midlife.* New York: W. W. Norton. This book is based on interviews of a large group of women who have never married. The contents take the form of life stories.

Cate, R. M., and Lloyd, S. A. 1992. *Courtship*. Newbury Park, CA: Sage. This text covers the history of courtship, discusses its functions, and traces the development of the relationship. It also looks toward the future.

Laumann, E. O., et al. 1994. *The social organization of sexuality: Sexual practices in the United States*. Chicago: University of Chicago Press. This book presents survey results on sexual practices in heterosexuality as well as homosexuality, and in married as well as non-marital sex. This book covers everything you ever wanted to know about sex, but does it within a carefully executed sociological analysis.

Wu, Z. 2000. *Cohabitation: An alternative form of family living*. Toronto: Oxford University Press. This review book provides a comprehensive discussion of all aspects of cohabitation and can be useful both for this and the next chapter.

Suggested Weblinks

For a more detailed discussion of cohabitation and same-sex marriage, consult

www.arts.yorku.ca/soci/ambert/writings/ cohabitation.html

and

www.vifamily.ca

and click on the section on Contemporary Family Trends.

PFLAG (Parents, Families and Friends of Lesbians and Gays) has several chapters across the country.

www.pflag.ca

Sex Information and Education Council of Canada also supports the *Canadian Journal of Human Sexuality*.

www.sieccan.org

CHAPTER 9

Patterns of Family Formation and Planning

"I come from a single-parent family and I wouldn't recommend it to anyone. My poor mom had too much of a hard time raising us three all alone, with no help and no respect from any one."

"My father left my mother before I even knew he existed so that I haven't missed out on much. The only drawback is that we weren't very well off, but outside of this I often think that I may just end up a single mother too one day if the right man doesn't come along. Beats not having children and besides I am very much like my mother and I would do very well thank you."

"I had an abortion two years ago and that was rather draining emotionally at the time because it would have been nice to have had the baby, but it would also have ruined my plans for school and perhaps getting married. So now I am thankful for it."

"Abortion is much easier than birth control." [from a student who had had three abortions]

"I hope to have had two children by then [in 10 years]. I guess it would be too much to think of having three because I'll need to keep my job."

"I don't see children on the horizon. I've got too many plans for my life and all that I can fit in there is a wife to share these projects with. Children are too time consuming nowadays."

These students' reflections on marriage, single motherhood, and some aspects of family planning set the tone for this chapter in which we look at *family* formation, including alternative modes such as adoption and recourse to reproductive technologies. Family formation has different starting points (Aldous, 1996): marriage and cohabitation (including same-sex), and single parents. Although adults are present in this chapter, its focus is on children's well-being within the various alternatives for family formation.

OVERVIEW OF FAMILY STRUCTURE

The 2001 census indicates that the proportion of "traditional" families—those composed of a mother, father, and at least one dependent child—has continued to decline while other forms of family structure are increasing. This parallels the steep decline in marriage rates in the 1990s (described in the previous chapter). This decline is in part driven by the exceptionally low rate of marriage (and remarriage) in Quebec, which had dropped to 3.1 per 1,000 population by 1998, compared to 5.0 in Canada as a whole.

In Table 9.1, we see that married-couple families (with and without children) constituted 70 percent of all families in 2001. What is not shown is that this is down from 83 percent in 1981—a substantial change. At the same time, the proportion of cohabiting families increased from 5.6 percent in 1981 to 14 percent in 2001. This change is particularly salient in Quebec, where only 58 percent of families fall into the married-couple category, compared with 74 to 75 percent for most of the other provinces. However, Nunavut, Yukon, and the Northwest Territories also have a low rate of families headed by married couples. These same provinces and territories have the highest percentages of families that are common-law. Furthermore, Nunavut and the Northwest Territories also have the highest percentages of one-parent families, perhaps as a result of the greater poverty of these regions. Statistics Canada (2002e) also informs us that the proportion of married couples with children younger than 25 at home declined from 60 percent of all couples in 1981 to 44 percent in 2001. However, common-law couples with children increased from 2.1 percent of all couples to 7.4 percent in 2001.

A cross-cultural perspective on family structure compares the prevalence of cohabiting couples in various western countries with Sweden as a baseline: This country has a longer history of consensual unions. Table 9.2 shows that Quebec has the same

TABLE 9.1 | **Distribution of Canadian Families by Provinces and Territories, 2001**

	% Married	% Cohabiting	% One-Parent
Canada	70.5	13.8	15.7
Newfoundland and Labrador	75.4	9.6	14.9
Prince Edward Island	74.1	9.4	16.4
Nova Scotia	71.8	11.4	16.8
New Brunswick	71.0	12.9	16.1
Quebec	58.2	25.2	16.6
Ontario	75.4	9.4	15.2
Manitoba	74.0	9.8	16.2
Saskatchewan	74.7	9.5	15.8
Alberta	74.1	11.6	14.4
British Columbia	73.4	11.1	15.5
Yukon	57.2	23.0	19.8
Northwest Territories	52.7	26.3	21.0
Nunavut	43.0	31.3	25.7

Source: Statistics Canada, *The Daily*, October 22, 2002e.

TABLE 9.2	Proportion of Cohabitational Couples for Selected Countries and Regions

Country	Year	As % of All Couples
Sweden	2000	30.0
Norway	2000	24.5
Iceland	2000	19.5
Finland	2000	18.7
Mexico	2000	18.7
New Zealand	2001	18.3
France	1999	17.5
Canada	2001	16.0
Quebec	2001	29.8
Other provinces/territories	2001	11.7
United States	2000	8.2

Source: Statistics Canada, *The Daily*, October 22, 2002e.

proportion of cohabiting couples as Sweden. When Quebec is excluded, only 11.7 percent of Canadian couples are common-law. Hence, the cohabitation rate for the rest of Canada more closely resembles the American rate than the Quebec one. Furthermore, the phenomenon is not a French one because, in France, the percentage of cohabiting couples is lower than that of Quebec. It should also be added that Québécois marry even less than people in France: In 2001, France had the same marriage rate as that of Canada at 5.0 per 1,000 population (Doisneau, 2002). Thus, Quebec constitutes a specific "francophone" cultural phenomenon related to its own evolution rather than to its cultural attachments to France. Reasons that are generally given for Quebec francophones' low marital and even fertility rates include a reaction to centuries of dominance by the Catholic Church's teachings on nuptiality, chastity before marriage, and high natality.

At least in the short term, in the life course of young couples, cohabitation is delaying marriage. It is also delaying marriage in yet another way: Cohabitants are less likely to be actively searching for a marital partner than others (Wu, 1999). However, among young adults aged 20 to 29, the proportion of those who are *neither* cohabiting nor married has increased—a trend that was already noticeable by 1996 (Bélanger and Dumas, 1998). This means that fewer adults are living in unions than in the past; therefore, it is not only cohabitation which is delaying marriage but also a **longer period of singlehood**. For instance, from 1981 to 2001, the proportion of 25- to 29-year-old Canadians living in a union of any type decreased from 64 to 45 percent for men and from 73 to 57 percent for women (Statistics Canada, 2002e). A longer period of singlehood results from the necessity of pursuing an advanced education, establishing oneself in the employment sector, and getting settled economically (Beaujot and Bélanger, 2001)—all of which take a longer time than was the case 20 years ago (Clarkberg, 1999). In turn, coresidence with parents contributes to delaying marriage, a phenomenon also found in Japan (Raymo, 2003). As we see later, a longer period of singlehood is also a result of the fact that sexual relationships outside marriage are now more socially acceptable. Nevertheless, it is expected that a majority of young persons will eventually marry, although this majority will be smaller than in the past—approximately 75 percent in Canada compared to the traditional 90 percent (Turcotte, 2002).

FAMILY FORMATION VIA MARRIAGE

The double focus of this section is to examine the status of children living with married parents and the role that marriage plays for society as a whole.

Marriage and Children

In subsequent sections, we see that the research demonstrates how, on average, parental cohabitation and solo parenting carry fewer advantages for children than parental marriage. Furthermore, in Chapter 5, we have documented how children who live with their married parents have the lowest poverty rate. In Chapter 14, the effect of parental divorce and remarriage will be studied. The overall conclusion from these various sources of information is that children benefit more unequivocally than adults from their parents' marriage.

However, children who experience a conflictual parental marriage benefit less than children living with a well-balanced single parent (Jekielek, 1998). But, on the whole, highly conflictual marriages do not last long because of the acceptability of divorce as an alternative. Even among those who divorce, at best one-third have highly conflictual marriages and many of those are childless. Therefore, a relatively small proportion of marriages are detrimental to children and an even smaller proportion of divorces are beneficial to them (Amato and Booth, 1997). Furthermore, conflict aside, even when parents do not judge their marriage to be the happiest, children still benefit from it. What is important to children above all else is family solidarity and the care they receive from their parents—not whether their parents are madly in love with each other. The latter is an adult perspective.

In a society with a nuclear family system, children who have two parents—whether natural or adoptive, whether of the same or opposite sex—are at an advantage because they have two rather than one person **invested** in their well-being, responsible for them, and acting as **authority figures.** Children in married families also tend to be better supervised than others (Fischer, 1993). Additionally, two parents provide a greater repertoire of behaviours, attitudes, and knowledge from which children can draw and learn. In James Coleman's theory, two parents constitute a greater source of social capital, which then translates into more human capital for the children. With two parents, children have an alternative when the other has less time, is ill, or is otherwise preoccupied. Two parents can also provide moral support to each other in their coparental duties, and this benefits children (Grossbard-Shechtman, 1993).

Infant mortality is lower in married families, and this advantage is even found in Scandinavian countries, where there is less poverty among single mothers and where cohabitation is more institutionalized than it is in Canada (Bennett et al., 1994; Oyen et al., 1997). Children also benefit from marriage in terms of economic security, school achievement, emotional stability, leisure activities, prosocial behaviour, and later on as adults, in terms of work (Cooksey et al., 1997; Langille et al., 2003).

Marriage and Society

Inasmuch as the institution of marriage contributes to the emotional stability and over-all well-being of adults and children, it becomes an institution beneficial to society. It produces a great deal of social capital and serves as an **agency of social control** (Laub et al., 1998). For instance, children in two-parent families on average get more edu-cation and are less often on welfare (McLoyd, 1998). Later on, they contribute more in taxes than children who are not raised within the context of parental marriage. From a societal point of view, marriage contributes to the successful socialization of citizens, which does not mean, however, that a majority of children in other forms of family are less adequately socialized. It means that *proportionally more* children from married families are successfully socialized. From this perspective alone, it has been suggested that the legalization of marriage for same-sex couples who have children would be beneficial rather than detrimental to society. The legalization of these unions would contribute to the couples' stability and to better outcomes for their children (Bell and Weinberg, 1978).

Many people have come to believe that marriage is merely a matter of choice and has few social consequences. The preceding chapter clearly indicated that marriage, particularly a good and equitable marriage, carries many benefits for the spouses. It is, above all, highly beneficial to children, whether it is equitable or not between the par-ents. There is a school of thought whose proponents argue that what is important is not family structure (one versus two parents), but healthy family processes. Although it is certainly true that healthy family dynamics explain a part of children's positive out-comes, the fact remains that such dynamics are more likely to occur in married fami-lies. Consequently, for society as a whole, marriage is an institution that deserves more encouragement. This topic is revisited in the last chapter.

COHABITATIONAL FAMILY FORMATION

A substantial proportion of cohabitations involve children (Seltzer, 2000). In 2001, 13 percent of Canadian children aged 0 to 14 lived in common-law households—in-cluding in Quebec, where 29 percent lived in such households. When Quebec is ex-cluded, the Canadian rate falls to 8.2 percent of children. In the U.S., it is estimated that 3.5 percent of children live in cohabiting families. However, American statistics often underestimate the number of consensual unions. For instance, perhaps as many as 40 to 50 percent of babies born to single mothers begin life in a cohabitational unit (Sigle-Rushton and McLanahan, 2002). Overall, it is estimated that 40 percent of all American children will live with their single mother (never-married or divorced) and her boyfriend at some point before their sixteenth birthday (Bumpass and Lu, 2000).

Cohabitational Stability and Children

Cohabiting couples with their own children have a higher level of stability than others (Wu, 1995) and are more likely to marry. However, marriage does not occur equally among all ethnic groups. Furthermore, even children whose parents cohabit will experience more instability than those whose parents marry before they are born (Lerman, 2002), and this holds true in most countries, including Sweden and Norway (Jensen, 1995). Marcil-Gratton (1998) found that 60 percent of children born to cohabiting parents had experienced family disruption by age 10, compared to 14 percent of those children whose parents had not cohabited. We also know that couples who cohabit before marriage have a higher divorce rate (Axinn and Thornton, 1992). Thus, overall, children are more likely to experience a parental divorce when their parents began their union as cohabitants or when a single mother cohabits and then marries. In some families, there is a "revolving door" situation, whereby serial partners succeed each other over the years. In a nutshell, children born to cohabiting parents are not at a large advantage compared to those in one-parent families, especially when a mother cohabits with a man who is not the children's father (Graefe and Lichter, 1999).

However, when a single mother begins to cohabit, **family poverty is reduced** by as much as 30 percent, which benefits children—although this benefit is often of short duration because of the fragility of these unions (Raley and Wildsmith, 2004). This advantage is furthermore mitigated by the fact that male cohabitants often earn less than married men. Thus, parental cohabitation does not make children well-off, but rather less poor (Morrison and Ritualo, 2000). Better-off cohabitants tend to marry when or before they have children (Manning and Smock, 1995).

Cohabitation and Children's Well-Being

Results are contradictory as to whether older children living with their parents, married or cohabiting, have fewer or more behaviour and emotional problems (Brown, 2002; Manning, 2002). Brown (2004b) has documented more problems among adolescents whose biological parents are cohabiting. Complicating matters is the fact that 80 percent of children in cohabiting families have an absent parent and have been part of a transition (Bumpass and Lu, 2000). Manning and Lamb (2003) have found that **instability** rather than structure is a more important factor in adolescent well-being in terms of mothers' marital lives. Furthermore, more research is needed on small children whose mothers cohabit with a man who is not the natural father. These couples are generally quite young and often disadvantaged. Unemployment is common. Such mothers are in a precarious situation both conjugally and economically (Brown, 2002). In some instances, the mothers themselves enter into these unions for short-term benefits and do not commit themselves to marry a man whose economic situation is unstable. In other instances, the mothers are the most committed partner but they are in a weaker bargaining position because they have a child who does not belong to the partner. Thus, the selection factor in cohabitation certainly accounts for some differences in children's well-being (Brown, 2002).

The potential instability of these women's unions and the instability of the level of support they receive result in stressors that can disrupt their parenting activities (Kalil,

2002). The mother's partner is not as likely to compensate for this neglect as a married father or even stepfather might do because the partner's attachment to the children is often low. Physical abuse is also more likely (Gelles, 1989). Girls are at risk of being sexually abused (Gordon, 1989); this is especially so in homes where males are transient. In instances where the mother is obviously sexually active with a series of men, the transmission of poverty, early pregnancy, and behavioural problems may become a long-term characteristic of the families.

After divorce, cohabitation instead of remarriage may bring in a less involved stepparent (Manning and Lamb, 2003). Furthermore, when a divorced father cohabits, he visits his children less often than a father who is remarried (Cooksey and Craig, 1998). This phenomenon may be less evident in Quebec and in countries where cohabitation after divorce is more prevalent and more institutionalized. In these cultures, cohabitants are less different from married spouses. Nevertheless, at this time in North America, cohabitation is not a situation that signals investment in children as much as does marriage, although there are many exceptions (Landale and Fennelly, 1992). Commitment and stability are at the core of children's needs; yet, in a great proportion of cohabitations, these two requirements are absent, which may have consequences well into adulthood (Teachman, 2003b).

SAME-SEX-PARENT FAMILY FORMATION

The following presentation complements the sections on same-sex couple formation in the previous chapter. The focus here is on family formation by two gay men or two lesbian women.

An Overview of Same-Sex-Parent Families

At least 3,000 same-sex couples are raising children in Canada today. The 2001 census revealed that 15 percent of households headed by lesbian couples had children, compared to three percent of households headed by gay couples (Statistics Canada, 2002a). These numbers underestimate the situation to some extent. Furthermore, they omit lesbians and gays who are single and have a child living with them, as well as those who are married heterosexually and have a child at home: Black et al. (2000) estimate that over 28 percent of all American lesbians and 14 percent of all American gays have children living with them. But even these numbers omit those whose heterosexual ex-spouse has custody of their children following a divorce. Thus, overall, more gays and lesbians have children than is apparent in the general statistics.

A majority of children in same-sex couples were born to a mother-father unit that ended in divorce and the lesbian or gay parent obtained custody. Thus, a majority of these children have another parent who is heterosexual. But more and more lesbian couples give birth via donor insemination or adoption (Gartrell et al., 2000). Some gay couples also adopt, and in the U.S., particularly California, a few have had recourse to surrogate mothers. In other cases, a gay couple cooperates with a lesbian couple in producing children (via donor insemination) and raising them jointly, an arrangement that allows children to have parents of both sexes (Patterson and Chan, 1997). Lesbian women prefer committed relationships far more than do gay men and are more monogamous sexually (Fowlkes, 1994). As women, they are socialized to be "kin-keepers." This characteristic leads to the formation of a greater number of lesbian-based families than gay-based and may also lead to higher parenting compatibility and skills than among heterosexual parents (Stacey and Biblarz, 2001).

The lesbian parental role and parental cooperation differs depending on the timing of family formation. When partners decide to have children together, the child "is the new member being incorporated into an existing unit" (Slater, 1995:94). Both partners can be free to parent equally and the child may bolster their intimacy. For many, however, despite their efforts, differences remain between the roles of the biological and the nonbiological mother (Nelson, 1996). The family challenges are different when one partner comes to the couple as a parent; the other partner, then, is the new family member and may not always agree on parenting style (Nelson, 1996). There are instances when both partners bring children from previous relationships. These situations are similar to those of stepparenting among heterosexuals, but they may also differ depending on whether the children came from a heterosexual marriage or from another lesbian union. One problem specific to same-sex parents is that they have to keep explaining their situation, they have to repeatedly "come out," and they have to challenge individuals (teachers, physicians) who do not accept their families as real ones (Nelson, 1996).

Consequences of Same-Sex Parenting for Children

In the population at large, there are three main concerns regarding the children of same-sex parents: the fear that the offspring will grow up to be psychologically maladjusted because of social stigma; that they will be molested by their parents or parent's partners; and that they will become homosexual themselves. None of these concerns have been supported by the research so far (Ross, 1994), except perhaps the last one. Although same-sex-parent families have been excluded from large, representative surveys on family life, all the small studies put together arrive at fairly similar, positive results. In interpreting these results, it is important to remember that the young adults and most adolescents in these studies were originally born in heterosexual families that ended in divorce. These studies have failed to separate the effects of the two variables—divorce and parents' sexual identity—and have not included a wide range of developmental outcomes; nor have they examined such situations as child abuse and the effect of spousal conflict on children (Stacey and Biblarz, 2001).

A structural-functional analysis suggests that society would benefit if all family types were equally supported. Children in same-sex-parent families need stability and security, as do other children, in order to grow up to become functional members of society.

Psychological Adjustment

Tasker and Golombok (1995, 1997) initiated a longitudinal study to compare children whose single mother was lesbian with those whose mother was heterosexual. At the time, the children were, on average, 9 1/2 years old, and they were reinterviewed 14 years later. The young adults with a lesbian mother reported a better relationship with her and with her partner than did young adults whose mother was heterosexual and brought in a stepfather. The children of lesbians even had a better relationship with their fathers, perhaps because a mother's female partner does not "compete" with a father. Hence, there is a possibility that children with a lesbian mother experience a less difficult time before and after their parents' divorce compared to children with two heterosexual parents: There may be less parental conflict, jealousy, and feelings of personal rejection. However, a divorce between two same-sex parents may be no less difficult. These hypotheses deserve to be researched.

Children living in same-sex-parent families are often teased by peers and shunned by their peers' parents, and thus their lives may be more stressful (Morris et al., 2001:151). Yet they do not seem to grow up disadvantaged emotionally and may even possess certain strengths of character such as tolerance, empathy, and contentment (Laird, 1993; Patterson, 2000). However, other evidence points to difficulties experienced by adolescents who feel embarrassed by their parents' homosexuality, a situation which may be attenuated in later cohorts (DeAngelis, 2002; Nelson, 1996).

A study comparing lesbian and heterosexual mothers, some single, some in couples, found no difference in children's adaptation and development around age seven, even though all had been produced by donor insemination—which is certainly an additional complication in a child's self-definition (Chan et al., 1998). Overall, as parents, lesbian mothers are similar to heterosexual mothers; it is not their sexual orientation that emerges as an important variable but their identity as mothers (Lewin, 1993). Their children show few differences from other children (Parks, 1998), and whatever differences exist stem largely from the social stigma attached to homosexuality and consequent social rejection outside the home. However, the values of some gay and lesbian parents may later translate into differences in adult children compared to children of heterosexual couples (Stacey and Biblarz, 2001).

Sexual Behaviour and Identity

Children of homosexual partners usually adopt heterosexual identities (Bailey and Dawood, 1998). Bailey et al. (1995) compared adult sons who had spent many years with their gay father to sons who had lived only briefly with a gay father. The rate of homosexuality among the offspring with longer contact with their father was not higher. A small research by Costello (1997) found that many homosexual partners consciously avoid pressuring their children to conform to their sexual preference. Nevertheless, young people raised in same-sex-parent families are more tolerant of same-sex experimentation, and they develop a homosexual identity more often than do children in other families—whether heredity and learning are interrelated causal factors is impossible to evaluate at this point (Stacey and Biblarz, 2001).

Tasker and Golombok (1995) found that, when mothers had had more lesbian partners and were more open about their sexuality when the children were young, there was a greater likelihood that, as young adults, these children would have a homosexual identity. However, we do not know to what extent a mother's serial same-sex relationships pose developmental problems similar to those found among children whose heterosexual mothers have had serial relationships, particularly multiple cohabitations (Dunifon and Kowaleski-Jones, 2002). As far as worries over child sexual abuse are concerned, gay men are no more likely than heterosexual men to abuse children, and the same applies to lesbian women (Jenny et al., 1994). Homosexuality is not synonymous with pedophilia.

SINGLE PARENTING

Single-parent families are of interest to sociologists because the cultural values of most societies dictate that children should have two parents rather than one—and that, preferably, these parents should be married by the time the child is born. Second, families that deviate from this norm often differ from two-parent families in other ways as well, especially in terms of a higher poverty rate (Wu and Schimmele, 2003). Thus, single-parent families are also a concern for policy-makers, although one can as easily say that policy-makers are a "risk" to these families (Wong and Checkland, 1999). However, not all these families suffer from adversities, and a great proportion do not differ from two-parent families in any meaningful way. The main problem with the generic concept of "single parenting" is that it actually is a gendered one, because women, not men, give birth, and often do the caring work, have financial responsibility, and are blamed by society—and by the welfare system in particular (Ambert, 2002c).

Trends and Numbers

The number of **births** to unmarried mothers has increased continuously since 1921, when only two percent of all Canadian births were outside marriage. This number reached five percent by the end of the Second World War. Births to single mothers accounted for nine percent of all births in 1971, 14 percent in 1981, and 27 percent in 1991 (Belle and McQuillan, 1994). However, after 1985, a growing proportion of these births were to cohabiting women, and such women are now generally considered to be partnered, thus no longer single.

In Canada, there were over 1.3 million single-parent families in 2001, or 16 percent of all families with dependent children (refer to Table 9.1). In the U.S., there were over nine million such families in 1997, or 27 percent of families with children. Using children as the unit of analysis, in 2001, 19 percent of Canadian children and 28 percent of American children lived in one-parent families. Overall, a majority are headed by a female parent, generally a divorced one. In Canada, 25 percent are headed by a single woman as a result of a nonmarital birth, compared to 35 percent in the U.S. As is the case in the U.S. and in many Caribbean nations, black children (aged 0 to 14) belong to one-parent families more often (46 percent) than other children do (Milan and Tran, 2004).

Contrary to what is often believed, single-parent families do not represent a new phenomenon (Lynn, 2003). In 1941, for instance, single-parent families accounted for 14 percent of all families. In the past, because life expectancy was shorter, large proportions of children lost one parent and then another to death. What has changed over time is the **composition** of such families: By the 1970s, a majority of these families had divorced rather than widowed parents. As the years went by, a larger proportion of nonmarital one-parent families occurred as sexuality outside marriage became more acceptable and as single mothers increasingly kept their babies rather than have them adopted.

Teen Birth Rates and the Structure of Teen Motherhood

As explained further on, fertility always refers to women. However, the study of masculine fertility is equally important, yet it is a neglected topic (Kaufman, 1999), particularly in terms of single parenting. This is because most of the fathers are largely absent and take on few responsibilities, which is part of young women's and their children's problem (Ambert, 2002b).

Teen Birth Rates

In 1998, nearly 20,000 women aged 15 to 19 gave birth, while a little over 21,000 had an abortion. Thus, in 1998, for Canada as a whole, the pregnancy rate per 1,000 teen women stood at 41.7 and the birth rate at 20 (see Figure 9.1). The latter had decreased to 17.3 by the year 2000—an all-time low. In all cases, the rates are far higher for teens aged 18 and 19 and lower for younger teens. In 1974, only 10 percent of teens who gave birth were single, but now about 80 percent are and it is this fact that has led to the concept of "teen" pregnancy in the early 1970s. Thus, "teen" pregnancy and births are historically grounded social constructs. Furthermore, births to single teen mothers have never represented more than 20 percent of nonconjugal Canadian births and 33 percent of nonconjugal American births. As well, abortions to teens constitute 20 percent of all abortions in Canada, thus not the majority. The U.S. birth rate for single teen mothers is more than double the Canadian one: In 2001, it stood at 45.9 (versus 20 in Canada), which is nevertheless a drop from the high rate of 60 in 1990 (U.S. Department of Health and Human Services, 2002b). Consequently, Americans more than Canadians have held a moral and social problems-oriented discourse on this issue (Caragata, 1999). Nevertheless, the sources and consequences of unmarried teen parenting are similar in both countries, as they are in other western countries as well.

As indicated in Figure 9.1, large provincial differences exist: Quebec, British Columbia, and Ontario have particularly low teen birth rates, in part because of the availability of abortions. Nevertheless, the fact remains that, for Canada as a whole, nearly half of pregnant teens give birth, in great part because they, their parents, or their boyfriends prefer to have a baby or object to abortion; for others, abortions are out of reach. As well, many realize that they are pregnant or accept that fact too late in the gestation period to have recourse to an abortion. Since 1974, the proportion of teens choosing or being able to access an abortion has climbed steadily, while the proportion of those giving birth has declined accordingly. This trend reflects another factor: the generally unplanned character of unmarried pregnancies (Clark, 1999).

The Structure of Teen Motherhood

The structure of teen motherhood—generally associated with poverty (Chapter 5)—contains the seeds of disadvantages, often for several years (Turner et al., 2000). It is difficult in our society to be both an adolescent and a mother or a father. Adolescence is socially constructed as a period during which children acquire rights and independence as well as formal education, whereas motherhood involves assuming responsibilities and being tied down. The two may conflict to the girl's detriment, but particularly to the infant's disadvantage, and this is often problematic for the entire

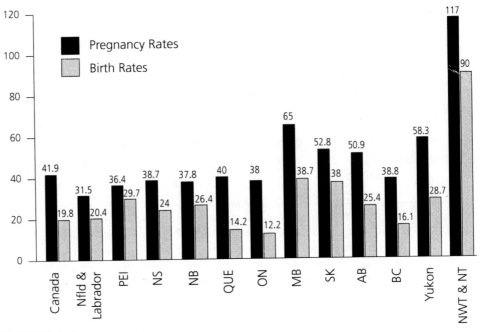

FIGURE 9.1

Teen Pregnancy Rates and Birth Rates per 1,000 Women Aged 15 to 19 for Canada, Provinces and Territories, 1998

Source: Dryburgh, 2002.

kin group (Cramer and McDonald, 1996), especially for mothers and siblings (East, 1999; East and Jacobson, 2000), as illustrated in the following student's quote:

> *"My sister had her first baby at 15, the second at 16, and the third at 18. She 'loves' babies but we've always had to take care of them and now she lives in our basement. I really resent her because sometimes I have to write a paper and there are these babies that I have to babysit. And now guess what, my brother's girlfriend is pregnant too and she's only 17. My mother should have never set a precedent by helping my sister."*

Undoubtedly, teen mothers do not remain teenagers forever (Davies et al., 1999). But, even as they pass into the ranks of adults, for many, this early beginning with motherhood leaves long-term consequences.

Nevertheless, single-teen motherhood is far from a homogeneous situation resulting in similar outcomes for all mothers and children. A source of difference among teen mothers resides in their overall socioemotional development. From Montreal, Serbin and colleagues (1998) report that childhood aggressiveness is related to early pregnancy and dropping out of school. Before having a baby, adolescent mothers average more instances of suspensions, truancy, drug use, and fighting in school than other adolescent girls. Thus, single parenting is part of a non-normative life course for a *subgroup* of adolescents who were problematic children long before becoming pregnant (Woodward et al., 2001). Even though these adolescent mothers are still antisocial and impulsive, as are many of the fathers, they now have the responsibility of a helpless baby. *The teens' babies' fathers* often have a background similar to that of the young mothers (Hardy et al., 1998). For instance, Moffit et al. (2002) found that young men who are highly antisocial father nearly three times the percentage of babies than do less antisocial young men by the time they reach the age of 26. For them, the practice and meaning of fatherhood is probably very different from that of married fathers (Ambert, 2002b for a review of this topic).

Children Born to Single Mothers

I summarize only some of the general consequences for children living in a single-mother-headed family because a more extensive discussion is readily available to students on my website (Ambert, 2002b,c), and some of these consequences overlap with the effects of divorce on children detailed in Chapter 14. It is first necessary to point out that the main explanation for the negative consequences that exist resides in poverty, especially when it is intergenerational (Chapter 5). Suffice it to repeat here that the daily life of disadvantaged children tends to be very different from that of children whose families are economically comfortable (Bradley et al., 2001). Furthermore, the consequences for children of having a single mother depend greatly on:

- mother's characteristics: income, education, mental health, social conformity, social support
- parenting quality: warmth, involvement, supervision
- child's characteristics: birth weight, health, abilities, and temperament
- father's characteristics, contribution, and relationship with mothers

On average, children of single mothers are more likely than children living with both parents to exhibit behavioural problems including hyperactivity, aggressiveness, fighting, and hostility (Stevenson, 1999). They are also more at risk of becoming young offenders (Willms, 2002b). Emotionally, they are more at risk of suffering from depression, anxiety, and other disorders, as well as having relationship problems, in part due to their difficult behaviours. They do less well in school and repeat grades more often. Adults who have spent part of their childhood in a single-mother-headed family are more likely to have a child nonmaritally, particularly during adolescence, to have achieved lower educational levels, to be unemployed, and to do less well economically than those adults who have spent their entire childhood in a two-parent family. They are also at greater risk of having a criminal record for violent and serious property offences and to have marital problems and experience divorce.

For its part, single teen parenting, depending on the circumstances, may have consequences that are specific to this situation and that are related to the structure of adolescent motherhood, as explained by a mature student:

> "I had my only child when I turned 17 and although I had a lot of support from my mother our family situation became precarious because I was too young and saw my son as a doll that I could leave behind when I went out with my friends or at other times I would take him out with me at all hours. The friends I had were not very good as you can imagine and we were all school dropouts. The

clincher in all of this is that I didn't nurture my son, he had no regular life and became hyperactive and out of control by age 2. He was no longer a live doll and I often resented him. He is now 13 and the problems are endless.... I have no life because of him...[but] when he was small he had no life and no luck because I was an irresponsible adolescent who only wanted to have a good time."

Furthermore, because they initiate life course transitions younger, teen mothers are more likely than older women to experience **multiple transitions**, such as successive cohabitations and separations, that make lives, including those of small children, less stable and therefore more vulnerable. Outcomes for the babies of difficult teen mothers are more negative than for the babies of conforming teen mothers (Stevens-Simon et al., 2001). For instance, difficult teen mothers are often unable to meet even basic child needs. As a consequence, their small children are more frequently brought to hospital emergency rooms because of injuries that suggest both neglect and abuse (Serbin et al., 1996). One would also expect that this type of "delinquent" motherhood is more related to poverty, both as a source and as an effect, thus to its intergenerational transmission as well as to the intergenerational transmission of delinquent behaviours from mother and father to offspring.

However, some previously difficult teens change for the positive after the birth of their child (Davies et al., 1999). They may, however, have much catching up to do in terms of acquiring habits necessary for the survival of a young parental unit. The corollary is that parenting by older and well-balanced adolescents is less detrimental for all involved and may actually be based on a rational decision. Adolescent mothers' educational level is the best predictor of small children's outcomes (Clark, 1999; Serbin et al., 1998). Young mothers who are able to remain in school and continue on to higher education probably possess other positive characteristics—such as maturity and emotional stability—that are helpful to their parental role. We need more research on the role of the children's fathers when discussing both single mothers' and their children's outcomes as well as the relationships between mothers and fathers (Davies et al., 1999). It would be highly desirable to hold a discourse on teen fathers and single fathers to counterbalance the focus on mothers alone.

FAMILY PLANNING AND FERTILITY

Family planning changed a great deal during the past century, aided in great part by advances in medical technology in the domain of contraception. Furthermore, the changing roles of women and children have drastically altered couples' and individuals' desired family size.

Family Planning

Family planning refers to individuals' or couples' decisions concerning the number and spacing of children they desire. Although anyone can now obtain contraceptives, family planning still remains a more difficult goal to achieve among singles. It is particularly problematic for adolescent women whose first intercourse is not voluntary (Abma et al., 1998). Family planning has become easier within the marital unit because couples are more open on this subject and family size is an important topic of discussion between spouses. Research is needed concerning the extent to which such concerns apply to same-sex couples (Nelson, 1996).

We now benefit from a wider availability of contraceptive techniques—from condoms and the contraceptive pill, to injectables (the "shot"), implant (Norplant), the "morning-after pill," as well as vasectomies and tubal ligations. Natural methods of birth control have declined, as has the use of the pill, while the number of vasectomies has increased (Bélanger, 1998). Fewer sexually active women than in the past report not using any method.

Couples' family planning intentions change over time, depending on circumstances such as health, finances, and work requirements (Heaton et al., 1999). Only seven percent of Canadians aged 20 to 34 do not intend to have children (Stobert and Kemeny, 2003). However, 12 percent of those who have no religious affiliation wish to remain childless. Men generally want to have slightly fewer children than women—2.28 versus 2.46 (Dupuis, 1998). The desired fertility is therefore higher than the achieved one, as indicated below. Therefore, many individuals are unable to achieve their ideal family size because of instability in conjugal relationships and the difficulty of linking production with reproduction (Beaujot, 2004). Couples now show a preference for a two-child family—ideally, one boy and one girl. Couples who have reached this goal stop childbearing more often than those who have two same-sex children (Yamaguchi and Ferguson, 1995). For example, some couples with two or three girls "try one more time" in order to have a son.

Fertility

Fertility or birth rates refer to the number of births per 1,000 women during their fertile years (ages 15 to 44). The *total* fertility rate, which is an estimate, refers to the lifetime average number of children per woman (McVey and Kalbach, 1995). Currently, it is at a low 1.5 in Canada (for 2002). Lower rates of 1.3 to 1.4 are found in the Maritimes, higher rates of 1.8 in Manitoba, Saskatchewan, and the Northwest Territories, and still higher at 3.0 in Nunavut. In the western world, family size began declining in the 19th century. In Canada, the downward trend began after the 1880s, as illustrated in Figure 9.2. This decline continued throughout the decades, only to reverse temporarily during the **baby boom** of the late 1940s and 1950s. Indeed, after the Second World War, there was a sharp increase in fertility, in part because of the social and economic optimism then generated. This increase was also fuelled by a return home of soldiers and young women who had been employed during the war. Thereafter, the downward trend resumed and has continued to this day.

These trends can be examined in terms of total fertility per woman, which stood at 4.6 children in 1901 and had already declined to 3.5 by 1921, then dropped to a further 2.6 in 1937 during the recession (Milan, 2000). While over half of women currently aged 65 to 69 have had three children, less than a quarter of women in the 35 to 39 age group have (Bélanger and Oikawa, 1999). Women who have their first child when they are less than 25 years old are the most likely to have a third one, while those who are over 30 when their first child is born are the least likely to do so. Thus, smaller family size is in part related to a greater proportion of women than before waiting un-

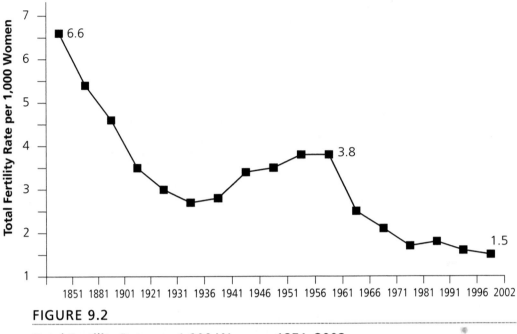

FIGURE 9.2

Total Fertility Rate per 1,000 Women, 1851–2002

Sources: Milan, 2000; McVey and Kalbach, 1995; Statistics Canada, 2004i.

The total fertility rate is an estimate of the average number of children that women aged 15 to 44 will have in their lifetime.

til later to have their first child. In 1997, 31 percent of all first births were to women aged 30 and over, versus only seven percent in 1971 (Wu and MacNeill, 2002).

Recently, most western European nations have experienced fertility rates below the 2.1 replacement value needed to maintain a population. Ireland's and Norway's rates are close to 1.9; for its part, France's fertility has risen in 2000 to 1.8 (Daguet, 2004). Several European nations have a rate below 1.3: Spain, Greece, Austria, Germany, Italy, and Russia (Doisneau, 2002). In comparison, China's rate is around 2.0, South America's 2.7, and Africa's 5.3 (Beaujot and Kerr, 2004). The American rate is 2.1.

The very low fertility rate experienced in all western societies and in others as well, such as Japan (1.3), is a result of the combination of industrialization, urbanization, individualism, female labour force participation, and later age at marriage (Krull and Trovato, 2003a; Lesthaege, 1998). Parents respond to the economic situation by increasing the number of wage earners in their family unit and decreasing childrearing costs (Li, 1996). Indeed, children are less useful to the family unit and more costly in industrialized and technological societies (Zelizer, 1985). In contrast, families tend to be larger in horticultural and agricultural societies or in the countryside more than in the urban zones of these societies. Agrarian children contribute to the familial economy in ways that are often substantial (LeVine and White, 1994). In these same societies, large families, particularly those with many sons, are a source of masculine pride.

For its part, *involuntary infertility*, or the inability to conceive, affects approximately 15 percent of all couples (Achilles, 1995). In the U.S., the number of women who report some form of fertility impairment increased from 4.6 million in 1982 to 6.2 million in 1995 (Chandra and Stephen, 1998). Although such statistics do not exist for Canada, this upward trend is largely the result of **delayed childbearing** among the baby boomers who then have difficulty conceiving when they finally try to do so during their less fertile reproductive years (Heaton et al., 1999). Involuntary infertility may lead to "feelings of guilt, anger, frustration and depression, and to marital disputes" (Baker, 2001b:129). Eventually becoming a mother erases earlier distress (McQuillan et al., 2003). Women are generally more affected than men emotionally because, until now, the onus has been placed on their reproductive role. Furthermore, it is only recently that medicine has discovered that men are equally implicated. Despite this fact, women more than men are the target of assisted reproductive technologies.

Childlessness by Choice

Although we have no solid information on the number of couples or individuals—whether gay or heterosexual—who remain childless by choice, it is a more common phenomenon than in the recent past. It is, however, difficult to know at which point in their life course women, or couples, reach such a decision, which is certainly facilitated by the recognition that women can occupy roles other than that of mother (Wu and MacNeill, 2002). The same sociocultural factors which have lowered fertility are implicated in childlessness by choice.

Although childless couples are more likely to divorce, controlling for number of years in a marriage, they experience greater marital satisfaction on some dimensions of their relationship than do parenting couples (Twenge et al., 2003). Couples are also happier before childbearing and after childrearing is completed. This has been called the **U-curve phenomenon** because levels of marital happiness start from high, then dip, then come up again. This U-curve phenomenon is not universally accepted among scholars. Some large-scale studies indicate that marital quality diminishes after a few years of marriage, children or no children, and that, on average, it does not pick up again after children are gone (Glenn, 1998). This question will be settled only when longitudinal studies of couples in their mid- to later years are carried out, comparing those who have children with those who are childless by choice. Similar research will be needed for same-sex couples.

Childless couples retain a more egalitarian division of household labour, for, as we see in Chapters 10 and 11, the transition to parenthood leads to more traditional roles between husbands and wives. A couple alone has far less housework and does not have a schedule revolving around children. Consequently, the spouses do not have to renegotiate the terms of their relationship concerning who does what after the arrival of the first child, as is the case among couples who form a family. Childless couples have more freedom for work and leisure and fewer economic constraints. Their sexuality may be more spontaneously expressed. Their life choices as individuals are more numerous. For instance, they can more easily move without concerns about school and child care availability and the quality of the neighbourhood population.

Overall, there are costs and rewards associated with having children (Ambert, 2001). However, the balance of costs and rewards weighs differentially, depending on the gender and marital status of parents as well as other variables. A longitudinal study found a balance of costs and rewards for married men and women but more costs to unmarried men and women, including at the emotional level (Nomaguchi and Milkie, 2003). The effect of childlessness at older ages largely depends on attitudes (Koropeckyj-Cox, 2002). However, at the societal level, both low fertility and childlessness present a problem for the future of the workforce and the tax base (Beaujot, 2004).

Abortion

Induced abortion is an extreme form of birth control and occurs after other methods have failed or because no precautions were taken. In 1969, a law was passed allowing abortions to be performed by a qualified medical practitioner in a hospital after approval by a Therapeutic Abortion Committee. In 1988, the Supreme Court of Canada gave women more freedom in this domain. Abortion clinics outside of hospitals existed only in Quebec (initiated by Dr. Henry Morgentaler) but, by 1995, other clinics were in existence in all the other provinces except Prince Edward Island (Health Canada, 2002). In the U.S., therapeutic abortions became legal in 1973, with the famous *Roe* v. *Wade* case, but the topic has remained mired in political minefields and emotional rhetoric far more than is the case in Canada.

Abortion rates increased dramatically after 1969, dropped and stabilized at a lower level in the early 1980s, and increased again after the 1988 Supreme Court decision. Between 1990 and 2001, the rate rose slowly from 14.6 to 15.6 per 1,000 women aged 15 to 44 years. This corresponds to 106,418 abortions in 2001, which is 22 percent of reported pregnancy outcomes (Statistics Canada, 2004f). In 2001, the Northwest Territories, Nunavut, and Quebec had the highest abortion rates at 28.3, 22.7, and 19.6 respectively. The following percentages indicate the age at which women obtained an abortion in 1995 (Health Canada, 2002; Statistics Canada, 2002c):

- 20% were younger than 20 years of age
- 52% were between 20 and 29 years of age
- 26% were between 30 and 39 years of age
- 2% were older than 40 years of age

There is agreement in the research that the decision to terminate an unwanted pregnancy, while not lightly made, rarely leads to serious and lasting psychological distress (Russell and Zierk, 1992), as expressed by a student:

> *"My boyfriend didn't want a baby so I had an abortion and I really hated myself for it eventually. I hated him because he could have left me with the baby; my parents would have helped. But he had said that no man should be forced to be a father against his will and that one day I'd ask for support when he couldn't afford it or the child would bounce up and sue him.... So it broke up the relationship.... Now with hindsight I know I am better off all around."*

When abortion is accompanied by a great deal of lasting distress, there generally are preexisting emotional problems. In fact, among adolescents, the long-term consequences of childbearing are more salient than those of abortion (Zabin and Hayward,

1993). Furthermore, children who were unintended at times suffer from negative outcomes (Hummer et al., 2004). The mechanisms involved in this link are not known (Axinn et al., 1998). This being said, however, it is quite likely that abortion can result in lasting distress when the woman's moral beliefs, or those of her family, are opposed to it. Therefore, abortion is both a matter of conscience and practicality. But the matter of conscience is often ignored in research.

REPRODUCTIVE ALTERNATIVES

For women and men who are infertile, medical advances now offer a wide range of reproductive alternatives generally labelled "reproductive technologies." The issues surrounding these technologies are sociologically interesting beyond the relatively small number of persons who have recourse to them. First, these scientific advances are problematic because they generally occur without any social planning and legal protection. For medical researchers, biologists, and geneticists, discoveries represent progress as well as a source of income. However, governments are not given a chance to evaluate the social merits of these discoveries before they are implemented (Strathern, 1995:33). Second, critics argue that children may become commodities themselves, made to order in a catalogue; better-to-do women and couples are advantaged in this process (Rothman, 1999). Another criticism is that, although single women as well as a few gay and lesbian couples have recourse to them, reproductive technologies and surrogacy are more available to married couples; they reinforce the traditional family structure (Cole, 1995). We now review what is already available in reproductive technologies and conclude with a section on surrogate mothers.

Donor Insemination

Donor insemination is a relatively simple and accepted procedure that was practised by the end of the 19th century. Although sperm donors are occasionally friends or relatives, organized donor insemination now predominates: Males donate their sperm to a physician or to a sperm bank. In this instance, which constitutes one large step from the usual biological family, the husband is not the biological father; he is technically the *social father.* Prospective parents can also request "designer" sperm by choosing a donor with certain characteristics, such as high IQ. One potential complication resides in the child's being half-adopted, half-biological. Ethical questions that result are multiple:

- Should parents divulge to the child his or her biological background? After all, only one parent is not biological and this factor can easily be kept secret. Indications are that most heterosexual parents do not tell their child about his or her different genetic origins. Unfortunately, many confide in other people and this creates the risk of the child learning about it from someone else (Golombok et al., 2002).
- What are the child's rights in knowing the biological father's identity?
- What is in the child's and the donor's best interest if the child, upon reaching adulthood, wants to locate the biological father?

A few European countries have already legislated on these three questions. For instance, in Sweden, when he or she reaches age 18, a child born as a result of insemination has the right to know the identity of the sperm donor. The donor has no paternity rights or duties, however (Almond, 1995). Other questions are:

- What about multiple donations by the same man within a narrow geographic area? The possibility exists, however remote, that two half-siblings of the opposite sex could meet and have a child who may then suffer from a birth defect. In France, only two or three donations per man are allowed.
- With the North American inclination to litigate, could a mother sue the donor for child support if the social father died or left?

In Vitro Fertilization and Transplantation

Another step in reproductive technologies occurred in Great Britain in 1978 with the birth of the first *test-tube baby*, Louise Brown. Her mother's egg was fertilized in vitro (in a test tube) by her father's sperm, and was then implanted into her mother's womb. Other kinds of IVF then followed, each involving a degree of biological distancing and pushing the boundaries of the "nature" of parenthood:

- The mother's egg is externally fertilized by donor sperm and then transplanted into her uterus. The birth mother is the biological mother, whereas her spouse is the social father.
- A donor's egg is fertilized by the father's sperm and then transplanted into the wife's uterus. The wife becomes a nonbiological birth mother to her husband's and donor's biological child.
- A donor's egg is fertilized by a donor's sperm and transplanted into the birth mother's uterus. Neither the birth mother nor the birth father are biological parents. They are very similar to adoptive parents, except that the mother has carried the baby and given birth.

The last technique has recently been applied for women over age 55; one birth mother was 63 years old. These cases have raised many questions concerning the future of a child who may be left orphaned at a young age. But it has been pointed out that older men often have children without encountering social disapproval (Schwartz and Rutter, 1998); older women, the argument goes, are discriminated against simply on the basis of their gender (van den Akker, 1994). Furthermore, there is no evidence that older women are less able mothers than women in their thirties (Berryman and Windridge, 1991).

IVF carries higher risks of premature delivery, miscarriage, multiple births, and low birth weight even to single infants (Schieve et al., 2002). In turn, low birth weight is associated with an increased risk of cerebral palsy and developmental delay (Stromberg et al., 2002). IVF has a high failure rate and it can be a stressful and physically debilitating treatment (Eugster and Vingerhoets, 1999). So far, indications are that mothers whose embryos have been implanted are not negatively affected by their experience in terms of their parenting skills subsequent to the birth of *one* baby (Golombok et al., 1995). Nor are the children growing up differently compared to children conceived naturally (Golombok et al., 2002; McMahon et al., 1995). Nevertheless, these methods can raise legal issues in terms of paternity and donor protection, as already anticipated in some European countries (Achilles, 1995).

Frozen Embryos

Couples wishing to delay parenthood can freeze their embryos (i.e., fertilized eggs) so that they may have children of their genetic background when they are in their late thirties or early forties. However, there have already been cases in France and the U.S. of the death and divorce of the potential parents. In France, despite sexual liberalism, single women are not regarded as ideal mothers. A widowed woman requested to have one of her and her late husband's frozen embryos implanted in her uterus. The medical establishment refused; the courts upheld the decision, stating that it was not in the child's best interest to have a single mother. In the U.S., a divorced couple is fighting for the "custody" of their embryos because the ex-wife wants to have a baby. Her ex-husband is afraid that he will be held responsible for children he does not want, particularly not from "that woman."

Multiple Births

Fertility treatment, including drugs and transplants of multiple embryos, are probably the main cause of the many multiple births that currently occur. Women who have recourse to fertility drugs have a 25 percent chance of giving birth to more than one baby (Wright, 1998). Furthermore, women are more likely to release multiple eggs when they are older. Delaying parenthood consequently causes a rise in the number of multiple births. Normally, twins and higher-order births occur in the population at the rate of 1 or 2 percent:

- one set of twins per 90 births
- one set of triplets per 9,000 births
- one set of quadruplets per 500,000 births

However, between 1972 and 1989, triplet births increased by 156 percent, quadruplets by 386 percent, and higher-order births by 182 percent among white women, who

Twins and higher-order births occur more frequently than in the recent past because of fertility treatment and delayed conception. These infants are generally born prematurely, weigh much less, and require more care from their parents than do singletons.

constitute the majority of fertility clinics' clientele (*Santa Barbara New Press*, 1992). In 1995 alone, 57 American infants were born who were quintuplets or sextuplets, although not all survived (Adler, 1997). After the 1997 birth of the McCaughey septuplets and the less publicized 1998 birth of octoplets, the medical establishment finally began considering the ethical ramifications of such births following the implantation of multiple embryos or drug fertility treatment that allows the release of several ova. These pregnancies place the mothers' lives in serious danger.

Furthermore, nearly all multiple births have two immediate health consequences for infants: The fetuses have to compete for scarce resources in the womb, and a majority are born prematurely because the womb becomes too crowded. Twins therefore have low birth weight, and babies of higher-order births can have extremely low birth weights—as little as or less than half a kilogram. These infants are then at a far higher risk of neonatal death than singletons, particularly as a result of respiratory failure or the shutdown of some other part of their tiny, immature systems. The danger period may last several months, during which the infants are kept in neonate intensive care units. Prematurely born infants are also far more likely than others to suffer from neurological deficits, whether learning disabilities or muscle coordination problems, although most of them make remarkable progress. For parents, twin and multiple births require a far greater adjustment to parenting than does a single birth: more time demands; less economic resources available per capita; the necessity to seek and accept help, even from total strangers; and more health-related concerns.

Surrogate Mothers

A surrogate mother is a woman who carries a baby to term for a fee plus medical expenses, and relinquishes the child to the married couple or, more rarely, gay couple. However, payments are not allowed in Canada following *The Assisted Reproduction Act* of 2004. Traditionally, the surrogate is inseminated with the father's sperm (Bartholet, 1993). Other surrogate mothers carry a woman's ovum fertilized by either the father or a donor; such surrogates are not biologically related to the child.

The surrogate mother phenomenon can be analyzed both from class and feminist perspectives, although there is a great deal of overlap between the two perspectives on this particular topic. Couples or gay men who avail themselves of a surrogate's services are unavoidably well off financially, whereas the surrogate is usually in some degree of financial need. Even though many surrogates may enjoy being pregnant, there is a social class gap between the parties involved, and this is seen as exploitative (Rothman, 1999). The effects of the 2004 Act remain to be studied. Feminists point out that this "rent-a-womb" arrangement exploits women and uses their bodies, although until now, another woman (the mother) has benefited. Furthermore, surrogacy with embryo transplant involves medical treatment that may affect a woman's health (Eichler, 1988).

On the other side of the coin, there have been cases of a mother carrying her daughter's baby because the daughter had no uterus (or of sisters doing the same). In South Africa, for example, a mother carried all her daughter's children; in other words, she gave birth to her three grandchildren. The motives in these cases are purely altruistic. Therefore, although surrogacy is questionable from some analytical perspectives, it can also be analyzed from an altruistic perspective. Many surrogates describe their act as a gift to another woman. Compared to women who relinquish their child for adoption, the surrogates have planned the pregnancy and its conclusion (Ragoné, 1994). Nevertheless, with the advances of IVF, surrogacy may be morally acceptable only in situations where a prospective mother's health would be seriously compromised by a pregnancy or when she does not have a uterus.

FAMILY FORMATION VIA ADOPTION

In the late 1990s, 1.2 percent of Canadian children under 12 years of age had been adopted, or 57,300 children (Vanier Institute of the Family, 2002). In the U.S., 2.5 percent of all children under 18 are adopted, for a total of 1.6 million (E.B.D. Adoption Institute, 2002). However, we have no information on the proportion of the entire Canadian population which is adopted—the estimate is around two percent. Most adoptions involve adults who are already related to the child (Daly and Sobol, 1994). But the focus here is on non-kin adoption because the issues which surround it allow for a deeper sociological analysis of family formation using a social constructionist perspective.

The Social Construction of Adoption

In North America and other societies of European origin, family is equated with biology and this cultural bias leads to ambivalence concerning adoption (March and Miall, 2000)—even though, in general, a majority of Canadians and Americans express favourable views toward adoption in public opinion surveys (Miall and March, 2004). Yet, adoption is now rarely offered as an option to young single women who have an unwanted pregnancy (Caragata, 1999). Blood ties and their symbolism have long been important in shaping attitudes toward adoption (Christensen, 1999; March, 1995a). In more recent years, advances in the fields of **genetics and medicine** have given rise to a "genetic consciousness" that reinforces negative stereotypes of adoption. What Lebner (2000) includes under the rubric of medicalization and geneticization of our life stories—of our medical risks based on our parents' histories—increases adoptive parents' anxieties when they do not have a full account of their adopted children's background. Yet, these anxieties are only rarely justified because, for the majority of human beings, the environment is far more influential than genes in the domain of health (Lippman, 1998). Furthermore, very soon, a person's own genetic profile will be mapped and will be used in preventive medicine.

A woman's fertility is still considered an important mark of self-esteem and social recognition despite the liberalization of gender role norms (Letherby, 1994). **Biological motherhood** is often considered superior to adoptive motherhood, even by a few feminists (Chesler, 1989). This alliance of biology with feminism presents an anomalous situation at the ideological level because feminist theories generally reject gender roles based on biological constraints (Rothman, 1989). We have all heard the well-known feminist slogan that "biology is not destiny." Yet, as Bartholet (1993) points out, infertility is stigmatized even from these same quarters. Arlene Skolnick (1998) rightly criticizes this "new biologism" as a cultural phenomenon with policy implications. As well, Rothman (1989:39) points out that "we can recognize and appreciate the genetic tie without making it the determining connection."

The more recent development of reunions of adopted children with their birth mothers well illustrates the theme of the social construction of adoption. Search-movement activists have depicted the psychological need to search as a universal one, although not every adoptee has this need and will remain "incomplete" without a reunion (Wegar, 1997). What "incomplete" entails is also a social construction but it is an effective imagery: It has high value in current pop psychology. This presumed universal need to locate one's biological roots has arisen from our concerns over genetic connectedness. This need is then packaged within other very **modern psychological themes** such as "the need to find oneself," self-fulfillment, freedom, choice, human rights, and the presumed personal problems and "repression" of those who do not search (Griffith, 1991). It is a need that has been created by our culture (Ambert, 2003c).

However, once created, *it exists* and becomes salient in many adoptees' lives. Thus, the recognition of the social construct aspect of this phenomenon is not synonymous with shrugging the created need aside. Bartholet (1993) points out that the search movement has inadvertently contributed to further stigmatize adoption and particularly adoptive parents as well as adult adoptees who are not interested in finding their birth parents. This is well illustrated in a student's autobiography: She had been adopted along with her (non-biological) sister:

> *"Last year has been a difficult year in my family because my sister [age 19] was reunited with her birth mother.... My parents were apprehensive because my sister has always been a more easily influenced child than me and my brother. The school counsellor had put it in her head that she'd feel 'whole' only after she was able 'to make peace with her past.' Lisa and me had long arguments over this because we were both adopted within a month of our birth and I said, 'What past? Our past is here.' You may ask, Am I not curious about my birth family? Only to the extent that I could finally tell my physician that there is or there is not breast cancer or heart problems or diabetes in my background.... I have had parents practically from Day One and I don't see what finding a woman who is supposed to be my mother just because I got a set of genes from her and she carried me would do for me.... So my sister located her birth mother and she doesn't look a thing like her and the woman is not sure who the father is on top of it all. So now because my sister got brainwashed by this school counsellor about being 'whole' she is still recovering from the shock of these discoveries and she even thinks that the Children's Aid located the 'wrong mother' because she has it in her mind that she should have looked just like her and so on.... My parents have to deal with all of this of course."*

Adopted Children's Development

Some researchers have not found any significant difference in adjustment between adopted and non-adopted persons while others have (for a review, see Sharma et al., 1998). A few studies report that adopted children show certain ego strengths and resilience (Benson et al., 1994). The deficits and strengths that are found largely depend on the methodology used, the type of adopted children included in the sample, the comparison group, and the outcomes measured. For instance, adoptive mothers report more child problems, whereas adoptive fathers and adopted children's reports are more similar to those in biological families (Lansford et al., 2001). But, overall, adoptees and their parents do not show any consistent deficit that would warrant concern (Bartholet, 1993). Two studies of young adult adoptees concluded that whatever differences existed between them and non-adopted adults were small; as well, these differences were not identical in both studies (Feigelman, 1997; Smyer et al., 1998). A study by Borders et al. (2000) focused on adoptees who ranged from 35 to 55 years of age with a similar comparison group of non-adopted adults. Both groups were experiencing their adult years similarly, but the adoptees had a slightly lower level of self-esteem and a slightly higher level of depression. One study has shown that adopted children fare equally well across a variety of family structures—when they are only children, have younger or older adopted siblings, or have younger or older biological siblings (Brodzinski and Brodzinski, 1992).

Parents often experience more stress when they have adopted **older children** (Bird et al., 2002). In part, this can be explained by the fact that older children often have special needs or suffer from problems related to difficulties in their original families and/or foster placements (Barth and Berry, 1988). They may also have had more problematic parents than children adopted at birth and thus have inherited more difficult predispositions (Miller et al., 2000). Therefore, older children who are adopted bring with them genetic, emotional, and contextual baggage which may make it more difficult to form an attachment to their adoptive parents and to be parented successfully (Barth and Miller, 2000).

There is a greater proportion of adopted than non-adopted children among psychologists' and psychiatrists' clientele (Brodzinski, 1993). Why is this so? The explanations that have been offered are twofold. First, some adopted children may have a more difficult time growing up because of identity problems or because their parents have not properly bonded with them. Second, there may be no actual developmental difference between adopted and non-adopted children, but adoptive parents are of higher socioeconomic status and are more familiar with mental health services. Consequently, they may be more inclined to consult professionals as soon as their children evidence some problems (Warren, 1992). Thus, adopted children are overrepresented among clinical samples. Furthermore, more children with various disabilities are adopted (about 12 percent) while only about five percent of biological children suffer from similar problems.

But there is another explanation that has not been sufficiently explored. Although adopted children may feel as loved and as accepted by their parents as non-adopted children, their **peers** and even adults often openly express doubts to them on this topic (Leon, 2002):

> An adopted respondent in March's (1995a:656) study said that outside the family, people "never believe that your adoptive parents love you like their parents love them. Because you aren't biological." One of my students recalls returning home one day quite distressed and asking her mother, "Is it true that you can't love me as much because I am adopted?" Another student reported that, upon learning she was adopted, her peer on the school bus shrieked, "Oh, you poor poor child! You don't have any real parents."

A student recalled the following causality chain in her autobiography:

> *"When I was 6 one day I proudly told one of my friends that I was adopted. To me, this had been a source of joy because I had always been told by my parents how much they had wanted me.... My little friend didn't say much and with hindsight I gather that she probably didn't know what I was talking about. The next day she and another girl turned around me in a funny way and my friend finally said, 'My mom feels sorry for you.' I was puzzled and asked why. 'Because you're 'dopted [sic] and you don't have real parents. You're not their real little girl and you don't look like them.' I didn't understand any of this at first but it sounded awful and I started bawling out and the teacher had to call my mother to come and console me. It did the trick but I never thereafter talked about being adopted to any other child until I was in university. It didn't change my feelings about my situation at home but this incident definitely made me feel different, more socially anxious, and less self-assured."*

This theme of not being a "real" child and not having "real" parents is an excellent example of the social construction of adoption and is a recurring one in the autobiographies of students who have been adopted. It is not their theme but that of others. This stigmatization may constitute a heavy mental burden on adoptees (Leon, 2002). Children are especially vulnerable to what their peers think. If their peers present them with questionable notions of their adoptive status, then these children are at risk emotionally. This may explain why, in some studies, adolescence is the time when adopted children begin to show a higher rate of behavioural problems compared to other children (Miller et al., 2000). In this respect, children conceived by donor insemination and who are not told about their status constitute an excellent comparison group because their social environment is not aware of their half- or fully adopted status: Studies reveal that they are no different than other children (Golombok et al., 2002). For their part, professionals who "treat" troubled adopted children or adolescents may be too hasty to attribute the problems to the adoption itself (Miall, 1996). This social construction of adoption may prevent these youngsters from being treated for the real problems that affect them.

The view on adoptive parents is equally mixed (Groze, 1996). Some writers have suggested that adoptive parents may be less confident, more anxious, and stigmatized because of their infertility, whereas other researchers have not found any support for this "at-risk" perspective (for a review, see Borders et al., 1998). (Parenthetically, not all adoptive parents are infertile.) Adoption often resolves the psychological distress associated with infertility (McQuillan et al., 2003). Adoptive parents are in a dilemma: On the one hand, they are expected to "accept the fact that their family is not biological"—not to be "in denial." On the other hand, they are expected to love their children as much as non-adoptive parents do. Most adoptive parents have no problem with either point and at least one study has found that the transition to parenthood was easier for them than for biological parents (Cebello et al., 2004). However, in order for such parents to build a normal family life, they cannot be obsessive about their adoptive status, and they must go through their daily lives with their children as any other parent does.

The Diversity of Adoption

Stepchild Adoption

We do not have recent information about stepchild adoption in Canada. However, over 50,000 American stepchildren are adopted by their stepparents, generally a stepfather, each year (Flango and Flango, 1994). Although there are a few similarities between regular adoptions and adoptions by a stepparent, there are important differences as well as motives specific to each situation (Ganong et al., 1998). The main reasons for step-adoptions after divorce reside in a desire to be a "regular" family, to legitimize the roles and relationships within the reconstituted family, and to sever the relationship with the nonresidential parent, particularly when the latter does not contribute child support or is uninvolved with the child (Marsiglio, 2004). The nonresidential parent either consents to the adoption or the case can go to court. A judge will rule in favour of the adoption only if the nonresidential parent is deemed unfit or if it is in the child's best interest to sever the relationship (Mahoney, 1994). A better model might be that of the *British Children Act of 1987*, whereby stepparents can have responsibilities for children without obliterating noncustodial parents' responsibilities and rights (Mason, 1998). The long-term consequences of stepchild adoption have yet to be studied (Ambert, 2003c).

Transracial and Transnational Adoption

We do not have solid information on transracial adoption in Canada. The U.S. 2000 census indicates that 17 percent of adoptions are transracial (Adoption Council of Canada, 2003). Overall, there is absolutely no indication in the American research literature that black children adopted by white parents turn out much differently than those adopted in black families (Silverman, 1993). The same results have been replicated in Great Britain (Bagley, 1993). Vroegh (1997) reports from a longitudinal study that, by adolescence, these children are still well adjusted and enjoy a high level of self-esteem—as is the case for children born to interracial couples (Stephan and Stephan, 1991). Most interracially adopted children grow up identifying as black, and most parents conscientiously promote their children's African-American heritage (Vroegh, 1997). In Canada, the adoption of Native children by non-Native parents has been and continues to be an issue, in great part because cultural genocide indeed took place as it did in the U.S. However, in the U.S., the First Nations represent a smaller proportion of the population than in Canada and are less visible politically so that this topic is less researched. But, again, we do not have statistics on transadoptions of Native children in Canada, and the numbers are relatively small—despite the large number of these children in foster care.

As the number of *young* children available via foster care and especially private agencies declined, international adoptions increased. Canadians have recently adopted between 1,890 and 2,220 children internationally each year (Adoption Council of Canada, 2003). Quebec and Ontario are the provinces with the most transnational adoptions (Ouellette and Belleau, 2001), particularly from China, with a preponderance of girls over boys: 68 percent and 32 percent respectively (Adoption Council of Canada, 2003). The same situation occurs in the U.S. where, in 2002, Americans adopted 20,000 children internationally (Tarmann, 2002). This sex ratio imbalance in part stems from the fact that so many children originate from China where most of the available children are female because of the one-child family policy and preference for male children. Over 70 percent of the children are younger than five years of age, so that Canadians who wish to adopt infants often find international adoptions, if not easier, at least faster and more likely to result in a young child than would be the case within their country. However, adoption of children who had been very deprived in their country of origin often leads to stressful parenting, especially when behavioural problems emerge (Judge, 2003).

Open Adoption

Grotevant and McRoy (1998) have categorized adoptions along a continuum ranging from confidential to mediated and then to fully disclosed. Confidential adoptions provide anonymity but generally disclose parents' backgrounds. In the mediated category, the adoption agency may transmit pictures, letters, and gifts, or even arrange meetings between parents without full identification. In the fully disclosed category, both parties know each other's identity and may meet (Miall and March, 2004). Thus, many single mothers now relinquish their infant only under circumstances that allow them greater control over the adoption process and even access to the child (Sobol et al., 2000). At the extreme continuum of openness, biological parents more or less enter the adoptive parents' family system as they exchange regular visits and participate in decision-making concerning their child's health (Grotevant et al., 1994). The concept of open adoption generally subsumes the mediated and fully disclosed categories; Miall and March (2004) have shown that the public in general is more accepting of mediated than fully open adoption.

Studies on the outcomes of open adoption are still embryonic, do not include a wide range of ages, are not longitudinal, and are highly selective (Ambert, 2003c). But, overall, many studies indicate that most of the adoptive and biological parents are satisfied with their relationship with each other (Etter, 1993). However, more biological than adoptive parents are happy about this arrangement, which concurs with Berry's (1991) conclusion that benefits accrue to biological parents. McRoy et al. (1998) found that semi-open (or mediated) adoptions might be more functional than fully open ones. For instance, in fully open cases, adoptive parents reported feeling burdened by meetings with birth parents. Berry et al. (1998) noted that, in nearly half of the open adoptions, the level of contact between the two families had decreased after four years. Frasch et al. (2000) reported similar results. Along these lines, the 1987–1992 longitudinal study by Grotevant and McRoy (1998) of 190 adoptive families and 169 birth mothers indicated that openness does not threaten adoptive parents' sense of entitlement to parenthood but does not necessarily ensure that birth mothers will be successful in their grief resolution or that children's curiosity will be satisfied when they reach adolescence (Wrobel et al., 1996).

At least two studies have found no difference on measures of child adjustment between open and confidential adoptions (Berry et al., 1998; Grotevant and McRoy, 1998). The concept of boundary ambiguity (Boss, 1993) leads to the possibility of problems when children are attached to two sets of parents, as is the case in foster families (Leathers, 2003). Furthermore, Kohler et al. (2002:100) concluded that adolescent "preoccupation with adoption is not an inherent outcome of confidential adoptions." They also found that adolescents who were extremely preoccupied with their adoption felt somewhat more alienated from their parents—although one can only offer hypotheses concerning the direction of causality.

Reunions with Birth Parents

Today, many adoption agencies provide basic information to adult children about birth parents, whereas others openly encourage search and reunion (March, 1995b). Registries exist in which birth parents as well as children and even siblings can enter information about themselves and indicate for whom they are searching. One example is the Canadian Adoptee Registry Inc. on the Internet. Mothers and daughters are the most common clientele (Pacheco and Eme, 1993). This **gender difference** may be the result of women being more biologically involved in reproduction and birthing and because women are socialized to be more nurturant and family oriented than males. In some instances, young women search for their birth parents only after they have become mothers themselves.

The functions fulfilled by reunions and their consequences largely depend on which part of the family unit is considered: the child, the birth parent, the birth parent's family, and the adoptive family. (See Ambert, 2003c, for a more complete presentation.) The few studies that exist on this topic indicate that a majority of adoptees who have been reunited with their biological family see this as a positive experience (March, 1995a), although March (1995b) also documents many cases of rejection. Yet, in most instances, the adoptee acquired a stronger sense of being their adoptive parents' child. However, a mismatch between the respective motivations and expectations of the two parties may develop over time (Gladstone and Westhues, 1998). As Pacheco and Eme (1993:55) point out, the high success rate is somewhat inflated; there is the possibility that the individuals who refuse to participate in surveys have had a negative experience. Furthermore, all reunions studied are initiated by the adoptees, and when biological parents initiate the reunion, the adoptees' response is less positive (Sachdev, 1992). As well, many of the studies have obtained their samples from support groups with a strong advocacy position in favour of reunions. Adoptees who might believe otherwise or do not search are excluded. As a last note, I should mention that it is very difficult to study birth mothers and their families (March, 1995b).

FOSTER FAMILIES: FAMILY RESTRUCTURING

Fostering is really a form of family restructuring rather than family formation and it is far more common than adoption. But the number of children in need of foster care far exceeds the availability of suitable families. In 1999, there were nearly 66,000 children in care, at least 20,000 who could be adopted (Ross, 2000; Vanier Institute of the Family, 2004). In the U.S., well over 550,000 children are in the foster care system at any point in time in comparison to 200,000 in the 1980s. One of the problems of foster children is that a great proportion have at least one sibling, yet many siblings are fostered separately because it is too difficult to find families willing to take in more than one child at a time (Phillips, 1998). As a consequence, these children face a second loss after that of their parent(s). They are also deprived of the social support they could provide each other. However, large age disparities may lead teens to wish to be placed separately from their younger siblings (Drapeau et al., 2000). In many cases, some siblings fare better separately, especially when one is abusive or suffers from behavioural problems (Staff and Fein, 1992).

Children who have been in foster care and group homes generally have more negative outcomes than other children, particularly in terms of delinquency, mental health, and adult criminality (Orme and Buehler, 2001). These children were neglected or abused in their families and the foster care placement represents for many an additional dislocation (Harden, 2004). Above all, many of the older ones find themselves on their own without a support group when they are discharged or run away from foster care. Intermediary programs are being established in some regions to help them acquire skills for independent living and to provide them with peer social support (Mallon, 1998).

There is little research on children's and parents' lived experience with foster care (Desetta, 1996). Some children call their foster parents "Mom" and "Dad" and perceive them as family, whereas their biological parents may be referred to by name or as the "other mother." Some foster children believe that they are much better off than in their parents' homes and are even grateful to have been removed from the home when they were small (for a review, see Berrick et al., 1998). Others rebel against their foster family and the fact of being in foster care (Whiting and Lee, 2003). Length of care brings greater closeness and a sense of identity with the foster family (McAuley, 1996). On the other hand, regular contact and hopes of reunification with the natural family decrease closeness with foster parents (Leathers, 2003). Children who are to be reunited with their original families do better when their parents visit them regularly (McWey and Mullis, 2004). In the U.S., slightly over half of children are reunited with their parents; however, nearly a third eventually return to foster care, often within one year (Wulczyn, 2004). More are being adopted than a decade ago.

Foster families grow and shrink in size depending on external circumstances. They are scrutinized by child welfare agencies and receive occasional visits from the children's parents (Berrick et al., 1998). Adaptation is constantly required and equilibrium takes up to 18 months to be reestablished when a new child arrives (Seaberg and Harrigan, 1997). Somewhat like stepparents, foster parents lack clearly defined behavioural guidelines about their relationships with the children in their care (Erera, 1997). Furthermore, they do not receive sufficient support and have no safety net for their later years (Barth, 2001).

CONCLUSIONS: FAMILY FORMATION ALTERNATIVES IN CONTEXT

Are cohabitation, marriage, and solo parenting equivalent modes of family formation? Despite divorce, marriage seems to be the *current* optimal alternative when children are present. Since a good proportion of divorces do not involve children, the number of children benefiting from their parents' marriage is far greater than those who will be harmed by it. Most importantly, the research is unanimous to the effect that married fathers invest far more in their children than fathers either in cohabitation or as single parents (Cooksey and Craig, 1998; Doherty et al., 1998).

What about single mothering? Under the current economic and political system, absolutely nothing in the extensive research literature recommends unmarried motherhood for adolescents and adults alike (Kaufman, 1999). For established and mature adults, however, single parenthood may well be a positive alternative for parent and child. This alternative is socially advantageous when an adult, generally a woman, adopts a child who would not otherwise have a family. A feminist analysis suggests that women (and men) should not have to depend on marriage and should have the option of forming one-parent families that function well and contribute to society's social capital (Coontz, 2000). Thus, single parenting could become a far better alternative for children and adults in the future under the following circumstances:

1. If young males were socialized to be nurturing and equally responsible for their offspring, then even children in single-mother families would have two parents investing in them and supporting them.

2. If women earned incomes equal to those of men, then the poverty rate of families headed by women would diminish substantially, and so would children's problems.

3. If society was willing to invest in children, regardless of their parents' marital status, such a policy would prevent these children from even coming near the poverty line.

4. If social reproduction was valued by society and if what is now unpaid work was remunerated, mothers and their children would have more options.

5. Once all these conditions are in place, delaying motherhood until adulthood and attaining greater maturity would be the last necessary ingredient to making single parenting more functional for children and their parents than it currently is.

Thus, overall, while much of the research literature documents the disadvantages that single mothering *on average* brings, disadvantages are not inevitable (Ruspini, 2000). Rather, they are tied to the economic and urban structure of our societies, thus to deprivation, lack of a supportive community, and the culture of feminine inequality that pervades all domains of life (Vosko, 2002). Nevertheless, I would be derelict in my duties as a researcher were I to romanticize single parenting as an alternative to free women from marriage—for, indeed, as a few feminists have pointed out, women end up paying the price, not society nor the fathers (Folbre, 1994; Walby, 1990, 1997). Cohabitational parenting and single-mothering currently present a risk element for women and their children, especially within the context of poverty. Thus, it could be argued that educated individuals who promote the equivalency with marriage of these parenting situations, without taking the economic system into consideration, may actually be promoting a perspective that is linked to their advantaged social situation: They are not the ones who will ever suffer from the consequent problems.

Summary

1. Recent changes in family structure in Canada include a decrease in marriage and increases in cohabitational and one-parent families. A longer period of singlehood and more cohabitation among young cohorts are delaying marriage.

2. Marriage as an institution is advantageous for children and society. Children who live with their married parents have the best outcomes of all categories of children. The only exception occurs in highly conflictual marriages. These, however, are a minority, as most end in divorce. Furthermore, a marriage that is not quite satisfactory to the parents still usually benefits children.

3. Cohabitations involving children have increased. Children of these unions are more similar to those in single-parent than married families. Although cohabitation boosts a mother's income, cohabiting couples are less economically secure than married couples. Small children's well-being is less well served by such unions, particularly when a mother cohabits with a man who is not their natural father.

4. So far, most children who are raised in same-sex-parent families were born in a mother-father family that was disrupted by divorce. But more and more, same-sex couples are having children by donor insemination and

adoption. Overall, the results indicate that the public's concern for these children is unwarranted: They grow up normally, are not sexually molested by either parent, and most are heterosexual.

5. Nonmarital fertility has increased dramatically since the 1960s. Although one-parent families are not a new phenomenon, their composition has changed over time and most are now the result of divorce. Nonmarital teen births have increased and then stabilized at a lower rate. The life course of adolescent mothers generally contains more transitions, and a proportion of them, as is the case for fathers, are truant, aggressive, and use drugs. The babies' fathers tend to come from the same background as that of mothers. Children born to single mothers tend to be the most disadvantaged in their outcomes, but much depends on mothers' and children's characteristics.

6. There has been a general decrease in fertility in all industrialized countries, and Canada's current fertility rate of 1.5 is no exception. Various factors have contributed to this decrease, including urbanization and later age at marriage.

7. Childlessness by choice has also increased as have abortion rates. Half of abortions are sought by women in the 20 to 29 years age bracket.

8. New reproductive technologies range from various forms of donor insemination, embryo implantation, and surrogate motherhood. Children's and donors' rights are discussed, as are other ethical considerations. With fertility treatment, multiple births have increased astronomically. They do not represent an ideal developmental context for children, particularly while they are in the womb.

9. Adoption is an alternative form of family formation that has been socially constructed as less "natural" than biological parenting. The literature on the consequences of adoption for children tends to be divided between studies that show no disadvantage and those that indicate small deficits. Were the latter to be real, they would be most likely created by the less than optimal social climate surrounding adoption, particularly in children's peer groups. There are no indications that children adopted by single parents fare worse.

10. Stepchild adoption is the most common type of adoption. On the whole, indications are that transracially adopted children succeed as well as others and identify with their own racial group. It is difficult to evaluate the research on open adoption because of a variety of methodological considerations ranging from sample size and type as well as researchers' joint role as advocates and researchers. The same remark applies to the consequences of reunions of adoptive children with birth parents. In this case, reunions can have consequences for the child, the birth parents, and the adoptive parents.

11. Foster children generally have poor outcomes, mainly because of prior neglect or abuse and because of the dislocation in their young lives as they are shifted around.

12. Currently, marriage is the pattern of family formation that is in the best interest of children. Single parenting could become a more appropriate alternative with cultural and economic changes at the systemic level.

Key Concepts and Themes

Abortion, p. 253
Adoption, pp. 257–263
Agency of social control, p. 240
Authority figures, p. 239

Birth parents, pp. 258, 263
Birth rates, pp. 246, 250–251
Childlessness by choice, p. 252
Cohabitation and children, pp. 241–242

Analytical Questions

1. It is said in the media that cohabitation is replacing marriage. Discuss the pros and cons of such a statement.

2. Academics often believe that, for children, cohabitation and single parenting are equivalent modes of family life to that of parents' marriage. Yet, the research literature across the world points to a different conclusion. How can you reconcile these two perspectives?

3. Children in same-sex-parent families fare as well as other children, contrary to what many people think. Explain why this is so. (The answers are not necessarily all in the text.)

4. The teen birth rate was far higher in the 1950s than it currently is. How can this be, given the statistics presented in the text?

5. Currently, the Canadian fertility rate stands at 1.5, while the American one is at 2.1. This is a relatively large difference. What factors can explain it?

6. Discuss the "nature" of parenthood within the context of adoption and reproductive alternatives.

Suggested Readings

Beaujot, R., and Kerr, D. 2004. *Population change in Canada*, 2nd Ed. Toronto: Oxford University Press. This comprehensive overview of population trends in Canada includes a great deal of discussion on fertility and family composition.

Booth, A., and Crouter, A. C. (Eds.) 2002. *Just living together*. This collection of articles well documents the diversity of cohabitation and the need for research on children and adults who live in cohabitational units.

Nelson, F. 1996. *Lesbian motherhood*. Toronto: University of Toronto Press. This book provides interesting research results on the entire process of becoming and being a lesbian mother. The couple relationship between the two women is examined within the context of mothering.

Nock, S. L. 1998. *Marriage in men's lives*. New York: Oxford University Press. The author uses surveys to study the role that marriage plays in men's lives and in terms of their well-being. One of his theses is that marriage is at the root of adult masculinity.

Wong, J., and Checkland, D. (Eds.) 1999. *Teen pregnancy and parenting: Social and ethical issues*. Toronto: University of Toronto Press. This small volume presents a well-balanced and critical series of analyses and policy suggestions on the topic outlined in its title.

Wu, Z. 2000. *Cohabitation: An alternative form of family living*. Toronto: Oxford University Press. This text presents a comprehensive review of the literature on cohabitation.

Suggested Weblinks

Government websites provide some of the best information on family formation trends. For Canada, consult

www.statcan.ca

especially *The Daily*. For the U.S.:

www.fedstats.gov

for general statistics. Click on *A to Z* to obtain an alphabetical list of topics; **Bureau of the Census:** Click on *People* and an index will appear.

www.census.gov

Canada Health Network has sections on reproduction and related issues.

www.Canadian-health-network.ca

Health Canada also has sections on reproductive and genetic technologies.

http://hc-sc.gc.ca

For a more ample discussion of one-parent families, see

www.arts.yorku.ca/soci/ambert/writings/oneparent_1.html

and

www.arts.yorku.ca/soci/ambert/writings/oneparent_2.html

For adoption, the **Adoption Council of Canada** provides research as well as general information and links to various services.

www.adoption.ca

For a more detailed description of material presented on adoption in this chapter, see

www.arts.yorku.ca/soci/ambert/writings/adoption.html

For a thorough discussion of the implications of reduced fertility, see R. Beaujot's article, "Delayed life transitions: Trends and implications," at

www.vifamily.ca/library/cft/delayed_life.html

as well as several articles from the Population Studies Centre at the University of Western Ontario at

www.ssc.uwo.ca/sociology/popstudies

CHAPTER 10

Families' Life Courses

Leslie and George Hawkins, born in 1945 and 1942 respectively, grew up near Vancouver and met in university. They married five years later in 1970 after Leslie had established herself as a teacher and George professionally. At the birth of their first child in 1976, they were 31 and 34 years old. When the children were four years and one year old, Leslie entered graduate school part-time at the age of 35. She completed her degree five years later and has been employed ever since. In her autobiography, their daughter Bev recalls that her father would come home from work when she was small and read stories to her and her brother so that their mother would have some free time to study. After dinner, both parents would retreat to the sunroom and have a cup of coffee before watching a program with the children and putting them to bed. The family went camping during the summer and eventually bought a cottage in the interior of B.C. Bev, who is 24 years old, is doing a B.A. in Ontario after having spent a year working on a cruise ship and another two years as a ski instructor. Her younger brother will enter medical school next year. Bev plans on teaching abroad for a few years before returning to Vancouver. In 10 years from now, she anticipates teaching, skiing, "and hopefully being married and planning on having my first child." Her parents are active in outdoor activities and the family still regularly spends time at the cottage.

Maria and Antonio Milano were born in 1949 and 1945 respectively, in two villages in southern Italy. Both grew up on small pieces of farmland in crowded relatives' houses. They worked in the fields and Maria also did house chores so that they attended school irregularly. Their families immigrated to Toronto when they were 12 and 14 years old and again lived in relatives' houses. The two fathers worked in construction and the mothers in factories. Maria and Tony met at a relative's wedding and married in 1968, aged 19 and 23 respectively. They lived with Maria's parents and had their first child a year later. Tony had long ago followed his father in construction. When their second child was born in 1972, they moved into their own modest semi-detached house and Maria left her cleaning job and became a full-time mother. Their third child was born three years later. When all the children were in school, Maria became a part-time receptionist for a building contractor, where she is still employed, while Tony and a brother started a small but profitable business. When Anna, the oldest child, who is 24 (writer of the autobiography), began high school, the family moved into their larger suburban "dream home" of which they are extremely proud. During a rebellious adolescence, this student married against her parents' will at age 18. Her son is nearly six years old. She left her abusive husband and took her son to live with a cousin downtown so as not to embarrass her parents. Her father was very angry at her for several years but her mother helped her so that she could complete high school and begin university. Anna writes that her parents used to lead largely separate lives with their male and female relatives: "It's not that they were unhappy with each other but they were very busy and they had a lot of obligations. Now things are more relaxed and they do more things together. But my mother still does the housework alone."

The two families in these vignettes lived through the same historical period but in different cultural environments. The parent couples married and started their families at different ages and followed divergent educational and socioeconomic paths. Consequently, although these families' life courses share some common transitions, their dynamics and the life courses of individual members in the second generation are quite different.

Ideally, within the life course perspective, family stages are studied in conjunction with parents' age and the stage in their relationship and work history (Luxton and Corman, 2001). The interweaving of family transitions with the life trajectory of each member is analyzed within its historical context (Hareven, 1994b). That is, as the culture and the economic situation of the decades change, so do the roles attached to certain family transitions such as marriage, and especially the timing of these transitions as well as their sequencing (Ravanera and Rajulton, 2004). Other vignettes could have shown the life course of families from two different time periods, in which case we would have seen another set of differences emerge based on the effect of cohort or time period (Ravanera et al., 2004).

Adults now live longer and the sequencing of familial events has changed to include births to nonmarried women, cohabitation, divorce, and the extension of adult children's dependence on parents, at least in terms of housing. Thus, family developmental stages have become more varied; some have become longer (e.g., adult children who remain at home) while others have become briefer (e.g., marriage) and even succeed each other at a more rapid pace than was the case just 30 years ago (Beaujot, 2004). Family development has become more complex and less linear (Ravanera and Rajulton, 2004). Aside from employment, the precursors to family development include dating, having sexual relations, cohabiting, and marrying. This is what we referred to as *couple* formation in Chapter 8. Then, in Chapter 9, we saw that there are different ways of starting a *family*.

In this chapter, we focus on the family from first pregnancy all the way to the death of aged grandparents, all the while keeping in mind various lifestyle alternatives: There is no universal or proper developmental trajectory that applies to everyone (Laszloffy, 2002). There are, as well, differences by ethnicity, but these have yet to be researched—although Chapter 4 indicates that new immigrants more often than not have a family development trajectory which resembles more the traditional Canadian one than the postmodern ones. Furthermore, there are differences by social class, and the timing of the first transitions reverberates throughout a family's entire trajectory, as well illustrated in the vignettes (Ravanera and Rajulton, 2004).

THE GENDERED SOCIAL CONSTRUCTION OF PARENTHOOD

One of the most important influences on individuals' experiences of family development stems from the gendered social construction of parenthood (McMahon, 1995). The overall social stratification by gender dictates that mothers and fathers fulfill different functions in their respective parenting roles. The household division of labour is largely unequal and gives far more flexibility to males in the activities they choose to engage in at home (Fox, 2001). However, as seen in Chapter 5, changes in the economy and at the cultural level have considerably altered the framework within which fathers and mothers interpret their roles.

Motherhood

Probably the most salient metamorphosis that occurs in the formation of a new nuclear family is the transformation of a girl or a woman into a mother. Motherhood is not only a biological state but is, above all, a social and cultural phenomenon (Arendell, 2000): It is socially constructed to serve the culture of the time and the economic system of a society. It is also defined according to the prevailing definition of childhood and of children's needs and roles within a particular economic system (Wall, 2004). The "nature" of childhood is socially constructed and thus differs from culture to culture and from century to century (Prout and James, 1990). Parenting, and particularly mothering, is defined along with the nature of childhood, as the "needs" of children differ culturally (Ambert, 1994b). For instance, in North America, it is believed that small children need to be talked to, given affection, allowed some autonomy, and prepared for school (LeVine, 1994). As well, their self-esteem has to be nurtured. More and more, the emphasis is placed on the development of intellectual abilities from a young age (Nadesan, 2002). Such beliefs about children's needs place specific demands on how women mother (Pitt, 2002; Hays, 1996). In other societies, such as the Efe foragers and the Lese farmers of Zaire, small children are defined as needing assistance from older children, having to learn how to help in and around the house and to get along with others (Morelli and Tronick, 1991). Such needs place fewer demands on mothers.

Once there is agreement in a society on what is "in the best interest of the child," what mothers should do and should be is implicitly and explicitly constructed. For instance, LeVine (1994) has found that the Gusii in East Africa, an agrarian people, focus on the health and survival of their infants because of high mortality. The role of caregivers is accordingly scripted around child safety and feeding. Notions pertaining to the development of self-esteem, attachment, and intellectual abilities simply do not exist. Thus, the role description of Efe, Lese, and Gusii mothers does not include activities and concerns about these aspects of child development. For instance, Whiting and Edwards (1988:94) have found that, in some societies, mothers initiate very few nurturing acts, such as cuddling; they leave these aspects of child care to older children. This observation led Whiting and Edwards to suggest that current stereotypes regarding the nature of the maternal role should be revised.

Furthermore, in western societies, it is believed that mothers are absolutely essential to children's well-being, and that women have a natural, rather than learned, aptitude for mothering (Eyer, 1992). Although it may be that mothers are indeed the most important persons and parents in a majority of children's lives in modern societies, this should not be taken to mean that *one* mother is a necessity of human nature. Indeed, the western focus on individual mothers at the core of children's development is not universal. Many anthropologists question it as an *ethnocentric phenomenon* (LeVine, 1990). That is, motherhood is defined according to western criteria. The reality is that multiple mothering and even **multiple parenting** are in the majority in many agrarian and gathering societies such as the Efe of Zaire (Morelli and Tronick, 1991). This means that several women in a small community share in the care and supervision of children (Rogoff et al., 1991); the members of the village are responsible for all the children; older siblings or other youngsters are often small children's caregivers as well as their main source of psychological comfort and discomfort (Harkness and Super, 1992). To some extent, one encounters multiple parenting among blacks in Canada and the U.S. (Collins, 1992) and even more so in some Caribbean communities. As well, the care of small children by older ones was widely practised in black families during slavery (Alston, 1992).

In contrast, many western societies require **intensive mothering**—mothering that is expert-guided, is labour intensive at the middle-class level, and emphasizes the child's psychological development, particularly the promotion of self-esteem and individualism (Lareau, 2003). The child is seen as a project that has to be perfected (Blum, 1999; Wall, 2001). Hays (1996) discusses the cultural contradictions of what is involved in this type of motherhood. She points out that this social construct requires mothers to expend a tremendous amount of time, energy, and money in raising their children. Yet, in expensive western economies, two salaries are often necessary, so mothers can no longer afford to stay home and care for their children 24 hours a day.

Thus, at the same time that the economy propels men and women into an ever-competitive workplace, it also requires of these parents that children be raised intensively at the psychological level and prepared to become efficient workers later on (Eichler, 1988). The end result is that the requirements of the current social constructions of motherhood and childhood compete. Furthermore, this cultural mothering perpetuates outdated assumptions regarding the "proper" relationship between mothers and children (Hays, 1998:782).

Another anomaly inherent to the social construction of intensive motherhood in a society where women are employed resides in the division of labour between fathers and mothers (Luxton and Corman, 2001). As we see in Chapter 5, even a mother who has a career as demanding as that of her husband spends more time in child care and housework than he does (Nelson and Robinson, 2002). This division of labour includes 24-hour-a-day maternal availability if the child is ill or needs special attention. Even the task of hiring nannies or locating daycare facilities are usually a woman's responsibility. Mothers also worry more about their children (Hays, 1996:104) and are blamed when a child "goes wrong" or develops problems (Ambert, 2001). Children themselves internalize the cultural definition of motherhood and behave accordingly: They demand more of their mothers than of anyone else in society, including their fathers. Therefore, the transition to parenthood presents a complex situation for both parents, however much a child is wanted. But this transition affects a **woman's role** in terms of daily activities and preoccupations far more than a man's role. A new father retains his primary identity as a worker, whereas a new mother acquires another identity that may supersede identities that she has devoted years to acquire by going to professional school, for instance.

Fatherhood

The social construction of fatherhood has evolved substantially, particularly among researchers (Bouchard, 2001; Le Camus, 1997). However, it is still affected by the ethnic and educational status of families, as illustrated in the two opening vignettes (Coley, 2001). Although fathers are still defined as the chief breadwinners in two-parent families, the reality that mothers contribute heavily to the family's economy contradicts this traditional social construction and brings considerable unease to a segment of men. Thus, there has been a shift in the social construction of fatherhood, in great part as a result of women's increased participation in the labour force (Lamb, 1997). The ideal father is now often described as the one who is involved with his children and shares household responsibilities with the mother (Dubeau, 2002). But reality clashes with this cultural shift, as paternal involvement in children's daily lives remains comparatively low (Acock and Demo, 1994).

Furthermore, a dual practice of fatherhood exists: one for intact families and one for what are called absent fathers (Eggebeen and Knoester, 2001). The more remote the *legal* paternity linkage to children, the less involved fathers are. Most are less involved after divorce, even though they may share custody, and are even less involved when the custody is not shared (Seltzer, 1998). When fathers remarry and have other biological children, their first set of children is often displaced or, as Cooksey and Craig (1998) put it, "crowded out." After separation, common-law fathers are far less likely to support their children than are divorced fathers (Mandell, 2002). Finally, men who father children nonmaritally, especially when they have not lived with the mother, are the least involved of all parents.

The male peer group encourages involvement with and support of children when the familial context is a *traditional* one and a fully legal one. Thus, the social practice of fathering, and fathers' self-definitions, which influence their level of involvement with their children and even with their children's mothers, suffer from a double standard: one for traditional paternity within the two-parent family versus one for "new" paternities after divorce, in cohabitation, or in mother-headed families. This double standard is problematic in view of the increase in alternate lifestyles, such as cohabitation and single parenting. "New" paternity includes same-sex male couples: Will these fathers also become more or less delinquent when their unions dissolve?

Generally, mothers maintain a high level of emotional investment with children, even during marital conflict and divorce. In contrast, the role of fathers is less "scripted" (Parke, 1995) and is consequently more influenced by situational variables (Doherty et al., 2000). Thus, **fathers' investment** in children decreases as fathers' relations with mothers deteriorate: Mothers constitute a key context for fathering (Madden-Derdich and Leonard, 2000). A husband who perceives that his wife has confidence in his parenting ability is far more involved in the care of their children (McBride and Rane, 1998). These results clearly show another set of differences between motherhood and fatherhood. The latter depends to a large extent on the relationship with the children's mother (Pasley et al., 2002). In contrast, motherhood exists on its own: A good relationship with the father helps, but does not determine the presence or absence of mothering. Fathering is "a more contextually sensitive process than mothering" (Doherty et al., 1998:207).

This phenomenon is not a North American aberration. Throughout history and across cultural zones, men have favoured the children of their preferred wives or even mistresses. In polygamous societies, men prefer the sons of a favourite wife. This wife is then in a good position to see to it that scarce resources are bestowed upon her children. Her sons receive more affection, attention, and wealth. This was particularly evident when polygamous kings chose a successor.

Much media attention has been devoted to "house husbands," or fathers who stay home and care for their children. However, this occurrence is more one where mothers and fathers have different work shifts and share child care (Casper, 1997). Furthermore, fathers are more likely to take care of their children when their own job schedule allows it (Brayfield, 1995). Casper and O'Connell (1998) also document that, in periods of recession, even though both spouses may still be employed, the spectre of economic insecurity leads couples to economize: Child care by fathers is one form of economy. Nevertheless, when fathers spend time with their children, they provide them with more emotional support. But, if the father is in a "bad mood," more conflicts arise (Almeida et al., 2001). Thus, research is needed on factors that increase both time and quality of father involvement.

THE PRE-BIRTH OR PRE-ADOPTION STAGE

Life during the months preceding the first baby's birth or adoption differs from family to family because there is such a wide variety of situations involved. The following structural arrangements are presented in their order of frequency in the population, first for married couples and then for other types of family structure.

Married Couples

For married couples, I follow the typology derived from the Cowans' (1997) longitudinal study of couples experiencing their first pregnancy. This typology, illustrated in Figure 10.1, consists of the following situations:

- Spouses who have planned the pregnancy and welcome it: Cowan and Cowan (1997) report that 50 percent of their couples were "planners."
- Spouses who are expecting as a result of an unplanned pregnancy, which they accept (acceptance of fate): Also included are ambivalent couples who are uncertain as to whether they want to pursue the pregnancy. For both sets of prospective parents, the pregnancy is an unscheduled or off-time event. One-third of the Cowans' sample fell in this combined category.
- Spouses who experience serious disagreement about the pregnancy: One spouse is enthusiastic or determined to have the baby, while the other accepts it reluc-

tantly in order to save the relationship. Some 17 percent of the Cowans' couples belonged to this category.

I have added the following two situations to the Cowans' typology:

- Married couples—whether heterosexual or homosexual—who are expecting as a result of various fertility methods, including in vitro fertilization and surrogate motherhood, or who are still in the process of negotiating such births. These couples, had they been included in the Cowans' sample, would have fallen under the rubric of "planners" (Chabot and Ames, 2004; Nelson, 1996).
- Married couples who are awaiting the arrival of an adopted child, a stage that may last many months and even years: These couples are also "planners" (Cebello et al., 2004).

Cohabiting Couples

- Cohabiting couples may fall in any one of the Cowans' first three preceding categories of expectant married couples but are less likely to be planners. The union may be more or less stable, and plans for marriage may be under way. Some of these cohabitants have been married before and one may already have at least one child from the previous union.
- Lesbian couples who are expecting via childbirth or adoption
- Gay couples who are expecting via adoption or surrogacy

Single Women

- Single women who become pregnant accidentally: This category is varied because it includes women who subsequently cohabit with or marry the child's father, others who remain with their parents, and yet others who will be on their own. Poverty is a frequent accompaniment to this transition.

FIGURE 10.1

A Typology of Married Couples Expecting Their First Child

Source: Based on Cowan and Cowan, 1997, 1998.

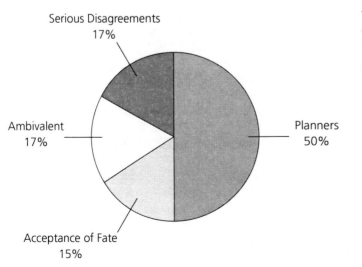

Serious Disagreements
17%

Ambivalent
17%

Acceptance of Fate
15%

Planners
50%

- Single women who have planned a pregnancy in the hope of marrying the father
- Single women, generally over 30 years old, who have planned a pregnancy or an adoption on their own

This simplified classification represents a vast array of family planning activities and adaptations to the forthcoming arrival of a baby. Therefore, the mental health consequences and the readiness to parent vary. Among couples, the conjugal relationship may be weakened or strengthened as a result of the pregnancy (Cowan and Cowan, 1998). The baby then arrives in a family that is prepared or ill-prepared, harmonious or conflictual, well adapted or weakened by stressors. The pre-birth level of readiness, in turn, affects how parents relate to each other and to the baby, as well as to the baby's subsequent development, particularly when the infant is frail (Crockenberg and Leerkes, 2003).

THE INFANT'S ARRIVAL

The infant's arrival, which constitutes the real beginning of a family, similarly differs in terms of impact and adaptation, depending on the marital status, the gender combination, and the number of available parents.

Among Married Heterosexual Couples

Longitudinal studies that have followed couples through the transition to parenthood find that about 50 percent of spouses experience stress and many experience some disenchantment with their marriage (Cowan and Cowan, 1992). In a society where companionship and romantic love are so highly prized, the infant may place a certain strain on these aspects, at least temporarily. During the pregnancy, the couple's sexual relations are less frequent (Call et al., 1995). Similarly, the household division of labour becomes more traditional (Fox, 2001) and couples experience a steep decline in joint activities that lasts throughout early childhood (Kurdek, 1993). The demands of child care, particularly in the middle of the night, exert a physical toll; fatigue may be the norm rather than the exception for several months.

The level of adaptation required of parents in general is underestimated (Demo and Cox, 2000). Obviously, the simple shift from that of being a couple to becoming a family with a tiny infant is not without inherent problems. This transition is smoother for couples who were well adjusted before and for those who had planned the timing of their family. Variables that are particularly conducive to a smooth transition are a husband's expression of fondness for his wife, his attitude of "we-ness," and the private, psychological time the couple retains (Gottman, 1998).

In the Cowans' study (1997:24), "the couples who stayed together but remained childless showed remarkable stability over the 7 years of the study in all five aspects of life that we assessed. By contrast, the couples who became parents described significant and often unexpected or disturbing shifts in every domain." Nevertheless, by the time the children had reached age five, 20 percent of the parenting couples had separated or divorced compared to 50 percent of the couples who had remained childless during the seven years of the study. Either being parents reduces the risk of divorcing (social causation) or couples who decide to have children have a more stable relationship to begin with (social selection). There is evidence supporting both explanations.

New mothers often wish that their husbands participated more in child care than they do (Belsky and Kelly, 1994). In a longitudinal study of couples who were interviewed the first two months after their weddings and then two years later, preferences about the division of child care tasks were evaluated and compared over time. Johnson and Huston (1998) found that, when wives' love was strong, their preferences changed in the direction of their husbands', but husbands' love for their wives did not translate into similarly accommodating changes in preferences. Thus, the traditional social constructions of motherhood and fatherhood are maintained and reinforced throughout the transition to parenting by the emotional work that mothers put in (Fox, 1997). Furthermore, many couples experience a substantial level of disagreement on how to parent, which particularly undermines mothers' sense of well-being (Invest in Kids, 2002).

For most women today, the arrival of the first baby interrupts their employment trajectory. Mothers stay at home after the birth for varying lengths of time. In another longitudinal pre- and after-birth study of couples in the U.S., Volling and Belsky (1993) found that mothers who returned to work within the first three months after birth had higher levels of education, more prestigious occupations, and larger prenatal incomes than mothers who delayed returning to work. They stressed their career development and enjoyment as reasons for resuming work more often than those who were less educated. In Canada, women who have lower salaries tend to return earlier when maternity leaves are available because lower-income women need the financial resources (Mitchell, 2003:16).

In Other Family Structures

The family development literature has largely focused on the two-parent unit, including families who divorce and then remarry. We know very little about the transition to parenthood in other types of family structure, particularly in cohabitational units. Even though much has been written about unmarried teen mothers, little is known of their family development and even less is known about this transition for the fathers. But the majority of women who are single mothers are not teenagers, yet even less is said about their own transition into parenthood.

Young Unmarried Mothers

Many young mothers at first bask under the sun of family attention and love for the baby, peer support or curiosity, as well as the young father's temporary interest. For many, the baby represents someone who will love *them* unconditionally (Carlip, 1995). As well, for many mothers, including single ones, becoming a parent represents a transition away from the manner in which they themselves were mothered. Both Carlip (1995) and Higginson (1998) have found that teen mothers often wanted to be very different from their parents. They wanted to be more permissive and described their own parents as too restrictive. Others, however, felt that their mothers had neglected them or had not paid sufficient attention to them. Either of these themes should herald a great deal of mother-daughter tension among teens who continue living at home and who may be dependent on their families for support (Burton, 1996b).

For many teen mothers, the transition to motherhood is overlaid with the usual transitions that adolescents in this society make as they become more independent from their parents. Teen mothers thus experience a double transition. Based on the literature we reviewed in Chapter 9, it is more likely that many teen mothers had long emancipated themselves from their parents and had done this earlier than comparable girls who led a more normative life course. This premature disaffection from parental rules may actually have been one of the immediate causes of their becoming sexually active and pregnant.

Young single mothers begin life transitions earlier than older mothers and experience more life transitions than mothers in two-parent families. Little is known about how women who mother on their own most of their lives and then become **single grandmothers** experience their personal development, identity, and old age. Their personal transitions may be far more linked to those of their children, grandchildren, and even great-grandchildren than is the case for mothers whose fertility transitions occurred later on in life and even mothers who were young at first birth but spent most of their lives with a husband.

Mature Unmarried Mothers

Births to educated, professional women constitute only 5 percent of all unmarried births (Musick, 2002). But for these women who are well established and have *planned* the pregnancy or the adoption, the arrival of a baby may actually require less adaptation than is the case among couples. To begin with, there is no conjugal relationship that needs readjustment and the household division of labour does not become less egalitarian as generally occurs among couples after the baby's birth. The older single mother may already have adjusted to a larger dwelling, have made contact with potential child caregivers, have assured herself of social support from friends and parents, and may expect far more difficulties than a couple generally does (Miller, 1992). Consequently, the mature single mother may actually find that the difficulties she encounters are less numerous than what she had been warned against. A mature student well illustrates this situation—two years earlier, she had adopted together two infant girls abroad, aged one month and 11 months, respectively:

> "Right now is the happiest stage in my life [around age 35]. Everything is perfect. I have returned to school and I am completing the requirements so that I can apply for a M.A. program. As I mentioned before, I have inherited quite a lot of money from my great aunt and that's what allowed me to fulfill my lifelong dream of having children. I had it all planned and everything is working like a charm even though everyone had warned me that I would have a difficult time, you know, the usual b.s. But I have a wonderful daycare and a nice elderly woman who babysits when I go out, which is rarely. I don't even have to ask anything from my parents, which they were afraid would happen I am sure, so seeing this they now volunteer to help me out.... Sure the girls have cried as is usual but I was ready and I wanted them so much that for me it's simply living in a dream."

The older single mother may experience fewer internal pressures than couples do, although external pressures on family boundaries may be greater. But she may welcome the latter when they result in instrumental help and social support.

Two research questions regarding same-sex-parent families in which a child is born or adopted are, Will they be more or less stable than heterosexual-parent families? and, Will male and female same-sex-parent families be equally stable?

Same-Sex Couples

Same-sex couples have to do far more planning than heterosexual couples, both before and after a child's arrival (Nelson, 1996). They may, for instance, arrange for a cooperative childrearing environment with another homosexual couple of the opposite sex. Overall, little research exists on the adjustment process that takes place among lesbian couples when one of the two has a child or they adopt together. There are potentially both structural advantages and ambiguities in this situation compared to heterosexual families. In terms of advantages, much evidence suggests that the role of the father is often problematic these days. This is a pitfall that lesbian couples avoid, because they can more easily share roles (Koepke et al., 1992).

However, two potential structural ambiguities exist in same-sex-parent families. First, the child is the biological child of only one of the two women (or men), although creative alternatives, such as the insemination of one woman with her partner's brother's semen, alleviate this biological ambiguity (Stacey, 1998). The second structural ambiguity resides in the fact that two persons play the same role toward the child: Both are mothers, regardless of the terminology used in each household. The biological mother may be the "mom" and her companion the "other mother" or called by her first name (Nelson, 1996). The same structural problem arises in the case of gay couples: Both are father figures.

Although a child may prefer his or her father or mother in a heterosexual arrangement, the less favoured parent may not be much affected by this preference, as many explanations based on gender roles are readily available. Fathers who realize that their children are more attached to their mothers, as is generally the case, can easily accept this situation as a normal outcome of the mothers' primary caregiver role (Noller, 1994). But this rationalization may not be available in a same-sex-parent family. Thus, the potential for jealousy exists or, at the very least, the feeling can arise that the child plays too much of a role in the biological mother's life (Nelson, 1996). Research is needed in these domains.

Delayed Parenthood

Not all parents are at the same stage of their own lives when the transition to parenthood occurs. For instance, a woman's average age at the birth of her first child is 27.7 years—28.5 in Ontario and British Columbia (Statistics Canada, 2004i). As well, the proportion of women who have their first child in their thirties has increased spectacularly: Nearly a third of first births in 1997 were to mothers aged 30 and over compared to 19 percent a decade earlier (Milan, 2000). There is also a large difference in educational status: Among women born between 1961 and 1980, the median age at first birth is 30.3 for those with the most education compared to 26.5 for those with the least (Ravanera and Rajulton, 2004).

In the *traditional* life course theories, adults who have their first child before age 30 are considered "on time," whereas those who are older or very young are considered "off time." But the entire life cycle has since shifted upwards in terms of what is considered the young adult stage. This stage now lasts into individuals' early thirties. Even "old age" has shifted to later years as longevity has increased (Sheehy, 1995). Overall, the results are mixed but generally indicate a lower level of parenting stress, greater nurturing, and fewer interparental childrearing conflicts among older than younger first-time parents (Cebello et al., 2004; Garrison et al., 1997). Varied results are also illustrated in the following student quotes:

> "At the time of my birth my mother was 33 and my father 38 years old. Today, people my parents' [current] age have grandchildren and this is one reason why my parents regret marrying late in their lives. My father often complains that he is getting too old to have to worry about supporting us.... My mother does not want me to follow in her footsteps."

> "In 10 years from now? I will probably be thinking of getting married and having children but not before. I want to do like my parents and have children late when there is more time for them and more money. I just don't envy people my age who are getting married. I wouldn't be a good mother, not until I am older, satisfied with my life, more experienced, have seen the world. My parents did all of that and then after gave so much more of themselves to us, they had more time for us two than my friends' parents who were much younger had because they were struggling financially and were often impatient with their lives and their children."

Heath (1995) replicated the positive results of late parenting and added that late-timing fathers are more nurturing and hold higher behavioural expectations for their children than young fathers. Cooney and colleagues (1993) report that late-timing fathers are more positive about their role, more involved with their children, and more satisfied with their marital relationship. By their late thirties and early forties, fathers are better established in their employment, more secure, and may be more able to devote time to their children without experiencing role conflict. Older parents often feel more competent, and their self-esteem is less tied to the vagaries of parenting (Cowan and Cowan, 1992). Greater personal maturity during the transition to parenthood implies a more stabilized sense of self, one that is less easily bruised by "failures" in the exercise of the parenting role. Older parents offer more material and social capital to their children (Lockhead, 2000) as well as a more stable marital union (Martin, 2000).

The study of late-timing parenthood is a neglected field; delayed first births on a large scale is a relatively new phenomenon; thus, some of its consequences are likely to change as society gets used to "older" mothers and fathers and even older grandparents. Furthermore, as illustrated in Figure 10.2, delayed parenthood decreases the number of generations present in a family. One also has to consider that many of the postponed first births may be so for only one of the two spouses when one of them had already been married before. In many of these families, however, the issue of stepparenting presents a confounding variable that makes it difficult to study the impact of the first birth as a life transition and a family development stage.

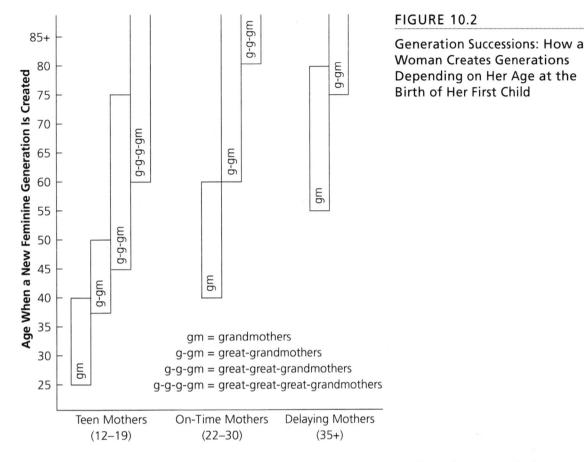

FIGURE 10.2

Generation Successions: How a Woman Creates Generations Depending on Her Age at the Birth of Her First Child

gm = grandmothers
g-gm = great-grandmothers
g-g-gm = great-great-grandmothers
g-g-g-gm = great-great-great-grandmothers

Teen Mothers (12–19)   On-Time Mothers (22–30)   Delaying Mothers (35+)

Age Condensed and Age Gapped Generational Successions

Whether one looks at delayed or youthful generation creation, the life course perspective shows the extent to which the "circumstances experienced by one member of the family impact on the lives of other family members and create change for them" (Martin-Matthews, 2000:335). For instance, when a 16-year-old has a baby, she initiates a generational chain of events in her family if she is her mother's first child to have a baby. She creates a young grandmother, as described in Figure 10.2, and may be creating a young great-grandmother and so on up the generational line (Burton and Bengtson, 1985). In other words, the family is "age condensed": it has multiple generations closely succeeding each other. In the case of an on-time or yet older mother, the opposite occurs and the family has an "age gap" as the generations are less close in age (Milan and Hamm, 2003; Rosenthal, 2000).

For their part, early births accelerate family stages and stack up several generations of *young* people within a same family—young people who have had little time to devote to their own developmental tasks (Burton, 1996a). They also have had little time to accumulate social and material resources that could benefit both the youngest and the oldest generations (see East and Jacobson, 2000). Early fertility that is repeated across generations contributes to an increase in social inequalities between families (Beaujot,

2004). The opposite is more likely to occur when adults become grandparents at an older age. The generations have had more time for education and asset accumulation, and exchanges can benefit the young as well as the frail elderly.

As well, with a young mother, the generational gap between mother and child is blurred: As the child ages, his or her young mother may be more like a peer or a sibling. Unless another adult takes over, this child then lacks the benefit of having a parent who assumes moral authority and who can serve as a guide. A 12-year-old child may have a 27-year-old mother who dates and is obviously sexually active with men who are not the child's father. Under such circumstances, the child may become a peer who is not monitored nor guided, so that the risks of delinquency and the transmission of nonmarital births are high (Levine et al., 2001:369). Such a child has a very different life compared to a child in a two-parent family and compared to a child whose single mother is older, more mature, and authoritative. On the other hand, for some young grandmothers whose teenage daughters largely relinquish their maternal duties to them, it may be the first opportunity that they have to be able to enjoy parenting without the burden of youthful transitions and insecurities that had marred their own early mothering (Harvey, 1993).

SUBSEQUENT STAGES

Subsequent stages of family development include, in a majority of families that remain intact, the arrival of a second child. It may even involve incorporating pets into family life—pets that more or less become the children's companions and present additional responsibilities and joys to parents.

The Early Years

The early years of childrearing, including the school years, consolidate gender differences in how fathers and mothers live their roles. As well, the early years of childrearing temporarily draw men into greater contact with kin without diminishing the size of their overall network (Munch et al., 1997). However, women's social networks decrease substantially, especially around the time the youngest child is age three. This period seems to be very demanding in terms of parenting investment because of the requirements of the child's developmental stage as defined by society. Mothers' social networks generally return to their previous volume when the last child enters school. Therefore, the arrival of children and their young age present a multitude of transitions for mothers, which include not only an increase in workload but also changes in their employment patterns, as well as a reduction in social contacts.

Parents' Transition to a Second Child

In most families today, but less so than in the past, another stage is reached with the arrival of the second child. Many adults choose to have their children in rapid succession so that siblings can form close bonds, and the labour-intensive period of parenting takes place over a shorter period of time. This preference is often motivated by long-term family or conjugal goals and by employment or career considerations. For instance, a mother who has two children in two or three years interrupts her career only once if she chooses to stay home until the children reach kindergarten age. If she depends on her mother for child care, she has to consider the grandmother's age and needs to resume her own life more freely.

The transition required for a second child is probably easier than for the first one. The structure of the family is not affected because the partners have already crossed over the parenthood threshold. Furthermore, the second child presents less of an enigma, as parents already have some experience in caring for an infant and have accumulated social resources such as pediatricians and caregivers. The arrival of a second infant, however, does further intensify the traditional division of labour, particularly when mothers remain at home, at least for a period of time.

The Older Child's Transitions

The transition to a two-child family is one that parents have to help the first-born negotiate (Kramer and Ramsburg, 2002). The latter now has to share his or her parents so that the newborn is not always a welcome addition to the first-born's life (Baydar et al., 1997a,b). Children who are between two and four years of age are particularly affected, because their entire life has been spent as their parents' only child (Dunn, 1994). Older children are more competent cognitively and can understand the situation better. Parents may be able to appeal to their sense of being "grown up," as explained by this student:

> "What I like best to remember when I was 5 is the birth of my little sister. I had wanted a brother to play hockey with but you can't be too choosy. What I liked best was that my parents made me feel so important, so grown up to be the big brother. I just loved to take care of her even though the novelty wore off after a while."

Another milestone in the life of a family is the oldest child's entry into the school system. For each child individually, his or her first school day (generally kindergarten) is of momentous importance. The child's transition also constitutes one for the entire family, particularly for mother and the younger siblings. Students recall this day with a wide range of emotions:

> "This was the worst day of my life. I cried and clung to my mother. I didn't want to go to school. I wanted to stay home with my brother."

> "At age five my best memories are of going to kindergarten. I had wanted this ever since my older sister had gone. I thought she looked so grown up and I couldn't wait to be just like her so that when the day arrived no one had to force me to go. I went marching proudly."

Transition to Child Schooling

Formal schooling is certainly the most potent new context that young children encounter. It transforms their developmental path and affects the parent-child relationship. Children's social and cultural worlds expand and become more diversified. Thus, the fabric that constitutes the parent-child relationship is woven with threads of more varied colours and texture than was the case in early childhood. Several changes take place in the family's routine.

Today, children often attend preschool or a daycare centre before kindergarten, so the transition to school may be less momentous both for parents and children than in the recent past. However, for mothers who resume work when their last child enters school, this may be the most important stage for the young family since the first child's birth. With the resumption of maternal employment, the family routine is substantially altered for mother and children. It may well be at this stage that the couple renegotiates its daily practices concerning the division of labour on matters such as child care, housework, grocery shopping, and cooking. Research indicates, however, that even when negotiations do take place, they do not substantially alter the father's routine (Doherty et al., 1998).

Pets as New Family Members

One half of Canadian families have a pet—most often dogs or cats—which are usually introduced into the family as companions to young children or even adolescents (Bibby and Posterski, 2000). Pets fulfill several functions for children. In fact, an only child who has a pet spends more time with it than a child who has both a sibling and a pet (Melson and Fogel, 1996). These same researchers even found that interest in pets was often a substitute for interest in babies in general, particularly among boys. Children establish a parallel between babies and pets: Both have to be taken care of and are somewhat entertaining. But babies become less interesting when a pet is available! Pets can serve as agents of socialization to teach nurturance (Davis and Juhasz, 1995). An animal requires care and grooming, and is, in many ways, at the mercy of its owner for survival, somewhat as a small child is. Thus, children can learn to put their pets' needs after their own wants, which is a form of altruism. Unfortunately, violence against animal companions is frequent; it is often accompanied by other forms of family problems, such as conflict and abuse (Flynn, 2000).

Students often noted that being given a pet when they were small had been interpreted as a very special token of their parents' love; this gift was on a higher level than receiving even a large toy. The following quote from a student describes her delight upon receiving a pet and the opportunity to network afforded by the kitten's arrival:

> *"Dad said to go to my room. I did. When I got there, I found my mother sitting on my bed with the cutest, sweetest, softest little white kitten that one could ever see. I named her Fluffy (how original!) and I knew I'd love her for life. It felt great to care for something so helpless and gentle. I could feel the kitten respond to me and that felt so nice. I kept repeating 'She loves me!' I phoned all my little friends to tell them I just had a baby."*

Some students recounted how they used their pets to apologize to their parents after having been disobedient. They would carry the pet to the mother or father, and when the parent picked up the cat or dog or patted it affectionately, the child took this as a sign of having been forgiven and that all was well again. A student recalled taking her cat with her in her mother's bed. The sharing of the fluffy creature was a symbol of love and security. Molnar (1996) describes how each year the assorted Freud family dogs presented birthday poems to Sigmund Freud. These poems had been written by his daughter, the future child psychoanalyst, Anna Freud. They were a means of communicating feelings that might not have been otherwise acceptable in that family.

Research indicates that pets have a positive effect on adults' well-being. Although children are generally attached to their furry friends, there is little research on pets' effects on children's well-being by gender, age, and family structure.

Thus, pets can become symbols of affection between children and parents or even between parents, as when a child asks quarrelling parents to take turns patting the dog. The child seeks reassurance that the parents still love each other while at the same time trying to pacify them.

The Adolescent Years

Pasley and Gecas (1984) found that around 62 percent of the mothers and fathers in their study perceived adolescence as the most difficult and stressful stage of parenting. Gecas and Seff (1990:943) conclude that for "the parents of adolescents, therefore, adolescence may indeed be a time of storm and stress, at least in modern times." This study finds resonance in students' autobiographies: Approximately one-third recalled experiencing a psychologically and socially painful adolescence. Another third described this period as a happy one both for themselves and their parents; the remaining third recalled an adolescence that included happy as well as unhappy periods. A majority of the adolescents' sources of unhappiness were located at the peer-group level. This was followed by school problems, and further down in the hierarchy of stressors were family problems. Interpersonal difficulties experienced with parents tended to have resulted from the adolescents' state of mind and particularly from peer-driven stressors (Ambert, 1994a):

> "My behaviour toward my parents during this period [ages 11–14] was that of resentment.... I blamed my parents for making me ugly.... I still blamed them for what was happening in my life. In this way, I had a negative impact on my parents. They had to deal with a child who was impossible."

The adolescent years may require as much adaptation in terms of family dynamics as has so far occurred during the entire life span of the family. But the extent of this adaptation depends on the quality of the parent-child relationship during preadolescence as well as on the various temperaments and frailties involved. It also depends on the experience that parents have gained with a first adolescent (Whiteman et al., 2003). As well, familial adaptation to adolescence is contingent on the family's economic situation and race, because these two factors situate the family in neighbourhoods, schools, and peer groups, all of which influence the course of adolescent development. The adolescent years are discussed at greater length in Chapter 12.

The Young Adult Years

In centuries past, the nest was never empty as women continued childbearing to the end of their reproductive years. When parents lived into old age, a substantial proportion remained in their home with one adult child or moved in with a married one.

For instance, in 1900, 59 percent of the elderly resided with a grown child, compared to 14 percent in 1990 (Schoeni, 1998). The reasons elderly parents live with a grown child today differ from those in 1900. In those days, an adult male child lived with an elderly parent because the farm property had passed to him and the mother remained in what was her own home (Demos, 1974). In other cases, a child stayed with or took in elderly parents to care for them. In contrast, today it is as likely that a parent takes in an adult child because of that child's dependency as because of the older person's own needs (Hareven, 1994a).

As indicated in Table 10.1, young adults stay home longer than was the case just 20 years ago and provincial differences are apparent. There are also large differences between various metropolitan areas in terms of the proportion of young adults who are still living at home, although no one single explanation can account for these differences:

St. John's	46.5%	Halifax	30.7%
Montreal	30.7	Toronto	54
Winnipeg	38	Regina	32.6
Edmonton	34	Vancouver	45.7

For Canada as a whole, the number of young adults at home has jumped from 27.5 percent in 1981 to 41.1 percent in 2001 (Statistics Canada, 2002a). This change is even more obvious among the 25–29 age bracket, an age by which youths have nearly all

TABLE 10.1 | Proportion of Young Adults Aged 20 to 29 Living with Their Parent(s) for Provinces and Territories

	1981	2001
Canada	27.5%	41.1%
Newfoundland and Labrador	35.9	50.9
Prince Edward Island	33.5	42.1
Nova Scotia	30.8	38.0
New Brunswick	31.3	38.5
Quebec	31.9	39.2
Ontario	29.8	47.1
Manitoba	24.4	36.1
Saskatchewan	18.9	29.8
Alberta	15.6	30.6
British Columbia	21.8	40.2
Yukon	12.9	30.9
Northwest Territories	22.1	30.8
Nunavut	n/a	32.2

Source: Statistics Canada. *The Daily,* October 22, 2002e.

completed their education. In 1981, only 11.8 percent were still at home, compared to twice as many in 2001, or 23.7 percent (Beaupré et al., 2002). The reasons for this lengthened parent-child coresidence are detailed in Chapter 5 and differ somewhat by ethnicity (Gee et al., 2003): They largely centre around economic change and requirements as well as a consequent delay of age at marriage. This historic context, in turn, postpones parents' transition to the empty nest. It also delays grandparenting. Young adults whose parents are still together, as well as those with an employed mother, leave home later because their parents are better able to help them through higher education (Ravanera et al., 2003).

A second change that has occurred in recent decades is that the family may go through **transition reversals**: Approximately one-third of young Canadians aged 20–29 have returned home at least once after an initial departure (Mitchell, 2004). This return may occur because of unemployment and other financial problems, or because a relationship has ended (Mitchell and Gee, 1996). This has been referred to as the *revolving-door family* and the "boomerang" children. These situations—one of a delayed or postponed transition, and the other of a reversal transition—affect not only the development of family stages but also the quality of life of parents and children. There is agreement in the research that these situations are beneficial to the children first, although most parents report a reasonable level of satisfaction with the presence of their adult offspring at home (Veevers and Mitchell, 1998). Parents, however, are more likely to feel stressed when the young adults are financially dependent and are lagging in the completion of adult roles (Mitchell, 1998). As well, coresident children contribute little in terms of housework (Mitchell, 2004).

Thus, for many adults, active parenting has become a lifelong occupation. Social and cultural changes put their adult children and their grandchildren at the mercy of difficult circumstances such as unemployment, drug addiction, divorce, single parenthood, criminality—not to omit lack of social support for the mentally ill and the disabled. This situation represents yet another refutation of the pessimistic point of view of the family's loss of functions. Rather, active parenting is maintained well beyond what used to occur and is even reactivated, often repeatedly after all the children have left home for the first time. As Mitchell (2004:121) points out, mothers have become the new "unpaid social workers" as the welfare state continues to retrench.

THE GRANDPARENT STAGE

In the 19th century, adults who became grandparents for the first time were often still busy raising their younger children. Today, grandparenting tends to be a separate family developmental stage for over half of adults. As age at marriage is delayed, age at first grandparenting will also go up in the forthcoming decades. In 1995, women were becoming grandmothers on average at age 53.6 and men were becoming grandfathers at age 56.8—about 8 years later than in the U.S. This cross-cultural difference stems in part from the different racial composition of Canada, with fewer blacks and Latinos who tend to become grandparents at younger ages (Kemp, 2003). In Canada, 79 percent of all adults aged 65 and over are grandparents and the average grandparent has 4.7 grandchildren (Statistics Canada, 2003i). This has led to more generations present in families but with fewer members in each generation. This phenomenon is called the "bean pole" family because its structure is long and thin (Bengtson, 2001; McPherson, 1998).

The role of grandparents is not rigidly scripted; it is dynamic and fluid (Rosenthal and Gladstone, 2000). Overall, it has been qualified as a stabilizing force and as a source of family continuity. Grandmothers enjoy their role more than grandfathers and are also more involved. They have been described as **kin-keepers** and as persons who open the kin system so as to support members in difficulty (Dilworth-Anderson, 1992). The role that grandparents play differs according to their age, health, and ethnic group, as well as the age, gender, and location of their grandchildren. That role may differ for each grandchild; thus, as Mueller and Elder (2003:413) point out, the grandparent-grandchild relationship should be studied within the context of the entire network of family ties.

King and Elder (1995) indicate that the quality of the relationship between grandparent and adult child significantly impacts on the grandparent-grandchild relationship. Adult children who do not feel close to their parents or who perceive them to be meddlesome are less likely to encourage their children to visit them and to form close bonds with them (Rossi and Rossi, 1990). Similarly, it is possible that when children feel that their parents are not well treated by their grandparents, they may be reluctant to form close bonds, and may not trust the older generation as much (Hodgson, 1992). For instance, Whitbeck et al. (1993) found that the relationship between adolescents and their grandparents was described by the youths as less close when their parents recalled that their own parents had been emotionally distant toward them during their own adolescence. These and other results indicate that parents act as mediators in the grandparent-grandchild relationship. One area of research that should soon be addressed is the family relationships of grandparents who are gay or lesbian (Connidis, 2003b).

Grandparents Who Provide Child Care

For many women who become grandmothers, this transition constitutes an **extension** of their **maternal role.** Slightly over 40 percent of U.S. grandmothers provide care for at least one grandchild on a regular basis (Baydar and Brooks-Gunn, 1998). Grandmothers often babysit while their daughters are at work, whether they live with them or nearby. African-American grandmothers fill this role even more than their white counterparts, particularly when their daughters are single (Hogan et al., 1990).

We do not know whether more or fewer grandmothers are babysitting than was the case in the past. In the past, fewer young mothers were in the labour force and the necessity for regular child care was less urgent. On the other hand, more grandmothers are now employed themselves, thus precluding extensive babysitting. Some even care simultaneously for their older mothers. Grandmothers who have several children and grandchildren have more opportunities to become caregivers. This opportunity increases when a teenage daughter who lives with them has a baby. But in Canada, only three percent of grandparents live in a three-generation household (Kemp, 2003).

Grandparents Who Raise Grandchildren

In 1995 in the U.S., nearly six percent of all black children and two percent of white children were in the custody of grandparents (Pebley and Rudkin, 1999). In a national survey, 11 percent of grandparents reported that they had raised a grandchild for at

More young grandmothers are employed than in the past. Therefore, it is necessary for research to address the issue of change in their roles, particularly as babysitters, in families where two generations of women who are mothers are now employed simultaneously.

least six months in their lifetime (Pearson et al., 1997). In some states, and particularly among African Americans, over a quarter of children in foster care are living with grandparents, generally a grandmother (Bonecutter and Gleeson, 1997). In Canada, the numbers are more modest, in part because there are proportionally fewer never-married and divorced mothers, and drug addiction is not as prevalent. In 2001, only 0.4 percent of all Canadian children were in the care of their grandparents, for a total of 25,200 children between the ages of 0 and 14 (Milan and Hamm, 2003). The highest proportion is in Nunavut, or 2.3 percent of all the children.

Jendrek (1993) reports that, in 73 percent of their sample, grandchildren live with their grandparents because the child's mother suffers from emotional problems. Maternal drug problems are also involved in half of the cases, and alcoholism in 44 percent of the cases (Burton, 1992). In half of the cases, mothers suffer from a multiplicity of problems—not to omit the fact that fathers are absent. Obviously, such grandparents are taking charge of children who have lived in deteriorating family circumstances, a situation well described in this student's autobiography:

> *"I was raised by my grandparents who took me and my little brother in after my mother flipped after my father left her. We had had a hard life and all I remember about it is that my parents were scary [they were alcoholic]. Anyways we were better off with my grandparents and we knew them because they had often kept us over weekends.... Now that we're older it's harder on them in a way because my brother grew up with lots of problems but at least I turned out just fine and this just makes up for it.... I love them like my own parents and we owe them everything and I am planning on making a lot of money to take care of them because they are getting on in years."*

In Canada, grandparents who single-handedly assume the financial responsibility of their grandchildren tend to be younger, healthier, and more educated than grandparents who live with their adult children and grandchildren (Milan and Hamm, 2003). In contrast, in the U.S., those who raise one or more grandchildren tend to be poorer than the average for their age group, more often unemployed, and less educated (Solomon and Marx, 1995). In Strawbridge and colleagues' (1997) longitudinal study, many of these grandparents had experienced negative life events in their own past, such as problems with marriages, finances, and health. The life course of many of these caregiving grandparents had differed from that of other grandparents for several decades, probably as a result of poverty. This is an example of how the consequences of poverty carry through the generations—from the grandparents to their children and their grandchildren, and back to the grandparents again.

Solomon and Marx (1995) used the large National Health Interview Survey that included 448 American households headed by grandparents to see how this type of family structure affected children's school and health outcomes. Children raised by grandparents were compared to children living with both biological parents and to children in single-parent families. In terms of behaviour at school as well as indicators of school achievement, children in two-parent families had an advantage over the other two groups. However, children raised by grandparents were doing better than those raised in single-parent families, despite the generally low educational level of these grandparents. In terms of health, there were few differences between children in two-parent and grandparent families, but children in single-parent families were less healthy. Grandparents who raised girls had an easier time than those who raised boys.

In a nutshell, these results indicate that children raised by grandparents do quite well, considering the fact that many were often neglected or mistreated by their parents before. Thus, while being raised by a grandparent is a reasonable alternative for children, it is a more problematic one for the grandparents (Burnette, 1999); this is especially so when they are middle-aged and are encountering high demands from several generations as well as employment (Sands and Goldberg-Glen, 2000). Jendrek (1993) has studied the impact that this caregiving role has on grandparents' lifestyles, especially the changes that grandparents have to bring to their own lives, the dreams they have to postpone or abandon altogether, and the physical and emotional demands that such a role places on them. They often have a multiplicity of roles to fulfill in addition to childrearing. Overall, foster grandparents find themselves out of synchrony with the normal developmental stage of family life: People of their age do not raise children. This anomaly deprives them of moral as well as instrumental support at their grandchildren's schools and in the neighbourhood (Pruchno, 1999). Hence, it is not surprising that support groups now exist for foster grandparents; these groups constitute an indicator of changing times (Beltran, 2001).

Grandparenting after Divorce

Maternal grandparents often help their divorcing daughters both emotionally and instrumentally, especially in terms of child care. But many other grandparents lose touch with grandchildren after a divorce, either because the custodial parent moves too far away or is not cooperative, or because their son, who is the visiting parent, more or less relinquishes his responsibilities. This is yet another example of how adult children's marital or parental transitions create related transitions in the older generation: In the latter instance, grandparents lose their grandchildren (Ganong and Coleman, 1999).

In theory, in-laws, who are one's children's grandparents, should be a prime source of help. However, in my study, less than 20 percent of custodial parents actually talked to their former in-laws in a week's time, had visited them in a month's time, or had received some help from them (Ambert, 1989). Grandparents' visitation rights were opposed by over 90 percent of the divorced respondents, including those who had excellent relationships with their own parents and their former affines (in-laws):

> *"Then what? I would have to juggle visitations with their father, their grandparents on his side, and why not my own parents? That's ridiculous. I couldn't survive so much stress, my life would be a nightmare and we would all end up hating*

each other. Whose welfare do they have in mind anyway? Theirs; not mine, not my children's." (Remarried custodial mother, age 38, with two children)

Custodial parents often pointed out that their former in-laws had stopped seeing them or saw their grandchildren only when the latter were visiting with the noncustodial parent. Some 60 percent of respondents talked of former in-laws who were hostile toward them, or potentially hostile; 35 percent of the respondents felt that their former in-laws projected their negative attitude, either verbally or behaviourally, *to their grandchildren.* The most prominent difficulties were situations in which the ex-in-laws openly accused the custodial parent of having caused the failure of the marriage (48 percent). The second difficulty most frequently mentioned was ex-in-laws' comments concerning custodial parents' fitness as parents (46 percent).

> These accusations, gossips, and remarks ranged from stating that the parent was "unfit," was a "bad mother" or father, did not spend enough time with the children, left them alone too much, and was unfair or cruel to the father (or mother). These accusations were often extended into other areas of life, such as "poor money manager," "sexually loose," or "unable to hold down a job." Or grandparents would ask their grandchildren: "Does she go out? Whom with?" "Is she home when you come home from school?" "Does she drink?" One 14-year-old girl shouted at her mother, "Grandma says you sleep with anyone so I don't see why you can tell me that I can't go out tonight!"

Even when words were not spoken, grandparents' refusal to talk to or see the other parent was a behavioural indicator that did not go unnoticed by the children. It has been suggested that, where relevant, grandparents should visit their grandchildren at both their homes. Such visits would contribute to legitimize the two-home nuclear family. Grandchildren would retain a psychologically intact family and would not feel torn between the two sides of their kinship group. It is regrettable that not enough research has been carried out on grandparenting after an adult child's divorce (Henderson and Moran, 2001).

Another gap in the research exists in terms of grandparents who have themselves divorced. There are indications that divorced or remarried grandparents have a lower frequency of contact with their children (Uhlenberg and Hammill, 1998). They, and especially grandfathers, are less involved with their grandchildren than nondivorced ones but, in part, a good relationship between parents and grandparents compensates for the negative effect of grandparental divorce (King, 2003a). In other words, these studies confirm the long-term consequences of divorce on family life later on and across generations (Pezzin and Schone, 1999).

Step-Grandparenting

Step-grandparenting is a role that is even less culturally delineated than that of regular grandparenting, although many Canadian families include a step-grandparent. The few existing studies on this topic indicate that a child's young age upon entering a stepfamily facilitates the establishment of a true grandparenting situation and attachment (Ganong and Coleman, 1994). This relationship may become particularly useful and close if the child has more or less lost contact with one set of grandparents, generally on the father's side. A functional substitution can then take place.

However, when stepchildren do not accept their parent's remarriage, they may not wish to participate in family activities that include the stepparent's kin. It is particularly easy for a child to avoid contact with step-grandparents when it is the nonresidential parent, generally the father, who remarries. The child usually spends little time with his or her father, even less with the stepmother, and none with her kin (Henry et al., 1993). In my research, stepmothers often went to see their own parents when their husband's children were visiting. In part, there was the desire to allow these children to receive as much attention as possible from their father without interference from the stepmother and her own children. In some cases, women knew that stepchildren and their mother resented them and they preferred to distance themselves from the situation. Thus, in many instances of nonresidential fathers' remarriage, the stepmother and her kin effectively remain in the background. Her parents are grandparents in name only, and the termination of her marriage to him affects them very little as step-grandparents (Ganong and Coleman, 1999).

On the other side of the coin, it may be far easier for children and adolescents to accept a step-grandparent when they rebel against having a stepparent at home. This is a less threatening and far more benign relationship. When the remarried custodial parent visits with the new in-laws and brings the children along, the latter may indirectly acquire a sense of normalization of family relationships. In this respect, step-grandparents may contribute to the integration of the reconstituted family and fulfill the same functions as actual grandparents (Connidis, 2001:199).

THE DEATH OF ADULTS' PARENTS

At least 50 percent of adults become great-grandparents and a few others see the birth of a fifth generation (Johnson and Barer, 1997). As they age, parents are transformed into patriarchs and matriarchs. When their health falters, their role vis-à-vis their children may change, as seen in Chapter 12. A transitory period often occurs during which the elderly parent, generally the mother, resides in a retirement home. At that stage, the older person may renegotiate her sense of self in terms of what it means to be old and healthy (Hurd, 1999), as one adult describes it:

> "My mother is 90 and she is totally dependent for her care as she cannot stand up or walk, has Parkinson's in her hands, is in a wheelchair. But she thinks of herself as healthy because she has no illness, no cancer or heart problem, even though she is on medications. She is happy and accepts her dependency with good grace and considers herself lucky. Ten years ago, she would have felt very sorry for a person in her situation."

After seniors die, the mantle is passed on to their adult children who, if they themselves are grandparents, form a new branch of the family, each with the generations that descend from them. The very large family reunions that used to take place around the now deceased generation become smaller gatherings as the grandparent couples or singles head their own extended families separately from those of their siblings. The families become smaller because the birth rate has declined. The average 70-year-old grandparent today has 3 to 10 fewer grandchildren than his or her own parents' cohort had. The family tree becomes leaner.

Even though middle-aged and young senior adults fully expect their parents' death, this is an event that represents a transition both in their own individual lives and in the life course of the entire family system (Rossi and Rossi, 1990). Compared to the past, children and parents have a longer relationship because of a general increase in life expectancy (Connidis, 2001). This means that both generations go through family transitions together or witness each other's transitions more often than in the early 1940s, for instance. A century ago, many parents did not even live long enough to see all their children marry (Martel and Bélanger, 2000). Most now do and even watch their children become parents; an increasing proportion see them become grandparents (Silverstein and Long, 1998). Thus, the relationship is not only longer but it also involves more shared life transitions than in the past.

The end result is that adults, particularly females, have a more extended period of time during which to identify with their parents and delay the rupture of the knot by death than in the past. The death of the elderly parents is equally momentous among all ethnic groups, but is expressed differently by men and women (Umberson, 2003). However, this death was probably a more significant passage in previous centuries when people's life expectancy was much shorter: The first generation left young adults and even dependent children orphaned, and the remaining spouses often quickly remarried, especially fathers.

CONCLUSIONS: FAMILY DEVELOPMENT IN CONTEXT

The family development perspective focuses on the intersection of the life course of the family with that of parents and children (Elder, 1998). Two families may experience exactly the same stage—that of the birth of a first grandchild—yet the transition carries different meanings and consequences for each family. In one family, for instance, the new grandparents are 45 years old and are employed. They may still have a child at home. In another family, the new grandparents are 60, beginning their retirement, have only one child, who is the infant's mother, and they are both keeping an eye out for an older mother who lives alone. The life course of these two families intersects with two very different personal stages in the life course of its adult members.

A second aspect of the developmental perspective is that the socioeconomic context of families largely dictates the timing and multiplicity of the transitions they experience. As we have seen, a proportion of the disadvantaged actually experience accelerated generational transitions, beginning with early motherhood that may repeat itself across three generations. Family development in Canada is therefore contingent on socioeconomic status. Not only is there an increasing economic gap between the rich and the poor, but this gap creates a divergent pattern of family development between the disadvantaged and the rest of the population. Family development is also contingent upon ethnicity and especially immigration status, and many new Canadians' family stages are more similar to those of several decades ago in Canada than those of the postmodern family that is the main topic of textbooks.

Finally, the historical context or the decades in which a family is formed and experiences its transitions also sets limits or widens opportunities both on the timing of the stages and on their consequences. For instance, after the 1970s, women's greater educational opportunities and widespread employment contributed to adults' delayed passage into parenthood as well as a later timing of grandparenthood. At the same time, a longer life expectancy means that a family can now accumulate more generations and transitions in its developmental trajectory, unless a late passage into parenthood among families where a university education is the norm cancels out the results of the longer life expectancy.

Summary

1. A family's life course is influenced by its social context. It is interwoven with parents' age, stage in their relationship, and work history. Familial sequences are now more varied and less linear than in the past.

2. The social construction of motherhood and fatherhood greatly influences how family developments are experienced by men and women. Mothers are believed to have natural abilities to nurture children, who are socially constructed as needing their mothers on an intensive basis. Fathers have been defined mainly as breadwinners, although paternal involvement with children is a positive element in their development. Furthermore, there is a dual practice of fatherhood: Fathers in families other than intact and legally married are less invested in their children. Even married fathers are less involved when the conjugal relationship is difficult.

3. The stages of family development begin during pregnancy. This situation is experienced differentially, depending on the family structure involved (i.e., number, sex, and marital status of parents). About half of couples experience stress and some marital disenchantment after the birth of a first child. This transition is smoother for couples who were well adjusted before and for those who had planned the birth. In other types of family structure, young, unmarried mothers generally experience more family transitions than married ones. Older, single mothers who plan the birth or who adopt may face far fewer disruptions than generally believed. More research is needed for same-sex-parent families.

4. Delayed parenthood is becoming more common. Overall, the results are mixed but generally indicate a lower level of parenting stress, fewer interpersonal conflicts, and greater father investment.

5. A birth to an adolescent parent often leads to age-condensed generations whereby the young mother effectively creates premature grandmothers and great-grandmothers. Such families have rapidly succeeding generations that have had little time to accumulate social and material resources that could benefit both the youngest and the oldest generations.

6. The transition to a two-child family is less spectacular than the first transition into parenthood. However, it is a key transition in the life of the older child. The early years of childrearing consolidate gender differences in how fathers and mothers live their roles. Children's passage into the school system has traditionally been an important family transition that may be mitigated now by early daycare and nursery experience. Another passage occurs when families acquire pets for their children. Pets fulfill functions of socialization and interaction. The adolescent years are generally perceived by a majority of parents as the most difficult stage of parenting.

7. Young adults now stay home longer than was the case in the 1970s; thus, parents are older at the transition to what used to be called the

empty nest stage. Furthermore, the family often undergoes transition reversals as adult children return home following unemployment or divorce. The parenting role and family functions are extended over the family's life span.

8. The grandparenting role is not as culturally scripted as is the parental one. Grandmothers are more involved as kin-keepers and a substantial number provide some form of care for at least one grandchild on a regular basis. In addition, some grandparents raise a grandchild for at least six months in their lifetime. A proportion of custodial grandparents experience a great deal of stressors because, more often than not, they have already been through poverty, divorce, and single parenthood in earlier family stages. Children raised by grandparents do better than children raised in a single-parent family, but less well than those with two parents.

9. Grandparenting after an adult child's divorce may again involve a further extension of familial duties, or, if a son rarely sees his children, grandparents may lose contact with the grandchildren. Grandparenting visitation rights carry both advantages as well as difficulties, the latter particularly for custodial parents. Step-grandparenting is the least culturally scripted role. It is a situation that can be beneficial to children, especially those who have lost touch with their original grandparents.

10. Compared to the past, children and parents have a longer relationship because of a general increase in life expectancy. Furthermore, they share more transitions together as several generations often succeed each other within a person's life span.

11. The age at which transitions occur reflects different meanings and brings different experiences. The socioeconomic context of families largely dictates the timing and the multiplicity of their transitions. Finally, the historical context in which a family is formed and develops sets limits or widens opportunities both in the timing of the stages and on their consequences.

Key Concepts and Themes

Delayed parenthood, pp. 280–281
Ethnocentric phenomenon, p. 274
Extension of maternal role, p. 290
Father's investment, p. 275
Generational gap, pp. 283–284
Grandparenting role, p. 290
Intensive mothering, p. 274
Kin-keepers, p. 290
Life course, p. 272

Multiple parenting, p. 274
"Off time," pp. 276, 282
Older mothers, p. 280
"On time," p. 282
Single grandmothers, p. 280
Social construction of fatherhood, pp. 275–276
Social construction of motherhood, pp. 273–274
Step-grandparenting, pp. 293–294
Transition reversals, p. 289

Analytical Questions

1. What are some cross-cultural findings that cast doubt on the universality of motherhood as understood in North America?

2. Discuss paternal investment contextually.

3. Analyze family stages from a developmental and historical perspective.

4. Can you give one theoretical link between parts of this chapter and parts of Chapter 9?

5. Chapter 10 is more dynamic than Chapters 8 and 9 (which are more "static"). What does this mean?

Suggested Readings

Aldous, J. 1996. *Family careers: Rethinking the developmental perspective.* Thousand Oaks, CA: Sage. The author utilizes the developmental perspective within a very broad range of family situations and contexts.

Chappell, N., et al. 2003. *Aging in contemporary Canada.* Toronto: Prentice Hall. This textbook provides an overview of all aspects of individuals' senior years, including substantial sections pertaining to their families.

Connidis, I. A. 2001. *Family ties and aging.* Thousand Oaks, CA: Sage. This book by a Canadian scholar presents the only comprehensive review and discussion of the literature with a focus on family ties as they evolve during the last decades of individuals' lives.

Hays, S. 1996. *The cultural contradictions of motherhood.* New Haven, CT: Yale University Press. This book offers a critical feminist analysis, reviews of the literature, as well as qualitative sociological data on motherhood. The substantive focus is on intensive mothering.

LaRossa, R. 1997. *The modernization of fatherhood: A social and political history.* Chicago: The University of Chicago Press. This book combines a history of fatherhood, motherhood, and childhood. It presents unusual information on the history of the social construction of fatherhood, particularly in the 20th century.

Rosenthal, C. G., and Gladstone, J. 2000. *Grandparenthood in Canada.* Ottawa: The Vanier Institute of the Family (www.vifamily.ca). This article, part of the collection on Contemporary Family Trends, presents a thorough review of the literature on grandparenting.

Rossi, A. S., and Rossi, P. H. 1990. *Of human bonding: Parent-child relations across the life course.* New York: Aldine de Gruyter. This research on three generations in a family includes recollections of relationships with one's parents as well as current data. The research allows for the study of family transitions in the life cycle of individuals belonging to different cohorts.

The July 2001 issue of the *Journal of Family Issues* contains several articles on grandparents who raise grandchildren.

Suggested Weblinks

Canadian Association of Retired Persons. The website offers practical information on the later stages of family development, including grandparents who raise grandchildren as well as the care of elderly parents by their adult children. Regional resources are indicated.

www.50plus.com

Familles en mouvance. Dynamiques intergénérationnelles is a Quebec website that contains research results as well as reports from various agencies concerning family life, family policy, and aging.

http://partenariat-familles.inrs-ucs.uquebec.ca

Population Studies Centre is a University of Western Ontario website which provides research and position papers on demography, many of which are relevant to families' development.

www.ssc.uwo.ca/sociology/popstudies

PART 4

Couple and Family Relationships

Family relationships are examined within a largely interactional-transactional perspective that includes strong elements of gender-role analysis as well as some aspects of behaviour genetics. In other words, although the emphasis is on interactions, it is again obvious that families, in their intimate relationships, are impacted by their genetic inheritance and environment. The latter includes the society's gender stratification.

Chapter 11 examines the diversity and dynamics of marital and partner relationships. This chapter includes a focus on the division of domestic labour along gender lines.

Chapter 12 focuses on the parent-child relationship and child socialization across the life span. It also investigates the role that parents and children play in each other's lives when parents are older and at times more frail.

Chapter 13 looks at sibling relationships and situations in a variety of familial contexts. This topic also allows us to study how differences and similarities between siblings arise, affording us a more in-depth understanding of the complementary roles of genes and the environment.

CHAPTER 11

Spousal and Partner Relationships

"Right now, I'd rate myself as somewhat unhappy despite the fact that I just got married, which is what I wanted to do most in my life. It's just that marriage is so different than dating and becoming engaged. We used to do things together, special things, and had all the time in the world to talk. Now we're married and it's just like things are all settled for my husband; he has to work. I work, and I am finishing school and there's no time for the nice things in a relationship. Last year we were equally busy but he could find the time. I know that I may be too romantic and that I have to get used to this, but it is so disappointing."

"The past two years have certainly been the happiest of my life and mainly because I got married and even though I felt I was too young at the time it's the best decision I ever made. It's just the little things that make me happy like when I come home and he has the supper ready for me because he knows I have had a hard day and he knows that I am not used to cooking on a regular basis. What I like best probably is that we have so much to talk about, and we still talk about loving each other after two years but now we're also seriously planning the future as in having children. I can tell him that I am afraid to be cooped up in the house with two kids and no one to talk to and he takes it seriously and he says we'll have to find a way to keep me working and him doing a lot of fathering."

These two women students are at the beginning of their marriages and are of the same age—around 24 years old. Yet, their experience, level of happiness, and the extent to which their conjugal expectations are met are entirely different. Their autobiographies also indicate that they are fairly similar on many personal aspects, such as personality and values. They have, however, married young men with radically different conceptions of conjugal life. As a social category, men are more powerful agents of the construction of reality than women (Ferree and Hall, 1996). This macrosociological advantage, as we see in this chapter, carries into intimate relationships.

Throughout the last half of the 20th century, the relationship between spouses has become far more diverse than it used to be. To begin with, the explosion of divorce on the familial scene has meant that marital stability can no longer be taken for granted. Couples now enter marriage with a less secure feeling of permanency than was the case in the past, when only death could separate them. Second, the massive entry of women on the labour market has resulted in more complex feminine expectations and often more complex forms of masculine cooperation or resistance in terms of the household division of labour. Couples now have to negotiate who does what at various stages of family development, and this situation can result in a tense relationship. Third, couples' expectations of marriage concerning love, sexuality, and companionship have heightened. More is demanded of marriage in terms of relationship than in the past, while, at the same time, couples may be less patient when their expectations are not met (Amato and Booth, 1997). The cultural focus of marriage as an institution has shifted to an individualistic axis emphasizing needs and gratification.

The relationship between spouses has also become more diverse for the simple reason that it now includes more categories of couples. Today, the term spouse or partner has been extended to all couples involved in living-together relationships, whether cohabitants, same-sex couples, or remarried couples. Despite this diversity, marriage is still the predominant demographic basis of family formation. Even though couples are now delaying marriage, a majority of Canadians are still expected to marry at least once. This demographic reality, combined with the fact that comparatively more research exists on the marital relationship than on any other form of partner relationship, means that a majority of the pages of this chapter are devoted to heterosexual marriage.

TYPES OF MARRIAGES AND HOW THEY CHANGE

I wanted to begin this chapter with an overall classification of marital relationships, but I could not find recent in-depth studies of marriage types. Rather, I noted two trends in the research on marriage and married life. First, usually sociologists do not themselves interview or even observe couples but have recourse to large-scale surveys designed by other researchers. (This is called "secondary analysis" on p. 24.) Second, these surveys, dominated by multiple-choice questions, do not provide sufficiently detailed, dynamic, and complete descriptions, and generally focus on only one of the two spouses. The result, as pointed out by Huston (2000), is that research on marriage (and on other areas of family life, for that matter) tends to present isolated bits and pieces rather than overall perspectives. In other words, research on marital and partner relationships very much needs a qualitative and holistic perspective.

In 1965, using a qualitative approach, John Cuber and Peggy Haroff proposed a classification of marriage. Their typology was derived from in-depth interviews with 107 men and 104 women who had been married for *at least 10 years* and had never considered divorcing. The five types of marriage derived from the interview material were named on the basis of their central and distinguishing themes. They represent different configurations taken by the couples' relationships. This typology still applies today. However, the influx of immigrants from countries that are more patriarchal and, in other cases, where marriage is less a matter of companionship than a matter-of-fact relationship for reproductive and economic purposes, a sixth type should be added. I have taken the liberty of calling it "The reproductive-familial relationship" for want of a better term; this addition is tentative and subject to improvement if and when research is carried out. Furthermore, far more research should be carried out on same-sex marital relationships (Ambert, 2003a).

The Conflict-Habituated Relationship

The main characteristics of the conflict-habituated relationship are tension and unresolved conflict, some of which is overt and appears in the form of nagging and quarrelling. The spouses seem to argue for the sake of it. When on their best behaviour, these couples are polite, particularly in the company of others. But they do not conceal their differences from their children and, during the interviews, emphasized their incompatibility and how tense they were in each other's presence. Today, we would, in this category, include marriages in which spousal abuse occurs. Many of these couples had already been conflictual at the dating stage. What holds their marriage together may be force of habit, the fact that the spouses have personalities that are combative or have been so chiselled by the relationship that they might have difficulty adjusting to a more peaceful situation were they to divorce. In other cases, they cannot afford to divorce because of poverty or shared wealth and/or social position.

Among *young* couples today, this type of marriage is generally conflictual rather than conflict-habituated because conflicted relationships are likely to end soon (Gottman and Levenson, 2000). Even in the Cuber and Haroff sample in the early 1960s, this type of marriage was not the most frequently encountered. Today, it might cover 10 to 20 percent of long-term marriages. This is not a marital interaction that is valued in Canada, although it is far more acceptable in other cultures, especially when people appreciate arguing for the sake of arguing and when a "macho" code of conduct encourages marital spats in public, especially at the expense of women.

The Devitalized Relationship

In a devitalized relationship, the spouses had been deeply in love early on in their marriage, had enjoyed their sex lives, and had shared much together. Over time, the relationship lost its original "shine" and vitality. Now these couples simply take each other for granted but conflict is rare. Most of the time spent together is a matter of duty, to fulfill parental roles, to present a united front to the world, and to take care of each other's careers. These couples are often exemplary parents.

The relationship continues because of their commonly shared duties as well as the absence of conflict. There generally are other rewarding aspects in their lives, in which they invest much. They celebrate anniversaries and appreciate each other as parents or as workers. Some hold values that supersede those of individual happiness and they respect marriage as an institution. Cuber and Haroff found this type of marriage to be common in their sample, and may today constitute about one-third of all marriages of long duration.

However, these couples are susceptible to divorce because this type of marriage is considered less than ideal in our culture and the lack of positive affect takes a toll (Gottman and Levenson, 2000). It is a breach of romantic expectations of marital bliss. The risk of divorce is particularly high in view of the fact that these couples have, in the past, experienced greater companionship and pleasure in each other's presence. They are able to make comparisons with what they had before so that expectations for a happier relationship can arise and strain the status quo. Such expectations can also lead to extramarital affairs.

The Passive-Congenial Relationship

The passive-congenial relationship may be quite similar to the devitalized relationship, with the exception that couples do not have an early exciting past that has been hollowed out through the years. They harbour deep affection and especially respect for each other and are not disillusioned as are the devitalized couples. In fact, they are quite comfortable with their situation. They emphasize what they share, such as their total agreement on a variety of political or religious issues, or the fact that they have similar leisure interests, parenting goals, and social network.

These couples' dating lives were generally uneventful, and a strong element of level-headedness rather than passionate love was at the basis of their decision to marry. For them, marriage is a secure platform from which to explore and develop other deep and even passionate interests, whether in parenting, politics, careers, or even volunteer work. Compatibility of background is often important. Many of these spouses believe that society is placing too much emphasis on sex and passionate love. Although some of these marriages end in divorce, the risk is not as high as for the two previous categories. This marriage fulfills many culturally acceptable functions for the spouses and their families. These unions may also be cemented by strong principles and these couples may rate their marital happiness quite highly.

The Reproductive-Familial Relationship

The reproductive-familial relationship is added to the Cuber and Haroff typology to include marriages that are more or less arranged and do *not* become emotionally intimate. This type can, to some extent, cover those marriages that are not truly arranged but have been encouraged for familial, rational, or social reasons rather than for romantic purposes. Reproductive-familial marriages are characterized by a lack of romanticism and affectionate companionship and a focus on tradition or practicalities. The spouses tend to lead largely separate lives: Wives take care of the children and spend their leisure time with other women, often kin. Men are the breadwinners and their family's representatives in the community at large, and they spend their leisure time with other men. The extended family system is generally important and family visits usually result in men and women sitting and conversing separately.

The spouses interact with each other for sexual purposes but with a minimum of feelings involved. Wives are faithful sexually while men may or may not be. Spouses may have long conversations when alone or in the presence of their children. These conversations are cordial, may involve a great deal of mutual respect, may be supportive, but their focus tends to be on matters related to the family, children, business, jobs, and forthcoming celebrations. These conversations do not relate to mutual feelings nor do they involve discussions of the relationship nor negotiations concerning the household division of labour. When wives are employed, they may be so in their husband's or kinsmen's businesses or even in a professional setting. These marriages can also be conflict-habituated.

The Vital and Total Relationships

The essence of a *vital* relationship is sharing and togetherness. Couples value their relationship, regularly discuss it, and, when alone, often think about it. When they encounter conflict, they resolve it rapidly and move on. Differences are settled easily, even though with much discussion, but without verbal insults or humiliating put-downs, as would take place among the conflict-habituated couples. This type of marriage comes very close to conforming to Canadians' perception of an ideal marriage. Yet, it probably typifies only about one-third of couples who have been married for over 10 years. The vital marriage is not immune to divorce, although divorce is certainly less frequent among this category. But when a long-term vital relationship moves to a less involved one, such a marriage may become intolerable to one or both partners, even though it may still be a far better marriage than average. Divorce, rather than adjustment, may follow.

The vital marriage probably typifies the first years of a great proportion of western marriages as well as many marriages that are past the childrearing years. In other words, it is not only a type of marriage but, for many couples, it represents a stage in their relationship: the honeymoon.

For their part, couples in a *total* relationship form a minority and are the "stuff of novels." They are in many ways similar to the vital couples—the main difference being that there is more sharing at the intellectual and psychological levels, and more discussions taking place for the sake of sharing their interests verbally as well as physically. In many instances, the couples have professional interests in common and help each other, attend conventions together, and confer on a wide range of issues. Whereas vital couples retain their individual existences, total couples melt into the same existence, like identical twins.

These couples' sexual relationships are very important and are expressed in a multitude of settings and forms. Total couples define each other as lovers and best friends. Despite this, some do divorce because they have very high romantic and companionable standards. Experiencing less than what they have had, often after two or three decades, is not tolerable.

Marriages Change

Most students who have read these pages probably think that only the last two types of marriages would be good enough for them. This expectation is well expressed in the first quote opening this chapter, where the young woman is devastated by what appears to be a rapid passage from a dating honeymoon into a devitalized marriage. Few approve of the conflict-habituated relationship and most hope that their marriage will never become devitalized. Although some see merits in the passive-congenial type, it certainly does not appear "very exciting," particularly in comparison to media portrayals in soaps and movies. The reproductive-familial marriage, for its part, is generally encounterd among certain immigrant groups and, at least for the time being, is becoming more frequent in Canada. The studies of people who have divorced indicate that the first two types are at high risk for dissolution (Chapter 14).

But marital relationships evolve over time. Most middle-class couples probably begin at the vital stage, but a great proportion rapidly become conflictual or devitalized. At that point, marital satisfaction plummets and divorce rates soar. In today's cultural climate, only a minority of marriages survive constant conflict. The others make a conscious effort to change or seek counselling. Arranged marriages, for their part, may also evolve into a passive-congenial or even a vital relationship or they may degenerate into a conflict-habituated one, often very early on. Divorce may also follow.

One of the possible sequences between types that may occur throughout the years consists in a revitalization of the marriage after childrearing is completed. This is illustrated in the following student quote. She had described how the burdens of parenting and jobs had dulled her parents' marriage during her adolescence:

> *"Since then, my parents' happiness with their marital situation has been steadily rising. The business is great and my father's working less hours, Mary [a problematic adolescent] has a job, and I'm in college. They're happy with the whole family in general and they're like best friends. They're always getting all dressed up and they go out here, there, and everywhere. In fact, as I'm writing this down, they're on their way to Florida for a 2-week vacation—both from work and us kids. They're as close as a couple could be and are celebrating their 26th anniversary this year. They've made a lot of plans for the near future and they seem very happy and excited about it. Neither would be whole without the other."*

A devitalized marriage can also become a conflictual one over the years. At any point during these sequences, the marriage may break down, particularly when conflict and abuse occur. Furthermore, if we recall Cuber and Haroff's typology, marriages may remain of the same type throughout the years, except for the devitalized, which by definition represents a change from good to less satisfactory.

DIVISION OF LABOUR AND INEQUALITY

One very important aspect in the spousal relationship is the household and child care division of labour as well as its perceived equity, an element that was lacking in Cuber and Haroff's typology. When they did their research, gender roles and the domestic division of labour had not yet become salient social concerns. These themes were soon to become far more discussed under the convergence of two trends occurring in the 1970s. One trend was the influence of feminism as a theoretical perspective and the second was the massive entry of wives on the employment market, thus placing into question the traditional division of labour that had prevailed up to that point. Men had been (and are still generally so considered) the families' heads and breadwinners, and most women stayed at home with the children. This situation resulted from the social stratification by gender and conformed to its accompanying cultural values of feminine dependence and domesticity. The domestic division of labour is a perfect example of what was meant in Chapter 1 when I pointed out that microsociological phenomena (here, intimate domesticity) are closely related to macrosociological ones (in this instance, the overall social stratification by gender which pervades the entire society's organization, including the work environment).

A Classification of the Domestic Division of Labour

A classification of the division of labour between spouses has been derived from the sum of the research carried out on this topic. The terms used are frequently encountered in the literature. The domestic division of labour involves two elements: who does what, and who is responsible for planning or management—in other words, chores and responsibilities or availability. The classification is one based on *behaviours* rather than attitudes because far more couples believe in an egalitarian system than practise it (Pleck and Pleck, 1997). In other instances, daily necessities force cou-

When both spouses are employed, couples with a companionable marriage are more likely to share equally in terms of housework. In turn, equal sharing of work and responsibilities reinforces mutual feelings of satisfaction and companionship.

ples to share child care equally, yet this egalitarian practice is not necessarily accompanied by egalitarian beliefs, in particular by husbands (Coltrane, 1996). Thus, the gap between attitudes and behaviours makes it preferable to focus on the latter. This classification includes mothers who are not employed. But mothers who are employed are often forced to make adjustments to their work life because of familial constraints (Kempeneers, 1992).

The Egalitarian and Nongendered Division of Labour

In the egalitarian and nongendered division of labour, both spouses or partners are employed and participate equally in all aspects of the functioning of the household and in the care of the children. They come close to what Schwartz (1994) describes as **peer marriage,** and these couples are more likely to be encountered among the vital and total categories discussed earlier. Such couples may grocery shop and cook together, or they may alternate, with the husband cooking one week and the wife the next. Similarly, they may dress the children, get them ready for school, help them with breakfast, and so on together, or they may alternate—one week the father does morning duties while the mother does evening duties. If researchers went into such a household, they would add up the hours done by each parent on chores and responsibilities and would arrive at near identical totals.

Although many childless couples fit this description, relatively few couples with children do. As we have seen in the previous chapter, the arrival of the first child is generally the structural element that contributes to a shift in the spousal division of labour toward the traditional end of the continuum. At that point, it is generally the mother who takes a parental leave, thus further entrenching the gendering of caring and working (Beaujot, 2000).

The Equitable but Gendered Division of Labour

The equitable but gendered division of labour involves a similar number of hours of work (paid and unpaid) and child care but each spouse does different tasks largely based on what is considered appropriately male or female by this couple. It is another form of peer marriage but based on gender roles. For instance, the father may take care of the outside of the house, and he may cook and do the dishes, but his partner does the cleaning and the child care and buys the groceries. They may both visit with their children's teachers; however, the father participates in coaching while the mother is responsible for sick days.

Researchers observing such a family would again arrive at a comparable number of hours for each spouse, but they would note that fathers and mothers generally engage in different tasks and have different responsibilities. Despite trends in this direction, relatively few families fit this description. Although gendered, this division of labour is deemed fair by employed mothers, even those who earn high salaries, because what is important to them is that fathers participate equitably (Lennon and Rosenfield, 1994).

The Specialist Division of Labour: Equitable and Inequitable

The specialist division of labour may be gendered or not: It resides in the recognition that one of the two spouses is better at cooking, while the other is more enthusiastic about cleaning or doing the laundry. One spouse or the other is better at putting the children to bed, while the other is more competent at supervising or helping with homework. In other words, things get done by the partner who is defined by the other or who self-identifies as the most qualified for the job. Some tasks may be occasionally shared or rotated depending on who is present when the necessity arises.

Researchers studying such families may come up with two vastly different sets of results. In one group of families, both spouses spend the same number of hours on their different tasks. This would be an equitable specialist situation, and is often encountered in lesbian-headed families (Nelson, 1996; O'Brien and Goldberg, 2000). Many of these women describe themselves as very conscious of problems stemming from the traditional division of labour and want to make sure that neither of the partners will become the traditional mother. In the other group of families, one spouse has specialized in minor chores (e.g., washing the car and taking out the garbage) so that the other is left doing everything else on a daily basis. The other could be the wife or the husband, depending perhaps on which spouse earns the most, is the stronger, or has the most power in the relationship. Here we see the beginning of inequity and of the potential for dissatisfaction by the spouse who carries most of the burden, generally the wife.

The Husband-Helper Division of Labour

The husband-helper takes *no responsibility* to ensure that dinner is ready, that a babysitter is available, that the children do their homework, and so on. The mother takes all the responsibilities and remains on a permanent state of availability for these duties. In some cases, it can be the reverse and it is the wife who is the helper, particularly if her job is demanding or if she has more power in the relationship. But the scenario that typifies so many Canadian families sees the wife attending to most of the chores and child care responsibilities. She may ask, "Dear, I have left the grocery bags in the car, can you get them?" Or perhaps her husband may come in and ask what he can do to help or he simply does it. For instance, he might set the table or chop the onions. The mother's total number of hours devoted to child care and house chores will constitute 60 to 90 percent, and the father's will constitute the balance, after the work the children may do is factored in (Hofferth and Sandberg, 2001).

This division of labour typifies situations where the wife is not employed, as well as cases of dual-earner couples. In families where the wife is employed, the husband's help is often perceived as fair because she feels that he appreciates her role by offering to pitch in. Husbands of unemployed wives may, however, find their own help very generous and less fair. Thus, fairness in this respect is defined in a gendered way. When there is a discrepancy in perceptions, husbands' beliefs and perceptions are more likely to affect wives' than the reverse (Wilkie et al., 1998:592)—a reflection of the greater masculine power in society at large. Husbands can generally choose the timing of their help, but wives are more bound to a schedule of tasks that have to be performed on a daily basis. Fathers often choose activities they like. This may be why Larson and Richards (1994) have found that mothers' moods are at their lowest when they engage in housework. In contrast, fathers often feel relaxed and cheerful.

The Traditional and Delegated Divisions of Labour

With the *traditional division of labour*, the mother does nearly everything and the father either watches television, tinkers with his car, or has a beer with his buddies after work. More often than not, the wife is unemployed or holds a part-time job. If she is employed full-time, her husband may have objected to the decision. In his mind, and perhaps in hers as well, her place clearly is in the home. This division of labour is becoming less frequent but still occurs, particularly at the working-class level (see Harvey, 1993, for an ethnographic description). It also characterizes many families that have emigrated from countries where gender roles are patriarchal and the relationships are reproductive-familial.

For its part, the *delegated division of labour* is a phenomenon observed among affluent families that can afford a housekeeper, a nanny, or even a gardener. Although neither spouse actually does the work, and child care consists of engaging in leisure activities with the children and visiting their teachers, the wife is usually responsible for finding, hiring, training, and keeping the help (Marshall, 1994). This division of labour is a fairly traditional one. The wife may or may not be gainfully employed. When she is not, she engages in extensive community and volunteer work, organizes her husband's social activities, travels, and spends time shopping. It should be added that there is no research that looks at couple and family dynamics when a low-wage female employee contributes her labour to the household or takes care of the children in her home (Coontz, 2000).

The Overall Perspective

When all these types of division of labour are considered, the husband-helper and the specialized division of labour are probably the most common ones now, while the totally traditional one was still the rule in the 1960s (Luxton, 2001b). Whether the mother is married, divorced, part of a stepfamily, or single, she does most of the housework and child care (Coltrane, 2000)—and she does so even when both spouses are employed (Marshall, 1993), although perhaps less so in Quebec (Brayfield, 1992). Bianchi (in Bianchi et al., 1999) has estimated, on the basis of time-diaries, that women do three times more housework and child care than husbands. Furthermore, unless they belong to the egalitarian, equitable, or specialist categories, fathers devote little mental energy worrying about household and children's daily needs or planning activities for them (Larson and Richards, 1994).

All these observations are reflected in the 2001 Canadian census which found that over three times as many women as men spend over 60 hours a week on housework. Overall, among those who do housework, women and men spend respectively 4.3 and 2.8 hours daily in this activity. In the category of primary child care, 2.4 and 1.8 hours are spent daily respectively by women and men who engage in this activity (Statistics

Canada, 2004d). Furthermore, even among dual-career couples, mothers spend more time with their children than fathers, as indicated in Figure 11.1, including while engaging in housework and shopping (Silver, 2000). However, studies indicate that fathers who participate in the care of small children tend to maintain their involvement as the children get older (Aldous et al., 1998).

FIGURE 11.1

Average Minutes per Day Spent by Fathers and Mothers on Child Care and Housework/Shopping, with and without Child

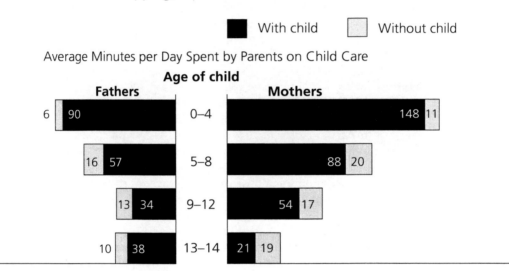

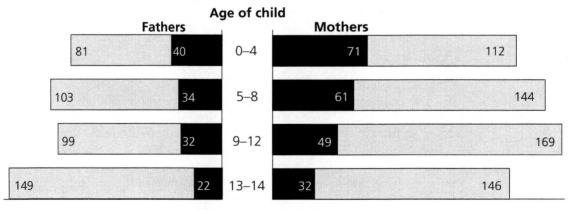

Source: Statistics Canada, General Social Survey, 1998; Silver, 2000.
Note: Both parents are employed full-time.

The Effect on Marital Quality: Overview of Recent Changes

In the 1950s and even in the early 1960s, middle-class wives' employment contributed to reduce marital satisfaction, especially among husbands, because it was then an infrequent and unusual phenomenon (Burke and Weir, 1976). Changes in gender roles at the cultural level had not yet occurred. In those days, there was no social support available to wives engaged in paid work. For their part, husbands suffered a lowered sense of self-worth because wife employment often signalled that husbands earned too little and could not support their families on their own. Although this is currently still one of the main reasons why mothers work for pay, today it is a culturally recognized fact that two paycheques are necessary. Therefore, husbands do not generally feel diminished by their wives' employment, as used to be the case 40 to 50 years ago. Most take it for granted and are as proud of their wives' achievements as wives are of their husbands'.

By the 1980s, a cultural shift had occurred, particularly among women, so that employed wives, especially highly educated ones, were more satisfied with their marriages than housewives (Houseknecht and Macke, 1981). Not surprisingly, husbands who held conventional beliefs about the division of labour and preferred to see wives at home reported lower levels of marital happiness when their wives were employed and earned high salaries (Perry-Jenkins and Crouter, 1990; Voydanoff, 1988). As time went by, husbands became more accepting of their wives' employment and started contributing more to housework, perhaps reluctantly. At the same time, researchers began to focus on the perception of fairness in the division of labour as it relates to marital happiness. The relative earnings of the spouses became an important factor influencing the power dynamics. In the 1990s, wives who were employed full-time were less satisfied than their husbands and than other wives concerning the equity of the work-family balance (White, 1999).

At the close of the 20th century, researchers were observing a correlation between marital satisfaction and the perception that the division of labour at home *and* at work is fair. In women's overall evaluation of the quality of their marriage, the division of labour at home is much more important, whereas the division of labour at work is considered more frequently by husbands (Wilkie et al., 1998). Furthermore, an American study has shown that, as husbands' share of housework increased (from 1980 to 2000 in two surveys), husbands reported less marital happiness and wives more (Amato et al., 2003). Thus, the division of domestic and paid work has positive and negative effects on marital satisfaction for both spouses, although the effects are still stronger for wives than husbands. These effects also have important implications for women's health (Bird, 1999; Brisson et al., 1999; see Family Research 11.1). It is not only the relative amount of work that counts in affecting marital satisfaction but the perception of fairness or equity as well as the feelings that one's overall contribution to the family is appreciated (Wilkie et al., 1998). Perceptions of inequity reduce marital happiness and may lead to divorce (Frisco and Williams, 2004). Finally, more longitudinal studies are needed to see how the division of labour changes over time within couples—cohabiting or married—and what it looks like among older couples (Szinovacz, 2000).

FAMILY RESEARCH 11.1

Blood Pressure, High Job Strain, and Large Family Responsibilities among Women

This research method (Brisson et al., 1999) combines traditional sociological techniques with medical research. It was designed to test the effect of job strain and family work on women's health, and on blood pressure in particular. Samples of married women holding jobs with high versus low levels of strain, as well as high versus low levels of family responsibilities, were selected in Montreal. Large family responsibilities were defined by the number of children at home, particularly young children, and much domestic work. All these were measured by means of questionnaires. The women's weight and height were also verified. They wore Spacelab monitors, and their blood pressure was recorded every 15 minutes as they went about their usual activities.

Division of Labour in Remarriages with Stepchildren

Some research indicates that decision-making tends to be shared more equally in remarriages, yet studies on the division of labour itself show that it tends to remain traditional (Demo and Acock, 1993). With stepchildren present, the division of labour may constitute a key aspect of the spousal relationship. Stepchildren who visit often cause an enormous amount of work to stepmothers in terms of cooking and cleaning up. In some reconstituted families, fathers tend to contribute more. But in many others, the father simply entertains his visiting children, or he leaves with them after lunch for an outing while his wife inherits a load of dirty dishes. The following is a quote from a woman reminiscing about the problems created by visiting stepchildren in her previous (second) marriage:

> *"His kids kept coming here because he didn't want to visit them at their place, of course, because he hated his ex-wife. We had six kids here at times and his are the rough type; after they'd gone, the whole house was a mess for us to clean and the fridge was empty and I had to pay."*

This theme of inequity recurred throughout my interviews with stepmothers and was often exacerbated by complaints from the custodial mother to the father. Some complained that the children had not slept enough, had not been properly fed, or had watched too much television while visiting at their father's place. The stepmother felt particularly targeted because, after all, she was the one responsible for the smooth functioning of the household (O'Connor and Insabella, 1999).

> *"I feel like a glorified babysitter. I mean, she brings her boys here so that she can have a nice weekend of rest and go out. It's nice for her but I get nothing out of this except work, work, and more work, and the boys order me around like a slave."* [Their father?] *"Oh, he's so afraid of having further problems with her or that the boys won't want to visit that he says nothing. He pretends it's not there."* [This stepmother did not intend to "stick around much longer."]

In short, the matter of the division of labour seemed to bring in a great deal of conflict among these couples who had been together for only a few months or years at most. The wife's feelings of inequity may have been greater than in a first marriage with her own children: In a remarriage, the wife is labouring for another woman's children—those of the ex-wife. Furthermore, Vinich and Lanspery (quoted in Walker and McGraw, 2000) found that wives of remarried men over the age of 60 often work to establish friendly contact with his adult children with whom he may be more or less estranged.

THE SILENT DIVISION OF LABOUR: EMOTIONAL WORK

Another aspect to the division of labour resides in that, generally, women do more emotional or "love" work than men. Most exceptions to this rule would be found among the vital and total couples. We have seen in Chapter 8 that girls and women who date have more invested emotionally than males in the relationship. They work harder at maintaining it (Sacher and Fine, 1996), they initiate more conversations about the relationship, they express their love more frequently, they divulge more of themselves to their partner in order to show him their commitment, and they plan more of their activities together than he does, often including their wedding ceremonies (Humble, 2003). This pattern continues during cohabitation or marriage. We see in subsequent chapters that females nurture their relationship with their parents, siblings, children, and grandchildren more than males. Thus, all in all, whatever the familial roles they assume, from the time they are very young, females are socialized to become the kin-keepers, the expressive partners, and the emotional workers.

According to Hochschild, in *The Managed Heart* (1983), "emotion work" is a capital or an asset that women exchange for security in a relationship. In subordinate positions, the role occupants tend to rely on emotional capital. There are couples where the husband is subordinate because he wanted the marriage more than she or because she has more alternatives than he. This analysis fits very well with the exchange theories outlined in Chapter 1. In general, women have fewer alternatives, either because their maternal investment restricts their ability to work or to find other partners, or because there are many other women competitors "on the market." In other cases, women are disadvantaged because of the double standard of aging (note in Chapter 14 the tendency for men to remarry women younger than their previous wives).

For men, their marriage is a haven, yet for women, it is often both a haven and a source of work and insecurity (Hochschild, 1997). Wives are not necessarily more invested in the stability of their marriage than husbands, but they are more invested in its *quality maintenance*. This differential investment is a source of emotional insecurity for women, thus of subordination. It is also a source of marital dissatisfaction. Men are not as observant as their wives are concerning the quality of their relationship. They tend to take it for granted, because they are not the emotional worker. In general, because of socialization and culture, women are more invested and sensitive in interpersonal relationships, and are particularly so in their marriage and cohabitation. However, women get more intrinsic rewards from these relationships—again a matter of gender-role socialization.

For instance, Larson and Richards (1994) report wives' moods to be more positive when they are with their husbands. Husbands' moods are also more positive when with their wives, but less so. Rook et al. (1991) have found that a husband's mood affects a wife's mood far more than the reverse. When spouses arrive home unhappy from stressors at work, it is the husband who is more likely to transmit this state of mind to his wife (who is more attuned to his feelings and more dependent on them), than is the wife who returns home unhappy. If a husband has any argument at work, this increases substantially the probability that he will have an argument with his wife later on (Bolger et al., 1989). In her autobiography, a mature student explains how deeply affected she is by this situation:

> "The only reason that I take one course each year is that it gives me something to escape to when my husband comes home in a bad mood because of pressure at work.... He wants all of us to feel it or to suffer with him; he takes it out on us. But the few times that I have done this, he laughed it off and walked out. It's so unfair [when husband ignores her own bad mood]. I just hop in my car and come to the library to work on my paper. If I stayed home and went downstairs to type he would follow me and manage to pick a fight."

Already 30 years ago, the reputed sociologist, Jessie Bernard (1972), talked of the two separate realities contained within one marriage—what she called a "his" and "hers," or two marriages in one. This differential still persists today and it is not a phenomenon specific to a particular social class or ethnic group; rather, it applies across the board.

ASPECTS OF SPOUSAL RELATIONSHIPS

The type of relationship, including the division of domestic labour, that characterizes a union involves elements of happiness or disaffection as well as potential for conflict and conjugal problems. Furthermore, these elements have a threefold time dimension. First, they can be studied throughout the life span of a *couple* well into the later years. Second, within a *person's* life span, marriages can succeed each other so that the sequencing of marital types, division of labour, and marital happiness constitutes an important research theme. Third, marital quality can be studied by *cohort*—that is, among couples born and raised in different decades who, consequently, may have different expectations (Amato et al., 2003).

Marital Happiness, Satisfaction, and Success

The concepts of marital happiness, satisfaction, and success have been very popular in the North American marriage literature ever since Burgess and Locke began their studies in the mid-1940s (Burgess et al., 1963). The goal of this domain of research is to define what a successful marriage is and compare the characteristics of couples who are satisfied and happy to those of couples who are not. These various concepts are often used interchangeably, but there are different meanings attached to them. Marital happiness is an emotional state and is totally subjective and individual. In contrast, marital adjustment and success, while also subjective, depend much more on how the persons in the dyad perceive how they have achieved their goals, how well they communicate, and how companionable their relationship is (Glenn, 1998:570; see also

Family Research 11.2). Furthermore, what makes for a happy marriage changes with the centuries and even the decades as couples' expectations evolve under various cultural influences that provide different social constructions of the conjugal relationship. It should also be mentioned that the emphasis on marital happiness as the foundation of a union is rather unique to western countries. In most societies, the notion itself does not even exist.

Overall, studying marital happiness is a complex undertaking, for it depends on a multitude of variables and it is impossible to include even most of them in research. The variables that help individuals achieve marital happiness can be found at several levels. Some, including economic situations, are derived from the macrosociological context and may help explain the lower marital satisfaction among blacks, who, on average, are economically disadvantaged (Aldous and Ganey, 1999). Others are psychological and involve personality characteristics, communication styles, and coping mechanisms. For instance, Miller et al. (2003) have found that being expressive toward one's spouse promotes marital satisfaction because expressiveness leads spouses to engage in affectionate behaviours and to interpret their partner's behaviour in a favourable light.

One can study what types of couples are happy together and what contributes to their dyadic satisfaction and even success. But it is also important to follow the trajectory of marital happiness longitudinally—that is, over time. Studying couples over time allows researchers to pinpoint types of interactions existing in, say 2000, that may predict dyadic success or yet unhappiness by the year 2005 when they are reinterviewed. **Longitudinal studies** indicate to what extent marital happiness at Time 1 predicts happiness at Time 2 and what has happened in the interval to explain change or stability.

FAMILY RESEARCH 11.2

How Is Marital Satisfaction Measured?

Several measuring instruments have been devised to quantify marital adjustment and satisfaction. These instruments are generally called *scales* and are used during phone and face-to-face surveys designed to evaluate a couple's or even a family's functioning. Among the best-known is Spanier's Dyadic Adjustment Scale, which can be used for couples in general (see Spanier, 1976). The scale contains 32 close-ended questions testing for dyadic satisfaction and happiness, dyadic cohesion (shared activities and communication), dyadic consensus or perceived level of agreement, and perceived agreement on demonstration of affection, including sexuality. Examples of questions are:

- How often do you kiss your mate?
- How often do you confide in your mate?
- How often do you work together on a project?
- How often do you quarrel?

The methodological issue to be addressed in this type of research is how one would measure marital satisfaction in cultures where husbands and wives lead largely separate lives and where romantic love is not valued, even though it may happen.

Currently, researchers are able to predict with reasonable accuracy which relationships will end in divorce and to verify this prediction with a follow-up study of the couples (Gottman, 1994). Furthermore, both psychologists and sociologists are interested in measuring parents' marital happiness to see how it relates to children's own development and adjustment. As well, longitudinal research has found that, over time, marital quality spills over into job satisfaction, so that increases in marital satisfaction relate to increases in work satisfaction for both men and women (Rogers and May, 2003). However, Larson and Goltz (1989) have argued that **commitment** may be a better predictor of marital quality and stability than marital satisfaction.

In view of the importance of the parenting role in adults' self-identity (Thoits, 1992), it is surprising how few researchers have examined the effect of **parenting satisfaction** on marital happiness. In other words, not all adults are happy as *parents*, particularly when they have serious difficulties with their children (O'Connor and Insabella, 1999). Is it not possible that when parents are happy in their roles this will reflect positively on their marital happiness? Sociologists Stacey Rogers and Lynn White (1998) have explored this question. They found reciprocal effects between marital happiness and parenting satisfaction, both for mothers and fathers. (*Parenting satisfaction* was defined as parents' satisfaction with their relationship with their children.) Rogers and White (1998:305) conclude that "success in one family role primes an individual for success in other family roles...parents may include their own success as parents as one component of their marital evaluation."

Marital Quality through the Decades

Indications are that the quality of marriages has been declining, at least since 1969. In 1991, sociologist Norval Glenn first showed that the proportion of people reporting their marriages to be very happy had declined between 1973 and 1988. This finding was unexpected because divorce rates had increased during the same period. One would think that the surviving marriages would be happier than in the past when even unhappy couples were forced to stay together. A complementary study carried out by Amato et al. (2003) used data gathered previously through two national phone surveys of couples 55 years of age or less, one survey in 1980 and the other in 2000.

Members of the 2000 survey reported less marital interaction, more conflict and problems in their marriage, but marital happiness and divorce proneness remained constant. Generally, there was greater conflict and less interaction when both spouses were employed and when there were small children at home. There was also more conflict when the spouses had fewer economic resources and the marriage had been preceded by cohabitation. The researchers concluded that the lives of husbands and wives are becoming more separate and couples are less likely to share activities such as eating meals, shopping, working on projects around the house, visiting friends, and going out for leisure activites (Amato et al., 2003:19).

Partner Conflict and Marital Problems

Researchers evaluate the frequency of spousal conflict via self-reports and, at times, observations in homes or in a laboratory. They also investigate the mechanisms used by couples to resolve their conflicts. Overall, most of what is known about marital conflict and resolution comes from self-reports as well as spousal appraisals of the other partner's behaviour. Same-sex and opposite-sex couples engage in similar conflict-resolution mechanisms (Kurdek, 1994). All report a relatively low level of conflict. Lesbian women report using more constructive conflict-resolution styles. They also report making greater effort to resolve conflict, perhaps because as women they have been socialized to be attuned to a partner's distress more than is the case among other couples that include at least one man (Metz et al., 1994).

Partner Conflict

Conflict between partners arises from issues pertaining to the division of labour, communication, lack of attention to each other, sex, children, finances, and leisure time (Vangelisti and Huston, 1994). Finances involve not only how money is spent but who controls it as well as who earns it. On average, the presence of children increases the frequency of disagreements (Hatch and Bulcroft, 2004). In a marriage, there are usually more reasons for wives than for husbands to be dissatisfied, because women have invested more in their marital and parental relationships than men; also, when there is inequity in the division of labour, it usually favours husbands. Furthermore, in their role of emotional workers, wives are more involved in problem resolution (Gottman, 1998). For all these reasons, wives are generally less satisfied with their current and past marriages than husbands. Furthermore, wives are compelled to express more dissatisfaction to their husbands than the reverse and are therefore in the unpleasant position of initiating more conflict (Kluwer et al., 1997).

Styles of conflict resolution appear to form during the first year of marriage (Schneewind and Gerhard, 2002). Constructive outcomes occur when the communication of the dissatisfaction results in a better understanding of each other's feelings with a mutual search for a solution, including compromise. Egalitarian couples tend to be more responsive to each other's disclosure of dissatisfaction and are more likely to engage in mutually satisfactory solutions (Rosenfeld et al., 1995). Traditional couples are more likely to avoid discussing their dissatisfaction, particularly with the division of labour. As well, conflicts are least likely to be resolved constructively when, for instance, the husband withdraws from the interaction and thus maintains the status quo (Gottman, 1994): Conflict avoidance does not resolve problems and may decrease marital happiness. However, were a researcher to ask these "avoiding" couples about conflict, the answer might be that little conflict exists—compared to what the researcher would find among couples containing at least one nontraditional spouse. Thus, a lack of reported conflict in this case simply refers to *overt* conflict; such couples may actually have a very high level of what could be called *covert* or simmering conflict, as described by a divorced woman about her previous marriage:

> *"My ex-husband always said to whoever would be present that we never had problems or quarrels. That's true, we never fought verbally and certainly not physically. But we could never talk about our disagreements and problems. As soon as I'd mention something, he'd smile, or laugh, or joke and walk away. He just left and things just kept getting bottled up; I mean we couldn't talk about money, about sex, about going out or not, his mother, nothing. Sure, we had no quarrels, we had no communication."*

Marital Problems

Marital problems are more encompassing than conflict. However, the two overlap in the sense that disagreements and conflict constitute one type of problem reported by spouses. As is the case for the division of labour, there is a **gendered aspect** to marital problems: Wives report problems more than husbands and say that more problems are created by their husbands, both during marriage and after divorce (Kitson, 1992). Furthermore, marital problems affect women's health more negatively than they do men's (Hetherington, 2003). Not surprisingly, the quality of relationships in wives' own family of origin may have a greater effect on their perception of marital quality (Sabatelli and Bartle-Haring, 2003).

A longitudinal study of married persons spanning the years 1980 to 1992 provided respondents with a list of problems and asked them to indicate which existed in their marriage and which person had the problem: the respondent, his or her spouse, or both. Amato and Rogers (1997) used this information to see if there were specific marital problems that could predict that a couple would be divorced at each subsequent reinterview. They found six problems, at times occurring as far back as nine years earlier, that predicted divorce. These were infidelity, spending money foolishly, drinking or using drugs, jealousy, having irritating habits, and moodiness. However, there might have been other equally good precursors to divorce that had not originally been included in the study. Examples might include problems related to an unequal division of labour, or physical abuse, both of which are often mentioned by people after a divorce.

The Conjugal Relationship in Later Life

Although a proportion of older couples live a conflict-habituated or a devitalized relationship, on average, they experience relatively high levels of marital satisfaction, with a great deal of closeness and little conflict (Carstensen et al., 1995). At this point in time, it is difficult to determine if this elevated level of happiness in the later years is the result of the **U-curve phenomenon** or if it is a matter of cohort. The U-curve refers to those studies that have found a dip in the quality of marriages during the childrearing years, followed by an upward trend after late adolescence. Such studies imply that the quality of a marriage varies during a couple's life course and is particularly affected by the negative aspects of the parental role. There is a great deal of support for this perspective: As we have seen in the previous chapter, companionship diminishes after the birth of a first baby.

But, in the case of a **cohort effect,** it would mean that older couples who married 30 to 70 years ago began their relationship in a social climate that emphasized mutuality or duty rather than personal gratification in marriage. These couples may have had lower expectations to begin with in terms of what marriage could do for them, focusing instead on what they can do for the relationship. They may, as a result, have been happier maritally (Glenn, 1998). When the U-curve applies, higher marital satisfaction in later years could reflect relief from the stress of active parenting as well as work-related problems (White and Edwards, 1990). Rather than being mutually exclusive, it is likely that both the U-curve and the cohort effect are implicated in the longitudinal dynamics of marital quality.

Retirement presents both opportunities and potential strains on the conjugal relationship (Davey and Szinovacz, 2004). It reduces the pressure of commitments related to work, as well as time constraints. Couples can then engage in more activities together and make plans that cannot be derailed because of role conflicts. However, increased togetherness may be stressful for some, particularly when their entire lives had revolved around parenting and working, and their relationship had become hollow. They may find themselves with too much time on their hands and too little to say to each other, and thus some divorces occur at this stage. Many wives actually dread the day their husbands retire because "he won't know what to do with himself and I'll lose my freedom." A French study of couples found that women are more likely than men to consider their spouse's work and retirement situation when making plans for the time of their own retirement (Sedillot and Walraet, 2002). Thus, even in late mid-life, women still do more relationship maintenance work than men.

In an in-depth study, Robinson and Blanton (1993) asked 15 couples who had been married for at least 30 years to give their perception of the qualities that had sustained their relationship. The first qualities mentioned were intimacy and closeness, which resulted in the sharing of joys and activities and in mutual support in difficult times. These couples had enjoyed doing things together. They closely resembled the vital couples described earlier. The other quality that made their marriage endure was commitment to the relationship, to the spouse, or even at some points in the past to their marriage and children. The third aspect was communication or the sharing of thoughts and feelings so as to know the other's perspective. The fourth was called "congruence" by the researchers. This refers to the fact that most of these couples had similar perceptions regarding various domains of their lives, from commitment to religious orientation. Finally, the last salient quality was religiosity, which returns us to the contents of Chapter 7 indicating a positive effect of religiosity on the marital relationship and family life in general.

When both spouses live into very old age, one of the two may become frail. Physical impairment, such as difficulties walking, does not diminish closeness between the spouses. But a spouse's **cognitive impairment** lowers the degree of closeness between them, as perceived by the caregiving spouse (Townsend and Franks, 1997). This spouse also perceives that his or her efforts are less effective. Cognitive disabilities—such as dementia, senility, and Alzheimer's disease—bring changes in personality and behaviours that constitute a discontinuity in the pattern of the relationship. The caregiving spouse becomes more socially isolated because of the demands of his or her new role (Barber and Pasley, 1995). It is then more difficult to cope with the conflicts engendered by the new dependency, such as when the afflicted spouse criticizes the efforts of the other, refuses the help offered, or even becomes aggressive. In contrast, when the frail spouse is supportive of the partner's efforts, the caregiver feels more efficient, less stressed, and is more satisfied with the caretaker role (Dorfman et al., 1996).

The Next Time Around: Remarriage

Remarriages are as happy as first marriages, once duration is taken into consideration (Ganong and Coleman, 1994). Yet, remarriages end in divorce more than first marriages. How can this paradox be explained? First, Kurdek (1990) has found that marital satisfaction decreased more in remarriages than in first marriages. Then, Booth and Edwards (1992) suggest that it takes less deterioration in marital quality to precipitate a divorce among remarried than married couples.

In a remarriage, the spouses enter the union with more emotional baggage than in a first one. Their previous union may have raised or depressed their expectations and it may have made them more or less tolerant when expectations are not met. So far, the higher redivorce rate suggests that couples are less tolerant the second time around. Remarried spouses may be less willing to cope with what are considered by others to be smaller disappointments; these disappointments then bring ideas of divorce that might not occur so rapidly in a young couple who has never had to contemplate divorce. Obviously, there are processes involved in the second marital relationship that bring about a dissolution more readily than the first time around. Consequently, remarriages that are successful may require a deeper commitment and a conscious effort to avoid the downward spiralling trend. A re-evaluation of what is and is not important in life is required, as expressed by a remarried man during his interview:

> "I came to the conclusion that if marriage is to be successful, both partners have to work at it or at least spend time enjoying it. I had to rework my priorities and since I can't imagine myself married to your average Jane Doe, I knew I was in for another career woman and I had to learn to give in a bit. Point of fact, my wife is very similar to my first wife and the reason is obvious: My first wife was fine. It's just that we failed to live our married lives. Now my career's less important, my marriage more.... It's a shame that it took a divorce to come to this realization."

Furthermore, redivorces occur even more rapidly than first divorce, as we see in Chapter 14. This rapid breakup may reflect the inability of many remarried spouses to establish a satisfying relationship very early on because of the complications of the structural factors involved (Tzeng and Mare, 1995). The presence of stepchildren, ex-spouses, and ex-in-laws represents for some couples a force that diverts their attention from the task of building their relationship and hampers their ability to invest in the dyad. A man reflects a similar perspective when trying to evaluate the quality of his remarriage during an interview:

> "I think it's very difficult to start a remarriage on the right footing even with the best of intentions. There's always someone ready to make you trip over, especially her children. I find it hard to commit to this relationship—and I love her deeply, don't take me wrong here—because her children are so hostile. I can't separate them from her; they come in a package deal. One minute we're happy and I feel that I belong and the next minute they come in, throw stuff around, just ignore me, and it's so awkward."

Thus, when studying remarried couples' conjugal quality, it would be important to distinguish between those who have dependent stepchildren and those who were childless when they remarried.

SAME-SEX-PARTNER RELATIONSHIPS

The research on the quality of the dyadic relationship among cohabiting same-sex partners is scant, and much of what exists is flawed methodologically. To begin with, it is impossible to draw large random samples of same-sex couples. Therefore, most of the studies on same-sex couples have been small and many have relied on self-selection (i.e., researchers have placed ads in gay/lesbian newsletters and clubs to solicit couples' cooperation). Obviously, such an approach draws relatively educated couples who maintain links to the homosexual community, may be activists, and are fairly young. Less educated same-sex couples who have little to do with the homosexual subcultures or who are older will not be represented in these samples (but see Yip, 1997). Moreover, gays and lesbians have suffered from stigmatization and may not wish to share the intimate details of their lives with researchers for fear of being further victimized or categorized (Nelson, 1996:10). As a result, only couples who are happy together may respond to such ads.

For instance, Kurdek (1998) admits to his sample's lack of representativeness. Nevertheless, despite this sampling deficiency, his research is well designed. He compared married heterosexual couples to gay and lesbian couples on several dimensions of dyadic satisfaction. Gay couples reported more autonomy from each other in terms of activities, friendships, and decision-making than married dyads. Lesbian couples reported more intimacy, autonomy, and equality than married dyads. (However, the researcher did not present comparisons between gay and lesbian couples.) Both gay and lesbian couples had higher rates of dissolution than married ones. In provinces where same-sex marriage is legalized, it would be important to compare those couples who married to a group of similar cohabiting same-sex couples to see if the married ones will stay together longer—as is the case among heterosexual couples.

For instance, as Kurdek (1998) points out, there are no legal barriers preventing the dissolution of gay and lesbian relationships, and the same occurs for cohabiting couples who do not have children. Socially, a same-sex relationship is already labelled deviant by many, and few—particularly in their families—object if the relationship breaks up. Despite this lack of social barriers, around 85 percent of the same-sex couples remained together for the duration of the five-year longitudinal study. But they had already been together for an average of 10 and 7 years, respectively, for gay and lesbian dyads. In other words, they had survived the most unstable years, which are the first ones.

In the domain of conflict, Kurdek (1994) compared gay, lesbian, and heterosexual couples and found little difference in the rank order of frequency of conflict in six global areas: power, social issues, personal flaws, distrust, intimacy, and personal distance. Issues pertaining to intimacy and power were the most frequently mentioned sources of conflict by all three types of couples. This is interesting in itself because it indicates that problems related to power are not entirely explainable in terms of gender roles or the patriarchal order, for they exist in same-sex couples as well. For all three types of couples, conflict over intimacy and power was more related to either partner's lower satisfaction with the relationship than other conflict topics. During the one-year duration of the study, conflict over power was the most predictive of later relationship deterioration. These findings are in agreement with those of Gottman (1994) as well as Vangelisti and Huston (1994) for married heterosexual couples.

As is the case among heterosexuals, saying "I love you," showing physical affection, giving gifts, and cooking for the other are frequently mentioned expressions of love among same-sex partners (Stiers, 1996). Gift-giving is more often mentioned among males than females, perhaps as a substitute for verbal expressions of affection. Overall, as herein indicated and as seen in other chapters, there are more similarities than differences in the way homosexual and heterosexual couples live their relationships. The structure and requirements of daily life place similar demands on them.

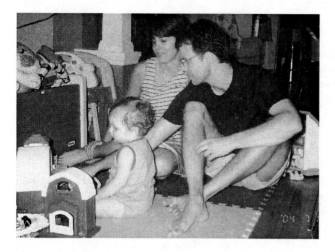

The quality of the spousal relationship is one of several key ingredients in a child's development. Parents in a secure and happy relationship transmit feelings of security to their children. Such parents are also more likely to agree in terms of socialization goals, thus again benefiting their children. Therefore, a child's home environment depends in great part on his or her parents' relationship.

THE EFFECT OF THE PARENTAL RELATIONSHIP ON CHILDREN

Researchers are particularly interested in finding a theoretical explanation for the observed link between the quality of parents' relationship and children's well-being. So far, the research has focused on parental conflict. This emphasis is understandable in view of the fact that children who live with openly conflictual parents are often less well adjusted than children in well-functioning single-parent families (Seltzer, 1994); as well, interparental conflict is related to harsh discipline and rejection on the part of parents (Krishnakumar and Buehler, 2000). Children are more disturbed when the content of the conflict pertains to them. For instance, parents who openly fight about their children upset them more than if they are quarrelling about money; the children may even blame themselves, especially when they are small (Grych and Fincham, 1994).

Parental disagreement by itself does not affect children negatively (Cummings et al., 2003). In fact, children can learn functional ways of solving human problems by listening to their parents iron out their difficulties in a cooperative manner. However, constant disagreement that is left unresolved or that simmers may be detrimental. Parental conflict of the hostile type has the most negative effects (Buehler et al., 1998). Children exposed to repeated hostility between parents fail to learn adaptive modes of conflict resolution and this pattern of interaction may spill into their own relationships (Jenkins, 2000). But, as Fincham (1998:551) correctly remarks, there is more to a marriage than absence of conflict. Above all, "there has been no research on the impact of the spouses' supportive behavior on child development." When parents enjoy a good marriage, the mother's relationship with her small child is warmer and she is more nurturing. Fathering is even more affected than mothering by the quality of the marriage. All in all, when parents get along well, children exhibit far fewer behavioural difficulties than they do when parents are in a conflictual marital situation (Morrison and Coiro, 1999). The advantage extends to adolescence and adulthood (Hetherington, 2003). Furthermore, a happy parental relationship is related to greater parent-child affection and consensus (Amato and Booth, 1997).

Several complementary explanations exist for the correlation between the quality of parents' relationship and their children's outcomes; these are illustrated in Figure 11.2. But before we examine them, it is important to mention that such a correlation may not exist in cultures where the reproductive-familial marriage is the norm—that is, where fathers and mothers, men and women, live largely separate lives; where the marital interaction might revolve around patriarchal authority and kin relationship; and where the relationship is an institutional one rather than one that is largely personal. It is not known what effect, if any, the quality of the marital interaction has on child development or on parenting in these societies, or in Canada, in these types of marriage.

Marital Quality Fosters Supportive Parenting

The most frequently mentioned explanation is that the supported and loved mother lives in a warm environment that translates into a close and attentive relationship with her child (arrow from left to centre and right in Figure 11.2). In contrast, when conflict exists, parents are stressed, feel unappreciated, and may be less able to transfer loving feelings to their child (Belsky et al., 1991). Childrearing is disrupted and parents agree less with each other in terms of child care (Jodl et al., 1999). It becomes more difficult to use authoritative socialization practices. Parents' hostility toward each other often results in harsh parenting and rejecting behaviour toward children (Krishnakumar and Buehler, 2000). Parents may become so absorbed in their marital problems that they are less available to their children (Buehler and Gerard, 2002). In some cases, parents use their children to get at each other, as had occurred to a student who, in his self-description, grew up to be "out of control":

> "I was more attached to my father because I always turned to him when my mother said no and he usually said yes so that I always ended up doing what I wanted. At other times he'd say, 'Ah, don't worry about her, she doesn't know what boys are like,' and I think that after a while my mother gave up on me. I remember that my father used to just ignore her or would tell her off and I didn't mind at the time because I was getting my way. It worked great during my adolescence, well, at first, but then it turned sour because I had become way out of control and it took my last girlfriend's leaving me before I finally realized what had happened to me. She just hated my father and she said I'd turn out just like him as a husband and she wasn't going to live with this."

The Role of Learning and Personality

With the second explanation, the focus shifts on what children can learn in this context: that quarrelling and even being abused is a normal way of living and of resolving conflicts (Grych and Fincham, 1994). (This is expressed by the line from quality of marriage to child outcomes in Figure 11.2.) Small children who are already predisposed to hyperactivity, nervousness, or aggression may be especially vulnerable to parental conflict; they may be particularly susceptible to acquiring maladaptive behaviours by observing and modelling their parents' conflictual interaction.

The third explanation also resides in assumptions about personality and temperament, as shown at the top of Figure 11.2 (Erel and Burman, 1995). A conflictual marriage may arise because the two parents have problematic personalities, are difficult to

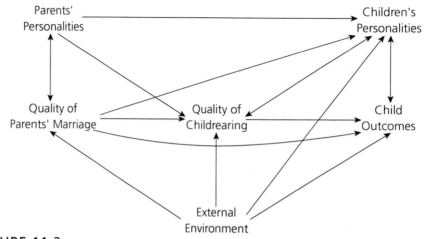

FIGURE 11.2

Variables Explaining the Correlation between the Quality of Parents' Marriage and Child Outcomes

get along with, do not like to compromise, or are aggressive. Even if only one of the two parents is so, the marriage is likely to be unstable. Furthermore, if a mother is impatient, irritable, and has little tolerance for frustration, she may exhibit these patterns in her parenting practices as well, and the same holds true for the father. This would explain why, in conflictual marriages, the parent-child relationship is less warm and more erratic *and* why the babies and children in these families experience more adjustment difficulties, anxiety, and behavioural problems. In contrast, in a peaceful and supportive marriage, there is a strong chance that the parents' personalities are conducive to good relationships, and the child's environment is accordingly regulated (Papp et al., 2004).

Genes and Within-Family Environment

A fourth and complementary explanation flows from the preceding one. It resides in joint genetic and environmental considerations (Reiss, 1995). Parents who are aggressive, have little tolerance for frustration, are impatient, or are not easy to get along with may well pass at least some of these unfortunate traits via genetic inheritance to their children (Plomin, 1994; Rowe, 1994). The result is that some of these babies may themselves be more fussy and irritable, and may later become more oppositional, hyperactive, and aggressive than children who are born to parents who are warm, patient, and cooperative, and who consequently have a stable relationship.

Each person in a family constitutes part of the others' environment. Thus, the behavioural manifestations of parental characteristics become part of the children's environment, both as childrearing styles and as marital styles (Rutter, 2002). At the negative level, children's own behavioural manifestations of their partly inherited traits, such as hyperactivity, elicit a negative reaction from parents, and this reaction then also becomes part of the children's environment. These partly genetically driven environments interact with each other and result in inadequate parent-child relationships as well as negative child outcomes or adjustment (Reiss, 1995).

The Larger Environment Affects Marriage and Childrearing

Finally, as shown in the lower part of Figure 11.2, marriages and childrearing can be strained by the environment external to the family—poverty and unemployment come to mind here. Thus, children's personalities and outcomes may be indirectly affected by these environmental strains. Furthermore, as they age, children whose parents have a conflictual marriage may be more at the mercy of deleterious neighbourhood, school, and peer influences. A student unwittingly puts her finger on this chain of circumstances when she points out the following:

> "I stayed home as little as I could between the ages of 10 and 18 because my parents weren't easy to get along with and were fighting all the time, more my father than my mother, and a lot of the time they'd get mad at me or yell at me or it would upset me to see my mother cry. My parents were too busy fighting and maybe it was a relief for them when I was out so that I was on the streets most of the time by [age] 10. Of course, I got into all kinds of trouble but they became aware of little of it and I ran around with much older children.... I think that all of this affected my personality because I am somewhat difficult to be with and I don't put up with much. I don't know if I got that from my parents [genes] or because I ran around [with] peers who were like that or because the teachers gave me a hard time (after I gave them a hard time), I don't know. But the fact is that I'd like to have a nice relationship with a male but it's an uphill battle because I tend to fly off the handle."

CONCLUSIONS: DEFINITIONS OF RELATIONSHIP QUALITY ARE CULTURE SPECIFIC

A spousal relationship consists of several dimensions, from the affective level to its power-sharing aspect. Some of these dimensions tend to be given a greater emphasis in different cultures, at different historical periods, and, within each couple, at different times in their life course. For instance, the romantic or love aspect considered so important in North America is not even taken into consideration in many countries of the world. In other countries, love often develops among a proportion of married couples, but it is not an aspect of marriage deemed necessary. The sexual satisfaction dimension was not given much emphasis in this country a hundred years ago, particularly for women. Sex was certainly not something openly discussed concerning marriage. Within couples in western countries, romantic love may be considered far more important at the beginning of the relationship, for instance, and so may sexual satisfaction. As time goes by and as the relationship develops, these domains may become less salient than value consensus, shared activities, the division of labour, and parenting.

Culture is a key factor in teaching men and women what to expect in marriage and in determining what constitutes a satisfying conjugal relationship. As culture changes, so do cultural definitions of marital happiness to some extent. Currently, the media are a key source of cultural definitions, including books written by experts and articles in popular magazines, as well as what is depicted in films and on television.

The media focus entirely on heterosexual dating, cohabiting, and marriage. Thus, the general public inherits the cultural representations that depict ideal partner relationships only as opposite-sex couples. Yet, we have learned that there is a great deal of overlap between what makes a homosexual and a heterosexual couple satisfied with their respective relationships. What differs, naturally, are the mechanics of sex. But, otherwise, there is much similarity between gay, lesbian, and heterosexual couples. It would be interesting to gain a better understanding of how and from where homosexuals develop expectations concerning relationship satisfaction in view of the fact that they grow up in a heterosexual culture.

Summary

1. The Cuber and Haroff typology of couples married for at least 10 years includes the conflict-habituated, the devitalized, the passive-congenial, the vital, and the total. To this is added the reproductive-familial marriage. Changes in marital quality over the conjugal life may lead to conflict and divorce—or revitalization can occur.

2. The spousal division of labour includes not only who does what in the household and in child care but also who is responsible for what. The classification suggested includes the egalitarian and nongendered division of labour; the equitable but gendered; the specialist (which can be equitable or inequitable); the husband-helper (fairly widespread but typical in husband-earner families); the traditional; and the delegated among the more affluent. In general, gender roles dictate that the wife-mother does far more housework and child care and that she remain available for these responsibilities. Statistics are presented.

3. The effect of this unequal division of labour on marital quality seems to have changed during the last decades of the 20th century along with the evolution of the cultural and economic climate concerning the employment of women. The spousal division of labour becomes a particularly thorny issue for stepmothers of live-in or frequently visiting stepchildren. An important aspect of the spousal division of labour resides in emotional work: Women generally work harder at maintaining the relationship and are more sensitive to its quality and to their partners' moods than are men.

4. The concepts of marital happiness, satisfaction, and success are defined and differentiated. Marital adjustment and success is a predictor of stability. There are reciprocal effects between marital happiness and spouses' satisfaction with their parenting role. The quality of marriages may have been declining since the 1970s as a result of changes in the social context of marriage.

5. Same- and opposite-sex couples engage in similar types of conflict and conflict-resolution mechanisms. Conflict arises from issues pertaining to the division of labour, communication, lack of attention to each other, sex, children, and finances. In marriages, wives are generally less satisfied than husbands and perceive more problems.

6. Older couples experience relatively high levels of marital satisfaction. At this time, it is not known if this is a matter of cohort or of revitalization of marriages after mid-life (the U-curve phenomenon). Qualities that sustain long-term unions are closeness, commitment, communication, and similarity of perceptions and beliefs. The relationship is altered when one spouse becomes disabled, particularly at the cognitive level.

7. Remarriages are as happy as first marriages but satisfaction decreases more easily in remarriages. Remarried spouses may be less willing to cope with disappointments. Furthermore, the structure of remarriages (e.g., stepchildren and ex-spouses) complicates the relationship.

8. The study of the relationship among same-sex couples is still in its infancy and requires

methodological refinements. Lesbian couples report more intimacy, autonomy, and equality than married heterosexual couples, whereas gay couples report more autonomy. Same-sex couples have higher rates of dissolution than married couples. This may, in part, be due to an absence of barriers, particularly at the legal level, to leaving the relationship. All types of couples, however, experience similar sources of conjugal conflict.

9. The parental relationship affects children's development. Parental conflict that is perceived by children is detrimental. Happy marriages are related to healthy child development. This may be explained by the secure environment provided by such parents; the children have more positive role models; parents' personalities are less problematic in happy marriages; the children may have inherited easier predispositions; and, finally, external environmental influences affect parents and children.

10. Culture is a key factor in teaching men and women what to expect in marriage and in determining their level of happiness.

Key Concepts and Themes

Child well-being, pp. 322 ff.
Cohort effect, p. 318
Conflict, pp. 317, 321
Conflict-habituated marriage, pp. 302–303
Delegated division of labour, p. 309
Devitalized marriage, p. 303
Egalitarian division of labour, p. 307
Emotional work, pp. 313–314
Equitable division of labour, p. 307
Gendered aspect, pp. 306–310, 313
Genes, p. 324
Husband-helper, p. 308
Marital adjustment, p. 314
Marital happiness, pp. 314–315
Marital quality, pp. 311–316

Parenting satisfaction, p. 316
Passive-congenial marriage, pp. 303–304
Peer marriage, p. 307
Personality, p. 324
Remarriage, pp. 312, 320
Reproductive-familial marriage, p. 304
Relationship maintenance, p. 313
Retirement, pp. 318–319
Same-sex-partner relationship, pp. 320–321
Specialist division of labour, p. 308
Stepchildren, p. 312
Total marriage, p. 305
Traditional division of labour, p. 309
U-curve phenomenon, p. 318
Vital marriage, p. 304

Analytical Questions

1. Why did Cuber and Haroff study couples who had been married for a long time rather than newly married ones to arrive at a typology of marriages?

2. Considering the classification of the domestic division of labour, what can be concluded on the basis of exchange theory? (A return to Chapter 1 may help in answering this question.)

3. Which explanation do you prefer for the correlation between the quality of parents' marriage and their children's outcomes? Justify your choice.

4. How does culture play a role in the definition of what constitutes marital happiness? You may want to reexamine Chapter 2.

Suggested Readings

Alford-Cooper, F. 1998. *For keeps: Marriages that last a lifetime*. Armont, NY: Sharpe. The author reports on a study of couples belonging to two cohorts. One was married during the Great Depresssion and the other during the Second World War. She looks at the problems specific to each cohort of couples as well as their relationships.

Blumstein, P., and Schwartz, P. 1983. *American couples*. New York: Pocket Books. This is a relatively old but still relevant study on four types of couples: married, cohabiting, gay, and lesbian. Issues pertaining to their relationships are examined comparatively, including sexuality, money, and work.

Potuchek, J. L. 1997. *Who supports the family? Gender and breadwinning in dual-earner marriages*. Stanford, CA: Stanford University Press. This book presents a few statistics but is largely designed around the presentation of case studies of couples. The author studies husbands' and wives' social construction of breadwinning.

Schwartz, P. 1994. *Peer marriage: How love between equals really works*. New York: Free Press. The author presents the results of a qualitative study of couples who are in an egalitarian marriage. The relationships are examined, with a focus on the compromises and the necessity to radically alter traditional marriage patterns.

Suggested Weblinks

Canadian Research Institute for the Advancement of Women (CRIAW) presents research, statistical data, as well as activities on issues pertaining to women. Some of these issues are useful with respect to the spousal relationship.

http://criaw-icref.ca

National Council on Family Relations provides several sources and articles on topics related to marriage and spousal relationships. Their major journals, such as *Family Relations* and the *Journal of Marriage and Family,* are accessible on their website.

www.ncfr.org

The Vanier Institute of the Family provides several links and sources on topics related to marriage in Canada.

www.vifamily.ca

CHAPTER 12

The Parent-Child Relationship and Child Socialization

If you stay awhile in the nursery of a hospital maternity ward, you will see that each newborn is different from the very beginning of life. For instance, you may see one neonate such as Lucia, who cries constantly, even when picked up, and who is agitated and resists feeding. In the next crib, Jack is a total contrast: He sleeps contentedly, nurses avidly, and cries but stops as soon as he is fed or changed. A third baby, Latitia, is small, quiet, does not cry, sleeps most of the time, and drinks little milk.

Each baby needs different types of care. Baby Lucia requires more attention because she calls for more of it with her cries (what is called a child-driven stimulus). In contrast, Baby Jack demands little attention and is easy: All he needs is to be fed, changed, and cuddled. Jack's parents have more free time and feel competent because it seems to them that everything they do for him is rewarded with success. From the beginning of his life, Jack and his parents establish a smooth relationship that is likely to continue in the future.

Lucia's temperament presents at the outset the potential for problems. Her parents may feel less competent and more tense, especially if she is their first child. If they are poor and experience marital conflicts, Lucia may constitute an additional challenge. Her parents' reactions may not always be positive because they are already frazzled by other preoccupations. As a result, she might grow up with less positive interactions and may not find interpersonal relations as rewarding as Jack will.

For her part, Baby Latitia arouses her caregivers' concern because of her low birth weight and minimal appetite. At the same time, her parents are likely to feel comfortable because she is an easy baby. If fed regularly, she will eventually thrive and will not make too many demands on them. But when a mother does not know much about infant care, a neonate such as tiny Latitia may deteriorate and waste away because she may not cry enough to indicate that she is hungry.

This chapter continues and complements Chapter 10 on family development. The parent-child relationship is studied within a combined interactional-transactional and life course perspective (Elder, 1995). Our three fictive newborns illustrate some of the mechanisms at the origin of this relationship. What emerges from these vignettes are **interactions** or transactions (Clark et al., 2000). On a basic level, each baby has different needs to which parents (generally mothers) respond; this means that infants unwittingly initiate many of the parental gestures that form the cornerstone of the relationship. For instance, a baby who cries constantly (see Family Research 12.1) may elicit less positive reactions from his or her parents (Sanson and Rothbart, 1995). In turn, this reaction depends on parents' gender, personalities, perceptions, and life circumstances (Crockenberg and Leerkes, 2003). One particularly salient characteristic affecting parental responsiveness is depression (Onyskiw and Hayduk, 2001). Then, these reactions (being fed, changed, cuddled, or discouragingly ignored) become part of the babies' environment and contribute to the shaping of their subsequent behaviours and, later on, their attitudes and beliefs.

A small child who is blessed with positive characteristics, such as having a good attention span and low impulsivity, finds it easier to comply to parents' socialization requests as he or she internalizes family rules and norms more easily. In turn, this child requires less supervision and less repetition, and receives fewer negative reactions from his or her parents. That child is less frequently disapproved of and scolded. Such children may form stronger attachments to their parents, both as a result of their personalities and of the way parents react to them. This attachment then further reinforces their willingness and ability to be socialized (Kochanska, 1995). Thus, within the interactional and transactional perspective, parents and children interact with and influence each other's behaviours and attitudes (Magnusson and Allen, 1983). Utilizing the Canadian National Longitudinal Survey of Children and Youth, Elgar et al. (2003) found that maternal depression and children's behavioural problems interacted, one worsening the other over time in a bidirectional pattern.

Thus, from the very beginning, children contribute to the way their parents see them and treat them (Veevers, 1979). Second, these interactions between parents and children become part of the children's environment (Ambert, 2001). Third, these interactions are in turn affected and shaped by sociostructural variables (Bronfenbrenner, 1979; Lewis, 1997). These include the number of children and adults in the family, the family's economic situation, and how society defines children and good parenting as well as motherhood and fatherhood.

This perspective stands in contrast with traditional views on socialization describing children's personalities and behaviours as the product of their parents' childrearing—particularly their mothers'. Although parental practices are indeed important, children and even more so adolescents contribute to the formation of their environment and of their own development. In other words, **children are coproducers** of their

---

FAMILY RESEARCH 12.1

Can Mothers Accurately Judge Their Babies' Fussiness?

Lounsbury and Bates (1982) taped the hunger cries of infants who had already been described by their mothers as being either difficult, average, or easy. The tapes were played to other women, also mothers, who were unaware of the ratings. These women judged the cries of the infants who had been described by their own mothers as difficult to be more irritating than the cries of the other infants. The correlations between the biological mothers' judgments of their baby's difficultness and the observers' ratings were quite substantial.

own development (Lerner and Busch-Rossnagel, 1981). They are coagents in their socialization process: They help their parents teach them the ways of behaving and thinking that are acceptable within their status group and society at large (Corsaro, 1997). Furthermore, as we see in Chapter 13, children's genetic background may be at least as important as parenting (Rutter, 2002). Finally, many of the preceding and following chapters also point to factors in the extra-familial environment as key variables in human development: human qualities valued by society, media-influenced peer cultures, schools, religion, neighbourhoods, and economic forces.

PARENTS' SOCIALIZATION PRACTICES

Professional standards are applied to how parents, and especially mothers, should interact with their children (Eichler, 1988). This is part of current trends to standardize and rationalize lives in a postmodern economy, with emphasis on individualism and the development in children of qualities such as independence, self-sufficiency, and academic achievement (Ambert, 1994b; Wall, 2004). Parenting practices and parent-child interactions are **social constructs** (Smith, 1993). North American societies stress "democratic rather than authoritarian relations, including autonomy, psychological well-being, and emotional expressiveness" as the ideal (Pyke, 2000:241). These values are shared by family theorists and clinicians alike. This social construct of proper family relations also makes it difficult for many immigrant children to value their own family's style of interaction, which they see as deficient compared to the model presented to them by television, books, and peers (Pyke, 2000).

Much of the vast literature on parents' socialization practices purports to link proper ways of parenting causally to positive child outcomes (Ambert, 2001). This literature generally ignores the role of genes, the dynamics of the interactional perspective, as well as the social construction of motherhood, fatherhood, and childhood. Furthermore, there is no research on "character" and moral or ethical outcomes of children or, for that matter, on parents. In other words, the research does not address the moral context of our society—even if many of the concerns pertain to delinquency and early sexuality. Morality is a domain that is strangely absent from sociological inquiry. Also absent is the fact that socialization practices support the values of the technological capitalist system (Nadesan, 2002). In the presentation that follows, we begin with Baumrind's (1967) initial typology of parents' socialization practices: authoritative, authoritarian, and permissive styles of parenting. This typology is expanded to meet criteria of cultural diversity.

Authoritative Parenting

Parents who are authoritative combine warmth, respect for their children's individuality, and psychological autonomy with monitoring of their activities and whereabouts (Gray and Steinberg, 1999). Authoritative parents are firm, yet loving, and involved. Such parents explain to their children the reasons behind their demands and the consequences of not complying. They insist on obedience and then follow through with enforcement of rules and appropriate punishment. Some evidence shows that punishment, when necessary, increases the effectiveness of reasoning for small children. It may increase their ability to internalize rules of behaviour so that, when older, they will no longer need to be punished (Larzelere et al., 1998).

Warmth and monitoring have been correlated with successful child and adolescent outcomes in all types of family structures in Canada, the U.S., and other countries (Steinberg and Darling, 1994). More specifically, monitoring is related to lower rates of risky sexual activities among adolescents (Miller et al., 1999; Rodgers, 1999), fewer behaviour problems among early adolescents (Pettit et al., 1999), and higher academic achievement (Mounts, 2001). The authoritative pattern correlates the most with good adjustment on all dimensions of development, but its various components (psychological autonomy, monitoring, and involvement) contribute in unique and independent ways to diverse child outcomes (Gray and Steinberg, 1999). However, parental monitoring is often affected when adolescents' problematic and delinquent behaviours increase (Laird et al., 2003). Thus, within an interactional perspective, authoritative parenting cannot prevent *all* problems, as illustrated here in a male student's autobiography:

> "I had continued to do drugs through Grade 9 and managed to keep a decent average in school. Pete's, John's and my parents had been comparing incidents and behavioural changes for a little while and finally figured that we were doing drugs. The straw that broke the camel's back was when Pete's mother found drugs in his room (I am sure my parents had searched mine). Pete admitted everything, including my participation. What followed was what was most painful to me and that was reality. I had hurt my family, my reputation, and who knows what else during my drug times and now I had to deal with all of this. Firstly, my parents sat down and talked to me. They were crying and told me I was not allowed to see any of those people again, that I was grounded, that I would be much more accountable now, and that I would improve my marks in school to meet my potential."

In this incident, the parents could not detect drug use that was taking place behind their backs. But vigilance, communication with other parents, and then a firm but loving stand contributed to the adolescent's redress—along with his cooperative personality. Thus, again, one sees the interaction between parental efforts and child characteristics. This had led Kerr and Stattin (2003) to advance that it is actually an adolescent's willingness to disclose information to parents that allows them to be authoritative. Using this critique, Fletcher et al. (2004) reanalyzed data and, in so doing, provided what is probably the best "unpacking" of the variables constituting authoritative parenting: parental knowledge, monitoring, control, and warmth. They found that parental monitoring and control still remain important components of adolescents' behaviours.

Authoritarian Parenting

In contrast, what predominates in the authoritarian parenting style is the dimension of control, restriction, and, at the extreme, coercion. This type of discipline is not so effective for most North American adolescents, perhaps in part because it is not socially constructed as suitable within the broad cultural context. Control and restrictions, however, are better accepted in other cultures, where they are seen as guidance (Gorman, 1998). Other authoritarian parents are characterized by inconsistency. They are arbitrary and erratic; they tell their children what to do and punish severely and indiscriminately, or they threaten, then harshly punish one day, but fail to follow through the next day. They "order" this and that without explaining why. They are often quick with slaps. They "natter" a lot. This type of discipline is not as effective because children can take advantage of its inconsistencies; it neither stimulates the development of self-control nor does it respect children as persons (Stevenson, 1999). At the extreme, it can lead to child abuse.

"No-Nonsense" Parenting

If Baumrind rewrote her typology today, she would probably include a socialization practice that falls between the authoritative and the authoritarian: no-nonsense parenting, often seen in African Canadian and American as well as in Caribbean samples. Brody and Flor (1998) describe this style as higher on control than in the authoritative pattern but also involving more warmth and nurturance than is the case in the authoritarian style. Control includes physical punishment that occurs within an otherwise affectionate context.

This no-nonsense pattern, first described in an ethnographic study by Young in 1974, "represents a functional adaptation to contexts that are more dangerous" (Brody and Flor, 1998:813); it signals to the child that the parent is vigilant and cares. So far, studies have found that this style of parenting promotes black children's sense of competence and regulation, and results in lower rates of detrimental behaviours and attitudes (Brody and Murry, 2001). These findings apply both in one- and two-parent families. This style of parenting is related to black teenagers' better school outcomes and taking personal responsibility—even though these adolescents may find that their parents "hassle" them (Spencer et al., 1996).

Permissive and Uninvolved Parenting

For their part, permissive parents place very few maturity demands on their children, who can behave very much as they wish. Such parents do not actively socialize their children, because they fail to set rules concerning school, behaviour at home, or activities with peers. Neither do they supervise their children. Permissiveness can be combined with either a high level of warmth and acceptance or with disinterest and even rejection.

Subsequent to Baumrind's description of permissive childrearing, another style of parenting was added: uninvolved parents (Maccoby and Martin, 1983). Such parents are either permissive and indifferent or permissive and rejecting. They do not pay much attention to their offspring and do not fulfill their socialization function (Steinberg et al., 1996). Low parental control and rejection are the opposite of support and monitoring. They are a combination that has been consistently related to a host of negative outcomes, including delinquency and drug use (Baumrind, 1991b). Adolescents raised in such a context tolerate frustration poorly and are more likely than others to be underachievers. They lack emotional control and long-term goals as well as purpose in life (Lamborn et al., 1991). At one extreme, such parents are called *neglecting*: Chao and Willms (2002) refer to them as irresponsible. Others are *abusive*.

The well-known developmentalist Urie Bronfenbrenner (1985), as well as Noller and Callan (1991), points out that parental permissiveness has more negative consequences than authoritarianism in times when there is cultural and social instability. In such a fluid context, norms of behaviour change rapidly, and a child needs far more guidance than in times when the entire community agrees on what constitutes proper and moral behaviour. Baumrind (1991a:114) notes that "in a context of social instability, caregivers are required to sustain a higher level of supervision than would be needed in a period of stability." Today, there are more dangers that confront adolescents than was the case 50 years ago. Consequently, "premature emancipation is perhaps a greater threat to mature identity formation than delayed separation from family attachments" (Baumrind, 1991a:115).

A perfect example of permissive but warm parenting is described by a student whose parents were both highly trained professionals. She had initiated sexual intercourse at age 12, had had two abortions, had been "stoned" throughout high school, had sold drugs, and had lived on the streets by choice—all experiences she recalled fondly. Her parents allowed drug use and sex at home and finally bought a condominium to give her more freedom while she was a drugged teenager:

> "We were allowed to toke in the house and grow pot plants in the basement.... My parents were completely straight, but extremely liberal. They allowed all manner of goings on.... School at this point was a joke. I was stoned every single day. I sat in the girls' washroom, the "English Can" because of its location, and smoked and toked. I had company since boys also partied in there.... I spent nine months as a street kid. My experiences were, for the most part, fun. I think this is partly because I knew that I could always go home. I still don't know why I kept it up for so long.... From age 15 to 18 I simply didn't have any notably painful experiences. This was partly because I was constantly stoned and partly because I was having such an adventurous life.... I was now having the time of my life in a close-knit subculture."

The two students quoted in this section shared one problem: drugs. However, the two sets of parents' and the offsprings' reactions to this problem are dramatically opposite. The results are also entirely different. These different outcomes and student appraisals of their situations are not caused just by their parents' socialization practices. They are also the result of environmental factors that both parents and adolescents created as well as of the interaction between parents' and adolescents' personalities. In these quotes, one detects some similarities of character traits that each set of parents and their individual adolescent share (Plomin, 1994). The male adolescent and his parents seem more duty bound and emotionally connected. As a young man, he describes himself as cooperative and stable. The female adolescent and her parents are less tied to conventions, less emotionally involved, as well as more individualistic and gratification oriented. As a young woman, she describes herself as unstable, "depressed," and "highly critical" of other people's ways of living.

Additional Parenting Styles

There may yet be at least one other type of parenting style that has not been discussed by researchers. It overlaps somewhat with the permissive, and is tentatively called the **wavering-negotiating** pattern, for want of a better term. Parents who exhibit this style do not guide their children, even their toddlers, or make demands of them. Rather, they consult with their children about every step they undertake, even when the child is very small. When the parents make suggestions, they change them as soon as the child objects or disagrees. Such parents never punish but are very involved and loving. Here are two examples I recently observed:

> The mother and a 2-year-old boy are getting in line at one of the checkout counters of a large food store. *M: You want to follow the lady? B: No, no, want to leave! M: If you wait a minute, you'll get to ride the conveyor belt. B: Want a candy bar. M: OK, what about this one? B: No, this one. M: OK, now let's follow the lady. B: Want belt right away (stamps foot). M: Ask the lady [me] if she can push her cart.* The conversation went on like this for the approximately three minutes I stood at the checkout counter. When I turned around to leave, the child was on the conveyor belt, to the clerk's obvious dismay.

> The mother of a 4-year-old girl is trying to buy a blouse in a department store. *G: It's ugly, I don't like it. M: Of course, honey, you're right, but I really don't need a pretty one. G: This one is nicer [grabs one from the rack. Note that she is eating ice cream that is running down her hands]. M: All right, I'll try it on if you want. G: No, I'm tired, I want to see the dollies. M: All right, sweetie, let's go and see the dollies.* The mother patiently follows.

In all the numerous instances when this pattern of interaction was observed, the mothers appeared well educated and upper-middle class. Mother-child negotiating went on for extended periods and the mothers unavoidably lost each round with a weary smile or sigh. The children never appeared satisfied and, when the mothers finally drew the line somewhere, several of the children threw loud temper tantrums—all in public places. These observations are anecdotal, but it is my guess that if researchers carried out systematic observations in large food stores and malls in certain middle-class metropolitan areas, they would encounter this pattern regularly. This is not a pattern that less advantaged parents can afford because it would be too disruptive to their lives: As so many researchers point out, working-class parents and poor parents focus on the primary tasks of sheltering, feeding, clothing, and teaching basic skills and values to their children (Lareau, 2003). The rest is a "luxury" that only better-off families can afford.

DETERMINANTS OF PARENTS' SOCIALIZATION PRACTICES

How do parents develop their socialization practices? What influences parents to adopt an authoritative or permissive approach? Three types of influence come to mind. They are complementary rather than mutually exclusive, and *interact* with each other: contextual and cultural influences, parents' personalities and beliefs, and parents' adaptation to their children's personalities and behaviours. However, we have already seen that society entertains vastly different social constructions of motherhood and fatherhood. The gendered division of domestic labour may have led to what Jensen (1995) calls the feminization of childhood. It is therefore entirely possible that mothers and fathers develop their parenting styles somewhat differently. The mechanisms described here may not apply equally well to both genders at the same time. Furthermore, there is evidence of substantial disagreement among parents, at least of young children, around parenting practices (Invest in Kids, 2002).

Contextual and Cultural Determinants

Childrearing practices can become ineffective or harsh because of environmentally induced stressors. Examples are poverty, unemployment, marital conflict, and divorce. These stress-inducing circumstances tend to disrupt parental practices and make parents less responsive to children's needs. For instance, fathers' warmth decreases and irritability increases following unemployment (Elder et al., 1994a). Stress experienced by mothers because of marital problems or economic hardships often leads to a more erratic, punishing, and disciplinary relationship with their children (Conger et al., 1995). Lenton (1990:173) suggests that harsher disciplinary practices "are explained by insufficient resources and because parents may also experience an erosion of their authority." They then try to recoup their authority by becoming less flexible. Adults who experience work and stress overload feel easily harassed and impatient; they may therefore parent less effectively and happily (Galambos et al., 1995). Thus, the quality of childrearing may change over the life course, not simply in response to the different needs of growing children but also as a consequence of evolving contextual factors.

The Question of What Constitutes "Proper" Parenting

A particularly sensitive issue when discussing impoverished families as well as families from other cultures is the matter of what constitutes "proper" childrearing practices: the **social construction of proper parenting.** In North America, good parenting is synonymous with the authoritative style. This approach is endorsed by professionals, especially psychologists and social workers as well as child advocates. However, some practices may be more acceptable in certain cultural contexts than others: "What may be experienced by adolescents as parental intrusiveness in some cultural groups may be experienced as concern in others" (Steinberg et al., 1992:729). Poor mothers, particularly those living in disadvantaged neighbourhoods, are, on average, more disciplinarian or no-nonsense than authoritative, as seen earlier (Mason et al., 1996).

This stricter type of discipline generally has positive behavioural outcomes among black children (Deater-Deckard et al., 1996). In dangerous neighbourhoods, this style of parenting may be appropriate to secure compliance and to ensure safety and may be perceived as a form of concern (Lamborn et al., 1996). Hanson et al. (1997:213) have found that poor children are less "negatively affected by yelling and spanking and more positively affected by hugging and praising and by living with parents who have high aspirations for them." When peers are problematic, more controlling measures are adaptive and act as a deterrent to detrimental behaviours (Mason et al., 1996). Proper monitoring of children, especially by single parents, later results in far fewer difficult behaviours among adolescents (Amato and Fowler, 2002).

Therefore, one needs to evaluate "proper" parenting practices within the context in which they are applied. Rather than value independence and creativity in their children, impoverished minority mothers frequently value obedience and respect for authority—as is the case in most countries of the world. For instance, in the U.S., this is reflected in Latina mothers' preferences for obedience (Harwood et al., 1996). The valuation of independence and creativity is a western phenomenon, a consequence of education, relative affluence, and safe environments (Chao, 1994).

The Debate over Physical Punishment

There is a related debate as to whether physical or corporal punishment leads to maladjustment in children and adolescents. Some research, in fact, documents a relationship between corporal punishment and low self-esteem as well as delinquency, aggressiveness, and other problems (Straus and Donnelly, 1994). However, this research corpus has several limitations. The first stems from the fact that most studies are not longitudinal; thus, one has no way of knowing if physical punishment "caused" the delinquency, alcoholism, and behavioural problems in some of the adolescents and adults who report having been spanked as children. A life course perspective suggests that some of the adults were probably difficult children: Parents of children with behavioural difficulties generally use more disciplinary methods of *all* kinds, including reasoning, grounding, withdrawal of privileges, and spanking (Robert Larzerele, quoted in *The Globe and Mail*, October 5, 1999). Thus, parents may have been responding to children who were already problematic and are still so as adults. Similarly, it is possible that troubled young adults recall their parents' behaviours more negatively than they were in reality.

These studies also fail to provide valid results because they have little to say about parents' level of stress as well as psychological adjustment—all factors that could have contributed more substantially to their children's future problems. Furthermore, this research rarely inquires about the remainder of the parents' socialization practices. For instance, it rarely considers whether parents are or have been loving or rejecting in their punitive approach (Florsheim et al., 1996:1229). Finally, this research does not tell us whether children perceive the punishment as a sign of parental rejection or concern (Baumrind, 1994; Simons et al., 1994a).

In English-speaking western countries, there are indications that physical punishment is harmful psychologically when the child perceives it as a form of parental rejection (Rohner et al., 1996) or when the overall parent-child relationship is negative (Larzelere et al., 1998). It is important to distinguish between parents who hit in anger and impulsively "at the drop of a hat," and parents who spank with regret and after having explained repeatedly to the child how he or she disobeyed. In other words, physical punishment does not take place in a vacuum—its consequences will depend greatly on the *totality of the familial climate*. McLoyd and Smith (2002) have found a longitudinal increase in behavioural problems among children who had been spanked; but this increase nearly disappeared in situations of high maternal support of the child. Unfortunately, as they point out, "our measure does not reflect the extent to which spanking episodes are or are not preceded by the use of reason to gain the child's compliance" (p. 52). Nevertheless, there are no indications that corporal punishment *prevents* serious antisocial behaviour in North America (Simons et al., 2002)—nor that it causes it.

Baumrind (1996) emphasizes that it is not a particular disciplinary practice that is important but the broader parenting context within which it occurs. She mentions Sweden, where corporal punishment was legally abolished in 1979 (the *aga* law). In the following years, Sweden saw an increase rather than a decrease of adolescent violence: "The ban on corporal punishment in Sweden has not resulted in cultural spillover of the adult culture's nonviolent values to a segment of the youth" (p. 412). Baumrind concludes that "the root causes of youth violence are to be found elsewhere than in the use of disciplinary physical punishment in the home" (p. 413). In summary, it is unlikely that occasional and fair corporal punishment of young children in itself causes any of the ills with which it has been associated. Nevertheless, even light physical punishment is not a parenting practice that is appropriate on a regular basis and it is certainly detrimental for adolescents and children younger than 2. Harsh physical punishment, in contrast, is dangerous because it too often veers into abuse, is unfairly painful, and is likely to be perceived as an act of rejection and aggressiveness by the victims. It may also provide children with an example of a violent style of interaction.

Parents' Personalities and Beliefs

Parents' personalities and beliefs constitute the second element that influences how they raise their children. A wide range of adult personality characteristics can lead to authoritative parenting. For instance, parents who are patient, calm, and affectionate, who have a sense of humour, or who are businesslike may be more inclined to use authoritative or even no-nonsense techniques. By the same token, another range of personality configurations makes it impossible for adults to become authoritative or no-nonsense parents. For example, think of a man who is easily frustrated, impatient, and impulsive. Such a man is more likely to become a harsh, rejecting, and perhaps abusive parent than an authoritative one. In turn, there is a good chance that his children will show some of these partly genetically influenced traits (Neiderhiser et al., 1999). Their irritating behaviours will trigger bouts of impulsive punishing, especially when he is under stress. Poor parenting results to a certain extent from parents' difficult personalities and deviant attitudes (Newcomb and Loeb, 1999).

Parents' beliefs about the proper ways of raising children are also important determinants. These beliefs may originate from the way parents were themselves raised. For instance, adults who felt unloved as children because their parents were cold and nonexpressive may react by becoming warm and supportive parents. Others may have been influenced by cultural constructs of children as naturally good ("If you let them lead the way, everything will be fine"). Yet others have learned that "sparing the rod spoils the child" and behave accordingly. Parents' beliefs and notions about proper childrearing can be learned from books, professionals, television, or friends.

Parental Adaptation to Children

A third factor influencing parents' socialization practices is suggested by the interactional and behavioural genetics perspectives: Many parents adapt their practices to fit their children's behaviours, personalities, and abilities (Bates et al., 1998). Several studies document this process of adaptation. For instance, when hyperactive children are successfully treated with the drug methylphenidate, or Ritalin, their hyperactivity diminishes substantially, and mothers become less controlling (Tarver-Behring and Barkley, 1985). Similar reactions have been observed among teachers (Whalen et al., 1980). In other studies, mothers of cooperative children and mothers of oppositional children were experimentally paired with a difficult child (not their own) and then with a cooperative child (not their own). Both types of mothers exhibited more controlling and intrusive behaviour with the oppositional child than with the cooperative one (Brunk and Henggeler, 1984). In other words, adults may adapt their parenting practices to children's behaviours, or adolescents may determine them (Kerr and Stattin, 2003).

Pursuing this interactional line of reasoning, one can see that children and adolescents may influence their parents to become coercive or rejecting, even if they do so unwittingly (Simons et al., 2002). As Hanson and colleagues (1997:208) state, "Parents may monitor children with behavior problems more closely than they do children without these problems." Yet, as Simons et al. (1994c:359) point out, "rebellious, antisocial children often punish parental efforts to monitor and discipline while reinforcing parental withdrawal and deviance." Early oppositional and defiant behaviours undermine later parenting practices and nurturance (Scaramella et al., 2002). In turn, diminished parenting can lead to affiliation with deviant peers and delinquency (Simons et al., 2001). Patterson et al. (1992:11) observe that it is difficult to monitor the whereabouts of an adolescent who is extremely oppositional. Nevertheless, parenting affects child behaviours more than child behaviours detrimentally affect certain aspects of parenting (Scaramella et al., 2002). Hanson and colleagues (1997) also write about the possibility that lower-income parents may receive less admiration and respect from their children—and we have seen such examples in previous chapters. This disadvantage reduces their effectiveness as parents, and in turn may lead them to adopt harsher practices or feel defeated and become permissive. From this perspective, it can be said that children coproduce the parental socialization practices of which they are the beneficiaries or the victims (see also Henderson et al., 1996).

THE PARENT-ADOLESCENT RELATIONSHIP

The parent-adolescent relationship is influenced not only by the social construction of parenthood but also by societal definitions of what adolescence is (Arnett, 2001). North American research emphasizes conflict as well as lack of parent-adolescent communication. In this section, we also examine the limits and contexts of parental influence on adolescents.

The Social Construction of Adolescence

Much research has been devoted to parent-adolescent conflict. In contrast, harmony is much less emphasized in western research. This interest in conflict derives in part from old-fashioned western notions that portray adolescence as being necessarily a period of turbulence—the idea of "storm and stress." At the beginning of the 20th century, the psychologist Stanley Hall was at the origin of this perspective on adolescence as a naturally turbulent stage. Sigmund Freud, who was very influential, reinforced this idea that adolescence is unavoidably a period during which all youths undergo emotional turmoil. Were this textbook written in Africa or in parts of Asia, this discussion on adolescence would either be absent or have a totally different focus.

The beginning of adolescence is generally determined by the onset of puberty—that is, hormonal changes and the development of primary and secondary sexual characteristics. The transition to adolescence exists in all cultures throughout the world, even though the age of onset varies depending on life conditions, such as nutrition. A poor diet, for instance, is likely to delay the onset of menarche. What is important to underscore is that this period of physiological puberty does not give rise to an identical psychological and *social* puberty throughout the world (Schlegel and Barry, 1991).

But, despite the fact that the "storm and stress" ideology concerning adolescence does not apply universally, it still remains a widely held belief (Holmbeck and Hill, 1988).

The famed anthropologist Margaret Mead (1928) was the first to document the fact that the problematic type of adolescence frequently encountered in North America, and which has become common in most western countries, is a cultural rather than a biological entity. At that time, her research was going against the grain of prevailing social constructions. But in the last three decades, most qualified specialists have reached the same conclusion. "Teenagehood" is a **historical phenomenon** (Modell and Goodman, 1990). Historians Kett (1977) and Demos (1971) have placed the invention of adolescence as a social category between 1890 and 1920—after most middle-class youngsters were pushed out of the labour market and into the school system, separated from the adult world of which they had until then been part (Côté and Allahar, 1994). Today, adolescence has been further extended because of early puberty, longer schooling, and more engagement in peer worlds (Larson et al., 2002).

It is important to distinguish between the fact that Canadian and American societies often present a perturbing context for adolescents and the supposition that adolescence is in itself "naturally"—thus necessarily—a period that is difficult, stormy, and in opposition to the adult world. Adolescent crisis is in great part created by the type of environment that has evolved in most western countries—not by the nature of adolescence in general (Tyyskä, 2001). Contributing factors are materialistic values, age segregation, lack of a meaningful role for adolescents in the productive aspects of the economy, schools with low standards, and media-oriented peer groups (Adams et al., 2002). In the U.S., Montemayor (1986) estimates that over one-third of adolescents pass through difficult times. However, it should be noted that a good proportion of these teenagers are experiencing problems that were already with them in childhood (Carlson et al., 1999). One cannot therefore blame adolescence for all the problems encountered by youths. Many of these youths will remain problematic as adults: They are problematic persons rather than problematic adolescents.

How Do Parents and Adolescents Get Along?

As stated earlier, much of the literature on the parent-adolescent relationship focuses on conflict. The research indicates that conflict generally pertains to daily routines rather than key value issues (Smetana and Gaines, 1999). Nevertheless, 15 percent of adolescents report daily arguments while 40 percent report weekly or more frequent arguments (Bibby, 2001). Both parents and adolescents mention more conflict now than in the past (Collins and Russell, 1991). Adolescents also report more conflict than do their parents. Furthermore, naturalistic studies based on day-to-day reports, such as the one described in Family Research 12.2, show higher levels of daily tension than survey questionnaires do (Larson and Richards, 1994).

Barber (1994:384) suggests that the absence of conflict over controversial topics such as sex and drugs most likely means that, although parents and adolescents differ in attitudes about them, they do not discuss these issues. In fact, a survey reported in *Time* magazine (June 15, 1998) supports the notion that parents and children rarely talk to each other about drugs and sex. When asked from what sources teenagers learn about sex, only 7 percent mentioned parents, but 45 and 29 percent, respectively, mentioned peers and television. In Canada, only 8 percent of adolescents turn to parents for guidance about sex (Bibby and Posterski, 2000:172).

FAMILY RESEARCH 12.2

Naturalistic Self-Reporting: Daily Activities

In a study conducted by Larson and Richards (1994), adolescents and their parents were asked to carry a pager for one week. When beeped, each completed a report on their current activities, indicating what they were doing, where and with whom they were, as well as their thoughts and emotional state at the time of each signal. They were beeped once at random within every two-hour block of time between 7:30 a.m. and 9:30 p.m. This method was called the *Experience Sampling Method*. The focus was on the daily activities of adolescents and parents from single- and married-parent families. Adolescents were sampled from the fifth through ninth grades of a middle- and working-class Chicago suburb. In addition, parents and adolescents filled out many questionnaires about their family life and themselves.

This combination of methods allowed the researchers to study daily activities and accompanying moods of all the family members individually. But above all, it allowed them to compare how each family member felt in the company of the others and how each felt while engaging in various activities together or separately, whether at school, work, home, with peers or co-workers. The researchers could also obtain on-the-spot reports of conflict, contentment, or boredom while family members were together. They could also, for instance, compare how each reported on the same conflict.

Another related explanation, provided by Demo (1992:115), is that parents and adolescents "spend very little time together, often not more than one hour per day of direct interaction." While parents' and adolescents' reports on time spent together are somewhat at odds, both mention spending only a few minutes each day talking (Larson and Richards, 1994). There may be a wide variety of situations that adolescents experience and parents never know about, thus reducing the potential for conflict, but at the same time depriving adolescents of proper guidance. It is at least logical that, when adolescents' behaviours go against parental expectations, they try to carry on as much of their lives as possible without their parents' knowledge.

Moreover, parents are busier than previous cohorts of adults used to be, are generally employed, and many work even longer hours than just a decade ago to make ends meet (Schor, 1991). This is especially the case for immigrant parents who also experience a reduction in their authority within the family (Anisef and Kilbride, 2003). High rates of divorce and other problems, such as alcoholism, spousal abuse, and mental illness, mean that many parents are so preoccupied with their own personal difficulties that they overlook those of their children. These factors diminish parenting availability and monitoring, and henceforth reduce parent-adolescent friction.

Larson and Richards (1994) report that adolescents experience less conflict with their fathers than their mothers, partly because mothers interact more with them concerning the basics of their daily lives. The household division of labour based on gender places mothers at a disadvantage over fathers in this respect. In this vein, Collins (1990) reviews studies illustrating that, when a mother interrupts her adolescent during a discussion, the youngster subsequently interrupts her even more, but does not do so for the father. Yet, all studies indicate that adolescents are closer to their mothers than their fathers (Noller, 1994), particularly in divorced families (Williams, 2001c; Zill et al., 1993). In married families, adolescents are both more attached to and in conflict with their mothers than with their fathers. They also seek her support and advice more.

Parental Influence

Parental influence or the ability to socialize children and affect their outcomes is a much discussed topic these days, particularly with regard to adolescents. This section discusses how parental effectiveness does not operate within a vacuum but is circumscribed by society and the child outcomes it values.

The Role of Historical Periods

Family relationships take place within a distinct cultural context, at a given historical period, and under specific economic conditions (Hareven, 1994a,b). Families' social and cultural context has altered drastically within the past 30 years (Elder, 1995): Technological changes have occurred with an extreme rapidity that has no precedent in history. The environment is now controlled by information technology, including the audiovisual media. The workplace, schools, homes, and leisure activities have all been affected by these changes and the evolution of the value systems that generally accompanies such transitions. Parents have had to adapt their role within this new context and raise their children accordingly, although much of this adaptation takes place unconsciously (Alwin, 1990). For instance, numerous parents have accepted television and video games as children's main sources of entertainment and often as babysitters. Many have become habituated to the violence and the values streaming out of these visual media.

For their part, children react to their parents according to what they learn through their environment. Their sources of information include their peer group and the messages they receive from the media as well as from professionals. Children are more aware of their rights than in the past. They have higher material expectations and requirements. They want more autonomy, and male children in particular are taught to separate themselves from their mothers and the feminine realm. As a result of all these changes, children's and adolescents' receptivity to parental socialization efforts has evolved. Many no longer see their parents as legitimate sources of information or even of authority for their behaviours. While a great proportion of adolescents report that their mothers (81 percent) and their fathers (70 percent) are influencing their lives to quite an extent, only 18 percent say that they turn to them when facing serious problems (Bibby, 2001).

As a general rule, the extent of parents' influence on their children, particularly on their adolescents, varies according to prevailing sociohistorical conditions (Bronfenbrenner, 1989). In other words, there are *historical eras* or time periods when it is easier for parents to influence their youngsters and others when it is far more difficult to do so. Social change ushers in new influences on children's lives while also reducing the impact of other influences (Adams et al., 2002). Just 50 or so years ago, there was no television, but that medium has long since been considered to be a prime agent of socialization or of influence. Often, as seen in Chapter 3, the contents of television and related media do not support parental efforts and may even undermine their moral and practical teachings. In contrast, religion, which generally supports parents and upholds their moral authority, used to be a more powerful influence than it is now throughout all regions and social classes. Thus, parents have lost a degree of legitimacy through these two changes alone.

The Role of the Human Qualities That Are Valued

As society evolves, it places a premium on certain specific human outcomes. Thus, parents are emphasizing autonomy and self-reliance in their socialization practices both because of society's value orientation toward individuality and because parents who are employed need more self-reliant children (Rossi and Rossi, 1990). Mainstream technological society also values the development of self-esteem and educational achievement (Varga, 1997). Although all of these outcomes are, to some extent, affected by parents, these outcomes are particularly influenced by peer interaction and the school situation. For instance, self-esteem is peer driven after a certain age (Ambert, 2003d). Television may also affect self-esteem, for that matter, as teenagers probably find it difficult to compare themselves favourably to their idols who are invariably rich, attractive, popular, and well developed physically while remaining slim (Ambert, 2003e; Spitzer et al., 1999). Furthermore, self-esteem, achievement, and ability to be self-reliant are also affected by innate factors such as cognitive ability, hyperactivity, and locus of control. Self-esteem is a partly personality- and peer-driven element, and thus less easily influenced by parents.

In contrast, a few decades ago, the development of politeness, obedience, conformity, service to others, and patriotism was given more importance in the socialization of children (Alwin, 2001). These outcomes are more culturally influenced; they are thus subject to direct teaching and example and are more amenable to parental socialization. Therefore, parents were more influential in these respects than is the case for outcomes that are more personality driven, such as self-esteem and the ability to be independent. The topic of parental influence is continued at the end of Chapter 13, where we will take a critical look at the conclusions reached by some behaviour geneticists in this respect.

THE ROLE OF PEERS IN THE PARENT-ADOLESCENT RELATIONSHIP

I have chosen to focus on the role of peers in the parent-adolescent relationship because it is a topic that is less researched than the role that parents play in the facilitation of their children's relationships with their peers (Updegraff et al., 2001)—a topic favoured by psychologists. Today's parents have less control than in the past over whom their child associates with after a certain age, and they are also concerned about the quality of their children's peers. More peer interactions, especially among boys, take place outside the home than used to be the case. When children attend schools outside their neighbourhood, or have a car, or live in a spread-out suburb or in an area where gangs rule, parents are fairly helpless (Brown and Huang, 1995). They cannot monitor what takes place and with whom their child or adolescent associates.

Peer Groups and Parental Isolation

The peer group may support parental teachings, but it may also conflict with parents' values. Children whose peers' behaviours and values are so different from what they are taught within their families experience **cross-pressures.** A child's socialization is considerably easier when both peers and parents agree, and is difficult, at best, when fundamental contradictions exist between the two systems. The greater the similarity between parents' values and those of their children's peers, the lower the level of parent-child conflict. Youngsters whose parents approve of their peers, and particularly of their close friends, will get along better with their parents. Not only do they have more in common, but parents need to exert less direct control over them, thus pre-empting conflict. In contrast, when parents disapprove of their adolescents' friends, a great deal of tension may exist if parents voice their concerns.

What parent has not heard, "But all the others are going!" "Everybody is doing it" and "Everybody has one." These are powerful and often intimidating messages handed to parents (Ambert, 1997). Thus, each parenting couple and, more and more, each single mother or father has to face what is presented by their child as a normal entitlement among youngsters. Parents are made to feel that, if they do not conform, they will do a grave injustice and deprive the child. This alleged consensus among youngsters allows them to speak with great authority to their parents, because parents are generally more isolated than children when it comes to tactical and moral support. Adolescent groups and subcultures are much more cohesive and less fragmented for each child than are adult subcultures for each individual parent. In reality, there is no such thing as a parental subculture or peer group, and this constitutes a disequilibrium that is detrimental to parents' role (Small and Eastman, 1991). A single mother expresses the situation thusly when attempting to understand with hindsight how her teenage daughter became delinquent without her noticing it:

> *"My daughter has a lot of friends, some I know, some I don't. They talk on the phone on a daily basis even after they have been to school together, they make plans, they exchange clothes, they cover for each other, they watch each other's back against their parents. They come and they go and it's impossible to keep track of all of this. New clothes that she wears are borrowed from Mindy and if I ask Mindy, she'll say, 'Don't I got good taste!' If Mindy's mother calls to find out where she is, all I can say is that they went to the movies together. That's what I was told. But they actually went to this boy's place. If Mindy's mother calls about clothes, I say that they exchange a lot while in reality they are all shoplifting. So you see you have to be a very very clever parent to keep track of all of this and to add it all up together to one conclusion: My child is a shoplifter and she's barely 15 and she's screwing around. But don't think for one minute that I added this up on my own; the police did it for me. These girls just protect each other. Protect for what? They're the ones who need protection against each other. Now I tell you that Mindy's mother, Jessie's mother, and I have all been fooled."*

Along these lines, Steinberg and colleagues (1995:453) find that, when adolescents' peers have authoritative parents, the latter contribute to positive developmental outcomes above and beyond the adolescents' own parents' authoritativeness: "We believe that this may be due in part to the higher level of shared social control provided by a network of authoritative parents." Yet, in the preceding quote, the parents are exhibiting all the "symptoms" of being authoritative, but their children's delinquent peer group is far more clever and better organized.

Many parents, especially more educated ones, make it a point of knowing their children's friends' parents (Muller and Kerbow, 1993). **Parent networks** can fulfill several functions both for parents and their children. When these are school based, they can contribute to a smoother socialization process, norms that are more closely adhered to, and better-informed parents. It is, however, far more difficult for adolescents' parents than for young children's parents to know their children's peers' parents and form an effective community—at a time when such a context would be the most helpful.

Peer Spillover Effect

Countless students' autobiographies underscore the continued impact of the peer group even after the child returns home from school at the end of the day. Once at home, the youngster keeps on reacting to what the peers did or said or failed to say. In other words, children and adolescents bring home the stress experienced via their peers, and this stress spills over into their interactions with parents (Ladd, 1992). Students frequently pointed out that they had used their parents as "scapegoats" and taken their peer-related frustrations out on them as soon as one parent had said or done something that the youngster could react to: "I used to sulk up and down the stairs, just to make them as miserable as I was," or "I would blow my top," or "I used to cry and yell and storm out." These adolescents would lash out at the surprised parent, who then tried to reason out the situation, only to unwittingly provoke a sharper outburst from the youngster.

Furthermore, peer maltreatment, discussed more extensively in Chapter 15, creates additional spillover effect into the parent-child relationship. The ill-treated child's parents often suffer with their child when they learn of the victimization, but they especially suffer indirectly. That is, the frustrated child often takes it out on his parents and siblings (Ambert, 1994a). Parents inherit what one student called "the flak." In addition, parents can even be blamed by clinicians for traumas that actually have peers at their source. A student's recollections illustrate this latter phenomenon quite vividly:

> "Up to that age [11 years] I had been quite happy at school but then something happened to me, I stopped growing and I became in no time the shortest and skinniest and soon the pimpliest little runt at my grade level. The other boys used to pick on me, hide my coat, steal my lunches and would never include me in their games. They'd laugh at me openly and the girls started avoiding me too because it wasn't cool to be seen with the most unpopular boy.... You can't imagine how many times my mother had to keep me home because I'd start throwing up. I became scared shitless.... The funny thing is that my parents had to send me to a psychiatrist and he turned around and blamed them for not being supportive and for whatever else. That's kind of sad when you think that my problems had nothing to do with my parents. My parents were sort of being made miserable because of this little runt I was and now by this psychiatrist and to this day they have never blamed me and have always been supportive."

THE RELATIONSHIP BETWEEN PARENTS AND ADULT CHILDREN

There are both continuities and changes in the parent-child relationship throughout the various stages of family development, as well as throughout the life course of each family member. In these respects, the following sections complement Chapter 10.

When the Child Is a Young Adult

In North America, full adulthood has traditionally meant financial independence from parents and the establishment of a separate household, usually with a marital partner. However, as we have seen in other chapters, this life stage may be postponed. As a social stage, adolescence starts earlier and finishes later than it did 50 years ago. Whereas adolescence as a social construct was the invention of the dawn of the 20th century, young adulthood is the creation of the closing of that century (Côté, 2000). Young adults remain home (coresidence) more often than was the case two decades ago and many remain financially dependent on their parents for a longer period of time (Mitchell, 2000). First, young adults stay home because they remain in the educational system longer and this system is costly. Second, the development of the service economy and the shrinking of the manufacturing base have resulted in an increase in part-time and low-paying jobs for young people without higher education—these jobs force them to remain with their parents for financial reasons (Gee et al., 2003). Thus, coresidence enables better transfers of capital from parents to children (Beaujot, 2004). In contrast, children who leave home too early may be disadvantaged, especially over time (Goldscheider and Goldscheider, 1999).

A third reason for the lengthening dependence of young adults may be related to the finding that they are increasingly endorsing consumerist values (Bibby and Posterski, 2000; Crimmins et al., 1991). What were considered luxuries in previous cohorts—cars, home entertainment systems, and computers—have become necessities for current ones. Consequently, the earnings required to reach such heightened material expectations come later, and in the meantime young adults can afford them only when they remain with their parents. Fourth, in some cities, rents are out of reach for those on low incomes, which makes the parental home comparatively more appealing. As Hareven (1994b:448) points out, whereas in the late 19th century, children remained at home to help aging parents or widowed mothers, now "young adult children reside with their parents in order to meet their own needs." In fact, 20- to 29-year-old young adults are the age group of grown children most likely to receive parental support (Cooney and Uhlenberg, 1992).

While parents have to give freedom to their older adolescents earlier than before, for instance regarding sexuality, they have to remain active in a supportive role for a far longer period than was the case previously. This duality of freedom and dependence can result in ambivalence or even in a conflict-generating situation, both for young adults and their parents (Connidis and McMullin, 2002a,b). The research results are inconsistent and even contradictory when it comes to evaluating parental satisfaction with their adult children's coresidence. The reasons for lengthened coresidence probably affect parents' satisfaction. For instance, parental satisfaction is higher when children are "occupying a role that appears to lead to full independence" (Mitchell, 2000:91). Furthermore, the quality of the relationship is an important variable and parental stress is lower when interaction is positive and little conflict exists (Aquilino and Supple, 1991).

Mothers of adult children with mental delays are often close to these living-at-home children and benefit from the closeness. However, the father-child relationship is contingent upon more factors, such as his personality, his marital life, and the adult child's behaviour (Essex, 2002). There are indications that male offspring are more likely to expect help from parents than females and that there is often a gap between mothers' expectations and children's in terms of help (Goldscheider et al., 2001). There may be differences by social class and race in terms of satisfaction with parenting young adult children. For instance, American black mothers perceive their children to be less supportive than do white mothers (Umberson, 1992). This contrast is possibly a question of income and resource differentials between the two groups, or it may result from the fact that African-American parents have higher filial expectations than do whites (Lee et al., 1998).

As young adults leave the nest and enter roles that parents have occupied for years, particularly work and marriage, parents feel closer to their children (Aquilino, 1997:682). As young adults age, their relationship with both parents is still important for their psychological well-being (Barnett et al., 1992). Gender differences do exist, in the sense that females continue to feel more connected to their parents than males.

When the Child Is 40 to 60 Years Old

One key aspect of the *life course perspective* is that it brings attention to the development of the relationship over time as both parents and adult children age and as cohorts change (Martin-Matthews, 2000). For instance, only 8 percent of persons born in 1910 still had a surviving parent by age 60. This percentage rose to 16 for those born in 1930 and it is expected to rise to 23 for people aged 60 born in 1960 (Rosenthal, 2000). But whatever their age, a majority of adults and their parents report having a good relationship and being in contact with each other fairly regularly, as illustrated in Figure 12.1. Adult children, particularly daughters, often speak with their mothers, although they do so less frequently with fathers (Townsend-Batten, 2002). Generally, the affection that exists between parents and adult children is the chief motivator in continued contact and exchange with parents (Rossi and Rossi, 1990). The more parents and children see each other, the greater affection they have for each other, and vice versa (Lawton et al., 1994:65). But these researchers have found that this reciprocity of affectivity does not always apply to fathers. They concluded that "the motivations for interaction between adult children and their mothers and fathers are different."

Studies tend to present demographic characteristics to explain the quality of the parent-child relationship: gender and marital status of parent and child, socioeconomic status, geographic distance, and parents' health status (Connidis, 2001) and even religiosity (Townsend-Batten, 2002). The interactional perspective also suggests studies

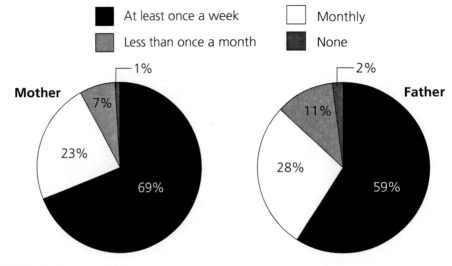

FIGURE 12.1

Frequency of Contact with Mothers and Fathers for Adults Aged 25 to 54 No Longer Living with Parents

Source: Statistics Canada, General Social Survey, 1995; Townsend-Batten, 2002.

Note: Percentages refer to population aged 25 to 54 with a parent living in another household.

that would look at a child's and a parent's personality characteristics that could affect the relationship. One might also look at the matter of fit between the personalities. Is the relationship between parent and adult child closer and warmer when the two have similar or complementary personalities? What if they are similar on traits that are not conducive to harmony, such as restlessness, aggressivity, and disagreeableness? What happens when the personalities are different but not complementary? Here, one could think of poised, warm, and peaceful parents whose son is irritable and verbally combative. Do these personality configurations produce a similar result whether the child is a son or a daughter? In other words, parents may have more difficulty getting along with a restless son than they would a restless daughter, or the reverse. Or children can have more difficulty getting along with an intrusive mother than an intrusive father, or the reverse. These interactional questions remain to be tested by researchers.

From a life course perspective, other researchers believe that, as adult children mature, their values become more similar to those of their parents because they have lived through similar experiences, such as getting married, having children, and shouldering work responsibilities (Rossi and Rossi, 1990). When children most closely resemble their parents in terms of values and beliefs, they have a better relationship with them, a phenomenon also observed between grandchildren and their grandparents (Giarrusso et al., 2001). In fact, Aldous and colleagues (1985) found that adult children who shared interests and values with their parents were favoured by them. How, then, does the parent-child relationship evolve over time when either the parent or the child lives in a homosexual union and there is a conflict of values in this respect? Does the relationship become closer or more distant as the years go by (Connidis, 2003b)? Or is the relationship simply ambivalent (Connidis and McMullin, 2002a,b)?

Finally, the interactional and life course perspectives accommodate structural variables in the parent-child relationship (Aldous, 1996). For instance, when there is a sharp distinction in professional standing, and therefore income, between father and adult child or mother and child, is the relationship affected? Rossi and Rossi (1990:299) comment that occupational success and social mobility may be attained at the expense of family solidarity and closeness between the generations. What happens, for example, when a child or several children have far surpassed their parents' social status—or, the reverse, when a child or all siblings have drifted downward socially? Do these families become fractured as a result of social mobility or does the generation with the most favourable position help the other? Differences among ethnic groups may exist in this respect, particularly when immigration is involved and parents expect their children to surpass them in occupational prestige.

Senior Parents Help Their Adult Children

In Chapter 10, we saw that a good segment of the senior generation contributes to their children's lives by babysitting or helping raise grandchildren. Generally, these are women whose maternal role is extended into their later years. They basically fulfill family functions that, given adequate social policies, should be dealt with by society—for instance, in the form of universal access to child care centres, longer parental leaves, and flexible work hours. In general, older parents, especially when they are still in reasonable health, provide a great deal of help to their adult children, including financial (Gee, 2000).

An intriguing result arose in a U.S. survey: Parents, particularly minority ones, tended to give more financial help to children who had a higher educational level and larger incomes. Researchers Lee and Aytac (1998:440) concluded that parents "concentrate their resources on promising children"—that is, children "who are likely to yield greater returns." However, it is equally plausible that parents help their needy children differently. They may do so by providing services such as babysitting, or giving them food, clothing, lodging, and gifts in kind rather than cash. In contrast, they may give more money to children who are doing well.

Another form of help that adult children benefit from is coresidence. About 30 percent of adults aged 25 to 54 who have never married and 13 percent of those who are divorced live in their parents' home (White and Peterson, 1995). The greater the number of children, the more likely senior parents are to have one who resides with them because of need. A few adult children have never left home, whereas others have returned. Parents over age 65 who have a coresident child (and about 15 percent do, according to Aquilino, 1990) usually receive relatively little in terms of household or financial help from that child. As male children are more likely to return home than female children and they do less housework than females, coresidence generally benefits adult children more than parents, and male children more than female children.

As parents age, they often do not or cannot disengage from the problems experienced by their adult children. Pillemer and Suitor (1991) report that a quarter of senior parents mention that at least one of their children is experiencing serious physical or mental health problems or a high level of stress. These children's problems correlate

Social policies concerning adults with special needs are so deficient that even frail elderly parents often have to continue assuming the entire responsibility for the care of their middle-aged children with disabilities. They receive little help, exhaust their meagre resources, and their own health may deteriorate.

significantly with depression in the older parents, and some studies find that older parents who have to provide a great deal of help to their children feel more depressed (Mutran and Reitzes, 1984). These parents may be particularly worried over children who fail to achieve a reasonable level of independence. In addition, when children have problems, they may receive advice that is not wanted or that they are unwilling or unable to put into practice. One can see that, at the very least, the potential for intergenerational ambivalence is high (Connidis and McMullin, 2002a,b).

Furthermore, a certain proportion of parents of troubled or distressed and unsuccessful adult children are themselves problematic persons: They were difficult persons as younger adults and may have had an unsatisfying relationship with their children when the latter were growing up (Reiss, 1995). In addition, these children might have inherited temperamental disadvantages from them, such as tendencies toward irritability or depression. Hence, it is to be expected that a segment of perturbed or difficult adults have parents who are or were similar to them. Research on such a theme would contribute additional perspectives on the family life course and adult development.

Adult Children Help Their Elderly Parents

When elderly parents become much older, a proportion experience diminished health as well as mobility limitations (see Family Research 12.3). At that point, adult children often become the parents' key instrumental and social support resources (Connidis, 2001). Nevertheless, the level of family care required by seniors has been overstated. For instance, in 2001, only 4.8 percent of males and 8.3 percent of females aged 15 and over had spent five hours or more a week caring or assisting a senior (Statistics Canada, 2004b). Caregivers themselves spend an average of 4.2 hours a week on assistance to seniors (Frederick and East, 1999). However, with shrinking social services and the shift away from institutionalized care, demand for family members to provide care for their elderly parents will increase (McDaniel and Gee, 1993). This government shortfall may be especially problematic for those women who are divorced

---

Natural Phenomena Can Be Used to Study Seniors' Families

Gignac, Cott, and Badley (2003) were interested in studying the impact of a single stressor on a group of seniors already burdened with one disability. They creatively utilized the 1998 ice storm in Ontario as a natural experiment to compare the responses of a group of 59 ice storm victims already suffering from osteoarthritis and/or osteoporosis. They compared these 59 persons with a similar control group of persons who were living in areas not affected by the storm. (The reader will recall that the storm in question left entire areas of Ontario and Quebec without power for many days and in some cases weeks; in addition, roads were impassable and many trees as well as power lines littered the ground.)

All the respondents (both the control and the experimental groups) were already part of a larger study of 247 community-dwelling seniors who were participating in a longitudinal study of people suffering from osteoarthritis and/or osteoporosis. Data on disability pain, self-reported health, helplessness, depression, and independence had been assessed prior to the storm and were assessed again 17 months after the first interviews. The researchers were then able to see how older adults with chronic physical illnesses may be particularly vulnerable when faced with additional stressors. From our perspective, similar research could be done to see how this situation affected family dynamics, particularly in terms of the help that adult children would have provided to their afflicted elderly parents.

---

or have been single all their lives and may have fewer social resources at their disposal (Abu-Laban and McDaniel, 2004). Aged lesbian women and gay men without partners also need to be studied in this context (Connidis, 2001).

For their part, elderly parents are happier when they give than when they receive, and they accept help more readily when they can contribute something in return, particularly to their sons. However, even this parental help may result in feelings of ambivalence in their mid-generation children (Ingersoll-Dayton et al., 2001). When parents require a great deal of support from their children, they are less satisfied with the relationship. In part, this can be explained by the fact that contact with the child is necessitated by the parents' needs rather than by the child's desire to see the parents or by the spontaneity of a visit just to socialize. It is not surprising, therefore, that when older parents are in better health, they report a more positive relationship with their children.

In some families, a process of status reversal begins to take place when parents fall prey to mental disabilities such as senility and Alzheimer's disease. The relationship is totally altered: The parent becomes the child and the child becomes the parent. This is when the responsibilities of caregiving multiply for the child, while meaningful verbal exchanges diminish until even recognition disappears. For the parent, the world, including his or her own children, fades away little by little until it has entirely evaporated. Children actually lose the parent long before biological death arrives. Adult children who help care for a parent are far more stressed when the parent suffers from cognitive-behavioural than physical disabilities (Starrels et al., 1997). In contrast, when the parent's challenges are physical only, the parent-child relationship generally continues to include most of its previous elements. (The same situation occurs when it is a parent who cares for a child.)

A popular but misleading concept is that of the **sandwich generation**: adults caught between raising their children and caring for frail parents. In reality, only a minority of adults provide care to both generations at the same time (Rosenthal, 2000). Their numbers may be increasing, particularly among those who have children late in life, or whose parent suffers from a premature disability, or who are grandparents caring simultaneously for a grandchild and a parent.

So far, the research literature has emphasized the stress experienced by adult children, especially daughters, as a result of their role as caregivers of disabled parents (Gerstel and Gallagher, 1993). This stress is real and is related to role overload, and more hours result in even greater overload (Frederick and East, 1999). In this respect, the concept of **burden** is frequently utilized. This, in itself, is yet another *social construct* worth analyzing, because it reflects cultural values about intergenerational relations. For instance, one does not encounter this concept when studying the care that parents give to their children, unless the latter are adults and quite problematic. The reason is that caring for their young children is considered to be part of parents' role. However, when these same parents age and their health falters, help extended to them by their children is analyzed in terms of burden—when in other societies it is simply a duty or an adult child's role, as illustrated in Chapter 2.

In great part, the notion of burden arises from the misuse of the word "care." Few adult children actually take care of their parents; rather, they **help** them (Rosenthal, 2000). Not surprisingly, there is also little research showing the positive side of caring for or helping one's elderly parents (Martin-Matthews, 2001). In this respect, Pruchno et al. (1997) have pointed out the importance of distinguishing between caregiving burden and caregiving satisfaction (Connidis 2001). Cranswick (1997) has found that Canadians who help their elderly parents tend to be more positive than negative about this experience, even though a substantial proportion have had to make adjustments in their own lives in order to fulfill this duty, such as sleeping less, changing working hours, and taking fewer vacations. Dupuis and Norris (2001) have found that "caregiving" daughters of parents in long-term care facilities adopt a wide variety of roles/attitudes in this respect.

Elderly adults who are childless are not less happy or in poorer health than those who have living children, although seniors receive more help when they have children. What seems to count for the emotional well-being of the elderly is not whether they have children but the quality of the relationship between them and their progeny (Connidis, 2001). For instance, Silverstein and Bengtson (1991) find that a warm relationship with adult children may increase parental longevity after widowhood.

Children's and Parents' Gender

Daughters are far more likely to become their elderly parents' helpers and caregivers than sons (Frederick and East, 1999). The time demands and emotional costs of help are also higher among daughters than sons (Raschick and Ingersoll-Dayton, 2004). However, when a son has the responsibility for his parents, his involvement is as stable as that of a daughter (Martin-Matthews, 2001). Often, his wife assumes this duty or, at the very least, contributes to it. Spitze and Logan (1991) point out that the key to receiving help resides in having one daughter. As a result, married couples are more likely to respond to the needs of the wife's parents (Shuey and Hardy, 2003). This situation reflects the fact that women are generally assigned nurturing roles in society and learn to be responsible for the well-being of others from the time they are young (Abu-Laban and McDaniel, 2004). Consequently, parents may also expect more help from their daughters than their sons—although the reverse occurs in many other societies, such as China or Japan.

Starrels and colleagues (1997) have found that elderly parents who receive help from their children tend to reciprocate more with sons than daughters and provide less assistance to daughters than sons. Parents seem to appreciate their sons' caregiving more than their daughters' caregiving, perhaps because sons are still more valued and also because it is taken for granted that daughters are nurturing. It is expected that they will help their elderly parents as part of their feminine role. This gender expectation and the greater reciprocity with or recognition accorded to helpful sons may be reasons why daughters experience more stress than sons in their helping role.

Gender is a factor not only in who gives help but also in who receives it. As their health deteriorates, widowed mothers in their seventies and older receive more attention from their children than do widowed fathers. Silverstein et al. (1995) report that affection is a stronger motivator for help to older mothers, while expectation of an inheritance is more frequently a factor for assistance to fathers, although this is more the case among sons than daughters. Overall, there is a certain degree of ambivalence in the relationship of adult children to aging parents, and this is especially so among women, toward in-laws, and when the relationship was not optimal during childhood (Connidis, 2001; Wilson et al., 2003).

CONCLUSIONS: THE MACRO AND MICRO ASPECTS IN THE PARENT-CHILD RELATIONSHIP

The parent-child relationship is best examined within the context of the life course of the two generations involved. Out of the small child's relationship with his or her parents is born the adolescent relationship and from both flow the adult child-parent involvement, closeness, or conflict and distancing. In addition, the life course is a road that is paved with both risks and successes, most of which originate in the extra-familial environment. Therefore, social and cultural changes as well as economic situations can influence both the quality of parenting (which, in turn, influences child socialization and development to some extent) and of the parent-child relationship.

At a more micro level of analysis, we consider the effect of personalities both on the quality of parenting and on the parent-child interaction. Parents' and children's personalities influence their behaviours and their subsequent reactions to each other. No longer are children considered a blank slate upon which parents write the script of their offspring's personalities and outcomes. Children are social actors who interact with their parents and contribute to the formation of their destinies (Corsaro, 1997). Children's personalities influence their familial environment just as do their parents' personalities. Personalities are the result of the interaction between nature and nurture and, in turn, the familial environment is also the result of this interaction between genetic and environmental forces (Reiss, 1995; Scarr, 1993). The future in the study of the parent-child relationship lies in the recognition of the combination of sociocultural and genetic influences on family members, a line of inquiry pursued in subsequent chapters.

Summary

1. The beginning of the parent-child relationship is rooted in the intersection between the infant's personality and needs, the parents' reactions to these needs, the feedback between the two levels of personalities and reactions, as well as the familial environment that they create.

2. The main types of parents' socialization practices are the authoritative, authoritarian, no-nonsense, permissive, uninvolved, neglecting, and even abusive. Socialization practices arise from the combination of (a) cultural and environmental determinants, including poverty and norms about what is considered "proper" parenting; (b) parents' personalities as well as beliefs; and (c) parental adaptation to children's behaviours, needs, and personalities. In this interactional perspective, children contribute to the development of their parents' socialization style. The matter of what constitutes proper parenting and corporal punishment is discussed.

3. The parent-adolescent relationship is largely based on social definitions of adolescence. Adolescence is a social construct dating back to the 1890–1920 period. It is a cultural invention rather than an unavoidable and universal period of stress and turmoil. Parent-adolescent conflict is generally about minor issues of daily living rather than crucial issues such as sex, drugs, and violence. This apparent paradox may stem from a lack of communication on these issues, the fact that adolescents and parents spend relatively little time daily in direct interaction, and the busy life of parents. Overall, about one-third of youths have a very difficult adolescence and parent-child relationship.

4. Eras or time periods as well as the human qualities that are valued within each make it easier or more difficult for parents to influence their adolescents.

5. Children's peers affect their relationship with their parents through the peer group spillover effect, the cross-pressures they place, and the relative solidarity of peer subcultures.

6. The timing of the passage into full adult independence is often postponed because of higher educational requirements. Therefore, young adults often remain home longer than was the case just 20 years ago. Coresidence is more difficult for parents when adult children remain financially dependent. Within the life course perspective, as children age and acquire new roles, the parent-child relationship generally remains strong, particularly with mothers. Several demographic variables contribute to the frequency of interaction, including the sex of both parent and child as well as geographic distance. Values, attitudes, and lifestyles may also be important variables.

7. Overall, elderly parents help their adult children substantially and are happier when they give than when they receive. Adult children help their elderly parents who become frail or disabled, but few actually undertake their entire care. The burden of care is highest when a parent becomes cognitively impaired, because the relationship is entirely altered. The concept of burden is discussed as a social construct. Daughters provide more help, particularly of a personal nature. Childless seniors are not less happy than others but they receive less help than those with children.

8. The parent-child relationship has to be examined within the context of the personalities involved and the sociocultural situation in which the family is embedded.

Key Concepts and Themes

Analytical Questions

1. How is social constructionism utilized in this chapter?

2. What does interactionism help explain in this chapter?

3. Are parents more or less influential in their children's lives than was the case in the 1950s, for instance?

4. Is there a new construction of young adulthood in the making? If yes, what are the consequences on family dynamics?

5. On the whole, which generation of adults benefits the most from the other in our type of society?

Suggested Readings

Ambert, A.-M. 2001. *The effect of children on parents*, 2nd Ed. New York: Haworth. This book discusses at greater length the parent-child relationship within a variety of contexts. The theoretical perspective amalgamates interactional, ecological, as well as genetic theories.

Bengtson, V. L., Schaie, K. W., and Burton, L. M. (Eds.) 1995. *Adult intergenerational relations: Effects of societal change*. New York: Springer. Collection of articles combining research results, commentaries, and perspectives on the adult parent-child relationship. There is an interesting section on African-American families that have teenage childbearers.

Connidis. I. A. 2001. *Family ties and aging*. Thousand Oaks, CA: Sage. This book by a Canadian scholar

presents an overview of the parent-child relationship as it evolves in adulthood and particularly in older ages.

Crouter, A. C., and Booth, A. (Eds.) 2003. *Children's influences on family dynamics*. Mahwah, NJ: Erlbaum. Collection of articles on this neglected aspect of family life. These articles present several discussions between the contributing authors.

Rossi, A. S., and Rossi, P. H. 1990. *Of human bonding: Parent-child relations across the life course*. New York: Aldine de Gruyter. The authors present the results of three-generational research on parents and children and their relationships.

Suggested Weblinks

Three scholarly organizations are the most pertinent for online information about the parent-child relationship and parenting:

American Psychological Association

www.apa.org

National Council on Family Relations

www.ncfr.org

and **Society for Research in Child Development**

www.srcd.org

Administration on Aging is a government agency offering information on the care of elderly parents, local resources, and other weblinks.

www.aoa.gov

Canadian Association of Retired Persons (CARP) has websites, information, and chat lines for elderly parents as well as grandparents.

www.carp.ca

Invest in Kids Foundation is a popular site, especially for parents; it includes a research section.

www.investinkids.ca

National Institute on Aging also has information on elder care, including care by children.

www.nih.gov/nia

National Parenting Center is a centre for parenting information services. It offers information as well as chat rooms, all with the goal of promoting parenting skills.

www.tnpc.com

CHAPTER 13

Sibling Relationships and Situations

At age seven, my family structure became more complex: I inherited four European siblings, whom I had never met, ranging in age from 15 to 21. At the time, I was merely affected by the mixed blessing that such a drastic family restructuring brings to the life of a child and also that of her 30-year-old mother. I was too little to understand how dislocated these fun-loving young people's lives had been. Their mother had died when they were small; my father had left them in the care of two of his sisters and had moved to Canada. When the Second World War arrived, they had to relocate to the south of France. Finally, two years after the war was over, they immigrated to Canada where they had to lead a more modest middle-class life shared with small siblings, one of whom had yet to be born.

Besides a large age gap, there were then and remain to this day striking differences between my father's two sets of children. For example, only one in the older group became a professional, whereas all of us younger ones did. We "little ones" had several advantages: We had stable lives and an energetic mother; we benefited from stimulating older siblings and our parents had a very happy marriage. True, we all shared one absent-minded, intellectual father who looked upon all of his children with some sort of "benign" annoyance. Nevertheless, whereas he was absent when the older children were growing up, we in the second group were able to prod him into helping us with our Latin and French homework, in which he would become as involved as we were. This engagement created bonds, stimulated our intellect...and led to great marks in school!

Our father had a gift for writing that ran in his family. A strange "coincidence" emerged: We children, so different from one another in terms of personality, life choices, and educational level, share one characteristic—all of us write well; five took up writing as a job in one form or another, and so far four of these have published books (in three different languages). I am sure that, somehow, this peculiar aspect of my adult family profile is responsible for my awareness of the combined impact of environmental and genetic forces on family dynamics. I have no doubt that we were born with this gift, but we would not have been able to develop it had our parents and the tradition in our family not encouraged us in this direction.

This autobiographical vignette—my own—introduces one of the key aspects of this chapter: the combined effect of the environment, including the familial one, and of genetic inheritance in the development of siblings' life course. Almost 80 percent of

Canadians have at least one sibling; thus, it is a very important type of familial relationship. It is also one that generally outlasts the parent-child relationship.

When children reach adulthood, the sibling relationship in industrialized societies, particularly those of western cultures, becomes discretionary. That is, continuing the relationship is a matter of choice and is secondary to the spousal and parent-child ones. Cicirelli (1994:16) points out that adult sibling interactions "do not have a major effect in family functioning or adaptation to the larger society." In contrast, in other societies, continuation of the sibling relationship into adulthood is the norm and is of fundamental importance for the family's integration into society at large. Sibling relationships, particularly between two brothers or two sisters, may actually be more consequential than their relationship with a spouse, both at the social and economic level (Ogbomo, 1997). Nevertheless, in Canada, most adults still perceive that they have obligations toward their siblings (Connidis, 2001).

THE SIBLING RELATIONSHIP BEGINS

Generally, whether the first-born child recognizes it or not, the birth of a second baby transforms his or her life entirely, as well as that of the family as a system. A new set of interactions is created, those between siblings. Each successive child enters the family at a different moment in its history and contributes to changing this environment (Zajonc, 2001).

The Only Child Becomes the Older Child

With the arrival of each baby, parents spend more time interacting with their children altogether, but they have less time for each child individually. Furthermore, the family's economic resources available per person diminish with each new child. On the positive side, the arrival of a second baby generally means that the older child has a lower chance of experiencing a parental divorce, compared to only children of the same age (Baydar et al., 1997a). The reason for this is that happily married couples are more likely to add another child to their family than couples who are not happy together (Myers, 1997).

But with the new arrival, parents cannot maintain their exclusive relationship with the first-born, a factor that may become paramount in this child's life experience if he or she feels a loss of status as well as affection. The survival requirements of an infant are more urgent and constant than those of an older sibling. As a result, parents give more attention to younger than older children. With the arrival of the second child, the mother-child relationship often becomes less affectionate, particularly if the spacing between the two children is small and the family experiences a reduction in income per person. The mother's parenting style at times becomes more punitive and the older child may feel less securely attached (Teti et al., 1996). As a result of all these changes, the first-born child occasionally suffers from a variety of problems of adjustment, including anxiety, clinging behaviour, bed-wetting, and even aggressiveness (Baydar et al., 1997a, b).

The child's reaction to the baby's arrival is largely tailored by his or her personality as well as by the steps that parents undertake to reassure and involve him or her.

Dunn (1994) points out that small children who are intense and less adaptable react more negatively to the baby's arrival than children with a sunnier and more content disposition. The former may even protest when the mother pays attention to the infant. The following amusing anecdote from a student portrays this situation:

> "When my little sister was born, I was three, and when my parents brought her home I asked them to return her to the hospital. I did not like to see all the fuss over this little red faced creature that cried all the time. Then one day, seeing that my parents were not returning her, I tried to wrap her in gift wrapping paper and my mother caught me in the act. It's funny to think of this now because we are best friends and often laugh over it. My sister has had my mother tell this story over and over: she just loves it."

Such an older child's reaction to the newborn often becomes part of the family culture: It constitutes a story everyone loves to hear.

Additional infants benefit from the experience that parents have acquired with their earlier-born children. Many first-born young adults, looking back on their past, feel that their parents acquired a great deal of skills at their expense:

> "If I could relive my life, I would have wanted to be the second oldest child in my family. I disliked having to be the first to 'test the waters.' I wish that I had had an older sibling whose errors would have served as warning posts on what lay ahead.... I was a learning experience for my parents."

> "I changed my parents' views on a lot of things. I had to fight to get what I wanted and when my sister reached the same point in life, she didn't have to fight as hard as I did. I was jealous of her for the longest time, but now I have come to learn to deal with it."

Obviously, the education that the first-born provides parents, while perhaps to the advantage of subsequent children, is often recalled as an injustice by the older child.

Consequences of Children's Spacing

During the newborn's first months, the infant's schedule is quite different from that of the older child, especially if the latter is already at school. With four years or more of spacing between the two children, the parents' relationship with the first-born may continue to be exclusive during a portion of the day as the baby sleeps. With this much spacing, each sibling is in a way an only child, and little competition takes place, especially if the older one likes to play at surrogate parenting:

> "Surely the happiest memory I have of my mid-teens is when my mother announced that she was pregnant. This took a bit to get used to, you know the idea that your parents are 'doing it' but my sister and I were really excited.... Then the best times arrived with my little sister. Oh how we loved that baby. She was spoiled as we would never leave her alone which somewhat worried my parents but then my mother was happy because she had less work to do as I always volunteered to take care of Kathy.... Now Kathy is seven and the brightest kid on the block because we provided her with an adult environment and each one of us in the family taught her different skills and she loved to learn from the time she was small. We read to her, made her read when she was three and took her skating,

biking, rollerblading, swimming. She became incredibly well coordinated. She is also very sociable because despite all the spoiling she got from us older sisters and our cousins, we still insisted on good manners and no temper tantrums or anything of the sort. She had a whole batch of parents to raise her."

In terms of educational achievement, children do less well, on average, when they are closely spaced, and this holds true both for two-children and larger families (Powell and Steelman, 1993). For instance, parents have less individual time for two children who are close in age, because they essentially follow the same routine. When one child is several years older, however, the two children have different needs at different times and receive more individual attention. The older child is an only child longer and the younger child then benefits both from having a sibling who is more developed and from parents who have more time for him or her. Much older siblings are more intellectually and socially stimulating for children than siblings closer to them in age (Zajonc and Mullally, 1997). A younger sibling benefits from a large age gap between him or her and older children simply because the latter know more, as is illustrated in the opening vignette and in the previous student quote. Smaller children tend to look up to their older brothers or sisters (Buhrmester and Furman, 1990).

Consequences of Family Size

In terms of number of children, those from large sibling groups generally do not do as well at school, on average, as children from small families (Downey, 1995). Neither do they advance as much professionally later on as do adults coming from smaller families. These results remain when parents' social class is taken into consideration: Even upper-class parents provide fewer resources per child in large than in small families. The concept used to explain this family size effect is the **dilution of parental resources**. In effect, this means that parents have fewer nonexpendable resources for each child individually, whether in terms of time, attention, and even economic means. In fact, mothers are less responsive to their children in larger families (Onyskiw and Hayduk, 2001). Therefore, a large sibling group often dilutes the quality of the home environment available to each child (Menaghan and Parcel, 1991). This occurs even more so when children are closely spaced in a large family, because they interact more among themselves and have less adult attention; they also learn less than they would with one or two much older siblings or alone with their parents. Aggressiveness also appears more often in larger families (Stevenson, 1999).

But, of course, there are plenty of exceptions to the rule and there are large families, particularly well-to-do ones, where all the children do very well at school or become high achievers in their professions later on. These families may benefit from other resources, such as the help of their relatives and the presence of a large community of parents' friends and colleagues who contribute to stimulate children's intellectual development and serve as individual role models. Some research supports such a perspective. For example, a large family size has a negative impact on most non-Orthodox Jews, but it has no effect for Muslim Arabs (Shavit and Pierce, 1991). For the latter, what counts is the *hamula*, or extended family, that supports the nuclear family. The extended family increases resources and compensates for the dilution of the resources at the nuclear level. These families, in other words, have more **social capital** to offer to each individual child.

Furthermore, as Zajonc and Mullally (1997:697) pointedly remark, there are advantages to large family size that are not measured by the traditional research perspective emphasizing achievement. For instance, it may well be that siblings growing up in a large family are more "affiliative, more affectionate, good leaders, less prone to depression, or otherwise healthier." They may be less individualistic and more cooperative. They are used to sharing everything and adjusting to a far greater number of personalities. They can compromise and overlook frustrating situations. However, the only reasonably recent and large-scale study on this topic has not found any family size advantage in terms of sociability and need to be with others (Blake et al., 1991). But this study did not test for the other possible advantages mentioned by Zajonc and Mullally (1997). Downey and Condron (2004) found that having one or two siblings was positively related to better social skills; additional siblings did not provide more advantage. It is equally possible that some siblings in a large family suffer from a lack of individual recognition, feel oppressed by all the social pressure within their intimate group, and are hampered by a lack of privacy. Such persons may grow up to be individualistic and may even distance themselves from the family group. However, despite having benefited from less individual attention, there is no indication that adult children from large families are less attached to their parents nor their parents to them than in small families (Spitze and Logan, 1991).

CHILD AND ADOLESCENT SIBLING RELATIONSHIPS

At the personal level, sibling relationships are determined by children's characteristics, their personality similarities and differences, parents' behaviour toward the children, and siblings' perception of such. Given that most of these factors are reasonably stable through each childhood, one can expect a certain degree of stability in the sibling relationship. However, the availability of peers as alternate playmates in later childhood and early adolescence is likely to bring change in the relationship. Munn and Dunn (1988) report that brothers and sisters whose personalities are compatible or complementary experience a more harmonious relationship than those who are temperamentally incompatible. When one child has an intense or unadaptable personality, sibling interactions are more conflictual (McCoy et al., 1994). As well, high-activity siblings get in each other's way and their requirements clash quickly and frequently.

Older and Younger Siblings

Furman and Lanthier (1996) gave personality tests and a relationship questionnaire to 56 triads of mothers and two siblings, one age nine and the other age 11. They found that it was the older child's personality that more strongly affected the distribution of power in the relationship. The dimensions of conscientiousness and agreeableness, particularly in the older child, were strong predictors of harmony and lack of power struggle.

To complement the above study, Dunn and colleagues (1994) found that older siblings tend to be fairly consistent over time in their behaviour toward their younger brother or sister: Aggressiveness or friendliness persists. This means that, in some families, younger children spend their entire childhood with a friendly and supportive sibling, whereas in others, they are in a relationship that is hostile, disparaging, and physically aggressive. The impact on child development may be substantial, but it is a question that is rarely raised in research, because traditional theories focus on parental rather than **sibling effect**. It is possible that negative effects that have been attributed to parents and to their harsh or rejecting treatment actually result from the rough handling that a child has received from siblings or from siblings and parents together. Such a possibility makes sense from the perspective of genetics alone. Intolerant and irritable parents may produce some offspring who are like them and may jointly have a negative impact on the sibling who is different at the outset.

Younger siblings show less stability of behaviour toward their older siblings than the older ones do toward them. As we have seen earlier, smaller children look up to their older siblings; the younger ones adapt their style of interaction in order to secure the older's good will. In contrast, the older child does not have to adapt, because it is the younger ones who do. Overall, older siblings tend to be more domineering, and younger ones are forced to be more compliant in the relationship. Putting these variables together, it is therefore not surprising that, in terms of development, the older child has a stronger effect on the younger one than vice versa (Dunn et al., 1994).

Gender and Class in the Sibling Relationship

By the time they were 12 or 13 years old, first-born boys in a longitudinal study by Dunn (1996) reported a more distant relationship with their younger siblings than did first-born girls. This difference was, in part, explained as a result of the older boys' growing ties with their peer group. As well, the second-born children were becoming more assertive and more willing to disagree with the older boys, and this in turn contributed to the cooler climate. These pitfalls were less in evidence with older sisters. Indeed, girls maintain more intimate relationships with both siblings and peers than do boys (Updegraff and Obeidallah, 1999). Thus, females begin at an early age their function of **kin-keepers** (Stack and Burton, 1993) and emotional workers, as described in Chapter 11.

For a girl, having an older brother often represents a precious social resource in male-dominated peer groups. Older brothers who are popular serve as protectors and may also enhance a child's status among peers at school:

> *"It was great having an older brother with so many friends. I remember playing foot hockey with them. I would give all to the game so that my brother would be proud of me.... After a few games of hockey with the guys, I gained my proud nickname, 'The little green monster.'...When I was in fifth grade I was known among all the grades.... It helps to have brothers who are both younger and older than you, since you become familiar with the students."*

Later on, the older brother's circle of friends may include males who can accompany a younger sister to a dance or party without her having to date. This circle of friends may, of course, also be a source of dates.

Another interesting aspect in the study of siblings is that they do not perceive their relationship similarly. Dunn and McGuire (1994:120) mention that only 23 percent of the siblings in their sample reported a degree of closeness similar to that reported by their brother or sister. This discrepancy may be explained by the age and gender differences between siblings. Smaller children may be more susceptible to feeling left out by older siblings who, for their part, may be more involved with peers and largely ignore the younger ones. Girls may find their brothers less supportive, whereas boys may not notice that they are being aloof from their sisters.

Dunn (1994) also found that, by early adolescence, a social class difference had emerged in the sibling relationship. The older children of higher-income families reported more warmth and closeness with their siblings than the older children of lower-income families. Negative behaviours toward younger siblings increased at the lower SES levels during the period of study. Dunn could not offer an explanation for this social class difference, but it could originate in the more stressful familial and neighbourhood environments in which many low-income families live. In such households, siblings may have to compete for scarce resources. Parents' stress and behaviours may also affect family harmony and feed back negatively onto the sibling relationship (Brody et al., 1999). But more research is needed in other cultural contexts because Lareau (2003) found quite the opposite in her research in terms of social class: Higher-income siblings were more competitive and quarrelsome.

Sibling Influence

As we have seen in the previous chapter, peers are a powerful source of influence on children and adolescents. In contrast, sibling influence and pressure are rarely acknowledged. McHale and Crouter (1996) report that preteens spend 33 percent of their out-of-school hours with siblings, compared to 13 percent with friends. These numbers alone should predict a great deal of sibling influence.

Older Siblings as Role Models

What information do researchers have? Overall, when an older sibling is competent, the younger one is positively affected (Brody and Murry, 2001). Contrariwise, when an older sibling is aggressive, the other tends to follow suit, even at a very young age (Baillargeon et al., 2002). Thus, siblings are important agents of socialization to each other in this respect, and probably in many others that have yet to be researched (Garcia et al., 2000). Patterson (1986) finds that the aggressive interaction style of the older boys in a family trains the younger boys to be equally coercive. There is a significant level of concordance among boys in a family in terms of delinquency: When one boy is delinquent, there is a good chance that the other one also is (Rowe and Gulley, 1992). The same has been found for girls (Slomkowski et al., 2001). Furthermore, when one adolescent abuses alcohol, the other is at risk of doing so (Conger and Rueter, 1996).

In terms of sexuality, Widmer (1997) reports that older siblings have an effect on the timing of first intercourse among their younger brothers and sisters. Adolescent girls who have a sexually active or childbearing adolescent sister, as well as similar peers, tend to be more sexually active, even when other family variables, such as education, are taken into consideration (East et al., 1993; Powers and Hsueh, 1997). East (1999) reasons that a birth to a teenager may make it more difficult for mothers to

Sibling relationships are more important to each child's well-being and development, particularly the younger one's, than is generally believed. Hence, not enough research has been devoted to the sibling role and influence when children are growing up.

supervise their younger children, as the grandchild increases the new grandmother's work level. Brothers are even more influential than sisters in the timing of sexual intercourse. When older brothers are virgins, their behaviour may reinforce parental teachings on sexual restraint by giving them validity in the mind of younger siblings. However, East et al. (1993) point out that this fraternal influence is less important than parental attitudes and teachings on this topic.

These results together indicate that older siblings act as role models for younger ones, that the sharing of activities leads to an indirect form of influence, and that an older sibling's treatment of the younger one serves as an incentive to adopt this interactional style in other relationships. These results could also indicate that siblings share an environment that encourages certain behaviours over others, whether at home, school, or in the neighbourhood. A complementary explanation is that siblings share certain personality characteristics that make them equally vulnerable or equally resilient to life's temptations and circumstances. The validity of this last explanation could be tested by studying siblings who are different. For instance, in situations where two brothers have different personalities and the younger one follows the example of the older one, a far more solid case of influence or modelling can be made than when two brothers have similar tendencies to begin with.

Older siblings are particularly important sources of information and general influence in families that have recently immigrated. This is especially so when parents do not speak English well (Perez-Granados and Callanan, 1997). In such instances, older siblings acquire an aura of authority as they are better able to introduce the Canadian culture, or even the subculture of a neighbourhood, to their younger siblings. This influence is strengthened when parents depend on their older children for translation, for instance, a phenomenon referred to in Chapter 4 as children assuming the role of cultural brokers.

Siblings Who Share Peers

Sibling influence can be compounded by the sharing of friends. During adolescence, and more in adulthood, siblings' similarity of characteristics seems to increase friendliness and contact as well as the sharing of friends. In turn, frequency of positive contact contributes to an increased resemblance between siblings over the long term, especially with regard to ideas, values, and leisure activities (Bouchard et al., 1990). One would expect that the sharing of a prosocial peer group by siblings enhances their own prosocial behaviours. This, in turn, greatly facilitates parental duties as these prosocial children are probably easier to raise. This network of peers becomes a form of **social capital** to both parents and children (Furstenberg and Hughes, 1995). Prosocial peers are also more likely to have authoritative parents; when a group of peers have similarly oriented parents, the burden of supervision is lessened for each individual set of parents, given that they all participate to some degree in the monitoring process (Fletcher et al., 1995). This refers us back to the concepts of the **effective community** and group or **collective socialization.**

By the same token, when siblings who are already predisposed to deviance share a delinquent or aggressive peer group, this raises the chance that they will commit delinquent acts (Rowe and Gulley, 1992). Consequently, parents must increasingly monitor such offspring and set more limits on their activities and whereabouts. This demanding level of supervision and alertness may go beyond the abilities of many parents, as indicated in the following passage from a female student's autobiography. It graphically illustrates the family dynamics that may occur during adolescence when siblings are closely spaced, get along with each other, and encourage each other and peers in activities that parents disapprove of:

> *"The problem with my family at that age is that there were four adolescent children, two boys, two girls, and we actually ran the house. There was nothing that our parents could do to control us. If we wanted some friends over for the night, we'd hide them and my parents would not notice. Anyway, they hated to come in our rooms which were an absolute mess.... My brother got a girl pregnant when he was only 15 and my sister became a drug addict at 16. The other two of us turned out all right, which is amazing considering the bad example we got from the other two and the fact that we used to encourage their misbehaviour, side with them, and help them out when in trouble. We had absolutely no solidarity with our parents. It was just among us children, as we were one or two years apart. Our second solidarity was for our friends."*

Supportive Sibling Relationships

The literature on the family is by necessity often oriented toward the study of problems rather than daily dynamics. One of the consequences of this orientation is that there is relatively little research on supportive sibling relationships during childhood and adolescence. The major exceptions pertain to children who have a sibling suffering from a disability, and to brothers and sisters whose parents are conflictual, divorce, or remarry.

When a Sibling Has a Disability

Parents usually shoulder the responsibility of caring for or coordinating the care of a child with a disability well into adulthood. A cooperative sibling can greatly lighten parents' burden; the parents often develop particularly warm feelings for that helpful adult child, as illustrated in this situation:

> *"My older sister is retarded and has some heart problems so that my relationship with her is one of role reversal. She is five years older than me but I take care of her a lot to give some breathing space to my parents. When I was a bit younger...once in a while our needs clashed with hers or the demands our parents placed on us because of her. She does look normal and my mother often asked us to take her out with us to see a movie or something of the sort. Jackie loved it but it was different for us because we wanted to be with our friends and felt unpleasantly 'special.'...*

My parents really appreciate what we do for her and for them because they say that they trust that we will take care of her after they are gone, which is the biggest worry that parents of delayed adult children have. My brother and I will take care of her for sure although thankfully our parents are still young. But I think that of the two of us I may end up having to do most of the caring because I noticed that my brother does less than he used to do—he is a male!"

However, in reality, there is no indication so far that siblings become the primary caregivers of their disabled brother or sister when parents are no longer able to do so. Many of these disabled individuals have to turn outside the family for help (Pruchno et al., 1996).

Horwitz (1993) suggests that therapists should encourage adults who are mentally ill to develop mutual relationships with their siblings, given that people are more willing to help someone who reciprocates. The results of Seltzer and colleagues' study (1997) further indicate the necessity to help the mentally ill develop less confrontational behaviours with their siblings. The researchers found that adults had a higher level of well-being and a closer relationship with a sibling who is mentally delayed than a sibling who is mentally ill. Siblings, like parents, are affected more negatively by behavioural and attitudinal problems than by intellectual limitations. In other words, adults who experience better psychological well-being are those whose mentally ill siblings are kept at a distance, which also means that the sibling with mental illness receives less support than the one with retardation, unless the latter also exhibits difficult behaviours.

During childhood and adolescence, having a brother or sister with special needs also carries costs (LeClere and Kowalewski, 1994). The literature is quite unanimous in this respect and the previous student quote nicely illustrates this dilemma. The siblings of special needs children generally get less parental attention because so much is demanded for the care of the disabled or chronically ill child. The family can less easily pursue leisure activities than other families, and friends cannot be invited home, lest they disrupt the routine of care. When a sibling with disabilities is aggressive toward the helping child or adolescent, the latter tends to be less well adjusted emotionally.

During Parental Conflict, Divorce, and Remarriage

Brothers and sisters, especially older ones who function well, can act as a buffer for their younger siblings at times of marital conflict or divorce, or in the event of a parent's illness or emotional problems. However, so far, the research indicates that this type of sibling support is not always forthcoming—for instance, divorce actually increases negative interactions between siblings (Kim et al., 1999). In fact, a conflictual relationship between parents is more likely to lead to, or be accompanied by, greater sibling conflict. Conger and Conger (1996:119) find that "it is the actual disruption of marriage rather than the degree" of parental conflict in intact marriages "that most adversely affects relations between brothers and sisters." This effect of divorce on the sibling relationship is one that is infrequently mentioned in the literature on the negative consequences of marital breakup.

This greater sibling conflict can be explained by a combination of variables. For one, conflict between parents, and even more so the divorce itself, dilutes familial resources so that stress and emotional deprivation pit each child against the other for scarce parental attention. Second, the stressors experienced by parents spill over into their childrearing practices and lead to brother-sister friction. Third, a portion of divorcing couples may have difficult personalities and their children may have inherited these predispositions so that the children develop conflictual relationships among themselves. Furthermore, the spacing between children has not been considered in these studies: Sibling friction may occur only when there is little age difference among them, because of competition for scarce resources such as parental attention.

Hetherington (1988) finds that the presence of a stepfather is often accompanied by fractious sibling interactions. Children, and especially boys, reaching adolescence disengage more from their siblings in remarried than in married families (Anderson and Rice, 1992). But among those siblings who remain cohesive, mutual support reduces the number of problems experienced when they are exposed to parental conflict (Jenkins and Smith, 1990). In families with two children, the presence of at least one girl enhances the chance that a cohesive sibling relationship is established (Conger and Conger, 1996). Thus, once again, the children's gender is an important variable in this respect.

DIFFERENTIAL PARENTAL TREATMENT

As seen earlier, parents treat children differently depending on each child's age. The focus of this section is on children and adolescents. However, differential parental treatment is probably even more common in adulthood. In fact, Suitor and Pillemer (2000) have found that children's personal problems stemming from their own acts (such as drug use or criminality) are related to relationships with parents that are less close. Thus, as children age and make life choices, differential treatment from parents may become more prevalent, although not necessarily more visible to the children themselves.

The younger child is favoured by both parents in some circumstances, yet the older one is in others (McHale et al., 1995). It is not uncommon, either, that by adolescence mothers are closer to one identical twin than the other (Crosnoe and Elder, 2002). Furthermore, fathers show more interest in sons, particularly first-borns, and in children who have a more expressive personality (Crouter et al., 1999; see Family Research 13.1 for other aspects of this study). There are also indications that parents who are stressed by poverty or marital conflict or who are depressed are more likely to treat one child less well than the other (Henderson et al., 1996). Differential treatment can also involve chore assignments as well as privileges (Tucker et al., 2003).

Birth Order and Development Stage as Factors

It appears that mothers treat their children similarly at a given age within relatively small sibling groups and spacing (Whiteman et al., 2003)—at least in the United Kingdom and North America. It is not known to what extent the following results apply in the case of larger families and other situations. A longitudinal study yielded high correlations between a mother's treatment of the older child at age two and her subsequent treatment of the younger child at the same age. That is, it appears that mothers treat children in a manner appropriate to each age level, so that both children are

---

Parents' Knowledge of Each Sibling's Daily Activities

Crouter and colleagues (1999) wanted to see if parents would be more aware of the older sibling's or the younger sibling's daily life, and whether this knowledge would depend on the children's sex, personality, as well as parents' employment hours. Letters were sent to the homes of fourth- and fifth-graders in 16 central Pennsylvania school districts. The 203 participating families were headed by two parents with at least two children, and the second sibling had to be younger by one to four years.

In a first step, family members were interviewed at home separately; parents and children also filled out questionnaires. Questions were read aloud when children's literacy skills required it. In a second step, both parents and children were interviewed over the phone on several different evenings during a two- to three-week period. Parents and children were queried about their daily activities. An interesting aspect of this research consisted of questions designed to measure parents' knowledge of their children's activities:

- Did child X have English homework today? What was the assignment?
- Did child X watch TV, videos, or movies at home today? What did he or she watch?
- Did child X have any conflict or disagreement with a friend today? Which friend?
- Was child X outside the home at 4 p.m. today? Where was he or she?

---

treated similarly at a given age, yet are treated differently in the present because they are of different ages (Dunn et al., 1986).

But the correlations between the maternal treatments of the children at the same age are not perfect. This suggests, first, that mothers adapt their behaviour to each child's individuality and developmental rhythm (Volling, 1997). Second, the later-born child enters the family system at a different point in the family's life course (Hoffman, 1991:193). The mother is now a more experienced parent; she may also be busier or more tired when the younger child is two years old than she was when the older one was the same age a few years earlier. This difference in treatment could also be explained by any other factor that may have changed in the child's and mother's lives and environment. For instance, when child B reaches age two, the parents may have separated and the mother may be under more (or less) stress than she was when child A was age two. Her higher or lower level of stress could affect her parenting vis-à-vis the younger child. Finally, it should be mentioned that parents often assign more responsibilities to a first-born (Tucker et al., 2003).

To sum up, it seems that mothers tend to treat their children similarly at a given level of child maturity. But they are not necessarily as consistent toward the same child while he or she is growing up because children change with age, and some become easier or more difficult; as well, the parental context evolves. In some families, it is obvious that parents treat their children differently, not simply because of age, but because one offspring may be less adaptive or need more encouragement or structure, as is illustrated in the following student quote:

"My parents have always treated my sister differently than they have me.... School came easier to her and my parents treated her as the smart one. They were much more concerned about whether I did homework or not and how my marks in school were; I was under much more scrutiny.... My sister was allowed to stay up later, go out for longer, do more things, and have more fun."

Information concerning parenting consistency during adolescence and later ages is lacking. As children grow older, it is quite possible that parents treat them increasingly differently so as to respond to their developmental needs. Children may contribute to this differential treatment as they try to differentiate themselves from their siblings in order to assert their own individuality.

Gender as a Factor

Gender is one of the most important variables in child socialization (Kimmel, 2000). Parents raise boys and girls to assume different roles in society, although families vary in the extent to which they socialize boys and girls differently. Overall, fathers are more likely than mothers to make a distinction between sons and daughters and are generally more involved with sons (Harris and Morgan, 1991). In the student autobiographies, parents are reported as treating sons and daughters increasingly differently as they age. Women students repeatedly complained that adolescent brothers were given much more freedom than they had been allowed at the same age. In some ethnic groups, a slightly older brother or even a younger one chaperones a sister whenever she goes out, especially in the evenings. Causing even more resentment is the fact that these girls have to do more housework, age for age, than their brothers, and some even have to clean up after them:

"In my family, there are two standards: one for my brother and one for my sister and I. We girls do everything in the house and work to pay for school whereas my brother does nothing and works to pay for his car and dates. I really resent it even though I try to rationalize it this way, that my parents come from a non-Christian background, but it does not erase the unpleasant reality. People who immigrate here should leave behind their unpleasant backgrounds and adapt to what families do here which is by and large to treat boys and girls the same."

"My brother gets to go out without even telling my parents where he is going. My sister and I have to tell my parents everything, where we are going, what time we will be home and so on."

The more males are valued in a culture, the greater the difference in parental treatment. (In fact, in some societies experiencing scarcity, sons are given the best food while daughters go hungry.) However, it is possible that, in large families, parents have less time to react to each child's gender and accordingly treat their offspring more similarly than do parents with fewer children. Or, alternatively, they may treat all the boys one way and all the girls the other way. In other instances, fathers feel closer to sons and mothers to daughters because they share same-sex interests, aspirations, and household chores.

Developmental Impact of Differential Treatment

Several studies have discovered that the sibling who receives the most favourable parental treatment seems to be doing better than the other. Daniels (1987) reports that the sibling who enjoys more affection from the father has more ambitious educational and vocational goals. Children who are more controlled by their mother or perceive receiving less affection than their siblings are more likely to be anxious or depressed. These children also tend to be more difficult.

The Interactional Perspective

It may not necessarily be the differential parental treatment that produces these observed outcomes (Feinberg et al., 2000). The interactional perspective suggests a reversed causality in many cases. For instance, a difficult child may require parents to become more controlling. It may also be that a more ambitious child attracts paternal attention and encouragement. That is, his or her ambitions *create* or evoke the favoured attention rather than vice versa. It is also possible that it is the perception and interpretation of differences rather than the actual differential treatment that cause the problems for the child who feels deprived (Reiss et al., 1995). In other words, children may not be adversely affected when their parents give more attention to a sibling if they find that this is justifiable on the basis of a younger siblings's needs, for instance.

In great part, except for gender roles, parents respond to their children according to their personalities and behaviours, as seen in the preceding chapter. Thus, Bank et al. (1996) find that parents behave differently with a boy who is aggressive and oppositional than with his easy-going sibling. In their experimental study, one group of families had both a difficult and an easy-going boy while the other set of families had two "easy" children. The researchers observed family interactions when the difficult son was present and then when he was absent. The two samples showed different parental treatment of their children when the difficult boy was included. But when only the parents and the easy-going child were considered together, there was no difference between the two samples of families in the way parents treated their children. This result illustrates the impact of a child on family dynamics and on the creation of differential parental treatment. Children contribute to create the differential treatment they receive from their parents—the concept of children as **coproducers** of their socialization experience (discussed in Chapter 12).

Situations That Cushion or Exacerbate the Impact

Volling (1997) makes a distinction between **differential favouritism**, which has negative consequences for family relationships, and **differential discipline**. Among preschoolers, she found that when the older child was disciplined more often than the younger one, the family functioned better than when it was the younger one who was more often disciplined. The reason for this observation is that, in the latter case, parents were not taking into consideration the children's respective developmental levels. They were probably as demanding of the younger as of the older one—a situation that creates difficulties because the younger child has not yet developed the ability to meet such maturity demands.

Differential parental treatment that does not appear fair to children causes jealousy and resentment on the part of the less favoured child, and may well give rise to feelings of entitlement on the part of the preferred child, who becomes the little king or queen. The less favoured offspring expresses his or her resentment toward the preferred one (Boer et al., 1992). This expression of negative feelings may be the result of justified jealousy or, alternatively, it may be the result of the more difficult personality of the less favoured child, who behaves less pleasantly toward siblings and parents alike.

McHale and colleagues (1995) as well as Volling (1997) went one step farther in this type of research on differential parental treatment and grouped families depending on whether both parents were *congruent* (displaying more affection for the same child) or *incongruent* (each parent preferring a different child). Congruent parents predominated. Incongruence tends to occur among couples whose relationship is distressed: These parents at times form a coalition with different children against each other (Reiss et al., 1994). When this occurs, the parent-child boundaries melt away while boundaries between parents rise. This situation, in turn, makes it difficult to raise children authoritatively. In contrast, parents who get along maintain the boundaries of the parental system and tend to agree on which child needs more support.

Thus, one sees the importance of studying parents' differential treatment in the context of other variables, such as marital happiness, as well as number and spacing of offspring. It is not known, for instance, if differential treatment has a more negative impact in a poor quality environment or in a more privileged environment, or in families that have children of only one sex or of both. Moreover, differential treatment may produce effects that vary according to parental personality, *relative parental power* within the family, and overall level of parenting involvement. For example, a parent who has little power or who is perceived to be weak may not have the same impact as one who is psychologically strong and is dominant in the family. Siblings may notice it more if they are treated differently by a dominant parent than by a weak one. As illustrated by the following mature student, some children seem to perceive their mother's lower social prominence and "shrug off" her differential behaviours toward them, yet are affected when the father does not treat them equally, however small the slight might be:

> *"At home, I am in a rather unfortunate situation: although I am always available to the children and am really their maid, when their father is around I am just as good as not there. They hang on to his every word and find him so interesting. He doesn't even have to ask them to do something, they just do it. One or the other children gets very upset if he doesn't talk to him or her or gives equal treatment. They're like courtesans around a king. Me, what am I? Nothing! So if I yell at one, that one doesn't even notice it. If I give him a compliment, they shrug it off. It has more or less always been like that: my husband is quite the social butterfly, looks good, and is known to a lot of people. In contrast, I am the somewhat mousy wife about whom people wonder, 'Whatever did he find in her?'"*

ADULT AND STEPSIBLING RELATIONSHIPS

Personalities and lifestyles are fairly important in determining the quality of adult sibling bonds, particularly in view of the fact that these relationships are largely optional (Connidis, 2001). Furthermore, the literature on remarriage has been so focused on problems of adult and child adjustment that little attention has been devoted to the new relationships that are formed among children from the merging families (Ganong and Coleman, 1994). Not only is there little information on the relationship between stepsiblings, but there is equally little on that between halfsiblings (i.e., when new children are born in a remarriage).

Adult Sibling Relationships

Among adults in North America, proximity increases contact between siblings and the potential for both conflict and closeness (Cicirelli, 1995). When no other family member lives nearby, proximity also increases the exchange of help between siblings (Miner and Uhlenberg, 1997). Cicirelli (1996) points out that older persons like to reminisce about the past. They can do so far better with like-minded siblings than with their adult children. Thus, siblings remain important confidants as well as sources of emotional support, especially after widowhood, but are less central in terms of companionship (Campbell et al., 1999; Connidis and Campbell, 1995). One area of sibling relationship that requires far more research at all age levels pertains to the homosexuality of one sibling, as well as her or his living in a same-sex union (Connidis, 2003b).

We return here to the theme of **gender** in the sibling relationship. Overall, bonds are closer between sisters than between brothers, although there are many exceptions (Weaver et al., 2004). Furthermore, sisters provide more help to each other as well as to other family members than do brothers (White, 2001); this pattern is more obvious in some ethnic groups than others (Johnson, 1985). For males, a good relationship with their sisters is also important for their morale. Cicirelli (1989) reports that elderly men who have more sisters feel happier and more secure. This result probably stems from the greater familial cohesiveness that exists in families that have females and from the nurturing role to which women are socialized (Baines et al., 1991). Sisters provide moral support to their brothers and this contributes to the latter's sense of well-being. Unfortunately, sisters may not benefit equally from fraternal support,

Although there is some research on middle-aged and older siblings, there is still relatively little literature devoted to sibling relationships during the young adult years, after siblings have established their own families, especially during the years of childrearing. Neither is the role and influence of cousins researched, in part because researchers in western societies do not pay as much attention to the extended family system as perhaps they should.

as brothers have not generally been socialized to be nurturing and supportive. For both genders, ties with siblings are particularly important after widowhood and in periods of crisis (Connidis, 2001).

However, differential parental treatment that was perceived to be unfair when the children were growing up often extends its negative consequences into adulthood and is reflected in the siblings' later relationships (Baker and Daniels, 1990). Siblings who were less favoured, or who perceived they were, may feel that they have been cheated and, as they age, may distance themselves from the others. They may find alternative sources of moral support. These relationships may even be more conflictual. In some cases, jealousy continues into old age, even though there never was any factual basis for it—it was simply a matter of perception, which one male student deplores:

> "I have never been able to understand why my older brother and sisters are still so jealous of me. It's very painful to me at this age [about 23] because I have never done anything and neither have my parents to attract this attitude. I was sick more often as a child and my parents had to worry about me more. But the older ones had a lot more freedom and they got much more financially: they didn't have to pay for school as I am doing. At my age they all had cars and I don't. I should be the one who is jealous, really. It's just in their heads and it's upsetting because they certainly don't go out of their way to encourage my little nephews and nieces to accept me."

Stepsibling Relationships

Remarriages are often brief and stepchildren do not always live in the same household, so that many of these relationships simply do not have the time or the opportunity to blossom. Each set of stepsiblings may simply be an element of curiosity for the other. A nonresidential father's children may feel some degree of animosity toward those stepsiblings who live with him and are his new wife's children. This animosity or jealousy can be provoked by the fact that many nonresident fathers see their own children rarely or do not support them unless forced to by the government:

> "My feelings for my father...I can't say with 100% certainty that I love him because we have always been his invisible children.... I can't stand his wife's children after all those years because they have it all: my father has been very good to them and they've always been in the way, like we can't see him without these two being there and grabbing all the attention."

> "So I have a stepsister who is two years older than I am. At first, we hated each other.... Now we are not close but we get along quite well now that we don't have to see each other often."

When the remarriage lasts, stepsiblings often become companionable and supportive (Anderson, 1999), and maintain some level of connectedness into adulthood.

> "My two stepbrothers were then 2 and 4 years younger than me and they looked up to me so that I soon ended up playing big brother. For a 10-year-old who is rather upset at what has happened to his parents, that was a great thing. We got along famously well and have been a team to this day."

Being black increases the likelihood of contact between stepsiblings (White and Riedmann, 1992)—so does being a female (and we note for the fourth time in this chapter the role that females play in sibling integration and solidarity). The stepsibling relationship is closer when there are no full siblings. Halfsiblings and stepsiblings may be better able to bond when the type of solidarity that generally exists between two full siblings, whether biological or adopted, is absent. The former may then serve as substitute siblings and all accept each other as such. Even among older cohorts, more conflict is reported between halfsiblings and stepsiblings than between full siblings, perhaps in part because they have at least one parent they do not share. Halfsiblings and stepsiblings also help each other less in old age than do full siblings.

All in all, in adulthood, the longer stepsiblings have lived together as children, the closer the bond. Having lived with one's mother and stepfather also leads to more contact than having lived with one's father and a stepmother—again indicating the salience of relationships that are maintained by a mother: Halfsiblings who share a mother tend to be closer than those who share a father (Bernstein, 1997).

HOW CAN SIBLINGS BE SO DIFFERENT?

As anticipated through the opening vignette, we now turn to investigate the ramifications of yet another aspect of the situation of siblings vis-à-vis each other: their differences. As I have already alluded to in Chapter 1, the issue of why siblings can be so different is linked to the investigation of the role that genes and the environment play in human development. Traditional socialization theories inform us that parents are extremely important in the formation of their children's personalities, behaviours, and well-being. Yet, most sociological and psychological studies based on this premise find only weak or moderate correlations between various child outcomes and parents' socialization practices. Furthermore, most results of behaviour genetic studies find the same.

These results combined put into question the validity of many past and current sociological interpretations of the parental role, particularly when it comes to *personality development* as opposed to *behaviours*. Geneticists correctly point out that the traditional research confounds genetic and environmental influences (Scarr, 1993): It studies the family as if it were only an environment and ignores the fact that genes play an important role in the interaction between parents and children. In essence, what in the past has been assumed to be the result of parenting is now better understood as an interplay between parents' and children's genetic predispositions as well as between these and the general environment in which families are located (Luster et al., 2000: 145). This perspective meshes well with the interactional-transactional theories that analyze causality from a multidirectional framework. For instance, Jaffee et al. (2003) have found that the less time fathers lived with their children, the more behaviour problems the children had (the role of family structure). But, when fathers exhibited antisocial behaviours, the reverse occurred: Their children had more behaviour problems the longer they lived with their father. These children received a "double whammy" of risks toward difficult behaviours: genetic (father's predispositions) and environmental (father's poor parenting).

What Are the Sources of Sibling Differences?

Dunn and Plomin (1990) have documented how dissimilar siblings generally are on at least some important personality characteristics and related behaviours. Everyday experience also presents the reader with many opportunities to observe such differences between two brothers or two sisters who are only one year apart. Yet, children in the same family are exposed to a **shared environment** that includes family structure, family routines and events, values and teachings emphasized by parents, as well as the effects of parents' personalities on family functioning (Plomin et al., 2001). The traditional socialization perspective predicts that this shared environment should make siblings quite similar in terms of personality characteristics, values, behaviours, and even adult lifestyles. Furthermore, each child inherits 50 percent of his or her genetic makeup from the mother and the other 50 percent from the father. Thus, siblings inherit their genetic makeup from the combined gene pool of a same mother and father—hence, one more reason for them to be similar. Why are they not? There are four reasons.

First, siblings are different because each inherits a different **combination** of their **parents' gene pool.** Let's take two sisters, Linda and Jenny. Linda looks like the father physically but is also sociable like the mother; in contrast, Jenny looks like the mother but is shy and reserved like the father is. We should add that the more different the biological parents are from each other, the more likely it is that siblings will be different because they do not inherit overlapping genes. Second, siblings are different because of the **nonshared environment,** which essentially refers to environmental influences or experiences that differ for each child. These include birth order, peers, school experiences, and accidents and illnesses that affect one sibling but not the other—and the timing of birth in the family life course (East and Jacobson, 2000). As we have seen, even their own relationship can constitute a nonshared experience: They often treat each other differently.

Children's Different Perceptions of Familial Environment

A third reason why siblings are different is that many transform much of their shared or familial environment into a nonshared one. Indeed, although siblings partake equally of their shared familial environment, such as parental teachings or even divorce, they attach **different meanings** (symbolic interactionism) to it because of their individual personalities and what they have learned outside the family (Monahan et al., 1993). For instance, Dunn and McGuire (1994) compared the impact on siblings of 256 events that had occurred in the families they had observed over a three-year period. These shared events affected the siblings differently in nearly 70 percent of the cases. Thus, only 30 percent of the events produced a common effect.

> Let's take the fictive example of two fraternal twins. Although their parents treat them similarly, twin Bob perceives that he receives less love, whereas twin Harry does not see any difference in the way they are treated. This perceptual gap is the result of twin Bob being more sensitive, anxious, and rebellious than Harry (Baker and Daniels, 1990). This perceptual difference produces another consequence: Bob's sense of resentment and then distancing from parents. In effect, because of his reaction, Bob is creating for himself a family climate different from that of his twin.

This divergent family climate will become part of their nonshared environment. In turn, this nonshared environment interacts with each twin's predispositions to create different ways of behaving toward others, including their parents. For instance, Bob becomes even more rebellious and anxious as a result of the nonshared environment he has in great part created—although he has done so unconsciously.

> Another hypothetical example, that of a disadvantaged family with three daughters, further illustrates this mechanism. One sister is good natured and easily satisfied. She does not feel deprived and makes the best out of a bad situation. The other sister is materialistic, envious, and demanding. Consequently, she reacts to their poverty with stress, dissatisfaction, behavioural problems, and lack of respect for their parents. The last sister is goal oriented and industrious; she is determined to improve her lot.

These siblings' **perceptions** based on their different personalities lead them to react differently to a shared environment of poverty. In turn, these disparate reactions not only strengthen their personality differences but also create a private environment—that is, one that they do not share with their two sisters. This nonshared environment contributes to maintaining or even widening the differences among these siblings. Such examples fit very well within the perspectives of symbolic interactionism and interactional theories. In summary, siblings are dissimilar to some extent in terms of personalities, appearance, and physical constitution because of a different combination of genes. (By the same token, however, they are more similar among themselves than to unrelated persons of the same age in their neighbourhood.) Second, siblings are also different because of the nonshared environment, such as different friends. And third, their different perceptions of and reactions to their shared environment reinforce their differences and create new ones. Finally, psychological traits are influenced by several genes combined (polygene), and the effect of genes can change over time (McCartney, 2003).

Families That Provide a More Powerful Shared Environment

The above having been said, the fact remains that some families provide more shared socialization experiences for their children than do most other families. This expanded family environment becomes more powerful and can make siblings similar, not necessarily in terms of personalities, but in terms of what is learned, leisure activities, lifestyle, beliefs, values, and even the skills they develop (Lykken, 1987). How do parents provide a more comprehensive or powerful shared environment?

To begin with, some fathers and mothers are quite similar to each other as a result of **assortative mating** (Chapter 8). Such parents pass on more similar genes to their children; they are also likely to reinforce each other's teachings and provide a more uniform home climate that leaves less room for differentiation among siblings than when parents hold different views. Second, we can use Thornton and Lin's (1994) theory of **family integration** as an explanation. Parents who engage in many activities with their children, both at home or elsewhere, provide siblings with a more cohesive and integrative learning experience. For instance, parents may take their children along on vacations and to the library or museums, and they may engage in specific sport activities as a family group. All these activities combined contribute to family integration, which enlarges the children's shared environment; the shared activities also limit the time the children spend in nonshared activities and in environments that could lead to different perceptions and learning experience.

Third, this shared effect becomes even more powerful when parents and children together engage in activities with other parents and their children as a group; the entire family then experiences more shared elements. These activities can include religious worship, sports, communal picnics, and visits to other families' homes. The end result is that parents and offspring interact with others their age within the same context that, in turn, reinforces parental teachings—a matter of collective socialization. Fourth, when parents are able to send their children to schools that replicate their own value system and lifestyle, siblings and parents have a more expanded, shared learning environment (Chapter 7). The school becomes an extension of the home, particularly when like-minded parents send like-minded children to the same schools. The school and the family essentially overlap in what the children learn, each agent of socialization reinforcing the other and, in rational theory's terms, offering **social closure** against the rest of the world.

Although each child in such families benefits from the common environment somewhat differently because of his or her personality, the fact remains that these siblings are surrounded by a "wrap-around" lifestyle that is shared by parents, relatives, friends, friends' parents, parents' friends, and even teachers. This shared environment becomes an effective community where everyone more or less pitches in and socializes its children similarly. **Collective socialization** is a far more powerful agent of socialization than isolated parental efforts at home, which can be diminished by different sets of values and behaviours as soon as children step outside. The shared environment becomes a more powerful source of influence on offspring. Siblings then become more similar, not necessarily in terms of personality characteristics, but with regard to lifestyle, education, values, beliefs, and occupational achievement.

One sees such examples among traditional Mafia families that interact among themselves and where the male children learn to engage in illegal activities; and among communities of rural Amish and Mennonite families where the children who remain home replicate their parents' specific rural and religious lifestyle. This expanded shared environment can also occur by default in geographically isolated pockets of rural poverty or even in distant Native villages, where all the children fall under the same influences that mould their perceptions and limit their life alternatives. They consequently grow up to replicate their parents' and their neighbours' poverty, despite having different personalities and innate abilities (Rowe et al., 1999).

SIBLING SIMILARITIES AND DIFFERENCES: TWIN STUDIES

Until the science of molecular or biological genetics is able to pinpoint exactly which sets of genes are related to specific health conditions, abilities, and to a lesser extent to personality predispositions, behaviour geneticists in the meantime have to rely on sophisticated statistical guesswork. The best natural experiment that life provides at this point is twins, as well as adoption situations.

Twins as Natural Experiments

The rationale behind research with twins and adopted siblings is to take advantage of degrees of genetic relatedness (Plomin et al., 1998; see Family Research 13.2). Identical twins share all of their genes; fraternal twins and other siblings share about 50 percent; halfsiblings about 25 percent; and stepsiblings as well as adopted children have no genetic background in common. The more closely related two persons are genetically, the more likely they are to be similar (Reiss, 2003). Furthermore, research designs comparing identical twins and fraternal twins reared apart in adoptive homes to twins raised together in their family of birth allow for the study of the separate and combined role played by genetics, shared environment, and nonshared environment (Kendler, 1996).

Thus, researchers "experiment" with degrees of genetic closeness along with degrees of shared environments: Twins who have been adopted into separate families present an ideal experimental situation. This particular twin research design is illustrated in Table 13.1. This table is fictive in the sense that the numbers are invented for teaching purposes (the statistics utilized by behaviour geneticists are too complex for a family textbook). However, the numbers presented follow the general line of reasoning of such studies. This table focuses on personality characteristics because they are somewhat more likely to be genetically influenced than are lifestyles and activities; the latter depend far more on the available environment.

To begin with, if genes were the main source of personality formation, the percentages for identical twins would be close to 90 percent to indicate near perfect similarity. But the highest figure in Table 13.1 is 40 percent, which more or less means that around 60 percent of the identical twins' personalities is produced by the environment,

---

FAMILY RESEARCH 13.2

Potential Problems in Twin Studies

The Colorado Adoption Project study compared pairs of adoptive siblings with pairs of biological siblings, including twins, on mild delinquency and aggressive behaviour. For our purposes here, we are interested in the potential problems of twin studies. For instance, Deater-Deckard (2000) wondered whether it is valid to assume that twins' family environment is equivalent to that of siblings who are not twins. The equivalency assumption is a necessary one if the results of behaviour genetics studies are to be valid. Yet, one can easily see that parenting two or more same-age children (twins) may create a different familial climate, which would violate the assumption of an equivalent family environment.

Furthermore, identical twins may be more likely to copy each other's behaviour than fraternal twins or even just regular siblings, a situation that could artificially increase, but not eliminate, the genetic influence. Twins, particularly when they are identical, are more likely to share a similar environment, which would again contribute to increasing their similarity. Thus, methodological problems may exist in the research on twins and *may* reduce researchers' ability to draw solid and generalizable conclusions about the role of genetics and environment in human development. However, studies of twins reared separately in different families do not suffer from this possible methodological complication.

| TABLE 13.1 | Fictive Percentages of Overall Personality Similarity among Identical and Fraternal Twins Who Were Raised Together or Separately* |

Identical Twins Raised Together (Group 1)	Identical Twins Raised Separately (Group 2)	Fraternal Twins Raised Together (Group 3)	Fraternal Twins Raised Separately (Group 4)
40%	35%	20%	15%

*The fictive subjects are four groups, each containing 100 pairs of same-sex twins aged 14.

both shared and nonshared. A second way of examining the role of genes and environment is to look at twins reared together (Groups 1 and 3). Identical twins are still much more similar than fraternal twins on personality characteristics: The percentages are 40 and 20 for identical and fraternal twins, respectively. This indicates a role played by genes. If genes played no role, identical and fraternal twins would be equally similar because of the environment they share: Their percentages would be the same.

However, one would expect no similarity between identical twins raised separately were the home environment the main determinant. Thus, a third way is to look at different family environments, in this case those in which twins have been raised separately (Groups 2 and 4). Identical twins reared apart are still more similar to each other in terms of personality than fraternal twins (35 versus 15 percent), but they are not quite as similar as identical twins who have been raised together (40 versus 35 percent). This indicates that genes are important but that the family environment also plays a role, although a small one, as can be seen by the mere five percent difference between twins raised apart and separately.

According to this line of reasoning, genes are more important than family influence, but less so than the nonshared environment. Behavioural geneticists calculate the influence of the nonshared environment as being nearly everything else that is not accounted for by genes and family (or around 55 percent for identical twins in this table). Thus, because the percentage difference attributed to the family environment is so small in these statistics (five percent), several behaviour geneticists have come to believe that the nonshared environment is more influential in siblings' development than the familial or shared environment is. The conclusions derived from this line of reasoning are critiqued later on.

Identical adult twins who have been adopted separately and thus raised apart give many similar answers when they are asked to describe the homes in which they have been reared (Hur and Bouchard, 1995:339). Their **perceptions** are more similar than are those of fraternal twins also raised apart. In view of the fact that the homes were different, how can this be? This similarity of perceptions is the result of a combined genetic and environmental effect. To begin with, it is likely that these identical twins' different sets of adoptive parents were reacting fairly similarly to the twins' identical physical appearances and relatively similar personalities when they were growing up.

Although living in different homes, the identical twins may then have developed more similar relationships with their two sets of parents and thus naturally perceive these homes more similarly than do fraternal twins. The latter were less alike in terms of appearance and personalities, and consequently elicited **different reactions** from their two sets of adoptive parents. As the reader can see, these processes are also easily understood through both symbolic interactionism and interactional theories: People create reactions that then become part of their environment, and this environment in turn helps create their personalities and perceptions. All in all, these studies indicate that genes indirectly play a role in the creation of a person's environment: Genes and environment act together.

Is Parental Influence Irrelevant?

As we have seen, the results of behaviour geneticists' studies have led many to emphasize the effect of the nonshared environment over the familial one in the shaping of siblings' personalities and related behaviours (Plomin and Rutter, 1998). Unfortunately, these statistical results and conclusions have led a few researchers and some popular writers (such as Harris, 1998) to conclude that parenting is largely irrelevant to children's development. Is this so?

No: This belief is a misunderstanding arising from the twin and adoption *methodology* (Monahan et al., 1993). The misunderstanding arises because the relative lack of similarity among siblings raised together is interpreted to mean that only a different, thus nonshared, environment is influential. Within this interpretation, parents (shared environment) consequently play practically no role in their children's development because, according to this way of thinking, parents should create similarity, not difference.

The fact is that whether siblings are similar or different is irrelevant in terms of parental influence. Parents influence their offspring, both biological and adopted, both similar and different, and they do so within the *limits* set by these children's genetic predispositions, perceptions, and reactions (Reiss, 2003). Think of it this way: If parents had no impact on their children, whether they are similar or different in terms of personality, children would arrive in daycare or kindergarten totally unsocialized—that is, as small, grunting animals. Yet, quite the contrary is true: Young children who have spent their first four years at home with their parents, even with no television and no peer group, arrive in kindergarten fully equipped with language, skills, beliefs, expectations, and attitudes. These can only come from parental effect or what is called the shared environment (Rutter, 2002).

As seen earlier, some parents are more successful than others at influencing their children, in part because they have more personal resources and the social context they live in is more compatible with their values (Lamborn et al., 1996). Furthermore, children unconsciously (and later consciously) filter their parents' teachings through their own predispositions or personalities. Rutter (1997:393), a sociologically influenced behaviour geneticist, correctly puts this into perspective when he points out that parents produce an effect but it is dissimilar or nonshared: It is different for each child because each child is different at birth.

For example, twin Mia is impulsive, quick to react, and pays little attention to what is said. With the help of her mother, Mia learns to become less impulsive than she would be were she living in a family that provides little structure. In the latter family, she would become more impulsive. Her twin Al is totally different:

He is quiet, shy, and learns quickly. With the mother's help, he becomes more engaging socially, thus less shy. Because he is a quick learner, the mother can teach him many skills, so that Al learns even better than he would in a family with a less invested mother.

Although both twins remain different, each improves under maternal influence, even though his or her basic personality remains (Fergusson et al., 1995:613). Unfortunately, this improvement (or worsening in other cases) is not measured by the behaviour genetic studies described earlier (see also Cherlin, 1999).

Thus, it is false to conclude that parents and the shared environment have no influence, and that, for instance, only peers matter (Scaramella et al., 2002). On the other hand, it is equally false to conclude, as sociologists and psychologists have done, that parents hold *the key* to their child's development: Both genes and the nonshared environment (siblings, peers, media, teachers, etc.) contribute the other keys (Bronfenbrenner, 1994). Difficult or aggressive peers, for instance, can have a great negative impact (Espelage et al., 2003). Yet, parents' firm behavioural control can be effective against such peer influence (Golombos et al., 2003). As well, one has to consider that certain parental effects on children are derived from their own genes; thus even the familial environment is partly genetic (Kim-Cohen et al., 2004).

Furthermore, as adolescents become adults, their environment changes and family influences are diluted (Udry, 2003). As we have seen when discussing parental influence in the previous chapter, environmental forces today are far more powerful in child socialization in different ways than they were a century ago: The family then constituted a larger part of a child's environment and the rest of the community tended to hold values that were generally compatible with those reflected in the family, thus providing a larger component of closure from other influences (Côté, 2000).

CONCLUSIONS: THE NATURE AND NURTURE OF PARENTAL INFLUENCE

In western countries, sibling interactions are far more varied and optional than parent-child relationships because they are less scripted culturally. The sibling relationship is affected by the familial context and later on by the peer network and other social alternatives. We have also seen that the influence of siblings on each other is underrated, and it is quite possible that, at least for the younger child in a family, it is greater than parental influence in many domains of life.

The study of siblings, particularly twins and adopted children, has been directed toward better understanding the role that genes and the environment jointly play in human development. For sociologists, this new knowledge can be utilized to soften traditional views on the presumably all-powerful role that parents play in their child's socialization—and consequently to rectify the blame parents have received when a child turns out "wrong." On the one hand, traditional sociological and psychological theories have overrated parental influence on children's personality development. On the other hand, geneticists' results often lead to the conclusion that parents have relatively little to do in terms of their children's behavioural development. In this respect, we have seen that the methodology used by geneticists is a stumbling block in understanding parental contribution to children's outcomes. The reality is that parents influence their children, but they do so within a specific context (their social class, neighbourhood, peer group, media), and in conjunction with the genetic material or predispositions inherited by their children as well as their children's interpretations of reality. The latter are also influenced by genetic and environmental factors. Thus, there is a constant, ongoing interplay between nature and nurture.

Summary

1. The mother-child interaction changes with the arrival of a second infant. The older child's personality and parents' initiatives largely affect the child's adaptation to the arrival. Each new baby dilutes parental resources, but this is particularly so in large families with closely spaced children. In such families, offspring do not do as well at school, on average. There are advantages, however, to being part of a large sibling group, but studies have yet to measure these adequately.

2. Sibling relationships are determined by siblings' characteristics, personality compatibility, and parental behaviours, as well as children's perceptions of how they are treated compared to their siblings. Older siblings tend to be fairly consistent over time in their behaviour toward younger ones, whereas younger ones show less stability because they are the ones who have to adapt to the older's behaviours. It is possible that effects that have been attributed to parental practices are actually the result of the handling a child has received from siblings. Gender plays a very important role in sibling relations, with girls being closer to their siblings than boys. Overall, siblings do not perceive their relationship similarly.

3. Siblings influence each other, particularly older ones toward younger ones. This is documented in studies on aggressiveness, delinquency, early sexual activity, and even early childbearing. The sharing of friends contributes to sibling similarity and influence.

4. When a child suffers from disabilities, siblings often help parents care for him or her. However, adults' well-being is often negatively affected when the sibling has emotional problems compared to physical or mental delay. Although siblings can act as a buffer for each other in times of family distress, the research indicates that divorce and the arrival of a stepparent is often accompanied by sibling conflict.

5. Differential parental treatment of siblings is in part related to children's age, developmental stage, gender, and child personality. Mothers tend to treat children similarly at a given age, but at any point in time, siblings are treated somewhat differently.

6. The adult sibling relationship is discretionary in western societies. In North America, proximity increases contact and the potential for both conflict and closeness. Gender continues to be an important variable: Sisters form closer bonds and benefit even brothers. Perceived differential treatment from parents while growing up often contributes to the tone of the adult sibling relationship. Stepsiblings do not usually bond as closely when full siblings are present. The longer stepsiblings have lived together as children, the closer the adult bond.

7. The study of sibling differences returns us to the issues raised by behaviour genetics. This theoretical perspective redressed some of the excesses of traditional socialization theories and meshes with the interactional framework. Despite a shared home environment and genes inherited from the same parents, siblings are different because each inherits a particular combination of their parents' gene pool and has a different nonshared environment, including

birth order as well as peer and school experiences. Furthermore, because of their individual personalities, children perceive and interpret their shared environment (such as parental teachings) differently. Certain families are able to extend the shared environment and to make its impact stronger so that siblings become more similar, not in terms of personalities, but in terms of values and lifestyles.

8. In order to study the joint and separate effect of genes and environment on human development, twin and adoption studies are used because they present degrees of genetic closeness. Twins reared apart also present degrees of environmental closeness. Identical twins show more personality similarities than fraternal twins, even when raised separately. The similarity is higher when they are raised together. The totality of the studies indicates that environmental forces are more important than biology. However, the calculations used by behaviour geneticists has led many to conclude that it is not the shared home environment that is the most important in human development but the nonshared one. They confuse a relative lack of similarity between siblings with a lack of parental influence. The fact is that parents influence their offspring, both biological and adopted, but they do so only within the limits set by the children's genetic predispositions, perception, and reactions.

Key Concepts and Themes

Assortative mating, p. 378
Birth order, pp. 365, 369
Collective socialization, pp. 367, 379
Combination of parents' gene pool, p. 377
Different meanings, p. 377
Different reactions, p. 382
Differential parental treatment, pp. 369 ff., 375
Dilution of parental resources, p. 362
Effective community, p. 367
Family integration, p. 378
Family size, p. 362
Gender, pp. 364, 371, 374
Interactional perspective, p. 372

Kin-keepers, p. 364
Nonshared environment, pp. 377, 381
Perceptions, pp. 377–378, 381
Shared environment, p. 377
Sibling differences, pp. 376 ff.
Sibling effect, p. 364
Sibling influence, pp. 365 ff.
Social capital, p. 362
Social class, p. 365
Social closure, p. 379
Social resource, p. 379
Spacing, p. 361
Stepsiblings, p. 375

Analytical Questions

1. Do you think there are advantages to large family size in terms of personality development? Would your answer differ for the 21st century compared to the 19th?

2. Families are becoming smaller (related to lower fertility). Analyze this development from a life course perspective.

3. Why are siblings different from each other? And are they more different from each other than the other kids in the neighbourhood?

4. What role do perceptions play in the distinction of what constitutes the shared versus the nonshared environment?

5. Do you agree or disagree with behaviour geneticists when they rule out parental influence (or the shared environment) as a key element in children's development?

Suggested Readings

Berk, L. E. 2000. *Child development,* 5th Ed. Boston: Allyn and Bacon. This comprehensive textbook on child development includes a clear introduction to behaviour genetics.

Brody, G. H. (Ed.) 1996. *Sibling relationships: Their causes and consequences.* Norwood, NJ: Ablex. This is a collection of scholarly articles from a wide range of disciplines focusing on diverse aspects of the sibling relationship. Some of the studies presented are longitudinal. Various ages are considered throughout the life span. Sibling influence, family contexts, and behaviour genetics are other aspects surveyed.

Hetherington, E. M., Reiss, D., and Plomin, R. (Eds.) 1994. *Separate social worlds of siblings: The impact of the nonshared environment on development.* Hillsdale, NJ: Erlbaum. As indicated by the title, this collection of articles is largely inspired by behaviour genetics theories. Reviews of the literature as well as new research data are presented.

Suggested Weblinks

Multiple Births Canada and **Multiple Births** are two websites that provide information, advice, and sources of support for parents of twins, including issues of sibling identity. Many links to other sites are listed.

www.multiplebirthsCanada.org

and

http://multiplebirthsfamilies.com

Family Challenges and Solutions

Part 5 emphasizes challenges that families encounter, including marital transitions and diverse forms of abuse and neglect. A focus on social policies that could prevent some family crises and alleviate family problems in general is also evident.

The topic of **Chapter 14** is marital transition, particularly divorce and remarriage. Widowhood is also discussed. A distinction is made between the outcomes of these transitions for adults and children.

Chapter 15 examines violence, abuse, and child neglect occurring within the family. The discussion proceeds in the developmental order of family life, beginning with dating violence and proceeding with abuse between spouses or partners who live together. Abuse of children by their peers, which is such a topical issue, is included. The theoretical perspective is largely structural but also includes elements of behaviour genetics, interactional-transactional theories, and gender roles.

Chapter 16 focuses on the future of families and on a reexamination of the main themes that have informed this text. Above all, this chapter returns to social policies affecting families and especially a critique of these policies. It also offers specific models of programs that could lead to a reduction in familial challenges, particularly poverty, and an increase in familial well-being.

CHAPTER 14

Divorce and Remarriage

"I really didn't see it coming [his marriage breaking up]. I guess I was too busy."

"Oh, I was so unhappy with him, you have no idea. He has no idea either." [The above man's ex-wife]

"My divorce was a pathetic waste, a waste of time and a psychological waste. We could have stayed together; instead we chose to subject each other to all manner of psychological warfare." [This man was happily remarried.]

"Am I better off now? I am not any happier. It's hard to raise children on your own when that wasn't in the planning. But at least I don't have to put up with his constant rejection and abuse."

"I couldn't afford a divorce but that's all I got in life, a lousy piece of paper that gives me no rights and all the burdens in the world." [Custodial mother on welfare]

"I used to think that a woman my age was too old for me. I dated much younger women, you know the stereotypical bachelor. I liked the ego boost these girls gave me. But when the party was over and time came to face life, I went for a woman my age...otherwise the life goals, long-term life goals, would have been too different."

"He shares in the upbringing of our children whereas I had to do it all in my previous marriage. He is thoughtful and we plan everything together. In my first marriage, it was all his life; his home was his castle. I was a fringe benefit."

"I love my stepchildren. Now I have a very large family and more grandchildren."

"I'd rather not have my stepsons. Mind you, I care for them and I am attached to them but I never set out to have children, and having someone else's children is a burden; I often resent it."

I have selected these quotes from the hundreds available in the files of my longitudinal study on divorce to represent the various stages from divorcing, to remarrying or remaining single, and to stepparenting. These quotes offer a glimpse into some of the issues that are discussed in this chapter. They also illustrate how the experience of divorce is one that is both very individual and yet carries some similarities across cases: A first divorce is, at the very least, a marking event in most persons' lives.

In previous centuries, single-parent families were a common occurrence. For instance, in 1900, 25 percent of all children under the age of 15 had lost a parent to death. Until the Second World War, the death of a spouse remained the leading cause of family disruption, at which point it was surpassed by divorce. It is because of this historical shift that divorce, rather than widowhood, is the main focus of this chapter. Divorce is a legal institution whose function is to separate spouses who can no longer live together. It also brings about, at least temporarily, the social relocation of the ex-spouses from one marital status category to another with consequently different opportunities for life as well as constraints (Cotten, 1999). Divorce carries implications for the life course of adults and children. As we have seen in Chapter 5, one of its results often includes family poverty, with consequently negative impacts on children. In this chapter, therefore, several pages are devoted to studying how divorce affects children, in addition to exploring its ramifications for adults.

The history of the legalization of divorce in Canada predates that of its colonial overseer, England, where it was only in 1857 that divorce was legislated, mainly on grounds of adultery. Nova Scotia, New Brunswick, and Prince Edward Island respectively enacted divorce laws in 1761, 1791, and 1837, generally on grounds of adultery. It was not until 1968 that Canada enacted its first unified federal Divorce Act, which was followed by the more liberal or "no fault" act of 1985 (Sev'er, 1992). But the history of divorce is still unfolding as, in the future, we will have to consider divorce among same-sex couples (Tyler, 2004).

DIVORCE RATES

Current estimates indicate that about 37 percent of Canadian marriages end in divorce, ranging from 48 percent in Quebec to a low of 22 percent in Prince Edward Island (Statistics Canada, 2004j). These estimates are based on divorce rates per 100 marriages followed up to 30 years after their wedding, as indicated in Table 14.1. However, **yearly** divorce rates are the numbers which are generally presented because they are easier to compile and they are the rates which are used for international comparisons and which the media present.

Table 14.2 presents yearly trends over time per 1,000 population and per 1,000 married couples. We see that rates had already begun climbing even before the Second World War, so that by the 1968 Divorce Act, divorce, although still rare, was more common. Rates then increased spectacularly after the 1968 Act and peaked in 1987 at 3.6 divorces per 1,000 population (compared to 5.2 American divorces in 1981 which was the peak year in the U.S.). Thereafter, the rates declined to the point where, in the 2000s, they were equivalent to those of the 1970s. Similar trends are evident in the U.S., although with rates always higher than Canadian ones. As indicated in Table 14.3, Canadian rates are comparable to those of France and are lower than British and especially American ones. The American rates are the highest in the western world. It is difficult to explain this American phenomenon, but it is possible that the sources of divorce discussed in a next section are more in evidence in the U.S. than elsewhere in the western world.

TABLE 14.1 | Total Divorce Rates, per 100 Marriages, by the 30th Wedding Anniversary Since 1998 by Provinces and Territories

	Per 100 Marriages				
	1998	1999	2000	2001	2002
Canada	36.1	37.3	37.7	37.9	37.6
Newfoundland and Labrador	23.2	22.5	22.9	19.6	21.8
Prince Edward Island	26.4	28.0	26.9	22.9	25.2
Nova Scotia	28.2	28.2	30.4	28.9	30.4
New Brunswick	26.9	30.4	31.9	29.1	27.2
Quebec	45.2	46.5	47.4	48.3	47.6
Ontario	33.0	34.4	34.6	35.3	34.9
Manitoba	30.1	31.9	34.6	31.1	30.3
Saskatchewan	31.5	31.7	31.4	28.4	28.7
Alberta	39.0	40.4	41.5	41.9	41.9
British Columbia	40.0	40.3	40.6	41.0	41.0
Yukon	55.2	51.8	33.6	44.1	43.4
Northwest Territories and Nunavut	37.5	34.0	40.7	37.1	31.2

Source: Statistics Canada, 2004J.

We have seen in Table 14.1 that divorce rates differ by geographic region. The low rates for the Maritimes, despite economic pressure, might be the result of a higher level of social integration, a more effective community, or demographic variables such as a smaller number of married couples or an older population. In contrast, the higher rates for Quebec may stem from a combination of variables such as widespread cohabitation before marriage, lower religiosity, and more liberal and individualistic attitudes. Another recent trend in divorce rests in that couples are now on average older at divorce than in the past: Women and men are 40.5 and 43.1 years old on average. This is partly the result of an increasing age at marriage and the fact that the average duration of a marriage before divorce is now 14.2 years, thus 1.4 years longer than a decade ago (Statistics Canada, 2004j).

Divorce rates are particularly complex to discuss. First, in Canada, we tend to think in terms of the higher American rates because of the omnipresence of their media in our lives. Second, different methods are used to compute rates and some of these are less adequate than others. Finally, a proportion of divorces are actually second or third divorces. Unfortunately, general statistics do not differentiate between first and subsequent divorces. The least that can be said is that repeat divorcers inflate the yearly rate; in turn, this means that there are fewer *first* marriages that ever end in divorce than the overall rate suggests.

TABLE 14.2 | Divorce Rates per 1,000 Population and Married Couples Over the Years

Years	Numbers	Divorce Rates per 1,000 Pop.	Divorce Rates per 1,000 Married Couples
1921	558	.06	N/A
1941	2,462	.21	N/A
1961	6,563	.36	N/A
1968*	11,343	.55	N/A
1970	26,093	1.23	N/A
1981	67,671	2.71	11.74
1985**	61,980	2.53	11.03
1986	78,304	2.99	13.02
1987***	96,200	3.62	15.86
1990	80,998	2.96	13.11
1995	77,636	2.62	12.22
1997	67,400	2.25	N/A
2000	71,144	2.31	N/A
2002	70,155	2.23	N/A

Source: Statistics Canada throughout the years; last one 2004j.
*Divorce Act
**Reform of Divorce Laws
***Peak Year

Thus, in Tables 14.1 to 14.3, there are two other missing ingredients that prevent us from grasping the entirety of the phenomenon of **marital dissolution**. The first concerns those couples who separate but never divorce and about whom there are no official statistics. The second involves cohabiting couples who separate—and over 50 percent do (Milan, 2000). Neither separation nor cohabitation breakups are included in divorce statistics. But we have seen in Chapter 8 that cohabitations are not always an equivalent to marriage. Therefore, many of these dissolutions may not unavoidably be equivalent to a divorce but more akin to the breakup of a dating relationship. However, while less than 30 percent of children in married families experience their parents' divorce, over 60 percent of children whose parents cohabit do (Marcil-Gratton, 1999).

Serial Divorces

There is no readily available information on Canadians who divorce several times, but I would estimate that at least 15 percent of all divorces are redivorces for at least one or both spouses. (In the U.S., the rate is closer to 30 percent.) For instance, 32

TABLE 14.3 | **Western Divorce Rates per 1,000 Population for 1996**

Country	Rates per 1,000 Population
Canada	2.6
Cuba	3.7
France	2.7
Germany	2.0
Italy	0.5
Mexico	0.4
Portugal	1.4
Spain	0.7
Sweden	2.2
United Kingdom	3.1
United States	4.3

Source: United Nations, 1998.

percent of marriages which took place in 1996 included at least one spouse who had been previously married compared to only 16 percent in 1970 (Vanier Institute of the Family, 2000:51). Table 14.4 indicates that even among very young American women (20 to 29 years), around 15 percent of their divorces were following a remarriage; that is, these women had been divorced and remarried at least once before. Naturally, the proportion of redivorces increases with age: As people age, they have lived more years during which several marital transitions could have taken place. Women aged 45 to 49 had the highest divorce rate after a remarriage; a small proportion of these remarriages might have followed a period of widowhood rather than divorce. This age bracket contains women who are older by 20 years than the first set of younger women. Their marital transitions have occurred later and perhaps at a less rapid pace. In contrast, young adults who go through multiple marital transitions experience them

TABLE 14.4 | **Percentages of All American Divorces That Follow a Remarriage (Women) in 1980 and 1990**

Age Bracket	1980	1990
20–24 years old	8.5%	13.1%
35–39	24.7	28.5
45–49	25.1	36.4

Source: U.S. Bureau of the Census, 1997, p. 107.

earlier and at a more accelerated pace. U.S. data show that, with each subsequent divorce, the time that elapses between marriage and divorce decreases remarkably (National Center for Health Statistics, 1995:19).

These statistics give the distinct impression that people who divorce more than twice may be in what South and Lloyd (1995) have called a state of permanent availability to any better alternative that comes along. Indeed, the serially divorced seem to differ on some dimensions from people who have divorced only once (Booth, 1999). For instance, they are more likely to suffer from emotional, alcohol, and drug-related problems (Counts, 1992). They may have more unstable personalities and may be more stressful to get along with (Kurdek, 1990). They are less committed to their relationship and the institution of marriage and have fewer ties to the community (Booth and Amato, 2001). They like being married but are not much willing or ready to make adjustments or concessions that could lead to stability, as illustrated in the quotes below:

"Women expect too much out of marriage. I sure as hell can't live out their dreams." [Man in his fourth marriage]

"My wife says I have to work at our marriage. I don't agree with her. Marriage is supposed to be pleasant and if it isn't, well, it's not my problem." [Man in his third marriage]

Such remarks were very different from whatever most respondents who had divorced only once said (Ambert, 1989). The latter expressed more feelings of hurt, guilt, and even regret. While interviewing persons who had divorced several times within a *short time span*, I often had the impression that their marriage was part of the throw-away culture: If it's of no use, then get rid of it. However, the serially divorced did not all unavoidably differ from those who had divorced only once. Some had simply had the misfortune of remarrying a "divorce-prone" spouse. Moreover, there are persons who make a mistake early on and divorce in their twenties, remarry, have children, and divorce again in their forties or fifties. There is no research comparing such persons who divorce a second time after years of stability with those, such as in my study, who had divorced two to four times within 15 years or less. One can reasonably assume that the former may be more stable and more responsible spouses and parents than the latter.

How Are Divorce Rates Measured?

Statisticians use four basic methodologies to measure or estimate divorce rates:

1. The most commonly used method to measure divorce both nationally and internationally is seen in Tables 14.2 and 14.3: It is the rate for every 1,000 or 100,000 people in the population. This is called the "crude" divorce rate. The problem is that the denominator (bottom figure of 1,000 or 100,000) includes the entire population—that is, children, widowed, single, and already-divorced persons. These people cannot divorce: They are not even married! Furthermore, this measure may obscure cohort differences. For instance, the presence of large numbers of seniors or of children in a population in effect lowers the overall divorce rate. It can, for example, hide the fact that young adults might be divorcing at a very high rate.

2. A more accurate method measures the rate of divorce per 1,000 or 100,000 *married* couples or even married women in the population: This method is also included in Table 14.2. The obvious advantage of this measure is that only those who are eligible to divorce are used as the basis of calculations.

3. An even more refined way of measuring divorce is illustrated in Table 14.1 and consists of looking at couples who married 30 years ago, to see what proportion have since divorced. This method gives the closest approximation to a lifetime divorce rate because, after 30 years of marriage, few divorces take place. However, this method is not practical for the purpose of producing yearly statistics across the world because it requires more complex calculations. Therefore, it is not widely utilized.

4. A ratio is used: The annual rate of divorces occurring in a year is placed over the rate of marriages contracted that same year. For instance, in 1994, the divorce rate per 1,000 population was 2.7 and the marriage rate was 5.5. With this ratio, it seems as if one out of every two marriages ends in divorce. This approach is misleading because, each year, both the numbers of divorces and marriages change, so that, if fewer marriages occur, for instance, the proportion or rate of divorce will rise even though the number of divorces may not have increased. Furthermore, those couples who marry in one year are not generally the ones who divorce that year (Statistics Canada, 2004j)! Unfortunately, this misleading approach is often used in the media and even in some textbooks.

All in all, the true proportion of new marriages in a year that will eventually end in divorce can be obtained only after one of the two spouses has died. The closest approximation of the true divorce rate resides in Method 3, illustrated in Table 14.1.

THE SOURCES OF DIVORCE

Multiple, interlocking factors contributed to the rise of divorce in Canada and other western countries in the second half of the 20th century and to its maintenance at a relatively high level. In this section, both sociocultural and demographic factors associated with an increase in divorce are considered. We also look at the reasons couples give to explain the breakup of their marriage.

Sociocultural Sources

Sociocultural factors are broad social and cultural variables that affect several aspects of people's lives and contribute to influence the ways in which families perceive and experience their relationships. Divorce rates were already slowly inching up in the 19th century as a result of secularization trends, the liberalization of norms concerning individual choice, and the lessening of religious influence. These sociocultural trends later came to influence the **liberalization of divorce laws** that ensued. In turn, easier divorce laws, such as those promulgated in 1968 and 1985, signal the normalization of divorce and are usually followed by an increase in divorce. Divorce lost its stigma and became socially accepted. These cultural and legal factors have made it easier for people to be less attached to marriage as an institution and consequently to turn to divorce.

Furthermore, although religion is still important in Canada, it does not influence as many aspects of personal life as in the past, and even less so in Quebec. Overall, religious prescriptions concerning the conjugal relationship are no longer paramount in couples' lives. This evolution is at times referred to as the **desacralization of marriage:** Marriage is no longer a covenant or sacrament contracted before God but has become an individual choice. This change has contributed to the acceptance of the temporal nature of marriage.

Individualism is an ideology emphasizing rights as opposed to responsibilities. Affective individualism emphasizes the emotional bonds among family members over reciprocal responsibilities (Stone, 1977). In the past, responsibilities were more important than emotions, particularly in terms of marriage. When individualism is coupled with an ideology of gratification, particularly sexual and psychological, where people are encouraged to be "happy" and "fulfilled," it follows that spouses' mentality about their marriage is affected (Glenn, 1996). As well, more is demanded of marriage in terms of personal gratification than was the case in the past and than is still the case in many countries of the world (Fowers, 2000). As Simons et al. (1996:219) put it, "If the raison d'être for marriage is mutual love and support, it is difficult for people to justify staying in a relationship where this is no longer present." In other words, marriage is deinstitutionalized (Cherlin, 2004).

Along with individualism and the pursuit of gratification, westerners have developed a **lower threshold of tolerance** when their marriage does not meet with their expectations for personal fulfillment (Amato, 1999). They are less likely to put up with unpleasantness than their grandparents' generation was. All things considered, while more is expected of marriage, couples are also less tolerant about its failings and less willing to shoulder the sacrifices it may require (Shorter, 1975). At the positive level, the lower threshold of tolerance also means that women now leave abusive relationships that would have kept them captive 40 years ago and fewer children live in marriages riddled with acrimonious conflict.

Demographic Sources

Given the cultural variables facilitating divorce, we now look at demographic factors through which vulnerability to divorce is expressed. Although this is not a source of divorce, let's mention that the first four years of marriage are by far the most vulnerable to disruption. Statistics Canada indicates that the highest rates of divorce occur in year three and four of marriage with over 25 divorces per 1,000 marriages. Early divorces carry both advantages and disadvantages. The advantages reside in the fact that fewer children may be included; as well, the spouses are young and have a higher probability of remarrying if they so wish. On the other hand, when children are involved, these early divorces may create more poverty, as parents may be less well established on the labour market.

Low Income, Youthful Marriage, and Parental Divorce

Low-income couples are at a higher risk of divorcing (Amato and Previti, 2004; Smock et al., 1999). We have seen in Chapter 5 how poverty multiplies individual risks in general, reduces life opportunities, and increases stressors. All of these factors impact negatively on the marital relationship. But we have also seen that divorce contributes to poverty. This means that these two variables reinforce each other in the causality chain.

Youthful marriage also increases the risk of divorcing (Feng et al., 1999). This variable is partly related to the previous one; couples who marry during their teens are less likely to benefit from reasonable means of support. Moreover, they often marry for reasons that differ from those of couples who are more mature. For instance, Forthofer and colleagues (1996) find that adolescents who suffer from emotional problems are more likely to marry (and, now, to cohabit). Although comparatively few now marry because of a pregnancy, others marry to get away from an unhappy home situation. These youthful reasons for marrying do not form a solid foundation for a lasting marriage. We also see later on in this chapter that parents' divorce during childhood or adolescence is a factor that is related to more elevated divorce rates among children when they reach adulthood (Amato and DeBoer, 2001). However, a wife's closeness to her in-laws may reduce the risk of divorce, especially when her own parents had divorced (Timer and Veroff, 2000).

Prior Cohabitation

On average, couples who have cohabited before marriage are more likely to divorce (Berrington and Diamond, 1999; Bumpass and Lu, 2000; Wu and Balakrishnan, 1995). Bélanger and Dumas (1998) report a doubling of the divorce rate for marriage preceded by cohabitation. Wu (2000) even found that simply being married to a spouse who has previously cohabited raises one's risk of divorcing. In one U.S. study, a woman's cohabitation with her future husband did not increase her chance of divorcing, but prior cohabitations did (Teachman, 2003a). The Canadian General Social Survey also found that, in the 20-to-30 age group, 63 percent of women whose first relationship had been cohabitational had separated by 1995 compared to 33 percent of women who had married first without cohabiting (Le Bourdais et al., 2000). (The cohabitational figure included women who had cohabited with one man and had separated from him before marrying another man, and other women who had cohabited with their future husband.) Overall, largely because of cohabitation and divorce, people are experiencing more life transitions of the conjugal and near conjugal type, thus greater instability in family life than in the past (Smock and Gupta, 2002).

Why does cohabitation currently increase the risk of divorce?

1. A first explanation may reside in **selection effects**: Some individuals choose cohabitation because it does not require, in their opinion, sexual fidelity and, particularly among men, it represents a lesser commitment than marriage (Clarkberg et al., 1996). Therefore, within this selection effect, many of these less committed couples do move on to the next stage, which is marriage, and then later divorce when a crisis arises because their level of commitment is not sufficient enough to motivate them to overcome their differences. Furthermore, some studies actually indicate that married persons who cohabited before marriage are less sexually exclusive both before and after marriage (Forste and Tanfer, 1996)—a lack of sexual exclusivity is related to a higher rate of marital dissolution. Thus, it is possible that some of the couples who select themselves into marriage via cohabitation already present a higher risk of relationship dissolution.

2. Still in terms of selection, we have seen in Chapter 7 that, on average, persons who are not religious are more willing to cohabit (Turcotte and Bélanger, 1997a), and that several studies indicate a correlation between religiosity and marital happiness as well as stability (Call and Heaton, 1997). If couples who are both less religious and less committed to each other and to the institution of marriage cohabit and then go on to marry, it is not surprising that they will have a higher divorce rate. They experience multiple risks: low religiosity, low commitment, and prior cohabitation. Furthermore, cohabitants are more approving of divorce as a solution to marital problems than non-cohabitants. They are also more likely to come from a divorced family and to have less education (Bumpas and Lu, 2000).

3. For others, **causality effects** may be more at play. For instance, it is possible that the experience of a less faithful and committed cohabitation shapes subsequent marital behaviour (Dush et al., 2003). Such couples continue to live their marriage through the perspective of the insecurity, low commitment level, and lack of fidelity of their prior cohabitation. Others simply learn to accept the temporary nature of relationships (Smock and Gupta, 2002). The result is a marriage which is at risk (Wu, 2000).

4. Cohan and Kleinbaum (2002) report that, in the first two years of their marriage, couples who had cohabited had somewhat less positive problem-solving behaviours and were less supportive of each other on average than those who had not cohabited. McLaughlin et al. (1992) have found that newly married couples who had cohabited before marriage had substantially higher rates of premarital violence than those who had not lived together. Premarital violence is in turn followed by more marital violence than when none has taken place before, and we know that domestic violence is causally related to divorce (Ambert, 2002a).

Reasons People Give for Divorcing

Couples who are asked what led to their divorce mention "irreconcilable differences," "didn't get along," "no longer loved each other," fighting and quarrelling about money, children, and their relationship. In the U.S., Amato and Previti (2004) found that infidelity was the reason most often given. Frequently mentioned also are physical abuse, mental cruelty, religious differences, and alcoholism. Drug addiction, gambling, mental illness, criminality, "he's never home," and child-related problems, such as the stress of caring for a child with a disability, are occasionally mentioned. The spouse who has not initiated the divorce (and often very much wants to remain married) generally has a less extensive list of reasons or motives: "You ask me why I divorced? Ask *her! She* wanted it," replied one man bitterly, even though he was happily remarried. Generally, in cases of divorce and unhappy marriage, one spouse is happy with the relationship (Waite and Gallagher, 2000). Often it is the husbands who are surprised when their marriage breaks down (Hetherington, 2003).

Marriages are less likely to last when wives complain to their husbands, and the latter, instead of sympathizing with their wives' problems, escalate the interaction into a full-blown conflict (Gottman, 1998). A proportion of couples who eventually divorce threaten to do so or talk about it for a few acrimonious months or years before finally separating. Generally, one of the two partners is more active in this process. In most cases of divorce, one spouse wants out far more than does the other (Hopper, 2001). Women generally find more problems with their marriage than husbands do and decide to divorce more often than men, even though they are the ones who carry the larger burden afterwards (Furstenberg and Cherlin, 1991). Already in 1956, William Goode had explained this apparent contradiction as follows:

> "*Women have been socialized to be the expressive and emotional partner. For their part, many husbands disengage from or avoid discussions pertaining to marital problems. Conflicts are thus not resolved and this situation often leads to divorce.*
>
> "*We suggest, then, that in our society the husband more frequently than the wife will engage in behavior whose function, if not intent, whose result, if not aim, is to force the other spouse to ask for the divorce first. Thereby the husband frees himself to some extent from the guilt burden, since he did not ask for the divorce. A by-product of this process frees him still more: the wife's repeated objections to this behavior will mean that there are family squabbles, and one almost constant result of repeated family squabbles is a lessened affection between husband and wife.*" (Goode, 1956:136–137)

Many of the results and insights of Goode's pioneer study are still applicable. Today, though, the dynamics described by Goode can also be initiated by women, particularly when they stand to lose relatively little and gain much from the divorce. Women who would fit Goode's explanation are more likely to be young, financially independent, and marriageable.

South and Lloyd (1995) report that in over a third of divorces there has been at least one extramarital affair for one or both partners. In the study I conducted, there were several cases in which casual and unplanned extramarital affairs, such as those occurring at an out-of-town convention, caused an enormous blow-up when the other spouse accidentally learned of it; separation was practically immediate. I refer to these as "accidental" or "useless" divorces (Ambert, 1989). These divorces may never have otherwise occurred because the relationships were sound and both ex-spouses reported a high level of marital happiness (see Family Research 14.1). It is commonly believed, with probably a great deal of truth, that only marriages that are not sound disintegrate following a casual affair. In many cases, however, the offended spouse simply cannot cope with this dilemma, even in a good marriage. An affair plants seeds of doubt and insecurity that are too difficult to overcome for persons who may have fewer psychological resources or may have other alternatives.

The Sources of Divorce Are Linked

Many of the self-reported reasons for divorce stem from larger sociocultural factors described in a previous section. For example, without an emphasis on individualism, people would not divorce because they "fell out of love" or because they did not get along. In cultures where marriage is strongly institutionalized within a context of family solidarity, these reasons would be considered frivolous. In a society where divorce is more difficult to obtain and less acceptable, only "strong" reasons, such as abuse

Asking Both Ex-Spouses about Their Past Marital Happiness

You may recall reading in Chapter 11 that few studies examine the marital happiness of a *couple*. Generally, only one spouse is interviewed and then husbands and wives are compared as two separate groups. But these are husbands and wives who are *not* married to each other. Therefore, little can be said about the couple. The same problem occurs in studies of divorce. In order to compensate for this deficit, I have interviewed both new spouses when my respondents had remarried. I also interviewed both ex-spouses, which allowed me to derive a classification of ex-couples depending on both ex-spouses' reported level of marital happiness in their past marriage:

High happiness ex-couples	13%
Mid-level happiness ex-couples (mixture of near high, average, near low)	52%
High unhappiness ex-couples	35%

At the time, these results surprised me, but they have since been replicated in the U.S. In other words, in only one-third of the cases did both ex-spouses recall having been very to fairly unhappy in their past marriage. Furthermore, at least one divorce in 10 occurred to couples in which both partners had been happy or very happy (Ambert, 1989). Analyses at the couple level could be used to study many questions that, until now, have used only one or the other spouse as the basis.

---

and abandonment, are tolerated. Therefore, before people decide to divorce because of personal reasons, a **social and cultural climate** has to exist that offers a legitimate framework for their reasons. Furthermore, personal grounds for divorce such as "didn't get along" and "fighting" tend to be mentioned more by couples with some of the demographic characteristics discussed in the previous subsection, such as youthful marriage and prior cohabitation. Thus, sociocultural and demographic factors related to divorce "push" people out of marriage into divorce via their own personal reasons.

THE AFTERMATH OF DIVORCE FOR ADULTS

There is a great deal of diversity in the post-divorce experience (Hetherington, 2003). Nevertheless, the ex-spouse who has the least personal, financial, and social resources, while at the same time having the most responsibilities, encounters more difficulties and may take longer to adjust to divorce and to life in general, especially when he or she has not initiated the divorce (Wang and Amato, 2000). The ex-spouse who has ample resources adapts more successfully. This does not mean, however, that he or she is less hurt than the other. In fact, the stronger person may suffer the most, yet be able to overcome the pain more effectively. Often, as soon as separation or divorce occurs, a relationship that was rather placid becomes conflictual, and statistics show that, during this period, women are at greater risk of being assaulted and even killed by their former partner (Fleury et al., 2000; GSS, 2000; Kurz et al., 1996). As we see in Chapter 15, cohabiting women are more often abused than married women. This has led Sev'er (2002) to wonder if the dissolution of their unions might not also place them at a particularly high risk for violence.

Factors Associated with Adjustment

In a nutshell, *adjusting to divorce is easier when:*

- A couple does not have dependent children.
- A couple does not share many assets, such as a house or a car (the division of assets constitutes one of the most rancorous aspects of divorce).
- The marriage has been brief—less than five years: The spouses have had less time to invest themselves in the relationship and less time to become habituated to being married.

For a *woman*, adjusting to divorce is easier when:

- She is under age 30, which gives her a much higher chance of remarrying and of having a family in her second marriage.
- She has been employed throughout her marriage or, at the very least, fairly recently: Her economic situation will be less precarious and she may have a work-related social network.

In contrast, *divorce is much more stressful and requires a great deal of adjustment,* at least for *one* spouse, when:

- A couple has children who still live at home.
- A couple jointly owns a home and shares other assets.
- A marriage was long and many habits have to be changed.
- A couple is older, thus less flexible, and perhaps no longer employed.
- A husband and wife share all their friends.
- One or both spouses is in ill health, an alcoholic, or a drug abuser.
- Respective families take sides: Each ex-spouse then loses half of her or his extended kin group.
- Friends are lost: Social support deteriorates at a time of emotional need.
- There is a loss of financial resources and economic status.

For a *woman*, it is generally more difficult to adjust when:

- She has not been employed in the past five years.
- She is over age 40: At that age, a woman is less likely to remarry and it is more difficult to rebuild her social life.

Divorce drastically reduces the mental health of many adults (Aseltine and Kessler, 1993). This may be particularly so for men compared to women in the long term, in part because men have fewer close friendships, seek support less, and have not been socialized to take care of their domestic needs. The first two years after divorce are the most difficult for women (Kitson, 1992), but many grow personally and feel empowered as a result of their divorce (Sev'er, 1992).

Changes in Ex-Spouses' Social Networks after Divorce

Persons' social networks after divorce are rarely studied. In order to modestly remedy this lack of information, I am using qualitative data from my longitudinal study of divorce. With divorce, most couples lose the in-law kin system, so that each ex-spouse now has a reduced kin network until remarriage. Women become single mothers and their supportive network is generally smaller (Cross, 1990). In my research, more women than men reported losing friends after separation. This may reflect the fact that women have more close friendships than men to begin with. Women tended to suffer the greatest loss of friendships in long-term marriages during which friendships had been shared as a couple (Sev'er, 1992). Mutual friends remained with the ex-husband more often than with the ex-wife. Two women explained this situation thusly:

> *"His wife [a friend's wife] feels more secure with Paul I think than with me. As a single woman, I am a threat to her.... I just never realized that she'd be so jealous the minute her husband looked at me."*

> *"My ex-husband is more fun to be with because he has more money to do things and go out."*

Women reported a sharp decline in social activities involving friends they had while married: fewer phone calls, visits, outings, and movies, for instance. Men reported either little change or an increase in visiting, particularly being invited over for dinner and for outings when their children were with them. Custodial fathers definitely received more offers of help from friends and colleagues, and even from their children's teachers, than custodial mothers. Friends seem to presume that a father needs more help because it is relatively unusual for men to have sole physical custody of their children. They received far more sympathy than custodial mothers.

However, very few women had lost those friends whom they had already had before their marriage or had maintained separately during the marriage. The workplace became an important source of moral support at that time. As pointed out in the next quote, in a couple-oriented society, social support is more readily extended to coupled individuals and, after divorce, to men, unless women have a strong, independent network of female friends. Married men seem less threatened by their divorced male friends than married women are by their divorced women friends.

At Time 2, and particularly Time 3, of the follow-up, three and six years later respectively, a great proportion of respondents had remarried. These remarriages provided an excellent opportunity to see if changes in social networks had occurred. Remarried women had seen a substantial increase in their social activities involving new friends. This increase was more salient for women who had lost their friends to their ex-husbands. The change had been practically instantaneous for many. One woman sarcastically put it this way:

> *"Remarriage puts a woman back where she belongs; she's no longer a threat to other women, no longer a temptation to their husbands. But I also think that socially a woman has value because of her married status; I could feel it. I mean, I felt so bitter about it when I was divorced, it was so obvious. From a couple's point of view a divorced woman is more than useless, and all adults are couples so that leaves you nowhere." [Now?] "I am part of a couple again."*

Remarried men also reported an increase in social activity but a less noticeable one when they had maintained their original network. When adults remarry, they gain another set of in-laws; then, they often acquire each other's friends and this explains in part their increased social network and activities. Again, to paraphrase the last woman's quote, this increase is also in part explained by the fact that a couple is a safer and more valued unit for friendship than a divorced individual for other couples. The **status** of marriage or **of being part of a couple** certainly enhances a person's social acceptability. Therefore, adults who need friends less (the married) have more, while those who could benefit from friends' social support, such as divorced mothers and the poor, often have fewer (Hughes et al., 1993). These are social inequities based on gender and coupling status. We need similar research for cohabiting couples who separate.

Custodial Fathers and Mothers

A substantial increase has occurred in the number but not the proportion of fathers who have physical custody. In 2002, only 8.5 percent of custody awards went to husbands exclusively—down from a high of 15 percent in 1986. However, 42 percent were joint legal custody, while 49.5 percent went to wives—an all-time low for wives (Statistics Canada, 2004j). However, in most of these instances, children live with their mother. Overall, custodial fathers have fewer children in their care, and fewer younger ones, than custodial mothers. Fathers who have small children or many of them tend not to seek their custody. When a father has custody, he may have only one or two of the children and not all of them (Drapeau et al., 2000). Furthermore, compared to custodial mothers, custodial fathers are more likely to have another adult living with them, whether a cohabitant, their own mother, or a housekeeper (Bianchi, 1995).

For men, coresidence with their child after divorce results in a better father-child relationship than would otherwise be the case, and contributes to fathers' mental health (Arendell, 1995). Fathers are less subjected to feelings of lack of control over their paternal situation, as is the case among nonresidential fathers (Umberson and Williams, 1993). However, fathers find their role constraining—they have less freedom and more demands are placed on them—and are less happy than visiting fathers (Shapiro and Lambert, 1999).

Fathers are particularly satisfied with **joint legal custody** (Arditti, 1992). Joint custody may involve children living on alternate weeks or months with each parent, but it may also simply involve equal rights for both parents while the children remain with one parent. Children prefer equal time with each parent as do young adults retrospectively (Fabricius, 2003). Mothers prefer sole custody, but are favourable to joint custody when they perceive their ex-husbands to be good parents (Wilcox et al., 1998). The evidence so far accumulated indicates that father and mother custody have equivalent results for children (Downey and Powell, 1993). This means that children who live with their mother, compared to those who live with their father, do not do worse or better overall, although they may fare slightly better or less well on specific dimensions of their lives. For instance, adolescents who live with their father value family life somewhat less than those who live with their mother: 48 versus 57 percent

(Bibby, 2001). Actually, children in single-father and single-mother families are *both* outperformed in school by children in two-parent families. Single fathers have more financial resources available for their children than single mothers (Hao, 1996), but the latter compensate with a higher level of interpersonal resources (Downey, 1994). This includes more time spent with children (Maccoby, 1999).

There does not seem to be any specific overall advantage of **same-sex matching** between parent and child. Boys and girls by age 16 do as well or as poorly whether in a father's or a mother's custody (Powell and Downey, 1997). Similarly, there is no difference in well-being among adults depending on the sex of the single parent with whom they grew up (Downey et al., 1998). But the research is not unanimous, as some studies have found an advantage for children who live with a parent of their own sex (Zill, 1988). This may be a question of having a same-gender role model or of parental ability to understand a same-sex child better (Gately and Schwebel, 1991).

Both in terms of numbers and the social construction of motherhood, noncustodial mothers are nonnormative (Walker and McGraw, 2000). Among them are mothers who relinquish custody because of financial hardship and a few who do so in order to have more freedom or to remarry someone who does not want children at home. In other cases, the father has won custody after a lengthy and often costly legal battle. Other noncustodial mothers are involuntary as a result of ill health, mental problems, drug addiction, criminal conviction, child neglect, or because the child has been kidnapped by the father.

In the U.S., nonresident mothers have more frequent telephone, letter, and extended visitation contacts with their children than nonresidential fathers (Stewart, 1999b). However, both sets of parents tend to engage largely in leisure activities with their children (Stewart, 1999a). Furthermore, neither mothers nor fathers pay all the child support they owe. Fathers who have new biological children are less able to support their nonresidential ones (Manning and Smock, 2000). In Canada, Marcil-Gratton (1999) indicates that about 15 percent of fathers never visit their children while another 25 percent do so only irregularly. As well, common-law unions that dissolve with children are far less likely to provide child support than formerly married ones (Child Support Team, 2000). Some researchers suggest that there is something in the structure of being a nonresidential parent, including the presence of "new" children, that inhibits active parenting as well as economic support for children outside of marriage (Doherty et al., 1998; Manning et al., 2004).

WHAT ARE THE EFFECTS OF DIVORCE ON CHILDREN?

In 1998 in Canada, there were 36,252 *dependent* children involved in a parental divorce (the total number of divorces had been 69,088) compared to over one million in the U.S. Couples who divorce are less likely to have children or to have as many children as those who do not divorce—in great part because a good proportion divorce within the first few years of marriage.

How Does Divorce Affect Children?

In a nutshell, although most children do not experience developmental problems, divorce is certainly a strong risk factor (Cherlin, 1999) and a source of stressors (Emery, 1999). Divorce is, above all, an emotionally painful transition and, as Kelly and Emery (2003:359) point out, it can "create lingering feelings of sadness, longing, worry, and regret that coexist with competent psychological and social functioning." Connidis (2003a) remarks that relationships are changed after divorce and have to be renegotiated many times over the years, and the effects are felt across several living generations within a family.

Although *average* differences are not very large, children and adolescents whose parents are divorced tend to do less well in school and have more behavioural and emotional problems than children in intact families (Zill et al., 1993). They are also at greater risk for delinquency (Ambert, 1999; Coughlin and Vuchinich, 1996) and for premarital births (Wu, 1996). Furthermore, their educational and occupational levels are, on average, lower than those of children whose parents have not divorced. As indicated in Table 14.5, when children who have experienced their parents' marital dissolution reach adulthood, their relationship with their parents is less likely to be warm. Amato and Booth (1997) have found that adult children of divorce fare even less well in this respect than children whose parents remained in an unhappy marriage. Indeed, many adult children have lost contact with their father (Amato, 2003).

They also tend to have higher cohabitation (Turcotte and Bélanger, 1997b) and divorce rates themselves (Hetherington, 2003). However, children whose parents divorce after a low-conflict marriage are more likely to divorce in adulthood than those whose parents' marriage was highly conflictual—probably because a low-conflict marriage ending in divorce transmits an attitude of lack of commitment to marriage in general (Amato and DeBoer, 2001). A new couple's risk of divorcing is even higher when their two sets of parents had divorced during their childhood or adolescence

TABLE 14.5 | Recalled Childhood Quality for Men and Women Who Experienced Parental Structure Change Versus Those Who Did Not*

	Men		Women	
	No change	Change	No change	Change
Very happy childhood	93%	74%	91%	71%
Very close emotionally to mother	92	83	87	76
Very close emotionally to father	73	53	75	49

Source: Statistics Canada; Williams, 2001c.

* Includes all individuals who began life with two parents (biological or adoptive).

(Amato, 1996). When they reach young adulthood, children of divorced parents leave home earlier (Boyd and Norris, 1995). They generally do so as a consequence of their custodial parent's remarriage or cohabitation; they often cite family conflicts as the reason for leaving (Kiernan, 1992).

Longitudinal studies following children up to age 33 indicate that, *when* emotional problems develop, the effect of parental divorce may last and can even intensify (Cherlin et al., 1998). Because these studies were longitudinal, the researchers were able to measure other family and child characteristics that could have influenced the development of emotional problems. Yet, even after they had considered these other influences, their results still showed that the divorce itself had increased the likelihood of emotional problems, even later on in adulthood.

Do the Effects Vary by Age and Gender?

The effects of divorce differ by the child's age and gender, depending on the outcomes that are measured. For instance, boys' behaviour often becomes much more difficult after divorce than that of girls (Morrison and Cherlin, 1995). Despite this difference, after divorce, both boys and girls tend to exhibit more acting-up problems than other children and more so during adolescence than during childhood (Baumrind, 1991a).

In terms of age, small children are not mentally equipped to make sense of what is essentially an adult transition (Jenkins and Smith, 1993). As a result, they may believe that the departure of a parent is their fault. Adolescence may be a particularly difficult period for a parental divorce to occur, but at least adolescents are able to see reasons for divorce and in some cases appreciate its benefits. Furthermore, teenagers often distance themselves from family turmoil (Aseltine et al., 1994). Their interactions with peers can serve to insulate them from family upheavals, if these relationships are supportive. However, children of divorce and remarriage are, as are those in unmarried families, more at risk of falling in with a negative peer group (Kim et al., 1999).

What Are the Effects of Multiple Divorces?

There is little information on the effect of repeated parental divorce on children. But we know that the more marital transitions parents experience, the less well adjusted children are in some domains of life (Amato and Sobolewski, 2001). However, it is possible that most of the hardships caused to children stem mainly from their own parents' divorce. Remarriages end more quickly than first marriages, thus children may not have had the time to bond with their temporary stepparent to suffer from this loss. However, repeated divorces affect adults, which in turn may affect their ability to parent adequately (Hetherington, 2003; Seltzer, 1994). Moreover, multiple divorces may constitute a **socialization experience** for children who see their parents divorce so rapidly and so often: They may fail to learn adequate conflict resolution techniques. Such children may learn to quarrel or to give up without resolving differences. They may also learn to think that marriage is a personal choice of a temporary nature. In turn, they could later on experience more difficulties and instabilities in their own marital lives.

THEORIES EXPLAINING HOW DIVORCE AFFECTS CHILDREN

Several theories explaining the negative consequences of divorce for children receive some support in the research. These explanations are complementary rather than mutually exclusive, because each fits some children better than others.

Economic Explanation

One of the theories that receives the greatest research support is that of economic or material resources (Ross and Mirowsky, 1999a). As documented in Chapter 5, a majority of children experience a reduction in their standard of living after divorce and many become poor. When all variables are considered, the studies reviewed by McLanahan (1997:47) led her to conclude that postdivorce poverty is at least as strong a source of lower cognitive ability and school achievement as is the divorce itself. Hence, when poverty does not occur along with divorce, children may not be so adversely affected, at least in terms of cognitive development, depression, and school success (Aseltine, 1996).

A 20 to 40 percent income loss for women and children after divorce leads to many concurrent changes. For instance, the family often has to move to a more disadvantaged neighbourhood in a small and crowded apartment. This means that children go to a different school, where many students may also be disadvantaged or less well supervised, and where the rates of juvenile delinquency and teen pregnancy may be higher. The sudden, reduced standard of living is often accompanied by a less than plentiful diet, fewer clothes, and little pocket money. In a consumer-oriented society, such a downfall may be felt acutely by children, particularly in the age group of 10- to 16-year-olds. All of these changes are a lot to ask of children, including adolescents who are simultaneously undergoing physiological puberty with its accompanying socioemotional risks (Hines, 1997).

Disruption of Parenting

The economic theory is not in itself sufficient to explain divorce effects: Living in a single-parent family still produces an independent negative effect of its own (Wu, 1996). Thus, a second theory that also receives a great deal of research support sees parenting behaviours as either a direct causative variable or as a mediator variable (McLanahan, 1997). In a nutshell, this theory posits that parents who divorce experience a great deal of stressors and have to adjust to a new lifestyle that gives them less social support as individuals and as parents (Simons et al., 1996:89–91). As a consequence, their parenting skills and availability suffer (Lee, 1993). Many become less tolerant of misbehaviour and are more prone to have screaming fits, while others become depressed and withdraw from their children (Forgatch et al., 1996). Divorced parents tend to be preoccupied or busy, which means less time for children—less time for advice, for love, and for monitoring children's activities. Sons often become defiant, disobedient, disrespectful, and even abusive (Hetherington et al., 1992).

Amato and Gilbreth (1999) suggest that children of divorce have better outcomes when nonresidential fathers are more than friends and entertainers and behave as parents—that is, when they provide emotional and instrumental support, make behavioural demands, place limits on what can be done, and administer consistent discipline. When nonresidential fathers remain **active parents**, as opposed to "Sunday daddies" or their children's "pals," they complement and reinforce custodial mothers' socialization efforts. Children receive the same message of support and authority from both parents, an ideal situation rarely achieved. Basically, what counts in child outcomes is neither the custodial arrangement nor the frequency of visitation, but the quality of parenting and parents' psychological functioning (Wallerstein, 1998).

The Role of Parental Conflict

The third theory overlaps with the second theory to some extent. It focuses on parental conflict both during marriage and after divorce. Conflict is so detrimental that children who remain in a conflict-ridden family have more negative outcomes than those whose parents divorce to eliminate the tension (Amato et al., 1995). Parental conflict is particularly painful when adolescents or children hear their parents fight about them: They feel caught in the middle (Maccoby et al., 1993). In at least one study looking at situations of high parental conflict, boys who were in regular contact with their nonresidential parent tended to have more problems than boys for whom this contact was limited (Amato and Rezac, 1994). As expressed in the following male student quote, conflict is extremely painful for children of all ages, both while parents are married and after the divorce:

> "When I was 11, my parents separated. This has been the most difficult period of my short life until now and it still hurts to this day. But when I was 11 it was worse because my life became so different. My sister seemed to cope better but I just couldn't stand the fighting. They'd fight over the phone about everything and when my father would pick us up for the weekend they'd go at it some more and I'd be shaken up for the entire weekend and it would start all over when he would drop us off and on top of it all, they used to talk against each other and say awful things about each other in front of me. To this day, my skin crawls when I know that they'll talk to each other which is rare now that we're older. My sister's wedding was a nightmare of tension and as far as I'm concerned I'll just elope one day because I just couldn't go through with it. I have been a nervous wreck since that time [age 11]."

In fact, Buchanan et al. (1996) have found that the worst thing that can happen to a child is that his or her parents remain locked in conflict after divorce. In such cases, divorce fulfills no positive function for the child; rather, it exacts a heavy price for which there is no compensation. Parental conflict also means lack of authoritative and guiding parenting. In contrast, low parental conflict *after* divorce may shield children from the stressors of divorce (Amato and Booth, 1997). As we saw, low-conflict marriages that end in divorce appear to have a strong negative effect on children, whereas divorce for high-conflict couples may have a beneficial effect (Booth and Amato, 2001). In many cases, "intense anger and conflict is ignited by the separation itself and the impact of highly adversarial legal processes" (Kelly and Emery, 2003:353; Hopper, 2001). Overall, there is research consensus that pre- and postdivorce conflict is detrimental to children but that the divorce itself contributes an additional source of potential problems (Hanson, 1999).

Preexisting Child Conditions

A fourth explanation has evolved from longitudinal studies of children who were in intact families at the time of the first interview, or Time 1. Throughout the years, some of these children's parents divorced. This family development allowed the researchers at subsequent stages of the study to return to what they had observed at Time 1 and compare the behaviour and mental health of children whose parents stayed together to those of children whose parents eventually divorced. Two of these studies found that long before the divorce occurred, children of divorce already exhibited more problems than children whose parents stayed together (Block et al., 1988). This led these authors to warn that some of what is interpreted to be consequences of divorce may have actually existed before the divorce or have been consequences of conflict within the marriage (Elliott and Richards, 1991).

Subsequent studies, however, have established that the functioning of children and adolescents often changes negatively *after* their parents' separation, even when researchers control for the child's predivorce characteristics or difficulties (Aseltine, 1996; Morrison and Cherlin, 1995). In other words, the pre- and postdivorce differences "can be attributed to parental divorce and its accompanying disruption of family processes" (Forehand et al., 1997:157). This conclusion is reaffirmed by Cherlin and colleagues (1998) whose data indicate that predivorce characteristics cannot entirely explain children's problems after divorce. Nevertheless, it appears that, in many cases, children are already more difficult before the divorce, which makes sense, considering that their parents may have been fighting or were at the very least preoccupied.

Genetic Influence

A fifth theory relates to the genetic inheritance of problematic predispositions. Offspring of divorce "are more likely to have an interpersonal style marked by...problems with anger, jealousy, hurt feelings, communication, [and] infidelity" (Amato, 1996:638). These interpersonal behaviours may be both learned and genetically transmitted. Indeed, Hetherington (2003) found moderate correlations between parents' personality risks and offspring's personality risks. Genetic transmission would be particularly relevant to the offspring of parents whose divorce is caused by alcoholism, mental illness, and difficult personality characteristics (Kendler, 1995). When children are already genetically vulnerable, the environment created by the divorce exacerbates their vulnerabilities. They receive less attention, monitoring, and guidance, so that their genetic liabilities often find a fertile ground upon which to grow (Plomin and Rutter, 1998). In contrast, children who have more positive predispositions (Garmezy and Masten, 1994) and also have more stable parents are far less likely to develop problems after divorce.

Overview of the Effects of Divorce on Children

In summary, most children survive their parents' divorce quite well developmentally, even though they may be worried and unhappy (Emery, 1999). But when children are adversely affected in terms of mental health, sociability, behaviour, school and work achievement, and later on in their own marital lives, a combination of factors enters into play to explain these consequences. To these, one may add that a parental re-marriage often contributes another set of stressors.

WIDOWHOOD AND BEREAVEMENT

There were 1,245,000 widowed women but only 287,000 widowed men in Canada in 2001. (These numbers pertain only to those who were not remarried in 2001 so that, in reality, far more women are *ever* widowed than men—Novak, 1997.) At all age levels, women are more likely to be widowed than men and this difference widens after age 55. Norland (1994) showed that 72 percent of all the marriages among people aged 65 and over that end in widowhood are the result of the husband's death. Widows comprise 45 percent of all women aged 65 and over (Statistics Canada, 2004o).

Men's life expectancy is shorter than that of women and they tend to marry women younger than they. Furthermore, widowhood is less likely to be followed by repartnering among women than men. For instance, in 2001, 61 percent of senior men lived with a spouse or partner compared to only 35 percent of senior women (Statistics Canada, 2002e). As well, widowed men remarry or initiate a cohabitation far sooner than do widowed women, and this is so even within the younger age groups (Wu, 1995). Widowhood is therefore a **gendered stage** that affects women far more than men. Widowed women are also more likely than their male counterparts to become poor, especially elderly women who are living alone (McDonald, 1997). However, they may have long-term friendships and are more likely than men to acquire new acquaintances (Martin-Matthews, 1991). Because widowhood occurs later in life than it did even 50 years ago, most young children are spared the loss of a parent by death. In Bibby's (2001) survey of adolescents, only 3 percent had a deceased parent while 25 percent had parents who were no longer living together.

Stages of Bereavement

The death of a partner requires much readjustment in addition to the great emotional pain it brings. Age, health status, and level of independence may prolong or shorten bereavement. Adaptation to widowhood also depends on the income that is available, as a drop in income may add a tremendous burden to the afflicted person (Statistics Canada, 2004o). The widowed partner and his or her children go through stages of bereavement (McPherson, 1994). These stages can include an initial period of shock and disbelief, particularly following a sudden death, and even denial. The grieving family members may then experience guilt if they feel that they did not show enough love for the deceased while he or she was alive. "If only I had..." is a recurrent thought. Others go through a period of anger, especially when the death was accidental or was caused by another party, as in the case of drunk driving. The anger may actually galvanize them into social activism that can benefit other members of society later on.

The period of grief can include a stage of idealization of the deceased, even if the latter had caused much suffering. Among seniors, the loss of a spouse is often followed by some mental confusion, helplessness, depression, illness, and general physical vulnerability, as well as a loss of interest in life. Health care costs generally rise following widowhood (Prigerson et al., 2000). The length of the grieving period depends on personal resources, the social support received, and how well prepared the bereaved spouse was for the death. With a long terminal illness, the spouse often begins mourning before death occurs and may be more resigned to it. In addition, the loss of a spouse may bring feelings of relief and newly acquired freedom among older women (Hurd, 1999).

The quality of the relationship with the deceased partner is also an important element in the grieving process, but may produce different results. Some spouses may be relieved by the death of a partner who has made their lives miserable, whereas others may feel guilty. When a good relationship existed, some spouses miss their partners and are inconsolable for a long period, yet others are thankful for the years they shared. At least one longitudinal study has found that happy marriages are associated with more traumatic grief symptoms (Prigerson et al., 2000). Another study found that men and women who had been quite dependent on their spouse during marriage experienced a great deal of personal growth in widowhood (Carr, 2004).

Consequences of a Parent's Death for Children

In terms of outcomes, children and adolescents of widowhood do as well as those in two-parent families or, at the very least, far better than children of divorced and single parents (Biblarz and Gottainer, 2000). This is not to say that children do not grieve and miss their deceased parent. But they may benefit from several social, familial, and personal advantages over children of divorce (Teachman, 2004). First, they are less likely to have been subjected to parental conflict before the death and are certainly not affected by it after. Second, the remaining parent is often left in a more favourable economic situation and may also be helped by life insurance benefits so that poverty occurs less frequently. This relative economic security also protects children from a host of accompanying stressors, such as having to move and change school. Third, following death, there are social rites of bonding through which sympathy and feelings of community are bestowed upon children, which is quite a contrast to what happens to children in cases of parental divorce.

Fourth, the remaining parent's task of grieving, of caring for the children's own pain, and of behaving as a proper widow or widower delays his or her reentry on the dating and mating scene. Children are not immediately faced with a parent who is suddenly unavailable because of the demands of his or her social life (Seltzer, 1994). There is no immediate competition for the parent's love. A fifth element protecting children of widowhood is that a good proportion of the deaths occur to couples who had a stable marriage. Thus, the personalities involved may not have included so many parents with difficult personalities as may be the case in situations of divorce (Simons et al., 1996). Consequently, the children themselves have greater chances of being stable individuals.

Children of widowhood may also adapt better to their parent's remarriage later because this loss makes them more receptive to acquiring a substitute parent. Bereaved children no longer have another parent, whether visiting or custodial, whose place seems to be usurped by a stepparent. No visitations are involved; there is only one home, one set of rules, and one family. With peers and teachers, a formerly widowed parent with children and a new spouse more easily pass for a "real" family.

REMARRIAGE

Excluding Quebec, approximately 58 percent of divorced women and 70 percent of divorced men remarry. In the U.S., approximately 66 percent of women and 78 percent of men eventually remarry, generally two years after divorce (DeWitt, 1994). In Quebec, rates are closer to 35 percent for women and 45 percent for men because of a preference for cohabitation and for living independently. For Canadian women between the ages of 25 and 35, the probability of marriage is 66 percent and closer to 80 percent among men. Between the ages of 35 and 50, the probability for women declines to 48 percent and 61 percent for men (Ambert, 2002a). Similar declines by age are noted in France (Cassan et al., 2001) and the U.S. Naturally, these figures say nothing of cohabitation frequencies after divorce; furthermore, a proportion of the divorced cohabit for a time before remarrying and we have no statistics on this trajectory either.

The Aftermath of Remarriage for Spouses

A remarriage after divorce generally increases the quality of adults' lives, emotionally, socially, and financially—the latter especially for women. Many mother-headed families exit poverty through remarriage (Wilmoth and Koso, 2002). However, as pointed out by Baker (2001b:108), one should not ignore the idea that many divorced and widowed middle-aged and older women may prefer to remain single. These women's level of well-being should be quite high. When a remarriage or cohabitation endures, it may far outlast the first marriage. After years of remarriage or cohabitation, many spouses even forget that they have been married to someone else, particularly when there were no children from the first union. We do not have information on fertility after a remarriage nor about the proportion of remarriages which bring in stepchildren.

Adjustment to Remarriage: The Impact of Stepparenting

When neither spouse has children, adjustment to remarriage is no different than in a first marriage. It becomes more complex with stepchildren, and the complexity increases when there are both live-in and visiting stepchildren. The period of readjustment takes several years before a stepfamily is stabilized (Bray and Kelly, 1998)—however, we have no research data concerning cohabitational stepfamilies. Being a stepparent is not a role one expects to occupy and for which one is prepared—it is not an institutionalized one (Cherlin, 1978). Stepparenthood is also a vilified role when one thinks of the "wicked stepmother" in fairy tales. The role is considered inferior to that of mothers (Nielsen, 1999). No norms or rules guide the behaviour of

Remarriages are as happy as first marriages; they are, however, more fragile and likely to end in another divorce. The structural complexity of remarriages—including the presence of children belonging to each partner—certainly contributes to their instability.

a "good" stepparent, as is the case for a good parent. Each stepparent more or less has to reinvent the role and the relationship, which can be both an advantage and a disadvantage. These remarks also apply to stepparenting in same-sex marriages (Nelson, 1996).

With stepchildren, the newlyweds have to adapt to two key roles simultaneously, parent and spouse, while these two roles are generally initiated separately in first unions. The complexity of the adjustment requirements may contribute to making remarriages more unstable than first marriages (Booth and Edwards, 1992). Furthermore, when children are involved, their other parent constitutes an additional, structural complication for the newly remarried spouses.

The Impact of the Ex-Spouse

After divorce and remarriage, there is a wide spectrum in the quality of the parents' relationship and in the frequency of face-to-face and over-the-phone contact (Ahrons, 1994). Masheter (1997) has compared divorced persons along two dimensions: their level of preoccupation with and hostility toward their ex-spouse. She finds that the divorced who are better adjusted in terms of emotional well-being fall into two categories: those who are friendly but not obsessed or preoccupied with their ex-spouse, and those who are also little preoccupied but are high on hostility. In contrast, respondents who are very preoccupied and friendly with the ex-spouse do not adjust as well to divorce because their attachment prevents them from forging ahead. Anger, combined with low preoccupation, may mobilize divorced individuals against depression (Clapp, 1992). In terms of coparenting, friendliness without preoccupation is more functional. Ex-spouses need to be mutually supportive for the benefit of their children (Madden-Derdich and Arditti, 1999). Ex-husbands are more likely to remain involved if they feel supported by their ex-wives in their parenting role (Arditti and Bickley, 1996).

The New Spouse and the Ex-Spouse

Another effect of remarriage on adults resides in the fact that a remarried person whose spouse has children may need to relate to the children's other parent. Relatively little research exists on this complex relationship, so I have borrowed from my fieldwork. It is obvious from the quotes that follow as well as from the entire research data that the spouse's ex is not overly popular among current wives and husbands:

> "We don't socialize. It's strictly business for the children's sake. I didn't marry my husband to acquire his ex-wife or her new husband, and my husband certainly does not want to be saddled with my ex-husband and his girlfriend. No. These relationships are nice on a TV screen but not in real life."

The new husband or wife often resents the help the spouse has to give his or her ex, especially financial help (Nielsen, 1999). Noncustodial fathers frequently expressed serious concerns about their ex-wife's new partner who had become their children's live-in stepparent. They worry about the way the new stepfather treats the children, the example he provides, as well as the potential for sexual abuse:

> "My ex-wife's husband is a burden to me in a way [he is an alcoholic]. I told my wife, my ex-wife, that she's got to be very careful never to let the girls alone with him. She was offended but she got the point. I just don't trust him."

In some instances, the new wife and the ex-wife have to cooperate in order to raise the children and to arrange visitation schedules:

> "We have a lot of planning to do to arrange her children's visits.... So we have a lot to talk about. But I think she must appreciate me because I don't have to have his children over as often as I do especially so since I have three of my own, so actually I babysit for her. She doesn't [interfere], not exactly, but what can you expect with so many children, it's a real interference even if they're quite good."

In a few cases, a new wife and her husband's ex-wife will develop a warm and friendly relationship. But, overall, the study unearthed a great deal of uneasiness about the possibility of having a close relationship with that person, in part because of the threat of instability in the new marriage. For instance, a man's ex-wife more easily accepts his new wife when the latter has not been involved with him in an adulterous relationship. Obviously, boundary maintenance is a key element in the success of remarriages, and this issue arises more sharply than in first marriages (Ganong and Coleman, 1994).

When a friendship is involved, the two persons—ex and current spouse—generally avoid discussing the partner they have shared serially. Although there are no explicit ground rules that guide this relationship, respondents were very articulate and opinionated concerning what they should or should not do, should say or not say to their spouse's ex-husband or ex-wife. When the current spouse and the spouse's ex were asked what they talked about when they met, children were always mentioned first, especially by women. They exchanged information and gossip they believed could be mutually useful: recipes, television programs, films, or work. Men mentioned "sports, news, cars, and the like." Conversations between a woman's two "husbands" were less personal than those between a man's two "wives." But, overall, this was generally a relationship people wished they could live without.

What Are the Effects of Remarriage on Children?

Do children benefit from their parents' remarriage? Research yields mixed results, in part because it has focused on the short term—that is, the first years following remarriage. Although each case is different, one has to consider that most stepchildren have already undergone one difficult passage involving an incredible array of adjustments—their parents' divorce. They have lived in a single-parent family for a year or more during which they may have been exposed to their mothers' dating and sexuality and to models of masculine unreliability (Ellis et al., 2003). Then, their parents remarry or repartner, one after the other. Stepchildren do not generally have better outcomes than those who remain with their divorced parent, except perhaps financially while they live at home (Brown, 2004b; McLanahan, 1997). However, parental cohabitation rather than remarriage may be associated with more child problems (Buchanan et al., 1996). This may stem from a lower stepfather investment in situations of cohabitation. In contrast, there is a correlation between high stepfather involvement and mothers' reports of fewer behavioural problems among children (Amato and Rivera, 1999).

Boys and Girls May Adapt Differently

Some children who adjusted well to divorce with no or few adverse outcomes begin to deteriorate after the custodial parent's remarriage. This is particularly the case for girls who adjust better to divorce than boys, although the research is not unanimous on this point (see Cooksey et al., 1997). When girls had a close relationship with their single mother, they are more likely to fare poorly in the remarriage. They miss the attention their mother lavished on them and may resent the intruder. For them, the remarriage constitutes a loss (Vuchinich et al., 1991). As adults, estrangement from fathers also occurs more often among daughters than sons, and many daughters interpret this distancing to be the result of their father's remarriage (Ahrons and Tanner, 2003).

Moreover, stepdaughters are more at risk of being abused sexually by their stepfather or their mother's boyfriend than are daughters in intact families (for a review, see Giles-Sims, 1997). This may stem from the fact that roles are more blurred than in biological families. Furthermore, stepfathers have a low involvement in child care, and low involvement in care increases the risk for sexual abuse, even among fathers (cited in Giles-Sims, 1997). As well, in many cases, stepfathers become acquainted with the child only when she is older and can be perceived as an object of sexual attraction.

In contrast, boys adjust better than girls to being a stepchild, perhaps because they are at home less or because many benefit from the presence of a stepfather. However, Pagani et al. (1997) have found that boys living with a recently remarried parent were the most hyperactive at school of all categories of boys aged 12 to 16. This latter result was replicated in the U.S. by Coughlin and Vuchinich (1996), who documented higher rates of early delinquency among boys who had lived in either a single-parent or stepparent family at age 10. Cooksey and colleagues (1997) find that black children benefit more than white children from the presence of a stepfather (married to the mother). This may be because a live-in *male* parent is a more scarce, thus valued, person among African Americans than among whites; as well, a stepfather may be particularly helpful financially—black males who marry are more likely to have a steady employment than those who do not. Furthermore, African Americans are more flexible at integrating other kin within their families.

Children's Age May Matter

Stepchildren adapt better when they are very small and have more or less always known the stepparent, as the latter becomes more involved in these situations (Hofferth and Anderson, 2003). For their part, adolescents frequently resent the intrusion of one or more authority figures in their lives at a time when they may be seeking autonomy from their family (Hetherington and Kelly, 2002). In the autobiographies, there were students who "hated" the stepparent and had decided to break up their father's or mother's remarriage and succeeded. They made the stepparent's life so unpleasant that the newly married spouses were soon embroiled in conflict with each other as the adolescent played one against the other. One student admitted to being ashamed of her role in the breakup of her mother's remarriage,

> "...because it had been my mother's only chance to rebuild her life and I ruined it. Today my mother feels very vulnerable after two failed marriages and is quite lonely. I feel quite guilty and go out of my way to make her happy."

Advantages for Stepchildren

Stepchildren can harvest advantages, particularly in the long term. They belong to two nuclear families and, in times of illness or other emergencies, care can in theory be more easily arranged. They often acquire stepsiblings and even halfsiblings (Anderson, 1999). Children also acquire step-grandparents. The kin system expands and the potential for establishing other rewarding relationships increases. Stepgrandparents can be quite a resource for a child who has lost one set of kin, often the father's side of the family.

Many stepparents actually become de facto parents when noncustodial parents distance themselves from their duties, and others even adopt their stepchild (Ganong et al., 1998). Children who establish a good relationship with their stepfather benefit in terms of emotional and behavioural stability (White and Gilbreth, 2001). In some cases, stepchildren replace biological children. Therefore, if stepparents are in many instances a child's second best chance of acquiring a parent, stepchildren may bring unexpected joys to their parent's spouse.

CONCLUSIONS: THE FAMILIAL AND SOCIAL MEANINGS OF DIVORCE

According to Furstenberg and Cherlin (1991:28), divorce creates a **structural ambiguity** in that "the social and psychological tasks of divorce directly collide with the normal expectations of parenthood." Divorce represents a solution to conjugal unhappiness and misery. But what is a solution for adults is not necessarily one for their children (Beaujot, 2000). Nevertheless, results on the effect of divorce on children have to be interpreted with caution. First, not all children are affected by their parents' divorce, whether positively or negatively. Some children had no problems before and acquire none after. Others had problems before and have the same or worse ones after. Yet others do better after the divorce of highly conflictual parents (Jekielek,

1998). Second, among children who *are* affected, the magnitude and duration of the effect differ greatly. There is also a great deal of difference in terms of the domains of life that are touched. For instance, some children are affected emotionally, others socially, and still others in terms of school performance. The most affected are impacted on all these and other fronts. Therefore, although the results have to be interpreted cautiously, this is by no means to suggest that they are trivial.

Contrary to expectations from various corners, "the increase in marital instability has not brought society to the brink of chaos, but neither has it led to a golden age of freedom and self-actualization" (Amato, 2000:1282). Furthermore, the factors associated with divorce may be evolving. For instance, as young people delay marriage, youthful marriages become a less salient correlate of divorce. As cohabitations increase in frequency, their dissolution may replace some divorces, and, for others, cohabitation before marriage may become a factor associated with an increased propensity to divorce. At a more global level, media influences may change and affect adults' mentality concerning their marriage and thus contribute to encouraging or discouraging divorce. Any unforeseen religious revival might strengthen the institutional aspect of marriage for a segment of families and contribute to a reduction in divorce. In a nutshell, marital breakdown is a social phenomenon that evolves within the changing sociocultural context in which the family system is embedded. It cannot be understood fully without an appreciation of this larger context.

Summary

1. At 2.2 per 1,000 population in 2002, the Canadian divorce rate is half that of the American one. Rates vary by geographic region. Marriages last on average longer and take place at an older age than a few decades ago. Serial divorces have increased. Indications are that individuals who divorce several times within a decade may have deficits in terms of personality that translate into difficulties in getting along and being committed to the relationship. There are four methods to measure divorce rates: the rate per 1,000 population; per 1,000 married couples; for married couples within a given number of years after marriage (the most accurate but less frequently used method); and the annual ratio of new divorces over new marriages.

2. The sociocultural factors related to a high divorce rate are multiple and interlinked. They include the secularization of society; the desacralization and deinstitutionalization of marriage; the liberalization of norms and divorce laws; individualism; and a lower threshold of tolerance for marital failings combined with a high level of expectation of marital life.

3. At the demographic level, the first four years of marriage are the most vulnerable to divorce. Besides poverty, additional demographic risks include youthful marriage, prior cohabitation, and parents' divorce. Selection and causality effects of cohabitation help explain its relationship to divorce. Reasons for divorcing vary, but the most commonly mentioned are irreconcilable differences, conflict, and falling out of love.

4. The many factors associated with an easier adjustment to divorce among adults include a couple having no dependent children and no shared assets; a marriage that has been brief; and each spouse retaining friends individually. Women who are younger and have remained employed are advantaged in the process of adjustment. After divorce, changes occur in ex-spouses' social networks.

5. Joint legal custody of children is becoming much more common, even though the children still live with their mother. Father and mother custody seem to have equivalent results for children.

6. At the individual level, children exhibit a wide range of consequences of divorce, from being very negatively affected to benefiting from it. On average, however, children whose parents divorce experience higher rates of behavioural, emotional, and achievement problems, even into adulthood, than children raised by their two parents. The main theories explaining these negative consequences focus on the diminished family income and even poverty that too often follows divorce; disruption of parenting behaviours as a result of stressors; parental conflict both before and after divorce; and genetic inheritance of difficult personalities in some families. Preexisting negative child attributes and behaviours also contribute to problems after divorce, but problems specific to divorce arise, as well.

7. Early widowhood is far less common than it was even in the 1920s. But widowhood is more common among women than men in middle age and after. It is a gendered stage. The stages and length of bereavement vary. In the long term, children of widowhood have outcomes similar to those whose parents remain together.

8. Excluding Quebec, approximately 70 percent of men and 58 percent of women who divorce eventually remarry. Stepchildren complicate the dynamics of remarriages in part because their presence necessitates contact with the ex-spouses involved. The relationship between, say, a man's wife and ex-wife is generally difficult and there are no norms that guide interaction. Although remarriage usually raises parents' level of well-being and a mother's familial income, children benefit differentially from remarriage. For many, it requires even more negative adjustment than had been the case for divorce. For others, there are few benefits but no disadvantages. Still others, particularly adolescent boys, may benefit from the presence of a stepfather. The acquisition of step-grandparents may also be beneficial.

9. Divorce and remarriage are adult institutions that often create a structural ambiguity that collides with the requisites of effective parenting. The factors associated with divorce and remarriage may evolve over time.

Key Concepts and Themes

Analytical Questions

1. What relationships would you establish between the reasons people give for their own divorce and the sociocultural factors related to divorce?

2. What is the advantage of Table 14.1 over Table 14.3?

3. Of the theories meant to explain the negative effects of parental divorce on children, which would particularly apply to children whose parents have remarried and why?

4. Some politicians, especially south of the border, want to return to a time when divorce was difficult to obtain. What do you think the consequences would be?

Suggested Readings

Amato, P. R., and Booth, A. 1997. *A generation at risk: Growing up in an era of family upheaval.* Cambridge, MA: Harvard University Press. This book presents the results of a longitudinal study including intact families and families of divorce. This study considers, among other things, the quality of the parent/child relationship, along with the quality of the parents' marriage and timing of divorce.

Ganong, L., and Coleman, M. 1994. *Remarried family relationships.* Newbury Park, CA: Sage. This volume presents a thorough review of the literature on the relationships that develop after remarriage, including stepparenting.

Mandell, D. 2002. *"Deadbeat dads": Subjectivity and social construction.* University of Toronto Press. This research on a small group of seven fathers includes thorough discussions, information, and a well-balanced perspective on the payment/nonpayment of child support after divorce.

Matthews, A. M. 1991. *Widowhood in later life.* Toronto: Butterworths/Harcourt Brace. The author discusses bereavement and how people rebuild their lives following the death of a spouse. Comparisons are brought by gender with other marital statuses and by the presence or absence of children.

Simons, R., and Associates (Eds.) 1996. *Understanding differences between divorced and intact families.* Thousand Oaks, CA: Sage. Several researchers present the results of their studies. The topics covered are diverse and even include sibling relations after divorce.

Suggested Weblinks

BC Council for Families provides articles on a wide range of topics, including stepfamilies.

www.bccf.bc.ca

Bureau of the Census. For the U.S., click on *People* and an index of topics will appear, including divorce.

www.census.gov

Statistics Canada contains information relevant to this chapter, some of which can be found through the Search option.

www.statcan.ca

CHAPTER 15

Family Violence, Abuse, and Child Neglect

A man stalks his wife after she leaves him for battery. Despite a restraining order preventing him from coming within 300 feet, he savagely stabs her as she returns home from work. She leaves two children. (Source: 2003 newscast)

Social workers are called to a home where they find five children ranging in age from two to 10 in a filthy and barely furnished home. The children are hungry and cold, and the level of functioning of all but the oldest one indicates delay due to neglect. The two parents involved have been out on a crack-induced "trip" for three days. (Source: 1998 newscast)

A man is beaten up by his gay partner so severely that he requires emergency surgery. The battering has been going on for two years. (Source: 1998 newscast)

A 16-year-old rapes his 15-year-old girlfriend in his car on the way back from the movies. He felt that they had been going out long enough and it was time "to go all the way." (Source: Abstract from student autobiography)

A police officer brings a 14-year-old girl back home after finding her doing drugs with two older males at a strip mall. It's 3 a.m. She lives in an affluent suburban home. Her parents did not know that she was out. (Source: Abstract from student autobiography)

A 10-year-old girl has been fondled, kissed in the genital area, and convinced to "touch" the genitals of her father's best friend. He is "part of the family," and often babysits the two children, a boy and a girl. One day, he forces the girl to practise oral sex on him when the boy, age 11, walks in. [He] later tells his parents who call the police. (Source: Abstract from student autobiography)

What these vignettes share in common is either violence or neglect. To these situations, one can add sibling violence and peer abuse—which are the most common types of maltreatment—and child-to-parent abuse in order to form a more complete picture of abuse and neglect affecting Canadian families (Duffy and Momirov, 2000). In 2001, family violence constituted one-quarter of all violent crimes reported to the police (Statistics Canada, 2003e). In this chapter, various forms of family violence and neglect are analyzed as reflections of general cultural norms that foster such behaviours. However, not everyone in our society is equally vulnerable to being an abuser and/or a victim: Social inequalities by class, race/ethnicity, and especially gender and age come to the fore.

DATING AND COURTSHIP VIOLENCE

Family violence and partner abuse have belatedly become more socially and politically visible in the last four decades. For its part, dating abuse is only beginning to emerge in the public consciousness. For a substantial segment of Canadian youths, dating is a fertile ground upon which to continue their aggressive behaviours toward their peers. For others, it is an opportunity to discover a new arena in which to exercise **power**. Few incidents of courtship or dating violence are reported to authorities or to parents, but DeKeseredy and Kelly (1993a) and Johnson (1996) estimate that over 20 percent of women students are assaulted in a broad sense each year. Many youths actually consider acts of violence a normal part of the dating process (Sleek, 1998):

> *"We both have strong personalities and don't let people walk all over us and that goes for each other. I don't mind punching him in the stomach or kicking his legs if he's too fresh and he does the same, except that he's bigger and it hurts more. My mother goes on my nerves about this because she says, 'if that's the way the both of you behave now think what it's going to be like in 5 years.'"*

But other women students are not so complacent:

> *"I'd rate myself as unhappy at this point because I have to decide if I'll stay with my boyfriend of three years. Once in a while he calls me names but recently he's grabbed me and shoved me in the car and once against the wall another time and I am afraid that I'll end up a battered wife."*

Dating violence predicts domestic abuse later on in married life. Perhaps the most surprising aspect of courtship violence, as is the case for spousal abuse, is that both men and women are involved in inflicting harm (Makepeace, 1997; Swinford et al., 2000). However, women sustain most of the injuries (Stets and Henderson, 1991) and much of the violence carried out by women is in self-defence (DeKeseredy et al., 1997).

Date Rape

Date rape is an issue that has belatedly received attention. In Canada, DeKeseredy and Kelly (1993a) found a 28 percent sexual abuse rate among female university students, albeit within a broad definition. About 20 percent of American female college students surveyed mention having been forced to have sexual intercourse (Brener et al., 1999). Most of these students never report anything to the authorities, as is the case for the following young woman:

> *"The most painful event in my entire life is having been raped. Wayne was a good friend. I had known him for a long time. One winter day I decided to call Wayne from school. He invited me to come over to watch movies, and seeing as I didn't feel like going to class, I went. When I got to Wayne's apartment everything seemed to be running smooth. We were watching movies. Wayne then suggested that I check out his bedroom, so, out of stupidity and perhaps curiosity, I went. He then locked the door and raped me. I really did try to fight him off but he's a football player.... I couldn't tell my parents, and they still don't know."*

The situation of date and even acquaintance rape may have worsened in the 1990s with the arrival of readily available chemicals that, when dropped in a woman's drink, secure her full "cooperation." The woman cannot later recall much of what occurred. These situations happen on campuses as well as in bars and nightclubs where the purpose is to meet members of the opposite sex. They include gang rape, even in college fraternities (Sanday, 1990). Gang rape is the ultimate in terms of a "power trip" and **patriarchal dominance**. These instances well illustrate young males' readiness to circumvent decency and legality in order to secure their own sexual gratification and to be able to justify their acts within a masculinist mentality (Sanday, 1996). In November 1999, newscasts reported that 30 percent of male students admitted that they would force sex on a woman if they felt that they could get away with it (see also Totten, 2000).

Sources of Dating Violence

The sources of dating violence are still debated in the research literature. Most studies have turned to **psychological** and **familial explanations** while excluding extra-familial and cultural influences. This omission of influential factors at the macrosociological level distorts reality and prevents us from acquiring a full understanding of how particular behaviours emerge (Sev'er, 2002). For instance, in certain peer groups, including athletes, the **social construction of masculinity** includes violent attitudes toward females as well as a mentality of sexual entitlement (Sanday, 1996). Thus, a feminist perspective indicates that, among heterosexual couples, the overall gender stratification provides an open-door policy for violence against women. This type of cultural climate is reflected in the *media*. As well, pornographic materials, to which many men and boys are exposed, do contain violent sex. Similarly, as we soon see, children engage in a great deal of peer abuse that can easily be transposed into dating relationships.

Studies on childhood exposure to interparental violence as the key factor in the origins of dating violence are inconclusive: Some find a relationship between the two but others do not (Simons et al., 1998a). The least that can be said is that exposure to parental violence during adolescence and young adulthood as well as having been harshly treated by one's parents certainly constitute **risk factors**. Furthermore, on average, males who assault their dates were more aggressive as boys (Capaldi and Clark, 1998). Many exhibited behavioural problems as children and may still be out of control; the same pattern occurs among some abusive females. Simons and colleagues (1998b) find that males who engage in dating violence are more likely to have engaged in delinquent acts and drug use than other males. These results corroborate those of other researchers who report two categories of abusers among the married: those who limit their abuse to the home and those who are violent in other contexts as well (Delsol et al., 2003).

VERBAL AND PSYCHOLOGICAL ABUSE OF PARTNERS

Verbal abuse consists of repeatedly referring to one's partner with epithets; using much foul language; using berating and demeaning put-downs; and threatening and criticizing, even in public (DeKeseredy, 2000). Its purpose is to dominate, to exercise *power,* and to show who is "the boss." It is also used to rationalize or excuse one's bad behaviour by demeaning the other. Calling one's date an "idiot" once is unfortunate but it does not constitute verbal abuse; however, if such a behaviour is repeated, then it is abusive. Verbal abuse marks the erosion of civility and sets a precedent upon which physical abuse can be added in the relationship. Indeed, physical abuse is generally accompanied or preceded by verbal insults and attempts by one partner or both to intimidate the other (Sugarman et al., 1996). Males particularly tend to practise both types of abuse in severe cases of psychological and physical assaults (Hamby and Sugarman, 1999).

Verbal abuse may be on the increase. For instance, it is quite salient in music videos favoured by youths, and it is nearly always directed against women because, in a subtle way, culture defines women as legitimate targets of male violence. The word *bitch* is widespread in a growing segment of younger cohorts; it is often used as soon as a quarrel erupts. It is not unusual to hear young couples calling each other foul and demeaning names; such insults were rarely overheard just a decade ago. These exchanges represent a dangerous escalation, a **lack of civility,** part of what Garbarino (1995) refers to as the "toxic" environment in which people raise children. Such toxic verbal exchanges are common occurrences on the *Maury Show* on television.

As Renzetti (1997b) has discovered among same-sex couples, psychological abuse is often tailored to fit a partner's vulnerabilities. During my own study on divorce, ex-spouses, particularly ex-wives, frequently mentioned that such verbal violence had been a pattern in their past marriage:

> One woman who was obese was repeatedly called a "fat slob" and a "pile of lard" by her husband. He would tell her to "move your fat ass" or order her to "sit on your god-damn fat ass, I have something to tell you." At the dinner table, she had to eat like a bird lest he observed to the children, "There goes your mother, stuffing her fat face." Or he would yell, "You're just adding one pound of lard to your fat ass." The more he emphasized her weight, the more she ate, and the larger she became, until her health was threatened.

This tailoring of verbal abuse can focus on facial features, body shape, clumsiness, lack of mental agility, as well as unemployment and financial difficulties: One ex-wife had repeatedly taunted her unemployed husband in front of their children as "good for nothing" and "you're no real man."

Verbal abuse can also take the form of threats and become a form of psychological blackmail:

> One divorced woman recalled that her ex-husband used to threaten to tell her children that she had given up her first-born for adoption—disregarding the fact that the infant had been his and he had not wanted it (this was before they married). Another was constantly threatened by her ex-husband of losing custody of her children: She suffered from bouts of depression, and the threats, which terrorized her, merely increased her sad condition. One ex-husband was threatened by his ex-wife of legal exposure if he did not "cough up" more monthly support; at some point in the past, he had defrauded his former employers in order to meet his wife's extravagant demands but had never been caught. Now that she was his ex-wife, she used his illegal past activities as leverage.

Psychological abuse can turn into life threatening situations. Renzetti (1997b:74) writes of two women with physical disabilities:

"Their partners would abandon them in dangerous settings (i.e., an isolated wooded area) without their wheelchairs. Another woman who was diabetic stated that her partner would punish her by forcing her to eat sugar."

Verbal and psychological abuse is an issue that is particularly important among adolescents who begin dating at an early age. Young girls are easy prey to being manipulated, ordered around, having their whereabouts controlled, and may even consider their boyfriends' over-possessiveness and extreme jealousy as proofs of love. Thus, the dating process may have negative effects on the personal development of some teenagers and on the dynamics of their intimate relationships later. There is little research on these aspects of dating.

SPOUSAL AND PARTNER PHYSICAL ABUSE

Interpartner violence is a matter of **power** or an attempt at regaining power when one thinks it is slipping away. This may be one reason why women are at risk of being battered when they try to separate or after they have separated from their boyfriend or husband (Ptacek, 1997). As a result, women often have to seek a restraining court order (Mahoney, 1991). Yet, many are killed. (For a review, see Duffy, 2004.) This is a reflection of a patriarchal ideology concerning intimate relations and abuse of women (DeKeseredy and Kelly, 1993b). Men who lack the material and status ability "of expressing and maintaining power within their intimate relationships may engage in violence as a means of reestablishing their domestic position" (Anderson, 1997:668). The cultural framework allows them to have recourse to violence as an ego booster (Renzetti, 1997a). Men in stressful occupations may compensate against their partners while others in physically violent occupations may use the techniques at home (Melzer, 2002). Furthermore, among some groups with different cultural backgrounds, the prerogatives of patriarchy include violence against female kin—in order to keep them "in line" and to save the family's honour (Sev'er, 2002)—and this may include murder.

Many batterers are actually quite pathological (Coleman, 1994). But here as well, one has to consider that pathology is culturally influenced or even created. In our society as in many others, pathology can lead to interpersonal violence or abuse. As was the case for dating, both men and women who engage in spousal violence are more likely than nonviolent spouses to have been involved in delinquency and to have been considered troublemakers when adolescents (Giordano et al., 1999). Gottman (1998:153) found that violent men tended to reject their wives' influence in an experimental laboratory situation: They not only rejected their wives' complaints but they also escalated any attempt at discussion into a full-blown conflict. Batterers who continue their abuse tend to be younger and are more likely to be cohabiting than married. University-educated women are often victims of spousal abuse for a longer period because they do not report it out of shame (Johnson, 2003).

Delsol et al. (2003) as well as others have proposed a typology consisting of three types of violent men based on the frequency and severity of their violence, wives' fears of the husbands, and men's attitude toward violence. These types are violence-in-family-only; the medium-violent; and the generally violent, psychologically distressed types. The latter is also more likely to conform to Johnson's (1995) concept of intimate terrorism than the other two types.

Range of Violent Acts

Spousal or partner physical abuse covers quite a range of acts, so that one has to exercise caution when interpreting statistics. The Conflict Tactics Scale (CTS) devised by Straus (1979) is commonly used and includes the following acts, in descending order of severity:

1. Threw something at spouse
2. Pushed, grabbed, or shoved spouse
3. Slapped spouse
4. Kicked, bit, or hit spouse with fist
5. Hit or tried to hit spouse with something
6. Beat up spouse
7. Choked spouse
8. Threatened spouse with a knife or gun
9. Used a knife or a gun on spouse

However, this scale has several drawbacks. For instance, it is not a valid instrument for determining whether an act is committed in self-defence or what its consequences are (Kelly, 1997; Propper, 1997). Most acts of violence committed by intimate partners tend to be at the less severe end of the scale. But once a wife becomes a target of abuse, she is likely to be a repeat victim—about three times each year. This is particularly the case when physical injury results (Brookoff et al., 1997). Women are even attacked during pregnancy, which, of course, does not show in the CTS (Sev'er, 2002).

Eight percent of Canadian women and seven percent of men report that they have experienced spousal abuse in the past five years (Patterson, 2003). The fact that wives also commit acts of violence does not mean that they are more violent than or even as violent as husbands or dates (Browne, 1997). Women who are truly and forcefully violent and abuse their male partners are still the exception. Above all, women may fear painful retaliation if they hit their partners. They attack with far less force and energy than men. They are less muscular, tall, heavy, and strong, thus the results of their aggressiveness are generally inconsequential physically and their partners may not even take these assaults seriously. In contrast, when men attack, the effect on women is far more lethal and results in bruises, concussions, and broken bones (Feldhaus et al., 1997). For instance, in 1994 in the U.S., 204,000 women and 39,000 men were treated in emergency rooms for injuries resulting from partner violence (Rand, 1997). At least one large survey has found that being the victim of domestic violence is a "qualitatively different experience for women and men" (Umberson et al., 1998:449). For instance, it results in a loss of feelings of personal control among women but not men. Women are also likely to become depressed, which in no way negates the fact that many men who are victims are also negatively impacted (Anderson, 2002).

Rape is one aspect of spousal violence (Duffy, 2004). Men who are very violent toward their wives often combine physical battering with sexual assault (Browne, 1997). This is the ultimate way of establishing one's power over the other. Browne points out that women whose partners are sexually aggressive are also at a higher risk of suffering more severe physical aggression than women with male partners who are physically but not sexually violent.

Factors Related to Spousal Abuse

Spousal abuse, as with dating abuse, is facilitated by our culture of violence and particularly by ideologies of masculine dominance over women. As pointed out at the outset of this section, spousal abuse is in large part the result of a desire to control women (Daly and Chesney-Lind, 1988), although women are not exempt from this motive, as we see below (Migliaccio, 2002). Within this broad cultural context, other factors come into play. For instance, a proportion of dating and domestic violence is committed under the influence of **alcohol** or other substance. Many batterers and even their victims construct alcohol as a socially acceptable excuse for violence (Gelles, 1993:184). The belief that men batter because drinking "pushes" them to it is so well ingrained in the collective mentality that cases have even been thrown out of courts because "he was so drunk that he didn't know what he was doing." Alcohol facilitates abuse because it deinhibits control. When both the batterer and the victim have been drinking, they may not even notice the presence of their children (Hutchison, 1999). In other cases, alcohol use follows a battering incident rather than precedes it (Gelles, 1993). Alcohol and drugs are involved in a majority of the cases when the police are called, perhaps because women are more afraid of the violence and, if they have also been drinking, they may be less inhibited and less inclined to excuse their partner (Brookoff et al., 1997).

Cohabiting couples have the highest rate of partner violence (Brownridge and Halli, 2001) and cohabiting women often suffer more severe abuse (GSS, 2000), a fact that undermines the claim of those who portray *marriage* per se as a "licence to hit." Magdol et al. (1998) have reported that, in a group of 21-year-olds, cohabitants were even more likely than daters to be abusive. We do not know what causes the relationship between abuse and cohabitation: Is it the fact of cohabiting itself (with its lesser commitment and absence of norms to guide the relationship)? Or do some individuals with a tendency for aggressiveness channel themselves more into cohabitation than marriage? As we have seen in Chapter 8, cohabitation is not institutionalized: There are fewer rules governing it. Thus, it may not be a structural situation that is as efficient as marriage at preventing domestic violence (Faurre and Maddock, 1994).

Very **low-income** couples and women with relatively little schooling are at an increased risk for partner violence (DeKeseredy, 2000). A lack of social control may in part explain the following (DeMaris et al., 2003): Poor couples who live in **disadvantaged neighbourhoods** are more at risk of spousal abuse (and, as seen later, child abuse) than similar couples who live in economically secure environments (Miles-Doan, 1998). The presence of social problems in some neighbourhoods and lack of an effective community described in Chapter 6 are highly applicable to partner violence (Browning, 2002). In contrast, the absence of visible violence in relatively comfortable areas may act as a deterrent against domestic abuse. In fact, poor neighbourhoods exhibit higher rates of violence of all sorts, and this includes spousal abuse. Children in low-income households witness physical violence twice as often as others (Statistics Canada, 2003h). However, this should not be taken to mean that domestic abuse does not occur among the more affluent. It does.

Few studies focus on **ethnicity.** Yet, in the U.S., one study indicates substantial levels of cohabitant and spousal abuse among blacks (Uzzell and Peebles-Wilkins, 1989). In Canada, a large percentage of First Nations women are abused by their partners (McGillivray and Comaskey, 1998): approximately 25 percent of women and 13 percent of men (Patterson, 2003). Domestic violence among oppressed minorities may have sources compounding those among whites (Baskin, 2003). For instance, blacks are differentially located in society because of their devalued colour. Prejudice and discrimination may be internalized among a segment of black males, who then demean black women and express their general rage toward them rather than projecting it onto society (Crenshaw, 1994). Nevertheless, as pointed out earlier, one cannot overlook the fact that, in some countries with a more rigid patriarchal structure, women are more likely to be abused by men—and this pattern is pursued once they settle in Canada (Sev'er, 2002). This is a topic that has been addressed to some extent in the U.S. but not yet in Canada.

Same-Sex-Partner Violence

Same-sex-partner violence is as much a matter of power and control as it is in heterosexual couple violence, except that gender or patriarchal ideologies are not an issue. The rate of violence among same-sex couples approximates that of heterosexuals, between 12 and 33 percent, depending on the sample and measures (Straus and Gelles, 1990a). The research carried out strictly on gay and lesbian samples shows slightly higher rates (Elliott, 1996). Depending on the studies, as many as 50 percent or as few as 17 percent of lesbians admit having been abused by a female partner. Of those who have been victimized, the same proportion report having also practised abuse. But 30 percent of those who have not been abused report having been abusive.

These statistics are tentative, because no reliable study of the prevalence of same-sex-partner abuse exists yet (Renzetti, 1997a). Estimating same-sex-partner abuse is difficult because homosexuals may be reluctant to talk about their personal lives for fear of being misunderstood and further stigmatized. Domestic abuse is also a problem that the homosexual community often avoids discussing and redressing, because it is frequently believed that it occurs only in male-female couples. In addition, same-sex-partner violence receives less attention from the police, both because it is less reported and may be interpreted as violence of one man against another rather than as domestic violence.

Bars have often been important to this point in the social life of homosexuals, leading to alcohol-related problems, including partner abuse. However, as happens among heterosexual couples, alcohol is merely a facilitator and is utilized as an excuse, both for one's actions and for those of the abuser by the victimized partner (Renzetti, 1997a). Renzetti also found that partner abuse often went hand in hand with child abuse, particularly toward the child of the victimized partner. These cases, however, have been documented only among lesbian couples whose children were from a previous marriage. Thus, one major drawback of the literature on same-sex domestic violence is that it does not study its effects on children. Lesbian and homosexual couples who have children together represent a new phenomenon and it will take a few years before these children are grown. However, it is reasonable to assume that same-sex couples who are involved in physical abuse are less likely to have children than similar heterosexual couples. Most cohabit, and cohabitation is more fragile than marriage; thus, same-sex couples who do not get along and quarrel violently probably separate even before the thought of having children occurs to them.

Moreover, reproducing children is a far more complicated project to carry out among homosexuals than among heterosexuals. It is not something that happens accidentally, for instance. Therefore, it is possible that a process of **social selection** is at work: Those who decide to have children and are then able to achieve this goal may be a select group of more stable and devoted couples than are average heterosexual couples. Consequently, they would not fall prey to deviances, especially spousal abuse, that could endanger their relationship and their children's well-being. This hypothesis deserves to be tested empirically.

The Effect of Spousal Violence on Children

We have already discussed, in the previous chapter, the effect that parental conflict has on children, and we saw that it is an important factor in the negative outcomes of children before and after divorce. Here, we will explore what happens to children when they watch or hear their father beat their mother or both parents throw projectiles at each other and engage in mutual slapping and punching, with much yelling and name calling. Some effects are immediate; others are delayed until certain life transitions occur; and many are long lasting (Sev'er, 2002). One immediate effect is fear, an urge to run away or to help the victimized parent. Children may throw themselves between parents, and often older sons try to fend off a father; many children are injured in the process (Brookoff et al., 1997). Other children call for neighbours' help or even the police. A few others take the abuser's side, and it may be them that society has to fear, as explained by an older woman student:

> *"Ever since I can recall, my father always beat up my mother and in those days (1960–70) women had to put up with it. I used to hide when it would start and then I would run to my mother and hug her and kiss her and cry with her. As a result, I have always been a sad child and to this day I tend to be anxious and easily pessimistic. But perhaps the saddest part is that my older brother never felt sorry for my mom. He used to tell her like my father did, 'That serves you right, next time do as he says.' My brother used to kiss my father's ass and really worship the ground he walked on. He grew up just like him and he often beat me up too and a couple of times he slapped my mother.... [He] beat up his ex-wife and he's tried it on many women but he's such a hypocrite: At work he's a model citizen."*

On average, children of abused mothers have more behavioural and psychological problems (Moss, 2004) and exhibit less interpersonal sensitivity (Rosenberg, 1987). Other long-lasting effects include lower psychological well-being in adulthood, increased risk for depression, as well as poor parent-child relationships (McNeal and Amato, 1998). These consequences on children may be exacerbated by the negative effect of battering on the mothers themselves. Women who are repeatedly abused have high rates of sleep disorders, depression, illness, and even suicide attempts (Birns and Birns, 1997). It would be surprising if these severe maternal symptoms did not disrupt mothers' ability to parent and, consequently, negatively affect at least some aspects of many children's personal development.

The greatest negative impact of interparental violence occurs in those families where parents are the most violent toward each other and engage in the entire spectrum of abusive activities (Jouriles et al., 1998). By the age of 18, offspring from these dysfunctional families have generally been exposed to other adversities, including poverty, divorce, parental alcoholism, and even criminality and childhood abuse (Birns and Birns, 1997). Once these contextual circumstances are controlled for, the direct negative effect of interparental violence is substantially reduced but does not disappear entirely (Fergusson and Horwood, 1998). The Canadian follow-ups from the National Longitudinal Survey of Children and Youth showed that children who had witnessed some physical violence (parents, siblings) at home were more aggressive at the time, especially boys, and that their chance of being aggressive and/or anxious was still higher two and four years later (Statistics Canada, 2003h).

The matter of the **intergenerational transmission of violence**—that is, from witnessing parental violence to committing dating and partner violence later on—is much discussed. As we have seen, the evidence is not unanimous, and some researchers do not find more violence in the family background of spousal abusers than nonabusers (Delsol et al., 2003). Others who find a relationship still point out that "the most typical outcome for individuals exposed to violence in their families of origin is to be nonviolent in their adult families" (Heyman and Slep, 2002:870). Even researchers who support the cycle of violence theory recognize that "the mechanisms by which violence is transmitted appear to be complex and multidimensional" (O'Keefe, 1998:41). O'Keefe distributed questionnaires to 1,012 high school students in the Los Angeles area. She asked them about parental violence, their own dating experience, their attitude toward dating violence, and the type and frequency of violence they witnessed in their community and at school. She then centred her research on the 232 students who reported a *great deal* of interparental violence in order to see what would characterize those who followed the parental example.

She found that 51 percent had never inflicted violence against a dating partner, and 49 percent had done so at least once. As well, 55 percent reported having been victimized at least once. Among males, those who had inflicted or been the victim of dating violence tended to be of lower SES and reported more exposure to community and school violence. Among females, those who had followed the parental example or who had been victimized were characterized by exposure to community and school violence, poor school performance, and having been abused as a child.

Therefore, the exposure to a *high* level of parental violence places youths at a great risk of committing similar acts and/or being themselves victimized. But there are other risk factors at the social level that increase the likelihood of such occurrences in the students' own lives (Onyskiw and Hayduk, 2001). The variable of exposure to community and school violence is particularly significant because it appears as a risk factor for both genders. Conversely, the protective factors that intervene to prevent the transmission of violence across the two generations are higher SES and low community and school violence. Thus, O'Keefe's results on dating violence confirm those of studies finding more spousal and child abuse in disadvantaged areas where other types of violence exist.

CHILD ABUSE AND NEGLECT BY PARENTS

In Canada, Children's Aid Societies were given the right to remove abused or neglected children from their homes for the first time in Ontario in 1893 (Baker, 1995). The latest set of Canada-wide data on child abuse is from the year 1998: The incidence of cases investigated by welfare agencies was estimated to be 21.5 per 1,000 children— 40 percent of which constituted neglect, particularly failure to supervise (Health Canada, 2001). Another estimate of child physical abuse at home yielded a rate of nearly six cases per 1,000 children for 1993 (Kaplan et al., 1999). The Ontario Health Supplement Study found that 31 percent of male and 21 percent of female respondents aged 15 and over reported some abuse that had occurred while they were growing up (MacMillan et al., 1997) and 31 percent of adolescents in Bibby's (2001) study reported that a close friend had been physically abused at home.

It is customary in textbooks to begin discussions of child abuse with abuse by parents, even though, as they enter the school system, children are far more likely to be maltreated by their siblings and peers (lower part of Figure 15.1). Only very small children who are abused are abused mainly by their parents or a caregiver (upper part of Figure 15.1)—more by mothers than fathers, although more by fathers in terms of neglect when they are absent. But the latter situation is never entered in the statistics. Figure 15.1 presents a reasonable estimate of the overall sources of child abuse up to age 16 in terms of who tends to maltreat children the most frequently.

Child Abuse by Parents

There are, unfortunately, many methodological problems in surveys intended to measure child abuse by parents. First, when children are very small, they cannot report their own abuse; at a slightly older age, many may not know what constitutes abuse. As adolescents and adults, problems of recollection set in, exacerbated by current states of mind and relationships. Furthermore, parents are not likely to report all of their own abusive behaviours, and abuse that comes to the attention of authorities represents the tip of the iceberg. Finally, what the researchers include in definitions of abuse makes it often impossible to compare the results of various studies.

Furthermore, with toddlers and preschool-age children, it is often difficult to distinguish a *first* occurrence of abuse from an accidental circumstance. For instance, daycare workers or kindergarten teachers may notice bruises or a child who is limping. The child may not be able to establish a cause and effect between these physical symptoms and the fact that he or she was punched or thrown against a piece of furniture the day before. Parents generally explain that the child fell into the bathtub, off the toilet seat, or down the staircase. These explanations are plausible because nearly all small children sooner or later have such accidents and some are more accident prone than others, particularly when they are active as well as impulsive (Schwebel and Plumert,

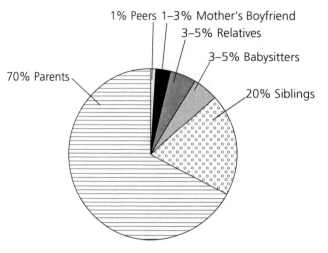

Ages 0–5

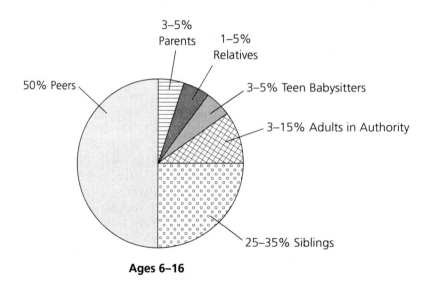

Ages 6–16

FIGURE 15.1

Estimates of the Main Sources of Child Maltreatment up to Age 16

1999). Trocme et al. (2003) describe the injury aspect of various forms of child abuse. At the more lethal level, between one-third and one-half of deaths due to abuse and neglect could have been prevented, as these children had already been brought to the attention of law enforcement and child protection agencies (Emery and

Laumann-Billings, 1998). Infants are at a higher risk of fatal abuse from their mothers up to age four months, from their fathers between four to 10 months, and from their mothers' boyfriends or stepfathers from 10 to 25 months.

Factors Related to Child Abuse by Parents

Child abuse and neglect are more common in *low-income* families, especially in **neighbourhoods** with a high concentration of **poverty** and **violence** (Bell and Jenkins, 1993). It is possible that child abuse is more easily detected among the poor—particularly those who are clients of social agencies—than among other income groups who may also harbour this problem (Appell, 1998). Despite this cautionary remark, a true relationship still exists between poverty and child abuse (McLoyd, 1995). In fact, two decades ago, Garbarino and Sherman (1980) had already found that living in a high-risk neighbourhood correlated with child abuse, even after controlling for family characteristics. In these neighbourhoods, the lack of an effective community means that each set of parents, or each single parent, is more socially isolated, lacks support, and is deprived of elements of social control (Garbarino and Kostelny, 1992). Were all these missing elements present, parents would be prevented from lashing out at their children as often and cruelly as some do.

Many studies link parents' daily stressors and psychological distress to distant, rejecting, and punitive parenting. McLoyd (1995) shows that, among single mothers, the adverse effects of poverty increase maternal depression and, in turn, punishment of adolescents. All in all, the daily stressors of poverty exacerbate difficult temperaments and may activate predispositions to violence, while simultaneously inhibiting controls against violence. In conditions of poverty, coping mechanisms are unduly taxed by daily irritants that cumulate to form an explosive situation. Depending on the temperament of the individuals affected and the characteristics of the child who is targeted, either explosive or apathetic behaviours may result (Elder et al., 1994a). Poverty aside, a parental history of severe mental illness and especially antisocial behaviour may increase the risk of child abuse (Walsh et al., 2002).

Physical Punishment: The Question Mark

Corporal punishment is part of a continuum, from harsh to mild, and also from disciplining to vindictive or particularly violent. Spanking is used by 84 to 97 percent of all parents at some point in their offsprings' lives (Straus and Donnelly, 1994). Most spankings occur to children below age 10. Mothers are more often the agents than fathers because they are the primary caregivers (Day et al., 1998), and because children are more difficult with mothers than they are with fathers (Ambert, 2003d). Light spanking is considered abusive by some but appropriate by a majority (Flynn, 1994). Over 80 percent of American college students, and even more so among blacks than whites, judge spanking as appropriate (Flynn, 1998). Canadian mothers are more accepting of corporal punishment than are Swedish mothers and are more likely to practise it (Durrat et al., 2003). Spanking was banned in Sweden in 1978, and other European countries followed in 1989 and later on in 2000. In 2003, the Supreme Court of Canada upheld parents' rights to fair corporal punishment, as spelled out in Section 43 of the Criminal Code, but set some guidelines, including the inappropriateness of having recourse to such punishment for a child younger than 2. This is an important step because perhaps as many as 40 percent of parents of infants under the age of one use some physical punishment (Invest in Kids, 2002).

Overall, the labelling of "fair" corporal punishment as a form of child abuse is controversial, as we have seen in Chapter 11. Reports of negative consequences for occasional and light spankings are probably unfounded, unless there are other risk factors present (Rosellini, 1998). These could include lack of overall parenting warmth, parenting aggressiveness, parents who are generally antisocial or criminal, detrimental peers, poverty, and child frailties, such as low impulse control or high anxiety and sensitivity.

Consequences for Children of Abuse by an Adult

The literature on child abuse unavoidably focuses on children's developmental outcomes rather than on their current suffering, struggles, and small victories—as researchers could not ethically study these children without intervening to help them. Hence, the everyday life of these children is not well documented. What is known is that, on average, children who have been or are abused do less well in school (Eckenrode et al., 1993), are more frequently delinquent (Sternberg et al., 1993), have more peer-related problems (Howes, 1988), and are less reciprocal in their relations (Salzinger et al., 1993). Understandably, they become hypervigilant to danger and threat, and as a result are often more aggressive and tend to attribute hostile intent to others (Dodge et al., 1990). They frequently experience conflict with authority figures (Stouthamer-Loeber et al., 2001). As adults, they are also likely to suffer from psychological problems (MacMillan et al., 2001).

In other words, these children share some of the characteristics mentioned earlier about children who witness interparental violence. Fathers who abuse their wives physically are more likely to abuse their children (McCloskey et al., 1995). In turn, abused mothers use harsh punishment more often than nonabused mothers (Straus and Smith, 1990). Women who have been abused as children have a higher chance of marrying an abusive husband. Together, these factors mean that child abuse often **coexists** or overlaps with spousal abuse and related difficulties. This combination of factors may explain the similarity between the long-term effects of child abuse and those of interparental violence. It also makes it difficult to determine the effects specific to child abuse alone. However, children who have been abused generally fare less well than those who witness interparental violence (see Margolin, 1998) but they are also at risk of being abusive later on in romantic relationships (Swinford et al., 2000). Miller et al. (2002) have found that harsh parenting is related to greater anxiety among young children of low SES than children of high SES. Thus, when children are small, low SES makes them even more vulnerable to the consequences of ill treatment.

Instead of becoming aggressive, adults who have been abused as children at times become depressed, withdrawn, and addicted to drugs (McCauley et al., 1997). Others may become warm and particularly altruistic. Certain types of abuse and degree of severity affect personal development, whereas other types of abuse affect subsequent parenting behaviours or interpersonal relations. Still other patterns of abuse are linked to antisocial behaviour or are causally linked to all such negative outcomes. However, the initial "causative" factor (the abuse) may be outweighed by personality resilience, happy circumstances in the person's life course, and a general lack of subsequent stressors.

Therefore, the path between a variable believed to be causal and its resulting outcome depends on many other factors along the life course. Salzinger et al. (1993) pointedly remark that protective factors must exist for severely abused children who turn out well, whereas risk factors must exist for children who are not abused but go on to become abusive as adults. These protective and risk factors may be found at the microsociological level (the child's personality), at the family level (supportive siblings or one parent who is warm), or at the macrosociological level (good schools and a neighbourhood that is largely prosocial).

Do Abused Children Become Abusive Parents?

Just as is the case for interparental violence, one of the consequences of child abuse that is much studied and debated involves its reproduction in the next generation. As it turns out, abusive parents themselves, compared to nonabusive parents, have, on average, been more frequently abused or harshly treated as children (Pears and Capaldi, 2001). Abusive parents, especially those who are sexually exploitative, lack empathy for their child and entertain unrealistic expectations of what the child can do for them (Pianta et al., 1989). Despite these parental drawbacks, most abused children do not grow up to be abusive, although severe and persistent child abuse probably always leaves long-term traces of psychological misery.

Kaufman and Zigler (1987) and Widom (1990) have estimated the transmission rate of family violence to be about 30 percent or lower. Abuse is not unavoidably transmitted because several factors enter into play in the chain of transmission. This includes the meaning that people attach to having been abused (Korbin, 1986): Some children who are beaten interpret this as justifiable punishment, yet, because it has hurt them, decide later on to utilize other forms of punishment with their own children. Attachment to a partner and children as well as the perceived disapproval of friends and relatives concerning family violence also prevent individuals who suffered or witnessed violence in their families from committing it themselves. This explanation is related to social bonding theory (Lackey and Williams, 1995). In other instances, a spouse intervenes and resocializes the potential abuser into utilizing more appropriate punishment.

Although some violent parents are more at risk of transmitting this pattern than others, the mechanisms through which this occurs are still poorly understood. In this respect, Simons and colleagues (1995) propose that a **parent's antisocial orientation** may well be one mediating factor in the transmission of violence to the next generation. Thus, it is possible that abusive parents who have other antisocial characteristics are more likely to transmit various abusive and violent behaviours to their children than adults who, except for being abusive parents, are otherwise prosocial (Frick et al., 1992). Antisocial parents might abuse their spouse, pick fights with others, or engage in criminal activity, for instance. In other words, they provide a stronger negative socialization experience for their children. In a small core of families, it may also be that physical abuse as well as other antisocial activities are transmitted across generations by **heredity**—that is, parents pass on to their children severe predispositions for aggressiveness or for other partly genetically influenced traits, such as low self-control or high impulsivity. However, one should be careful not to think that heredity means unavoidability or that it excuses the behaviours. Most people born with a predisposition to aggressiveness are not condemned or forced to act it out. But they are more likely to act it out when their environment encourages violence.

Parental stress induced by a child's disruptive behaviour often precipitates abuse (Pianta et al., 1989). Hence, another pathway to the transmission of abuse in some families is through a child's difficult behaviour, to which impulsive parents respond inappropriately, and that children pursue later on as adults. In a previous section, we have seen that exposure to community and school violence represents risk factors in the transmission of violence. We have also noted earlier that spousal and child abuse more frequently occur in poor neighbourhoods, along with many other forms of violence and antisocial behaviours. It is therefore quite likely that children who were abused *and* still live in a high-crime area will be more at risk of reproducing this pattern of violence in their own families than similar children who grow up in peaceful neighbourhoods where visible violence is practically nonexistent.

Child Neglect by Parents

Neglect involves not so much what parents do to their offspring but what they fail to do; it is a passive form of maltreatment (Barnett et al., 1993). This includes failing to feed children, not clothing them adequately in cold weather, allowing toddlers to roam outside without supervision, failing to keep dangerous substances and firearms out of their reach, and not sending them to school. At the more psychological level, neglecting parents fail to give their children a chance at getting an education or they neglect them emotionally by ignoring them most of the time and not interacting with them. Other parents fail to reprimand their children and their adolescents when they engage in antisocial or badly inappropriate behaviours.

Neglect is a situation that is less easily detected and less reported than abuse. For instance, adolescents are neglected when they are given all the freedom they want to experiment with sex, alcohol, drugs, and even criminal activities. Not surprisingly, many of these youths do not define their parents as neglectful; they often see them as being "understanding" and "cool." Parents may actually define themselves along the same lines. In fact, I heard one child advocate arguing that permissive parents "are simply respecting their children's rights." What was meant here were "rights" to engage in early sex, to abuse drugs, and to exploit other children. Adolescents are far more likely to complain about supervisory than permissive parents, even though the former are more invested parents. Although child neglect, particularly at the adolescent stage, is less discussed than child abuse, it involves more children and it may carry consequences that well-intentioned persons do not think of linking to it.

> In the course of my fieldwork on divorce, one of the dilemmas I encountered as a researcher involved a young deserted mother of three children below age eight. Julie was, by all measures, an excellent mother and the children were well adjusted, happy, and pleasant. She was a recent arrival to Toronto and had no one who could help her. A strikingly attractive young woman, she had staved off poverty and solved child care during the day by becoming a highly paid stripper at night. She was ashamed of this but, without a high school diploma, she had had no other alternative. She had entirely childproofed the apartment, and left for work in the evening after the children were sound asleep to return at 3 a.m.

She was constantly terrified that something would happen to the children (particularly fire) or that they would be discovered alone and taken away from her. Alarmed, and with Julie's obvious relief at being helped, I immediately contacted another much older woman interviewee who was reliable and for whom babysitting at night was a great opportunity because she was on welfare. Officially, and in one respect, Julie was a seriously neglecting mother; terrible harm could have come to the children. But all she needed was help. Indeed, the young family continued to do well and, by the last follow-up six years later, Julie had become a secretary after taking day classes. She was also considering marriage.

Child neglect by parents is more common than child abuse (Health Canada, 2001). In the U.S., it accounts for nearly half of child deaths related to maltreatment (McCurdy and Daro, 1994). *Physical* child neglect is related to parents' drug addiction and mental illness (DiLeonardi, 1993). Above all, it stems from **poverty** as well as the stressors and social isolation created by poverty (Pelton, 1994). Furthermore, when families are forced to remain in or move to a poor neighbourhood with social problems, children are immediately at risk of physical and psychological harm as well as bad example. The dangers are so numerous that parents have to be extremely vigilant, which is not a normal state—for parents or for children (Garbarino et al., 1991). Therefore, it is easy for such parents to not be vigilant enough, although they may be doing everything they can. Pelton (1991:3) points out that poverty sets up a double standard of parenting "in that we implicitly ask impoverished parents to be *more* diligent in their supervisory responsibility than middle-class parents, because greater protection is required to guard children from the dangerous conditions of poverty than from the relatively safer conditions of middle-class homes and neighbourhoods."

When parents are under stress or hold jobs that keep them away from home a great deal of the time, children go unsupervised. In other societies, leaving children home alone is not a problem. But this is often not the case here due to the potential risks involved. This, then, becomes child neglect unless parents supervise their children's activities by phone, for instance, and set strict rules of safety and behaviours to be followed during their absence. Dangers are less likely in a "good" area because the neighbourhood offers fewer harmful activities for children to engage in and because the presence of other supervising parents helps (Kupersmidt et al., 1995). In a disadvantaged and dangerous area, however, such neglect can have serious consequences: It can lead to peer abuse and excessively premature motherhood, for instance.

Too few studies document the negative effects of child neglect (Crouch and Milner, 1993). Children often suffer from abuse and neglect together or from physical and emotional neglect combined (Ney et al., 1994). This overlap makes it nearly impossible to attribute specific effects. The consequences of neglect range from insecurity to aggressiveness toward peers, behaviour problems, and lack of school readiness (Eckenrode et al., 1993). In general, neglectful families function less adequately than other families. They often receive less social support from their immediate kin network, as was the case with Julie, and mothers perceive their children to be more difficult (Harrington et al., 1998). Yet, in spite of all these and their own problems, children who are neglected do not necessarily perceive their family differently than other children. They may have no basis for comparison, particularly if other families around them are similar to theirs. In other instances, children do not wish to report neglect to social workers because they fear being placed out of their homes (Gable, 1998).

Is Child Abuse by Parents Increasing?

Child abuse was brought to the public's attention only in the 1960s by doctors who coined the concept of the *battered-child syndrome* (Kempe et al., 1962). It is therefore impossible to estimate how widespread a phenomenon it was before that date. Although some researchers have registered an increase in the U.S. (Kaplan et al., 1999), according to Straus and Gelles (1990b), the period between 1975 and 1985 saw a decrease in the rate of child abuse. All estimates are somewhat lower than reality, but the increases recently apparent in statistics and social work caseload may reflect the fact that society has become sensitized to child and wife battery as well as sexual exploitation, so that more cases are now reported than in the past. Therefore, social agencies are swamped by **reported cases** at a time when the rate of occurrence may be lower than in those days when no one spoke about the problem and it was more widely tolerated and practised.

Demographic changes alone are consonant with the notion of a decrease. Families have fewer children and especially fewer unplanned children than in the past. They are less burdened demographically and are less overcrowded. Parents, particularly mothers, spend fewer hours per week with their children, a situation that lowers the potential for child abuse—but not neglect. Women now have their first child when they are older and more mature, and can put their children's needs ahead of theirs. Parents are more aware of some of the literature on child development, at least at the middle-class level, and may try to avoid any situation that could traumatize their children. Furthermore, parents certainly perceive that there is a greater likelihood that they could get caught and punished severely, including losing their children, and this perception may act as a deterrent.

However, there are three caveats. Child abuse may soon increase when children who are violent toward their peers become parents later on. As well, child *neglect* may be on the rise because parents often suffer from role strain and spend too many hours employed away from home. Second, one of the reasons that may have contributed to a decrease in child abuse—parental fears of being labelled as abusers—may have contributed to lower the authority of parents in general and have led to a reluctance on their part to intervene in some domains of their children's lives. This situation would leave youths unsupervised and unprotected, which are forms of neglect.

CHILD SEXUAL ABUSE BY ADULTS

Sexual abuse is the commission of a sex act with a person who does not want it or is too young or immature to understand what is asked of or done to him or her. This broad definition involves inappropriate touching as well as penetration for the perpetrator's sexual gratification.

Who Are and Where Are the Abusers?

The incidence of child sexual abuse is even more complex to estimate than that of physical abuse because of the element of victims' shame or ignorance, perpetrators' complete secrecy, and lack of visible physical symptoms. It is estimated that 90 percent of sexual offences are never reported to the police. But of those reported in 2002, 61 percent were of persons younger than 18 years of age, and girls constituted 85 percent of these. The peak age for the reported sexual victimization of girls is 13 (Statistics Canada, 2003f). Overall, the consensus is that about one out of every four females is sexually abused before she reaches age 16. A late-1980s American national survey revealed that 27 percent of the women and 16 percent of the men interviewed reported having been sexually abused as children (Finkelhor et al., 1990). Although no question was asked about this topic, the female students' autobiographies nevertheless revealed a range from 15 to 25 percent, depending on the year; rare instances surfaced among males. In the U.S., substantiated cases of child sexual abuse have declined by a third between 1992 and 1999 (Jones et al., 2001)—although the verdict is still out as to whether this constitutes a real decline or a reporting bias (Leventhal, 2001).

Young girls are more often sexually abused within the family, and boys more often outside the family. Although estimates vary, parents (mainly fathers) are the prime suspects in 20 percent of the cases reported to the police for children younger than age 11, but even fewer parents are involved for older ages (Statistics Canada, 2003f). Other perpetrators within the family include stepfathers or mothers' boyfriends, as well as older sisters' boyfriends, more frequently than fathers. These are followed by siblings, grandparents, uncles, and cousins, as well as other relatives. Children are also sexually abused by fathers' friends; in foster care, daycare and group care institutions; by babysitters and coaches; as well as by peers. A majority of the perpetrators are males, but victimization by a mother, a sister, or a female babysitter, as well as a stepmother, occasionally occurs. In the students' autobiographies, only four cases of father-daughter incest came to light. It is possible, however, that students did not want to discuss it because it was too painful and private—but I doubt this because a great deal of other very sensitive material was divulged. Rather, such cases probably occur more in school-age and clinical samples than in university student samples, because this is a type of abuse that carries the most serious consequences (see also Hyman, 2000). Three of the four reported cases had occurred in immigrant families in which many problems co-existed or who originated from patriarchal societies (Duffy, 2004).

In a clinical intervention for 50 adolescent girls who had been sexually abused, the fathers had been the offenders in 16 percent of the cases, whereas stepfathers and mothers' boyfriends had been in 32 percent of the cases (Morrison and Clavenna-Valleroy, 1998). Furthermore, over half of these girls' mothers also reported having been sexually abused as a child, an extremely high rate that coincides with a high rate of these mothers' partners having abused their daughters. This double female victimization relates to other research findings showing that a proportion of women who are abused as girls marry partners who abuse them and may also abuse their daughters. The abuse carries from one generation to the next through the **transmission of victimization** from mother to daughter. In fact, children who live with an abused mother are over 12 times more likely to be sexually abused (McCloskey et al., 1995).

Once again, children from low-income families are more likely to be sexually victimized than others (Hollingsworth, 1998). This brings us back to Chapter 9, where we saw that a proportion of girls who became mothers by age 15 had been coerced into sex, and most were poor. Furthermore, males who have been sexually abused as boys are more likely to impregnate a teenager at some point in their lives (Rosenberg,

2001). In addition, Chapter 6 indicates that, in areas with a high level of poverty, children may be less well supervised and thus more at risk of victimization. The presence of transient male adults in a family as well as overcrowding can also contribute to explain this difference in child sexual abuse by social class.

Consequences of Sexual Abuse for the Child

The consequences for the sexually abused child are generally analyzed within a psychogenic model of trauma: The more severe the abuse, the more negative the consequences (Kendall-Tackett et al., 1993). Probably the most dramatic results follow **incest,** particularly if a father, mother, sibling, or grandfather is the culprit. The child is at his or her most vulnerable within these situations because of daily availability, longer duration, and more extensive harm (Fischer and McDonald, 1998). Perhaps worst of all is the reality that the child is emotionally attached to and trusts the abuser. The abuser should be the protector and an agent of socialization but instead becomes the tormentor.

> A student devoted many pages detailing the sexual abuse she began suffering at age six when her grandparents were babysitting her. Although her grandmother was nearby in the kitchen, the grandfather regularly coerced the child into performing oral sex in the family room because "it made him feel good and he used to tell me that I was his special girl." The poor little girl gagged and gagged and had to submit to further indecencies. "At the time I was convinced that I was special and he had me promise not to tell anyone so that I was essentially isolated and didn't know any better." As she grew up, she became more and more repulsed and begged her mother to find her another sitter. The abuse stopped when she was 10 years old. By early adolescence, she feared men, and by late adolescence, she had to seek therapy because sex disgusted her. She began suffering from depressive episodes. "I will never let any old man babysit my children."

The conjugal unit and even the entire family can be destroyed by incest. Mothers may leave the perpetrator, although cases of mothers who turn against their daughters are not unheard of in clinical practice or among delinquents and street kids. In these instances, the daughter is seen as the trespasser within the conjugal subsystem; yet, in reality, it is usually the father or boyfriend who initiated the coalition with the daughter. When mothers are not supportive or do not believe the daughters, the latter risk becoming very depressive, even during treatment (Morrison and Clavenna-Valleroy, 1998). Mothers who have been sexually abused themselves when they were children experience greater emotional distress than other mothers when they learn of their child's abuse. This maternal turmoil in itself reflects the long-term effects of child sexual abuse; these mothers are forced to relive their own abuse, which is very traumatic for them (Hiebert-Murphy, 1998).

The Life Course Perspective

Within a life course sociological framework, sexual abuse constitutes **inappropriate sexual socialization.** One immediate consequence is that sexual contact with an adult focuses the child on his or her own sexuality from a less than healthy perspective very early on in life. The abuse constitutes a precocious initiation into sex. This life course brings a premature foreclosure in identity: The young girl begins to define herself in terms of sexuality and perhaps material gains. This opens the door to deviant opportunities and closes the door to a normal life course. In turn, these "opportunities" may lead to early sexual relations with older peers and pregnancy (Roosa et al., 1997). These children have more sexual partners among older peers, and are at greater risk of contracting sexually transmitted diseases and becoming homeless (Seidman et al., 1994). The same path may lead to prostitution.

As Browning and Laumann (1997:557) explain, adult sexual contact with a young girl "seems to provide access to sexuality without cultivating the emotional and cognitive skills to manage sexual experiences." The subsequent deviant behaviour of the girls often arises from the fact that their self-perception has been distorted as a result of the abuse (Dalenberg and Jacobs, 1994). Some of these young girls may grow up believing that others have the right to their body or that early sexuality is normal. As we have just seen in the previous case study, this is actually one of the *discourses* that child abusers hold with their victim. They explain that the act is "normal" or that the relationship is a "special" one in order to convince the child to be victimized and, later on, to justify the abuser's behaviour (Gilgun, 1995; see Family Research 15.1). Browning and Laumann (1997) find that, when child abuse does not give rise to an early, risky sexual life, the victims are less likely to experience adverse outcomes later in life. The authors conclude that the long-term effects of child sexual abuse are probably indirect through the negative life course that they often generate; redirecting sexual trajectories at an early age might cancel most of the severe and long-term negative consequences of sexual abuse.

Fortunately, most children who are sexually abused do not follow a deviant life course. Parental or peer support, personal strength, as well as appropriate psychotherapy may be instrumental in resocializing children and helping them build their lives constructively. Nevertheless, many such children develop emotional and behavioural problems, both as children and later on as adults (Briere and Runtz, 1993). As illustrated in the student vignette, depression is a common sequel that can appear as

---

FAMILY RESEARCH 15.1

In-Depth Interviews with Incest Perpetrators

Jane Gilgun (1995) recruited 11 incest perpetrators, 10 men and 1 woman, from two prisons and referrals from community-based treatment centres. Her goal was to use in-depth conversations with these informants to test hypotheses derived from the literature and to modify these hypotheses if they did not fit her data. Each informant was interviewed an average of six times for a total of 12 hours. The author proceeded through open-ended life history interviews.

Open-ended interviews tend to be conversational in style and the researcher is free to probe issues more in depth, which is not possible to do with a fixed set of multiple-choice or close-ended questions. With the respondents' consent, Gilgun tape-recorded and transcribed the contents of the interviews. She then analyzed the interviews to identify themes and variations within each theme. "My intent was to create as complete a picture of the moral discourse of the perpetrators in this study" (p. 270).

early as adolescence (Heger and Lytle, 1993). Sexual abuse may trigger problems in a child who may not otherwise be at risk, or it may increase preexisting problems, even later on in life (Mancini et al., 1995).

Many children grow up to forget or repress the abuse. For instance, Williams and Banyard (1997) followed up with men and women who, in the early 1970s, had been examined in a hospital emergency room for sexual abuse. After 17 years, 38 percent of the women and 55 percent of the men had no recollection of the abuse. Widom and Morris (1997) found similar numbers when they followed up court-substantiated instances of child sexual abuse that had taken place 20 years earlier. Perhaps the fact that the abuse has been forgotten means that, at the time, it had not been vested with tragic overtones by the child. Perhaps children who grow up to forget have particular strengths. But, above all, as Browning and Laumann (1997) indicate, perhaps children who grow up to forget are also more likely to have had a normal life course.

SIBLING ABUSE

As is the case for child abuse, in general, sibling violence is divided between physical and sexual. (Psychological abuse was covered to some extent in Chapter 13.)

Sibling Violence

Straus and colleagues (1980) sampled 1,224 pairs of siblings ranging in age from three to 17 years. Pushing and shoving were the most frequently mentioned acts of physical violence at the less serious end of the continuum. At the other extreme, 14 percent reported having beaten up their sibling and five percent reported using a gun, either to threaten or to hurt. This survey took place in 1975. The level of violence among children in general has since risen, and, because adult presence at home has diminished, these figures could be higher today. The result that sister pairs were the least aggressive of all sibling pairs is probably still true today, but here as well, one can expect higher frequencies than in the 1970s because there has been an increase in violence perpetrated by girls.

The media, the public, professionals, and researchers have all paid a great deal of attention to child abuse by parents when, actually, sibling abuse is more common (Wallace, 1999). This selective inattention to sibling abuse stems from widespread beliefs that it is simply part of growing up. It is considered normal (Gelles, 1997). Siblings hurt each other so frequently that no one pays much attention to it (Wieke, 1997). Parents are very concerned, however, about sibling conflict. They do not like the name calling, fighting, shoving, slapping, and hair pulling, but generally do not intervene (Perozynski and Kramer, 1999). Frequently heard comments from parents run like the following:

- "It drives me crazy; they're always at it."
- "I'm always afraid they'll really hurt each other one day, but it's better to let them resolve their problems on their own."
- "Parents shouldn't interfere in their children's lives; they have to learn on their own."

Sibling violence and abuse is a neglected topic of research, both in terms of its incidence and its consequences. Negative consequences may exist for the younger child who is victimized. But one also has to consider that the abusive child is allowed to socialize himself or herself into a role that may repeat itself later on in other aspects of life and against other victims such as dates and spouses or even children. Is sibling violence a "phase" or is it likely to be a lasting phenomenon in a person's life?

This type of reasoning leads to the conclusion that sibling violence is not "real" violence that one has to prevent (Gelles, 1997). These parents' beliefs about nonintervention are reinforced by the lack of professional concern. Because of this widespread **adult tolerance**, children are far less likely to report sibling abuse to their parents or other authority figures than is the case for abuse by adults (DeKeseredy and Ellis, 1997). The stronger of the two siblings is encouraged on this path because he or she benefits from advantages over the other and no one intervenes. As a result, later on, adults who are asked about victimization in their past often fail to equate sibling beatings with assault. Once more, this leads to the underrepresentation of sibling violence in official surveys (Bachman, 1994). Furthermore, very little is actually known about the developmental consequences of everyday sibling abuse; nor is it known how it affects their relationship as adults or their parenting practices, if at all.

Sibling Sexual Abuse

The following student quote serves as an introduction to a topic that is equally overlooked: sibling sexual abuse or sibling incest, which is probably more common than parent-child incest (O'Brien, 1991):

"The most painful time in my life is the period between the ages of 6 to 10: my brother was six years older than me and my parents counted on him to babysit me.... At first I did not understand what was happening to me, however difficult this is to explain with hindsight, but my brother got me into performing intimate acts for him and later on after a year of this his best friend used to come over and they would both share me. This is all I can write here because this is very painful. This went on for two years until I became strong enough to resist and threaten to tell my parents which of course I never did because I was too ashamed. At school I was ashamed too because I saw this boy.... Now I harbour intensely negative feelings about my brother who seems to have forgotten all about these years.... It would kill my parents if I told them. I went into therapy when I got to this university and have come to terms with the situation, which is not to say that I accept it but I can live with it and go on with my life. But I know that I will be very very careful with my own children later on in life. Very careful."

Sibling incest is a predominantly brother-to-sister initiated or coerced phenomenon, but incest between siblings of the same sex also occurs (Smith and Israel, 1987). Ascherman and Safier had placed the incidence of sibling incest at about 13 percent in

1990. A 1982 study found that it had occurred in 60 percent of psychiatric outpatients (Bess and Janssen, 1982). As is the case for all types of sexual abuse, sibling incest is found more in clinical than in survey populations. This would indicate that sibling incest results in serious psychological consequences for many abused brothers and sisters. Sibling sexual abuse may perhaps occur more among malfunctioning families where other problems already exist, or among families that simply cannot supervise their children because of various burdens (DiGiorgio-Miller, 1998). It can also result from the way parental roles are carried out. Extramarital affairs, open sexuality between parents that children observe, for instance, are related to sibling incest (Smith and Israel, 1987): Children may copy what they see. A lack of parental supervision and involvement is especially evident in many of these families.

O'Brien (1991) compared adolescent sex offenders whose victims were siblings with other adolescent sex offenders whose victims were children outside the family. Adolescents who had sexually abused a sibling had done it more often and for a much longer period of time (one year) than adolescents who had abused a child outside the family, because of the availability of the little brother or sister at home (as illustrated in the student quote). As well, their sibling victim was much younger, between four and nine years of age, than the victims of other abusers. This young age allowed for greater accessibility, because a small child can more easily be coerced than an older child. The frequency of the abuse resulted in nearly half of the sibling cases progressing to anal or vaginal penetration. This occurred rarely when the victim was not a sibling, for it is easier to progress to penetration within the context of long-term availability and within the secrecy of home.

In families of sibling incest, O'Brien uncovered a phenomenon we have already encountered for child sexual abuse by a father or a stepfather, where both mother and daughter have been abused: (1) Parents of incest perpetrators, particularly mothers, had been more often abused sexually as children than was the case among the parents of the other sex offenders and (2) 42 percent of the incestuous offenders had been abused sexually, although generally outside the family. Thus, in these families, many parents had themselves been vulnerable during their childhood. Furthermore, some of their sons had also been sexually abused, and of those many had gone on to abuse their siblings. The transmission from one generation to the next was one of *vulnerability* for sexual victimization in many of these families.

PEER ABUSE

As we have seen in Figure 15.1, older children are more likely to be abused by their peers than by anyone else. Examples of cruel, destructive, and even violent peer behaviours are mentioned in the newscasts on a weekly basis, and in some cases, the results are deadly. Peer abuse is a situation that severely depletes a child's social capital outside the home and often endangers the development of his or her human capital. It also affects family dynamics.

A conservative estimate might be that a minimum of 20 percent of all children are *seriously* abused by peers during their young lives—and this does not refer to normal conflicts, disagreements, and teasing (Eder, 1991). Moreover, recent surveys reported in the news media, both in Canada and the U.S., present much higher estimates, often as high as 75 percent. Such a rate implies that most adolescents are both victims and abusers, although not necessarily at the same time. A third of Bibby's (2001) adolescent respondents had a close friend who had been attacked at school.

In the autobiographies, students recalled far more peer maltreatment that they described as having had detrimental and *lasting* consequences on their development than was the case for parental treatment. That is, these experiences had affected them for several years, often up to the present time (Ambert, 1994a). Furthermore, there was an increasing trend over a decade. In the autobiographies, as well as in magazines (*Time* and *Newsweek*, May 1999), one reads about students who had been happy and well adjusted, but quite rapidly began deteriorating psychologically, sometimes to the point of becoming physically ill and incompetent in school or even delinquent. For many, the impact of peer maltreatment leads to avoidance of school (Kochenderfer and Ladd, 1996). In other instances, it contributes to poor school performance (Hodges et al., 1997) as well as anxiety and depression (Egan and Perry, 1998). As one student recalls it, even school work can be disrupted, as young victims become too distraught and often too fearful to focus on anything else:

> "The years between 12 and 16 were the worst in my life. I was surely the most unpopular boy at my school. There was a group of boys with some girls too who used to pick on me and no one would have dared be nice to me after that. They'd steal my lunch, force me to hand over my pocket money, they'd laugh and snicker when I passed by.... It got to the point where I felt so terrorized that I couldn't even pay attention to what the teacher said in class and my marks suffered and of course my parents weren't too sympathetic because they hadn't a clue that this was going on until I got really sick with chronic stomach problems, but by then the years had gone by and my life had been ruined. I feel insecure to this day and always sit at the back to avoid being noticed."

There have been many studies describing *victims'* personal characteristics. This is akin to inquiring about the personal life of rape victims rather than prosecuting the rapist for his actions. Nowadays, a child can become the victim of peer abuse through no fault of his or her own or of his or her family (Garbarino, 1999). In other words, peer abuse is not merely a psychological situation created by a victim and an abuser because of two sets of personality characteristics. Nor is it merely a consequence of a victim's parents' childrearing practices, as often described in the literature (Finnegan et al., 1998).

Rather, peer abuse is influenced by the clique structure of schools and by what children have learned elsewhere, including the media—whether television or video games—and siblings. For instance, Espelage and colleagues (1996) find that adolescent bullies watch more violent television, are more difficult at home, spend less time with adults, and have more exposure to gang activities than other children. A third had a single parent and another third lived with a stepparent. Thus, it would seem that serious bullies escape adult influence and control. Their family structure is burdened in terms of its ability to provide supervision. Instead, they surround themselves with negative, virtual (as in videos), and real role models. At a more macrosociological level, the **culture of violence** in the society at large is implicated along with reduced social control. It is a situation created by opportunity. Peer abuse is, above all, a cultural phenomenon and a reflection of a lack of an effective community (Coleman and Hoffer, 1987).

Peer Sexual Harassment and Abuse

Sexual harassment, mainly by boys toward girls, is a particularly pernicious form of abuse that may begin early (Stein, 1995). It generally goes undetected, may even be approved of by boys' parents ("he's *all* boy"), and some girls may be led by their peers to believe that it is flattering ("he likes you, silly") or simply the normal price one has to pay for popularity. It is the forecaster of date and partner abuse. Many adolescents and even preadolescent girls are coerced into sexuality by male peers. The degree of coercion ranges from outright rape to subtle pressure in a relationship where the girl is afraid to lose her date. Adolescents are particularly at risk when they score high on scales of conformity to peers (Small and Kerns, 1993): They become vulnerable because they need their peers' approval more than a less conforming adolescent does. While many girls are not raped, they nevertheless do not want sexual intercourse but comply because of peer pressure (Laumann, 1996). Some of this pressure comes from female peers who may already be sexually active or pretend to be. This creates a **cultural climate** that is very potent; as a result, a teenager eager for peer acceptance will follow suit.

Victimization from severe forms of sexual abuse, rape, or coercion into unwanted sexuality is more likely to occur to adolescents who live in neighbourhoods that have a high rate of social problems and whose parents cannot supervise or protect them adequately. Girls from single-parent families, particularly when they are disadvantaged, as well as those who have parents who suffer from alcoholism, for instance, are at a higher risk of sexual victimization in general, including by peers (Moore et al., 1989). Peer sexual abuse, as is the case for peer abuse in general, is very much a **crime of opportunity.** It is done by and occurs to children and adolescents while they are unsupervised by adults, whether at school, at home, in an abandoned building, or in a car. Peer sexual abuse is the result of media influences and disengagement from adults, including teachers and parents—in other words, a generalized lack of an effective community.

ABUSE OF PARENTS BY CHILDREN

Two additional types of familial abuse exist: ill treatment of parents by their young children and the abuse of elder parents by their adult offspring. The literature is thin concerning both topics; yet, the matter of parent abuse by children may be timely because children and adolescents are, on average, less disciplined, more aggressive, and exhibit more behavioural problems than before (Ambert, 2003d). One could well argue that parents can easily become victims of aggressive and out-of-control children, particularly because respect for parents is less valued than in the past, even by parents themselves (Alwin, 1986), and because peer groups, often of the aggressive type, have become more influential.

Physical Abuse of Parents by Children and Adolescents

The relative absence of research on this topic is perplexing in view of the fact that small children, Canadian and American, are generally more physically aggressive than older ones (Onyskiw and Hayduk, 2001) and spend more time with parents; furthermore, people often witness verbal abuse of parents by children and even adolescents and young adults. For instance, several teens in one of my studies repeatedly yelled at their mother that she was "stupid" and even a "bitch." (Yet, if the mothers were the ones doing the name-calling, they would be censured by professionals.) One can also witness physical assault of mothers by children as young as age three (Straus and Ulma, 2003). These observations are made in public areas—such as sidewalks, parks, and subway plat-forms—for everyone to see, a sign that children are no longer sensitized against this be-haviour and that they do not have to fear public condemnation in this respect.

I observed the following scene in a subway train. A well-dressed mother, age 25 to 30, walked in with an equally well-groomed little boy, age four or five. The lit-tle boy was screaming at his mother at the top of his lungs:

B: *You hurt my feelings!*

M: *(bending down to soothe him) I'm so sorry, honey, I apologize.*

B: *I hate you, I hate you! (He was red in the face with rage and was hitting his mother with his fists.)*

M: *(softly) Again, I'm sorry honey; it won't happen again.*

B: *You're stupid. (He kicked her with his booted foot.)*

The mother had tears in her eyes. The boy was not in the least bit deterred by the staring disapproval from passengers as he continued punching and yelling.

Moreover, my fieldwork for two separate studies has revealed mothers who were regularly assaulted by their adolescents, and even bore marks of recent beatings. The mothers were single and poor; one was in a wheelchair. The latter was also called a "scumbag" by her 16-year-old son. Several studies in the U.S. and Great Britain have obtained self-reports by adolescents of child-to-parent abuse, with a trend for mothers to be a more frequent recipient of physical violence than fathers (Straus and Ulma, 2003). In Massachusetts, between September 1992 and June 1993, nearly one-third of all restraining court orders issued were requested by parents against children, mainly by mothers against sons (reported in Gelles, 1997). In a 1996 British Crime Survey, one in 10 mothers reported having been assaulted by her children—some of these offspring were over age 18 (Mirrlees-Black et al., 1996).

Among American university students, some mutuality of parent and young adult violence exists. There is some continuity of behaviour from parents who have physi-cally maltreated their children to the children who then maltreat parents (Browne, 1998). On the other side of the equation, Gelles (1997:112) points out that clinical ob-servations of abusive adolescents reveal deficiencies in the authority structure of fam-ilies whereby adolescents have been granted too much control and decision-making power. There may be a connection between permissive parenting and abuse of parents by their offspring.

Abuse of Elderly Parents by Adult Children

Women outlive men, and one of the consistent findings on elder abuse is that most victims are women (Whittaker, 1995). Until now, explanations for elder abuse have emphasized the dependent elderly's caregivers: The line of reasoning is that the frustrated and burdened caregiver lashes out at the frail dependent parent (Steinmetz, 1993). However, elderly parents are often abused by an adult child who lives with them because of that child's own dependency (Carp, 2000). In that case, the adult child depends on the parent financially or for shelter, because he or she is unemployed or is mentally delayed, physically challenged, or emotionally disturbed. Indeed, after discharge from hospital care, 85 percent of unmarried adult children who are mentally ill move in with their elderly parents (Greenberg et al., 1993). The potential for abuse certainly exists (Lefley, 1997). Hence, researchers may have placed too much emphasis on the dependence of the elderly as a source of abuse; the elderly who have a dependent and physically stronger spouse or child living with them should be considered at risk (Carp, 2000). Other explanations propose that elder abuse is spousal abuse "grown old" or that it stems at least in part from prejudicial attitudes and beliefs toward the elderly (Harbinson, 1999).

Police-reported data for the year 2000 showed that Canadian men are the most frequent perpetrators of violence against an older family member—80 percent of such cases. Older men were more frequently victimized by their adult children whereas older women were as likely to be abused by their spouse or adult children. In the 1999 General Social Survey, seven percent of seniors reported emotional abuse, while one percent reported financial abuse and another one percent physical or sexual violence (Dauvergne, 2003). Material forms of abuse by adult children are motivated by greed, personal debts or addictions, or a spouse's or children's demands. Material abuse includes siphoning off parental revenues, walking out with parents' possessions, or controlling the parents' house (Korbin et al., 1995). Medical abuse is at times perpetrated when the caregiving adult child does not seek assistance for a sick or suffering elderly parent—to safeguard the entirety of the inheritance or precipitate its occurrence.

Elderly parents who are abused by their adult children rarely report the situation. They feel ashamed and may fear retaliation. Furthermore, they are often socially isolated and have no one in whom to confide.

This problem has very low visibility: Elderly parents may be less likely to report abuse than would a maltreated adolescent or even a child. Actually, perhaps as few as five percent report it (Tatara, 1993). Elderly parents may be ashamed of their situation and may have no one else to turn to for help. An attempt to report the abuse might fail and result in dreaded retaliation. Moreover, while abused children grow up and may eventually denounce their parents, the elderly parent dies with the secret. Thus, abuse of elderly parents is a relatively easy act to commit and can have even less social visibility than abuse of school-age children. The elderly who are most at risk are often socially isolated: They are no longer connected to their social networks, such as church, work, or even friends (Duffy and Momirov, 1997). No one may notice the abuse, and physicians who see bruises may be told that the senior person fell, something which occurs quite often in old age. (The parallel with small children is obvious here.)

It is not known if the model of the intergenerational transmission of violence is a valid explanatory framework for elder abuse. As well, this perspective does not address larger sociological issues (Whittaker, 1995). Some of these issues relate to the parallel facts that, among the elderly, women are poorer than men and most of their caregivers are other women, generally their daughters. As well, both sets of women belong to two generations with a different history of employment and dependency, yet both suffer from structural gender inequalities.

CONCLUSIONS: THE LARGER CONTEXT OF FAMILY VIOLENCE

The literature on neglect, and particularly physical and sexual abuse, is one largely oriented toward the psychological sources of maltreatment of a family member by another. One cannot deny that these sources are present. However, from a sociological perspective, violence within the family is a reflection of violence within society, including its media. To begin with, difficult and out-of-control temperaments that lead to abusive situations would not be so prevalent in a society where civility, altruism, and a sense of communal responsibility were the valued forms of behaviour. Second, within such a civilized and less competitive-aggressive environment, even impulsive parents, spouses, and children would learn to respect others rather than maltreat them.

Other larger sociocultural forces that are implicated in family violence include discrimination and poverty, as well as the fact that the family is the only institution that is single-handedly responsible for the well-being of its dependent members—whether children, the disabled, or the frail elderly. The family fulfills too many functions—and particularly too many caregiving functions—while it receives too little social support from the very complex, expensive, and competitive society in which it lives. In other words, we have come full circle, and these remarks return us to the discussion on multiple family functions in Chapter 3.

Summary

1. Few incidents of courtship violence are reported to authorities and many youths consider such incidents a normal part of the dating process. Both sexes participate in this phenomenon; however, women sustain most of the injuries. Most of the studies of the origins of dating violence fail to consider extrafamilial influences. Indeed, violence and abuse are greatly affected by the sociocultural context in which families live, including the social construction of masculinity. Date rape is the ultimate form of violence in terms of patriarchal dominance.

2. Verbal and psychological abuse of partners is not as easy to measure as physical abuse is. It has also been less researched. It is quite salient in music videos favoured by adolescents. This form of abuse is often tailored to fit partners' vulnerabilities.

3. At the spousal level, along with cultural influences, physical violence by a partner is an issue of power and covers a wide range of acts from mild to lethal. Cohabiting couples have the highest rate of partner violence. Poor couples, particularly those living in unsafe neighbourhoods, have a higher risk of partner

violence. Domestic violence among oppressed minorities may have causes that do not exist among whites. Same-sex-partner violence is as much a matter of power and control as it is in heterosexual couple violence, except that gender is not an issue. The rate of violence approximates that among heterosexual couples.

4. On average, children of abused mothers have more behavioural and psychological problems. However, the intergenerational transmission of violence depends on many variables, and only a minority of these children grow up to repeat the pattern in their own families. Factors that contribute to transmission include high levels of interparental violence as well as exposure to community and school violence.

5. Many statistics are presented on child and adolescent abuse, but these are merely estimates. Physical punishment is a much debated issue in this context and occurs occasionally in most families. Children who have been or are abused, on average, have more behavioural problems, particularly in terms of aggressiveness. Abused children are often surrounded by a climate of violence. Child abuse and neglect are more common in low-income families, especially in areas with a high concentration of poverty and violence. Approximately 30 percent of abused children grow up to repeat this pattern with their own offspring. Many variables enter into the risk of transmission. Parental stress often precipitates abuse, including stress caused by a child's disruptive behaviours. In some families, heredity may be a factor.

6. Child neglect is more widespread and involves not so much what parents do to their offspring as what they fail to do. It ranges from malnutrition to failure to supervise properly, and is not as easily detected nor as reported as abuse. Physical neglect is particularly related to poverty, and its consequences include early motherhood as a result of a lack of supervision.

7. There may have been a decrease in child abuse by parents in the last two decades of the 20th century, although there has been an increase in reporting. However, child neglect has probably increased.

8. Child sexual abuse tends to occur more within the family among girls and outside the family among boys. A proportion of women who are abused as girls marry partners who abuse them or their daughters. Again, children from low-income families are at a higher risk of sexual abuse. The consequences for the child depend on the nature of the abuse and who the perpetrator is. Father-daughter incest is probably the most damaging. Sexual contact with an adult prematurely focuses the child on his or her sexuality, and this focus in turn often initiates a series of events in the life course of the child that deviate from the norm of other young persons' life courses. Sexual abuse constitutes an inappropriate sexual socialization.

9. Sibling violence ranges from mild to severe and is fairly common. Relatively little attention has been paid to it, and parents rarely intervene even though many are concerned. Children rarely report it. Sibling incest is predominantly a brother-to-sister situation. It is reported more in clinical than in survey populations: It may happen more in families that are malfunctioning in other respects.

10. Abuse of children by their peers is probably the most common form of abuse in society. It carries many negative consequences and can be explained by sociocultural factors. Peer sexual abuse also arises out of society's general cultural climate of violence and exploitation of women.

11. A number of children and adolescents assault their parents, particularly their mothers, both verbally and physically, but this topic is not given much attention in the research. Among the elderly who are abused by their adult children, many are mothers. Some elderly are abused by their frustrated caregiving children,

but perhaps even more are abused by children who depend on them because the children have various disabilities. Furthermore, verbal as well as material forms of elderly parent abuse exist; the latter may be motivated by greed. Elder abuse is a relatively easy act to commit and may be less reported than child abuse.

12. Violence within the family is a reflection of violence in the society at large. It also results from the fact that the family is burdened with functions for which it receives little societal support.

Key Concepts and Themes

Adult tolerance, p. 443
Alcohol, pp. 427–428
Antisocial parents, p. 435
Cohabiting couples, p. 427
Community and school violence, p. 430
Concentration of violence, p. 433
Culture of violence, pp. 423, 446
Disadvantaged neighbourhoods, pp. 427, 433, 436
Ethnicity, p. 428
Inappropriate sexual socialization, pp. 440–444
Incest, pp. 440–443
Intergenerational transmission, pp. 430, 435

Lack of civility, p. 424
Life course, pp. 440–442
Media, p. 423
Patriarchal dominance, pp. 423, 428
Poverty, pp. 427, 433, 435
Power, pp. 422, 425
Psychologized, p. 423
Reported cases, p. 438
Risk factor, p. 423
Social constructs of masculinity, p. 423
Transmission of victimization, p. 439

Analytical Questions

1. The intergenerational transmission of violence and abuse is a recurrent theme in this chapter. It is also much emphasized in the media. How are the contents of this chapter different from the media emphases?

2. What role does culture play in partner abuse?

3. Cohabiting couples have high rates of partner violence. Explain why this is so, using infor-

mation from this chapter and perhaps Chapters 8 and 14.

4. Make a case for and against physical punishment being a form of child abuse.

5. Why is permissiveness a form of child or adolescent neglect?

Suggested Readings

Cardarelli, A. P. (Ed.) 1997. *Violence between intimate partners.* Boston: Allyn and Bacon. This collection of research articles focuses on violence in heterosexual marriage and cohabitation, between same-sex partners, and during courtship.

Duffy, A., and Momirov, J. 1997. *Family violence: A Canadian introduction.* Toronto: James Lorrimer. This small textbook offers an integrated presentation on violence against women, children, youth, and elders within the family context.

Renzetti, C. M., and Miley, C. H. (Eds.) 1996. *Violence in gay and lesbian domestic partnerships*. New York: Harrington Park Press. Several studies and reviews of the literature form the contents of this book.

Sev'er, A. 2002. *Fleeing the house of horrors: Women who have left abusive partners*. Toronto: University of Toronto Press. This book, although presenting a sophisticated and well-balanced discussion, is easy to read. It is based on a qualitative study of a small group of battered women.

Suggested Weblinks

Canadian Council on Social Development includes a section on violence by partners of women who are immigrant and belong to visible minorities.

www.ccsd.ca

Health Canada contains a section on violence that can be found through the A to Z directory. This site also contains the **National Clearinghouse on Family Violence** and the **Child Maltreatment Division**.

www.hc-sc.gc.ca

Let's Stop Domestic Violence provides many sites of interest on the topic, both research and personal.

http://famvi.com

CHAPTER 16

Family Futures and Social Policies

The first chapter opened, at my publisher's suggestion, with an autobiographical vignette which was pursued in Chapter 13. It may be fitting that this concluding chapter begins with a personal note as a teaching device. I am concerned with the problems facing families and am critical of the lack of social policies that could prevent or alleviate these hardships. But I did not have these concerns at the beginning of my research career. How, then, did this orientation arise? The answer: It probably was the result of career "accidents"—that is, the result of what I researched. For instance, much marital dissolution is detrimental to children and adolescents. However, long ago, such a conclusion would not have occurred to me because I was (pathetically) libertarian on this subject: I had had an "easy" early divorce after a brief, childless marriage. In fact, back then, I thought that divorce was "inconsequential" and had "no intellectual interest"—a point of view I expressed to the astonished publisher who wanted me to write a book on this topic!

After a few years of his nagging, I finally relented and agreed to do a book on divorce. I began reading and then interviewed divorced parents and did some semi-participant observation. Although many families were doing well, nothing had prepared me for the problems I was encountering among the others, particularly when these families were poor. The evidence I was gathering and what I was reading went overwhelmingly against my initial beliefs and personal experience.

By then, the students' autobiographies had been going on for years and many contained unexpected challenges not well documented in the literature. All of this evidence expanded my framework well beyond the realities of my own life. Indeed, I have come to the conclusion that one's personal situation and lifestyle are not necessarily a good base upon which to ground research and draw sound sociological conclusions and related policy implications, although I am sure that there are exceptions. Looking back now, I am relieved that, early on in my career, I was not interested in doing research on topics that pertained to my life. So doing might have influenced the types of questions I would have studied. At the very least, it would have kept me away from important concerns about matters such as poverty and family structure and functions.

This concluding chapter builds on the material presented in the entire book. It opens with a return to the key themes that inform this text and that were initially outlined in the first chapter. The reader is now familiar with the contents of the book and can therefore more meaningfully integrate these themes within the overall context. The opening is followed by a section in which future trends in family life are predicted on a modest scale. Family-related policies are then suggested within the context of some of the main themes outlined, as well as some of the problems defined in previous chapters.

SALIENT THEMES REVISITED

The key sociodemographic variables of social class, gender, and race/ethnicity are part of the fabric of the various themes that recur throughout this text. These variables constitute undercurrents in many of the chapters and are the key topics of other chapters and sections.

Social Inequalities

This interweaving of salient variables is most evident with the theme of social inequalities, particularly those created by the economy (social class and poverty), ethnic and racial divides, and gender stratification. The theme of social inequalities is the cornerstone of the contextual chapters (Chapters 4 through 7). This theme informs some of the social policies discussed later.

The theme of social inequalities is important in my own sociological perspective on families and, along with other themes, it offers a framework for this text's emphasis on problems faced by families. These challenges can be at the level of economic survival, racial discrimination, or are the result of the difficulties faced by certain parents with regard to child socialization or couple dynamics. Basically, families' major problems are largely, but not exclusively, created by economic, ethnic, and gender inequalities. Gender inequalities cut across ethnic and class divides. Indeed, so long as women are chiefly responsible for the care of family members, this situation reinforces their economic dependence and their inability to earn equal incomes (Beaujot, 2000). In turn, the types of jobs to which women have access reinforce inequality at home (Duffy and Pupo, 1996). Inequalities are also created by the fact that, *as an institution,* the family suffers from its own inequality: That is, compared to other social systems (corporations, the army, and political parties, for instance), it is underfunded and deprived of resources.

Diversity of Families

The theme of family diversity resides not only at the ethnic and racial level but also at the cultural level, including religion and ideologies. Family diversity also encompasses structure and modes of formation: stepfamilies, single-mother-headed units, foster families, same-sex-parent families, and families created by adoption or with the help of reproductive technologies. The theme of family diversity is well captured by social constructionism and its links with inequalities: Not all diversity is socially acceptable and treated equally. Accepted definitions of what constitutes a family, a "normal" family, a "natural" family, often stigmatize nonnormative ones (Bartholet, 1993; Wegar, 1992).

On the basis of available research, two conclusions have been reached with respect to family diversity. First, so long as certain types of families exist and do a good job at loving and raising their children, it becomes functional for society as a whole to support them. Second, because of current socioeconomic conditions, certain types of family structures—namely, single parent and, to some extent, cohabiting structures—are less well equipped than others to invest in children's well-being and future. At this point in time, marriage is the context that is the most favourable to child development (Coley and Chase-Lansdale, 1998) and adult well-being, especially for men's (Nock, 1998c). Hence, extending the right to marriage to same-sex-parent families is in children's best interest as this right will increase family stability in general (Bell and Weinberg, 1978; Kurdek, 1998). Furthermore, we have seen that, in great part, difficulties faced by mother-headed families stem from gender inequalities arising from work and pay inequity and the gendered division of parenting responsibilities (Eichler, 1997; Luxton, 1997a).

A Surfeit of Family Functions

The third theme arose from the recurring observation that the family has not lost its functions but, rather, has acquired new ones—in great part because a lack of effective social policies is forcing family care and dependency (Beaujot, 2000, 2004). This multiplication of family functions was documented in many chapters, whether we discussed neighbourhood and school quality, peer and media influences, or the lack of adequate care provided by society to its frail seniors. Parents and adult children have to step in to provide care, assistance, guidance, coordination of services, and to exert vigilance. Accordingly, we have seen that families are burdened with responsibilities imposed by the deficits of the social structure and the poverty of the political culture. This situation in great part explains why single parents as well as poor parents (who are often the same) encounter so many roadblocks to the fulfillment of their responsibilities.

Furthermore, our documenting the burden of functions that are fulfilled by the family has led us to question what is often seen as the "decline of the family" in some circles. Certainly, the traditional family—or, rather, what people think the traditional family was—no longer exists, because the society that had given rise to it has changed radically. Rather, the new social structure based on the market economy, technology, and cutbacks to helpful policies has bestowed upon the family a new set of responsibilities or functions. Thus, too great a proportion of families are ill equipped to fulfill their functions, particularly in terms of supervising, guiding, and educating their youths. It is only in this sense that one could think of a decline of the family. This inability of nuclear families to care for their members, protect them, and maintain them within a normative life course stems from five major causes.

First, at the juncture of the microsociological and macrosociological levels of analysis is the absence of an effective community surrounding families. A second cause, at the macrosociological level of analysis, resides in the lack of social and political support that would provide more resources to parents, children, and other family members with special needs. A third cause, also systemic, refers to those countless families that are forgotten by society and relegated to segregated enclaves. The fourth source of individual families' inability to fulfill their functions is related to the previous ones: Too many families are headed by parents, often young and single, who do not have the financial, educational, and maturity resources to raise children (Coley and Chase-Lansdale, 1998). Finally, at the micro level, parents often become so burdened by their own personal dramas and the need to make a living for their fractured family that their children are not sufficiently supported, even if only for a brief but crucial period of time. Other families are too burdened with simply making ends meet. Negative consequences can be lifelong, particularly within the context of social inequalities (Cherlin et al., 1998).

The Effective Community

We have seen in many chapters that more and more research points to the necessity of having parents supported by a community that cares for its children—*all* of its children, regardless of social class, race, and parents' gender. There is convergence among researchers from several disciplines as to the necessity of *collective* forms of *socialization* (Brooks-Gunn et al., 1995; Frempong and Willms, 2002; Sampson, 1997; Steinberg et al., 1995). An effective community links parents together and prevents them from being isolated and ignorant of their children's activities. In turn, within such a context, what children learn at home is reinforced at their friends' homes or in schools. Adolescents then realize that other parents (and teachers) have expectations similar to theirs. This collectivity lends an aura of legitimacy to their parents' teachings and example. It adds credibility to the parenting effort in the children's eyes. Furthermore, within the shelter of this effective community and *informal social control,* there are fewer opportunities for nonnormative behaviours that would take adolescents off the path of prosocial development.

This description of the effective community is one that fits reality less and less, particularly in cities and their new suburbs. Thus, the past decades have seen the erosion of the community (Bellah et al., 1985; Etzioni, 1994). This is one of the reasons why too many problems experienced by families and their children are so intractable. The erosion of the effective community has occurred as a result of urbanization, individualism, dependency on expert knowledge, interest groups, and the technological market economy. All of these forces have contributed to weaken *community.*

The Cultural Context

The fifth theme informing the text was particularly evident in Chapter 3, which focused on the cultural revolution constituted by the audiovisual media (television, videos, Internet). Concerns about the advisability of exposing children to physical violence, verbal abuse, foul language, exploitative sexuality, and low-quality programming have not been taken seriously by the industries in question. The net effect is that perhaps much of the nastiness, aggressiveness, lack of compliance, and at times lack of morality that is now encountered among some children, adolescents, and even young adults may in great part originate from the media (Garbarino, 1995). Parental roles become far more difficult to fulfill within such a cultural climate—a conclusion that reinforces the previous theme of families' inability to fulfill their functions adequately and to raise their children according to their values and not those of a consumerist society (Doherty, 2000).

The theme of cultural context was also reflected in the recourse to social constructionism as an explanatory framework. It is the sociocultural context that defines what is proper behaviour and what are masculine and feminine roles. The evolving culture has constructed and reconstructed people's perceptions of the roles of children and adolescents throughout the centuries and has done so even more recently. These are only some of the most salient examples of the role of *social constructs* in family studies encountered in this book. As well, the cultural context was reflected in the chapter on education and religiosity.

Interactional and Genetic Themes

The interactional nature of family relations and the contribution of genetic inheritance to family members' development and relationships is a theme running through several chapters, particularly Chapters 11 through 15 (Ambert, 2001). Both the environment and a person's genes interact to produce personality, relationship styles, child socialization patterns, and family environment (Plomin and Rutter, 1998).

Overall, next to its macrosociological framework of contexts and inequalities arising from the social structure, the questions of how and why family members interact toward each other as they do certainly characterize much of this text. The combination of the interactional perspective with behavioural genetics complements and even corrects sociological theories that pay absolutely no attention to the fact that human beings are genetic as well as cultural entities.

Gender Stratification and Roles

The last theme, that of gender stratification and roles, was in evidence in most chapters. Thus, feminist perspectives influenced the course of these discussions. The text highlighted the extent to which females, at all age levels, are the nurturers and kin-keepers and how much more invested in various family domains they generally are, compared to males. Basic child socialization and care, as well as familial problems and interactions, affect mothers more than fathers, wives more than husbands, sisters more than brothers, and grandmothers more than grandfathers. Furthermore, social inequalities based on gender stratification mean that women are paid less than men for equivalent work; as well, women often channel themselves into part-time work and less well paid jobs (with no benefits) because of the unequal household division of labour (Crompton and Harris, 1998). This double factor contributes to keeping a large proportion of mother-headed families at or under the poverty level (Baker, 1997).

WHAT DOES THE FUTURE HOLD?

No responsible sociologist can peer into a crystal ball and predict the future of the family beyond the *next five to ten years*. The reason for this caution is that rapid change, rather than stability, is the landmark of our society. We live in a *technol-*

ogy-driven rather than a socially or morally driven world. The pace of technology is rapidly distancing humanity's ability to control it, plan for it, and adjust to it (Noble, 1995; Talbott, 1995). The family is immersed in a global economy where technology and profits are paramount and where the less educated become a surplus population (Rifkin, 1995; Schiller, 1996). Under such circumstances, there are not a great deal of rules; therefore, predictions of the distant future are impossible. A few demographic trends constitute the field's only secure source of predictions for the next decade.

Age Distribution and Fertility

As more seniors live longer and are in better health, they will constitute a larger *proportion* of the population, because their growing numbers are not accompanied by similar numbers of births at the other end of the age structure. As is the case in many other western countries with a low fertility rate, the Canadian population is aging. For instance, the 2001 census indicated that the median age has reached an all-time high of 37.6 years compared to 25.4 years in 1966. Seniors aged 65 and over accounted for 13 percent of the population, and it is projected that this segment will reach the 15 percent mark by 2011. Nova Scotia and Quebec have the oldest median ages at 38.8, and Alberta the youngest at 35 years (Statistics Canada, 2002b). Furthermore, the group that is increasing the fastest is the 80-and-over age bracket, which is expected to surpass 1.3 million by 2011. Because of longevity, families will often include more generations than in the past. The family then takes the "bean-pole" form: great-grandparents, grandparents, one or two middle-aged children, and a few great-grandchildren.

Unless governments quickly adopt policies more favourable to youths and young families (Lutz et al., 2003), one can predict that young families will continue having few children and perhaps more couples will choose to remain childless. These trends are evident in all western societies as well as in technologically advanced Asian countries such as Japan, Korea, and even China (the latter because of the one-child family policy). The Canadian fertility rate, currently standing at 1.5, could dip even lower. Or it could increase slightly if structural conditions that could reduce the costs of having children were put in place (Beaujot and Kerr, 2004)—that is, if policies for accessible and affordable child care were enacted, if the government paid a universal child credit, and corporations and other employers became more family friendly (Beaujot, 2004). A substantial change in social policies that would provide financial compensation for middle-class and low-income parents might serve as an incentive (Phipps and Burton, 1996). Under such circumstances, the interests of adults would compete less with those of children, and parents would find their situation more equitable than is currently the case, especially women (Buggarf, 1997; Matthews and Beaujot, 1997). Fertility rates also depend on stable marital unions and on the age at first marriage (Beaujot and Kerr, 2004). But it would be unrealistic to expect any upward shift that might go beyond a rate of two children per woman—even though women *desire* more children. However, even such an increase would result in large-scale, positive demographic consequences for several generations to come. Above all, it would reduce or stabilize the *proportion* of the population that is elderly.

But the aging of the population need not represent a doomsday scenario. Indeed, what concerns people is the cost of dependency. However, children are dependents to a greater extent than most seniors are: Most of the elderly live on their own and are in reasonably good health. Thus, a dependency ratio that includes both seniors and children is projected to be stable at least through 2011 (Beaujot and Kerr, 2004; Gee, 2000). This being said, however, policies will have to be devised so that the frail elderly are well taken care of and do not become the sole responsibility of families (McDaniel and Gee, 1993). Furthermore, we know that people would want more children if social and economic circumstances were more favourable. Beaujot (2004:22) suggests a world that is less centred on work and where family has priority.

Cohabitation, Marriage, and Divorce

Will cohabitation rates increase? Probably, at least in the short term, because the current trend in this direction may not have peaked yet (Turcotte, 2002). At the same time, marriage rates will dip accordingly among young adults. But over the entire life span, people will continue to marry at least once, although at a later age, and this majority will be smaller than it currently is. Factors that could halt this trend toward cohabitation are increased immigration from Muslim countries or a swing toward greater religiosity—which could also increase marriage and decrease single parenthood (Biles and Ibrahim, 2005). Better economic opportunities for the relatively unskilled might also foster marriage rather than cohabitation (Smock and Manning, 1997). This would be especially important among the less affluent segments of the population for whom marital commitment is not an option because of poverty (Goldstein and Kenney, 2001).

One also has to consider the possibility that cohabitational relationships may one day become as committed and as stable as marriages. Were this to occur, couples' and children's well-being would be equally well served in both types of unions. From a structural standpoint, cohabitations would no longer be a concern. However, they would remain a concern at the cultural level in terms of values for those who have moral/religious objections to this form of partnering; these objections are more likely to come from persons with strong religious preferences.

What about the Canadian divorce rate? Some factors would predict lower rates in the future while others may bring higher rates. In the balance, the next decade should not bring a marked decline or increase in divorce. Delaying marriage may act as a preventive measure to those divorces that are related to youthful marriages. Divorce, like marriage and cohabitation, is culturally and economically driven. Thus, the media may be influential in this respect: A predominance of individualistic and materialistic values accompanies high divorce rates. Furthermore, the presence of so many adults whose parents have themselves divorced might lead to an increase. We have also seen that marriages that are preceded by cohabitation are more likely to end in divorce (Wu, 2000). Thus, a higher level of cohabitation might actually raise the divorce rate. On the other hand, greater religiosity might decrease both cohabitation and divorce. However, there is no indication that any large-scale religious revival is close at hand even though many immigrants are more religious than Canadian-born citizens (see Bibby, 2002; Biles and Ibrahim, 2005).

As women continue to make gains on the labour market, the financial burden of divorce for men may slowly increase over time as they will stand to lose more than previous cohorts of men whose wives depended nearly entirely on them (McManus and DiPrete, 2001). Whether this trend would contribute to reducing divorce remains to be seen because there are also indications that wives' employment may be more related to divorce in current cohorts of women, and especially so among those with marriages of longer duration (South, 2001). Thus, were men to behave more equitably at home, and were the cultural assumptions about men's and women's roles changed in society at large, women would be more rewarded by and more inclined to remain in their marriage (see Pupo, 1997).

Nonmarital Family Formation

The rates of births to women who are neither cohabiting nor married have decreased recently, particularly among adolescents, both in Canada and the U.S. This decrease seems to be related to more widespread recourse to contraception and, in the U.S., to a greater level of abstinence. It could be related to a greater emphasis on higher education and to higher employment rates, which encourage couple formation before the birth of a child. The current rates of births to single women are also artificially decreased in comparison to past years by the exclusion of births to cohabiting couples which used to be listed as births to single mothers.

What is the future of nonmarital family formation? Recall here that nonmarital motherhood is generally neither in the best interest of a mother or a child, at least economically. On the other hand, nonmarital fatherhood is not immediately detrimental to individual men (Nock, 1998a). So long as this gender-role imbalance remains, women remain entirely responsible for the reduction of nonmarital fertility. This inequity makes it more complicated to alter the pattern because women's good intentions may be thwarted by men's desire for immediate gratification without consequent responsibilities. It is difficult to predict if this downward trend will persist when such other factors that encourage single motherhood are in the equation, such as more permissive sexual attitudes and media influences. Factors that could reduce the rate of births to single women include higher educational attainment, better job prospects in pockets of poverty, a change in cultural values, more adequate utilization of contraception, and male cooperation. Fertility needs to be de-gendered in terms of responsibilities.

Same-Sex Parenting

Same-sex parenting may actually become somewhat less frequent as the number of lesbians and gays who procreated in the past within heterosexual unions will decrease (Stacey and Biblarz, 2001). Unless same-sex parents are highly self-selected among the very committed, which is a possibility that has not been studied, same-sex "divorces" will become more frequent and so will same-sex stepparenting. However, these trends are self-limiting because homosexuality is a minority demographic phenomenon (Hewitt, 1998). It is furthermore constrained by the fact that it is difficult for homosexual couples to reproduce children. Hence, even with more liberal adoption laws, these families will still remain a minority phenomenon. They will, however, be more visible and better accepted socially because they do not present a threat to the social order.

Interracial Unions

Interracial unions have steadily increased and this trend is expected to continue, especially as visible-minority-group immigrants, particularly Chinese, become second- and third-generation Canadians. Interracial marriages with one black partner account for nearly half of all unions that include a black person. Any increase in interracial unions is structurally functional only to the extent that both sexes of a same race marry out equally. Currently, black men marry out more than black women; this demographic imbalance limits black women's marital options (Milan and Tran, 2004). Furthermore, it devalues them, because it often leads black males to judge black women unfavourably compared to white or Asian ones.

Domestic Division of Labour

It is difficult to predict what the future holds in terms of the domestic division of labour and child care. Women will continue to be needed on the labour market and, as their salaries are raised to meet equity requirements, they will contribute a greater share of the household income. This will be accompanied by either the current situation of inequality or an increase in husbands' participation in housework and child care. Furthermore, the fact that fathers are currently more involved in housework than those of the past could lead to higher rates of participation among their sons later on (Cunningham, 2001). However, new immigrants originating from patriarchal societies may slow down this process until their children are assimilated at that level. Overall, fathers will become more involved with their children when there is a more substantial shift in *their* gender role ideology (Bulanda, 2004). Such a shift could be fostered by social policies that take some of the burden of child care out of families and facilitate women's employment on a basis equal to that of men (Skrypnek and Fast, 1996).

Parenting

Aside from the issue of the gendered role of parenting, which is addressed throughout this chapter, there are several other problems facing parents. We have seen that in English-speaking western countries, childrearing has become professionalized to help children learn traits that are valued in our type of society. These traits include individualism, self-esteem, self-sufficiency, and independence. At the same time, children's lives have become more structured in terms of extracurricular activities and less spontaneous. Parents are encouraged to use an authoritative style, and many parents, afraid of assuming their role, extend this pattern into either a permissive or a "negotiating/wavering" style. These trends are pronounced mainly at the middle-class and upper-class levels which are the social strata that are the most successfully embedded in the economic system of production and consumerism. Working-class and disadvantaged parents, in general, hold somewhat different values of obedience and familism (the degree to which different groups think family is important), as do many immigrants; are more group oriented; and use childrearing practices that fit within the exigencies of their more constrained lifestyles. Sociologist Annette Lareau (2003) calls this the "accomplishment of natural growth" in contrast to the "process of concerted cultivation" enacted by middle-class parents.

However, as middle-class parents, especially mothers, become more stressed by the regimentation of their children's lives, many yearn to return to a situation whereby their children can enjoy, along with them, more free time and especially more family time. As well, as our economy is polluting and depleting the environment of its non-renewable resources in order to meet a spiralling series of consumer "needs," countermovements of minimalist living and environmental protection are emerging. These movements, along with the limitations of our planet, will eventually have to put a break on consumerism and change children's "needs." Furthermore, when one sees the recent trends toward violence and unbridled sexuality in the media, all of which are totally self-centred, one can well wonder whether a backlash may not occur among parents and whether a movement toward a more simple life oriented around the group rather than the individual may not emerge. Thus, at this point, the parent-child relationship and, especially, child socialization and the organization of children's lives may be nearing a turning point: Changes may be needed if adults are going to desire to have any children at all—or be able to raise the ones they have so that a humane rather than robotic society emerges.

The Longer Time Frame

The possible trends just presented pertain to a future that is nearly here. Surely within a longer time frame, perhaps 20 years, more momentous changes in family life and structure may take place. Consider the domains of the division of labour at home (more egalitarian?); children's increased or decreased familialization; reproductive modes and technologies (in vitro wombs? cloning?); and families' growing dependency on or rejection of technology (virtual sex? robotic companions?). Most of the changes that will occur in families in general will be largely dictated by technoeconomic forces—that is, the combination of technological developments with the structure of the economy.

However, a point may be reached whereby unplanned technology so saturates life and degrades its humaneness that other societal forces might reassert themselves, including social planning, humanitarian philosophies, religion, morality, and community rather than economic values. What one must not forget is that technology and the market economy are ideologies; in theory, such ideologies could be rejected as *determinants* of people's lives. Rather, people could more judiciously choose technologies that can enhance rather than ruin the environment and family life. This is a choice that humanity will have to make at some point if it is to remain humane. Therefore, social policies may become more relevant to fostering a healthier and more egalitarian family life.

SOCIAL POLICIES PERTAINING TO FAMILIES

The reader will note that this section is not entitled "Family Policies" because Canada (as well as the U.S. and Great Britain) really does not have a coherent and purposive set of family policies (Beaujot, 2000). In fact, there is no equivalent to a Ministry of the Family, except in Quebec, which is the province that is also the most advanced in this domain. Rather, what we have in Canada are social policies that directly or indirectly affect families. Policies in general and family policies in particular are social choices (Zimmerman, 1995). Such choices are heavily influenced by the ideologies and the values espoused by a political system at a given time (Blank and Blum, 1997). For instance, there are generally vast differences in the policies enacted by a Conservative-versus a Liberal-controlled Parliament (or a NDP one) both at the federal and the provincial levels. There are also vast differences between various western countries because of their ideologies as well as their historical backgrounds (Gauthier, 1996). In Canada, as mentioned, there are differences between Quebec and other provinces.

Furthermore, some consequences of planned policies are unintended. For instance, mothers who are dropped from the welfare rolls because of time limitations may not find jobs and may not have enough to eat because their salaries are too low. Furthermore, policies aimed at other aspects of social organization or of any of its systems, such as the justice system, can have indirect and unintended consequences for the family. One instance from the U.S. is the incarceration of small-time drug traffickers, which has had devastating results for black families in inner cities. It has led to a severe reduction in the number of young black males available to support their families: Over 25 percent of young black males have a criminal record, which limits their access to jobs, and many are incarcerated (Tonry, 1995). As a further consequence, a great number of young, American black mothers have been left single and without support (Blank, 1997).

A true family policy would cover several domains of family life in an interrelated rather than piecemeal fashion and would be proactive or intended. The welfare state is a recent phenomenon historically and, in Canada, despite several amendments to the *British North America Act* of 1867, family policies are divided between the federal and the provincial governments (Baker, 1995). In previous centuries, hard work, families, and religious institutions were considered the sources of prevention of problems, and the remedy once problems occurred. Thus, it is only in the early 20th century that some federal and provincial initiatives arose to help injured and older workers, the needy, and especially disadvantaged mothers (Eichler, 1988).

Focus of "Family Policies"

Overall, social policies that can be termed "family policies" largely focus on five areas of family life.

1. **Family creation:** An example is the bonus for families that the Quebec government initiated at the birth of each child, with a larger amount for subsequent children, in order to raise the fertility rate. The bonus was more recently replaced by a different system. Laws pertaining to adoption would also fall in this category (Baker, 1995).

2. **Family reunification or reconstitution:** Examples are the emphasis in the *Immigration Act* on reuniting immigrants with their immediate families and the emphasis of children's aid societies on returning children who have been abused or severely neglected to their original families.

3. **Childrearing and care:** The creation of daycare centres and the legislation of parental leave would fall in this category. Partly paid parental leave is a Canadian social policy that is very useful to parents before and after the birth of a child and may prevent poverty in some families. The *Unemployment Insurance Act* of 1940 was amended in 1971 to allow mothers up to 15 weeks of maternal leave, with a proportion of their salaries paid. In 1990, another 10 weeks of leave were added for either parent and, in December 2000, this parental leave was increased to 35 weeks (Marshall, 2003). Currently, mothers can take from six months to a year off. Furthermore, parents must have worked 600 hours rather than the previous 700 in order to qualify—an advantage for parents who work seasonally. However, mothers who are unemployed, are self-employed, or work too few hours cannot receive these benefits. They constitute 39 percent of all mothers, down from 46 percent in 2000 (Marshall, 2003). Mitchell (2003:16) also found that women with salaries below $20,000 tended to return to work more rapidly than others—probably because their maternal benefits are too low to sustain their family.

   Between 2000 and 2001, the median maternity leave increased from six to 10 months. The proportion of fathers who also took some parental leave jumped from about three percent in 2000 to 10 percent in 2001. This makes Canada comparable to Holland and Denmark but lower than Sweden (where 36 percent of fathers take some parental leave) and especially Norway where 78 percent of fathers take parental leave. In Norway, fathers' leave is independent of that of mothers and, therefore, does not reduce the mothers' own time off. For very small children, subsidized parental leave may be a more appropriate social policy in large cities than subsidized child care centres (Maccoby and Lewis, 2003). However, if parental leave is taken only by mothers, the gendered division of child care remains and women may have less access to promotions and salary increases (Beaujot, 2000).

4. **Caregiving for the frail and elderly:** Governments in the recent past undertook steps toward strong contributions in this domain. However, budget cuts are resulting in increased reliance on family members (Connidis, 2001:253). The provision of free time to attend to the care of the elderly and the sick, as well as the availability of services such as visiting homemakers, also falls in this category, as does the maintenance of subsidized seniors' homes.

5. **Economic support** includes such initiatives as the Child Tax Benefit and Old Age Security, as well as the Canada Pension Plan. For instance, for 67 percent of senior families, government transfers constitute their principal source of income (Williams, 2003). Without this income, a high proportion of seniors, particularly single women, would be poor.

Inertia of Political Systems

On the whole, it is safe to advance that our political system makes it very difficult to adopt preventive policies (Baker, 1995). Such policies require a great deal of planning and a certain level of consensus on the definition of the family, what family policy means, and what the goals are (Bogenschneider, 2000). Political will to invest in the

Government budget cuts will more and more require that the entire care of frail seniors be subsidized by families, thus extending family functions throughout the generations. Adult grandchildren become particularly helpful in this intergenerational chain and contribute to the senior generation's well-being and happiness.

future is also a prerequisite. The future needs of families clash with the current political reality of getting votes (Bogenschneider et al., 2000:328). Political expediency forces the adoption of stop-gap policies to solve a few problems that are identified by public opinion polls. But even remedial policies can take a very long time to produce a visible effect that can be assessed and appreciated by the public. In contrast, politicians need immediate or foreseeable results if their party is to remain in power. Thus, politics conducted on the basis of media appeal and ability to raise huge sums of money from lobby groups to fund campaigns do not favour constructive family policies. Finally, it should be emphasized that social policies pertaining to families should be the object of evaluation or research to ascertain the extent to which the explicit goals have been reached and to seek unintended (negative or positive) consequences.

One should point out that human nature is flawed and even the best family policies cannot eliminate all problems for families and for individuals. Our scientifically minded century often leads us to believe that there is a solution for all problems. This is an overly idealistic notion. Thus, while alleviating poverty is a must, it cannot solve all problems. Other structural and cultural factors have to be considered along with individual variables that include negative genetic predispositions that have yet to be mapped. Society needs more adequate social policies to offer a protective structure for individuals who are challenged at the psychological level. Indeed, countries such as

Sweden and Norway could serve as models for Canada, as they have to some extent for Quebec. But even these countries' policies have not, for instance, achieved full parenting equality between men and women nor equity on the labour market.

REDUCING POVERTY

We have seen throughout the text that social inequalities brought by poverty are the root cause of a multiplicity of social problems, family misery, and individual deficits. Poverty prevents and destabilizes marriage and increases the divorce rate. It creates social isolation, delinquency, behavioural problems, school dropouts, and teenage motherhood, and it encourages drug abuse and trafficking. These are only a few of the costly human results of poverty—overall, it makes families vulnerable. Mothers and their small children, as well as elderly women living alone, are particularly affected. Although the Canada Pension Plan narrows the gap in terms of income among the elderly (Prus, 2002), pension plans do not take into consideration the fact that women enter and exit the labour force during their employment years, a factor that contributes to their later inequality (McDonald, 2000).

This gendered situation holds across all cultures, except perhaps Sweden and the Netherlands, and has given rise to the concept of the *feminization of poverty*. Nevertheless, even in Sweden, poverty is transmitted from generation to generation when families have single mothers and/or criminal fathers (Stenberg, 2000). France also has a higher poverty rate among mother-headed families, despite more aggressive *prestations sociales* (Dell et al., 2003).

A Critique of Current Policies

Policies aimed at truly preventing and reducing poverty rather than simply displacing it (to jails, for instance) or shifting it to private agencies and food banks or discriminating against single mothers would benefit the entire society (Baker and Tippin, 1999; Lindsey and Martin, 2003). Pong et al. (2003) have shown that the academic achievement gap between children from one- and two-parent families narrowed in those countries that have policies aimed at equalizing economic resources between families. For example, families should receive higher rather than lower welfare payments until they are able to be self-sufficient (Gennetian and Morris, 2003). Welfare should be socially constructed as a form of salary given to families that have been marginalized by the economy or discrimination. It is an investment in the nation's youths and education (Sherman, 1994). Sufficient assistance could lift children and their parents out of poverty and give them better life chances (Hannon, 1997).

Adequate welfare payments that raise families above the poverty level can prevent the transmission of poverty, rather than perpetuating it, by enhancing children's cognitive development, which later contributes to their economic success (Duncan and Brooks-Gunn, 1997). In turn, this situation could lower the rates of unmarried motherhood for, as we have seen, this is largely a poverty-related phenomenon (Orton, 1999). As well, adequate welfare support may actually be correlated with lower homicide rates

(DeFronzo, 1997). Such programs are preferable to investing in prisons (Davey, 1995), which are merely a temporary or stop-gap remedy.

Low wages also create poverty, and many families living on such wages hold two or three jobs to make ends meet. For instance, in 2003, minimum wages ranged from $5.90 an hour in Alberta to $8.00 in British Columbia (Statistics Canada, 2004g). There is a great deal of political and business-community resistance to raising wages to acceptable levels because this would reduce corporations' profits and affect small employers. This returns us to Chapter 5 where we saw that the ease with which companies relocate their plants and services abroad, where wages are very low, is probably one of the main factors that prevent the provincial governments from raising wages. Under these circumstances, raising the minimum wage might result in layoffs and thus create poverty.

However, governments could make up the difference by topping low wages so that they reach a minimum that is sufficient—according to the cost of living in different areas. In other words, **wage supplements** might allow families a release from overtime or three jobs that prevent some couples from spending enough time together and others from having another child. Such a program has been shown to bring behavioural and school-related benefits to children (Gennetian and Miller, 2002). Society should provide a **guaranteed minimum income** to all men and women who are employed, including those who work part-time, and extend it to men and women who remain home to care for children or frail family members. Furthermore, a universal child tax benefit would help reduce child poverty and women's dependence.

One component of poverty is the lack of affordable housing, especially in Toronto and Vancouver, which are the two metropolitan areas where poverty has increased in the 1990s (Statistics Canada, 2004h). Governments promise to build more social or affordable housing, yet we have seen in Chapter 6 that neighbourhoods that have high proportions of low-income families are related to more problematic family dynamics and child outcomes. For instance, Kohen et al. (2002a) have found that disadvantaged children benefit from living in a neighbourhood that has a greater proportion of economically secure residents. Social housing tends to increase an area's already existing poverty.

Thus, one suggestion is that poor families receive subsidies that would allow them to find lodgings in a range of neighbourhoods. This could be accompanied by subsidies that would offer a proportion of low-income families the opportunity to buy a housing unit in any neighbourhood of their choice. Individual development accounts would assist families by providing them with monthly supplements to pay their mortgage and/or a downpayment (Boyle, 2002). These policies would have the double advantage of mixing social classes and empowering the poor via home ownership. Furthermore, governmental costs for building, managing, and maintaining public housing would no longer be necessary. Green and White (1997) suggest that the demands of home ownership force people to acquire new management skills related to property maintenance, financial planning, and interpersonal functioning that, in turn, may be transferred to more successful parenting practices. Indeed, there are indications that children whose parents are homeowners benefit in terms of behaviours and that these parents become more hopeful and future oriented (Boyle, 2002).

Expansion of Child Care Programs

The availability of inexpensive and quality child care for the entire population is a step required in order to lower the burdens of parenting in an economy that necessitates two salaries. It is also needed to redress the gender imbalance against women in the domain of child care. Furthermore, universal child care would be particularly important in the prevention of poverty and as a remedy when it occurs. Since the 1990s, the federal commitment to universal child care has dwindled along with reduced funding (Friendly, 2000).

As a first step, child care should be available to all low-income families, especially the youngest children, because early poverty is the most detrimental over time both for child, family, and society (Caspi et al., 1998; Duncan et al., 1998; McLoyd, 1998). This step has already been widely suggested (Zigler and Styfco, 1996), and it consists of providing care of the Head Start type to *all* children aged one to five in poor and near-poor families, *all day long* (Rushowy, 2004). (More intensive programs are more effective than half-day ones; see St. Pierre and Layzer, 1998.)

Two immediate results would follow. First, we know from Chapter 7 that children in such programs develop more human resources, both behaviourally and cognitively, that prepare them for school (Barnes et al., 1996; Barnett, 1995). Second, since child care constitutes mothers' main roadblock to self-sufficiency, this program would make it easier for mothers to find and retain jobs. For mothers on welfare, pursuing some postsecondary training would be an excellent investment (Gleason et al., 1998), which current welfare policies do not necessarily encourage, but which extended child care programs could make feasible.

The results of Head Start programs in the U.S. vary depending on their duration (Reynolds and Temple, 1998). One of the reasons why Head Start children soon lose the gains they have made after they enter school is that their one-year stay in the program is too brief or limited to overcome the cognitive and behavioural deficits created by poverty. Furthermore, upon arriving in Grade 1, these children are deprived of any support that would perpetuate whatever gains they have already made.

After-School Care and Improved Schooling

To extend the benefits of early childhood education, a second phase of the program would provide after-school care and tutoring through junior high school. This would, at the same time, provide children with much needed supervision and reduce opportunities for delinquency that too frequently occur from 3 p.m. to 6 p.m. (i.e., between the end of the school day and a parent's return home from work). Extended after-school hours already exist in Quebec.

As well, the quality of schools should be improved in areas of poverty. Such a policy might be initiated in primary school, and when the "improved" cohort of children moves on, then the program would be extended throughout high school. Each high school at risk should include incentive programs, at least on a trial basis, as exist in some American states (Mauldon, 1998:56). For instance, adolescents from low-income families could be given a "salary" to remain in school in good standing (no truancy, no disruptive conduct, and all homework done). As well, students who achieve an A or B+ could be guaranteed scholarships for higher education. Such incentives might have the unanticipated result of creating a school and peer culture that values rather than denigrates education. If this were to happen, material incentives would no longer be needed in the next cohort of children.

Consequences and Limitations of Programs

Each one of the preceding policies in isolation is insufficient to lift a sizable number of children out of poverty (St. Pierre and Layzer, 1998). It is the total configuration that counts. The financial costs of such multipronged, proactive, preventative policies may appear high initially, but their long-term results would make them cost effective. To begin with, welfare outlays would rapidly diminish as parents who are better educated are able to secure and maintain jobs. At that point, guaranteed income supplements would need to be added. Since low income brings poor health, health costs would certainly be reduced after a while (Blank, 1997:164), and so would costs stemming from child abuse and foster care (Pelton, 1997). Over $40,000 a year is needed to maintain a young person in a correctional institution (Greenwood, 1995). Thus, within a few years, the costs incurred for law enforcement and penal institutions would fall along with delinquency and particularly drug trafficking (Tonry, 1995).

Furthermore, an unintended consequence of Head Start extension and school reform in disadvantaged areas might be a further reduction in the rate of family formation by young mothers. This could result from a greater interest of children in school achievement and extracurricular activities generated by school quality and financial incentives toward postsecondary education. As children mature into adolescents and are supported by appropriate structures since age one, their enhanced educational capital would lead to jobs. College and university fees should be lower to prevent heavy debt load early on in a youth's work career. In turn, we already know that increased income constitutes an incentive to marriage before procreation and that two-parent families are less likely to become poor (Blank, 1997).

Unfortunately, not all poverty can be eradicated. Some individuals are not sufficiently gifted by nature and need to be supported because they are in no way responsible for their deficits of human capital. Furthermore, the ideology that has contributed to the initial creation of poverty would still survive (Baker, 1995). Indeed, poverty is created, as we have seen in Chapter 5, by global socioeconomic forces that include "smart" technology requiring higher educational credentials. It is also created by corporations that are guided by an ever-increasing profit motive for shareholders, largely disregarding human costs. Some corporations even register in countries that are tax havens so as to avoid paying taxes through which wealth can be redistributed. They are part of the problem (see Frantz, 1999, for example). Government debts siphon off monies that could be used to help young families (OECD, 2000). The combined ideologies of racism and sexism also contribute to poverty (Roschelle, 1999)—poverty of minority women who cannot find employed males to help support their children. In turn, all women—single and married alike—are disadvantaged on the labour market and in terms of wages.

ENCOURAGING AND STRENGTHENING MARRIAGE: ECONOMIC FACTORS REVISITED

Another priority of family policies should reside in the encouragement of marriage as an institution and the promotion of *happy* marital relationships (Emery, 1999). Three caveats exist, however. First, I am not suggesting that divorce be made less accessible: Whether one likes it or not, divorce is necessary. Second, neither am I suggesting that marriage is necessary to all adults. And third, as pointed out at the end of Chapter 9, a time may come when women (and men for that matter) will not have to depend on marriage or cohabitation in order to have a family that is beneficial to themselves and to their children. However, the fact of the matter is that the research reviewed in this text clearly indicates that this time has not arrived yet. Currently, cohabiting partners and their children as well as never-married mothers and their children are family forms that are more related to poverty and problematic child outcomes than are married families (Coley and Chase-Lansdale, 1998). These two forms of family are currently neither in the best interest of the child or the mother (Cooksey et al., 1997; Waite and Gallagher, 2000); nor do they promote responsible fatherhood (Nock, 1998a). Thus, by encouraging marriage, paternal involvement is also strengthened, and research indicates that the latter benefits children (Harris et al., 1998). In a nutshell, marriage fosters parental involvement in children, particularly when the marital relationship is positive (McBride and Rane, 1998). By encouraging the formation of *happy* marital units and strengthening existing ones, the family would be in a better position to fulfill its traditional functions as well as the new ones it has been invested with by current technoeconomic changes.

The topic of the *formation* of marital units relates to the previous section on poverty and to Chapter 5, where we have seen that poverty, including male unemployment and low wages, prevents marriage. For instance, better-off cohabitants are more likely to marry when or before they have children (Manning and Smock, 1995). Poverty deprives males of their potential ability to support children or even to contribute to the economic functioning of a couple living on its own. As a consequence, low-income or unemployed males are not ideal marriage prospects in young women's minds—neither are these men inclined to shoulder family responsibilities. Within the current *cultural climate of tolerance* (Pagnini and Rindfuss, 1993), women have no option except to have children in temporary cohabitations or on their own. As an additional result, the likelihood of these women ever marrying is reduced (Bennett et al., 1995). Hence, a great proportion of these children are deprived of paternal investment for life; furthermore, appropriate maternal socialization practices are more difficult to sustain under circumstances that involve poverty (Driscoll et al., 1999). Reducing unemployment and subsidizing low wages would contribute to the formation of marital units among all ethnic groups in society. Thus, the policies described earlier aimed at reducing poverty would have the secondary advantage of encouraging the formation of marital units or, at the very least, of mother-headed families that have adequate resources.

Furthermore, inasmuch as economic uncertainty creates or exacerbates marital conflict (Chapters 11 and 15), the alleviation of poverty would contribute to the *strengthening* of the conjugal bond once it is formed. As we have seen in Chapter 9, happy, stable marriages are functional for adults, children, and society. Were marital happiness promoted via cultural and antipoverty measures, divorce rates might possibly decrease as a result. More children would be spared the negative effect of parental conflict, divorce, and subsequent poverty. This is not to say, however, that divorce would disappear, because it exists at all social class levels. But it is particularly detrimental for poor families and it is a source of poverty in itself (Smock, 1994).

It should also be reemphasized here that **proper gender-role socialization** that would define boys as equally nurturing as girls, and fathers as equally responsible as mothers, would substantially reduce the gap in paternal investment that currently exists between married and unmarried fathers. Basically, it is the faulty socialization of boys that leads to their later disinvestment as fathers (Garbarino, 1999). Were the father-child bond accorded the same importance as the mother-child bond, then a father's relationship with his children would remain, even after his relationship with the mother has ended (Silverstein and Auerbach, 1999). In other words, the problematic aspects of nonmarital motherhood are largely created by paternal failures and the social construction of fatherhood.

PLANNING FOR DIVORCE

About two-thirds of divorces occur to low-conflict couples (Amato and Booth, 1997) and a number of couples divorce for what others would consider benign reasons and simply as a result of lower investment in their marriage (Amato and Rogers, 1999). These couples are generally good parents when married. *Any* decrease in the rate of such divorces involving children would be very effective, for these homes are not usually conflictual and are in the best interest of the child and the adults as well. When a divorce occurs in such families, children stand to lose a great deal on all fronts. In contrast, children whose parents are locked in constant conflict can benefit from the divorce (Booth, 1999).

Step 1: Before Marriage

Patterns of marital interaction and satisfaction are often set early on in marriage (Johnson and Booth, 1998); consequently, the best medicine against divorce might well begin *before* marriage. All couples applying for a marriage licence should receive a mandatory preparation course covering financial and family planning, marital communication, health, and basics of child development. This is not a new idea, but one that is frequently discussed. The Catholic Church, for instance, has had such courses for decades in most dioceses, although the form they take differs widely. The program herein suggested might consist of four to six classes or workshops of a two- or three-hour duration, available in *all* neighbourhoods, free of charge, with flexible hours, and might include child care where relevant and even transportation for those who live too far. Furthermore, these workshops would be culturally sensitive. One might consider providing a per-hour fee to help the disadvantaged who attend.

It is difficult to predict whether couples at risk would choose not to marry and would cohabit to avoid taking the course. But these couples might, at any rate, be the least likely to benefit from such a program. The reader may well say, But how do we know if such a policy would work? At this point, we backtrack to the list of research methods in Table 1.3 (page 24). One category of methods fell under the rubric of **evaluation research.** The purpose of such research is to evaluate the effectiveness of policies and programs. Sound sociology research principles would dictate that such programs begin randomly. That is, every other couple applying for a marriage licence would be enrolled in the program. This would constitute an experimental group. The other couples who are not enrolled could then serve as the control or comparison group. (In effect, this would become a natural experiment, Table 1.3, page 24.) To evaluate the effectiveness of the program, a random sample of couples from both groups would be interviewed three to five years after the marriage licence has been granted.

If the explicit goal of the program is to reduce divorce, then an effective program should show a lower rate of separation and divorce in the experimental group compared to the control group. Another indicator of effectiveness might be fewer children involved in the divorces of the couples who are in the experimental group. This would mean that the couples who were headed for an early divorce had at least learned to postpone having children. The program could have other worthwhile consequences such as raising the overall level of marital happiness in the experimental group. The quality of the marriages that have not dissolved would be examined.

Thus, a successful program would not only reduce divorce but would also increase the quality of remaining marriages. Once a policy is judged successful with the help of evaluation methods, then it can be extended to the entire population. In contrast, a program that shows no difference between the experimental and control groups has to be revamped and reevaluated. In such cases, researchers also have to look for larger sociocultural variables that were not controlled for (such as media influences) and that might have prevented the program from being successful.

Step 2: When Divorce Occurs

As a second part of divorce policy, parents who apply for a divorce should provide the judge with a plan for the care and education of their offspring—in more detail than what is currently done. If they are unable to arrive at an agreement, they would then be required to take a course to become more aware of the effects of divorce on children. The goal is to improve children's quality of life after divorce and lower their risks in terms of negative outcomes (Bartlett, 1999). Another goal is to encourage paternal involvement after divorce beyond merely being "Sunday daddies" so that fathers become more than friends and entertainers (Simons et al., 1996:16). Such a plan might force soon-to-be ex-spouses to coparent or at least set their differences aside for their children's well-being.

Such a policy would also need to be evaluated, but this could be done after a year or even six months, and also include randomized trials with experimental and control groups to compare the two sets of divorced families. Although such a policy, and the premarital policy suggested earlier, might not prove all that successful at the beginning, a structure for improvement would have been created (Zimmerman, 1995). First, a structure would be in place for procedures, trained personnel, and budget, whereas no such structure currently exists. Second, procedures could be improved because the study results would pinpoint areas of deficiencies and failures. In contrast, as things currently stand, nothing can be improved because no structure is in place. Furthermore, no evaluative or outcome research is available from those jurisdictions where related programs have been implemented, such as in Quebec where mediation is mandatory for all families with children. It would also be important to learn if mediation increases support payments for children; so far, research indicates a 73-percent compliance when parents have reached a private agreement (Mandell, 2002).

SUPPORTING THE PARENTAL ROLE

Most "family" functions are actually fulfilled by parents, especially females. The parenting role itself has numerous constitutive elements, not to mention the additional roles occupied by most parents outside the home. Parents are still believed to be the main agents of socialization, even when other agents, such as peers and the media, often have a greater influence on children, particularly during adolescence and in certain neighbourhoods. However, despite this belief in parents' importance, society does not generally support them, although blame is often lavished upon them (Lefley, 1997). Indeed, Canadian parents of young children do not feel supported in their role, and only 42 percent agree that "Canada values its young children" (Invest in Kids, 2002). Hence, it is necessary that parents regain an effective moral authority (Doherty, 2000). This is not synonymous with antiquated notions of property over children—behaving as if children were "owned" by their parents.

Based on these data and those presented in several chapters, I suggest that parents should be respected and supported by schools, professionals, welfare agencies, and law enforcement personnel (see also Adams et al., 2002). In other words, the parental role should be more adequately **institutionalized** and more positively reconstructed socially. Invest in Kids (2002) also found that parents were not confident in their role and often lacked knowledge, that many were distressed and too many utilized ineffective parenting practices. Chao and Willms (2002) noted that only about a third of parents are authoritative. All parents should receive training.

But also recall that interactional theories view children as coproducers in their development (Corsaro, 1997). Within this perspective, it is suggested that professionals help youngsters **cooperate** in their upbringing rather than evade their responsibilities (Brody et al., 2004). If children were encouraged from all quarters, including the media, to value their parents' moral authority, the family would become a more effective institution, whatever its structure and size (Ambert, 2001). Within such a context, children would more easily accept and internalize norms of behaviour and would be more inclined to cooperate in their upbringing (Ambert, 1997). This means that parental investment and monitoring would be facilitated, with the result that behavioural problems, drug and alcohol use, as well as delinquency would diminish substantially.

Faced with often contradictory how-to advice, constrained by a variety of professionals whose blame they fear, and muzzled by media and peer influences, many parents become indecisive, unsure of themselves, and unable to make maturity demands on their offspring (Damon, 1995). They no longer dare try to pass on their values to their children, give them guidance, or punish them for transgressions. Others are disempowered by poverty (Sampson and Laub, 1994). Still others, particularly nonresidential fathers, are disaffected because of their familial context (Doherty et al., 1998). Many adults find it easier to disengage from the parental role and to reduce it to one of being their child's friend (Adams et al., 2002). This role configuration may work well with adolescents who are self-controlled, have an easy temperament, or are achievement oriented, and especially with those who benefit from a prosocial peer group. But adolescents who are blessed with all these advantages are in the minority, so that egalitarian parenting, which is akin to the permissive style discussed in Chapter 12, is often disastrous (Baumrind, 1991a; Bronfenbrenner, 1985; Noller and Callan, 1991). Finally, fewer households than before have children, so that the parents' vote is less substantial than in the past, thus preventing parents from playing a larger political role on their own behalf and that of their children (Rankin, 2001).

One should not, however, interpret this discussion to imply tolerance for child abuse and neglect on the part of parents. Nor is this a sanctification of parents as *individuals;* rather, it is a call for the reinstitutionalization of parenting in general. It would be unrealistic to disregard the fact that many adults today are less than ideal parents in terms of the values they pass on to their children, the examples they set, as well as the behaviours they allow. For instance, parents who are excessively oriented toward material gain and acquisition have little time for their children and encourage materialism. In the long run, materialism is destructive of human values based on altruism,

Family research is contingent on the structural and cultural situation of a society at a given point in time. For instance, the effects of poverty on children differ, depending on the era in which it occurs.

the natural environment, and the enjoyment of simple and more direct pleasures of life. A second type of less than ideal parent is those who, either by their example or simply because of permissive attitudes, allow or encourage their children to engage in risky sex, to use drugs (including alcohol), to steal, behave aggressively, or, for boys, act exploitatively toward girls.

The types of adults just discussed may well constitute 10 to 20 percent of the parent population in certain areas. Policies aimed at supporting the parental role do not address all these parents. However, these policies would help conscientious parents and those who want to be. The ranks of the "less than ideal" parents would, in the long run, thin down as a result of the pressure of the effective community that would arise with the **empowerment of conscientious parents**—who constitute the majority (see, also, Steinberg, 2001).

CONCLUSIONS: THE FAMILY IN CONTEXT

The family represents an experience lived by all people, making each individual an "expert" on the topic. But as we have seen, this personal expertise is insufficient, for family life has many faces, speaks many languages, harbours a multitude of cultures, and involves different cohorts and dynamics. It entails great happiness and cradles painful dramas. It appears so simple but in its totality it is so very complex.

Family Research and Historical Context

The chapters in this book have highlighted many areas of family life and its relationship with the other social systems that have yet to be researched. Thus, despite the giant steps made by various disciplines in the advancement of knowledge on the family, much is still unknown. History also compounds this problem; knowledge that is applicable today may no longer be valid 10 to 20 years from now. This is due to the fact that, as the sociocultural context in which families are embedded changes, so does the family. Therefore, many topics of research will need to be revisited as the decades of the 21st century unfold, so that people do not draw conclusions and then implement policies based on results that are obsolete.

Some of the areas that may see change in research results in the near future are the statistical relationships between cohabitation and higher divorce rates. If cohabitants were to become more similar to married couples, then it is possible that premarital cohabitation would cease to be related to higher divorce rates. Similarly, if single parents, who are most often mothers, were to receive more adequate social and economic support, their children's well-being might become comparable to that of children in stable two-parent families. On another level, if the media that are accessible to children were regulated in terms of antisocial and materialistic contents, aggressiveness and consumerism might be reduced among children and adolescents. Thus, the results of current studies would no longer apply.

Family Functions and Their Environmental Context

The research summarized and evaluated in this book does not support the pessimistic view of a general family decline and loss of functions. Rather, the research supports pessimism concerning *individual families' ability* to fulfill their ever-increasing functions adequately, particularly that of the socialization of children. On the one hand, the family as an institution is highly valued, and exacting demands are placed on it in terms of its responsibilities in many domains. On the other hand, this same sociocultural context generally fails to provide individual families with equivalent moral support and practical help that could allow them to fulfill their functions.

For instance, society is choosing to embrace market capitalism and technology as a value and as a way of life (Allahar and Côté, 1998). Unavoidably, there are high costs to such a choice, and families bear a disproportionate burden in this respect, especially those that are marginalized by poverty and lack of access to the new types of jobs (Phillips and Phillips, 2000). As Blank (1997:198) phrases it, when a society "has chosen a market-oriented economy, it has a responsibility to those who cannot survive in the market on their own." This responsibility should not be displaced onto families. Unfortunately, this is exactly what is happening.

Above all, in western societies, the family is a small and relatively isolated unit that is much affected by its environment. In recent decades, this cultural and socioeconomic environment has broadened considerably because of globalization and a more pervasive as well as intrusive technology. At the dawn of this new millennium, families are experiencing change at a rapid pace and are contextualized in a larger world, but receive relatively fewer resources in terms of instrumental and effective moral support. Empowering families, no matter their structure, is one of the key social challenges of the 21st century.

Summary

1. The three key sociodemographic variables of social class, gender, and race are part of the fabric of the various themes that have recurred throughout this text. These themes are social inequalities, family diversity, the increase in family functions, the importance of the functional community, cultural influences, interactional and genetic themes, and gender roles.

2. Trends in the very near future of family life include more surviving generations, continuing low fertility, and consequent skewed age distribution toward the elderly; a temporary increase in cohabitation; the maintenance of the current divorce rate; a slightly reduced rate of family formation by single mothers; a small increase in the number of same-sex-parent families as well as interracial unions; the maintenance of the current household division of labour; and questions concerning the parental role.

3. Areas of family life addressed by policies are presented, and a critique of the political system is offered, including critiques of policies concerning poverty. Suggestions for the reduction of poverty are presented; expansion of daycare and after-school programs is suggested. The encouragement and strengthening of marriage through economic and cultural means is then

discussed. Another program involves planning for divorce both in terms of making marriage a more serious step and in terms of educating couples, as well as requiring divorcing parents to plan for the care of their offspring. A fourth suggestion consists of better support for the parental role, including a valorization and respect of parents.

4. Many areas of family life are lacking in research; other domains would benefit by being constantly studied as change occurs, because current results may no longer apply. The research presented in this book does not support the pessimistic view of a loss of family functions, but does support pessimism concerning families' ability to fulfill these ever-increasing functions adequately. The socioeconomic context in which the family evolves is problematic in terms of families' well-being.

Key Concepts and Themes

Cohabitation, p. 460
Collective socialization, p. 457
Conscientious parents, p. 476
Cultural context, p. 457
Divorce, pp. 460–461, 472 ff.
Effective community, p. 457
Empowerment, p. 476
Evaluation research, p. 473
Family functions, pp. 456, 477
Family policies, pp. 464–465
Feminization of poverty, p. 467
Gender roles, pp. 458, 462, 472

Informal social control, p. 457
Institutionalized parental role, p. 474
Interactional and genetic themes, p. 458
Marriage, pp. 460–461, 471 ff.
Media influence, p. 457
Parenting, pp. 462–463, 474 ff.
Political system, pp. 465–466
Race, p. 462
Reducing poverty, pp. 467 ff.
Social constructs, p. 458
Social inequalities, p. 455

Analytical Questions

1. Why are more and more families unable to meet their diverse functions?

2. The concept of the effective community has been used repeatedly in this text. What could be done to put it into practice and what would be the consequences?

3. Why should marriage be encouraged and strengthened? Why not cohabitation or one-parent families?

4. How does this chapter present a critique of our political system? How could this system be improved for the benefit of families and their members?

Suggested Readings

Baker, M. 1995. *Canadian family policies: Cross-national comparisons.* Toronto: University of Toronto Press. A thorough presentation of Canadian social policies that affect families, including a comparison with other countries.

Beaujot, R. 2000. *Earning and caring in Canadian families.* Peterborough, ON: Broadview Press. The last chapter contains a thoughtful discussion and critique of policies affecting families. Other countries such as Sweden are utilized in a comparative approach.

Crittenden, A. 2001. *The price of motherhood.* New York: Henry Holt. This popular and easy-to-read book presents many policy suggestions as well as a critique of the current system of gender inequality.

Danziger, S., and Waldfogel, J. (Eds.) 2000. *Securing the future: Investing in children from birth to college.* New York: Russell Sage. This collection of articles discusses policy suggestions that would increase investment in institutions that support children.

Eichler, M. 1997. *Family shifts: Families, policies and gender equality.* Toronto: Oxford University Press. The author presents an overview and a feminist critique of policies, which she categorizes along the lines of three models.

Mason, M. A., Skolnick, A., and Sugarman, S. 2003. *All our families: New policies for a new century,* 2nd Ed. New York: Oxford University Press. This text focuses on policy reform and covers a wide range of topics, such as teen pregnancy, child abuse, and divorce.

Zigler, E. F., Kagan, S. L., and Hall, N. W. (Eds.) 1996. *Children, families, and government.* Cambridge: Cambridge University Press. The many articles in this book contain wide-ranging discussions on various aspects of children's and their families' problems with a focus on policy.

Suggested Weblinks

American Psychological Association Policy Office presents information on policy activities as well as research. The office coordinates advocacy efforts at the federal level.

http://apa.org/ppo/topic.html

Future of Children is now published jointly by Princeton University and the policy- and research-oriented Brookings Institution. This site also contains the journal *The Future of Children.*

www.futureofchildren.org

Invest in Kids Foundation includes a national survey of parents of young children. The results of this survey are particularly relevant because they can lead to policy changes at various levels in order to revalue the parental role as well as provide parents with the knowledge and support they obviously need.

www.investinkids.ca

Glossary

Assortative mating: Refers to selecting spouses or mates in a nonrandom fashion; marrying persons who have similar given characteristics. The characteristics may be physical appearance, IQ, values, one or several personality traits, or even social class. The opposite of assortative mating is *random mating*.

Authoritarian parenting: Refers to parental behaviours and attitudes that are predominantly controlling and punishing. At the extreme, they can be even harsh and rejecting. The authoritarian approach does not appeal to a child's sense of reasoning or morality. It is a "do-as-I-say-or-you'll-get-smacked" type of upbringing. Authoritarian parents may also be inconsistent: They may threaten to punish but do not follow through with the punishment.

Authoritative parenting: Combines both warmth and monitoring of children's activities and whereabouts. Authoritative parents make maturity demands on their children. They explain the reasons behind their demands or rules. Once they have explained the reasons and the consequences, they consistently follow through with enforcement of those rules.

Cohort: A group of people who were born around the same time and who therefore go through life experiencing similar sociohistorical conditions. For example, people born during the Great Depression form a cohort.

Correlations: Correlations exist between two factors or variables, such as poverty and violence, when, as one increases or decreases, the other also changes. When both change in the same direction (e.g., both increase), this is a *positive* correlation. A *negative* correlation exists when one factor increases at the same time that the other decreases, as in the example of a decreasing number of cases of serious delinquency with an increasing level of socioeconomic status. Correlation is a statistical test, which is schematically illustrated in Figure 6.1 on page 152.

Critical mass: Refers to a proportion of wellfunctioning families that is necessary in a neighbourhood if that neighbourhood is to remain a good environment in which to raise children. The term can also refer to the proportion of children who are good students that is necessary in a classroom if learning is to take place. Researchers have not yet been able to determine what this exact proportion should be: 30 percent? 40 percent? 60 percent? (This term can also be used to refer to the negative as in "a critical mass of antisocial adolescents.")

Cross-pressure: A term used to signify that a child or an adolescent is subjected to influences that oppose each other. This concept applies particularly to parents and peers who may both influence a child toward opposite goals.

Defamilialization: Refers to the fact that children are increasingly being taken care of and socialized by nonfamily members; children spend less time at home interacting with their parents.

Dilution of parental resources: This concept is used to explain the finding that children in large families do less well, on average, than those in smaller families. The rationale is that, in large families, parents have fewer resources to place at the disposal of each child: The resources are scattered over several children, or diluted.

Dysfunction: See *Function*. Dysfunctional behaviours are those that impair a person's functioning and success. They are maladaptive either for society, the family, the person concerned, or all of these. Persons or groups can be dysfunctional for their family or society, for instance.

Effective community: Refers to parents' links to other parents and to members of the community who maintain a prosocial set of values and are in contact with each other. The sharing of values, socialization goals, instrumental help, and collective supervision of children are characteristics of an effective community.

Endogamy: When people date and marry within their own social class, race, religion, or even language group.

Ethnic group: A group that is set apart from others because of its unique cultural patterns, history, language, as well as its sense of distinctiveness.

Ethnocentric: Refers to the judgments of social situations and people that individuals make based on their experiences within the culture of their own ethnic or cultural group. It can also be the assumption that one's own way of life is superior to that of other cultures or groups in one's society.

Exogamy: The opposite of *endogamy*: marrying out of one's group. Interracial and interreligious marriages are examples of exogamy.

Function: What an institution or group does for society, for families, or for individuals.

Gender roles: Norms or rules that define how males and females should think and behave. Gender roles represent the social definition of what a society constructs as appropriately masculine or feminine in terms of behaviour.

Homogamy: See Assortative mating.

Homogeneity: Uniformity; similarity.

Human capital: The entirety of abilities, skills, education, and positive human characteristics that a person possesses or has achieved. Synonymous with *human assets*.

Hypothesis: A testable proposition or sentence. For instance, "Wives who have been employed all their married lives adjust better to divorce than do homemakers or women who have been employed irregularly." Hypotheses are often designed to test theories.

Indicator: Indicators are used to measure variables, such as conjugal conflict. They are sentences, numbers, or observations that serve to illustrate a variable. Indicators are often coded (given a number) to derive statistics. Indicators of conjugal conflict can be the number of times spouses say they quarrel and how long their quarrels last.

Individuation: A psychological concept referring to the process by which children gain a sense of identity separately from their connection to their parents.

Institution: A recognized area of social life that is organized along a system of norms (or rules) regulating behaviours that are widely accepted in a society. Examples of institutions are the family, schools, and the banking system. On a larger scale, institutions include the political, economic, and religious systems of a society.

Longitudinal studies: Consist of studying the same people over time. For instance, people may be interviewed at age 18 and restudied again at ages 25 and 35. This research design contrasts with *cross-sectional* or *one-time* studies and surveys. Synonymous with *panel study*.

Macrosociology: The study of the family within its broader sociocultural context to see how global forces such as the class system, the economy, and religion shape family structure and dynamics. In other words, "large" sociology or the study of large-scale phenomena and developments in a society, its social structure and organization.

Median: The middle number in a set of numbers that are arranged in order of magnitude.

Microsociology: The study of interactions between individuals within specific and generally smaller contexts, such as the family or a group of friends. It is also the study of the internal dynamics of small groups, including the family.

Minority group: A group that is given inferior status and less power in a society because of race, ethnicity, cultural practices, or religion. In Canada, this term generally refers to people other than white and Aboriginal.

Nonshared environment: Generally refers to experiences that differ for each sibling in a family. These can be different school, peer, and street experiences or environment. Within the home, the term refers to experiences that are specific to each child, such as differential parental treatment, the presence of the other siblings, or the chores given to a child because of his or her age or gender.

Polygenic: Refers to a trait, characteristic, or illness that can occur only when several specific genes are present.

Reference group: A group or category of persons whom people look up to, whose behaviour they imitate and emulate, and according to whose standards they evaluate themselves.

Shared environment: Generally refers to the home environment that siblings have in common or share. This could include parental behaviours, teachings, family routines and special occasions, and transitions, such as divorce or the death of a grandparent. It refers to the familial atmosphere. However, this shared environment is often perceived somewhat differently by each sibling, depending on his or her age, gender, and personality: The environment is shared but its impact differs.

Significant others: Persons who play an important role in an individual's life or with whom the individual identifies.

Social capital: A resource that resides in relationships, particularly family and community relations, that benefits child socialization. In Coleman's (1988) theory, social capital refers both to the positive interactions between a child's parents and between the child and his or her parents, as well as the relationships that parents maintain outside of the family that can benefit children or the entire family. Synonymous with *social assets*.

Social causation: Refers to theories that explain, for example, the high rates of well-being and economic success found, for example, among the married compared to the nonmarried, as a result of the benefits of marriage.

Social construct: A socially acceptable definition of a situation held by a group or a society, a social construct is a cultural creation or invention. Social constructs concerning a phenomenon such as adolescence generally differ across history and across cultures.

Socialization: Refers to the process whereby a child learns to think and behave according to the ways of the society and the group in which he or she is born.

Social mobility: The passage from one social stratum to another or from one social class to another. *Downward* mobility occurs when individuals fall below their parents' stratum (intergenerational mobility) or below the one they have themselves occupied earlier (intragenerational mobility). *Upward* mobility takes place when individuals achieve a higher socioeconomic status than that of their parents. In other words, they "move up" in the class system.

Social selection: Refers to theories that explain, for example, the high rates of well-being and economic success found among the married compared to the nonmarried, as a result of individuals being selected into the married status because they are better balanced and more motivated to begin with.

Socioeconomic status or SES: The ranking of people on a scale of prestige on the basis of occupation, income, and education. SES is often used as a synonym for *social class*.

Stratification: Refers to the ranking that people occupy in a system. Social stratification can be based on gender, race, or social class. For instance, families that belong to the higher social class have more resources, power, and prestige than the others.

Systemic: Refers to a problem that is built into a system, an institution, or a society. Solutions to such problems often require a restructuring of the institution, a difficult enterprise at best.

Theory: A set of interrelated propositions that explain a particular phenomenon. A theory is a sophisticated explanation that can be tested against facts to see if it fits. A good theory should withstand the test of research.

Bibliography and
Author Index*

*The boldfaced numbers are the pages on which these citations appear.

Abma, J., Driscoll, A., and Moore, K. 1998. Young women's degree of control over first intercourse: An exploratory analysis. *Family Planning Perspectives, 30*, 12–18. **227, 249**

Abler, T. S. 1970. Longhouse and palisade: Northeastern Iroquois villages of the seventeenth century. *Ontario History, 62*, 17–40. **34**

Abu-Laban, S., and McDaniel, S. A. 2004. Aging, beauty, and status. In N. Mandell (Ed.), *Feminist issues: Race, class, and gender*, 4th Ed. (pp. 100–126). Toronto: Prentice Hall. **74, 210, 352, 354**

Achilles, R. 1995. Assisted reproduction: The social issues. In E. D. Nelson and B. W. Robinson (Eds.), *Gender in the 1990s: Images, realities and issues* (pp. 346–364). Toronto: Nelson. **252, 255**

Acock, A. C., and Demo, D. H. 1994. Family diversity and well-being. Thousand Oaks, CA: Sage. **275**

Adams, G. R., Côté, J., and Marshall, S. 2002. *Parent/Adolescent relationships and identity development.* Ottawa: Health Canada. **341, 343, 474, 475**

Adler, J. 1997. Bundles of ... joy? *Newsweek*, December 1, p. 62. **256**

Adler, P. A., and Adler, P. 1998. *Peer power: Preadolescent culture and identity.* New Brunswick, NJ: Rutgers University Press. **66, 148, 168, 206**

Adoption Council of Canada. 2003. International adoptions steady: 1,891 in 2002. Ottawa: <www.adoption.ca>. **262**

Ahrons, C. 1994. *The good divorce.* New York: HarperCollins. **413**

Ahrons, C. R., and Tanner, J. L. 2003. Adult children and their fathers: Relationship changes 20 years after parental divorce. *Family Relations, 52*, 340–351. **415**

Aird, E. G. 2001. On rekindling a spirit of "home training": A mother's notes from the front. In S. A. Hofferth, N. Rankin, and C. West (Eds.), *Taking parenting public* (pp. 13–28). New York: Rowan & Littlefield. **14**

Aldous, J. 1996. *Family careers: Rethinking the developmental perspective.* Thousand Oaks, CA: Sage. **17, 236, 350**

Aldous, J., and Ganey, R. F. 1999. Family life and the pursuit of happiness: The influence of gender and race. *Journal of Family Issues, 20*, 155–180. **192, 315**

Aldous, J., Klaus, E., and Klein, D. M. 1985. The understanding heart: Aging parents and their favorite children. *Child Development, 56*, 303–316. **349**

Aldous, J., Mulligan, G. M., and Bjarnason, T. 1998. Fathering over time: What makes the difference? *Journal of Marriage and the Family, 60*, 809–820. **310**

Alexander, A. 1994. The effect of media on family interaction. In D. Zillman, J. Bryant, and A. C. Huston (Eds.), *Media, children, and the family* (pp. 51–59). Hillsdale, NJ: Erlbaum. **77**

Ali, J., and Avison, W. R. 1997. Employment transitions and psychological distress: The contrasting experiences of single and married mothers. *Journal of Health and Social Behavior, 38*, 345–362. **125**

Aliaga, D. E. 1994. Italian immigrants in Calgary: Dimensions of cultural identity. *Canadian Ethnic Studies, 26*, 141–148. **45, 101, 102**

Allahar, A. L., and Côté, J. E. 1998. *Richer & poorer.* Toronto: James Lorimer. **477**

Allen, K. R., and Baber, K. M. 1992. Starting a revolution in family life education: A feminist vision. *Family Relations, 41*, 378–384. **21**

Almeida, D. M., Wethington, E., and McDonald, D. A. 2001. Daily variation in paternal engagement and negative mood: Implications for emotionally supportive and conflictual interactions. *Journal of Marriage and Family, 63*, 417–429. **276**

Almond, B. 1995. Family relationships and reproductive technology. In C. Ulanowsky (Ed.), *The family in the age of biotechnology* (pp. 13–26). Aldershot, UK: Avebury. **255**

Alston, L. 1992. Children as chattel. In E. West and P. Petrick (Eds.), *Small worlds* (pp. 208–231). Lawrence, KS: University of Kansas Press. **274**

Alwin, D. F. 1986. From obedience to autonomy: Changes in traits desired in children, 1924–1978. *Public Opinion Quarterly, 52*, 33–52. **446**

Alwin, D. F. 1990. Cohort replacement and changes in parental socialization values. *Journal of Marriage and the Family, 52*, 347–360. **343**

Alwin, D. F. 2001. Parental values, beliefs, and behavior: A review and promulga for research into the new century. In S. L. Hofferth and T. J. Owens (Eds.), *Children at the millennium: Where have we come from, where are we going?* (pp. 97–139). Oxford, UK: Elsevier. **344**

Amato, P. R. 1996. Explaining the intergenerational transmission of divorce. *Journal of Marriage and the Family, 58*, 628–640. **406, 409**

Amato, P. R. 1999. The postdivorce society: How divorce is shaping the family and other forms of social organization. In R. A. Thompson and P. R. Amato (Eds.), *The postdivorce family* (pp. 161–190). Thousand Oaks, CA: Sage. *396*

Amato, P. R. 2000. The consequences of divorce for adults and children. *Journal of Marriage and the Family, 62,* 1269–1287. *417*

Amato, P. R. 2003. Reconciling divergent perspectives: Judith Wallerstein, quantitative family research, and children of divorce. *Family Relations, 52,* 332–339. *405*

Amato, P. R., and Booth, A. 1997. *A generation at risk: Growing up in an era of family upheaval.* Cambridge, MA: Harvard University Press. *239, 302, 322, 405, 408, 472*

Amato, P. R., and DeBoer, D. D. 2001. The transmission of marital instability across generations: Relationship skills or commitment to marriage? *Journal of Marriage and Family, 63,* 1038–1051. *397, 405*

Amato, P. R., and Fowler, F. 2002. Parenting practices, child adjustment, and family diversity. *Journal of Marriage and Family, 64,* 703-716. *337*

Amato, P. R., and Gilbreth, J. G. 1999. Nonresident fathers and children's well-being: A meta-analysis. *Journal of Marriage and the Family, 61,* 557–573. *408*

Amato, P. R., and Previti, D. 2004. People's reasons for divorcing: Gender, social class, the life course, and adjustment. *Journal of Family Issues, 24,* 602–606. *396, 398*

Amato, P. R., and Rezac, S. J. 1994. Contact with nonresident parents, interparental conflict, and children's behavior. *Journal of Family Issues, 15,* 191–207. *408*

Amato, P. R., and Rivera, F. 1999. Paternal involvement and children's behavioral problems. *Journal of Marriage and the Family, 61,* 375–384. *415*

Amato, P. R., and Rogers, S. J. 1997. A longitudinal study of marital problems and subsequent divorce. *Journal of Marriage and the Family, 59,* 612–624. *197, 318*

Amato, P. R., and Rogers, S. J. 1999. Do attitudes toward divorce affect marital quality? *Journal of Family Issues, 20,* 69–86. *472*

Amato, P. R., and Sobolewski, J. M. 2001. The effects of divorce and marital discord on adult children's psychological well-being. *American Sociological Review, 66,* 900–921. *406*

Amato, P. R., Spencer-Loomis, L. S., and Booth, A. 1995. Parental divorce, marital conflict, and offspring well-being during early adulthood. *Social Forces, 73,* 895–915. *408*

Amato, P. R., et al. 2003. Continuity and change in marital quality between 1980 and 2000. *Journal of Marriage and Family, 65,* 1–22. *311, 314, 316*

Ambert, A.-M. 1976. *Sex structure,* 2nd Ed. Toronto: Longman. *22*

Ambert, A.-M. 1989. *Ex-spouses and new spouses: A study of relationships.* Greenwich, CT: JAI Press. *292, 384, 399, 400*

Ambert, A.-M. 1994a. A qualitative study of peer abuse and its effects: Theoretical and empirical implications. *Journal of Marriage and the Family, 56,* 119–130. *27, 287, 346, 445*

Ambert, A.-M. 1994b. An international perspective on parenting: Social change and social constructs. *Journal of Marriage and the Family, 56,* 529–543. *273, 332*

Ambert, A.-M. 1997. *Parents, children, and adolescents: Interactive relationships and development in context.* New York: Haworth. *16, 345, 474*

Ambert, A.-M. 1998. *The web of poverty: Psychosocial perspectives.* New York: Haworth. *132, 145*

Ambert, A.-M. 1999. The effect of male delinquency on mothers and fathers: A heuristic study. *Sociological Inquiry, 69,* 621–640. *405*

Ambert, A.-M. 2001. *The effect of children on parents,* 2nd Ed. New York: Haworth. *16, 61, 225, 253, 274, 331, 458, 474*

Ambert, A.-M. 2002a. *Divorce: Facts, causes, and consequences.* Ottawa: The Vanier Institute of the Family. <www.vifamily.ca>. *398, 412*

Ambert, A.-M. 2002b. *One-parent families. Part 1: Characteristics and consequences.* Toronto: York University. <www.arts.yorku.ca/soci/ambert/writings/singleparent_1.html>. *61, 246, 248*

Ambert, A.-M. 2002c. *One-parent families. Part 2: Causes and issues of rights and responsibilities.* Toronto: York University. <www.arts.yorku.ca/soci/ambert/writings/single parent_2.html>. *245, 248*

Ambert, A.-M. 2003a. *Same-sex-parent couples and same-sex-parent families: Relationships, parenting, and issues of marriage.* Ottawa: The Vanier Institute of the Family. <www.vifamily.ca>. *221, 222, 302*

Ambert, A.-M. 2003b. *Cohabitation and marriage: Are they equivalent?* Toronto: York University. <www.arts.yorku. ca/soci/ambert/writings/cohabitation.html>. *222*

Ambert, A.-M. 2003c. *The negative social construction of adoption: Its effects on children and parents.* Toronto: York University. <www.arts.yorku.ca/soci/ambert/writings/adoption. html>. *258, 263, 264*

Ambert, A.-M. 2003d. *The rise in problematic behaviors among children and adolescents. Part 1: Personal and familial causes.* Toronto: York University. <www.arts.yorku.ca/soci/ ambert/writings/behavior_problems_pt1.html>. *14, 61, 344, 433*

Ambert, A.-M. 2003e. *The rise in problematic behaviors among children and adolescents. Part 2: Extra-familial causes.* Toronto: York University. <www.arts.yorku.ca/soci/ambert/ writings/behavior_problems_pt2.html>. *62, 344, 446*

Ambert, A.-M., et al. 1995. Understanding and evaluating qualitative research. *Journal of Marriage and the Family, 57,* 879–893. *26*

Anderson, A. L. 1998. Strength of gay male youth: An untold story. *Child and Adolescent Social Work Journal, 15,* 55–71. *207*

Anderson, C. A., and Bushman, B. J. 2001. Effects of violent video games on aggressive behavior, aggressive cognition, aggressive affects, physiological arousal, and prosocial behavior: A meta-analytic review of the scientific literature. *Psychological Science*, 12, 353–359. *75*

Anderson, E. B., and Rice, A. M. 1992. Sibling relationships during remarriage. In E. M. Hetherington and G. Clingempeel (Eds.), *Coping with marital transitions* (pp. 149–177). *Monographs of the Society for Research in Child Development*, 57, no. 227. *369*

Anderson, E. R. 1999. Sibling, half sibling, and stepsibling relationships in remarried families. In E. M. Hetherington, S. H. Henderson, and D. Reiss (Eds.), *Adolescent siblings in stepfamilies: Family functioning and adolescent adjustment* (pp. 101–126). *Monographs of the Society for Research in Child Development*, 259, 64, no. 4. *375, 416*

Anderson, K. J. 1991. *Vancouver's Chinatown: Racial discourse in Canada, 1875–1980*. Montreal, Kingston: McGill-Queen's University Press. *104*

Anderson, K. L. 1997. Gender, status, and domestic violence: An integration of feminist and family violence approaches. *Journal of Marriage and the Family*, 59, 655–669. *425*

Anderson, K. L. 2002. Perpetrator or victim? Relationships between intimate partner violence and well-being. *Journal of Marriage and Family*, 64, 851-863. *426*

Anderssen, E., and McIlroy, A. 2004. Starting from ten: Part 5. *Globe and Mail*. April 10. A1, A7. *99*

Andreasen, M. S. 1994. Patterns of family life and television consumption from 1945 to the 1990s. In D. Zillman, J. Bryant, and A. C. Huston (Eds.), *Media, children, and the family* (pp. 19–36). Hillsdale, NJ: Erlbaum. *68, 69*

Aneshensel, C. S., and Sucoff, C. A. 1996. The neighborhood context of adolescent mental health. *Journal of Health and Social Behavior*, 37, 293–310. *155*

Anisef, P., et al. 2000. *Opportunity and uncertainty*. Toronto: University of Toronto Press. *160, 184*

Anisef, P., and Kilbride, K. M. 2003. Overview and implications of the research. In P. Anisef and K. M. Kilbride (Eds.), *Managing two worlds: The experiences & concerns of immigrant youth in Ontario* (pp. 235–272). Toronto: Canadian Scholars' Press. *180, 186, 187, 342*

Ansen, J. 2000. Nationalism and fertility in francophone Montreal: The majority as minority. *Canadian Studies in Population*, 27, 377–400. *98*

Appell, A. R. 1998. On fixing "bad" mothers and saving their children. In M. Ladd-Taylor and L. Umansky (Eds.), *"Bad" mothers: The politics of blame in twentieth-century America* (pp. 356–380). New York: New York University Press. *433*

Aquilino, W. S. 1990. The likelihood of parent-adult child co-residence: Effects of family structure and parental characteristics. *Journal of Marriage and the Family*, 52, 405–419. *350*

Aquilino, W. S. 1997. From adolescent to young adult: A prospective study of parent-child relations during the transition to adulthood. *Journal of Marriage and the Family*, 59, 670–686. *215, 348*

Aquilino, W. S., and Supple, K. R. 1991. Parent-child relations and parents' satisfaction with living arrangements when adult children live at home. *Journal of Marriage and the Family*, 53, 13–28. *348*

Arditti, J. A. 1992. Differences between fathers with joint custody and noncustodial fathers. *American Journal of Orthopsychiatry*, 62, 186–195. *403*

Arditti, J. A., and Bickley, P. 1996. Fathers' involvement and mothers' parenting stress postdivorce. *Journal of Divorce and Remarriage*, 26, 1–23. *413*

Arendell, T. 1995. *Fathers and divorce*. Newbury Park, CA: Sage. *403*

Arendell, T. 2000. Conceiving and investigating motherhood: The decade's scholarship. *Journal of Marriage and the Family*, 62, 1192–1207. *273*

Argüelles, M. C. Z. 1999. Does a certain dimension of poverty exist in Cuba? In J. B. Lara (Ed.), *Cuba in the 1990s* (pp. 141–164). Havana: Instituto Cubano de Libro. *53*

Ariès, P. 1962. *Centuries of childhood: A social history of family life*. New York: Knopf and Random House. *18*

Armstrong, P., and Armstrong, H. 2003. *Wasting away: The undermining of Canadian health care*, 2nd Ed. Toronto: Oxford University Press. *61*

Arnett, J. J. 2001. *Adolescence and emerging adulthood: A cultural approach*. Upper Saddle River, NJ: Prentice Hall. *340*

Arnold, M. S. 1995. Exploding the myths: African-American families at promise. In B. B. Swadener and S. Lubeck (Eds.), *Children and families "at promise"* (pp. 143–162). Albany: State University of New York Press. *138*

Aseltine, R. H., Jr. 1996. Pathways linking parental divorce with adolescent depression. *Journal of Health and Social Behavior*, 37, 113–148. *407, 409*

Aseltine, R. H., Jr., Gore, S., and Colten, M. E. 1994. Depression and the social developmental context of adolescence. *Journal of Personality and Social Psychology*, 67, 252–263. *406*

Aseltine, R. H., Jr., and Kessler, R. C. 1993. Marital disruption and depression in a community sample. *Journal of Health and Social Behavior*, 34, 237–251. *134, 219, 401*

Astone, N. M., and McLanahan, S. S. 1994. Family structure, residential mobility, and school dropout: A research note. *Demography*, 31, 575–584. *167*

Atkin, C. 1978. Observation of parent-child interaction in supermarket decision making. *Journal of Marketing*, 42, 41–45. *77*

Audas, R., and McDonald, T. 2004. Rural-urban migration in the 1990s. *Canadian Social Trends*, 73, 17–24. *167, 168*

Austin, E. W. 2001. Effects of family communication on children's interpretation of television. In J. Bryant and J. A. Bryant (Eds.), *Television and the American family* (pp. 377–395). Mahwah, NJ: Erlbaum. *78*

Austin, E. W., Roberts, D. F., and Nass, C. I. 1990. Influences of family communication on children's television-interpretation processes. *Communication Research, 17,* 545–564. *73*

Axinn, W. G., Barber, J. S., and Thornton, A. 1998. The long-term impact of parents' childbearing decisions on children's self-esteem. *Demography, 35,* 435–443. *254*

Axinn, W. G., and Thornton, A. 1992. The relationship between cohabitation and divorce: Selectivity or causal influence. *Demography, 29,* 357–374. *241*

Aycan, Z., and Kanungo, R. N. 1998. Impact of acculturation on socialization beliefs and behavioral occurrences among Indo-Canadian immigrants. *Journal of Comparative Family Studies, 29,* 451–467. *108*

Bachman, J. G., et al. 1997. *Smoking, drinking, and drug use in young adulthood.* Mahwah, NJ: Erlbaum. *220*

Bachman, R. 1994. *Violence against women: A National Crime Victimization Survey report.* Washington, DC: Department of Justice, Bureau of Justice Statistics. *443*

Bagley, C. 1993. Transracial adoption in Britain: A follow-up study, with policy considerations. *Child Welfare, 72,* 285–299. *262*

Bagnell, L. 1989. *Canadese: A portrait of the Italian Canadians.* Toronto: Macmillan. *101*

Bahr, S. J., et al. 1998. Family, religiosity, and the risk of adolescent drug use. *Journal of Marriage and the Family, 60,* 979–992. *196*

Bailey, J. M., and Dawood, I. 1998. Behavior genetics, sexual orientation, and the family. In C. Patterson and A. R. D'Augelli (Eds.), *Lesbian, gay, and bisexual identities in families: Psychological perspectives.* New York: Oxford University Press. *245*

Bailey, J. M., et al. 1995. Sexual orientation of adult sons and gay fathers. *Developmental Psychology, 31,* 124–129. *244*

Baillargeon, R., Tremblay, R., and Willms, J. D. 2002. Physical aggression among toddlers: Does it run in families? In J. D. Willms (Ed.), *Vulnerable children* (pp. 71–103). Edmonton: University of Alberta Press. *365*

Baines, C., Evans, P., and Neysmith, S. 1991. Caring: Its impact on the lives of women. In C. Baines, P. Evans, and S. Neysmith (Eds.), *Women caring: Feminist perspectives* (pp. 11–35). Toronto: McClelland & Stewart. *374*

Bakan, A. B., and Stasiulis, D. (Eds.). 1997. *Not one of the family: Foreign and domestic workers in Canada.* Toronto: University of Toronto Press. *21*

Baker, L. A., and Daniels, D. 1990. Nonshared environmental influences and personality differences in adult twins. *Journal of Personality and Social Psychology, 58,* 103–110. *375, 377*

Baker, M. 1994. Family and population policy in Québec: Implications for women. *Canadian Journal of Women and the Law/Revue Femmes et Droit, 7,* 116–132. *98*

Baker, M. 1995. *Canadian family policies: Cross-national comparisons.* Toronto: University of Toronto Press. *175, 431, 464, 465, 470, 478*

Baker, M. 1997. Parental benefit policies and the gendered division of labour. *Social Service Review, 71,* 51–74. *458*

Baker, M. 2001a. Definitions, cultural variations, and demographic trends. In M. Baker (Ed.), *Families: Changing trends in Canada,* 4th Ed. (pp. 3–27). Toronto: McGraw-Hill Ryerson.

Baker, M. 2001b. *Families, labour and love.* Vancouver: University of British Columbia Press. *182, 252, 412*

Baker, M., and Tippin, D. 1999. *Poverty, social assistance, and the employability of mothers.* Toronto: University of Toronto Press. *467*

Bakker, I. (Ed.). 1996. *Rethinking restructuring.* Toronto: University of Toronto Press. *119*

Balakrishnan, T. R. 2001. Residential segregation and socio-economic integration of Asians in Canadian cities. *Canadian Ethnic Studies, 33,* 120–131. *104, 106*

Balakrishnan, T. R., and Hou, F. 1999. Residential patterns in cities. In S. S. Halli and L. Driedger (Eds.), *Immigrant Canada: Demographic, economic, and social challenges* (pp. 116–147). Toronto: University of Toronto Press. *157*

Banerjee, S., and Coward, H. 2005. Hindus in Canada: Negotiating identity in a "different" homeland. In P. Bramadat and D. Siljak (Eds.), *Religion and ethnicity in Canada,* (pp. 30–51). Toronto: Pearson. *191*

Bank, L., Patterson, G. R., and Reid, J. B. 1996. Negative sibling interaction patterns as predictors of later adjustment problems in adolescent and young adult males. In G. H. Brody (Ed.), *Sibling relationships: Their causes and consequences* (pp. 197–230). Norwood, NJ: Ablex. *372*

Bankston, C. L., III, and Caldas, S. J. 1998. Family structure, schoolmates, and racial inequalities in school achievement. *Journal of Marriage and the Family, 60,* 715–724. *180*

Bao, W.-N., et al. 1999. Perceived parental acceptance as a moderator of religious transmission among adolescent boys and girls. *Journal of Marriage and the Family, 61,* 362–374. *193*

Barber, B. K. 1994. Cultural, family, and personal contexts of parent-adolescent conflict. *Journal of Marriage and the Family, 56,* 375–386. *341*

Barber, E., and Pasley, B. K. 1995. Family care of Alzheimer's patients: The role of gender and generational relationship on caregiver outcomes. *Journal of Applied Gerontology, 14,* 172–192. *319*

Baril, R., Lefebvre, T., and Merrigan, P. 2000. Quebec family policy: Impact and options. *Choices: Family Policy, 6,* 4–52: IRPP. *98*

Barnes, H. V., Goodson, B. D., and Layzer, J. I. 1996. *Review of the research on family support interventions.* Cambridge, MA: Abt Associates. *469*

Barnett, D., Manly, J. T., and Cicchetti, D. 1993. Defining child maltreatment: The interface between policy and research. In D. Cicchetti and S. L. Toth (Eds.), *Advances in applied developmental psychology, Vol. 8: Child abuse, child development, and social policy.* Norwood, NJ: Ablex. *436*

Barnett, R. C., and Hyde, J. S. 2001. Women, men, work, and family: An expansionist theory. *American Psychologist, 56,* 781–796. *124*

Barnett, R. C., Marshall, N. L., and Pleck, J. H. 1992. Adult son–parent relationships and their associations with son's psychological distress. *Journal of Family Issues, 13,* 505–525. *348*

Barnett, S. W. 1995. Long-term effects of early childhood programs on cognitive and school outcomes. *The Future of Children, 5,* 25–50. *469*

Barnett, S. W. 1998. Long-term cognitive and academic effects of early childhood education of children in poverty. *Preventive Medicine, 27,* 204–207. *178*

Barrett, A. E. 1999. Support and life satisfaction among the never married. *Research on Aging, 21,* 46–72. *225*

Barrow, C. 1996. *Family in the Caribbean: Themes and perspectives.* Kingston, Jamaica: Ian Randle Publishers. *7, 8, 109, 125*

Barth, R. P. 2001. Policy implications of foster family characteristics. *Family Relations, 50,* 16–19. *265*

Barth, R. P., and Berry, M. 1988. *Adoption and disruption: Rates, risks, and responses.* New York: Aldine de Gruyter. *260*

Barth, R. P., and Miller, J. M. 2000. Building effective post-adoption services: What is the empirical foundation? *Family Relations, 49,* 447–455. *260*

Bartholet, E. 1993. *Family bonds: Adoption and the politics of parenting.* Boston: Houghton Mifflin. *257–259, 455*

Bartlett, K. T. 1999. Improving the law relating to postdivorce arrangements for children. In R. A. Thompson and P. R. Amato (Eds.), *The postdivorce family* (pp. 71–102). Thousand Oaks, CA: Sage. *473*

Baskin, C. 2003. From victims to leaders: Activism against violence towards women. In K. Anderson and B. Lawrence (Eds.), *Strong stories: Native vision and community survival* (pp. 213–287). Vancouver: Sumach Press. *428*

Bassuk, E. L., et al. 1996. The characteristics and needs of sheltered homeless and low-income housed mothers. *Journal of the American Medical Association, 276,* 640–646. *158*

Batalova, J. A., and Cohen, P. N. 2002. Premarital cohabitation and housework: Couples in cross-national perspective. *Journal of Marriage and Family, 64,* 743–755. *215*

Bates, J. E., et al. 1998. Interaction of temperamental resistance to control and restrictive parenting in the development of externalizing behavior. *Developmental Psychology, 34,* 982–995. *339*

Baumer, E. P., and South, S. J. 2001. Community effects on youth sexual activity. *Journal of Marriage and Family, 63,* 540-554. *154*

Baumrind, D. 1967. Child care practices anteceding three patterns of preschool behavior. *Genetic Psychology Monographs, 75,* 43–88. *332*

Baumrind, D. 1991a. Effective parenting during the early adolescent transition. In P. A. Cowan and M. E. Hetherington

(Eds.), *Family transitions* (pp. 111–163). Hillsdale, NJ: Erlbaum. *335, 406, 475*

Baumrind, D. 1991b. The influence of parenting style on adolescent competence and substance abuse. *Journal of Early Adolescence, 11,* 56–94. *334*

Baumrind, D. 1994. The social context of child maltreatment. *Family Relations, 43,* 360–368. *338*

Baumrind, D. 1996. The discipline controversy revisited. *Family Relations, 45,* 405–414. *338*

Bawin-Legrow, B., and Gauthier, A. 2001. Regulation of intimacy and love semantics in couples living apart together. *International Review of Sociology, 11,* 39–46. *8*

Baydar, N., and Brooks-Gunn, J. 1998. Profiles of grandmothers who help care for their grandchildren in the United States. *Family Relations, 47,* 385–393. *290*

Baydar, N., Greek, A., and Brooks-Gunn, J. 1997a. A longitudinal study of the effects of the birth of a sibling during the first 6 years of life. *Journal of Marriage and the Family, 59,* 939–956. *285, 360*

Baydar, N., Hyle, P., and Brooks-Gunn, J. 1997b. A longitudinal study of the effects of the birth of a sibling during preschool and early grade school years. *Journal of Marriage and the Family, 59,* 957–965. *285, 360*

Beaujot, R. 2000. *Earning & caring in Canadian families.* Peterborough: Broadview Press. *21, 23, 221, 253, 307, 416, 455, 456, 464, 465, 478*

Beaujot, R. 2004. *Delayed life transitions: Trends and implications.* Ottawa: Vanier Institute of the Family. <www. vifamily.ca/library/cft/delayed-life.html>. *17, 120, 250, 272, 283, 347, 456, 459, 460*

Beaujot, R., and Bélanger, A. 2001. Perspective on below replacement fertility in Canada: Trends, desires, accommodations. Paper presented at the International Union for the Scientific Study of Population, Tokyo, March 2001. <www.ssc.uwo.ca/sociology/popstudies/dp/dp01-6.pdf>. *238*

Beaujot, R., and Kerr, D. 2004. *Population change in Canada,* 2nd Ed. Toronto: Oxford University Press. *88–92, 94, 95, 111, 251, 268, 459, 460*

Beaujot, R., and McQuillan, K. 1982. *Growth and dualism: The demographic development of Canadian society.* Toronto: Gage Publishing. *35, 37*

Beaupré, P., et al. 2002. Junior is still at home: Trends and determinants in parental home leaving in Canada: Statistics Canada. *289*

Beavon, D., and Cooke, M. 2003. An application of the UN Human Development Index and registered Indians in Canada, 1996. In J. White et al. (Eds.), *Aboriginal conditions: Research as a foundation for public policy.* Vancouver, BC: University of British Columbia Press. *94, 95*

Beeghley, L. 1996. *What does your wife do? Gender and the transformation of family life.* Boulder, CO: Westview Press. *227*

Behar, R. 1998. *Cubana.* Boston: Beacon Press. *53*

Behiels, M. D. 1986. *Prelude to Quebec's Quiet Revolution.* Kingston and Montreal: McGill-Queen's University Press. *97*

Bélanger, A. 1998. Trends in contraceptive sterilization. *Canadian Social Trends, 50*, 16–19. *250*

Bélanger, A., and Dumas, J. 1998. *Report on the demographic situation in Canada 1997.* Ottawa: Statistics Canada. Cat no. 91-209. *238, 397*

Bélanger, A., and Oikawa, C. 1999. Who has a third child? *Canadian Social Trends, 53*, 23–26. *250*

Bell, A. P., and Weinberg, M. S. 1978. *Homosexualities: A study of diversity among men and women.* New York: Simon and Schuster. *210, 219, 240, 456*

Bell, C. C., and Jenkins, E. J. 1993. Community violence and children on Chicago's southside. *Psychiatry, 56*, 46–54. *433*

Bell, D., and Valentine, G. 1995. Queer country: Rural lesbian and gay lives. *Journal of Rural Studies, 11*, 113–122. *208*

Bell, R. Q. 1968. A reinterpretation of the direction of effects in studies of socialization. *Psychological Review, 75*, 81–85. *16*

Bellah, R. N., et al. 1985. *Habits of the heart: Individualism and commitment in American life.* Berkeley: University of California Press. *457*

Belle, M., and McQuillan, K. 1994. Births outside marriage: A growing alternative. *Canadian Social Trends, 33*, 14–17. *245*

Belliveau. J.-A., Oderkirk, J., and Silver, C. 1994. Common-law unions: The Quebec difference. *Canadian Social Trends, 33*, 8-12. *211*

Belsky, J., and Kelly, J. 1994. *The transition to parenthood: How a first child changes a marriage.* New York: Delacorte Press. *279*

Belsky, J., et al. 1991. Patterns of marital change and parent-child interaction. *Journal of Marriage and the Family, 53*, 487–498. *323*

Beltran, A. 2001. [A review of several books on] Empowering grandparents raising children: A training manual for group leaders/Grandparents raising grandchildren: Theoretical, empirical, and clinical.... *The Gerontologist, 41*, 559–563. *292*

Bengtson, V. L. 2001. Beyond the nuclear family: The increasing importance of multigenerational bonds. *Journal of Marriage and Family, 63*, 1–16. *60, 290*

Bennett, J. W., and Seena, B. K. 1995. *Settling the Canadian-American west, 1890–1915: Pioneer adaptation and community building. An anthropological history.* Lincoln, NE: University of Nebraska Press. *45*

Bennett, N. G., Bloom, D. E., and Miller, C. K. 1995. The influence of nonmarital childbearing in the formation of first marriages. *Demography, 32*, 47–62. *135, 471*

Bennett, T., et al. 1994. Maternal marital status as a risk factor for infant mortality. *Family Planning Perspectives, 26*, 252–256. *240*

Benson, P. L., Sharma, A. R., and Roehlkepartain, E. C. 1994. *Growing up adopted: A portrait of adolescents and their families.* Minneapolis, MN: Search Institute. *259*

Berardo, F. M. 1998. Family privacy: Issues and concepts. *Journal of Family Issues, 19*, 4–19. *166*

Berger, P. L., and Luckmann, T. 1966. *The social construction of reality: A treatise in the sociology of knowledge.* New York: Doubleday. *18*

Bernard, J. 1972. *The future of marriage.* New York: World. *20, 314*

Bernstein, A. C. 1997. Stepfamilies from siblings' perspectives. *Marriage and Family Review, 26*, 153–176. *376*

Berrick, J. D., et al. 1998. *The tender years: Toward developmentally sensitive child welfare services for very young children.* New York: Oxford University Press. *265*

Berrington, A., and Diamond, I. 1999. Marital dissolution among the 1958 British birth cohort: The role of cohabitation. *Population Studies, 53*, 19–38. *397*

Berry, M. 1991. The effects of open adoption on biological and adoptive parents and the children: The arguments and the evidence. *Child Welfare, 70*, 637–651. *263*

Berry, M., et al. 1998. The role of open adoption in the adjustment of adopted children and their families. *Children and Youth Services Review, 20*, 151–171. *263*

Berryman, J. C., and Windridge, K. 1991. Having a baby after 40: II. A preliminary investigation of women's experience of motherhood. *Journal of Reproductive and Infant Psychology, 9*, 19–33. *255*

Berthet, T. 1992. *Seigneurs et colons de Nouvelle France: l'émergence d'une société distincte au XVIIIème siècle.* Cachan, Éditions de l'E.N.S. *39*

Bess, B. E., and Janssen, Y. 1982. Incest: A pilot study. *Journal of Clinical Psychology, 4*, 39–52. *444*

Betcherman, G., and Lowe, G. S. 1997. *The future of work in Canada.* Ottawa: Renouf.

Bianchi, S. M. 1995. The changing demographic and socio-economic characteristics of single parent families. In S. M. H. Hanson et al. (Eds.), *Single parent families: Diversity, myths and realities* (pp. 71–98). New York: Haworth. *403*

Bianchi, S. M., and Casper, L. M. 2000. American families. *Population Bulletin, 55*. <www.prb.org>. *213*

Bianchi, S. M., Subaiya, L., and Kahn, J. R. 1999. The gender gap in the economic well-being of nonresident fathers and custodial mothers. *Demography, 36*, 195–203. *134, 309*

Bibby, R. W. 1995. *The Bibby Report: Social trends Canadian style.* Toronto: Stoddart. *209, 226*

Bibby, R. W. 2001. *Canadian teens: Today, yesterday, and tomorrow.* Toronto: Stoddart. *226, 227, 341, 343, 404, 410, 431, 445*

Bibby, R. W. 2002. *Restless gods: The Renaissance of religion in Canada.* Toronto: Stoddart. *190, 460*

Bibby, R. W., and Posterski, D. C. 2000. *Teen trends: A nation in motion.* Toronto: Stoddart. *226, 286, 341, 347*

Biblarz, T. J., and Gottainer, G. 2000. Family structure and children's success: A comparison of widowed and divorced single-mother families. *Journal of Marriage and the Family, 62, 533–548. 411*

Biles, J., and Ibrahim, H. 2005. Religion and public policy: Immigration, citizenship, and multiculturalism—Guess who's coming to dinner? In P. Bramadat and D. Seljak (Eds.), *Religion and ethnicity in Canada* (pp. 154–177). Toronto: Pearson. *22, 460*

Binda, K. P. 2001. Native diaspora and urban education: Intractable problems. In S. K. Binda and S. Calliou (Eds.), *Aboriginal education in Canada* (pp. 179–194). Mississauga: Canadian Educators' Press. *157, 187*

Binnema, T. 1996. Old swan, big man, and the Siksika bands, 1794–1815. *Canadian Historical Review,* 77, 1–32. *34*

Binnema, T. 2001. Migrant from every direction: communities of the Northwestern Plains to 1750. In T. Binnema (Ed.), *Common and contested ground: A human and environmental history of the northwestern plains.* Norman, OK: University of Oklahoma Press. *34*

Binstock, G., and Thornton, A. 2003. Separations, reconciliations, and living apart in cohabiting and marital unions. *Journal of Marriage and Family,* 65, 432–443. *8, 213*

Bird, C. E. 1999. Gender, household labor, and psychological distress: The impact of the amount and division of housework. *Journal of Health and Social Behavior,* 40, 32–45. *311*

Bird, G., and Melville, K. 1994. *Families and intimate relationships.* New York: McGraw-Hill. *165*

Bird, G. W., Peterson, R., and Miller, S. H. 2002. Factors associated with distress among support-seeking adoptive families. *Family Relations,* 51, 215–220. *260*

Birns, B., and Birns, S. 1997. Violence-free families. In S. Dreman (Ed.), *The family on the threshold of the 21st century* (pp. 129–146). Mahwah, NJ: Erlbaum. *430*

Black, D. A., et al. 2000. Demographics of the gay and lesbian population in the United States: Evidence from available systematic data sources. *Demography,* 37, 139–154. *207, 242*

Blake, J., Richardson, B., and Bhattacharya, J. 1991. Number of siblings and sociability. *Journal of Marriage and the Family,* 53, 271–284. *363*

Blank, R. M. 1997. *It takes a nation: A new agenda for fighting poverty.* New York: Russell Sage. *81, 464, 470*

Blank, S. W., and Blum, B. 1997. A brief history of work expectations for welfare mothers. *The Future of Children,* 7, 28–39. *464*

Blau, P. 1964. *Exchange and power in social life.* New York: Wiley. *13*

Block, J. H., Block, J., and Gjerde, P. F. 1988. Parental functioning and the home environment of families of divorce: Prospective and current analyses. *Journal of the American Academy of Child and Adolescent Psychiatry,* 27, 207–213. *409*

Blood, R. O., and Wolfe, D. M. 1960. *Husbands and wives. Dynamics of married living.* New York: The Free Press. *13*

Blum, L. 1999. *At the breast: Ideologies of breastfeeding and motherhood in the contemporary United States.* Boston: Beacon Press. *274*

Blumer, H. 1969. *Symbolic interactionism: Perspective and method.* Englewood Cliffs, NJ: Prentice Hall. *15*

Blumstein, P., and Schwartz, P. 1990. Intimate relationships and the creation of sexuality. In D. McWhirter, S. Sanders, and J. Reinisch (Eds.), *Homosexuality/heterosexuality: Concepts of sexual orientation* (pp. 96–109). New York: Oxford University Press. *231*

Boer, F., Goedhart, A. W., and Treffers, P. D. A. 1992. Siblings and their parents. In F. Boer and J. Dunn (Eds.), *Children's sibling relationships* (pp. 41–54). Hillsdale, NJ: Erlbaum. *373*

Bogenschneider, K. 2000. Has family policy come of age? A decade review of the state of U.S. family policy in the 1990s. *Journal of Marriage and the Family,* 62, 1136–1159. *465*

Bogenschneider, K., et al. 2000. Connecting research and policymaking: Implications for theory and practice for the Family Impact Seminars. *Family Relations,* 49, 327–339. *466*

Boivin, M. J., and Giordani, B. 1995. A risk evaluation of the neuropsychological effects of childhood lead toxicity. *Developmental Neuropsychology,* 11, 157–180. *164*

Bokemeier, J., and Maurer, R. 1987. Marital quality and conjugal labor involvement of rural couples. *Family Relations,* 36, 417–424. *162*

Bolger, N., et al. 1989. The contagion of stress across multiple roles. *Journal of Marriage and the Family,* 51, 175–183. *314*

Bond, J. T., Galinsky, E., and Swanberg, J. E. 1998. *The 1997 national study of the changing workforce.* New York: Families and Work Institute. *127*

Bonecutter, F. J., and Gleeson, J. P. 1997. Broadening our view: Lessons from kinship foster care. In G. R. Anderson, A. S. Ryan, and B. R. Leashore (Eds.), *The challenge of permanency planning in a multicultural society* (pp. 99–119). New York: Haworth. *291*

Booth, A. 1999. Causes and consequences of divorce: Reflections on recent research. In R. A. Thompson and P. R. Amato (Eds.), *The postdivorce family* (pp. 29–48). Thousand Oaks, CA: Sage. *394, 470*

Booth, A., and Amato, P. R. 2001. Parental predivorce relations and offspring postdivorce well-being. *Journal of Marriage and the Family,* 63, 197–212. *394, 408*

Booth, A., Carver, K., and Granger, D. A. 2000. Biosocial perspectives on the family. *Journal of Marriage and the Family,* 62, 1018–1034. *19*

Booth, A., and Edwards, J. M. 1992. Starting over: Why remarriages are unstable. *Journal of Family Issues,* 13, 179–194. *319, 413*

Borders, L. D., Black, L. K., and Pasley, B. K. 1998. Are adopted children and their parents at greater risk for negative outcomes? *Family Relations,* 47, 237–241. *261*

Borders, L. D., Penny, J. M., and Portnoy, F. 2000. Adult adoptees and their friends: Current functioning and psychosocial well-being. *Family Relations, 49,* 407–418. *259*

Borrell, K., and Karlsson, S. G. 2002. Reconceptualizing intimacy and ageing: Living apart together. Paper presented at the International Symposium on Reconceptualising Gender and Ageing, University of Surrey: Centre for Research on Ageing and Gender, June. *8*

Boss, P. 1993. Boundary ambiguity: A block to cognitive coping. In A. P. Turnbull, J. M. Patterson, and S. K. Behr (Eds.), *Cognitive coping,, families, and disability* (pp. 257–270). Baltimore: Brookes. *263*

Bouchard, B., and Zhao, J. 2000. University education: Recent trends in participation, accessibility, and returns. *Education Quarterly Review, 6. 175*

Bouchard, C. 2001. Etre père en 2001. *Revue Enfants Québec,* avril, 43–46. *275*

Bouchard, T. J., Jr., et al. 1990. Sources of human psychological difference: The Minnesota study of twins reared apart. *Science, 250,* 223–228. *366*

Bould, S. 2004. Caring neighborhoods: Bringing up the kids together. *Journal of Family Issues, 24,* 427-447. *153*

Bowlby, G. 2002. Farmers leaving the field. *Perspectives on Labour and Income, 3,* February 13–18. *160, 162*

Boyd, M., and Li, A. 2003. May–December: Canadians in age-discrepant relationships. *Canadian Social Trends, 70,* 29–33. *209, 210*

Boyd, M., and Norris, D. 1995. Leaving the nest? The impact of family structure. *Canadian Social Trends, 38,* 14–19. *406*

Boyle, M. H. 2002. Home ownership and the emotional and behavioral problems of children and youth. *Child Development, 73,* 883–892. *468*

Brabant, C., Bourdon, S., and Jutras, F. 2004. L'école à la maison au Québec: l'expression d'un choix familial marginal. *Enfances: Familles, Générations,* Fall. <www.erudit.org/revue/efg/2004>. *189*

Bradbury, B. 1996. *Working families: Age, gender, and daily survival in industrializing Montreal.* Toronto: Oxford University Press. *21, 119, 121*

Bradbury, B. 2000. Gender at work at home: Family decisions, the labour market, and girls' contribution to the family economy. In B. Bradbury (Ed.), *Canadian family history* (pp. 177–198). Toronto: Irwin Publishing. *66, 121, 145*

Bradley, R. H., et al. 2001. The home environments of children in the United States. Part l: Variations by age, ethnicity, and poverty status. *Child Development, 72,* 1844-1867. *248*

Bramadat, P., and Seljak, D. (Eds.). 2005. *Religion and ethnicity in Canada.* Toronto: Pearson. *195, 196, 201*

Brandáo, J. A., 2003. *Nation Iroquoise: A seventeenth-century ethnography of the Iroquois.* Lincoln, NE: University of Nebraska Press. *35*

Brauner, J., Gordic, B., and Zigler, E. 2004. Putting the child back into childcare: Combining care and education for children ages 3–5. *Social Policy Report, 18,* 3–15. *175*

Bray, J. H., and Kelly, J. 1998. *Stepfamilies: Love, marriage, and parenting in the first decade.* New York: Broadway Books. *412*

Brayfield, A. A. 1992. Employment resources and housework in Canada. *Journal of Marriage and the Family, 54,* 19–30. *309*

Brayfield, A. 1995. Juggling jobs and kids: The impact of employment schedules on fathers' caring for children. *Journal of Marriage and the Family, 57,* 321–332. *276*

Brendgen, M., et al. 2002. Same-sex peer relations and romantic relationship during early adolescence: Interactive links to emotional, behavioral, and academic adjustment. *Merril-Palmer Quarterly, 48,* 77–103. *206*

Brener, N. D., et al. 1999. Forced sexual intercourse and associated health-risk behaviors among female college students in the United States. *Journal of Consulting and Clinical Psychology, 67,* 252–259. *422*

Brewer, D. J., Eide, E. R., and Ehrenberg, R. G. 1999. Does it pay to attend an elite private college? Cross-cohort evidence of the effects of college type on earnings. *Journal of Human Resources, 34,* 104–123. *188*

Briere, J., and Runtz, M. 1993. Childhood sexual abuse: Long-term sequelae and implications for psychological assessment. *Journal of Interpersonal Violence, 8,* 132–133. *441*

Briggs, X. 1998. Brown kids in white suburbs: Housing mobility and the many faces of social capital. *Housing Policy Debate, 9,* 177–212. *154*

Bright, D. 1992. We are all kin: Reconsidering labour and class in Calgary, 1919. *Labour, 29,* 59–80. *45*

Brisson, C., et al. 1999. Effect of family responsibilities and job strain on ambulatory blood pressure among white-collar women. *Psychosomatic Medicine, 61,* 205–213. *311, 312*

Brody, G. H., and Flor, D. L. 1998. Maternal resources, parenting practices, and child competence in rural, single-parent African American families. *Child Development, 69,* 803–816. *334*

Brody, G. H., Murry, V. M. 2001. Sibling socialization of competence in rural, single-parent African-American families. *Journal of Marriage and Family, 63,* 996–1008. *334, 365*

Brody, G. H., et al. 1999. Sibling relationships in rural African American families. *Journal of Marriage and the Family, 61,* 1046–1057. *365*

Brody, G. H., et al. 2004. The strong African American families program: Translating research into prevention programming. *Child Development, 75,* 900–917. *474*

Brodzinski, D. M. 1993. Long-term outcomes in adoption. In R. E. Behrman (Ed.), *The future of children: Adoption* (pp. 153–166). Los Altos, CA: Center for the Future of Children, the Davis and Lucille Packard Foundation. *260*

Brodzinski, D. M., and Brodzinski, A. B. 1992. The impact of family structure on the adjustment of adopted children. *Child Welfare, 71,* 69–76. *259*

Bronfenbrenner, U. 1979. *The ecology of human development.* Cambridge, MA: Harvard University Press. *16, 331*

Bronfenbrenner, U. 1985. Freedom and discipline across the decades. In G. Becker, H. Becker, and L. Huber (Eds.), *Ordnung und unordnung (Order and disorder)* (pp. 326–339). Berlin: Beltz. *334, 475*

Bronfenbrenner, U. 1989. Ecologial systems theory. In R. Vasta (Ed.), *Six theories of child development* (pp. 185–246). Greenwich, CT: JAI Press. *16, 343*

Bronfenbrenner, U. 1994. Ecological models of human development. In T. Husen and T. N. Postlethwaite (Eds.), *International Encyclopedia of Education*, 2nd Ed. (pp. 1643–1647). Oxford, UK: Pergamon/Elseiver. *383*

Brookoff, D., et al. 1997. Characteristics of participants in domestic violence. *Journal of the American Medical Association*, 277, 1369–1373. *426, 427, 429*

Brooks-Gunn, J. 2003. Do you believe in magic?: What we can expect from early childhood intervention programs. *Social Policy Report* (Society for Research in Child Development), 17, 3–13. *178*

Brooks-Gunn, J., et al. 1993. Do neighborhoods influence child and adolescent development? *American Journal of Sociology*, 99, 353–395. *154*

Brooks-Gunn, J., et al. 1995. Towards an understanding of the effect of poverty upon children. In H. E. Fitzgerald, B. M. Lester, and B. Zuckerman (Eds.), *Children of poverty* (pp. 3–36). New York: Garland. *457*

Brooks-Gunn, J., Han, W.-J., and Waldfogel, J. 2002. Maternal employment and child cognitive outcomes in the first three years of life. The NICHD study of Early Child Care. *Child Development*, 73, 1052–1072. *125*

Brouillet, F. 2004. Une dirigeante de société gagne un tiers de moins que son homologue masculin, 2004. Paris: INSEE. <www.insee.fr>. *122*

Brown, B. B., and Huang, G.-H. 1995. Examining parenting practices in different peer contexts: Implications for adolescent trajectories. In L. J. Crockett and A. C. Crouter (Eds.), *Pathways through adolescence: Relation to social contexts* (pp. 151–174). Mahwah, NJ: Erlbaum. *344*

Brown, J., and Sime, J. 1981. A methodology for accounts. In M. Brenner (Ed.), *Social methods and social life* (pp. 173–187). London: Academic Press. *27*

Brown, J. K. 1970. Economic organization and the position of women among the Iroquois. *Ethnohistory*, 17, 151–167. *34*

Brown, S. L. 2002. Child well-being in cohabiting families. In A. Booth and A. C. Crouter (Eds.), *Just living together* (pp. 173-187). Mahwah, NJ: Erlbaum. *216, 241*

Brown, S. L. 2004a. Relationship quality dynamics of cohabiting unions. *Journal of Family Issues*, 24, 583–601. *213*

Brown, S. L. 2004b. Family structure and child well-being: The significance of parental cohabitation. *Journal of Marriage and Family*, 66, 351–367. *241, 415*

Brown, S. L., and Booth, A. 1996. Cohabitation versus marriage: A comparison of relationship quality. *Journal of Marriage and the Family*, 58, 668–678. *215*

Browne, A. 1997. Violence in marriage: Until death do us part? In A. P. Cardarelli (Ed.), *Violence between intimate partners* (pp. 48–69). Boston: Allyn & Bacon. *426, 427*

Browne, K. D. 1998. Physical violence between young adults and their parents: Associations with a history of child maltreatment. *Journal of Family Violence*, 13, 59–79. *447*

Browning, C. R. 2002. The span of collective efficacy: Extending social disorganization theory to partner violence. *Journal of Marriage and Family*, 64, 833–850. *427*

Browning, C. R., and Laumann, E. O. 1997. Sexual contact between children and adults: A life course perspective. *American Sociological Review*, 62, 540–560. *441, 442*

Brownridge, D., and Halli, S. S. 2001. *Explaining violence against women in Canada*. Lanham, NJ: Lexington Books. *427*

Broyles, P. A., and Drenovsky, C. K. 1992. Religious attendance and the subjective health of the elderly. *Review of Religious Research*, 34, 152–160. *196*

Brunk, M. A., and Henggeler, S. W. 1984. Child influences on adult controls: An experimental investigation. *Developmental Psychology*, 20, 1074–1081. *339*

Bryant, J., and Rockwell, S. C. 1994. Effects of massive exposure to sexually oriented prime-time television programming on adolescents' moral judgement. In D. Zillmann, J. Bryant, and A. C. Huston (Eds.), *Media, children, and the family*. Hillsdale, NJ: Erlbaum. *77*

Bryceson, D., and Vuorela, U. 2002. Transnational families in the twenty-first century. In D. Bryceson and U. Vuorela (Eds.), *The transnational family* (pp. 3–30). New York: Oxford University Press. *111*

Buchanan, C. M., Maccoby, E. E., and Dornbusch, S. M. 1996. *Adolescents after divorce*. Cambridge, MA: Harvard University Press. *408, 415*

Buchignani, N. 1987. Research on South Asians in Canada: Retrospect and prospect. In M. Israel (Ed.), *The South Asian Diaspora in Canada: Six essays* (pp. 113–141). Toronto: The Multicultural History Society of Ontario. *107*

Buchignani, N., and Armstrong, C. E. 1999. Informal care and older Native Canadians. *Ageing and Society*, 19, 3–32. *95, 96*

Buehler, C., and Gerard, J. M. 2002. Marital conflict, ineffective parenting, and children's and adolescents' maladjustment. *Journal of Marriage and Family*, 64, 78–92. *323*

Buehler, C., et al. 1998. Interparental conflict styles and youth problem behaviors: A two-sample replication study. *Journal of Marriage and the Family*, 60, 119–132. *322*

Buggarf, S. 1997. *The feminine economy and economic man: Revising the role of family in the post-industrial age*. Reading, MA: Addison Wesley. *459*

Buhrmester, D., and Furman, W. 1990. Perceptions of sibling relationships during middle childhood and adolescence. *Child Development*, 61, 1387–1398. *362*

Bulanda, R. E. 2004. Paternal involvement with children: The influence of gender ideologies. *Journal of Marriage and Family*, 66, 40–45. *462*

Bullen, J. 2000. Hidden workers: Child labour and the family economy in late nineteenth century urban Ontario. In B. Bradbury (Ed.), *Canadian family history* (pp. 199–219). Toronto: Irwin Publishing. *66*

Bumpass, L. 2001. The changing contexts of parenting in the United States. In J. C. Westman (Ed.), *Parenthood in America: Undervalued, underpaid, under siege* (pp. 211–219). Madison, WI: The University of Wisconsin Press. *63*

Bumpass, L. L., and Lu, H.-H. 2000. Increased cohabitation changing children's family settings. *Research on Today's Issues*, NICHD, 13, September. *211, 213, 240, 241, 397, 398*

Bumpass, L. L., Sweet, J. A., and Cherlin, A. 1991. The role of cohabitation in declining rates of marriage. *Journal of Marriage and the Family*, 53, 913–927. *211*

Bumpus, M. F., Crouter, A. C., and McHale, S. M. 1999. Work demands of dual-earner couples: Implications for parents' knowledge about children's daily lives in middle childhood. *Journal of Marriage and the Family*, 61, 465–475. *125*

Burgess, E. W., Locke, H. J., and Thomes, M. M. 1963. *The family: From traditional to companionship*. New York: American Book. *314*

Buriel, R., and De Ment, T. 1997. Immigration and sociocultural change in Mexican, Chinese, and Vietnamese American families. In A. Booth, A. C. Crouter, and N. Landale (Eds.), *Immigration and the family: Research and policy on U.S. immigrants* (pp. 165–200). Mahwah, NJ: Erlbaum. *105*

Burke, R., and Weir, T. 1976. Relationship of wives' employment status to husband, wife and pair satisfaction and performance. *Journal of Marriage and the Family*, 38, 279–287. *311*

Burnette, D. 1999. Social relationships of Latino grandparent caregivers: A role theory perspective. *The Gerontologist*, 39, 49–58. *292*

Burney, S. 1995. *Coming to Gum San: The story of Chinese Canadians*. Toronto: Health Canada (for the Multicultural History Society of Ontario). *104*

Burstyn, V. 1999. *The rites of men: Manhood, politics, and the culture of sport*. Toronto: University of Toronto Press. *78*

Burton, L. M. 1992. Black grandparents rearing children of drug-addicted parents: Stressors, outcomes, and the social service needs. *The Gerontologist*, 32, 744–751. *291*

Burton, L. M. 1996a. Age norms, the timing of family role transitions, and intergenerational caregiving among aging African American women. *The Gerontologist*, 36, 199–208. *283*

Burton, L. M. 1996b. The timing of childbearing, family structure, and the responsibilities of aging Black women. In E. M. Hetherington and E. A. Blechman (Eds.), *Stress, coping, and resiliency in children and families* (pp. 155–172). Mahwah, NJ: Erlbaum. *279*

Burton, L. M., and Bengtson, V. L. 1985. Black grandmothers: Issues of timing and continuity of roles. In V. L. Bengtson and J. F. Robertson (Eds.), *Grandparenthood* (pp. 61–80). Beverly Hills, CA: Sage. *283*

Burton, L. M., and Jarrett, R. L. 2000. In the mix, yet on the margins: The place of families in urban neighborhoods and child development research. *Journal of Marriage and the Family*, 62, 1114–1135. *156*

Bushman, B., J., and Huesmann, L. R. 2001. Effects of televised violence on aggression. In D. G. Singer and J. L. Singer (Eds.), *Handbook of children and the media* (pp. 223–254). Thousand Oaks, CA: Sage. *73, 74*

Buss, D. M., et al. 2001. A half century of mate preferences: The cultural evolution of values. *Journal of Marriage and Family*, 63, 491–503. *208–210*

Butler, A. C. 2002. Welfare, premarital childbearing and the role of normative climate: 1968–1994. *Journal of Marriage and Family*, 64, 295–313. *135*

Calhoun, C. 1998. Community without propinquity revisited: Communications technology and the transformation of the urban political sphere. *Sociological Inquiry*, 68, 373–397. *80*

Calixte, S., Johnson, J. L., and Motapanyane, J. M. 2004. Liberal, socialist, and radical feminism: An introduction to three theories about women's oppression and social change. In N. Mandell (Ed.), *Feminist issues: Race, class, and gender*, 4th Ed. (pp. 1–32). Toronto: Prentice Hall. *19, 20*

Call, V. R. A., and Heaton, T. B. 1997. Religious influence on marital stability. *Journal for the Scientific Study of Religion*, 36, 382–392. *196, 398*

Call, V., Sprecher, S., and Schwartz, P. 1995. The incidence and frequency of marital sex in a national sample. *Journal of Marriage and the Family*, 57, 639–652. *229, 230, 278*

Calliste, A. 2003. Black families in Canada: Exploring the interconnections of race, class, and gender. In M. Lynn (Ed.), *Voices: Essays on Canadian families*, 2nd Ed. (pp. 199–220). Scarborough, ON: Thomson Nelson. *42, 43, 108–110*

Campbell, L. D., Connidis, I. A., and Davies, L. 1999. Sibling ties in later life: A social network analysis. *Journal of Family Issues*, 20, 114–148. *374*

Cantor, J., and Nathanson, A. I. 2001. The media and parents: Protecting children from harm. In J. C. Westman (Ed.), *Parenthood in America: Undervalued, underpaid, and under siege* (pp. 232–241). Madison, WI: The University of Wisconsin Press. *62, 75*

Capaldi, D. M., and Clark, S. 1998. Prospective family predictors of aggression toward female partners for at-risk young men. *Developmental Psychology*, 34, 1175–1188. *423*

Caradec, V. 1997. Forms of conjugal life among the "young elderly." *Population: An English Selection*, 1997, 9, 47–73. *8*

Caragata, L. 1999. The construction of teen parenting and the decline of adoption. In J. Wong and D. Checkland (Eds.), *Teen pregnancy and parenting* (pp. 99–120). Toronto: University of Toronto Press. *134, 136, 246, 258*

Carbone, S. 1998. *Italians in Winnipeg: An illustrated history*. Winnipeg: University of Manitoba Press. *101*

Carey, E. 2001. Kids' special needs often unmet: Study. *The Toronto Star*, November 21. *141*

Carey, E. 2004. Homeless women "crisis." *Toronto Star*, April 13, A1, A4. *158*

Carey, N., and Farris, E. 1996. *Parents and schools: Partners in student learning* (NCES Publication No. 96–913). Washington, DC: U.S. Government Printing Office. *181*

Carlip, H. 1995. *Girl power: Young women speak out*. New York: Time Warner. *279*

Carlson, E. A., et al. 1999. Early environmental support and elementary school adjustment as predictors of school adjustment in middle adolescence. *Journal of Adolescent Research, 14*, 72–94. *341*

Carp, F. M. 2000. *Elder abuse in the family*. New York: Springer. *448*

Carr, D. 2004. Gender, preloss marital dependence, and older adults' adjustment to widowhood. *Journal of Marriage and Family, 66*, 220–235. *411*

Carstensen, L., Gottman, J., and Levenson, R. 1995. Emotional behavior in long-term marriage. *Psychology and Aging, 10*, 140–149. *318*

Casper, L. M. 1997. My daddy takes care of me! Fathers as care providers. *Current Population Reports*, Series P79–59. Washington, DC: U.S. Bureau of the Census. *276*

Casper, L. M., and O'Connell, M. 1998. Work, income, the economy, and married fathers as child-care providers. *Demography, 35*, 243–250. *276*

Caspi, A., et al. 1998. Childhood predictors of unemployment in early adulthood. *American Sociological Review, 63*, 424–451. *140, 469*

Cassan, F., Mazuy, M., and Clanche, F. 2001. Refaire sa vie de couple est plus fréquent pour les hommes. Paris: INSEE. <www.insee.fr>. *412*

Castaneda, C. 2002. *Figurations: Child bodies worlds*. Durham, NC: Duke University Press. *64*

Castellano, M. 2002. *Aboriginal family trends: Extended families, nuclear families, families of the heart*. Ottawa: Vanier Institute of the Family. *95*

Catasús Cervera, S. 1996. The socio-demographic and reproductive characteristics of Cuban women. *Latin American Perspectives, 23*, 87–98. *52*

Cavanaugh, C. 1993. The limitations of the pioneering partnership: The Alberta campaign for homestead dower, 1909–25. *Canadian Historical Review, 74*, 198–225. *45*

Cebello, R., et al. 2004. Gaining a child: Comparing the experiences of biological parents, adoptive parents, and stepparents. *Family Relations, 53*, 38–48. *261, 277, 282*

Ceci, S. J. 1991. How much does schooling influence general intelligence and its cognitive components? A reassessment of the evidence. *Developmental Psychology, 27*, 703–722. *179*

Chabot, J. M., and Ames, B. D. 2004. "It wasn't 'let's get pregnant and go do it'": Decision making in lesbian couples planning motherhood via donor insemination. *Family Relations, 53*, 348–356. *277*

Chafez, J. S. 1995. Chicken or egg: A theory of the relationship between feminist movements and family change. In K. O. Mason and A.-M Jensen (Eds.), *Gender and family change in industrialized countries* (pp. 63–81). Oxford: Clarendon Press. *121*

Chan, R. W., Raboy, R. C., and Patterson, C. J. 1998. Psychosocial adjustment among children conceived via donor insemination by lesbian and heterosexual mothers. *Child Development, 69*, 443–457. *244*

Chandra, A., and Stephen, E. H. 1998. Impaired fecundity in the United States: 1982–1995. *Family Planning Perspectives, 30*, 34–42. *252*

Chao, R. K. 1994. Beyond parental control and authoritarian parenting style: Understanding Chinese parenting through the cultural notion of training. *Child Development, 65*, 1111–1119. *337*

Chao, R. K., and Willms, J. D. 2002. The effects of parenting practices on children's outcomes. In *Vulnerable children* (pp. 149–166). Edmonton: University of Alberta Press. *334, 474*

Chappell, N. L., and Penning, M. J. 2001. Sociology of aging in Canada: Issues for the millennium. *Canadian Journal on Aging, 20*, 82–110. *21*

Chase-Lansdale, P. L., and Brooks-Gunn, J. 1995. Introduction. In P. L. Chase-Lansdale and J. Brooks-Gunn (Eds.), *Escape from poverty: What makes a difference for children?* (pp. 1–8). New York: Cambridge University Press. *141*

Chaves, M. 1991. Family structure and Protestant church attendance: The sociological basis of cohort and age effects. *Journal for the Scientific Study of Religion, 39*, 329–340. *198*

Cheal, D. 1996. *New poverty: Families in postmodern society*. Westport, CT: Greenwood Press. *120*

Che-Alford, J., and Hamm, B. 1999. Under one roof: Three generations living together. *Canadian Social Trends, 53*, 6–9. *6*

Cherlin, A. J. 1978. Remarriage as an incomplete institution. *American Journal of Sociology, 84*, 634–651. *412*

Cherlin, A. J. 1999. Going to extremes: Family structure, children's well-being and social science. *Demography, 36*, 421–428. *383, 405*

Cherlin, A. J. 2004. The deinstitutionalization of American marriage. *Journal of Marriage and Family, 66*, 848–861. *396*

Cherlin, A. J., Chase-Lansdale, P., and McRae, C. 1998. Effects of parental divorce on mental health throughout the life course. *American Sociological Review, 63*, 239–249. *406, 409, 457*

Chesler, P. 1989. *The sacred bond: The legacy of Baby M*. New York: Vintage. *258*

Chevan, A. 1996. As cheaply as one: Cohabitation in the older population? *Journal of Marriage and the Family, 58*, 656–667. *216*

Chi, P. S. K., and Laquatra, J. 1998. Profile of housing cost burden in the United States. *Journal of Family and Economic Issues*, 19, 175–193. *164*

Child Support Team. 2000. *Selected statistics on Canadian families and family law: Second edition*. Ottawa: Department of Justice. *404*

Children's Television Workshop. 1991. *What research indicates about the educational effects of Sesame Street*. New York: Children's Television Workshop. *70*

Christensen, C. P., and Weinfeld, M. 1993. The black family in Canada: A preliminary exploration of family patterns and inequality. *Canadian Ethnic Studies*, 25, 26–44. *108, 109*

Christensen, D. 2000. *Ahtahkakoop: The epic account of a Plains Cree head chief, his people, and their struggle for survival, 1816–1896*. Shell Lake, SK: Ahtahkakoop. *34*

Christensen, I. B. 1999. Is blood thicker than water? In A. L. Rygvold et al. (Eds.), *Mine—yours—ours—and theirs: Adoption, changing kinship and family patterns* (pp. 147–155). Oslo: Universiy of Oslo. *258*

Chung, A. 2003. Quebec parties make families a priority. *Toronto Star*, March 20. *98, 99*

Chunn, D. E. 2000. "Politicizing the personal": Feminism, law, and public policy. In N. Mandell and A. Duffy (Eds.), *Canadian families: Diversity, conflict, and change*, 2nd Ed. (pp. 225–259) Toronto. Harcourt Brace. *20*

CIC (Citizenship and Immigration Canada). 2003. International adoptions. *The Monitor*, Fall. <www.cic.gc.ca>. *262*

Cicirelli, V. G. 1989. Feelings of attachment to siblings and well-being in later life. *Psychology and Aging*, 4, 211–216. *374*

Cicirelli, V. G. 1994. Sibling relationships in cross-cultural perspective. *Journal of Marriage and the Family*, 56, 7–20. *360*

Cicirelli, V. G. 1995. *Sibling relationships across the life span*. New York: Plenum Press. *374*

Cicerelli, V. G. 1996. Sibling relationships in middle and old age. In G. H. Brody (Ed.), *Sibling relationships: Their causes and consequences* (pp. 47–74). Norwood, NJ: Ablex. *374*

Clairmont, D. H. J., and Magill, D. 1999. *Africville: The life and death of a Canadian black community*, 3rd Ed. Toronto: Canadian Scholars' Press. *43*

Clapp, G. 1992. *Divorce and new beginnings*. New York: Wiley. *413*

Clark, D. J. 2001. Surfing for seniors: Report of the National Council on Family Relations. March, F18, F20. *80*

Clark, L. A., Kochanska, G., and Ready, R. 2000. Mothers' personality and its interaction with child temperament as predictors of parenting behavior. *Journal of Personality and Social Psychology*, 79, 274–285. *330*

Clark, S. 1999. What do we know about unmarried mothers? In J. Wong and D. Checkland (Eds.), *Teen pregnancy and parenting* (pp. 10–24). Toronto: University of Toronto Press. *246, 249*

Clark, W. 1998. Religious observance, marriage and family. *Canadian Social Trends*, 50, 2–7. *191, 195, 196*

Clark, W. 2001. Kids and teens on the Net. *Canadian Social Trends*, 62, 6–10. *80*

Clark, W. 2002. Time alone. *Canadian Social Trends*, 66, 2–6. *127, 165*

Clark, W. 2003. Pockets of belief: Religious attendance patterns in Canada. *Canadian Social Trends*, 68, 2–5. *192, 193*

Clark, W. A. V., and Dieleman, F. M. 1996. *Households and housing*. New Brunswick, NJ: Center for Urban Policy Research. *164, 167*

Clarkberg, M. 1999. The price of partnering: The role of economic well-being in young adults' first union experiences. *Social Forces*, 77, 945–968. *239*

Clarkberg, M., Stolzenberg, R. M., and Waite, L. J. 1996. Attitudes, values, and entrance into cohabitational versus marital unions. *Social Forces*, 75, 609–633. *215, 397*

Clarke, J. 1991. Social integration on the Upper Canadian frontier: Elements of community in Essex County 1790–1850. *Journal of Historical Geography*, 17, 390–412. *39*

Clarke-Stewart, A. 1992. Consequences of child care for children's development. In A. Booth (Ed.), *Child care in the 1990s: Trends and consequences* (pp. 63–82). Hillsdale, NJ: Erlbaum. *176*

Clausen, J. A. 1986. *The life course: A sociological perspective*. Englewood Cliffs, NJ: Prentice Hall. *17*

Cleveland, H. H., and Wiebe, R. P. 2003. The moderation of adolescent-to-peer similarity in tobacco and alcohol use by school levels of substance use. *Child Development*, 74, 279–291. *180*

Clio Collective. 1987. *Quebec women: A history*. Toronto: Women's Press. *36, 57, 97*

Clydesdale, T. T. 1997. Family behaviors among early U.S. baby boomers: Exploring the effects of religion and income changes, 1965–1982. *Social Forces*, 76, 605–635. *126*

Coackley, J., and Donnelly, P. 2004. *Sports in society: Issues and controversies*. Toronto: McGraw-Hill Ryerson. *67, 78*

Coale, A. J., and Banister, J. 1994. Five decades of missing females in China. *Demography*, 31, 459–479. *49*

Cochran, S. D., et al. 2001. Cancer-related risk indicators and preventive screening behaviors among lesbians and bisexual women. *American Journal of Public Health*, 91, 591–597. *210*

Cohan, C. L., and Kleinbaum, S. 2002. Toward a greater understanding of the cohabitation effect: Premarital cohabitation and marital communication. *Journal of Marriage and Family*, 64, 180–192. *398*

Cohler, B. J., and Musick, J. S. 1996. Adolescent parenthood and the transition to adulthood. In J. A. Graber, J. Brooks-Gunn, and A. C. Petersen (Eds.), *Transitions through adolescence* (pp. 201–232). Mahwah, NJ: Erlbaum. *136*

Cole, P. 1995. Biotechnology and the "moral" family. In C. Ulanowsky (Ed.), *The family in the age of biotechnology* (pp. 47–60). Aldershot, UK: Avebury. *254*

Coleman, J. S. 1988. Social capital in the creation of human capital. *American Journal of Sociology, 94,* S95–S120. *14, 180, 184, 483*

Coleman, J. S. 1990a. *Foundations of social theory.* Cambridge, MA: Harvard University Press. *14, 126*

Coleman, J. S. 1990b. *Equality and achievement in education.* Boulder, CO: Westview Press. *14*

Coleman, J. S., and Hoffer, T. 1987. *Public and private schools: The impact of communities.* New York: Basic Books. *14, 153, 445*

Coleman, V. E. 1994. Lesbian battering: The relationship between personality and the perpetration of violence. *Violence and Victims, 9,* 139–152. *425*

Coley, R. L. 2001. (In)visible men: Emerging research on low-income, unmarried, and minority fathers. *American Psychologist, 56,* 743–753. *275*

Coley, R. L., and Chase-Lansdale, P. L. 1998. Adolescent pregnancy and parenthood: Recent evidence and future directions. *American Psychologist, 53,* 152–166. *137, 456, 457, 471*

Collins, P. H. 1990. *Black feminist thought: Knowledge, consciousness, and the politics of empowerment.* Boston: Unwin Hyman. *21, 342*

Collins, P. H. 1992. Black women and motherhood. In B. Thorne and M. Yalom (Eds.), *Rethinking the family* (rev. ed., pp. 215–245). Boston: Northeastern University Press. *125, 274*

Collins, W. A., and Russell, G. 1991. Mother-child and father-child relationships in middle childhood and adolescence: A developmental analysis. *Developmental Review, 11,* 99–136. *341*

Coltrane, S. 1996. *Family man: Fatherhood, housework, and gender equity.* New York: Oxford University Press. *307*

Coltrane, S. 1997. *Gender and families.* Thousand Oaks, CA: Sage. *20*

Coltrane, S. 2000. Research on household labor: Modeling and measuring the social embeddedness of routine family work. *Journal of Marriage and the Family, 62,* 1208–1233. *309*

Comeau, R. 1989. *Jean Lesage et l'éveil d'une nation: les débuts de la révolution tranquille.* Sillery, Quebec: Québec Presses de l'Université du Québec. *97*

Conger, R. D., and Conger, K. J. 1996. Sibling relationships. In R. Simons and Associates (Eds.), *Understanding differences between divorced and intact families* (pp. 104–121). Thousand Oaks, CA: Sage. *368, 369*

Conger, R. D., Ge, X.-J., and Lorenz, F. O. 1994. Economic stress and marital relations. In R. D. Conger and G. H. Elder, Jr. (Eds.), *Families in troubled times: Adapting to change in rural America* (pp. 187–203). New York: Aldine de Gruyter. *163*

Conger, R. D., Patterson, G. R., and Ge, X. 1995. It takes two to replicate: A mediational model for the impact of parents' stress on adolescent adjustment. *Child Development, 66,* 80–97. *337*

Conger, R. D., and Rueter, M. A. 1996. Siblings, parents, and peers: A longitudinal study of social influences in adolescent risk for alcohol use and abuse. In G. H. Brody (Ed.), *Sibling relationships: Their causes and consequences* (pp. 1–30). Norwood, NJ: Ablex. *365*

Connidis, I. A. 2001. *Family ties & aging,* 2nd Ed. Thousand Oaks, CA: Sage. *64, 294, 295, 298, 351–354, 356, 360, 373, 465*

Connidis, I. A., 2003a. Divorce and union dissolution: Reverberations over three generations. *Canadian Journal on Aging, 22,* 353–368. *405*

Connidis, I. A. 2003b. Bringing outsiders in: Gay and lesbian family ties over the life course. In S. Arber, K. Davidson, and J. Ginn (Eds.), *Gender and ageing: Changing roles and relationships* (pp. 79–94). Maidenhead, UK: Open University Press. *290, 350, 374*

Connidis, I. A., and Campbell, L. D. 1995. Closeness, confiding, and contact among siblings in middle and late childhood. *Journal of Family Issues, 16,* 722–745. *374*

Connidis, I. A., and McMullin, J. A. 1994. Social support in older age: Assessing the impact of marital and parent status. *Canadian Journal on Aging, 13,* 510–527. *225*

Connidis, I. A., and McMullin, J. A. 2002a. Sociological ambivalence and family ties: A critical perspective. *Journal of Marriage and Family, 64,* 558–567. *347, 350, 351*

Connidis, I. A., and McMullin, J. A. 2002b. Ambivalence, family ties, and doing sociology. *Journal of Marriage and Family, 64,* 594–601. *347, 350, 351*

Conrad, M. 1986. Sundays always make me think of home: Time and place in Canadian women's history. In V. Strong Boag and A. C. Fellman (Eds.), *Rethinking Canada: The promise of women's history* (pp. 67–81). Toronto: Copp Clark Pittman. *38*

Cook, C., and Beaujot, R. 1996. Labour force interruptions: The influence of marital status and presence of young children. *Canadian Journal of Sociology, 21,* 25–41. *220*

Cook, C., and Willms, J. D. 2002. Balancing work and family life. In J. D. Willms (Ed.). *Vulnerable children* (pp. 183–198). Edmonton: University of Alberta Press. *182*

Cook, D. A., and Fine, M. 1995. "Motherwit": Childrearing lessons from African-American mothers of low income. In B. B. Swadener and S. Lubeck (Eds.), *Children and families "at promise"* (pp. 118–142). Albany: State University of New York Press. *138*

Cooksey, E. C., and Craig, P. H. 1998. Parenting from a distance: The effects of paternal characteristics on contact between nonresidential fathers and their children. *Demography, 35,* 187–200. *242, 265, 275*

Cooksey, E. C., Menaghan, E. G., and Jekielek, S. M. 1997. Life-course effects of work and family circumstances on children. *Social Forces, 76,* 637–667. *125, 240, 415, 471*

Cooley, C. H. 1902. *Human nature and the social order.* New York: Scribner. *15*

Coombs, R. H. 1991. Marital status and personal well-being: A literature review. *Family Relations, 40,* 97–102. *218*

Cooney, T. M., and Dunne, K. 2001. Intimate relationships in later life. *Journal of Family Issues, 22,* 838-858. *216*

Cooney, T. M., and Uhlenberg, P. 1992. Support from parents over the life course: The adult child's perspective. *Social Forces, 71,* 63–84. *347*

Cooney, T. M., et al. 1993. Timing of fatherhood: Is "on-time" optimal? *Journal of Marriage and the Family, 55,* 205–215. *282*

Coontz, S. 1992. *The way we never were: American families and the nostalgia trap.* New York: Basic Books. *70*

Coontz, S. 2000. Historical perspectives on family studies. *Journal of Marriage and the Family, 62,* 283–297. *62, 68, 165, 265, 309*

Corak, M. 1998. Getting ahead in life: Does your parents' income count? *Canadian Social Trends, 49,* 6–10. *62*

Corcoran, M. 1995. Rags to rags: Poverty and mobility in the United States. *Annual Review of Sociology, 21,* 237–267. *141*

Corsaro, W. A. 1997. *The sociology of childhood.* Thousand Oaks, CA: Pine Forge Press. *15, 81, 175, 332, 354, 474*

Costello, C. Y. 1997. Conceiving identity: Bisexual, lesbian, and gay parents consider their children's sexual orientation. *Journal of Sociology and Social Welfare, 24,* 63–90. *244*

Côté, J. E. 2000. *Arrested adulthood: The changing nature of maturity and identity.* New York: New York University Press. *128, 347, 383*

Côté, J., and Allahar, A. L. 1994. *Generation on hold: Coming of age in the late twentieth century.* Toronto: Stoddart. *67, 76, 83, 341*

Cotten, S. R. 1999. Marital status and mental health revisited: Examining the importance of risk factors and resources. *Family Relations, 48,* 225–233. *390*

Coughlin, C., and Vuchinich, S. 1996. Family experience in preadolescence and the development of male delinquency. *Journal of Marriage and the Family, 58,* 491–501. *405, 415*

Counts, R. M. 1992. Second and third divorces: The flood to come. *Journal of Divorce and Remarriage, 17,* 193–200. *394*

Cowan, C. P., and Cowan, P. A. 1992. *When partners become parents: The big life change for couples.* New York: Basic Books. *278, 282*

Cowan, C. P., and Cowan, P. A. 1997. Working with couples during stressful transitions. In S. Dreman (Ed.), *The family on the threshold of the 21st century* (pp. 17–48). Mahwah, NJ: Erlbaum. *276–278*

Cowan, P. A., and Cowan, C. P. 1998. New families: Modern couples as new pioneers. In M. A. Mason, A. Skolnick, and S. D. Sugarman (Eds.), *All our families: New policies for a new century* (pp. 169–192). New York: Oxford University Press. *277, 278*

Cramer, J. C., and McDonald, K. B. 1996. Kin support and family stress: Two sides to early childbearing and support networks. *Human Organization, 55,* 160–169. *247*

Cranswick, K. 1997. Canada's caregivers. *Canadian Social Trends, 47,* 2–6. *353*

Crenshaw, K. W. 1994. Mapping the margins: Intersectionality, identity politics, and violence against women of color. In M. A. Fineman and R. Mykitiuk (Eds.), *The public nature of private violence.* New York: Routledge. *428*

Crimmins, E., Easterlin, R., and Saito, Y. 1991. Preference changes among American youth: Family, work, and goods aspirations, 1976–87. *Population and Development Review, 17,* 115–133. *347*

Crockenberg, S., and Leerkes, E. 2003. Infant negative emotionality, caregiving, and family relationships. In A. C. Crouter and A. Booth (Eds.), *Children's influence on family dynamics* (pp. 57–78). Mahwah, NJ: Erlbaum. *278, 331*

Crompton, R., and Harris, F. 1998. Explaining women's employment patterns: Orientation to work revisited. *British Journal of Sociology, 49,* 118–136. *458*

Crosnoe, R. 2004. Social capital and the interplay of families and schools. *Journal of Marriage and Family, 66,* 267–280. *179, 184*

Crosnoe, R., and Elder, G. H., Jr. 2002. Adolescent twins and emotional distress: The interrelated influence of nonshared environment and social structure. *Child Development, 73,* 1761-1774. *195, 369*

Cross, G. 1993. *Time and money: The making of consumer culture.* London: Routledge. *128*

Cross, W. E., Jr. 1990. Race and ethnicity: Effects on social networks. In M. Cochran et al. (Eds.), *Extending families: The social networks of parents and their children* (pp. 67–85). Cambridge: Cambridge University Press. *402*

Crotty, M. 1998. *The foundations of social research.* London: Sage. *18*

Crouch, J. L., and Milner, J. S. 1993. Effects of child neglect on children. *Criminal Justice and Behavior, 20,* 49–65. *437*

Crouter, A. C., et al. 1999. Conditions underlying parents' knowledge about children's daily lives in middle childhood: Between and within-family comparisons. *Child Development, 70,* 246–259. *125, 369, 370*

Crowder, K. D., and Tolnay, S. E. 2000. A new marriage squeeze for Black women: The role of racial intermarriage by Black men. *Journal of Marriage and the Family, 62,* 792–807. *209*

Csikszentmihalyi, M. 1999. If we are so rich, why aren't we happy? *American Psychologist, 54,* 821–827. *149*

Cuber, J., and Harroff, P. B. 1965. *The significant American.* New York: Hawthorn. *302–306*

Cummings, E. M., Goeke-Morey, M. C., and Papp, L. M. 2003. Children's responses to everyday marital conflict tactics in the home. *Child Development, 74,* 1918-1929. *322*

Cunningham, M. 2001. Parental influences on the gendered division of housework. *American Sociological Review*, 66, 184–203. *462*

Daguet, F. 2004. La fécondité dans les régions à la fin des années quatre-vingt dix. Paris: INSEE, April. <www.insee.fr>. *251*

Dalenberg, C. J., and Jacobs, D. A. 1994. Attributional analyses of child sexual abuse episodes: Empirical and clinical issues. *Journal of Child Sexual Abuse*, 3, 37–50. *441*

D'Alfonso, A. 2000. *En italiques: réflexions sur l'ethnicité*. Montréal: Éditions Balzac. *101*

Daly, K. 2000. It keeps getting faster: Changing patterns of time in families. Ottawa: The Vanier Institute of the Family. *123*

Daly, K. J. 2001. Deconstructing family time: From ideology to lived experience. *Journal of Marriage and Family*, 63, 283–294. *127*

Daly, K. 2003. Family theory versus the theories families live by. *Journal of Marriage and Family*, 65, 771–784. *12, 15, 129, 149*

Daly, K., and Chesney-Lind, M. 1988. Feminism and criminology. *Justice Quarterly*, 5, 497–538. *427*

Daly, K. J., and Sobol, M. P. 1994. Adoption in Canada. *Canadian Social Trends*, 32, 2–5. *258*

Damon, W. 1995. *Greater expectations: Overcoming the culture of indulgence in America's homes and schools*. New York: Free Press. *475*

Daniel, K. 1996. The marriage premium. In M. Tommasi and K. Ierulli (Eds.), *The new economics of human behavior* (pp. 113–125). Cambridge: Cambridge University Press. *219*

Daniels, D. 1987. Differential experiences of children in the same family as predictors of adolescent sibling personality differences. *Journal of Personality and Social Psychology*, 51, 339–346. *372*

Danvers, G. D. 2001. Gendered encounters: Warriors, women and William Johnson. *Journal of American Studies*, 35, 187–202. *34*

Darlington, J. W. 1997. Farmsteads as mirrors of cultural adjustment and change: The Ukrainian Canadian experience. *Great Plains Research*, 7, 71–101. *45*

Das Gupta, T. 2000. Families of Native people, immigrants, and people of colour. In N. Mandell and A. Duffy (Eds.), *Canadian families: Diversity, conflict, and change*, 2nd Ed. (pp. 146–187). Toronto: Harcourt Brace. *21, 41, 46, 93, 106, 107, 110*

Dauria, S. R. 1994. Kateri Tekakwitha: Gender and ethnic symbolism in the process of making an American saint. *New York Folklore*, 20, 55–73. *34*

Dauvergne, M. 2003. Family violence against seniors. *Canadian Social Trends*, 68, 10–14. *448*

Davey, A., and Szinovacz, M. E. 2004. Dimensions of marital quality and retirement. *Journal of Family Issues*, 25, 431–464. *318*

Davey, J. D. 1995. *The new social contract: America's journey from welfare state to police state*. Westport, CT: Praeger. *468*

Davies, A. A. 2002. Celebrating Alberta's Italian community. Heritage Community Foundation. <www.albertasource.ca/abitalian/>. *100*

Davies, L. 1995. A closer look at gender and distress among the never married. *Women and Health*, 23, 13–30. *225*

Davies, L. 2003. Singlehood: Transitions within a gendered world. *Canadian Journal on Aging*, 22, 343–352. *224, 225*

Davies, L., McKinnon, M., and Rains, P. 1999. "On my own": A new discourse of dependence and independence from teen mothers. In J. Wong and D. Checkland (Eds.), *Teen pregnancy and parenting* (pp. 38–51). Toronto: University of Toronto Press. *247, 249*

Davis, E. C., and Friel, L. V. 2001. Adolescent sexuality: Disentangling the effects of family structure and family context. *Journal of Marriage and Family*, 63, 669–681. *227*

Davis, J. H. and Juhasz, A. M. 1995. The preadolescent/pet friendship bond. *Anthrozoos*, 8, 78–82. *286*

Day, R. D., Peterson, G. D., and McCracken, C. 1998. Predicting spanking of younger children and older children by mothers and fathers. *Journal of Marriage and the Family*, 60, 79–94. *433*

DeAngelis, T. 2002. A new generation of issues for LGBT clients. *Monitor on Psychology*, 33, February. <www.apa.org/monitor/beb02/generation>. *210, 244*

Deater-Deckard, K. 2000. Parenting and child behavioral adjustment in early childhood: A quantitative genetic approach to studying family processes. *Child Development*, 71, 468–484. *380*

Deater-Deckard, K., et al. 1996. Physical discipline among African American and European American mothers: Links to children's externalizing behaviors. *Developmental Psychology*, 32, 1065–1072. *337*

Deater-Deckard, K., et al. 1998. Family structure and depressive symptoms in men preceding and following the birth of a child. *American Journal of Psychiatry*, 155, 818–823. *380*

DeFronzo, J. 1997. Welfare and homicide. *Journal of Research in Crime and Delinquency*, 34, 395–406. *468*

Dei, G. J. 1993. Narrative discourses of Black/African-Canadian parents and the Canadian public school system. *Canadian Ethnic Studies*, 25, 45–54. *110*

DeKeseredy, W. S. 2000. Current controversies on defining non-lethal violence against women in intimate heterosexual relationships: Empirical implications. *Violence Against Women*, 6, 728–746. *424, 427*

DeKeseredy, W. S., and Ellis, D. 1997. Sibling violence: A review of Canadian sociological research and suggestions for further empirical research. *Humanity & Society*, 21, 397–411. *443*

DeKeseredy, W. S., and Kelly, K. 1993a. The incidence and prevalence of woman abuse in Canadian university and college dating relationships. *Canadian Journal of Sociology, 18,* 137–159. *422*

DeKeseredy, W. S., and Kelly, K. 1993b. Woman abuse in university and college relationships: The contribution of the ideology of familial patriarchy. *Journal of Human Justice, 4,* 25–52. *425*

DeKeseredy, W. S., et al. 1997. The meanings and motives for women's use of violence in Canadian college dating relationships: Result from a national survey. *Sociological Spectrum, 17,* 199–222. *422*

Dell, F., Legendre, N., and Ponthieux, S. 2003. La pauvreté chez les enfants. Paris: INSEE. <www.insee.fr>. *467*

Del Negro, G. 2003. *Looking through my mother's eyes: Life stories of nine Italian immigrant women in Canada,* 2nd Ed. Toronto: Guernica. *102*

del Olmo, R. 1979. The Cuban revolution and the struggle against prostitution. *Crime and Social Justice,* Winter, 34–40. *52*

Delsol, C., Margolin, G., and John, R. S. 2003. A typology of maritally violent men and correlates of violence in a community sample. *Journal of Marriage and Family, 65,* 635–651. *423, 425, 430*

DeMaris, A., et al. 2003. Distal and proximal factors in domestic violence: A test of an integrated model. *Journal of Marriage and Family, 65,* 652–667. *427*

Demo, D. H. 1992. Parent-child relations: Assessing recent changes. *Journal of Marriage and the Family, 54,* 104–117. *342*

Demo, D. H., and Acock, A. C. 1993. Family diversity and the division of domestic labor: How much have things really changed? *Family Relations, 42,* 323–331. *312*

Demo, D. H., and Cox, M. J. 2000. Families with young children: A review of research in the 1990s. *Journal of Marriage and the Family, 62,* 876–895. *278*

Demos, J. 1971. Developmental perspectives on the history of childhood. *The Journal of Interdisciplinary History, 2,* 315–327. *341*

Demos, J., 1974. The American family in past time. *American Scholar, 63,* 422–446. *288*

den Boggende, B. 1997. Alone in the province: The Cobourg ladies' seminary of Burlington Ladies' Academy 1842–1851. *Ontario History, 89,* 53–74. *38*

Denzin, N. K., and Lincoln, Y. S. (Eds.). 1994. *Handbook of qualitative research.* Thousand Oaks, CA: Sage. *25*

Desetta, A. 1996. *The heart knows something different: Teenage voices from the foster care system.* New York: Perseus Books. *264*

Deveaus. 2000. Conflicting equalities? Cultural group rights and sex equality. *Political Studies, 48,* 522–539. *93*

Devine, J. A., and Wright, J. D. 1993. *The greatest of evils: Urban poverty and the American underclass.* New York: Aldine de Gruyter. *135*

DeWitt, P. M. 1994. The second time around. *American Demographics, 16,* 11–14. *412*

Diener, E., and Biswas-Diener, R. 2002. Will money increase subjective well-being? *Social Indicators Research, 57,* 119–169. *150*

DiGiorgio-Miller, J. 1998. Sibling incest: Treatment of the family and the offender. *Child Welfare, 77,* 335–346. *444*

DiLeonardi, J. W. 1993. Families living in poverty and chronic neglect of children. *Families in Society, 74,* 556–562. *437*

Dilla, H. (Ed.). 1999. *La democracia en Cuba y el diferendo con los Estados Unidos.* La Habana: Centro de Estudios Sobre América. *53*

Dilworth-Anderson, P. 1992. Extended kin networks in black families. *Generations, 17,* 29–36. *290*

Dion, K. 1996. Cultural perspectives on romantic love. *Personal Relationships, 3,* 5–17.

Dion, K. K., and Dion, K. L. 1993. Individualistic and collectivistic perspectives on gender and the cultural context of love and intimacy. *Journal of Social Issues, 49,* 53–69. *50, 217*

Dion, K. K., and Dion, K. L. 2001. Gender and cultural adaptation in immigrant families. *Journal of Social Issues, 57,* 511–521. *21*

Dittman, M. 2002. *Running on Ritalin.* New York: Bantam Books. *76*

Djider, Z. 2002. Femmes et hommes: les inégalités qui subsistent. Paris: INSEE. <www.insee.fr>. *122*

Dodge, K. A., Bates, J. E., and Pettit, G. S. 1990. Mechanisms in the cycle of violence. *Science, 250,* 1678–1683. *434*

Doherty, W. J. 2000. Family science and family citizenship: Toward a model of community partnership with families. *Family Relations, 49,* 319–325. *67, 275, 457, 474*

Doherty, J., Norton, E., and Veney, J. 2001. China's one-child policy: The economic choices and consequences faced by pregnant women. *Social Science and Medicine, 52,* 745–761. *49*

Doherty, W. J., Kouneski, E. F., and Erickson, M. F. 1998. Responsible fathering: An overview and conceptual framework. *Journal of Marriage and the Family, 60,* 277–292. *265, 276, 286, 404, 475*

Doherty, W. J., Kouneski, E. F., and Erickson, M. F. 2000. We are all responsible for responsible fathering: A response to Walher and McGraw. *Journal of Marriage and the Family, 62,* 570–574. *275*

Doisneau, L. 2002. Bilan démographique 2000: Le regain des naissances et des mariages se confirme. Paris: INSEE. <www.insee.fr>. *238, 251*

Donnerstein, E., and Linz, D. 1995. The media. In J. Q. Wilson and J. Petersilia (Eds.), *Crime* (pp. 257–266). San Francisco: CA: Institute for Contemporary Studies. *74*

Dorfman, L. T., Holmes, C. A., and Berlin, K. L. 1996. Wife caregiver of frail elderly veterans: Correlates of caregiver satisfaction and caregiver strain. *Family Relations, 45,* 46–55. *319*

Dorr, A., Kovaric, P., and Doubleday, C. 1990. Age and content influences on children's perception of the realism of television families. *Journal of Broadcasting and Electronic Media*, 34, 377–397. *72*

Dougherty, K., and Jelowicki, A. 2000. Night daycare to make debut: Pilot projects will offer $5 daily rate. *The Montreal Gazette*. August 31. *99*

Downey, D. B. 1994. The school performance of children from single-mother and single-father families: Economic or interpersonal deprivation? *Journal of Family Issues, 15*, 129–147. *404*

Downey, D. B. 1995. When bigger is not better: Family size, parental resources, and children's educational performance. *American Sociological Review, 60*, 746–761. *176, 362*

Downey, D. B., Ainsworth-Darnell, J. W., and Dufur, M. J. 1998. Sex of parent and children's well-being in single-parent households. *Journal of Marriage and the Family, 60*, 878–893. *404*

Downey, D. B., and Condron, D. J. 2004. Playing well with others in kindergarten: The benefit of siblings at home. *Journal of Marriage and Family, 66*, 333–350. *363*

Downey, D. B., and Powell, B. 1993. Do children in single-parent households fare better living with same-sex parents? *Journal of Marriage and the Family, 55*, 55–71. *403*

Dranoff, L. S. 2001. *Everyone's guide to the law*. Toronto: Harper Press. *8*

Drapeau, S., et al. 2000. Siblings in family transitions. *Family Relations, 49*, 77–85. *264, 403*

Driscoll, A. K., et al. 1999. Nonmarital childbearing among adult women. *Journal of Marriage and the Family, 61*, 178–187. *471*

Drolet, M. 2001. The male-female wage gap. *Perspectives on Labour and Income*, 2, December, 5–11. *122*

Drolet, M. 2003. Motherhood and paycheques. *Canadian Social Trends, 68*, 19–21. *121*

Dryburgh, H. 2002. *Teenage pregnancy*. Health Reports, Vol. 12, No. 1, Statistics Canada. *247*

Dua, E. 1999. Beyond diversity: Explaining the ways in which the discourse of race has shaped the institution of the nuclear family. In E. Dua (Ed.), *Scratching the surface: Canadian antiracist feminist thought* (pp. 237–260). Toronto: Women's Press. *21, 107, 110*

Dubeau, D. 2002. *Portraits of fathers*. Ottawa: The Vanier Institute of the Family. <www.vifamily.ca>. *275*

Duffy, A. 1997. The part-time solution: Toward entrapment or empowerment? In A. Duffy, D. Glenday, and N. Pupo (Eds.), *Good jobs, bad jobs* (pp. 166–188). Toronto: Harcourt Brace. *120*

Duffy, A. 2004. Violence against women. In N. Mandell (Ed.), *Feminist issues: Race, class, and gender*, 4th Ed. (pp. 127–159). Toronto: Prentice Hall. *425, 427, 439*

Duffy, A., Mandell, N., and Pupo, N. 1989. *Few choices: Women, work and family*. Toronto: Garamond. *122*

Duffy, A., and Momirov, J. 1997. *Family violence: A Canadian introduction*. Toronto: Lorimer. *448, 451*

Duffy, A., and Momirov, J. 2000. Family violence: Issues and advances at the end of the twentieth century. In N. Mandell and A. Duffy (Eds.), *Canadian families: Diversity, conflict, and change*, 2nd Ed. (pp. 290–322). Toronto: Harcourt Brace. *421*

Duffy, A., and Pupo, N. 1996. Family friendly organization and beyond: Proposals for policy directions with women in mind. In National Forum on Family Security, *Family security in insecure times*, vol. II. Ottawa: Canadian Council on Social Development. *455*

Dumas, J., and Bélanger, A. 1997. *Report on the demographic situation in Canada 1996*. Ottawa: Statistics Canada. *213*

Dumont, L. 1998. *Homo herarchicus: The caste system and its implications*. Delhi: Oxford University Press. *50*

Dumont, M. 1995. Women of Quebec and the contemporary constitutional issue. In F. P. Gingras (Ed.), *Gender politics in contemporary Canada* (pp. 153–175). Toronto: Oxford University Press. *98*

Dumont-Smith, C., and Sioui-Labelle, P. 1991. *National family violence survey: Phase 1*. Ottawa: Aboriginal Nurses of Canada. *94*

Dunaway, W. A. 2003. *The African-American family in slavery and emancipation*. Cambridge, New York: Maison des sciences de l'homme/Cambridge University Press. *42*

Duncan, G. J., and Brooks-Gunn, J. 1997. Income effects across the life span: Integration and interpretation. In G. J. Duncan and J. Brooks-Gunn (Eds.), *Consequences of growing up poor* (pp. 596–610). New York: Russell Sage. *140, 167*

Duncan, G. J., et al. 1998. How much does childhood poverty affect the life chances of children? *American Sociological Review, 63*, 406–423. *137, 140, 469*

Dunifon, R., and Kowaleski-Jones, L. 2002. Who's in the house? Race differences in cohabitation, single parenthood, and child development. *Child Development*, 73, 1249–1264. *244*

Dunn, J. 1994. Temperament, siblings, and the development of relationships. In W. B. Carey and S. C. McDevitt (Eds.), *Prevention and early intervention* (pp. 50–58). New York: Bruner/Mazel. *285, 361, 365*

Dunn, J. 1996. Brothers and sisters in middle childhood and early adolescence: Continuity and change in individual differences. In G. H. Brody (Ed.), *Sibling relationships: Their causes and consequences* (pp. 31–46). Norwood, NJ: Ablex. *364*

Dunn, J., and McGuire, S. 1994. Young children's nonshared experiences: A summary of studies in Cambridge and Colorado. In E. M. Hetherington, D. Reiss, and R. Plomin (Eds.), *Separate social worlds of siblings* (pp. 111–128). Hillsdale, NJ: Erlbaum. *365, 377*

Dunn, J., and Plomin, R. 1990. *Separate lives: Why siblings are so different*. New York: Basic Books. *377*

Dunn, J., Plomin, R., and Daniels, D. 1986. Consistency and change in mothers' behavior to two-year-old siblings. *Child Development*, 57, 348–356. *370*

Dunn, J., et al. 1994. Adjustment in middle childhood and early adolescence: Links with earlier and contemporary sibling relationships. *Journal of Child Psychology and Psychiatry*, 35, 491–504. *364*

Dupuis, D. 1998. What influences people's plans to have children? *Canadian Social Trends*, 48, 2–5. *250*

Dupuis, S. L. and Norris, J. E. 2001. The roles of adult daughters in long-term care facilities: Alternative role manifestations. *Journal of Aging Studies*, 15, 27–54. *353*

Duran, J. 1998. *Philosophies of science/feminist theories*. Boulder, CO: Westview Press. *20*

Durkheim, E. 1951 (1897). *Suicide*. New York: Free Press. *196*

Durrat, J. E., Rose-Krasnor, L., and Broberg, A. G. 2003. Physical punishment and maternal beliefs in Sweden and Canada. *Journal of Comparative Family Studies*, 34, 585–604. *433*

Dush, C. M. K., Cohan, C. L., and Amato, P. R. 2003. The relationship between cohabitation and marital quality and stability: Change across cohorts? *Journal of Marriage and Family*, 65, 539–549. *398*

Duvall, E. M. 1957. *Family development*. Philadelphia: Lippincott. *17*

Duvander, A. 1999. The transition from cohabitation to marriage. *Journal of Family Issues*, 20, 698–717. *213*

Eamon, M. K. 2002. Effects of poverty on mathematics and reading achievement of young adolescents. *Journal of Early Adolescence*, 22, 49–74. *140*

East, P. L. 1999. The first teenage pregnancy in the family: Does it affect mothers' parenting, attitudes, or mother-adolescent communication? *Journal of Marriage and the Family*, 61, 306–319. *247*

East, P. L., Felice, M. E., and Morgan, M. C. 1993. Sisters' and girlfriends' sexual and childbearing behavior: Effects on early adolescent girls' sexual outcomes. *Journal of Marriage and the Family*, 55, 953–963. *365, 366*

East, P. L., and Jacobson, L. J. 2000. Adolescent childbearing, poverty, and siblings: Taking new directions from the literature. *Family Relations*, 49, 287–292. *247, 283, 377*

Easterbrook, G. 2003. *The progress paradox: How life gets better while people feel worse*. New York: Random House. *128*

E. B. D. Adoption Institute. 2002. Overview of adoption in the United States. <www.adoptioninstitute.org>. *257*

Eckenrode, J., Laird, M., and Doris, J. 1993. School performance and disciplinary problems among abused and neglected children. *Developmental Psychology*, 29, 53–62. *434, 437*

Eder, D. 1991. The role of teasing in adolescent peer group culture. *Sociological Studies of Child Development*, 4, 181–197. *444*

Edin, K., and Lein, L. 1997a. *Making ends meet: How single mothers survive welfare and low-wage work*. New York: Sage. *135, 138*

Edin, K., and Lein, L. 1997b. Work, welfare, and single mothers' economic survival strategies. *American Sociological Review*, 62, 253–266. *133, 135, 136*

Edwards, M. E. 2001. Uncertainty and the rise of the work-family dilemma. *Journal of Marriage and Family*, 63, 83–196. *121*

Egan, S. K., and Perry, D. G. 1998. Does low self-regard invite victimization? *Developmental Psychology*, 34, 299–309. *445*

Eggebeen, D. J., and Knoester, C. 2001. Does fatherhood matter for men? *Journal of Marriage and Family*, 63, 381–393. *275*

Eichler, M. 1988. *Families in Canada today: Recent changes and their policy consequences*. Toronto: Gage. *10, 12, 20, 30, 66, 257, 274, 464*

Eichler, M. 1997. *Family shifts: Families, policies, and gender equality*. Toronto: Oxford University Press. *9, 21, 456, 479*

Eichler, M. 2001. Biases in family literature. In M. Baker (Ed.), *Families: Changing trends in Canada*, 4th Ed. (pp. 51–66). Toronto: McGraw-Hill Ryerson. *32*

Elder, G. H., Jr. 1991. Family transitions, cycles, and social change. In P. A. Cowan and M. Hetherington (Eds.), *Family transitions* (pp. 31–57). Hillsdale, NJ: Erlbaum. *17*

Elder, G. H., Jr. 1995. The life course paradigm and social change: Historical and developmental perspectives. In P. Moen, G. H. Elder, Jr., and K. Lüscher (Eds.), *Perspectives on the ecology of human development* (pp. 101–140). Washington, DC: American Psychological Association. *168, 330, 343*

Elder, G. H., Jr. 1998. The life course as developmental theory. *Child Development*, 69, 1–12. *17, 295*

Elder, G. H., Jr., Caspi, A., and Nguyen, T. V. 1994a. Resourceful and vulnerable children: Family influences in stressful times. In R. K. Silbereisen and K. Eyferth (Eds.), *Development in context: Integrative perspectives on youth development*. New York: Springer-Verlag. *337, 433*

Elder, G. H., Jr., Foster, E. M., and Ardelt, M. 1994b. Children in the household economy. In R. D. Conger, G. H. Elder, Jr., and Associates (Eds.), *Families in troubled times: Adapting to change in rural America* (pp. 127–146). New York: Aldine de Gruyter. *162*

Elder, G. H., Jr., Robertson, E. B., and Foster, E. M. 1994c. Survival, loss, and adaptation: A perspective on farm families. In R. D. Conger et al. (Eds.), *Families in troubled times: Adapting to change in rural America* (pp. 105–126). New York: Aldine de Gruyter. *162*

Elder, G. H., Jr., et al. 1992. Families under economic pressure. *Journal of Family Issues*, 13, 5–37. *139*

Elgar, F. J., et al. 2003. Antecedent-consequence conditions in maternal mood and child adjustment problems: A four-year cross-lagged study. *Journal of Clinical Child and Adolescent Psychology*, 32, 362–374. *331*

Elliott, B. J., and Richards, M. P. M. 1991. Children and divorce: Educational performance and behavior before and after parental separation. *International Journal of Law and the Family*, 5, 258–276. *409*

Elliott, P. 1996. Shattering the illusions: Same-sex domestic violence. In C. M. Renzetti and C. H. Miley (Eds.), *Violence in gay and lesbian domestic partnerships* (pp. 1–8). New York: Harrington Park Press. *428*

Ellis, B. J., et al. 2003. Does father absence place daughters at special risk of early sexual activity and teenage pregnancy? *Child Development*, 74, 801–821. *415*

Ellison, C. G. 1994. Religion, the life stress paradigm, and the study of depression. In J. S. Levin (Ed.), *Religion in aging and health: Theoretical foundations and methodological frontiers* (pp. 78–121). Newbury Park, CA: Sage. *195*

Ellison, C. G., and George, L. K. 1994. Religious involvement, social ties, and social support in a Southeastern community. *Journal for the Scientific Study of Religion*, 33, 46–61. *196*

Elze, D. E. 2002. Against all odds: The dating experiences of adolescent lesbian and bisexual women. *Journal of Lesbian Studies*, 6, 17–29. *208*

Emberley, J. V. 2001. The bourgeois family, Aboriginal women, and colonial governance in Canada: A study in feminist historical and cultural materialism. *Signs*, 27, 59–85. *41*

Emery, R. E. 1999. Postdivorce family life for children: An overview of research and some implications for policy. In R. A. Thompson and P. R. Amato (Eds.), *The postdivorce family* (pp. 3–27). Thousand Oaks, CA: Sage. *405, 410, 471*

Emery, R. E., and Laumann-Billings, L. 1998. An overview of the nature, causes, and consequences of abusive family relationships: Toward differentiating maltreatment and violence. *American Psychologist*, 53, 121–135. *432*

Engelbert, A. 1994. Worlds of childhood: Differentiated but different. Implications for social policy. In J. Qvortrup et al. (Eds.), *Childhood matters: Social theory, practice, and politics* (pp. 285–298). Aldershot, UK: Avebury. *67*

Engelbrecht, W. 2003. *Iroquoia: The development of a Native world*. Syracuse, NY. *35*

Engels, J. W. 1995. Marriage in the People's Republic of China: Analysis of a new law. In M. Rank and E. Kain (Eds.), *Diversity and change in families: Patterns, prospects and policies* (pp. 57–67). Englewood Cliffs, NJ: Prentice Hall. *47, 48*

England, P. 2000. Marriage, the costs of children and gender inequality. In L. J. Waite et al. (Eds.), *The ties that bind: Perspectives on marriage and cohabitation* (pp. 320–342). New York: Aldine de Gruyter. *220*

Entwisle, D. R., Alexander, K. L., and Olson, L. S. 1997. *Children, schools, and inequality*. Boulder, CO: Westview Press. *179, 182, 186, 202*

Erdwins, C. J., et al. 2001. The relationship of women's role strain to social support, role satisfaction, and self-efficacy. *Family Relations*, 50, 230–238. *178*

Erel, O., and Burman, B. 1995. Interrelatedness of marital relations and parent-child relations: A meta-analytic review. *Psychological Bulletin*, 118, 108–132. *324*

Erera, P.-I. 1997. Step- and foster families: A comparison. *Marriage and Family Review*, 26, 301–315. *265*

Errington, E. J. 1995. *Wives and mothers, schoolmistresses and scullery maids: Working women in Upper Canada, 1790–1840*. Montreal: McGill-Queen's University Press. *39*

Ertl, H. 2000. Parental involvement and children's academic achievement in the National Longitudinal Survey of Children and Youth, 1994–1996. *Education Quarterly Review*, 6, 35–50. *182*

Eshleman, J. R., and Wilson, S. J. 2001. *The family*, 3rd Can. Ed. Toronto: Pearson. *15*

Espelage, D., et al. 1996. Paper presented at the annual meeting of the American Psychological Association, reported in the APA *Monitor*, p. 41. *445*

Espelage, D. L., Holt, M. K., and Henkel, R. R. 2003. Examination of peer-group contextual effects on aggression during early adolescence. *Child Development*, 74, 205–300. *383*

Essex, E. L. 2002. Mothers and fathers of adults with mental retardation: Feelings of intergenerational closeness. *Family Relations*, 51, 156–165. *348*

Etter, J. 1993. Levels of cooperation and satisfaction in 56 open adoptions. *Child Welfare*, 72, 257–267. *263*

Etzioni, A. 1994. *The spirit of community: Rights, responsibilities, and the new communitarian agenda*. New York: Crown. *457*

Eugster, A., and Vingerhoets, A. J. J. M. 1999. Psychological aspects of in vitro fertilization: A review. *Social Science & Medicine*, 48, 575–589. *255*

Evans, P. M. 1996. Single mothers and Ontario's welfare policy: Restructuring the debate. In J. Brodie (Ed.), *Women and public policy*. Toronto: Harcourt Brace. *22*

Eyer, D. E. 1992. *Mother-infant bonding*. New Haven, CT: Yale University Press. *274*

Fabbi, N. 2003. Early Black Canadian history. Canadian Studies Center. Henry M. Jackson School of International Studies, University of Washington. <http://jsis.artsci.washington.edu/programs/Canada/edumodules/Early%20Black%20Canadian%20History.pdf>. *42*

Fabricius, W. V. 2003. Listening to children of divorce: New findings that diverge from Wallerstein, Lewis, and Blakeslee. *Family Relations*, 52, 385–396. *403*

Farnam, K. 1998. The westlings: Swedish pioneers. *Alberta History*, 46, 10–14. *45*

Fast, J., et. al. 2001. The time of our lives ... *Canadian Social Trends*, 63, 20–23. *79*

Faurre, L. C., and Maddock, J. M. 1994. Sexual meaning systems of engaged couples. *Family Relations*, 43, 53–60. *427*

Feigelman, W. 1997. Adopted adults: Comparisons with persons raised in conventional families. *Marriage and Family Review, 25,* 199–223. *259*

Feinberg, M. E., et al. 2000. Sibling comparison of differential parental treatment in adolescence: Gender, self-esteem, and emotionality as mediators of the parenting adjustment association. *Child Development, 71,* 1611–1628. *372*

Feldhaus, K. M., et al. 1997. Accuracy of 3 brief screening questions for detecting partner violence in the emergency department. *Journal of the American Medical Association, 277,* 1357–1361. *426*

Feldman, S. S., and Rosenthal, D. A. 1990. The acculturation of autonomy expectations in Chinese highschoolers residing in two Western nations. *International Journal of Psychology, 25,* 259–281. *106*

Feng, D., et al. 1999. Intergenerational transmission of marital quality and marital instablity. *Journal of Marriage and the Family, 61,* 451–463. *397*

Fenton, W. N. 1998. *The great law and the longhouse: A political history of the Iroquois confederacy.* Norman, OK: University of Oklahoma Press. *35*

Fergusson, D. M., and Horwood, L. J. 1998. Exposure to interparental violence in childhood and psychosocial adjustment in young adulthood. *Child Abuse & Neglect, 22,* 339–357. *430*

Fergusson, D. M., Lynskey, M., and Horwood, L. J. 1995. The adolescent outcomes of adoption: A 16-year longitudinal study. *Journal of Child Psychology and Psychiatry, 36,* 597–615. *383*

Fernandez-Kelly, M. P. 1995. Social and cultural capital in the urban ghetto: Implications for the economic sociology of immigration. In A. Portes (Ed.), *The economic sociology of immigration* (pp. 213–247). New York: Russell Sage. *136*

Ferraro, K. F., and Koch, J. R. 1994. Religion and health among black and white adults: Examining social support and consolation. *Journal for the Scientific Study of Religion, 33,* 362–375. *196*

Ferree, M. M., and Hall, E. J. 1996. Gender, race, and class in mainstream textbooks. *American Sociological Review, 61,* 929–950. *20, 301*

Ferree, M. M., Lorber, J., and Hess, B. B. (Eds.). 1999. *Revisioning gender.* Thousand Oaks, CA: Sage. *18*

Fincham, F. D. 1998. Child development and marital relations. *Child Development, 69,* 543–574. *322*

Fingard, J. 1992. Race and respectability in Victorian Halifax. *Journal of Imperial and Commonwealth History, 20,* 169–195. *44*

Finkelhor, D., et al. 1990. Sexual abuse in a national survey of adult men and women: Prevalence, characteristics, and risk factors. *Child Abuse & Neglect, 14,* 19–28. *439*

Finnegan, R. A., Hodges, E. V. E., and Perry, D. G. 1998. Victimization by peers: Associations with children's reports of mother-child interaction. *Journal of Personality and Social Psychology, 75,* 1076–1086. *445*

Fischer, D. G. 1993. Parental supervision and delinquency. *Perceptual and Motor Skills, 56,* 635–640. *154, 239*

Fischer, D. G., and McDonald, W. L. 1998. Characteristics of intrafamilial and extrafamilial child sexual abuse. *Child Abuse & Neglect, 22,* 915–929. *440*

Fiske, J., and Johnny, R. 2003. The Lake Babini First Nation family: Yesterday and today. In M. Lynn (Ed.), *Voices: Essays on Canadian families,* 2nd Ed. (pp. 181–198). Scarborough, ON: Thomson Nelson. *41, 95*

Flango, V., and Flango, C. 1994. *The flow of adoption information from the states.* Williamsburg, VA: National Center for State Courts. *261*

Fletcher, A. C., Steinberg, L., and Williams-Wheeler, M. 2004. Parental influence on adolescent problem behavior: Revisiting Statin and Kerr. *Child Development, 75,* 781–796. *333*

Fletcher, A. C., et al. 1995. The company they keep: Relation of adolescents' adjustment and behavior to their friends' perceptions of authoritative parenting in the social network. *Developmental Psychology, 31,* 300–310. *367*

Fleury, R. E., Sullivan, C. M., and Bybee, D. I. 2000. When ending the relationship does not end the violence. *Violence Against Women, 6,* 1363–1383. *401*

Florsheim, P., Tolan, P. H., and Gorman-Smith, D. 1996. Family processes and risks for externalizing behavior problems among African American and Hispanic boys. *Journal of Consulting and Clinical Psychology, 64,* 1222–123. *338*

Floyd, E. J., and Wasner, G. H. 1994. Social exchange, equity, and commitment: Structural equation modelling of dating relationships. *Journal of Family Psychology, 8,* 55–73. *206*

Flynn, C. P. 1994. Regional differences in attitudes toward corporal punishment. *Journal of Marriage and the Family, 56,* 314–324. *433*

Flynn, C. P. 1998. To spank or not to spank: The effect of situation and age of child on support for corporal punishment. *Journal of Family Violence, 13,* 21–37. *433*

Flynn, C. P. 2000. Why family professionals can no longer ignore violence toward animals. *Family Relations, 49,* 87–95. *286*

Folbre, N. 1994. *Who pays for the kids?* New York: Routledge. *266*

Fong, E. 1996. A comparative perspective on racial residential segregation: American and Canadian experiences. *Sociological Quarterly, 37,* 199–226. *156*

Fong, V. A. 2002. China's one-child policy and the empowerment of urban daughters. *American Anthropologist, 104,* 1098–1109. *47, 48, 49*

Forehand, R., Armistead, L., and David, C. 1997. Is adolescent adjustment following parental divorce a function of predivorce adjustment? *Journal of Abnormal Child Psychology, 25,* 157–164. *409*

Forehand, R., et al. 2002. African American childrens's adjustment: The roles of maternal and teacher depressive symptoms. *Journal of Marriage and Family, 64,* 1012–1023. *179*

Forgatch, M. S., Patterson, G. R., and Roy, J. A. 1996. Stress, parenting, and adolescent psychopathology in nondivorced and stepfamilies: A within-family perspective. In E. M. Hetherington and E. A. Blachman (Eds.), *Stress, coping, and resilience in children and families* (pp. 39–66). Mahwah, NJ: Erlbaum. *407*

Forste, R., and Tanfer, K. 1996. Sexual exclusivity among dating, cohabiting, and married women. *Journal of Marriage and the Family, 58,* 33–47. *208*

Forste, R., and Tanfer, K. 1996. Sexual exclusivity among dating, cohabiting, and married women. *Journal of Marriage and Family, 58,* 33–47. *215, 397*

Fortin, A. 1987. *Histoires de familles et de réseaux.* Québec: Saint-Martin. *6*

Forthofer, M. S., et al. 1996. The effects of psychiatric disorder on the probability and timing of first marriage. *Journal of Health and Social Behavior, 37,* 121–132. *219, 397*

Fournier, S., and Crey, E. 1997. *Stolen from our embrace: The abduction of First Nations children and the restoration of Aboriginal communities.* Vancouver/Toronto: Douglas and McIntyre. *94, 115*

Fouts, G., and Burggraf, K. 1999. Television situation comedies: Female body images and verbal reinforcements. *Sex Roles, 40,* 473–481. *71*

Fowers, B. L. 2000. *The myth of marital happiness.* San Francisco: Jossey-Bass. *396*

Fowlkes, M. R. 1994. Single worlds and homosexual lifestyles: Patterns of sexuality and intimacy. In A. S. Rossi (Ed.), *Sexuality across the life course* (pp. 151–184). Chicago: University of Chicago Press. *243*

Fox, B. 1997. Reproducing difference: Changes in the lives of partners becoming parents. In M. Luxton (Ed.), *Feminism and families* (pp. 142–161). Halifax: Fernwood. *279*

Fox, B. J. 2001. Reproducing difference: Changes in the lives of partners becoming parents. In B. J. Fox (Ed.), *Family patterns, gender relations,* 2nd Ed. (pp. 287–302). Toronto: Oxford University Press. *273, 278*

Fox, B., and Luxton, M. 2001. Conceptualizing family. In B. J. Fox (Ed.), *Family patterns and gender relations,* 2nd Ed. (pp. 22–33). Toronto: Oxford University Press. *18*

Fox, G. L. 1999. Families in the media: Reflections on the public scrutiny of private behavior. *Journal of Marriage and the Family, 61,* 821–830. *72*

Frank, R. H. 1999. *Luxury fever.* New York: Free Press. *128*

Frantz, D. 1999. Cruise lines profit from friends in Congress. *The New York Times,* February 19, A1, A16. *470*

Frasch, K. M., Brooks, D., and Barth, R. P. 2000. Openness and contact in foster care adoptions: An eight-year follow-up. *Family Relations, 49,* 435–446. *263*

Frazier, J. A., and Morrison, F. J. 1998. The influence of extended-year schooling on growth of achievement and perceived competence in early elementary school. *Child Development, 69,* 495–517. *179*

Frederick, J. 1995. *As time goes by: Time use of Canadians.* Ottawa: Statistics Canada. *123*

Frederick, J. A., and East, J. E. 1999. Eldercare in Canada: Who does how much? *Canadian Social Trends, 54,* 26–30. *351, 353*

Frempong, G., and Willms, J. D. 2002. Can school quality compensate for socioeconomic disadvantage? In J. D. Willms (Ed.), *Vulnerable children* (pp. 277–304). Edmonton: University of Alberta Press. *184, 457*

Frick, P. J., et al. 1992. Familial risk factors to oppositional defiant disorder and conduct disorder: Parental psychopathology and maternal parenting. *Journal of Consulting and Clinical Psychology, 60,* 49–55. *435*

Frideres, J. S. 2000. Revelation and revolution: Fault lines in Aboriginal-White relations. In M. A. Kalbach and W. E. Kalbach (Eds.), *Perspectives on Ethnicity in Canada* (pp. 207–237). Toronto: Harcourt Brace. *93, 95*

Friedman, B. M. 1999. The power of the electronic herd. *New York Review of Books,* July 15, 40–44. *128*

Friendly, M. 2000. Child care as a social policy issue. In L. Prochner and N. Howe (Eds.), *Early childhood education and care in Canada* (pp. 252–272). Vancouver: University of British Columbia Press. *97, 175, 178, 469*

Friendly, M., Beach, J., and Turiano, M. 2002. *Early childhood education and care in Canada in 2001.* Toronto: University of Toronto, Childcare Resource and Research Unit. *175*

Friesen, J. W. 1999. *First Nations of the Plains: Creative, adaptable, enduring.* Calgary, AB: Detselig Enterprises. *34*

Frisco, M. L., and Williams, K. 2004. Perceived housework equity, marital happiness, and divorce in dual-earner households. *Journal of Family Issues, 24,* 51–73. *311*

FSAT (Family Service Association of Toronto) and Community Social Planning Council of Toronto. 2004. *Falling fortunes: A report on the status of young families in Toronto.* Toronto. *61, 120, 130, 131, 133*

Fu, X., Tora, J., and Kendall, H. 2001. Marital happiness and inter-racial marriage: A study in a multi-ethnic community in Hawaii. *Journal of Comparative Family Studies, 32,* 47–60. *210*

Fuchs, V. R. 1990. Are Americans underinvesting in children? In D. Blankenhorn et al. (Eds.), *Rebuilding the nest: A new commitment to the American family* (pp. 53–72). Milwaukee, WI: Family Service America. *127*

Funk, J. B., Buchman, D. B., and Germann, J. N. 2000. Preference for violent electronic games, self-concept, and gender differences in young children. *American Journal of Orthopsychiatry, 70,* 233–241. *75*

Furman, W., and Lanthier, R. P. 1996. Personality and sibling relationships. In G. H. Brody (Ed.), *Sibling relationships: Their causes and consequences* (pp. 127–172). Norwood, NJ: Ablex. *363*

Furstenberg, F. F., Jr. 1992. Teenage childbearing and cultural rationality: A thesis in search of evidence. *Family Relations, 41,* 239–243. *135*

Furstenberg, F. F., Jr., and Cherlin, A. J. 1991. *Divided families: What happens to children when parents part?* Cambridge, MA: Harvard University Press. *399, 416*

Furstenberg, F. F., Jr., et al. 1994. How families manage risk and opportunity in dangerous neighborhoods. In W. J. Wilson (Ed.), *Sociology and the public agenda* (pp. 231–258). Newbury Park, CA: Sage. *156*

Furstenberg, F. F., Jr., and Hughes, M. E. 1995. Social capital and successful development among at-risk youth. *Journal of Marriage and the Family, 57,* 580–592. *366*

Gable, S. 1998. School-age and adolescent children's perceptions of family functioning in neglectful and non-neglectful families. *Child Abuse & Neglect, 22,* 859–867. *437*

Gable, S., and Lutz, S. 2000. Household, parent, and child contributions to childhood obesity. *Family Relations, 49,* 293–300. *69*

Gagnon, A. 1994. Our parents did not raise us to be independent: The work and schooling of young Franco-Albertan women, 1890–1940. *Prairie Forum, 19,* 169–188. *45*

Galambos, N. L., et al. 1995. Parents' work overload and problem behavior in young adolescents. *Journal of Research on Adolescence, 5,* 201–223. *337*

Galarneau, D., and Sturroch, J. 1997. Family income after separation. *Perspectives on Labour and Income, 9,* 18–28. *134*

Galloway, G. 2004. Black population growth dramatic, report shows. *Globe and Mail*, March 10: A11. *108, 109*

Gamble, T. J., and Zigler, E. 1989. The Head Start Synthesis Project. *Journal of Applied Developmental Psychology, 10,* 267–274. *178*

Games, A. 1999. *Migration and the origins of the English Atlantic world.* Cambridge, MA: Harvard University Press. *37*

Ganong, L., and Coleman, M. 1994. *Remarried family relationships.* Newbury Park, CA: Sage. *293, 319, 374, 414*

Ganong, L., and Coleman, M. 1999. *Changing families, changing responsibilities: Family obligations following divorce and remarriage.* Mahwah, NJ: Erlbaum. *292, 294*

Ganong, L., et al. 1998. Issues considered in contemplating stepchild adoption. *Family Relations, 47,* 63–71. *261, 416*

Garbarino, J. 1995. *Raising children in a socially toxic environment.* San Francisco: Jossey-Bass. *424, 457*

Garbarino, J. 1999. *Lost boys: Why our sons turn violent and how we can save them.* New York: Free Press. *21, 75, 445, 472*

Garbarino, J., and Kostelny, K. 1992. Child maltreatment as a community problem. *Child Abuse & Neglect, 16,* 455–464. *433*

Garbarino, J., Kostelny, K., and Dubrow, N. 1991. *No place to be a child: Growing up in a war zone.* Lexington, MA: Lexington Books. *437*

Garbarino, J., and Sherman, D. 1980. High-risk neighborhoods and high-risk families: The human ecology of child maltreatment. *Child Development, 51,* 188–198. *433*

Garcia, M. M., et al. 2000. Destructive sibling conflict and the development of conduct problems in young boys. *Developmental Psychology, 36,* 44–53. *365*

Gardner, M., and Herz, D. E. 1992. Working and poor. *Monthly Labor Review,* December, pp. 20–28. *121*

Garmezy, N., and Masten, A. S. 1994. Chronic adversities. In M. Rutter, E. Taylor, and L. Hersov (Eds.), *Child and adolescent psychiatry,* 3rd Ed. (pp. 191–208). Oxford: Blackwell. *409*

Garrison, M. E. B., et al. 1997. Delayed parenthood: An exploratory study of family functioning. *Family Relations, 46,* 281–290. *282*

Gartrell, N., et al. 2000. The National Lesbian Family Study: 3. Interviews with mothers of five-year-olds. *American Journal of Orthopsychiatry, 70,* 542–548. *242*

Gately, D. W., and Schwebel, A. I. 1991. The challenge model of children's adjustment to parental divorce. *Journal of Family Psychology, 5,* 60–81. *404*

Gauthier, A. H. 1996. *The State and the family.* Oxford: Clarendon. *464*

Gecas, V., and Seff, M. A. 1990. Families and adolescents: A review of the 1980s. *Journal of Marriage and the Family, 52,* 941–958. *287*

Gee, E. M. 2000. Voodoo demography, population aging, and social policy. In E. M. Gee and G. M. Gutman (Eds.), *The overselling of population aging* (pp. 1–25). Toronto: Oxford University Press. *350, 460*

Gee, E. M., and Mitchell, B. A. 2003. One roof: Exploring multi-generational households in Canada. In M. Lynn (Ed.), *Voices: Essays on Canadian families,* 2nd Ed. (pp. 291–311) Toronto: Thomson Nelson. *6*

Gee, E. M., Mitchell, B. A., and Wister, A. V. 2003. Home leaving trajectories in Canada: Exploring cultural and gendered dimensions. *Canadian Studies in Population, 30,* 245–270. *289, 347*

Gelles, R. J. 1989. Child abuse and violence in single parent families: Parent absence and economic deprivation. *American Journal of Orthopsychiatry, 59,* 492–501. *242*

Gelles, R. J. 1993. Alcohol and other drugs associated with violence—they are not its cause. In R. J. Gelles and D. R. Loseke (Eds.), *Current controversies in family violence.* Newbury Park, CA: Sage. *427*

Gelles, R. J. 1997. *Intimate violence in families,* 3rd Ed. Thousand Oaks, CA: Sage. *442, 443, 447*

Gennetian, L. A., and Miller, C. 2002. Children and welfare reform: A view from an experimental welfare program in Minnesota. *Child Development, 73,* 601–631. *468*

Gennetian, L. A., and Morris, P. A. 2003. The effects of time limits and make-work-pay strategies on the well-being of children: Experimental evidence from two welfare reform programs. *Children and Youth Services Review, 25,* 7–54. *467*

Gergen, K. J., et al. 1996. Psychological science in cultural context. *American Psychologist, 51,* 496–503. *18*

Gerstel, N., and Gallagher, S. K. 1993. Kinkeeping and distress: Gender, recipients of care, and work-family conflict. *Journal of Marriage and the Family*, 55, 598–607. *353*

Giarrusso, R. et al. 2001. Grandparent-adult grandchild affection and consensus: Cross-generation and cross-ethnic comparisons. *Journal of Family Issues*, 22, 456–477. *349*

Gignac, M. A. M., Cott, C. A., and Badley, E. M. 2003. Living with a chronic disabling illness and then some: Data from the 1998 Ice Storm. *Canadian Journal on Aging*, 22, 249–259. *352*

Giles-Sims, J. 1997. Current knowledge about child abuse in stepfamilies. *Marriage and Family Review*, 26, 215–230. *415*

Gilgun, J. F. 1995. We shared something special: The moral discourse of incest perpetrators. *Journal of Marriage and the Family*, 57, 265–282. *441*

Gilgun, J. F., Daly, K., and Handel, G. (Eds.). 1992. *Qualitative methods in family research*. Newbury Park, CA: Sage. *30*

Gilligan, C. 1993. *In a different voice: Psychological theory and women's development*. Cambridge, MA: Harvard University Press. *20*

Gillis, J. 1996. *A world of their own making: Myth, ritual and the quest for family values*. New York: Basic Books. *15*

Giordano, P. C., et al. 1999. Delinquency, indentity, and women's involvement in relationship violence. *Criminology*, 37, 17–37. *425*

Gladstone, J., and Westhues, A. 1998. Adoption reunions: A new side to intergenerational family relationships. *Family Relations*, 47, 177–184. *264*

Glass, J., and Fujimoto, T. 1994. Housework, paid work, and depression among husbands and wives. *Journal of Health and Social Behavior*, 35, 179–191. *124*

Glassner, B. 1999. *The culture of fear: Why Americans are afraid of the wrong things*. New York: Basic Books. *73, 78*

Gleason, P., Rangarajan, A., and Schochet, P. 1998. The dynamics of receipt of Aid to Families with Dependent Children among teenage parents in inner cities. *Journal of Human Resources*, 33, 988–1002. *469*

Glenday, D. 1997. Lost horizons, leisure shock: Good jobs, bad jobs, uncertain future. In A. Duffy, D. Glenday, and N. Pupo (Eds.), *Good jobs, bad jobs* (pp. 8–34). Toronto: Harcourt Brace. *119*

Glendon, M. A. 1989. *The transformation of family law: State, law, and family in the United States and Western Europe*. Chicago: University of Chicago Press. *65*

Glenn, N. D., 1991. The recent trends in marital success in the United States. *Journal of Marriage and the Family*, 53, 261–270. *316*

Glenn, N. D. 1996. Values, attitudes, and the state of American marriage. In D. Popenoe, J. B. Elshtain, and D. Blankenhorn (Eds.), *Promises to keep: Decline and renewal of marriage in America* (pp. 15–34). Lanham, MD: Rowan and Littlefield. *396*

Glenn, N. D. 1998. The course of marital success and failure in five American 10-year marriage cohorts. *Journal of Marriage and the Family*, 60, 569–576. *252, 314, 318*

Glenn, N. D., and Weaver, C. N. 1988. The changing relationship of marital status to reported happiness. *Journal of Marriage and the Family*, 50, 317–324. *221*

Glick, P. C. 1947. The family cycle. *American Sociological Review*, 12, 164–174. *17*

Goffman, E. 1959. *The presentation of self in everyday life*. New York: Doubleday. *15, 16*

Goldscheider, F. K., Thornton, A., and Yang, L.-S. 2001. Helping out the kids: Expectations about parental support in young adulthood. *Journal of Marriage and Family*, 63, 727–740. *348*

Goldscheider, F., and Goldscheider, C. 1999. *The changing transition to adulthood: Leaving and returning home*. Thousand Oaks, CA: Sage. *347*

Goldstein, J. R., and Kenney, C. T. 2001. Marriage delayed or marriage forgone? New cohort forecasts of first marriage for U.S. women. *American Sociological Review*, 66, 506–519. *460*

Golombok, S., et al. 1995. Families created by the new reproductive technologies: Quality of parenting and social and emotional development of the children. *Child Development*, 66, 285–298. *255*

Golombok, S., et al. 2002. Families with children conceived by donor insemination: A follow-up at age twelve. *Child Development*, 73, 952–968. *245, 255, 261*

Golombos, N. L., Baker, E. T., and Almeida, D. M. 2003. Parents *do* matter: Trajectories of change in externalizing and internalizing problems in early adolescence. *Child Development*, 74, 578–594. *383*

González, E. D. 1999. Cuban socialism: Adjustments and paradoxes. In J. B. Lara (Ed.), *Cuba in the 1990s* (pp. 53–72). Havana: Instituto Cubano del Libro. *52*

Goode, W. J. 1956. *Women in divorce*. New York: Free Press. *399*

Goode, W. J. 1963. *World revolution and family patterns*. New York: Free Press. *10*

Gordon, M. 1989. The family environment and sexual abuse: A comparison of natal and stepfather abuse. *Child Abuse & Neglect*, 13, 121–129. *242*

Gordon, T. 1994. *Single women: On the margins?* New York: New York University Press. *225*

Gorman, E. H. 1999. Bringing home the bacon: Marital allocation of income-earning responsibility, job shifts, and men's wages. *Journal of Marriage and the Family*, 61, 110–122. *219*

Gorman, J. C. 1998. Parenting attitudes and practices of immigrant Chinese mothers of adolescents. *Family Relations*, 47, 73–80. *333*

Gorman, T. 1997. Canadian television in transition. *Canadian Social Trends*, 44, 19–23. *68*

Gottman, J. M. 1994. *What predicts divorce? The relationship between marital processes and marital outcomes.* Hillsdale, NJ: Erlbaum. *316, 317, 321*

Gottman, J. M. 1998. Toward a process model of men in marriages and families. In A. Booth and A. C. Crouter (Eds.), *Men in families* (pp. 149–192). Mahwah, NJ: Erlbaum. *278, 317, 398, 425*

Gottman, J. M., and Levenson, R. W. 2000. The timing of divorce: Predicting when a couple will divorce over a 14-year period. *Journal of Marriage and the Family, 62,* 737–745. *303*

Goulet, L., Dressyman-Lavallee, M., and McCleod, Y. 2001. Early childhood education for Aboriginal children: Opening petals. In K. P. Binda and S. Calliou (Eds.), *Aboriginal education in Canada* (pp. 137–153). Mississsauga: Canadian Educators' Press. *178, 180*

Gove, W., Style, C. B., and Hughes, M. 1990. The effect of marriage on the well-being of adults. *Journal of Family Issues, 11,* 4–35. *219*

Graefe, D. R., and Lichter, D. T. 1999. Life course transitions of American children: Parental cohabitation, marriage, and single motherhood. *Demography, 36,* 205–217. *241*

Grant, J. N. 1973. Black immigrants into Nova Scotia, 1776–1815. *Journal of Negro History, 58,* 253–270. *42*

Grant, M. R., and Danso, R. K. 2000. Access to housing as an adaptive strategy for immigrant groups: Africans in Calgary. *Canadian Ethnic Studies, 32,* 3, 19–37. *108*

Gray, M. R., and Steinberg, L. 1999. Unpacking authoritative parenting: Reassessing a multidimensional construct. *Journal of Marriage and the Family, 61,* 574–587. *332, 333*

Green, R. K., and White, M. J. 1997. Measuring the benefits of homeowning: Effects on children. *Journal of Urban Economics, 41,* 441–461. *468*

Greenberg, B. S., and Busselle, R. W. 1996. Soap operas and sexual activity: A decade later. *Journal of Communication, 46,* 153–160. *77*

Greenberg, J. S., Seltzer, M. M., and Greenlay, J. R. 1993. Aging parents of adults with disabilities: The gratifications and frustrations of later-life caregiving. *The Gerontologist, 33,* 542–549. *448*

Greenwood, P. W. 1995. Juvenile crime and juvenile justice. In J. Q. Wilson and J. Petersilia (Eds.), *Crime* (pp. 91–117). San Francisco, CA: Institute for Contemporary Studies Press. *470*

Grewal, S. 2004. Sounds like trouble. *Toronto Star,* February 21, K1, K9. *76*

Griffith, J. 1996. Relation of parental involvement, empowerment, and school traits to student academic performance. *Journal of Educational Research, 90,* 33–41. *181*

Griffith, K. C. 1991. *The right to know who you are.* Ottawa: Katherine W. Kimbell. *258*

Grossbard-Shechtman, S. 1993. *On the economics of marriage: A theory of marriage, labor, and divorce.* Boulder, CO: Westview Press. *239*

Grotevant, H. D., and McRoy, R. G. 1998. *Openness in adoption: Exploring family connections.* Thousand Oaks, CA: Sage. *262, 263*

Grotevant, J. et al. 1994. Adoptive family system dynamics: Variations by level of openness in the adoption. *Family Process, 33,* 125–146. *263*

Groze, V. 1996. *Successful adoptive families: A longitudinal study.* Westport, CT: Praeger. *261*

Grunebaum, H. 1997. Thinking about romantic love. *Journal of Marital and Family Therapy, 23,* 295–307. *217*

Grych, J. H., and Fincham, F. D. 1994. Children's appraisals of marital conflict: Initial investigations of cognitive-contextual framework. *Child Development, 64,* 215–230. *322, 324*

Grzywacz, J. G., et al., 2002. Work-related spillover and daily reports of work and family stress in the adult labor force. *Family Relations, 51,* 28–36. *124*

GSS (General Social Survey). 2000. Family violence. *The Daily.* Ottawa: Statistics Canada. *216, 401, 427*

Habermas, J. 1987. *The theory of communicative action: Lifeworld and system: A critique of functionalist reason* (Vol. 2, translated by T. McCarthy). Boston: Beacon Press. *78*

Hagan, J., MacMillan, R., and Wheaton, B. 1996. The life course effects of family migration on children. *American Sociological Review, 61,* 368–385. *168*

Hamby, S. L., and Sugarman, D. B. 1999. Acts of psychological aggression against a partner and their relations to physical assault and gender. *Journal of Marriage and the Family, 61,* 959–970. *424*

Hamilton, R. 1995. Pro-natalism, feminism, and nationalism. In F.-P. Gingras (Ed.), *Gender and politics in contemporary Canada* (pp. 135–152). Toronto: Oxford University Press. *98*

Hamm, W. 1997. Guide for effectively recruiting African-American adoptive families. In G. R. Anderson, A. S. Ryan, and B. R. Leashore (Eds.), *The challenge of permanency planning in a multicultural society* (pp. 139–149). New York: Haworth.

Han, W.-J., et al. 2001. The effects of early maternal employment on later cognitive and behavioral outcomes. *Journal of Marriage and Family, 63,* 336–354. *125*

Hanawalt, B. A. 1993. *Growing up in Medieval London.* Oxford: Oxford University Press.

Hannon, L. 1997. AFDC and homicide. *Journal of Sociology and Social Work, 24,* 125–136. *467*

Handlin, O. 1951. *The uprooted.* Boston: Little, Brown and Company. *102*

Hansell, S., and Harmon, A. 1999. Caveat emptor on the web: Ad and editorial lines blur. *The New York Times,* 26, A1, A12. *79*

Hanson, T. L. 1999. Does parental conflict explain why divorce is negatively associated with child welfare? *Social Forces, 77*, 1283–1315. *409*

Hanson, T. L., McLanahan, S., and Thomson, E. 1997. Economic resources, parental practices, and children's well-being. In G. J. Duncan and J. Brooks-Gunn (Eds.), *Consequences of growing up poor* (pp. 190–238). New York: Russell Sage. *337, 340*

Hao, L. 1996. Family structure, private transfers, and the economic well-being of families with children. *Social Forces, 75*, 269–292. *134, 404*

Harbinson, J. 1999. Models of intervention for elder abuse and neglect: A Canadian perspective on ageism, participation, and empowerment. *Journal of Elder Abuse and Neglect, 10*, 1–17. *448*

Harden, B. J. 2004. Safety and stability for foster children: A developmental perspective. *The Future of children, 14*, 31–47. *264*

Hardy, C. 1990. Mormon polygamy in Mexico and Canada. In B. Card et al. (Eds.), *The Mormon presence in Canada* (pp. 186–209). Edmonton: The University of Alberta Press. *47*

Hardy, J. B., et al. 1998. Like mother, like child: Intergenerational patterns of age at first birth and associations with childhood and adolescent characteristics and adult outcomes in the second generation. *Developmental Psychology, 34*, 1220–1232. *248*

Hareven, T. K. 1987. Historical analysis of the family. In M. B. Sussman and S. K. Steinmetz (Eds.), *Handbook of marriage and the family* (pp. 37–57). New York: Plenum Press. *17*

Hareven, T. K. 1994a. Continuity and change in American family life. In A. S. Skolnick and J. H. Skolnick (Eds.), *Family in transition*, 8th Ed. (pp. 40–46). New York: HarperCollins. *60, 288, 343*

Hareven, T. K. 1994b. Aging and generational relations: A historical and life course perspective. *Annual Review of Sociology, 20*, 437–461. *272, 343, 347*

Harkness, S., and Super, C. 1992. Shared child care in east Africa: Socioculture origins and developmental consequences. In M. Lamb et al. (Eds.), *Child care in context: Cross cultural perspectives* (pp. 441–459). Hillsdale, NJ: Erlbaum. *274*

Harney, N. D. 1998. *Eh paesan!: Being Italian in Toronto.* Toronto: University of Toronto Press. *101*

Harrington, D., et al. 1998. Child neglect: Relation to child temperament and family context. *American Journal of Orthopsychiatry, 68*, 108–116. *437*

Harris, F. 2002. *Transformation of love.* Oxford, UK: Oxford University Press. *217*

Harris, J. R. 1998. *The nurture assumption. Why children turn out the way they do.* New York: Free Press. *382*

Harris, K. M., Furstenberg, F. F., Jr., and Marmer, J. K. 1998. Paternal involvement with adolescents in intact families: The influence of fathers over the life course. *Demography, 35*, 201–216. *471*

Harris, K. M., and Morgan, S. P. 1991. Fathers, sons, and daughters: Differential paternal involvement in parenting. *Journal of Marriage and the Family, 53*, 531–544. *371*

Harrison, T. W., and Friesen, J. W. 2004. *Canadian society in the twenty-first century: A historical sociological approach.* Toronto: Pearson-Prentice Hall. *41, 57, 92–95, 97*

Harvey, A. S., and Elliott, D. H. 1983. *Time and time again: Explorations of time use*, Vol. 4. Halifax: Employment and Immigration Canada. *128*

Harvey, D. L. 1993. *Potter Addition: Poverty, family, and kinship in a heartland community.* New York: Aldine de Gruyter. *284, 309*

Harvey, E. 1999. Short-term and long-term effects of early parental employment on children of the National Longitudinal Survey of Youth. *Developmental Psychology, 35*, 445–459. *124, 125*

Harwood, R. L., et al. 1996. Culture and class influences on Anglo and Puerto Rican mothers' beliefs regarding long-term socialization goals and child behavior. *Child Development, 67*, 2446–2461. *337*

Hatch, L. R., and Bulcroft, K. 2004. Does long-term marriage bring less frequent disagreements? Five explanatory frameworks. *Journal of Family Issues, 25*, 465–495. *317*

Haveman, R., and Wolfe, B. 1994. *Succeeding generations: On the effects of investments in children.* New York: Russell Sage. *131*

Hawkins, A. J., et al. 2002. Attitudes about covenant marriage and divorce: Policy implications from a three-state comparison. *Family Relations, 51*, 166–175. *197*

Hayes, D. S., and Casey, D. M. 1992. Young children and television: The retention of emotional reactions. *Child Development, 63*, 1423–1436. *73*

Hays, S. 1996. *The cultural contradictions of motherhood.* New Haven, CT: Yale University Press. *63, 122, 184, 273, 274*

Hays, S. 1998. The fallacious assumptions and unrealistic prescriptions of attachment theory: A comment on "Parents' socioemotional investment in children." *Journal of Marriage and the Family, 60*, 782–795. *274*

Hayward, M. D., Pienta, A. M., and McLaughlin, D. K. 1997. Inequality in men's mortality: The socioeconomic status gradient and geographic context. *Journal of Health and Social Behavior, 38*, 313–380. *160*

Health Canada. 2000. 1998/1999 Canadian sexually transmitted disease (STD) surveillance report. <www.hc-sc.gc.ca>. *228*

Health Canada. 2001. *The Canadian incidence study of reported child abuse and neglect.* <www.hc-sc.gc.ca>. *431, 437*

Health Canada. 2002. Induced abortion. <www.hc-sc.gc.ca>. *253*

Heath, D. H. 1994. *Schools of hope: Developing mind and character in today's youth.* San Francisco: Jossey-Bass. *74*

Heath, D. T. 1995. The impact of delayed fatherhood on the father-child relationship. *Journal of Genetic Psychology, 155,* 511–530. *282*

Heaton, T. B., Jacobson, C. K., and Holland, K. 1999. Persistence and chance in decisions to remain childless. *Journal of Marriage and the Family, 61,* 531–539. *250, 252*

Heger, A., and Lytle, C. 1993. Relationship of child sexual abuse to depression. *Child Abuse & Neglect, 17,* 383–400. *442*

Heimdal, K. R., and Houseknecht, S. K. 2003. Cohabiting and married couples' income organization: Approaches in Sweden and the United States. *Journal of Marriage and Family, 65,* 525–538. *214*

Helm, B., and Warren, W. 1998. Teenagers talk about cultural heritage and family life. *Transition, 28,* 4–7. *105, 106*

Henderson, S. H., Hetherington, E. M., Mekos, D., and Reiss, D. 1996. Stress, parenting and adolescent psychopathology in nondivorced and stepfamilies: A within-family perspective. In E. M. Hetherington and E. A. Blechman (Eds.), Stress, coping, and resiliency in children and families (pp. 39–66). Mahwah, NJ: Erlbaum. *340, 369*

Henderson, T. L., and Moran, P. B. 2001. Grandparent visitation rights: Testing the parameters of parental rights. *Journal of Family Issues, 22,* 619–638. *293*

Henripin, J., and Péron, I. 1972. The demographic transition of the province of Quebec. In D. V. Glass and R. Revelle (Eds.), *Population and social change* (pp. 213–231). London: Edward Arnold Publishers. *35, 98*

Henry, C. S., Ceglian, C. P., and Ostrander, D. L. 1993. The transition to stepgrandparenthood. *Journal of Divorce and Remarriage, 19,* 25–44. *294*

Hensen, K. A. 1993. Geographical mobility: March 1991 to 1992. *Current Population Reports* (Series P-20, No. 473). Washington, DC: U.S. Government Printing Office. *167*

Hensley, W. 1996. The effect of a Ludus love style on sexual experience. *Social Behavior and Personality, 24,* 205–212. *226*

HERI (Higher Education Research Institute). 2003. College freshmen spend less time studying and more time surfing the net, UCLA survey reveals. Los Angeles, CA: UCLA Graduate School of Education and Information Studies. *79*

Hertel, B. R. 1995. Work, family, and faith. In N. T. Ammerman and W. C. Roof (Eds.), *Work, family, and religion in contemporary society* (pp. 81–121). New York: Routledge. *192*

Hessing, M. 1993. Mothers' management of their combined workloads: Clerical work and household needs. *Canadian Review of Sociology and Anthropology, 31,* 37–63. *122*

Hetherington, E. M. 1988. Parents, children, and siblings: Six years after divorce. In R. A. Hinde and J. Stevenson-Hinde (Eds.), *Relationships within families: Mutual influences* (pp. 311–331). Oxford: Oxford University Press. *369*

Hetherington, E. M. 2003. Intimate pathways: Changing patterns in close personal relationships across time. *Family Relations, 52,* 318–331. *318, 322, 398, 400, 405, 406, 409*

Hetherington, E. M., Clingempeel, W. G., et al. 1992. Coping with marital transitions. *Monographs of the Society for Research in Child Development, 57,* 2–3. *407*

Hetherington, E. M., and Kelly, J. 2002. *For better or for worse: Divorce reconsidered.* New York: Norton. *416*

Hewitt, C. 1998. Homosexual demography: Implications for the spread of AIDS. *Journal of Sex Research, 35,* 390–396. *461*

Hewlett, S. A., and West, C. 1998. *The war against parents.* Boston: Houghton Mifflin. *81*

Heyman, R. E., and Slep, A. M. S. 2002. Do child abuse and interparental violence lead to adulthood family violence? *Journal of Marriage and Family, 64,* 864–870. *430*

Heyns, B. 1988. Schooling and cognitive development: Is there a season for learning? *Child Development, 58,* 1151–1160. *186*

Hiebert-Murphy, D. 1998. Emotional distress among mothers whose children have been sexually abused: The role of a history of child sexual abuse, social support, and coping. *Child Abuse & Neglect, 22,* 423–435. *440*

Higginson, J. G. 1998. Competitive parenting: The culture of teen mothers. *Journal of Marriage and the Family, 60,* 135–149. *279*

Hill, E. J., Hawkins, A. J., Ferris, M., and Weitzman, M. 2001. Finding an extra day a week: The positive influence of perceived job flexibility on work and family life balance. *Family Relations, 50,* 49–58. *127*

Hines, A. M. 1997. Divorce-related transitions, adolescent development, and the role of the parent-child relationship: A review of the literature. *Journal of Marriage and the Family, 59,* 375–388. *407*

Hirschl, T. A., Altobelli, J., and Rank, M. R. 2003. Does marriage increase the odds of affluence? Exploring the life course probabilities. *Journal of Marriage and Family, 65,* 927–938. *225*

Hobart, C. 1996. Intimacy and family life: Sexuality, cohabitation, and marriage. In M. Baker (Ed.), *Families: Changing trends in Canada,* 3rd Ed. (pp. 143–173). Toronto: McGraw-Hill Ryerson. *226*

Hochschild, A. R. 1983. *The managed heart.* Berkeley: University of California Press. *313*

Hochschild, A. R. 1997. *The time bind.* New York: Metropolitan Books. *122, 313*

Hochschild, A. R., with Machung, A. 1989. *The second shift.* New York: Avon. *122, 145*

Hodges, E. V. E., Malone, M. J., and Perry, D. G. 1997. Individual risk and social risk as interacting determinants of victimization in the peer group. *Developmental Psychology, 33,* 1032–1039. *445*

Hodgson, L. G. 1992. Adult grandchildren and their grandparents: The enduring bond. *International Journal of Aging and Human Development, 34,* 209–225. *290*

Hofferth, S., and Anderson, K. G. 2003. Are all dad equal? Biology versus marriage as a basis for paternal investment. *Journal of Marriage and Family, 65,* 213–232. *416*

Hofferth, S. L., Reid, L., and Mott, F. L. 2001. The effects of early childbearing on schooling over time. *Family Planning Perspectives, 33,* 259–267. *136*

Hofferth, S. L., and Sandberg, J. F. 2001. Changes in American children's time, 1981–1997. In S. L. Hofferth and T. J. Owens (Eds.), *Children at the millennium: Where have we come from, where are we going?* (pp. 193–229). Oxford, UK: Elsevier. *127, 308*

Hofferth, S., et al. 1998. Reported in *Time,* November 25, p. 44. *127, 148*

Hoffman, F., and Taylor, R. 1996. *Much to be done: Private life in Ontario from Victorian diaries.* Toronto: Natural Heritage/Natural History Inc. *39, 44*

Hoffman, L. W. 1991. The influence of the family environment on personality: Accounting for sibling differences. *Psychological Bulletin, 110,* 187–203. *38, 370*

Hogan, D. P., Hao, L., and Parish, W. L. 1990. Race, kin networks, and assistance to mother-headed families. *Social Forces, 68,* 797–812. *290*

Hollingsworth, L. D. 1998. Promoting same-sex adoption for children of color. *Social Work, 43,* 104–116. *439*

Holmbeck, G. N., and Hill, J. P. 1988. Storm and stress beliefs about adolescence: Prevalence, self-reported antecedents, and effects of an undergraduate course. *Journal of Youth and Adolescence, 17,* 285–306. *341*

Homans, G. C. 1961. *Social behavior: Its elementary forms.* New York: Harcourt, Brace, and World. *13*

Hondagneu-Sotelo A. P., and Avila, E. 1997. "I'm here, but I'm there": The meaning of Latina transnations motherhood. *Gender and Society, 11,* 548–571. *111*

Hopper, J. 2001. The symbolic origins of conflict in divorce. *Journal of Marriage and Family, 63,* 430–435. *399, 409*

Horney, J., Osgood, D. W., and Marshall, I. H. 1995. Criminal careers in the short term: Intra-individual variability in crime and its relation to local life circumstances. *American Sociological Review, 60,* 655–673. *220*

Horwitz, A. V. 1993. Adult siblings as sources of social support for the seriously mentally ill: A test of the serial model. *Journal of Marriage and the Family, 55,* 623–632. *368*

Horwitz, A. V., and Raskin White, H. 1998. The relationship of cohabitation and mental health: A study of a young adult cohort. *Journal of Marriage and the Family, 60,* 505–514. *220*

Hostetler, J. A. 1993. *Amish society,* 4th Ed. Baltimore: Johns Hopkins University Press. *63*

Hou, F., and Milan, A. 2003. Neighbourhood ethnic transition and its socio-economic connections. *Canadian Journal of Sociology, 28,* 387–410. *157*

Hou, F., and Picot, G. 2004. Visible minority neighbourhoods in Toronto, Montreal, and Vancouver. *Canadian Social Trends, 72,* 8–13. *156*

Houseknecht, S. K., and Macke, A. 1981. Combining marriage and career: The marital adjustment of professional women. *Journal of Marriage and the Family, 43,* 651–661. *311*

Housseaux, F. 2003. La famille, pilier des identités. Paris: INSEE. <www.insee.fr>. *62*

Hout, M., and Greeley, A. 1998. Comment: What church officials' reports don't show: Another look at church attendance data. *American Sociological Review, 63,* 113–119. *192*

Howell, N., Albanes, P., and Kwaku, O.-M. 2001. Ethnic families. In M. Baker (Ed.), *Families: Changing trends in Canada* (pp. 116–142). Toronto: McGraw-Hill Ryerson. *101, 103*

Howes, C. 1988. Abused and neglected children with their peers. In G. T. Hotaling et al. (Eds.), *Family abuse and its consequences* (pp. 99–108). Beverly Hills, CA: Sage. *434*

Hu, Y., and Goldman, N. 1990. Mortality differentials by marital status: An international comparison. *Demography, 27,* 233–250. *219*

Huesmann, L. R., et al. 2003. Longitudinal relations between children's exposure to TV violence and their aggressive and violent behavior in young adulthood: 1977–1992. *Developmental Psychology, 39,* 201–221. *75*

Hughes, M., and Thomas, M. E. 1998. The continuing significance of race revisited: A study of race, class, and quality of life in America, 1972 to 1996. *American Sociological Review, 63,* 785–795.

Hughes, R., Good, E. S., and Candell, K. 1993. A longitudinal study on the effects of social support on the psychological adjustment of divorced mothers. *Journal of Divorce & Remarriage, 19,* 37–56. *403*

Humble, A. M. 2003. *"Doing weddings": Couples' gender strategies in wedding preparation.* Oregon State University: Unpublished doctoral dissertation. *207, 313*

Hummer, R. A., et al. 1999. Religious involvement and U.S. adult mortality. *Demography, 36,* 273–285. *195*

Hummer, R. A., Hack, K. A., and Raley, R. K. 2004. Retrospective reports of pregnancy wantedness and child well-being in the United States. *Journal of Family Issues, 25,* 404–428. *254*

Hur, Y.-M., and Bouchard, T. J., Jr. 1995. Genetic influences on perceptions of childhood family environment: A reared apart twin study. *Child Development, 66,* 330–345. *381*

Hurd, L. C. 1999. "We're not old!": Older women's negotiation of aging and oldness. *Journal of Aging Studies, 13,* 419–439. *294, 411*

Huston, T. L. 2000. The social ecology of marriage and other intimate unions. *Journal of Marriage and Family, 62,* 298–320. *302*

Hutchison, I. W. 1999. The effect of children's presence on alcohol use by spouse abusers and their victims. *Family Relations, 48,* 57–65. *427*

Huttenlocher, J., Levine, S., and Vevea, J. 1998. Environmental input and cognitive growth: A study using time-period comparisons. *Child Development, 69*, 1012–1029. *180*

Hyman, B. 2000. The economic consequences of child sexual abuse for adult lesbian women. *Journal of Marriage and the Family, 62*, 199–211. *439*

Iannaccone, L. R. 1990. Religious practice: A human capital approach. *Journal for the Scientific Study of Religion, 29*, 297–314. *195*

Ingersoll, T. N. 1995. Slave codes and judicial practice in New Orleans, 1718–1807. *Law and History Review, 13*, 23–62. *42*

Ingersoll-Dayton, B., Neal, M. B., and Hammer, L. B. 2001. Aging parents helping adult children: The experience of the sandwich generation. *Family Relations, 50*, 262–271. *352*

International Labour Office. 1970. *Yearbook of labour statistics*, 37th Issue. Geneva: ILO. *52*

Invest in Kids. 2002. *A national survey of parents of young children*: Invest in Kids Foundation. June. <www.invest inkids.ca>. *127, 279, 336, 434, 474*

Ishii-Kuntz, M. 1997. Intergenerational relationships amongst Chinese, Japanese and Korean Americans. *Family Relations, 46*, 23–32. *105*

Jackson, P. A., and Sullivan, G. 1999. *Multicultural queen: Australian narratives*. New York: Haworth. *210*

Jaffee, S. R., et al. 2003. Life with (or without) father: The benefits of living with two biological parents depend on the father's antisocial behavior. *Child Development, 74*, 109–126. *376*

Jamal, A. 1998. Situating South Asian immigrant women in the Canadian/global economy. *Canadian Woman Studies, 18*, 26–33. *106*

James, C. E. 1999. *Seeing ourselves: Exploring race, ethnicity and culture*. Toronto: Thompson Educational Publishing. *187*

Jamieson, K. 1986. Sex discrimination and the Indian Act. In J. R. Ponting (Ed.), *Arduous journey: Canadian Indians and decolonization*. Toronto: McClelland & Stewart. *36*

Jamieson, L. 1998. *Intimacy: Personal relationships in modern societies*. Cambridge: Polity Press. *9*

Jansen, C. J. 1987. *Fact-book on Italians in Canada*, 2nd Ed. Toronto: York University. *101, 102*

Jekielek, S. M. 1998. Parental conflict, marital disruption and children's emotional well-being. *Social Forces, 76*, 905–935. *239, 416*

Jendrek, M. P. 1993. Grandparents who parent their grandchildren: Effects on lifestyle. *Journal of Marriage and the Family, 55*, 609–621. *291, 292*

Jenkins, J. M. 2000. Marital conflict and children's emotions: The development of an anger organization. *Journal of Marriage and the Family, 62*, 723–736. *322*

Jenkins, J. M., and Smith, M. A. 1990. Factors protecting children living in disharmonious homes: Maternal reports.

Journal of the American Academy of Child & Adolescent Psychiatry, 29, 60–69. *369*

Jenkins, J. M., and Smith, M. A. 1993. A prospective study of behavioral disturbance in children of parental divorce: A research note. *Journal of Divorce & Remarriage, 19*, 143–159. *406*

Jenny, C., Roesler, T. A., and Poyer, K. L. 1994. Are children at risk for sexual abuse by homosexuals? *Pediatrics, 94*, 41–44. *245*

Jensen, A.-M. 1995. Gender gaps in relationships with children: Closing or widening? In K. O. Mason and A.-M. Jensen (Eds.), *Gender or family change in industrialized countries* (pp. 223–242). Oxford: Clarendon. *21, 241, 336*

Jepsen, L. K., and Jepsen, C. A. 2002. An empirical analysis of the matching patterns of same-sex and opposite-sex couples. *Demography, 39*, 435–453. *210*

Jodl, K. M., et al. 1999. Relations among relationships: A family systems perspective. In E. M. Hetherington, S. H. Henderson, and D. Reiss (Eds.), *Adolescent siblings in stepfamilies: Family functioning and adolescent adjustment* (pp. 150–183). Monographs of the Society for Research in Child Development, 259, 64, no. 4. *323*

Johnson, B. R., et al. 2001. Does adolescent religious commitment matter? A reexamination of the effects of religiosity on delinquency. *Journal of Research in Crime and Delinquency, 38*, 22–44. *196*

Johnson, C. L. 1985. *Growing up and growing old in Italian-American families*. New Brunswick, NJ: Rutgers University Press. *374*

Johnson, C. L., and Barer, B. M. 1997. *Life beyond 85 years: The aura of survivorship*. New York: Springer. *294*

Johnson, D. R., and Booth, A. 1998. Marital quality: A product of the dyadic environment or individual factors? *Social Forces, 76*, 883–904. *472*

Johnson, H. 1996. *Dangerous domains: Violence against women in Canada*. Toronto: Nelson. *422*

Johnson, H. 2003. The cessation of assaults on wives. *Journal of Comparative Family Studies, 34*, 75–91. *425*

Johnson, J. K. 1994. Friends in high places: Getting divorced in Upper Canada. *Ontario History, 86*, 201–218. *38*

Johnson, M. E., and Huston, T. L. 1998. The perils of love, or why wives adapt to husbands during the transition to parenthood. *Journal of Marriage and the Family, 60*, 195–204. *279*

Johnson, M. P. 1995. Patriarchal terrorism and common couple violence: Two forms of violence against women. *Journal of Marriage and the Family, 57*, 283–294. *426*

Johnson, M. P. 1999. Personal, moral, and structural commitment to relationships: Experiences of choice and constraint. In W. H. Jones and J. M. Adams (Eds.), *Handbook of interpersonal commitment and relationship stability* (pp. 73–87). New York: Kluwar Academic-Plenum Press. *213*

Johnston, P. 1983. *Native children and the child welfare system*. Toronto: Canadian Council on Social Development, in association with James Lorimer and Company. *94*

Jones, C. (Chief), with Bosustow, S. 1981. *Queesto, Pacheenaht chief by birthright.* Nanaimo, BC: Theytus Books. *32*

Jones, F. 2000. Community involvement: The influence of early experience. *Canadian Social Trends, 57,* 15–19. *149, 196*

Jones, L. M., Finkelhor, D., and Kopiec, K. 2001. Why is sexual abuse declining? A survey of state child protection administrators. *Child Abuse & Neglect, 25,* 1139–1158. *439*

Jouriles, E. N., et al. 1998. Knives, guns, and interparent violence: Relations with child behavior problems. *Journal of Family Psychology, 12,* 178–194. *430*

Joy, L. A., Kimball, M. M., and Zabrack, M. L. 1986. Television and children's aggressive behavior. In T. M. Williams (Ed.), *The impact of television: A natural experiment in three communities* (pp. 303–360). Orlando, FL: Academic Press. *74*

Joyner, K., and Udry, J. R. 2000. You don't bring me anything but down: Adolescent romance and depression. *Journal of Health and Social Behavior, 41,* 369–391. *206*

Judge, S. 2003. Determinants of parental stress in families adopting children from Eastern Europe. *Family Relations, 52,* 241–248. *262*

Kaestle, C. E., Morisky, D. E., and Wiley, D. J. 2002. Sexual intercourse and the age difference between adolescent females and their romantic partners. *Perspectives on Sexual and Reproductive Health, 34,* 304–309. *227*

Kagan, S. L., and Neuman, M. J. 1998. Lessons from three decades of transition research. *Elementary School Journal, 87,* 365–379. *179*

Kaiser Family Foundation. 2003. *Sex on TV3.* Menlo Park, CA: H. J. Kaiser Family Foundation. <www.kff.org>. *77*

Kalbach, M. A. 2000. Ethnicity and the altar. In M. A. Kalbach and W. E. Kalbach (Eds.), *Perspectives on ethnicity in Canada: A reader* (pp. 111–121). Toronto: McClelland & Stewart. *209*

Kalbach, M. A., and Kalbach, W. E. (Eds.). 1999. *Perspectives on ethnicity in Canada: A reader.* Toronto: Harcourt Canada. *88, 102*

Kalil, A. 2002. Cohabitation and child development. In A. Booth and A. C. Crouter (Eds.), *Just living together* (pp. 153–159). Mahwah, NJ: Erlbaum. *241*

Kalmijn, M. 1998. Differentiation and stratification—Intermarriage and homogamy: Causes, patterns, and trends. *Annual Review of Sociology, 24,* 395–427. *208*

Kanner, B. 2001. From *Father Knows Best* to *The Simpsons*—on TV, parenting has lost its halo. In S. A. Hewlett, N. Rankin, and C. West (Eds.), *Taking parenting public* (pp. 45–56). New York: Rowan & Littlefield. *71*

Kaplan, S. J., Pelcovitz, D., and Labruna, V. 1999. Child and adolescent abuse and neglect research: A review of the past 10 years. Part 1: Physical and emotional abuse and neglect. *Journal of the American Academy of Child & Adolescent Psychiatry, 38,* 1214–1222. *431, 438*

Kasser, T. 2002. *The high price of materialism.* Cambridge, MA: MIT Press. *150*

Katz, L. F., Kling, J. R., and Liebman, J. B. 2001. Moving to opportunity in Boston: Early results of a randomized mobility experiment. *Quarterly Journal of Economics, 116,* 655–680. *154*

Katz, S., and Marshall, B. 2003. New sex for old: Lifestyle, consumerism, and the ethics of aging well. *Journal of Aging Studies, 17,* 13–16. *129*

Kaufman, J., and Zigler, E. 1987. Do abused children become abusive parents? *American Journal of Orthopsychiatry, 57,* 186–192. *435*

Kaufman, M. 1999. Issues in the care of young parents and their children. In J. Wong, and D. Checkland (Eds.), *Teen pregnancy and parenting* (pp. 25–37). Toronto: University of Toronto Press. *137, 226, 246, 265*

Kelley, J., and De Graaf, N. D. 1997. National context, parental socialization, and religious belief: Results from 15 nations. *American Sociological Review, 62,* 639–659. *193, 194*

Kelly, J. B., and Emery, R. E. 2003. Children's adjustment following divorce: Risk and resilience perspectives. *Family Relations, 52,* 352–362. *405, 409*

Kelly, K. D. 1997. The family violence and woman abuse debate. In A. Sev'er (Ed.), *Cross-cultural exploration of wife abuse* (pp. 27–50). New Jersey: Edwin Mellen. *426*

Kemp, C. 2003. The social and demographic contours of contemporary grandparenthood: Mapping patterns in Canada and the United States. *Journal of Comparative Family Studies, 34,* 187–212. *289, 290*

Kempe, C., et al. 1962. The battered child syndrome. *Journal of the American Medical Association, 181,* 17–24. *438*

Kempeneers, M. 1992. *Le travail au féminin.* Montréal: Presses de l'Université de Montréal. *307*

Kendall-Tackett, K. A., Williams, L. M., and Finkelhor, D. 1993. Impact of sexual abuse on children: A review and synthesis of recent empirical studies. *Psychological Bulletin, 113,* 164–180. *440*

Kendler, K. S. 1995. Genetic epidemiology in psychiatry: Taking both genes and environment seriously. *Archives of General Psychiatry, 52,* 895–899. *409*

Kendler, K. S. 1996. Parenting: A genetic-epidemiologic perspective. *American Journal of Psychiatry, 153,* 11–20. *19, 380*

Kenny, C. 2002. *North American Indian, Métis and Inuit women speak about culture, education and work.* Ottawa: Status of Women's Canada Policy Research Fund. *96*

Kerbow, D., and Bernhardt, A. 1993. Parental intervention in the school: The context of minority involvement. In B. Schneider and J. S. Coleman (Eds.), *Parents, their children, and schools* (pp. 115–146). San Francisco: Westview Press. *180*

Kerr, M., and Stattin, H. 2003. Parenting of adolescents: Action or reaction? In A. C. Crouter and A. Booth (Eds.),

Children's influence on family dynamics (pp. 121–152). Mahwah, NJ: Erlbaum. *333, 339*

Kessen, W. 1979. The American child and other cultural inventions. *American Psychologist, 34,* 815–820. *18*

Kett, J. F. 1977. *Rites of passage: Adolescence in America 1790 to present.* New York: Basic Books. *341*

Kiecolt, K. J. 2003. Satisfaction with work and family life: No evidence of a cultural reversal. *Journal of Marriage and Family, 65,* 23–35. *124*

Kiernan, K. 1992. The impact of family disruption in childhood on transitions made in young adult life. *Population Studies, 46,* 218–234. *406*

Kilbride, P. L. 1994. The principle: Celestial marriage among the Mormons. *Plural marriage for our times: A reinvented option?* (pp. 67–82) Westport, CT: Bergin and Garvey. *47*

Kim, J. E., Hetherington, E. M., and Reiss, D. 1999. Associations among family relationships, antisocial peers, and adolescents' externalizing behaviors: Gender and family type differences. *Child Development, 70,* 1209–1230. *368, 406*

Kimball, M. M. 1986. Television and sex-role attitudes. In T. M. Williams (Ed.), *The impact of television* (pp. 265–301). New York: Academic Press. *74*

Kim-Cohen, J., et al. 2004. Genetic and environmental processes in young children's resilience and vulnerability to socioeconomic deprivation. *Child Development, 75,* 651–668. *140, 383*

Kimmel, M. S. 2000. *The gendered society.* New York: Oxford University Press. *371*

King, V. 2003a. The legacy of a grandparent's divorce: Consequences for ties between grandparents and grandchildren. *Journal of Marriage and Family, 65,* 170–183. *293*

King, V. 2003b. The influence of religion on fathers' relationships with their children. *Journal of Marriage and Family, 65,* 382–395. *197*

King, V., and Elder, G. H., Jr. 1995. American children view their grandparents: Linked lives across three rural generations. *Journal of Marriage and the Family, 57,* 165–178. *290*

King, V., and Elder, G. H., Jr. 1999. Are religious grandparents more involved grandparents? *Journal of Gerontology: Social Sciences, 54B,* S317–S338. *197*

King, V., et al. 2004. Relations with grandparents: Rural Midwest versus urban Southern California. *Journal of Family Issues, 24,* 1044–1069. *161*

Kinsey, A. C., Pomeroy, W. B., and Martin, C. E. 1948. *Sexual behavior in the human male.* Philadelphia: Saunders. *207*

Kirkpatrick, L. A., and Davis, K. E. 1994. Attachment style, gender, and relationship status: A longitudinal analysis. *Journal of Personality and Social Psychology, 66,* 502–512. *206*

Kitson, G. C., with Holmes, W. M. 1992. *Portrait of divorce: Adjustment to marital breakdown.* New York: Guilford Press. *318, 401*

Klebanov, P. K., et al. 1998. The contribution of neighborhood and family income to developmental test scores over the first three years of life. *Child Development, 69,* 1420–1436. *154*

Kluwer, E. S., Heesink, J. A. M., and van de Vliert, E. 1997. The marital dynamics of conflict over the division of labor. *Journal of Marriage and the Family, 59,* 635–653. *317*

Knighton, T., and Mirza, S. 2002. Postsecondary participation: The effects of parents' education and household income. *Education Quarterly Review, 8,* 25–32. *182, 184*

Kochanska, G. 1995. Children's temperament, mother's discipline, and security of attachment: Multiple pathways to emerging internalization. *Child Development, 66,* 597–615. *331*

Kochenderfer, B. J., and Ladd, G. W. 1996. Peer victimization: Cause or consequence of school maladjustment? *Child Development, 67,* 1305–1317. *445*

Koepke, L., Hare, J., and Moran, P. B. 1992. Relationship quality in a sample of lesbian couples with children and child-free lesbian couples. *Family Relations, 41,* 224–229. *281*

Kohen, D. E., et al. 2002a. Neighborhood income and physical and social disorder in Canada: Associations with young children's competencies. *Child Development, 73,* 1844–1860. *148, 153, 468*

Kohen, D., Hertzman, C., and Willms, J. D. 2002b. The importance of quality child care. In J. D. Willms (Ed.), *Vulnerable children* (pp. 261–276). Edmonton: University of Alberta Press. *176*

Kohler, J. K., Grotevant, H. D., and McRoy, R. G. 2002. Adopted adolescents' preoccupation with adoption: The impact on adoptive family relationships. *Family Relations, 64,* 93–104. *263*

Kohler Riessman, C. 2000. Stigma and every day resistance practices: Childless women in South India. *Gender and Society, 14,* 111–135. *51*

Korbin, J. E. 1986. Childhood histories of women imprisoned for fatal child maltreatment. *Child Abuse and Neglect: The International Journal, 10,* 331–338. *435*

Korbin, J. E., Anetzberger, G., and Austin, C. 1995. The intergenerational cycle of violence in child and elder abuse. *Journal of Elder Abuse & Neglect, 7,* 1–15. *448*

Koropeckyj-Cox, T. 2002. Beyond parental status: Psychological well-being in middle and old age. *Journal of Marriage and Family, 64,* 957–971. *253*

Kotlowitz, A. 1991. *There are no children here.* New York: Anchor/Doubleday. *137*

Kowaleski-Jones, L., and Mott, F. L. 1998. Sex, contraception and childbearing among high-risk youth: Do different factors influence males and females? *Family Planning Perspectives, 30,* 163–169. *227, 228*

Krakauer, I. D., and Rose, S. M. 2002. The impact of group membership on lesbians' physical appearance. *Journal of Lesbian Studies, 6,* 31–43. *210*

Kralovec, E., and Buehl, J. 2001. End homework now. *Educational Leadership, 58,* 39–42. *183*

Kramer, L., and Ramsburg, D. 2002. Advice given to parents on welcoming a second child: A critical review. *Family Relations, 51,* 2–14. *285*

Kraut, R., et al. 2002. Internet paradox revisited. *Journal of Family Issues, 58,* 49–74. *80*

Kremarik, F. 1999. Moving to be better off. *Canadian Social Trends, 55,* 19–21. *167*

Kremarik, F. 2000a. The other side of the fence. *Canadian Social Trends, 57,* 20–24. *149*

Kremarik, F. 2000b. A family affair: Children's participation in sports. *Canadian Social Trends, 58,* 20–24. *78*

Kremarik, F. 2002. A little place in the country: A profile of Canadians who own vacation property. *Canadian Social Trends, 65,* 12–14. *164*

Kremarik, F., and Williams, C. 2001. Mobile homes in Canada. *Canadian Social Trends, 62,* 14–17. *165*

Krishnakumar, A., and Buehler, C. 2000. Interparental conflict and parenting behaviors: A meta-analytic review. *Family Relations, 49,* 25–44. *322, 323*

Krull, C. 2000. Fertility change in Quebec, 1931–1991. *Canadian Population Studies, Special Edition on Family Demography, 27,* 159B80. *97*

Krull, C. 2002a. Culture of resistance: Gender, intergenerational change and community development in Cuba. Paper presented at the annual meetings of the Canadian International Development Agency (CIDA). Toronto, ON. *52*

Krull, C. 2002b. Intergenerational differences amongst women living in revolutionary Cuba. Paper presented at the annual meetings of the Canadian Population Society. Toronto, ON. *52*

Krull, C. 2003. Pronatalism, feminism and family policy in Quebec. In M. Lynn (Ed.), *Voices: Essays on Canadian families,* 2nd Ed. (pp. 245–265). Scarborough, ON: Thomson Nelson. *36, 98*

Krull, C., and Kobayashi, A. Ongoing study. *Shared memories, common visions: Neighborhood, generation, and social organization among women in Havana, Cuba.* *53*

Krull, C., and Pierce, D. 1997. Behavior analysis and demograhics: Government control of reproductive behavior and fertility in the province of Quebec, Canada. In P. A. Lamal (Ed.), *Cultural contingencies: Behavior analytic perspectives on cultural practices* (pp. 107–132). Westport, CT: Praeger. *98*

Krull, C., and Trovato, F. 2003a. Collapse of the cradle: A comprehensive framework of fertility decline in Quebec: 1941–1991. *Canadian Studies in Population: Special Issue in Honor of Anatole Romaniuc, 40,* 193–220. *36, 38, 251*

Krull, C., and Trovato, F. 2003b. Where have all the children gone? Quebec's fertility decline: 1941–1991. *Canadian Studies in Population, 30,* 193–220. *39*

Krull, C., et al. 2003. La vida de las mujeres en San Isidro: Los patrones temporales y spatiales en una cultura de resisten-cia (Women's daily life in San Isidro: Time-space patterns in a culture of resistance). *Publicación de la Cátedra de la Mujer* (pp. 1–16). Havana: Universidad de Habana. *54*

Kubey, R. 1994. Media implications for the quality of family life. In D. Zillmann, J. Bryant, and A. C. Huston (Eds.), *Media, children, and the family* (pp. 61–69). Hillsdale, NJ: Erlbaum. *69*

Kupersmidt, J. B., et al. 1995. Childhood aggression and peer relations in the context of family and neighborhood factors. *Child Development, 66,* 360–375. *154, 437*

Kurdek, L. A. 1990. Divorce history and self-reported psychological distress in husbands and wives. *Journal of Marriage and the Family, 52,* 701–708. *319, 394*

Kurdek, L. A. 1993. Nature and prediction of changes in marital quality for first-time parent and nonparent husbands and wives. *Journal of Family Psychology, 6,* 255–265. *278*

Kurdek, L. A. 1994. Areas of conflict for gay, lesbian, and heterosexual couples: What couples argue about influences relationship satisfaction. *Journal of Marriage and the Family, 56,* 923–934. *317, 321*

Kurdek, L. A. 1998. Relationship outcomes and their predictors: Longitudinal evidence from heterosexual married, gay cohabiting, and lesbian cohabiting couples. *Journal of Marriage and the Family, 60,* 553–568. *321, 456*

Kurian, G. 1991. South Asians in Canada. *Intergenerational Migration, 29,* 421–433. *108*

Kurz, D., et al. 1996. Separation, divorce and woman abuse. *Violence Against Women, 2,* 63–81. *401*

Lackey, C., and Williams, K. R. 1995. Social bonding and the cessation of partner violence across generations. *Journal of Marriage and the Family, 57,* 295–305. *435*

Ladd, G. W. 1992. Themes and theories: Perspectives on processes in family-peer relationships. In R. D. Parke and G. W. Ladd (Eds.), *Family-peer relationships: Modes of linkage* (pp. 1–34). Hillsdale, NJ: Erlbaum. *346*

Ladd, G. W., Birch, S. H. and Buhs, E. S. 1999. Children's social and scholastic lives in kindergarten: Related spheres of influence? *Child Development, 70,* 1373–1400. *179*

Lai, D. C., Paper, J., and Paper, L. C. 2005. The Chinese in Canada: Their unrecognized religion. In P. Bramadat and D. Seljah (Eds.), *Religion and ethnicity in Canada* (pp. 89–110). Toronto: Pearson. *191*

Laird, J. 1993. Lesbian and gay families. In F. Walsh (Ed.), *Normal family processes,* 2nd Ed. (pp. 282–328). New York: Guilford Press. *244*

Laird, R. D., et al. 2003. Parents' monitoring-relevant knowledge and adolescents' delinquent behavior: Evidence of correlated developmental changes and reciprocal influences. *Child Development, 74,* 752–768. *333*

Lakey, J. 2001. Face of homelessness getting younger: Report. *The Toronto Star,* February 8, p. B4. *157*

Lam, L. 1982. The Chinese-Canadian families of Toronto in the 1970s. *International Journal of Sociology, 12,* 11–32. *105*

Lamb, K. A., Lee, G. R., and DeMaris, A. 2003. Union formation and depression: Selection and relationship effects. *Journal of Marriage and Family, 65,* 953–962. *216*

Lamb, M. E. 1997. *The role of the father in child development.* New York: Wiley. *275*

Lamb, M. E. 1998. Nonparental child care: Context, quality, correlates, and consequences. In W. Demon (Series Ed.), I. E. Sigel, and K. A. Renniger (Vol. Eds.), *Handbook of child psychology: Child psychology in practice,* 4th Ed. New York: Wiley. *175*

Lamborn, S. D., Dornbusch, S. M., and Steinberg, L. 1996. Ethnicity and community context as moderators of the relations between family decision making and adolescent readjustment. *Child Development, 67,* 283–301. *337, 382*

Lamborn, S. D., et al. 1991. Patterns of competence and adjustment among adolescents from authoritative, authoritarian, indulgent, and neglecting families. *Child Development, 62,* 1049–1065. *334*

Land, K., McCall, P., and Cohen, L. 1990. Structural covariates of homicide rates: Are there any invariances across time and space? *American Journal of Sociology, 95,* 922–963. *151*

Landale, N. S., and Fennelly, K. 1992. Informal unions among mainland Puerto Ricans: Cohabitation or an alternative to legal marriage? *Journal of Marriage and the Family, 54,* 264–280. *242*

Laner, M. R., and Ventrone, N. A. 1998. Egalitarian daters/traditionalist dates. *Journal of Family Issues, 19,* 468–477. *207*

Langille, D. B., et al. 2003. Association of socio-economic factors with health risk behaviours among high school students in rural Nova Scotia. *Canadian Journal of Public Health, 94,* 442–448. *240*

Langlois, S. 1992. Women's employment. In S. Langlois et al., *Recent social trends in Québec, 1960–1990* (pp. 120–128). Kingston: McGill-Queen's University Press. *97*

Lansford, J. E., et al. 2001. Does family structure matter? A comparison of adoptive, two-parent biological, single-mother, stepfather, and stepmother households. *Journal of Marriage and Family, 63,* 840–851. *259*

Lareau, A. 2003. *Unequal childhoods: Class, race, and family life.* Berkeley: University of California Press. *66, 180,182, 274, 336, 365, 463*

Laroche, M. 1998. In & out of low income. *Canadian Social Trends, 50,* 20–24. *135, 136*

LaRossa, R., and Reitzes, D. C. 1993. Symbolic interactionism and family studies. In P. G. Boss et al. (Eds.), *Sourcebook of family theories and methods: A contextual approach.* New York: Plenum Press. *15*

Larson, L. E., and Goltz, J. W. 1989. Religious participation and marital commitment. *Review of Religious Research, 30,* 387–400. *316*

Larson, R. 1995. Secrets in the bedroom: Adolescents' private use of media. *Journal of Youth and Adolescence, 24,* 535–550. *69*

Larson, R. W., and Richards, M. H. 1994. *Divergent realities: The emotional lives of mothers, fathers, and adolescents.* New York: Basic Books. *124, 309, 313, 341, 342*

Larson, R. W., Wilson, S., and Mortimer, J. 2002. Conclusions: Adolescents' preparation for the future. *Journal of Research on Adolescence, 12,* 159–166. *341*

Larzelere, R. E., et al. 1998. Punishment enhances reasoning's effectiveness as a disciplinary response to toddlers. *Journal of Marriage and the Family, 60,* 388–403. *333, 338*

Laszloffy, T. A. 2002. Rethinking family development theory: Teaching with the systemic family development (SFD) model. *Family Relations, 51,* 206–214. *17, 272*

Laub, J. H., Nagin, D. S., and Sampson, R. J. 1998. Trajectories of change in criminal offending: Good marriages and the desistance process. *American Sociological Review, 63,* 225–238. *220, 240*

Laumann, E. O. 1996. Early sexual experiences: How voluntary? How violent? In M. D. Smith et al. (Eds.), *Sexuality and American social policy.* Menlo Park, CA: Henry J. Kaiser Family Foundation. *446*

Laumann, E. O., et al. 1994. *The social organization of sexuality: Sexual practices in the United States.* Chicago: University of Chicago Press. *207, 214, 217, 229, 231*

Lavee, Y., and Katz, R. 2002. Division of labor, perceived fairness, and marital quality: The effect of gender ideology. *Journal of Marriage and Family, 64,* 27–39. *24*

Lavigne, M. 1986. Feminist reflections on the fertility of women in Québec. In R. Hamilton and M. Barrett (Eds.), *The politics of diversity: Feminism, Marxism and nationalism* (pp. 303–321). London: Verso. *98*

Lavoie, Y. 1981. *L'émigration des Québécois aux États-Unis de 1830 à 1840.* Québec: Conseil de la langue française, direction des études et recherches. *40*

Lawton, L., Silverstein, M., and Bengtson, V. 1994. Affection, social contact, and geographic distance between adult children and their parents. *Journal of Marriage and the Family, 56,* 57–68. *348*

Lawton, V. 2003. Food bank ranks swelling. *Toronto Star,* November 16, p. A8. *134*

Leathers, S. J. 2003. Parental visiting, conflicting allegiances, and emotional and behavioral problems among foster children. *Family Relations, 52,* 53–63. *263, 265*

Lebner, A. 2000. Genetic "mysteries" and international adoption: The cultural impact of biomedical technologies on the adoptive family experience. *Family Relations, 49,* 371–377. *258*

Le Bourdais, C., and Juby, H. 2002. The impact of cohabitation on the family life course in contemporary North America: Insights from across the border. In A. Booth and A. C. Crouter (Eds.), *Just living together* (pp. 107–118). Mahwah, NJ: Erlbaum. *213*

Le Bourdais, C., et al. 2000. The changing face of conjugal relationship. *Canadian Social Trends, 56,* 14–17. *211, 397*

Le Camus, J. 1997. *Le rôle du père dans le développment du jeune enfant.* Paris: Nathan. *275*

LeClere, F. B., and Kowalewski, B. M. 1994. Disability in the family: The effects on children's well-being. *Journal of Marriage and the Family, 56*, 457–468. *368*

Lee, C. M., and Duxbury, L. 1998. Employed parents: Support from partners, employers, and friends. *Journal of Social Psychology, 138*, 303–322. *123*

Lee, G. R., Peek, C. W., and Coward, R. T. 1998. Race differences in filial responsibility expectations among older parents. *Journal of Marriage and the Family, 60*, 404–412. *216, 348*

Lee, S. A. 1993. Family structure effects on student outcomes. In B. Schneider and J. S. Coleman (Eds.), *Parents, their children, and schools* (pp. 43–75). San Francisco: Westview Press. *407*

Lee, Y.-J., and Aytac, I. A. 1998. Intergenerational financial support among whites, African Americans, and Latinos. *Journal of Marriage and the Family, 60*, 426–441. *350*

Lefebvre, S. 2003. Housing: An income issue. *Canadian Social Trends, 68*, 15–18. *164*

Lefley, H. P. 1997. Synthesizing the family caregiving studies: Implications for service planning, social policy, and further research. *Family Relations, 46*, 443–450. *448, 474*

Lehrer, E., and Chiswick, C. U. 1993. Religion as a determinant of marital stability. *Demography, 30*, 385–403. *210*

Lennon, M. C., and Rosenfield, S. 1994. Relative fairness and the division of housework: The importance of options. *Journal of Sociology, 100*, 506–531. *124, 308*

Lenton, R. L. 1990. Techniques of child discipline and abuse by parents. *Canadian Review of Sociology and Anthropology, 27*, 157–185. *337*

Leon, I. G. 2002. Adoption losses: Naturally occurring or socially constructed? *Child Development, 73*, 652–663. *260, 261*

Leon, K. 2003. Risk and protective factors in young children's adjustment to parental divorce: A review of the research. *Family Relations, 52*, 258–270. *179*

Lerman, R. I. 2002. *Married and unmarried parenthood and economic well-being: A dynamic analysis of recent cohorts.* New York: The Urban Institute. <www.urban.org>. *220, 241*

Lerner, R. M. 1982. Children and adolescents as producers of their own development. *Developmental Review, 2*, 342–370. *16*

Lerner, R. M. 1995. *America's youth in crisis.* Thousand Oaks, CA: Sage. *16*

Lerner, R. M., and Busch-Rossnagel, N. A. 1981. Individuals as producers of their development: Conceptual and empirical bases. In R. M. Lerner and N. A. Busch-Rossnagel (Eds.), *Individuals as producers of their development: A life-span perspective* (pp. 1–36). San Diego, CA: Academic Press. *332*

Lesthaeghe, R. 1998. On theory development: Applications to the study of family formation. *Population and Development Review, 24*, 1–14. *251*

Letherby, G. 1994. Mother or not, mother or what? Problems of definition and identity. *Women's Studies International Forum, 17*, 525–532. *258*

Leventhal, J. M. 2001. Commentary. *Child Abuse & Neglect, 25*, 1137–1138. *439*

Levin, I., and Trost, J. 1999. Living apart together. *Community, Work, and Family, 2*, 279–294. *8*

Levin, J. S. 1994. Investigating the epidemiologic effects of religious experience: Findings, explanations, and barriers. In J. S. Levin (Ed.), *Religion in aging and health: Theoretical foundations and methodological frontiers* (pp. 3–17). Newbury Park, CA: Sage. *195*

Levine, J. A., Pollack, H., and Comfort, M. E. 2001. Academic and behavioral outcomes among the children of young mothers. *Journal of Marriage and Family, 63*, 355–369. *284*

LeVine, R. A. 1990. Infant environments in psychoanalysis: A cross-cultural view. In J. W. Stigler, R. A. Shweder, and G. Herd (Eds.), *Cultural psychology: Essays on comparative human development* (pp. 454–476). New York: Cambridge University Press. *274*

LeVine, R. A. 1994. *Child care and culture: Lessons from Africa.* Cambridge: Cambridge University Press. *273*

LeVine, R. A., and White, M. 1994. The social transformation of childhood. In A. S. Skolnick and J. H. Skolnick (Eds.), *Family in transition* (8th ed., pp. 273–293). New York: HarperCollins. *251*

Levinger, G. 1976. A socio-psychological perspective on marital dissolution. *Journal of Social Issues, 52*, 21–47. *13*

Lewin, E. 1993. *Lesbian mothers: Accounts of gender in American culture.* Ithaca, NY: Cornell University Press. *244*

Lewin, T. 1999. Union links women's pay to poverty among families. *The New York Times*, February 25, A12. *133*

Lewis, M. 1997. *Altering fate: Why the past does not predict the future.* New York: Guilford Press. *331*

Ley, D., and Smith, H. 2000. Relations between deprivation and immigrant groups in large Canadian studies. *Urban Studies, 37*, 37–62. *157*

Li, P. 1996. *The making of post-war Canada.* Toronto: Oxford University Press. *251*

Li, P., and Peng, X. 2000. Age and sex structures. In Y. Li and P. Xizhe (Eds.), *The changing population of China* (pp. 64–76). Oxford: Blackwell Publishers. *49*

Lichter, D. T., McLaughlin, D. K., and Cornwell, G. T. 1995. Migration and the loss of human resources in rural America. In L. J. Beaulieu and D. Mulkey (Eds.), *Investing in people: The human capital needs of rural America* (pp. 235–256). Boulder, CO: Westview Press. *160*

Lillard, L. A., and Waite, L. J. 1995. Til death do us part: Marital disruption and mortality. *American Journal of Sociology, 100*, 1131–1156. *219*

Lindsey, D., and Martin, S. K. 2003. Deepening child poverty: The not so good news about welfare reform. *Children and Youth Services Review, 25*, 165–173. *467*

Lindsey, E. W. 1998. The impact of homelessness and shelter-life on family relationships. *Family Relations, 47,* 243–252. *159*

Lincoln, C. E., and Mamiya, L. H. 1990. *The black church in the African American experience.* Durham, NC: Duke University Press. *192*

Lindsey, E. W. 1998. The impact of homelessness and shelter-life on family relationships. *Family Relations, 47,* 243–252. *159*

Link, B. G., et al. 1987. The social rejection of former mental patients: Understanding why labels matter. *American Journal of Sociology, 92,* 1461–1500. *219*

Lippman, A. 1998. The politics of health: Geneticization versus health promotion. In S. Sherwin (Ed.), *The politics of women's health: Exploring agency and autonomy* (pp. 64–82). Philadelphia: Temple University Press. *258*

Lipps, G., and Frank, J. 1997. The social context of school for young children. *Canadian Social Trends, 47,* 22–26. *184, 185*

Liu, C. 2000. A theory of marital sexual life. *Journal of Marriage and the Family, 62,* 363–374. *231*

Livingstone, S., and Bovill, M. 2001. *Children and their changing media environment: A European comparative study.* Mahwah, NJ: Erlbaum. *69*

Lockhead, C. 2000. The trend toward delayed first childbirth: Health and social implications. *ISUMA: Canadian Journal of Policy Research,* Autumn, 41–44. *282*

Loewen, R. 1994. The Mennonites of Waterloo, Ontario and Hanover, Manitoba, 1980s: A study of household and community. *Canadian Papers in Rural History, 9,* 187–209. *45*

Logan, J. R., Alba, R., and Zhang, W. 2002. Immigrant enclaves and ethnic communities in New York and Los Angeles. *American Sociological Review, 67,* 299–322. *157*

Logan, J., Fuquin, B., and Bian, Y. 1998. Tradition and change in the urban Chinese family: The case of living arrangements. *Social Forces, 76,* 3, 851–882. *49*

London, R. A. 1996. The difference between divorced and never-married mothers' participation in the Aid to Families with Dependent Children Program. *Journal of Family Issues, 17,* 170–185. *134*

Longhurst, B. 1995. *Popular music and society.* Cambridge, UK: Polity Press. *76*

Longmore, M. A., Manning, W. D., and Giordano, P. G. 2001. Preadolescent parenting strategies and teens' dating and sexual initiation: A longitudinal analysis. *Journal of Marriage and Family, 63,* 322–335. *206*

López Vigil, M. 1999. *Cuba: Neither heaven nor hell.* Washington, D. C.: EPICA. *53*

Lorber, J. 1994. *Paradoxes of gender.* New Haven, CT: Yale University Press. *20*

Lounsbury, M. L., and Bates, J. E. 1982. The cries of infants of differing levels of perceived temperamental difficultness: Acoustic properties and effects on listeners. *Child Development, 53,* 677–686. *331*

Lowry, D. T., and Towles, D. W. 1989. Soap opera portrayals of sex, contraception, and sexually transmitted diseases. *Journal of Communication, 39,* 76–83. *77*

Ludwig, J., Duncan, G., and Hirshfeld, P. 2001. Urban poverty and juvenile crime: Evidence from a randomized housing mobility experiment. *Quarterly Journal of Economics, 116,* 655–680. *154*

Luffman, J. 1998. When parents replace teachers: The home schooling option. *Canadian Social Trends, 50,* 8–10. *189*

Lukasiewicz, K. 2002. Ethnicity, politics and religion: Polish societies in Edmonton in the inter-war years. *Alberta History, 50,* 2–12. *45*

Lupri, E. 1991. Fathers in transition: The case of dual-earner families in Canada. In J. E. Veevers (Ed.), *Continuity and change in marriage and family.* Toronto: Holt, Rinehart, and Winston. *123*

Luster, T., and Oh, S. M. 2001. Correlates of male adolescents carrying handguns among their peers. *Journal of Marriage and the Family, 63,* 714–726. *152*

Luster, T., et al. 2000. Factors related to successful outcomes among preschool children born to low-income adolescent mothers. *Journal of Marriage and the Family, 62,* 133–146. *376*

Luthar, S. S. 2003. The culture of affluence: Psychological costs of material wealth. *Child Development, 74,* 1581–1593. *150*

Luthar, S. S., and Becker, B. E. 2002. Privileged but pressured: A study of affluent youth. *Child Development, 73,* 1593–1610. *150*

Luthar, S. S., and D'Avanzo, K. 1999. Contextual factors in substance use: A study of suburban and inner-city adolescents. *Development and Psychopathology, 11,* 845–867. *150*

Lutjens, S. L. 1994. Remaking the public sphere: Women and revolution in Cuba. In M. A. Tétreault (Ed.), *Women and revolution in Africa, Asia and the New World* (pp. 366–393). Columbia, SC: University of South Carolina Press. *52*

Lutz, W., O'Neill, B., and Scherbov, S. 2003. Europe's population at a turning point. *Science, 299,* 1991–1992. *459*

Luxton, M. (Ed.), 1997a. *Feminism and families: Critical policies and changing practices.* Halifax: Fernwood. *456*

Luxton, M. 1997b. Feminism and families: The challenge of neo-conservatism. In M. Luxton (Ed.), *Feminism and families* (pp. 10–26). Halifax: Fernwood. *21, 60*

Luxton, M. 2001a. Conceptualizing "families": Theoretical frameworks and family research. In M. Baker (Ed.), *Families: Changing trends in Canada,* 4th Ed. (pp. 28–50). Toronto: McGraw-Hill Ryerson. *12, 20*

Luxton, M. 2001b. Family coping strategies: Balancing paid employment and domestic labour. In B. J. Fox (Ed.), *Family patterns, gender relations,* 2nd Ed. (pp. 318–337). Toronto: Oxford University Press. *309*

Luxton, M., and Corman, J. 2001. *Getting by in hard times: Gendered labour at home and on the job.* Toronto: University of Toronto Press. *21, 272, 274*

Lykken, D. 1987. An alternative explanation for low or zero sib correlations. *Behavioral and Brain Sciences, 10,* 31. *378*

Lynn, M. M. 2003. Single-parent families. In M. Lynn (Ed.), *Voices: Essays on Canadian families,* 2nd Ed. (pp. 32–54). Toronto: Thomson Nelson. *245*

Ma, X., and Zhang, Y. 2002. *A national assessment of effects of school experiences on health outcomes and behaviours of children.* Technical Report. Ottawa: Health Canada. *179, 181*

MacBeth, T. M. 1998. Quasi-experimental research on television and behavior: Natural and field experiments. In J. K. Asamen and G. L. Berry (Eds.), *Research paradigms, television, and social behavior* (pp. 109–151). Thousand Oaks, CA: Sage. *75*

Maccoby, E. E. 1999. The custody of children of divorcing families: Weighing the alternatives. In R. A. Thompson and P. R. Amato (Eds.), *The postdivorce family* (pp. 51–70). Thousand Oaks, CA: Sage. *404*

Maccoby, E. E., and Martin, J. 1983. Socialization in the context of the family: Parent-child interaction. In E. M. Hetherington (Ed.), *Handbook of child psychology: Vol. 4. Socialization, personality, and social development* (pp. 1–101). New York: Wiley. *16, 334*

Maccoby, E. E., and Jacklin, C. N. 1983. The "person" characteristics of children and the family as environment. In D. D. Magnusson and V. L. Allen (Eds.), *Human development: An interactional perspective* (pp. 75–92). New York: Academic Press. *16*

Maccoby, E. E., and Lewis, C. C. 2003. Less day care or different daycare? *Child Development, 74,* 1069–1075. *176, 465*

Maccoby, E. E., et al. 1993. Post divorce roles of mothers and fathers in the lives of their children. *Journal of Family Psychology, 7,* 24–38. *167, 408*

MacDonald, M. A. 1990. *Rebels and royalists: The lives and material culture of New Brunswick's early English-speaking settlers, 1758–1783.* Fredericton, NB: New Ireland Press. *38*

Mackay, R., and Miles, L. 1995. A major challenge for the educational system: Aboriginal retention and dropout. In M. L. Battiste and J. Barman (Eds.), *First Nations education in Canada: The circle unfolds* (pp. 157–178). Vancouver: University of British Columbia Press. *187*

MacMillan, H. L., et al. 1997. Prevalence of child physical and sexual abuse in the community: Results from the Ontario Health Supplement. *Journal of the American Medical Association Abstracts, 9,* July 9. *431*

MacMillan, H. L., et al. 2001. Childhood abuse and lifetime psychopathology in a community sample. *American Journal of Psychiatry, 158,* 1878–1883. *434*

Madden-Derdich, D. A., and Arditti, J. A. 1999. The ties that bind: Attachment between former spouses. *Family Relations, 48,* 243–249. *413*

Madden-Derdich, D. A., and Leonard, S. A. 2000. Parental role identity and fathers' involvement in coparental interaction after divorce: Fathers' perspectives. *Family Relations, 49,* 311–318. *275*

Magdol, L., et al. 1998. Hitting without a license: Testing explanations for differences in partner abuse between young adults daters and cohabitors. *Journal of Marriage and the Family, 60,* 41–55. *427*

Magnusson, D., and Allen, V. L. (Eds.). 1983. *Human development: An interactional perspective* (pp. 75–92). New York: Academic Press. *331*

Magnusson, D. 1995. Individual development: A holistic, integrated model. In P. Moen, G. H. Elder, Jr., and K. Lüscher (Eds.), *Examining lives in context* (pp. 19–60). Washington, DC: American Psychological Association. *16*

Mahoney, M. M. 1994. *Stepfamilies and the law.* Ann Arbor, MI: University of Michigan Press. *261*

Mahoney, M. R. 1991. Legal images of battered women: Redefining the issue of separation. *Michigan Law Review, 1,* 43–49. *425*

Makepeace, J. M. 1997. Courtship violence as process: A developmental theory. In A. P. Cardarelli (Ed.), *Violence between intimate partners* (pp. 29–47). Boston: Allyn & Bacon. *422*

Mallon, G. P. 1997. Toward a competent child welfare service delivery system for gay and lesbian adolescents and their families. In G. A. Anderson, A. S. Ryan, and B. R. Leashore (Eds.), *The challenge of permanency planning in a multicultural society* (pp. 177–194). New York: Haworth. *157*

Mallon, G. P. 1998. After care, then where? Outcomes of an independent living program. *Child Welfare, 77,* 61–78. *264*

Malszecki, G., and Cavar, T. 2004. Men, masculinities, war & sport. In N. Mandell (Ed.), *Feminist issues: Race, class, and gender,* 4th Ed. (pp. 160–187). Toronto: Prentice Hall. *74, 78*

Man, G. 2001. From Hong Kong to Canada: Immigration and the changing family lives of middle-class women from Hong Kong. In B. Fox (Ed.), *Family patterns, gender relations,* 2nd Ed. (pp. 420–438). Toronto: Oxford University Press. *104, 105*

Mancini, C., Van Ameringen, M., and Macmillan, H. 1995. Relationship of childhood sexual and physical abuse to anxiety disorders. *The Journal of Nervous and Mental Disease, 183,* 309–314. *442*

Mandelbaum, D. J. 1979. *The Plains Cree: An ethnographical, historical and comparative study.* Regina: Canadian Plains Research Centre. *34*

Mandell, D. 2002. *"Deadbeat dads."* Toronto: University of Toronto Press. *275, 419, 474*

Mandell, N. 2001. Women, families, and intimate relations. In N. Mandell (Ed.), *Feminist issues: Race, class, and sexuality,* 3rd Ed. (pp. 195–218). Toronto: Prentice Hall. *20*

Mandell, N. 2004. Making families: Gender, economics, sexuality, and race. In N. Mandell (Ed.), *Feminist issues: Race, class, and gender,* 4th Ed. (pp. 188–225). Toronto: Prentice Hall. *30, 222, 223*

Mandell, N., and Momirov, J. 2000. Family history. In N. Mandell and A. Duffy (Eds.), *Canadian families: Diversity, conflict, and change* (pp. 17–47). Toronto: Harcourt Brace. *119*

Mandell, N., and Sweet, R. 2004. Homework as home work: Mothers' unpaid educational labour. *Atlantis, 28.2,* 7–18. *62, 180, 183*

Manlove, J., et al. 2002. Preventing teenage pregnancy, childbearing, and sexually transmitted diseases: What the research shows. Washington, DC: Child Trends Research Brief. May. <www.childtrends.org>. *180, 227*

Mannheim, K. 1936. *Ideology and Utopia.* London: Routledge & Kegan Paul. *18*

Manning, M., and Baruth, L. 2000. *Multicultural education of children and adolescents.* Toronto: Allyn & Bacon. *184*

Manning, W. D. 2002. The implications of cohabitation for children's well-being. In A. Booth and A. C. Crouter (Eds.), *Just living together* (pp. 121–152). Mahwah, NJ: Erlbaum. *241*

Manning, W. D., and Lamb, K. A. 2003. Adolescent well-being in cohabiting, married, and single-parent families. *Journal of Marriage and Family, 65,* 876–893. *241, 242*

Manning, W. D., and Smock, P. 1995. Why marry? Race and the transition to marriage among cohabitors. *Demography, 32,* 509–520. *241, 471*

Manning, W. D., and Smock, P. J. 2000. "Swapping" families: Serial parenting and economic support for children. *Journal of Marriage and the Family, 62,* 111–122. *404*

Manning, W. D., Stewart, S. D., and Smock, P. J. 2004. The complexity of father's parenting responsibilities and involvement with nonresidential children. *Journal of Family Issues, 24,* 645–667. *404*

March, K. 1995a. Perception of adoption as social stigma: Motivation for search and reunion. *Journal of Marriage and the Family, 57,* 653–660. *258, 260, 264*

March, K. 1995b. *The stranger who bore me.* Toronto: University of Toronto Press. *263, 264*

March, K., and Miall, C. 2000. Adoption as a family form. *Family Relations, 49,* 359–362. *258*

Marcil-Gratton, N. 1998. *Growing up with mom and dad? The intricate life course of Canadian children.* Ottawa: Statistics Canada, Cat. No. 89–566. *241*

Marcil-Gratton, N. 1999. Growing up with mom and dad? Canadian children experience shifting family structures. *Transition, 29,* September, 4–7. *392, 040*

Margolin, G. 1998. Effects of domestic violence on children. In P. K. Trickett and C. J. Schellenback (Eds.), *Violence against children in the family and the community* (pp. 57–101). Washington, DC: American Psychological Association. *434*

Marks, L. 2004. Feminism and stay-at-home motherhood: Some critical reflections and implications for mothers on social assistance. *Atlantis, 28.2,* 73–83. *21, 122*

Marks, N. F. 1996. Flying solo at midlife: Gender, marital status, and psychological well-being. *Journal of Marriage and the Family, 58,* 917–932. *220, 225*

Marks, N. F., and Lambert, J. D. 1998. Marital status continuity and change among young and midlife adults: Longitudinal effects on psychological well-being. *Journal of Family Issues, 19,* 652–686. *221*

Marks, S. R. 2000. Teasing out the lessons of the 1960s: Family diversity and family privilege. *Journal of Marriage and the Family, 62,* 609–622. *149*

Maroney, H. J. 1992. Who has the baby? Nationalism, pronatalism and the construction of a "demographic crisis" in Quebec, 1960–1988. *Studies in Political Economy, 39,* 7–36. *98*

Marshall, K. 1993. Dual earners: Who's responsible for housework? *Canadian Social Trends, 31,* 11–14. *309*

Marshall, K. 1994. Balancing work and family responsibilities. *Perspectives on Labour and Income, 6,* Spring, 26–30. *309*

Marshall, K. 2003. Parental leave: More time off for baby. *Canadian Social Trends, 71,* 13–18. *465*

Marsiglio, W. 2004. When stepfathers claim stepchildren: A conceptual analysis. *Journal of Marriage and Family, 66,* 22–39. *261*

Martel, L., and Belangér, A. 2000. Dependence-free life expectancy in Canada. *Canadian Social Trends, 58,* 26–29. *295*

Martin, G. 1974. British officials and their attitudes to the Negro community in Canada, 1833–1861. *Ontario History, 66,* 79–88. *42*

Martin, G. T., Jr. 1997. An agenda for family policy in the United States. In T. Arendell (Ed.), *Contemporary parenting: Challenges and issues* (pp. 298–324). Thousand Oaks, CA: Sage. *66*

Martin, S. P. 2000. Diverging fertility among U.S. women who delay childbearing past age 30. *Demography, 37,* 523–533. *282*

Martin, T. C. 2002. Consensual unions in Latin America: Persistence of a dual nuptuality system. *Journal of Comparative Family Studies, 33,* 35–55. *211*

Martin-Matthews, A. 1991. *Widowhood in later life.* Toronto: Butterworths/Harcourt. *410, 419*

Martin-Matthews, A. 2000. Change and diversity in aging families and intergenerational relations. In N. Mandell and A. Duffy (Eds.), *Canadian families: Diversity, conflict, and change* (pp. 323–360). Toronto: Harcourt Canada. *283, 348*

Martin-Matthews, A. 2001. *The ties that bind aging families* Ottawa: The Vanier Institute of the Family. <www.vifamily.ca>. *353*

Martoz-Baden, R., and Mattheis, C. 1994. Daughters-in-law and stress in two-generation farm families. *Family Process, 43,* 132–137. *162*

Masheter, C. 1997. Healthy and unhealthy friendship and hostility between ex-spouses. *Journal of Marriage and the Family,* 59, 463–475. *413*

Mason, C. A., et al. 1996. Neither too sweet nor too sour: Problem peers, maternal control, and problem behavior in African American adolescents. *Child Development,* 67, 2115–2130. *337*

Mason, M. A. 1998. The modern American stepfamily: Problems and possibilities. In M. A. Mason, A. Skolnick, and S. D. Sugarman (Eds.), *All our families: New policies for a new century* (pp. 95–116). New York: Oxford University Press. *262*

Matthews, B., and Beaujot, R. 1997. Gender orientations and family strategies. *Canadian Review of Sociology and Anthropology,* 34, 415–428. *459*

Mauldon, J. 1998. Families started by teenagers. In M. A. Mason, A. Skolnick, and S. D. Sugarman (Eds.), *All our families: New policies for a new century* (pp. 39–65). New York: Oxford University Press. *469*

Maxim, P. S., White, J. P., and Gyimah, S. O. 2003. Earnings implications of person years lost life expectancy among Canada's Aboriginal peoples. *Canadian Studies in Population,* 30, 271–295. *151*

Mayberry, M., et al. 1995. *Home-schooling: Parents as educators.* Thousand Oaks, CA: Corwin. *189*

Mayfield, M. 2001. *Early childhood education and care in Canada.* Toronto: Prentice Hall. *178*

McAuley, C. 1996. *Children in long term foster care.* Avebury, UK: Brookfield. *265*

McBride, B. A., and Rane, T. R. 1998. Parenting alliance as a predictor of father involvement: An exploratory study. *Family Relations,* 47, 229–236. *275, 471*

McCartney, K. 2003. On the meaning of models: A signal amidst the noise. In A. C. Crouter and A. Booth (Eds.), *Children's influence on family dynamics* (pp. 27–30). Mahwah, NJ: Erlbaum. *378*

McCartney, K., et al. 1997. Social development in the context of typical center-based child care. *Merrill-Palmer Quarterly,* 43, 426–450. *176*

McCarthy, E. D. 1996. *Knowledge as culture: The new sociology of knowledge.* London: Routledge. *18*

McCauley, J., et al. 1997. Clinical characteristics of women with a history of childhood abuse. *Journal of the American Medical Association,* 277, 1362–1368. *434*

McChesney, K. Y. 1995. A review of the empirical literature on contemporary urban homeless families. *Social Service Review,* 69, 429–460. *158*

McClare, D. (Ed.). 1997. *The 1815 diary of a Nova Scotia farm girl, Louisa Collins of Colin Grove, Dartmouth.* Dartmouth, NS: Brook House Press. *38*

McCloskey, L. A., Figueredo, A. J., and Koss, M. P. 1995. The effects of systemic family violence on children's mental health. *Child Development,* 66, 1239–1261. *434, 439*

McCollum, A. T. 1990. *The trauma of moving.* Newbury Park, CA: Sage. *168*

McCoy, J. K., Brody, G. H., and Stoneman, Z. 1994. A longitudinal analysis of sibling relationships as mediators of the link between family processes and youths' best friendships. *Family Relations,* 43, 400–408. *363*

McCracken, G. 1988. *Culture and consumption: New approaches to the symbolic character of goods and activities.* Bloomington, IN: Indiana University Press. *128*

McCurdy, K., and Daro, D. 1994. Child maltreatment: A national survey of reports and fatalities. *Journal of Interpersonal Violence,* 9, 75–94. *437*

McDaniel, S. 1996. The family lives of the middle-aged and elderly in Canada. In M. Baker (Ed.), *Families: Changing trends in Canada* (pp. 195–211). Toronto: McGraw-Hill Ryerson. *63*

McDaniel, S. A. 2000. What did you ever do for me?: Intergenerational linkages in a reconstructing Canada. In E. M. Gee and G. Gutman (Eds.), *The overselling of population aging* (pp. 129–152). Toronto: Oxford University Press. *89*

McDaniel, S. A., 2001. Family change and life course development: Social transformation on intimate frontiers. In A. Sales (Ed.), *Social transformations at the turn of the millennium: Sociological theory and current empirical research.* Madrid: International Sociological Association. *89*

McDaniel, S. A. 2002. Women's changing relations to the state and citizenship: Caring and intergenerational relations in globalizing Western democracies. *Canadian Review of Sociology and Anthropology,* 39, 1–26. *17*

McDaniel, S. A. 2003. Family/work challenges among midlife and older Canadians. In M. Lynn (Ed.), *Voices: Essays on Canadian families,* 2nd. Ed. (pp. 152–176). Toronto: Thomson Nelson. *18*

McDaniel, S. A., and Gee, E. M. 1993. Social policies regarding caregiving to elders: Canadian contradictions. *Journal of Aging and Social Policy,* 5, 57–72. *351, 460*

McDonald, K. B., and Armstrong, E. M. 2001. De-romanticizing Black intergenerational support: The questionable expectations of welfare reform. *Journal of Marriage and Family,* 63, 213–223. *136, 155*

McDonald, L. 1997. The invisible poor: Canada's retired widows. *Canadian Journal on Aging,* 16, 82–92. *410*

McDonald, L. 2000. Alarmist economics and women's pensions. In E. M. Gee and G. M. Gutman (Eds.), *The overselling of population aging* (pp. 114–128). Toronto: Oxford University Press. *467*

McDonough, S., and Hoodfar, H. 2005. Muslims in Canada: From ethnic groups to religious community. In P. Bramadat and D. Seljak (Eds.), *Religion and ethnicity in Canada* (pp. 133–153). Toronto: Pearson. *192*

McGillivray, A., and Comaskey, B. 1998. Everybody had black eyes ... Nobody don't say nothing: Intimate violence. Aboriginal women, and justice system response. In K. D.

Bonnycastle and G. S. Rigakos (Eds.), *Unsettling truths: Battered women, policy, and politics and contemporary research in Canada*. Vancouver: Collective Press. *428*

McHale, S. M., and Crouter, A. C. 1996. The family contexts of children's sibling relationships. In G. H. Brody (Ed.), *Sibling relationships: Their causes and consequences* (pp. 173–196). Norwood, NJ: Ablex. *365*

McHale, S., et al. 1995. Congruence between mothers' and fathers' differential treatment of siblings: Links with family relations and children's well-being. *Child Development, 66*, 116–128. *369, 373*

McHardie, D. 2000. Web-surfing teens turn off the TV. *Globe and Mail*, May 24, A1, A5. *79*

McIntyre, L., et al. 2002. Food insecurity of low-income lone mothers and their children in Atlantic Canada. *Canadian Journal of Public Health, 93*, 411–416. *140–141*

McLanahan, S. S. 1997. Parent absence or poverty: Which matters more? In G. J. Duncan and J. Brooks-Gunn (Eds.), *Consequences of growing up poor* (pp. 35–48). New York: Russell Sage. *407, 415*

McLanahan, S. S., and Casper, L. 1995. Growing diversity and inequality in the American family. In R. Farley (Ed.), *State of the Union: America in the 1990s. Vol. Two: Social trends* (pp. 1–46). New York: Russell Sage. *220*

McLaughlin, S. S., Leonard, K. E., and Senchal, M. 1992. Prevalence and distribution of premarital aggression among couples applying for a marriage license. *Journal of Family Violence, 70*, 309–319. *398*

McLeod, N. 2000. Plains Cree identity: Borderlands, ambiguous genealogies and narrative irony. *Canadian Journal of Native Studies, 20*, 437–454. *34*

McLoyd, V. C. 1995. Poverty, parenting, and policy: Meeting the support needs of poor parents. In H. E. Fitzgerald, B. M. Lester, and B. Zuckerman (Eds.), *Children of poverty* (pp. 269–298). New York: Garland. *433*

McLoyd, V. C. 1998. Socioeconomic disadvantage and child development. *American Psychologist, 53*, 185–204. *140, 141, 240, 469*

McLoyd, V. C., and Smith, J. 2002. Physical discipline and behavior problems in African American, European American, and Hispanic children: Emotional support as a moderator. *Journal of Marriage and Family, 64*, 40–53. *338*

McMahon, C. A., et al. 1995. Psychosocial outcomes for parents and children after *in vitro* fertilization: A review. *Journal of Reproductive and Infant Psychology, 13*, 1–16. *255*

McMahon, M. 1995. *Engendering motherhood*. New York: Guilford. *273*

McManus, P. A., and DiPrete, T. A. 2001. Losers and winners: The financial consequences of separation and divorce for men. *American Sociological Review, 66*, 246–268. *461*

McManus, S. 1999. Their own country: Race, gender, landscape, and colonization around the 49th parallel, 1862–1900. *Agricultural History, 73*, 168–182. *45*

McNeal, C., and Amato, P. R. 1998. Parents' marital violence: Long-term consequences for children. *Journal of Family Issues, 19*, 123–139. *429*

McNeil, J. 1975. Feminism, femininity and the television shows: A content analysis. *Journal of Broadcasting, 19*, 259–269. *71*

McPherson, B. D. 1994. Aging: The middle and later years. In L. Tepperman, J. Curtis, and J. Richardson (Eds.), *Sociology* (pp. 230–266). Toronto: McGraw-Hill Ryerson. *410*

McPherson, B. D. 1998. *Aging as a social process*, 3rd Ed. Toronto: Harcourt Brace. *96, 290*

McQuillan, J., et al. 2003. Frustrated fertility: Infertility and psychological distress among women. *Journal of Marriage and Family, 65*, 1007–1018. *252, 261*

McRoy, G. R., Grotevant, H. D., and White, K. L. 1998. *Openness in adoption: New practices, new issues*. New York: Praeger. *263*

McVey, W. W., Jr., and Kalbach, W. E. 1995. *Canadian population*. Toronto: Nelson. *250, 251*

McWey, L. M., and Mullis, A. K. 2004. Improving the lives of children in foster care: The impact of supervised visitation. *Family Relations, 53*, 293–300. *265*

Mead, G. H. 1934. *Mind, self and society*. Chicago: University of Chicago Press. *15*

Mead, M. 1928. *Coming of age in Samoa*. New York: William Morrow. *341*

Mekos, D., Hetherington, E. M., and Reiss, D. 1996. Sibling differences in problem behavior and parental treatment in nondivorced and remarried families. *Child Development, 67*, 2148–2165. *126*

Melson, G. F., and Fogel, A. 1996. Parental perceptions of their children's involvement with household pets: A test of a specificity model of nurturance. *Anthrozoos, 9*, 95–106. *286*

Melzer, S. A. 2002. Gender, work, and intimate violence: Men's occupational violence spillover and compensatory violence. *Journal of Marriage and Family, 64*, 820–832. *425*

Menaghan, E. G., and Parcel, T. L. 1991. Determining children's home environments: The impact of maternal characteristics and current occupational and family conditions. *Journal of Marriage and the Family, 53*, 417–431. *125, 362*

Menaghan, E. G., and Parcel, T. L. 1995. Social sources of change in children's home environments: The effects of parental occupational experiences and family conditions. *Journal of Marriage and the Family, 57*, 69–84. *136*

Menzies, H. 1996. *Whose brave new world?* Toronto: Between the Lines. *119*

Merkle, E. R., and Richardson, R. A. 2000. Digital dating and virtual relating: Conceptualizing computer mediated romantic relationships. *Family Relations, 49*, 187–192. *208*

Merten, D. E. 1996. Going-with: The role of a social form in early romance. *Journal of Contemporary Ethnography, 24*, 462–484. *208*

Merton, R. K. 1968. *Social theory and social structure*. New York: Free Press. *12*

Messner, M. 1997. *The politics of masculinity: Men in movements*. Thousand Oaks, CA: Sage. *20*

Meston, C. M., Trapnell, P. D., and Gorzalka, B. B. 1998. Ethnic, gender, and length of residency influences on sexual knowledge and attitudes. *Journal of Sex Research, 35,* 176–188. *106*

Metz, M. E., Rosser, B. R. S., and Strapko, N. 1994. Differences in conflict-resolution styles among heterosexual, gay, and lesbian couples. *Journal of Sex Research, 31,* 293–308. *317*

Miall, C. E. 1996. The social construction of adoption: Clinical and community perspectives. *Family Relations, 36,* 34–39. *261*

Miall, C. E., and March, K. 2004. Open adoption as a family form: Community assessment and social support. *Journal of Family Issues, 25,* in press. *258, 263*

Migliaccio, T. A. 2002. Abused husbands: A narrative analysis. *Journal of Family Issues, 23,* 26–52. *427*

Milan, A. 2000. One hundred years of families. *Canadian Social Trends, 56,* 2–12. *213, 230, 250, 251, 281, 392*

Milan, A. 2003. Would you live common-law? *Canadian Social Trends, 70,* 2–6. *211, 212, 214*

Milan, A., and Hamm, B. 2003. Across the generations: Grandparents and grandchildren. *Canadian Social Trends, 71,* 2–7. *6, 283, 291*

Milan, A., and Hamm, B. 2004. Mixed unions. *Canadian Social Trends, 73,* 2–6. *157, 209*

Milan, A., and Peters, A. 2003. Couples living apart. *Canadian Social Trends, 69,* 2–6. *8, 211*

Milan, A., and Tran, K. 2004. Blacks in Canada: A long history. *Canadian Social Trends, 72,* 2–7. *209, 245, 462*

Miles-Doan, R. 1998. Violence between spouses and intimates: Does neighborhood context matter? *Social Forces, 77,* 623–645. *427*

Mill, D., Bartlett, N., and White, D. 1995. Profit and nonprofit day care: A comparison of quality, caregiver behaviour, and structural features. *Canadian Journal of Research in Early Childhood Education, 4,* 45–53. *175*

Mill, D., and White, D. 1999. Correlates of affectionate and angry behavior in day care education of preschool-aged children. *Early Childhood Education Quarterly, 14,* 155–178. *175*

Millar, N. 1999. *Once upon a wedding*. Calgary: Barjeaux Arts.

Miller, B. C., et al. 2000. Comparisons of adopted and non-adopted adolescents in a large nationally representative sample. *Child Development, 71,* 1458–1473. *260, 261*

Miller, F., Jenkins, J., and Keating, D. 2002. Parenting and children's behaviour problems. In J. D. Willms (Ed.), *Vulnerable children* (pp. 167–182). Edmonton: University of Alberta Press. *434*

Miller, K. S., Forehand, R., and Kotchick, B. A. 1999. Adolescent sexual behavior in two ethnic minority samples: The role of family variables. *Journal of Marriage and the Family, 61,* 85–98. *228, 333*

Miller, N. 1992. *Single parents by choice: A growing trend in family life*. New York: Plenum Press. *280*

Miller, P. J. E., Caughlin, J. P., and Huston, T. L. 2003. Trait expressiveness and marital satisfaction: The role idealization processes. *Journal of Marriage and Family, 65,* 978–995. *315*

Miner, S., and Uhlenberg, P. 1997. Intragenerational proximity and the social role of sibling neighbors after midlife. *Family Relations, 46,* 145–153. *374*

Mirrlees-Black, C., Mayhew, P., and Percy, A. 1996. *The 1996 British Crime Survey: England and Wales*. London: Home Office Statistical Bulletin, No. 19–96. *447*

Mitchell, B. A. 1998. Too close for comfort? Parental assessments of "boomerang kid" living arrangements. *Canadian Journal of Sociology, 23,* 21–46. *129, 289*

Mitchell, B. A. 2000. The refilled "nest": Debunking the myth of families in crisis. In E. M. Gee and G. M. Guttman (Eds.), *The overselling of population aging* (pp. 80–99). Toronto: Oxford University Press. *347, 348*

Mitchell, B. A. 2003. Would I share a home with an elderly parent? Exploring ethnocultural diversity and intergenerational support relations during young adulthood. *Canadian Journal on Aging, 22,* 69–82. *7*

Mitchell, B. A. 2004. Home, but not alone: Socio-cultural and economic aspects of Canadian young adults sharing parental households. *Atlantis, 28.2,* 115–125. *63, 289*

Mitchell, B. A., and Gee, E. M. 1996. Young adults returning home. Implications for social policy. In B. Galaway and J. Hudson (Eds.), *Youth in transition: Perspectives on research and policy* (pp. 61–71). Toronto: Thompson. *289*

Mitchell, K. 2003. Parental leave: More time off for baby. *Canadian Social Trends, 71,* 13–18. *279, 465*

Mitchell, K. J., Finkelhor D., and Wolak, J. 2001. Risk factors for and impact of online sexual solicitation on youth. *Journal of the American Medical Association, 285,* June 20, 3011–3014. *77*

Modell, J., and Goodman, M. 1990. Historical perspectives. In S. S. Feldman and G. R. Elliott (Eds.), *At the threshold: The developing adolescent* (pp. 93–122). Cambridge, MA: Harvard University Press. *341*

Mody, P. 2002. Love and the law: Love-marriage in Delhi. *Modern Asian Studies, 36,* 223–256. *50*

Moffitt, T. E., et al. 2002. Males on the life-course-persistent and adolescence-limited antisocial pathways: Follow-up at age 26. *Development and Psychopathology, 14,* 179–206. *248*

Molnar, M. 1996. Of dogs and doggerel. *American Imago, 53,* 269–280. *286*

Monahan, S. C., et al. 1993. Sibling differences in divorced families. *Child Development, 64,* 152–168. *377, 382*

Montemayor, R. 1986. Family variation in parent-adolescent storm and stress. *Journal of Adolescent Research, 1,* 15–31. *341*

Moore, K. A., Nord, C. W., and Peterson, J. L. 1989. Nonvoluntary sexual activity among adolescents. *Family Planning Perspectives, 21,* 110–114. *446*

Moore, M. R., and Chase-Lansdale, P. L. 2001. Sexual intercourse and pregnancy among African American girls in high-poverty neighborhoods: The role of family and perceived community environment. *Journal of Marriage and Family, 63,* 1146–1157. *156*

Morelli, G. A., and Tronick, E. Z. 1991. Parenting and child development in the Efe foragers and Lese farmers of Zaire. In M. H. Bornstein (Ed.), *Cultural approaches to parenting* (pp. 91–114). Hillsdale, NJ: Erlbaum. *273, 274*

Morgan, C. 1996. *Public men and virtuous women: The gendered languages of religion and politics in Upper Canada, 1791–1850.* Toronto: University of Toronto Press. *39*

Morissette, R. 2002a. On the edge: Financially vulnerable families. *Canadian Social Trends, 67,* 13–17. *130, 137*

Morissette, R. 2002b. Families on the financial edge. *Perspectives on Labour and Income, 3,* July, 5–16. *130*

Morissette, R., and Zhang, X. 2001. Experiencing low income for several years. *Perspectives on Labour and Income, 2,* March, 5–15. *136, 137*

Morris, J. F., Balsam, K. F., and Rothblum, E. D. 2001. Lesbian and bisexual mothers and nonmothers: Demographics and the coming-out process. *Journal of Family Psychology, 16,* 144–156. *207, 244*

Morris, P. A., et al. 1996. American families: Today and tomorrow. In U. Bronfenbrenner et al. (Eds.), *The state of Americans* (pp. 90–145). New York: Free Press. *135*

Morris, S. N., Dollahite, D. C., and Hawkins, A. J. 1999. Virtual family life education: A qualitative study of father education on the World Wide Web. *Family Relations, 48,* 23–30. *80*

Morrison, D. R., and Cherlin, A. J. 1995. The divorce process and young children's well-being: A prospective analysis. *Journal of Marriage and the Family, 57,* 800–812. *406, 409*

Morrison, D. R., and Coiro, M. J. 1999. Parental conflict and marital disruption: Do children benefit when high-conflict marriages are dissolved? *Journal of Marriage and the Family, 61,* 626–637. *322*

Morrison, D. R., and Ritualo, A. 2000. Routes to children's economic recovery after divorce: Are cohabitation and remarriage equivalent? *American Sociological Review, 65,* 560–580. *241*

Morrison, N. C., and Clavenna-Valleroy, J. 1998. Perceptions of maternal support as related to self-concept and self-report of depression in sexually abused female adolescents. *Journal of Child Sexual Abuse, 7,* 23–40. *439, 440*

Morry, M. M. and Staska, S. L. 2001. Magazine exposure: Internalization, self-objectification, eating attitudes, and body satisfaction in male and female university students. *Canadian Journal of Behavioural Sciences, 33,* 269–279. *129*

Moss, K. 2004. Kids witnessing family violence. *Canadian Social Trends, 73,* 12–16. *141, 429*

Moss, M. H. 1998. *Manliness and militarism: Educating young men for war in the province of Ontario.* Ed. D. dissertation, University of Toronto. *44*

Mounts, N. S. 2001. Young adolescents' perceptions of parental management of peer relations. *Journal of Early Adolescence, 21,* 92–122. *333*

Mueller, M. M., and Elder, G. H., Jr. 2003. Family contingencies across the generations: Grandparent-grandchild relationships in holistic perspective. *Journal of Marriage and Family, 65,* 404–417. *290*

Muller, C., and Kerbow, D. 1993. Parent involvement in the home, school, and community. In B. Schneider and J. S. Coleman (Eds.), *Parents, their children and schools* (pp. 13–42). San Francisco: Westview Press. *75, 183, 346*

Munch, A., McPherson, J. M., and Smith-Lovin, L. 1997. Gender, children, and social contact: The effects of childrearing for men and women. *American Sociological Review, 62,* 509–520. *284*

Munn, P., and Dunn, J. 1988. Temperament and the developing relationship between siblings. *International Journal of Behavioral Development, 12,* 433–451. *363*

Murdie, R. A., and Teixeira, C. 2003. Towards a comfortable neighbourhood and appropriate housing: Immigrant experiences in Toronto. In P. Anisef and M. Lanphier (Eds.), *The world in a city* (pp. 132–191). Toronto: University of Toronto Press. *156*

Musick, K. 2002. Planned and unplanned childbearing among unmarried women. *Journal of Marriage and Family, 64,* 915–929. *135, 280*

Mutran, E., and Reitzes, D. G. 1984. Intergenerational support activities and well-being among the elderly: A convergence of exchange and symbolic interaction perspectives. *American Sociological Review, 49,* 117–130. *351*

Myers, D. G. 2000a. The funds, friends, and faith of happy people. *American Psychologist, 55,* 56–67. *150*

Myers, D. G. 2000b. *The American paradox: Spiritual hunger in an age of plenty,* New Haven, CT: Yale University Press. *150*

Myers, J. 2000. Notes on the murder of thirty of my neighbors. *The Atlantic Monthly,* March, 72–86. *75*

Myers, S. C. 1997. Marital uncertainty and childbearing. *Social Forces, 75,* 1271–1289. *360*

Myers, S. M. 1996. An interactive model of religiosity inheritance: The importance of family context. *American Sociological Review, 61,* 858–866. *192, 194, 195*

Myles, J., and Hou, F. 2004. Changing colours: Spatial assimilation and new racial minority immigrants. *Canadian Journal of Sociology, 29,* 29–55. *156, 157*

Nadesan, M. H. 2002. Engineering the entrepreneurial infant: Brain science, infant development toys, and governmentality. *Cultural Studies, 16*(3), 401–432. *273, 332*

Nakosteen, R. A., and Zimmer, M. A. 1997. Men, money, and marriage: Are high earners more prone than low earners to marry? *Social Science Quarterly, 78,* 66–82. *225*

Nanda, S. 1991. Arranging a marriage in India. In P. R. DeVita (Ed.), *The naked anthropologist: Tales from around the world.* Belmont, CA: Wadsworth. *217*

National Center for Health Statistics. 1995. Advance report of final divorce statistics, 1989 and 1990. *Monthly Vital Statistics Reports, 43*(9). *394*

National Televised Violence Study. 1998. *National televised violence study,* Vol. 3. Santa Barbara: University of California, Center for Communication and Social Policy. *74*

Nault, F., and Bélanger, A. 1996. *The decline in marriage in Canada, 1981–1991.* Ottawa: Statistics Canada. Catalogue no. 84-536-XPB. *8*

NCW (National Council on Welfare). 2004. Number of welfare recipients. <http://www.ncwcnbes.net>. *134*

Neff, C. 1996. Pauper apprenticeship in early nineteenth century Ontario. *Journal of Family History, 21,* 144–171. *38*

Neiderhiser, J. M., et al. 1999. Relationships between parenting and adolescent adjustment over time: Genetic and environmental contributions. *Developmental Psychology, 35,* 680–692. *339*

Neisser, U., et al. 1996. Intelligence: Knowns and unknowns. *American Psychologist, 51,* 77–101. *180*

Nelson, A., and Robinson, B. W. 2002. *Gender in Canada,* 2nd Ed. Toronto: Pearson. *30, 209, 274*

Nelson, F. 1996. *Lesbian motherhood.* Toronto: University of Toronto Press. *243, 244, 250, 269, 277, 281, 308, 321, 413*

Nelson, H. L. 1997. Introduction. In H. L. Nelson (Ed.), *Feminism and families* (pp. 1–9). New York: Routledge. *20*

Nett, E. M. 1993. *Canadian families: Past and present,* 2nd Ed. Toronto: Butterworths. *37*

Newcomb, M. D., and Loeb, T. B. 1999. Poor parenting as an adult problem behavior: General deviance, deviant attitudes, inadequate family support and bonding or just bad parents? *Journal of Family Psychology, 13,* 175–193. *339*

Ney, P. G., Fung, T., and Wickett, A. R. 1994. The worst combinations of child abuse and neglect. *Child Abuse & Neglect, 18,* 705–714. *437*

Ng, W. C. 1999. *The Chinese in Vancouver, 1945–80: The pursuit of identity and power.* Vancouver: University of British Columbia Press. *106*

NICHD (National Institute of Child Health and Human Development) Early Child Care Research Network. 1998. Relations between family predictors and child outcomes: Are they weaker for children in child care? *Developmental Psychology, 34,* 1119–1128. *176*

NICHD (National Institute of Child Health and Human Development) Early Child Care Research Network. 2003. Does amount of time spent in child care predict socioemotional adjustment during the transition to kindergarten? *Child Development, 74,* 976–1005. *176*

NICHD (National Institute of Child Health and Human Development) Early Child Care Research Network. 2004. Are child developmental outcomes related to before- and after-school care arrangements? Results from the NICHD Study of Early Child Care. *Child Development, 75,* 280–285. *176*

Nicholas, A. B. 2001. Canada's colonial mission: The great white bird. In K. P. Binda and S. Calliou (Eds.), *Aboriginal education in Canada* (pp. 933–947). Mississauga: Canadian Educators' Press. *187*

Nicholson, B. J. 1994. Legal borrowing and the origins of slave law in the British colonies. *American Journal of Legal History, 38,* 38–54. *42*

Nicholson, L. 1997. The myth of the traditional family. In H. L. Nelson (Ed.), *Feminism and families* (pp. 27–42). New York: Routledge. *60*

Nielsen, L. 1999. Stepmothers: Why so much stress? A review of the research. *Journal of Divorce & Remarriage, 30,* 115–148. *412, 414*

Noble, D. F. 1995. *Progress without people.* Toronto: Between the Lines. *459*

Nock, S. L. 1998a. The consequences of premarital fatherhood. *American Sociological Review, 63,* 250–263. *215, 219, 461, 471*

Nock, S. L. 1998b. Too much privacy? *Journal of Family Issues, 19,* 101–118. *166*

Nock, S. L. 1998c. *Marriage in men's lives.* New York: Oxford University Press. *197, 269, 456*

Noël, J. 2001. New France: Les femmes favorisées. In A. Prentice and S. Mann Trofimenkoff (Eds.), *The neglected majority,* Vol. 2 (pp. 18–40). Toronto: McClelland & Stewart. *36*

Noller, P. 1994. Relationships with parents in adolescence: Process and outcome. In R. Montemayor, G. R. Adams, and T. P. Gullotta (Eds.), *Personal relationships during adolescence* (pp. 37–77). Thousand Oaks, CA: Sage. *281, 343*

Noller, P. 1996. What is this thing called love? Defining the love that supports marriage and family. *Personal Relationships, 3,* 97–115. *217*

Noller, P., and Callan, V. 1991. *The adolescent in the family.* New York: Routledge. *334, 475*

Nomaguchi, K. M., and Milkie, M. A. 2003. Costs and rewards of children: The effects of becoming a parent on adults' lives. *Journal of Marriage and Family, 65,* 356–374. *253*

Noonan, M. C. 2001. The impact of domestic work on men's and women's wage. *Journal of Marriage and the Family, 63,* 1134–1145. *122*

Norland, J. A., 1994. *Profile of Canada's seniors.* Toronto: Statistics Canada and Prentice Hall. *410*

Novak, M. 1997. *Aging & society: A Canadian reader.* Toronto: Nelson. *410*

O'Brien, C.-A., and Goldberg, A. 2000. Lesbians and gay men inside and outside families. In N. Mandell and A. Duffy (Eds.), *Canadian families: Diversity, conflict, and change,* 2nd Ed. (pp. 115–145). Toronto: Harcourt Brace. *9, 308*

O'Brien, M. J. 1991. Taking sibling incest seriously. In M. Q. Patton (Ed.), *Family sexual abuse* (pp. 75–92). Newbury Park, CA: Sage. *443, 444*

O'Connor, T. G., and Insabella, G. M. 1999. Marital satisfaction, relationships, and roles. In E. M. Hetherington, S. H. Henderson, and D. Reiss (Eds.), *Adolescent siblings in step-families: Family functioning and adolescent adjustment.* Monographs of the Society for Research in Child Development, 259, 64(4) *312, 316*

OECD (Organization for Economic Co-operation and Development). 2000. *Reforms for an aging society.* Paris: OECD. *470*

Ogbomo, O. 1997. *When men and women mattered: A history of gender relations among the Owan of Nigeria.* Rochester, NY: University of Rochester Press. *360*

O'Keefe, M. 1998. Factors mediating the link between witnessing interparental violence and dating violence. *Journal of Family Violence,* 13, 39–57. *43, 431*

Oldman, D. 1994. Adult-child relations as class relations. In J. Qvortrup et al. (Eds.), *Childhood matters: Social theory, practice and politics* (pp. 43–58). Aldershot, UK: Avebury. *67*

Onyskiw, J. E., and Hayduk, L. A. 2001. Processes underlying children's adjustment in families characterized by physical aggression. *Family Relations,* 50, 376–385. *206, 331, 362, 430, 446*

Orme, J. G., and Buehler, C. 2001. Foster family characteristics and behavioral and emotional problems of foster children: A narrative review. *Family Relations,* 50, 3–15. *264*

Orton, M. J. 1999. Changing high-risk policies and programs to reduce high-risk sexual behaviours. In J. Wong and D. Checkland (Eds.), *Teen pregnancy and parenting* (pp. 121–150). Toronto: University of Toronto Press. *78, 132, 227, 228, 467*

Osmond, M. W., and Thorne, B. 1993. Feminist theories: The social construction of gender in families and society. In P. G. Boss et al. (Eds.), *Sourcebook of family theories and methods: A contextual approach* (pp. 591–623). New York: Plenum Press. *20*

Ouellette, F.-R., and Belleau, H. 2001. Family and social integration of children adopted internationally: A review of the literature. Montréal: Institut national de la recherche scientifique. Université du Québec. <http://partenariat-familles.inrs-ucs.uquebec.ca>. *262*

Owasu, T. 1999. Residential patterns and housing choices of Ghanaian immigrants in Toronto, Canada. *Housing Studies,* 14, 77–97. *157*

Owusu, T. Y. 2000. The role of Ghanaian immigrant associations in Toronto, Canada. *International Migration Review,* 34, 1155–1181. *109*

Oyen, N., et al. 1997. Combined effects of sleeping position and prenatal risk factors in Sudden Infant Death Syndrome: The Nordic Epidemiological SIDS study. *Pediatrics, 100,* 613–620. *240*

Pacheco, F., and Eme, R. 1993. An outcome study of the reunion between adoptees and biological parents. *Child Welfare, 72,* 53–64. *263, 264*

Pagani, L., Boulerice, B., and Tremblay, R. E. 1997. The influence of poverty on children's classroom placement and behavior problems. In G. J. Duncan and J. Brooks-Gunn (Eds.), *Consequences of growing up poor* (pp. 311–339). New York: Russell Sage. *140, 415*

Pagnini, D. L., and Rindfuss, R. R. 1993. The divorce of marriage and childbearing: Changing attitudes and behavior in the United States. *Population and Development Review, 19,* 331–347. *471*

Pallas, A. M. 2002. Educational participation across the life course: Do the rich get richer? *Advances in Life Course Research, 7,* 327–354. *184*

Palameta, B. 2003. Who pays for domestic help? *Perspectives on Labour and Income, 4,* August, 2–15. *124*

Palmer, H. 1990. Polygamy and progress: The reaction to Mormons in Canada, 1887–1923. In B. Card et al. (Eds.), *The Mormon presence in Canada* (pp. 108–135). Edmonton: The University of Alberta Press. *46, 47*

Papillon, B. M. (n.d.) Montreal's economy from 1851–1901. <http://is.dal.ca/~rogerssh/cea/Montreal.pdf>. *40*

Papp, L. M., Cummings, E. M., and Schermerhorn, A. C. 2004. Pathways among marital distress, parental symptomatology, and child adjustment. *Journal of Marriage and Family,* 66, 368–384. *324*

Pappano, L. 2001. *The connection gap—Why Americans feel so alone.* New Brunswick, NJ: Rutgers University Press. *165*

Parcel, T. L., and Dufur, M. J. 2001. Capital at home and at school: Effects on child social adjustment. *Journal of Marriage and Family,* 63, 32–42. *180*

Park, R. E., and Burgess, E. W. 1925. *The city.* Chicago: University of Chicago Press. *147*

Parke, R. D. 1995. Fathers and families. In M. Bornstein (Ed.), *Handbook of parenting* (Vol. 4). Mahwah, NJ: Erlbaum. *275*

Parks, C. A. 1998. Lesbian parenthood: A review of the literature. *American Journal of Orthopsychiatry,* 68, 376–389. *244*

Parr, J. 1980. *Laboring children.* London: Croom Helm. *121*

Parr, J. 2000. Rethinking work and kinship in a Canadian hosiery town, 1910–1950. In B. Bradbury (Ed.), *Canadian family history* (pp. 220–240). Toronto: Irwin Publishing. *121*

Parsons, T. 1951. *The social system.* New York: Free Press. *12*

Parsons, T., et al. 1955. *Family, socialization and interaction process.* Glencoe, IL: Free Press. *12*

Pasley, K., Futris, T. G., and Skinner, M. L. 2002. Effects of commitment and psychological centrality on fathering. *Journal of Marriage and Family,* 64, 130–138. *276*

Pasley, K., and Gecas, V. 1984. Stresses and satisfactions of the parental role. *Personal and Guidance Journal, 2,* 400–404. *287*

Patterson, C. J. 2000. Family relationships of lesbians and gay men. *Journal of Marriage and the Family, 62,* 1052–1069. *225, 230, 244*

Patterson, C. J., and Chan, R. W. 1997. Gay fathers. In M. E. Lamb (Ed.), *The role of the father in child development,* 3rd Ed. (pp. 245–260). New York: Wiley & Sons. *242*

Patterson, G. R. 1986. The contribution of siblings to training for fighting: A microsocial analysis. In D. Olweus, J. Block, and M. Radke-Yarrow (Eds.), *Development of antisocial and prosocial behavior* (pp. 235–261). Orlando, FL: Academic Press. *365*

Patterson, G. R., Reid, J. B., and Dishion, T. J. 1992. *Antisocial boys.* Eugene, OR: Castalia. *340*

Patterson, J. 2003. Spousal violence. In H. Johnson and K. Au Coin (Eds.) *Family violence in Canada: A statistical profile 2003* (pp. 4–20). Ottawa: Ministry of Industry. *426, 428*

Paul, P. 2004. The porn factor. *Time,* February 9, 75–76. *66, 80*

Paupanekis, K., and Westfall, D. 2001. Teaching Native language programs: Survival strategies. In K. P. Binda and S. Calliou (Eds.), *Aboriginal education in Canada* (pp. 89–104). Mississauga, ON: Canadian Educators' Press. *187*

Pearce, L. D., and Axinn, W. G. 1998. The impact of family religious life on the quality of mother-child relations. *American Sociological Review, 63,* 810–828. *196, 197*

Pearce, M. J., et al. 2003. The protective effects of religiousness and parent involvement on the development of conduct problems among youth exposed to violence. *Child Development, 74,* 1682–1696. *196*

Pears, K. C., and Capaldi, D. M. 2001. Intergenerational transmission of abuse: A two-generational prospective study of an at-risk sample. *Child Abuse & Neglect, 25,* 1439–1461. *435*

Pearson, J. L., et al. 1997. Grandmother involvement in child caregiving in an urban community. *The Gerontologist, 37,* 650–657. *291*

Pease, W. H., and Pease, J. H. 1962. Organized Negro communities: A North American experiment. *Journal of Negro History, 47,* 19–34. *44*

Pebley, A. R., and Rudkin, L. L. 1999. Grandparents caring for grandchildren: What do we know? *Journal of Family Issues, 20,* 218–242. *290*

Pelton, L. 1991. Poverty and child protection. *Protecting Children, 7,* 3–5. *437*

Pelton, L. 1994. The role of material factors in child abuse and neglect. In G. B. Melton and F. D. Barry (Eds.), *Protecting children from abuse and neglect: Foundations for a new strategy* (pp. 131–181). New York: Guilford Press. *437*

Pelton, L. H. 1997. Child welfare policy and practice: The myth of family preservation. *American Journal of Orthopsychiatry, 67,* 545–553. *470*

Pena, D. 2000. Parent involvement: Influencing factors and implication. *Journal of Educational Research, 12,* 68–89. *180*

Peplau, A., Cochran, S. D., and Mays, V. M. 1997. A national survey of the intimate relations of African American lesbians and gay men: A look at commitment, satisfaction, sexual behavior and HIV disease. In B. Greene (Ed.), *Ethnic and cultural diversity among lesbians and gay men* (pp. 11–38). London: Sage.

Perez-Granados, D. R., and Callanan, M. A. 1997. Parents and siblings as early resources for young children's learning in Mexican-descent families. *Hispanic Journal of Behavioral Sciences, 19,* 3–33. *366*

Perkins, D. F., et al. 1998. An ecological, risk-factor examination of adolescents' sexual activity in three ethnic groups. *Journal of Marriage and the Family, 60,* 660–673. *228*

Perozynski, L., and Kramer, L. 1999. Parental beliefs about managing sibling conflict. *Developmental Psychology, 35,* 489–499. *442*

Perry-Jenkins, M., and Crouter, A. 1990. Men's provider role attitudes: Implications for household work and marital satisfaction. *Journal of Family Issues, 11,* 136–156. *311*

Persell, C. H., Catsambris, S., and Cookson, P. W. 1992. Differential asset conversion: Class and gender pathways to selective colleges. *Sociology of Education, 65,* 208–225. *188*

Peters, A. 2002. Is your community child-friendly? *Canadian Social Trends, 67,* 2–5. *148, 152*

Peters, J. 1990. Cultural variations: Past and present. In M. Baker (Ed.), *Families: Changing trends in Canada,* 2nd Ed. (pp. 166–191). Toronto: McGraw-Hill Ryerson. *37*

Pettit, G. S., et al. 1999. The impact of after-school peer contact on early adolescent externalizing problems is moderated by parental monitoring, perceived neighborhood safety, and prior adjustment. *Child Development, 70,* 768–778. *155, 333*

Pettit, G. S., et al. 1996. Stability and change in peer-rejected status: The role of child behavior, parenting, and family ecology. *Merrill-Palmer Quarterly, 42,* 267–294. *142*

Pezzin, L. E., and Schone, B. S. 1999. Parental marital disruption and intergenerational transfers: An analysis of lone elderly parents and their children. *Demography, 36,* 287–297. *293*

Phillips, C. 1998. Foster care system struggles to keep siblings together. *APA Monitor,* January, 26–27. *264*

Phillips, P., and Phillips, E. 2000. *Women & work.* Toronto: James Lorimer. *119, 477*

Phipps, S. 1999. Economics and the well-being of Canadian children. *Canadian Journal of Economics, 32,* 1135–1163. *137*

Phipps, S., and Burton, P. 1996. Collective models of family behaviour. *Canadian Public Policy, 22,* 129–143. *459*

Pianta, R. C., Egeland, B., and Erickson, M. F. 1989. The antecedents of maltreatment: Results of the Mother-Child Interaction Research Project. In D. Cicchetti and V. Carlson (Eds.), *Child maltreatment* (pp. 203–253). Cambridge: Cambridge University Press. *435*

Pillemer, K., and Suitor, J. J. 1991. "Will I ever escape my children's problems?" Effects of adult children's problems on elderly parents. *Journal of Marriage and the Family, 53,* 585–594. *350*

Pitt, K. 2002. Being a new capitalist mother. *Discourse & Society, 13,* 251–267. *65, 174, 182, 273*

Pleck, E. H., and Pleck, J. H. 1997. Fatherhood ideals in the United States: Historical dimensions. In M. E. Lamb (Ed.), *The role of the father in child development* (pp. 33–48). New York: John Wiley & Sons. *306*

Plomin, R. 1994. *Genetics and experience: The interplay between nature and nurture.* Thousand Oaks, CA: Sage. *324, 335*

Plomin, R., et al. 1998. Adoption results for self-reported personality: Evidence of nonadditive genetic effects? *Journal of Personality and Social Psychology, 75,* 211–218. *19, 380*

Plomin, R., et al. 2001. *Behavior genetics.* New York: North. *19, 377*

Plomin, R., and Rutter, M. 1998. Child development, molecular genetics, and what to do with genes once they are found. *Child Development, 69,* 1223–1242. *382, 409, 458*

Pong, S. I. 1998. The school compositional effect of single parenthood on 10th-grade achievement. *Sociology of Education, 71,* 24–43. *180, 184*

Pong, S.-L., et al. 2003. Family policies and children's school achievement in single- versus two-parent families. *Journal of Marriage and Family, 65,* 681–699. *467*

Poonwassie, D. H. 2001. Parental involvement as adult education: A microstrategy for change. In K. P. Binda and S. Calliou (Eds.), *Aboriginal education in Canada* (pp. 155–165). Mississauga, ON: Canadian Educators' Press. *183, 187*

Porter, C. 2003. A wedding story. *Toronto Star* (a series of articles ending September 14, A1 and A8 following a Canadian-Pakistani male through the steps leading to his arranged marriage in Pakistan). *108*

Portes, A. 1998. Social capital: Its origins and applications in modern sociology. *Annual Review of Sociology, 24,* 1–24. *14*

Potter, J. 1996. *Representing reality: Discourse, rhetoric, and social construction.* London: Sage. *18*

Pothen, S. 1989. Divorce in Hindu society. *Journal of Comparative Family Studies, 20,* 378–392. *50*

Potter-MacKinnon, J. 1993. *While the women only wept: Loyalist refugee women.* Montreal, Kingston: McGill-Queen's University Press. *38*

Powell, B., and Downey, D. B. 1997. Living in single-parent households: An investigation of the same-sex hypothesis. *American Sociological Review, 62,* 521–539. *404*

Powell, B., and Steelman, L. C. 1993. The educational benefits of being spaced out: Sibling diversity and educational progress. *American Sociological Review, 58,* 367–381. *262*

Powers, D. A., and Hsueh, J. C.-T. 1997. Sibling models of socioeconomic effects on the timing of first premarital birth. *Demography, 34,* 493–511. *365*

Presser, H. 1995. Are the interests of women inherently at odds with the interests of children and the family? A viewpoint. In K. Mason and A.-M. Jensen (Ed.), *Gender and family change in industrialized countries* (pp. 297–319). Oxford: Clarendon. *21*

Presser, H. B. 2000. Nonstandard work schedules and marital instability. *Journal of Marriage and the Family, 62,* 93–110. *122*

Presser, S., and Stinson, L. 1998. Data collection mode and social desirability bias in self-reported religious attendance. *American Sociological Review, 63,* 137–145. *192*

Pribesh, S., and Downey, D. B. 1999. Why are residential and school moves associated with poor school performance? *Demography, 36,* 521–534. *167*

Prigerson, H. G., Maciejewski, P. K., and Rosenbeck, R. A. 2000. Preliminary explorations of the harmful interactive effects of widowhood and marital harmony on health, health service use, and health care costs. *The Gerontologist, 40,* 349–357. *411*

Prochner, L. 2000. A history of early education and child care in Canada, 1820–1966. In L. Prochner and N. Howe (Eds.), *Early childhood care and education in Canada* (pp. 252–272). Vancouver: University of British Columbia Press. *174*

Propper, A. 1997. Measuring wife assault by surveys: Some conceptual and methodological problems. In A. Sev'er (Ed.), *Cross-cultural exploration of wife abuse* (pp. 51–78). New Jersey: Edwin Mellen. *426*

Prout, A., and James, A. 1990. *Constructing and reconstructing childhood: Contemporary issues in the sociological study of childhood.* London: Falmer. *273*

Pruchno, R. 1999. Raising grandchildren: The experiences of Black and White grandmothers. *The Gerontologist, 39,* 209–221. *292*

Pruchno, R., Patrick, J. H., and Burant, C. J. 1996. Aging women and their children with chronic disabilities: Perceptions of sibling involvement and effects on well-being. *Family Relations, 45,* 318–326. *368*

Pruchno, R., Patrick, J. H., and Burant, C. J. 1997. African American and White mothers of adults with chronic disabilities: Caregiving burden and satisfaction. *Family Relations, 46,* 335–346. *353*

Prus, S. G. 2002. Changes in income within a cohort over the later life course: Evidence from income status convergence. *Canadian Journal on Aging, 21,* 475–504. *467*

Ptacek, J. 1997. The tactics and strategies of men who batter: Testimony from women seeking restraining orders. In A. P. Cardarelli (Ed.), *Violence between intimate partners* (pp. 104–123). Boston: Allyn & Bacon. *425*

Pupo, N. 1997. Always working, never done: The expansion of the double day. In A. Duffy, D. Glenday, and N. Pupo (Eds.), *Good jobs, bad jobs* (pp. 144–165). Toronto: Harcourt Brace. *128, 461*

Pyke, K. 2000. "The normal American family" as an interpretive structure of family life among grown children of Korean and Vietnamese immigrants. *Journal of Marriage and the Family, 62,* 240–255. *73, 332*

Pyper, W. 2002. Falling behind. *Perspectives on Labour and Income, 3,* July, 17–23. *135*

Quadagno, J. 1982. Italian American family. In C. H. Mindell, and R. W. Habenstein (Eds.), *Ethnic families in America: Patterns and variations,* 2nd Ed., (pp. 61–85). Oxford: Elsevier Science Publishing. *100*

Quane, J. M., and Rankin, B. H. 1998. Neighborhood poverty, family characteristics, and commitment to mainstream goals: The case of African American adolescents in the inner city. *Journal of Family Issues, 19,* 769–794. *154*

Quart, A. 2003. *Branded: The buying and selling of teenagers.* New York: Perseus. *76*

Qvortrup, J. 1995. From useful to useful: The historical continuity of children's constructive participation. *Sociological Studies of Children, 7,* 49–76. *67*

Rafferty, Y., and Rollins, N. 1989. *Learning in limbo: The educational deprivation of homeless children.* New York: Advocates for Children. ERIC Document Reproduction No. ED 312 363. *159*

Rafferty, Y., and Shinn, M. 1991. The impact of homelessness on children. *American Psychologist, 46,* 1170–1179. *158, 159*

Ragoné, H. 1994. *Surrogate motherhood: Conception in the heart.* Boulder, CO: Westview Press. *257*

Raley, R. K., and Wildsmith, E. 2004. Cohabitation and children's family instability. *Journal of Marriage and Family, 66,* 210–219. *241*

Ralson, H. 1997. Arranged, semi-arranged and love marriages among South Asian immigrant women in the Diaspora and their non-migrant sisters in India and Fiji. *International Journal of the Family, 27,* 43–69. *88, 106, 108*

Ramirez, B. 1989. *The Italians in Canada.* Montreal: Canadian Historical Society. *99–102*

Rand, M. R. 1997. *Violence-related injuries treated in hospital emergency departments.* Bureau of Justice Statistics Special Report, NCJ-156921. Washington, DC: U.S. Department of Justice. *426*

Rangarajan, A., and Gleason, P. 1998. Young unwed fathers of AFDC children: Do they provide support? *Demography, 35,* 175–186.

Rankin, N. 2001. The parent vote. In S. A. Hewlett, N. Rankin, and C. West (Eds.), *Taking parenting public* (pp. 251–264). New York: Rowan & Littlefield. *475*

Raschick, M., and Ingersoll-Dayton, B. 2004. The costs and rewards of caregiving among aging spouses and adult children. *Family Relations, 53,* 317–325. *353*

Ravanera, Z. R., and Rajulton, F. 2004. Social status polarization in the timing and trajectories to motherhood. Population Studies Centre, University of Western Ontario. <www.ssc.uwo.ca/sociology/popstudies>. *272, 282*

Ravanera, Z. R., Rajulton, F., and Burch, T. K. 2003. Early life transitions of Canadian youth: Effects of family transformation and community characteristics. *Canadian Studies in Population, 30,* 327–353. *289*

Ravanera, Z. R., Rajulton, F., and Burch, T. K. 2004. Patterns of age variability in life course transitions. *Canadian Journal of Sociology,* in press. *17, 272*

Raver, C. C. 2003. Does work pay psychologically as well as economically? The role of employment in predicting depressive symptoms and parenting among low-income families. *Child Development, 74,* 1720–1736. *125*

Raver, C. C., and Zigler, E. F. 1997. New perspectives on Head Start. *Early Childhood Research Quarterly, 12,* 363–385. *178*

Ray, B. D. 2001. Homeschooling in Canada. *Education Canada, 41,* 28–31. *189*

Ray, B. D., and Wartes, J. 1991. The academic achievement and affective development of home-schooled children. In J. A. Van Galen and M. A. Pitman (Eds.), *Home schooling: Political, historical, and pedagogical perspectives* (pp. 43–62). Norwood, NJ: Ablex. *190*

Raymo, J. M. 2003. Premarital living arrangements and the transition to first marriage in Japan. *Journal of Marriage and Family, 65,* 302–315. *239*

RCAP (Report of the Royal Commission on Aboriginal Peoples). 1996. *Gathering Strength,* Vol. 3. Ottawa: Canada Communication Group. *96, 178*

Reboucas, L. 2002. Brazil confronts adolescent sexual health issues. *Population Reference Bureau.* <www.prb.org>. *77*

Recht, M. 1997. The role of fishing in the Iroquois economy, 1600–1792. *New York History, 78,* 429–454. *34*

Reid, J. G. 1990. *Sir William Alexander and North American colonization: A reappraisal.* Edinburgh: University of Edinburgh, Centre of Canadian Studies. *37*

Reiss, D. 1995. Genetic influence on family systems: Implications for development. *Journal of Marriage and the Family, 57,* 543–560. *324, 351, 354*

Reiss, D. 2003. Child effects on family systems: Behavioral genetic strategies. In A. C. Crouter and A. Booth (Eds.), *Children's influence on family dynamics* (pp. 3–25). Mahwah, NJ: Erlbaum. *380, 382*

Reiss, D., et al. 1994. The separate worlds of teenage siblings: An introduction to the study of the nonshared environment and adolescent development. In E. M. Hetherington, D. Reiss, and R. Plomin (Eds.), *Separate social worlds of siblings* (pp. 63–110). Hillsdale, NJ: Erlbaum. *373*

Reiss, D., et al. 1995. Genetic questions for environmental studies: Differential parenting and psychopathology in adolescence. *Archives of General Psychiatry, 52,* 925–936. *372*

Ren, X. S. 1997. Marital status and quality relationships: The impact on health perception, *Social Science and Medicine, 44,* 241–249. *221*

Renzetti, C. M. 1997a. Violence in lesbian and gay relationships. In L. L. O'Toole and J. R. Schiffman (Eds.), *Gender violence* (pp. 285–293). New York: New York University Press. *425, 428*

Renzetti, C. M. 1997b. Violence and abuse among same-sex couples. In A. P. Cardarelli (Ed.), *Violence between intimate partners* (pp. 70–89). Boston: Allyn & Bacon. *424, 425*

Reynolds, A. J., and Robertson, D. L. 2003. School-based early intervention and later child maltreatment in the Chicago Longitudinal Study. *Child Development, 74*, 3–26. *179*

Reynolds, A. J., and Temple, J. A. 1998. Extended early childhood intervention and school achievement: Age thirteen findings from the Chicago Longitudinal Study. *Child Development, 69*, 231–246. *179, 469*

Reynolds, C. 2004. The educational system. In N. Mandell (Ed.), *Feminist issues: Race, class, and gender*, 4th Ed. (pp. 247–265). Toronto: Prentice Hall. *174*

Rezai-Rashti, G. 2004. Unessential women: A discussion of race, class, and gender and their implications in education. In N. Mandell (Ed.), *Feminist issues: Race, class, and gender*, 4th Ed. (pp. 83–99). Toronto: Prentice Hall. *21*

Rhodes, M. 1996. Globalization, the State and the restructuring of regional economies. In P. Gurnmett (Ed.), *Globalization and public policy* (pp. 161–180). Cheltenham, UK: Edward Elgar. *119*

Rifkin, J. 1995. *The end of work*. New York: Putnam's Sons. *459*

Riley, D., and Steinberg, J. 2004. Four popular stereotypes about children in self-care: Implications for family life educators. *Family Relations, 53*, 95–101. *127*

Rinehart, J. M. 1996. *The tyranny of work: Alienation and the labour process*. Toronto: Harcourt Brace. *119*

Ritzer, G. 2000. *The McDonaldization of society*. Thousand Oaks, CA: Pine Forge. *66*

Rizk, C. 2003. Le cadre des ménages les plus pauvres. Paris: INSEE. <www.insee.fr>. *166*

Roberts, D. F., and Foehr, U. G. 2004. *Kids & media in America*. Cambridge, UK: Cambridge University Press. *69*

Robinson, J. D., and Skill, T. 2001. Five decades of families on television: From the 1950s through the 1990s. In J. Bryant and J. A. Bryant (Eds.), *Television and the American family* (pp. 139–162). Mahwah, NJ: Erlbaum. *74*

Robinson, L. C., and Blanton, P. W. 1993. Marital strengths in enduring marriages. *Family Relations, 42*, 38–45. *319*

Rochère, B. 2003. La santé des sans-domicile usagers des services d'aide. Paris: INSEE. <www.insee.fr>. *158*

Rodgers, K. B. 1999. Parenting processes related to sexual risk-taking behaviors of adolescent males and females. *Journal of Marriage and the Family, 61*, 99–109. *333*

Rodgers, K. B., and Rose, H. A. 2002. Risk and resiliency factors among adolescents who experience marital transitions. *Journal of Marriage and Family, 64*, 1024–1037. *149*

Rodríguez Calderón, M. 1993. Domestic life as a sphere for the exercise of conscious political choice for Cuban women. *NWSA Journal, 5*, 3, 352–354. *54*

Rogers, E. S., and Updike, L. 1969. Plains Cree. *Beaver, 300*, 56–59. *34*

Rogers, S. J., and May, D. C. 2003. Spillover between marital quality and job satisfaction: Long-term patterns and gender differences. *Journal of Marriage and Family, 65*, 482–495. *316*

Rogers, S. J., and White, L. K. 1998. Satisfaction with parenting: The role of marital happiness, family structure, and parents' gender. *Journal of Marriage and the Family, 60*, 293–308. *316*

Rogoff, B., et al. 1991. Cultural variation in the role relations of toddlers and their families. In M. H. Bornstein (Ed.), *Cultural approaches to parenting* (pp. 175–184). Hillsdale, NJ: Erlbaum. *274*

Rohner, R. P., Bourque, S. L., and Elordi, C. A. 1996. Children's perceptions of corporal punishment, caretaker acceptance, and psychological adjustment in a poor, biracial Southern community. *Journal of Marriage and the Family, 58*, 842–852. *338*

Rook, K., Dooley, D., and Catalano, R. 1991. Stress transmission: The effects of husbands' job stressors on the emotional health of their wives. *Journal of Marriage and the Family, 53*, 165–177. *313*

Roosa, M. W., et al. 1997. The relationship of childhood sexual abuse to teenage pregnancy. *Journal of Marriage and the Family, 59*, 119–130. *441*

Roschelle, A. R. 1999. Gender, family structure, and social structure. In M. M. Ferree, J. Lorber, and B. B. Hess (Eds.), *Revisioning gender* (pp. 311–340). Thousand Oaks, CA: Sage. *470*

Rosellini, L. 1998. When to spank: For decades, parenting experts have said spanking irreparably harms kids. But a close look at the research suggests otherwise. *U.S. News & World Report, 124*, April 13, 52–53, 55. *434*

Rosenberg, J. 2001. Boyhood abuse increases men's risk of involvement in a teenager's pregnancy. *Family Planning Perspectives, 33*, 184–185. *439*

Rosenbaum, J. E. 1991. Black pioneers—Do their moves to the suburbs increase economic opportunity for mothers and children? *Housing Policy Debate, 2*, 179–213. *154*

Rosenberg, M. S. 1987. Children of battered women: The effects of witnessing violence on their social problem-solving abilities. *Behavior Therapist, 4*, 85–89. *429*

Rosenfeld, L. B., Bowen, G. L., and Richman, J. M. 1995. Communication in three types of dual-career marriages. In M. A. Fitzpatrick and A. L. Vangelisti (Eds.), *Explaining marital interactions* (pp. 257–289). Thousand Oaks, CA: Sage. *317*

Rosenthal, C. J. 2000. Aging families: Have current changes been "oversold"? In E. M. Gee and G. M. Gutman (Eds.), *The overselling of population aging* (pp. 45–63). Toronto: Oxford University Press. *283, 348, 353*

Rosenthal, C. J., and Gladstone, J. 2000. *Grandparenthood in Canada*. Ottawa: The Vanier Institute of the Family. <www.vifamily.ca>. *290, 298*

Ross, C. E., and Mirowsky, J. 1999a. Parental divorce, life-course disruption, and adult depression. *Journal of Marriage and the Family, 61*, 1034–1045. *407*

Ross, C. E., and Mirowsky, J. 1999b. Disorder and decay: The concept and measurement of perceived neighborhood disorder. *Urban Affairs Review, 34*, 412–432. *151*

Ross, C. E., Mirowsky, J., and Pribesh, S. 2001. Powerlessness and the amplification of threat: Neighborhood disadvantage, disorder, and mistrust. *American Sociological Review, 66*, 568–591. *153*

Ross, D. P., Scott, K., and Kelly, M. 1996. *Child poverty: What are the consequences?* Ottawa: Centre for International Statistics, Canadian Council on Social Development. *140*

Ross, E., et al. 2000. Adoption research review. Adoption Council of Canada, *Canada's Children, 2*, 31–34. *151, 264*

Ross, J. L. 1994. Challenging boundaries: An adolescent in a homosexual family. In F. Handel and G. G. Whitechurch (Eds.), *The psychosocial interior of the family*, 4th Ed. (pp. 158–175). New York: Aldine de Gruyter. *243*

Rossi, A. S., and Rossi, P. H. 1990. *Of human bonding: Parent-child relations across the life course*. New York: Aldine de Gruyter. *290, 295, 298, 344, 348*

Rossi, P. H., and Wright, J. D. 1993. The urban homeless: A portrait of urban dislocation. In W. J. Wilson (Ed.), *The ghetto underclass* (pp. 149–159). Newbury Park, CA: Sage. *158*

Rothblum, E. D. 2002. "Boston marriage" among lesbians. In M. Yalom and L. L. Carstensen (Eds.), *Inside the American couple* (pp. 74–86). Berkeley, CA: University of California Press. *207, 225*

Rothermel, P. 2000. The third way in education: Thinking the unthinkable. *Education, 28*, 3–13. *190*

Rothman, B. K. 1989. *Recreating motherhood: Ideology and technology in a patriarchal society*. New York: W. W. Norton. *258*

Rothman, B. K. 1999. Comment on Harrison: The commodification of motherhood. In S. Coontz (Ed.), *American families: A multicultural reader* (pp. 435–438). New York: Routledge. *254, 257*

Rowe, D. C. 1994. *The limits of family influence: Genes, experience, and behavior*. New York: Guilford Press. *324*

Rowe, D. C., Jacobson, K. C., and Van den Oord, E. J. C. G. 1999. Genetic and environmental influences on vocabulary IQ: Parental education level as moderator. *Child Development, 70*, 1151–1162. *379*

Rowe, D. C., and Gulley, B. L. 1992. Sibling effects on substance use and delinquency. *Criminology, 30*, 217–233. *365, 367*

Royal Commission on Aboriginal Peoples. 1996. Appendix E: Ethical guidelines for research, in *Report of the royal commission on Aboriginal peoples*. Vol. V: *Renewal: A twenty-year commitment*. Ottawa. *96*

Rubin, L. B. 1990. *Erotic wars: What happened to the sexual revolution?* New York: HarperCollins. *227*

Rubin, L. B. 1994. *Families on the fault line*. New York: HarperCollins. *139*

Rumberger, R. W., et al. 1990. Family influences on dropout behavior in one California high school. *Sociology of Education, 63*, 283–299. *184*

Rushowy, K. 2004. Pre-school crucial time. *Toronto Star*, March 27, pp. A1, A4. *176, 179, 469*

Ruspini, E. 2000. Lone mothers' poverty in Europe: The cases of Belgium, Germany, Great Britain, Italy, and Sweden. In A. Pfenning and T. Bahle (Eds.), *Families and family policies in Europe* (pp. 221–244). Frankfurt am Main: Peter Lang. *266*

Russell, N. F., and Zierk, K. L. 1992. Abortion, childbearing, and women's well-being. *Professional Psychology: Research and Practice, 23*, 269–288. *253*

Rutter, M. L. 1997. Nature-nurture integration: The example of antisocial behavior. *American Psychologist, 52*, 390–398. *19, 382*

Rutter, M. 2002. Nature, nurture, and development: From Evangelism through science toward policy and practice. *Child Development, 73*, 1–21. *324, 332, 382*

Ryan, R. M., et al. 1999. The American dream in Russia: Extrinsic aspirations and well-being in two cultures. *Personality & Social Psychology Bulletin, 25*, 1509–1524. *150*

Sabatelli, R. M., and Bartle-Haring, S. 2003. Family-of-origin experiences and adjustment in married couples. *Journal of Marriage and Family, 65*, 159–169. *318*

Sabatelli, R. M., and Shehan, C. L. 1993. Exchange and resources theories. In P. G. Boss et al. (Eds.), *Sourcebook of family theories and methods: A contextual approach* (pp. 385–417). New York: Plenum Press. *13*

Sachdev, P. 1992. Adoption reunion and after: A study of the search process and experience of adoptees. *Child Welfare, 71*, 53–58. *264*

Sacher, J. A., and Fine, M. A. 1996. Predicting relationship status and satisfaction after six months among dating couples. *Journal of Marriage and the Family, 58*, 21–32. *206, 313*

Salamon, S. 1992. *Prairie patrimony: Family, farming, and community in the Midwest*. Chapel Hill: University of North Carolina Press. *162*

Salazar Parreñas, R. 2001. Mothering from a distance: Emotions, gender, and intergenerational relations in Filipino transnational families. *Feminist Studies, 27*, 361–389. *112*

Salzinger, S., Feldman, R. S., and Hammer, M. 1993. The effects of physical abuse on children's social relationships. *Child Development, 64*, 169–187. *434*

Sameroff, A. J., and Seifer, R. 1995. Accumulation of environmental risk and child mental health. In H. E. Fitzgerald, B. M. Lester, and B. Zuckerman (Eds.), *Children of poverty* (pp. 223–253). New York: Garland. *140*

Sameroff, A. J., Seifer, R., and Bartko, W. T. 1997. Environmental perspectives on adaptation during childhood and adolescence. In S. S. Luthar and J. A. Burack (Eds.), *Developmental Psychopathology* (pp. 507–526). New York: Cambridge University Press. *16*

Sampson, R. J. 1993. The community context of violent crime. In W. J. Wilson (Ed.), *Sociology and the public agenda* (pp. 259–286). Newbury Park, CA: Sage. *151*

Sampson, R. J. 1997. Collective regulation of adolescent misbehavior: Validation results from eighty Chicago neighborhoods. *Journal of Adolescent Research, 12,* 227–244. *154, 167, 457*

Sampson, R. J., and Laub, J. H. 1994. Urban poverty and the context of delinquency: A new look at structure and process in a classic study. *Child Development, 65,* 523–540. *125, 137, 475*

Sampson, R. J., Morenoff, J. D., and Earls, F. 1999. Beyond social capital: Spatial dynamics of collective efficacy for children. *American Sociological Review, 64,* 633–660. *14, 153*

Sanday, P. R. 1990. *Fraternity gang rape: Sex, brotherhood, and privilege on campus.* New York: New York University Press. *423*

Sanday, P. R. 1996. *A woman scorned: Acquaintance rape on trial.* New York: Doubleday. *423*

Sandberg, J. F., and Hofferth, S. L. 2001. Changes in children's time with parents: United States, 1981–1997. *Demography, 38,* 423–436. *127*

Sands, R. G., and Goldberg-Glen, R. S. 2000. Factors associated with stress among grandparents raising their grandchildren. *Family Relations, 49,* 97–105. *292*

Sanson, A., and Rothbart, M. K. 1995. Child temperament and parenting. In M. Bornstein (Ed.), *Handbook of parenting* (Vol. 4, pp. 299–321). Mahwah, NJ: Erlbaum. *331*

Santa Barbara News Press. 1992. Study: Fertility drugs contribute to rise in costly multiple births, July 15. Associated Press. *256*

Sapolsky, B. S., and Tabarlet, J. L. 1991. Sex in prime time television: 1979 versus 1989. *Journal of Broadcasting and Electronic Media, 15,* 505–516. *77*

Sassen, S. 1994. *Cities in a world economy.* Thousand Oaks, CA: Pine Forge Press. *119*

Sassler, S. 2004. The process of entering into cohabiting unions. *Journal of Marriage and Family, 66,* 491–505. *213, 214*

Sassler, S., and Schoen, R. 1999. The effect of attitudes and economic activity on marriage. *Journal of Marriage and the Family, 61,* 147–159. *135*

Sastry, J. 1999. Household structure, satisfaction and distress in India and the United States: A comparative cultural examination. *Journal of Comparative Family Studies, 30,* 135–152. *50, 51*

Sauvé, R. 2002a. *Tracking links between jobs and families.* Ottawa: The Vanier Institute of the Family. <www.vifamily. ca>. *120, 219*

Sauvé, R. 2002b. *The current state of Canadian family finances 2001 Report.* Ottawa: Vanier Institute of the Family. <www.vifamily.ca>. *121, 123, 130, 132*

Scaramella, L. V., et al. 2002. Evaluation of a social contextual model of delinquency: A cross-study replication. *Child Development, 73,* 175–195. *340, 383*

Scarr, S. 1993. Biological and cultural diversity: The legacy of Darwin for development. *Child Development, 64,* 1333–1353. *354, 376*

Scarr, S. 1998. American child care today. *American Psychologist, 53,* 95–108. *125, 176*

Schellenberg, G., and Ross, D. 1997. *Left poor by the market: A look at family poverty and earnings.* Ottawa: Canadian Council on Social Development. *122*

Schieve, L. A., et al. 2002. Low and very low birth weight in infants conceived with use of assisted reproductive technology. *New England Journal of Medicine, 346,* 731–737. *255*

Schiller, H. I. 1996. *Information inequality: The deepening social crisis in America.* New York: Routledge. *459*

Schlegel, A., and Barry, H., III. 1991. *Adolescence: An anthropological inquiry.* New York: Free Press. *340*

Schneewind, K. A., and Gerhard, A.-K. 2002. Relationship personality, conflict resolution, and marital satisfaction in the first 5 years of marriage. *Family Relations, 51,* 63–71. *317*

Schneider, B., Waite, L., and Dempsey, N. P. 2000. Teenagers in dual-career families. *Family Focus,* December, F11, F13. *127*

Schoeni, R. F. 1998. Reassessing the decline in parent-child old-age coresidence during the twentieth century. *Demography, 35,* 307–314. *288*

Schor, E. L., and Menaghan, E. G. 1995. Family pathways to child health. In B. C. Amick et al. (Eds.), *Society and health* (pp. 18–45). New York: Oxford University Press. *132*

Schor, J. B. 1991. *The overworked American: The unexpected decline in leisure.* New York: Basic Books. *342*

Schor, J. B. 1999. *The overspent American: Why we want what we don't need.* New York: HarperCollins. *150*

Schor, J. B. 2001. Time crunch among American parents. In S. A. Hewlett, N. Rankin, and C. West (Eds.), *Taking parenting public* (pp. 83–102). New York: Rowan & Littlefield. *127*

Schteingart, J. S., et al. 1995. Homelessness and child functioning in the context of risks and protective factors moderating child outcomes. *Journal of Clinical Child Development, 24,* 320–331. *159*

Schvaneveldt, J. D., Pickett, R. S., and Young, M. H. 1993. Historical methods in family research. In P. G. Boss et al. (Eds.), *Sourcebook of family theories and methods: A contextual approach* (pp. 99–116). New York: Plenum Press. *26*

Schwartz, P. 1994. *Peer marriage: Love between equals.* New York: Free Press. *307, 328*

Schwartz, P., and Rutter, V. 1998. *The gender of sexuality.* Thousand Oaks, CA: Pine Forge. *222, 227, 255*

Schwebel, D. C., and Plumert, J. M. 1999. Longitudinal and concurrent relations among temperament, ability estimation, and injury proneness. *Child Development, 70,* 700–712. *431*

Seaberg, J. R., and Harrigan, M. P. 1997. Family functioning in foster care. *Families in Society, 78,* 463–470. *265*

Sedillot, B., and Walraet, E. 2002. La cessation d'activité au sein des couples: y a-t-il interdépendence des choix? *Economie et Statistique, 357–358,* 79–96. *319*

Seidman, S. N., Mosher, W. D., and Aral, S. D. 1994. Predictors of high-risk behavior in unmarried American women: Adolescent environment as a risk factor. *Journal of Adolescent Health, 15,* 126–132. *441*

Seiter, E. 1993. *Sold separately: Children and parents in consumer culture.* New Brunswick, NJ: Rutgers University Press. *76*

Seljak, D. 2005. Education, multiculturalism, and religion. In P. Bramadat and D. Seljak (Eds.), *Religion and ethnicity in Canada* (pp. 178–200). Toronto: Pearson. *188*

Seltzer, J. A. 1994. Consequences of marital dissolution for children. *Annual Review of Sociology, 20,* 235–266. *322, 406, 411*

Seltzer, J. A. 1998. Fathers by law: Effects of joint legal custody on nonresident fathers' involvement with children. *Demography, 35,* 135–146. *275*

Seltzer, J. A. 2000. Families formed outside of marriage. *Journal of Marriage and the Family, 62,* 1247–1268. *213, 215, 240*

Seltzer, M. M., et al. 1997. Siblings of adults with mental retardation or mental illness: Effects on lifestyle and psychological well-being. *Family Relations, 46,* 395–405. *368*

Serbin, L. A., et al. 1998. Intergenerational transmission of psychosocial risk in women with childhood histories of aggression, withdrawal, or aggression and withdrawal. *Developmental Psychology, 34,* 1246–1262. *247*

Serbin, L. A., Peters, P. L., and Schwartzman, A. E. 1996. Longitudinal study of early childhood injuries and acute illness in the offspring of adolescent mothers who were aggressive, withdrawn, or aggressive-withdrawn in childhood. *Journal of Abnormal Psychology, 105,* 500–507. *249*

Sered, S. S. 1999. "Woman" as symbol and women as agents: Gendered religious discourses. In M. M. Ferree, J. Lorber, and B. B. Hess (Eds.), *Revisioning gender* (pp. 193–221). Thousand Oaks, CA: Sage. *198*

Sev'er, A. 1992. *Women and divorce in Canada.* Toronto: Canadian Scholars' Press. *390, 401, 402*

Sev'er, A. 2002. *Fleeing the house of horrors: Women who have left abusive partners.* Toronto: University of Toronto Press. *216, 401, 423, 425, 426, 428, 429, 452*

Shane, P. G. 1996. *What about America's homeless children?* Thousand Oaks, CA: Sage. *157, 158*

Shapiro, A., and Lambert, J. D. 1999. Longitudinal effects of divorce on the quality of the father-child relationship and on fathers' psychological well-being. *Journal of Marriage and the Family, 61,* 397–408. *403*

Sharma, A. R., McGue, M. K., and Benson, P. L. 1998. The psychological adjustment of United States adopted adolescents and their nonadopted siblings. *Child Development, 69,* 791–802. *259*

Sharon, R. A. 1995. *Slaves no more: A study of the Buxton settlement,* Upper Canada, 1849–1861. PhD. dissertation. Buffalo, NY: State University of New York. *42*

Sharrock, S. R. 1974. Crees, Cree-Assiniboines, and Assiniboines: Interethnic social organization on the far northern plains. *Ethnohistory, 21,* 95–122. *34*

Shatzmiller, M. 1996. Marriage, family, and the faith: Women's conversion to Islam. *Journal of Family History, 21,* 235–246. *209*

Shavit, Y., and Pierce, J. L. 1991. Sibship size and educational attainment in nuclear and extended families. *American Sociological Review, 56,* 321–330. *362*

Sheehy, G. 1995. *New passages: Mapping your life across time.* New York: Dutton. *282*

Shephard, R. B. 1997. *Deemed unsuitable: Blacks from Oklahoma move to the Canadian Prairies in search of equality in the early twentieth century only to find racism in their new home.* Toronto: Umbrella Press. *43*

Shields, M. 2003. The health of Canada's shift workers. *Canadian Social Trends, 69,* 21–25. *122*

Sherman, A. 1994. *Wasting America's future.* Boston: Beacon Press. *467*

Sherry, J. L. 2001. The effects of violent video games on aggression: A meta-analysis. *Human Communication Research, 27,* 409–431. *75*

Shinn, M., Knickman, J., and Weitzman, B. C. 1991. Social relationships and vulnerability to becoming homeless among poor families. *American Psychologist, 46,* 1180–1187. *157*

Shoemaker, N. 1991. The rise or fall of Iroquois women. *Journal of Women's History, 23,* 39–57. *35*

Short, S., and Fengying, Z. 1998. Looking locally at China's one-child policy. *Studies in Family Planning, 29,* 373–387. *48, 49*

Shorter, E. 1975. *The making of the modern family.* New York: Basic Books. *396*

Shuey, K., and Hardy, M. A. 2003. Assistance to aging parents and parents-in-law: Does lineage affect family allocation decisions? *Journal of Marriage and Family, 65,* 418–431. *353*

Shumway, D. R. 2003. *Modern love: Romance, intimacy and the marriage crisis.* New York: New York University Press. *216*

Siegel, J. M. 1995. Looking for Mr. Right? Older single women who become mothers. *Journal of Family Issues, 16,* 194–211. *224*

Sigle-Rushton, W., and McLanahan, S. 2002. The living arrangements of new unmarried mothers. *Demography, 39,* 415–433. *240*

Silver, C. 2000. Being there: The time dual-earner couples spend with their children. *Canadian Social Trends, 57,* 20–29. *310*

Silver, C. 2001. From sun-up to sundown: Work patterns of farming couples. *Canadian Social Trends, 61,* 12–15. *162*

Silverman, A. R. 1993. Outcomes of transracial adoption. *The Future of Children, 3,* 104–118. *262*

Silverstein, L. B., and Auerbach, C. F. 1999. Deconstructing the essential father. *American Psychologist, 54,* 397–407. *472*

Silverstein, M., and Bengtson, V. L. 1991. Do close parent-child relationships reduce the mortality risk of older parents? *Journal of Health and Social Behavior, 32,* 382–395. *353*

Silverstein, M., and Long, J. D. 1998. Trajectories of grand-parents' perceived solidarity with adult grandchildren: A growth curve analysis over 23 years. *Journal of Marriage and the Family, 60,* 912–923. *295*

Silverstein, M., Parrott, T. M., and Bengtson, V. L. 1995. Factors that predispose middle-aged sons and daughters to provide support to older parents. *Journal of Marriage and the Family, 57,* 465–475. *354*

Simms, G. P. 1993. Diasporic experience of Blacks in Canada: A discourse. *Dalhousie Review, 73,* 308–322. *42*

Simons, R. L., Johnson, C., and Conger, R. D. 1994a. Harsh corporal punishment versus quality of parental involvement as an explanation of adolescent maladjustment. *Journal of Marriage and the Family, 56,* 591–607. *338*

Simons, R. L., et al. 1994b. Economic pressure and harsh parenting. In R. D. Conger, G. H. Elder, Jr., and Associates (Eds.), *Families in troubled times: Adapting to change in rural America* (pp. 207–222). New York: Aldine de Gruyter. *163*

Simons, R. L., et al. 1994c. The impact of mothers' parenting, involvement by nonresidential fathers, and parental conflict on the adjustment of adolescent children. *Journal of Marriage and the Family, 56,* 356–374. *340*

Simons, R. L., et al. 1995. A test of various perspectives on the intergenational transmission of domestic violence. *Criminology, 33,* 141–172. *435*

Simons, R. L., et al. (Eds.). 1996. *Understanding differences between divorced and intact families.* Thousand Oaks, CA: Sage. *396, 407, 411, 473*

Simons, R. L., Lin, K.-H., and Gordon, L. C. 1998a. Socialization in the family of origin and male dating violence: A prospective study. *Journal of Marriage and the Family, 60,* 467–478. *423*

Simons, R. L., et al. 1998b. A test of latent trait versus life-course perspectives on the stability of adolescent antisocial behavior. *Criminology, 36,* 217–244. *423*

Simons, R. L., et al. 2001. Quality of parenting as mediator of the effect of childhood defiance on adolescent friendship choices and delinquency: A growth curve analysis. *Journal of Marriage and Family, 63,* 63–79. *340*

Simons, R. L., et al. 2002. Community differences in the association between parenting practices and child conduct problems. *Journal of Marriage and Family, 64,* 331–345. *153, 338, 340*

Singer, J. D., et al. 1998. Early child-care selection: Variation by geographic location, maternal characteristics, and family structure. *Developmental Psychology, 34,* 1129–1144. *176*

Singh, S., Darroch, J. E., and Frost, J. J. 2001. Socioeconomic disadvantage and adolescent women's sexual and reproductive behavior: The case of five developed countries. *Family Planning Perspectives, 33,* 258–268. *135*

Skill, T. 1994. Family images and family actions as presented in the media: Where we've been and what we've found. In D. Zillman, J. Bryant, and A. C. Huston (Eds.), *Media, children, and the family* (pp. 37–50). Hillsdale, NJ: Erlbaum. *73*

Skolnick, A. 1998. Solomon's children: The new biologism, psychological parenthood, attachment theory, and the best interests standard. In M. A. Mason, A. Skolnick, and S. D. Sugarman (Eds.), *All our families: New policies for a new century.* New York: Oxford University Press. *258*

Skrypnek, B., and Fast, J. 1996. Work and family policy in Canada: Family needs, collective solutions. *Journal of Family Issues, 17,* 793–812. *462*

Slater, S. 1995. *The lesbian family life cycle.* New York: Free Press. *243*

Sleek, S. 1998. "Innocuous" violence triggers the real thing. *APA Monitor, 29,* April (pp. 1, 31). *422*

Slomkowski, C., et al. 2001. Sisters, brothers, and delinquency: Evaluating social influence during early and middle adolescence. *Child Development, 72,* 271–283. *365*

Small, S. A., and Eastman, G. 1991. Rearing adolescents in contemporary society: A conceptual framework for understanding the responsibilities and needs of parents. *Family Relations, 40,* 455–462. *345*

Small, S. A., and Kerns, D. 1993. Unwanted sexual activity among peers during early and middle adolescence: Incidence and risk factors. *Journal of Marriage and the Family, 55,* 941–952. *446*

Smetana, J., and Gaines, C. 1999. Adolescent-parent conflict in middle-class African American families. *Child Development, 70,* 1447–1463. *341*

Smith, D. E. 1974. Women's perspective as a radical critique of sociology. *Sociological Inquiry, 44,* 7–13. *21*

Smith, D. E. 1987. *The everyday world as problematic: A feminist sociology.* Toronto: University of Toronto Press. *21*

Smith, D. E. 1993. The Standard North American family: SNAF as an ideological code. *Journal of Family Issues, 14,* 50–65. *18*

Smith, D. S. 1993. *Parent-generated home study in Canada: The national outlook, 1993.* Westfield, NB: Francombe Place. *189, 332*

Smith, H., and Israel, E. 1987. Sibling incest: A study of the dynamics of 25 cases. *Child Abuse & Neglect, 11,* 101–108. *443, 444*

Smith, H. E. H., and Sullivan, L. M. 1995. Now that I know how to manage: Work and identity in the journals of Anne Langton. *Ontario History, 87,* 253–269. *38*

Smith, J. R., Brooks-Gunn, J., and Klebanov, P. K. 1997. Consequences of living in poverty for young children's cognitive and verbal ability and early school achievement. In G. J. Duncan and J. Brooks-Gunn (Eds.), *Consequences of growing up poor* (pp. 132–189). New York: Russell Sage. *137*

Smith, T. W. 1998. A review of church attendance measures. *American Sociological Review, 63,* 131–136. *191*

Smock, P. J. 1994. Gender and short-run economic consequences of marital disruption. *Social Forces, 74,* 243–262. *472*

Smock, P. J., and Gupta, S. 2002. Cohabitation in contemporary North America. In A. Booth and A. C. Crouter (Eds.), *Just living together* (pp. 53–84). Mahwah, NJ: Erlbaum. *215, 397, 398*

Smock, P. J., and Manning, W. D. 1997. Cohabiting partners' economic circumstances and marriage. *Demography, 34,* 331–341. *211, 460*

Smock, P. J., Manning, W. D., and Gupta, S. 1999. The effect of marriage and divorce on women's economic well-being. *American Sociological Review, 64,* 794–812. *134, 396*

Smyer, M. A., et al. 1998. Childhood adoption: Long-term effects in adulthood. *Psychiatry: Interpersonal and Biological Processes, 61,* 191–205. *259*

Sobol, M. P., Daly, K. J., and Kelloway, E. K. 2000. Paths to the facilitation of open adoption. *Family Relations, 49,* 419–424. *263*

Solomon, J. C., and Marx, J. 1995. "To grandmother's house we go": Health and school adjustment of children raised solely by grandparents. *The Gerontologist, 35,* 386–394. *291, 292*

South, S. C. 2001. Time-dependent effects of wives' employment on marital dissolution. *American Sociological Review, 66,* 226–245. *461*

South, S. D. 1996. Mate availability and the transition to unwed motherhood: A paradox of population structure. *Journal of Marriage and the Family, 58,* 265–280. *135*

South, S. J., and Lloyd, K. M. 1995. Spousal alternatives and marital dissolution. *American Sociological Review, 60,* 21–35. *394, 399*

Spanier, G. B. 1976. Measuring dyadic adjustment: New scales for assessing the quality of marriage and similar dyads. *Journal of Marriage and the Family, 42,* 15–27. *315*

Spencer, M. B., et al. 1996. Parental monitoring and adolescents' sense of responsibility for their own learning: An examination of sex differences. *Journal of Negro Education, 65,* 30–43. *334*

Spitze, G., and Logan, J. R. 1991. Sibling structure and intergenerational relations. *Journal of Marriage and the Family, 53,* 871–884. *353, 363*

Spitzer, B. L., Henderson, K. A., and Zivian, M. T. 1999. Gender differences in population versus media body sizes: A comparison over four decades. *Sex Roles, 40,* 545–565. *344*

Spitzer, D., et al. 2003. Caregiving in transnational context: My wings have been cut; where can I fly? *Gender and Society, 17,* 267–286. *106*

Sprechner, S. 2001. Equity and social exchange in dating couples: Associations with satisfaction, commitment, and stability. *Journal of Marriage and the Family, 63,* 599–613. *13*

Sroufe, L. A. 1996. *Emotional development.* New York: Cambridge University Press. *16*

St. Pierre, R. G., and Layzer, J. I. 1998. *Improving the life chances of children in poverty: Assumptions and what we have learned.* Ann Arbor, MI: Society for Research in Child Development. *469, 470*

Stacey, J. 1996. *In the name of the family: Rethinking family values in the postmodern age.* Boston: Beacon Press. *64, 65, 83*

Stacey, J. 1998. Gay and lesbian families: Queer like us. In M. A. Mason, A. Skolnick, and S. D. Sugerman (Eds.), *All our families: New policies for a new century* (pp. 117–143). New York: Oxford University Press. *222, 281*

Stacey, J., and Biblarz, T. J. 2001. (How) does the sexual orientation of parents matter? *American Sociological Review, 66,* 159–183. *243, 244, 461*

Stack, C., and Burton, L. 1993. Kinscripts. *Journal of Comparative Family Studies, 24,* 157–170. *364*

Stack, S., and Eshleman, J. R. 1998. Marital status and happiness: A 17-nation study. *Journal of Marriage and the Family, 60,* 527–536. *218*

Staff, I., and Fein, E. 1992. Together or separate: A study of siblings in foster care. *Child Welfare, 71,* 257–270. *264*

Stambrook, F., and Hryniuk, S. 2000. Who were they really? Reflections on East European immigrants to Manitoba before 1914. *Prairie Forum, 25,* 215–232. *45*

Stanley, S. M., Whitton, S. W., and Markman, H. J. 2004. Maybe I do: Interpersonal commitment and premarital or nonmarital cohabitation. *Journal of Family Issues, 25,* 496–519. *196, 215*

Stark, S. D. 1997. *Glued to the set: The 60 television shows and events that made us who we are today.* New York: Free Press. *70*

Starna, W. A., Hammel, G. R., and Butts, W. 1984. Northern Iroquoian horticulture and insect infestation: A cause for village removal. *Ethnohistory, 31,* 197–207. *34*

Starrels, M. A., et al. 1997. The stress of caring for a parent: Effects of the elder's impairment on an employed adult child. *Journal of Marriage and the Family, 59,* 860–872. *352, 354*

State Council Information Office of the People's Republic of China. 2000. White paper—Fifty years of progress in China's human rights. <www.chinesehumanrightsreader.org/governments/2000wp/html>. *47, 48*

Statistics Canada. 1997. 1996 Census: Marital status, common-law unions and families. *The Daily,* October 14. <www.statcan.ca>. *211*

Statistics Canada. 1999. Section "Keeping Track." *Canadian Social Trends, 52*, p. 23. *134*

Statistics Canada. 2000. *Perspectives on Labour and Income, 12*, December, Cat. No. 75–001. <www.statcan.ca>. *122*

Statistics Canada. 2001. *2001 Census: Immigrant population.* Ottawa, Canada. *88, 89, 91, 93, 100, 104*

Statistics Canada. 2002a. 2001 Census of Canada: Profile of Canadian families and households: Diversification continues. <www.statcan.ca>. *4, 129, 242, 288*

Statistics Canada. 2002b. Shifts in the population size of various age groups. Analysis Series. <www.statcan.ca>. *459*

Statistics Canada. 2002c. Therapeutic abortion. *The Daily*, January 18. <www.statcan.ca>. *253*

Statistics Canada. 2002d. Trends in Canadian and American fertility. *The Daily*, July 3. <www.statcan.ca>. *251*

Statistics Canada. 2002e. 2001 Census: Marital status, common-law status, families, dwellings and households. *The Daily*, October 22. <www.statcan.ca>. *165, 211, 223, 237, 238, 288, 391, 410*

Statistics Canada. 2002f. *Perspectives on labour and income. 12*, December, Cat. No. 75–001. <www.statcan.ca>. *120*

Statistics Canada. 2002g. *Citizenship and Immigration Canada. Facts and figures: Immigration overview.* Catalogue MP43-333/2003E. Ottawa: Statistics Canada. *89, 91, 92*

Statistics Canada. 2003a. *Longitudinal survey of immigrants to Canada: Process, progress, and prospects.* Statistics Canada Cat. No 89–611. <www.statcan.ca>. *90*

Statistics Canada. 2003b. *Labour force historical review 2003.* Ottawa: Cat. No. 71F0004XCB. <www.statcan.ca>. *121*

Statistics Canada. 2003c. Life after welfare. *The Daily*, March 26. <www.statcan.ca>. *134*

Statistics Canada. 2003d. Digital divide in schools: Student access to and use of computers. *The Daily*, June 23. <www.statcan.ca>. *79, 80*

Statistics Canada. 2003e. Family violence. *The Daily*, June 23. <www.statcan.ca>. *421*

Statistics Canada. 2003f. Sexual offences. *The Daily*, July 25. <www.statcan.ca>. *439*

Statistics Canada. 2003g. Household spending on domestic help. *The Daily*, August 26. <www.statcan.ca>. *123*

Statistics Canada. 2003h. Witnessing violence: Aggression and anxiety in young children. *The Daily*, December 1. <www.statcan.ca>. *428, 430*

Statistics Canada. 2003i. Grandparents and grandchildren. *The Daily*, Dec. 9. <www.statcan.ca>. *289*

Statistics Canada. 2003j. Family Income 2001. *The Daily*, December 17. <www.statcan.ca>. *120*

Statistics Canada. 2003k. Survey of household spending. *The Daily*, December 17. <www.statcan.ca>. *132*

Statistics Canada. 2003l. *Aboriginal peoples of Canada: A demographic profile.* Cat. No.96F0030X1E2001007. Ottawa: Statistics Canada. *93, 95*

Statistics Canada. 2004a. Study: How long do people live in low income neighbourhoods? *The Daily*, January 21. <www.statcan.ca>. *150, 151*

Statistics Canada. 2004b. Population 15 years and over by hours spent providing unpaid care or assistance to seniors, provinces and territories. Accessed January 22, 2004. <www.statcan.ca>. *351*

Statistics Canada. 2004c. Owner households and tenant households by major payments and gross rent as a percentage of 2000 household income, provinces, and territories. Accessed January 22, 2004. <www.statcan.ca>. *164*

Statistics Canada. 2004d. Families, households, and housing. Household activities. Accessed February 21, 2004. <www.statcan>. *309*

Statistics Canada. 2004e. Study: Student reading performance in minority-language schools. *The Daily*, March 22. <www.statcan.ca>. *186*

Statistics Canada. 2004f. Induced abortions. *The Daily*, March 31. <www.statcan.ca>. *253*

Statistics Canada. 2004g. Study: Minimum-wage workers. *The Daily*, March 26. <www.statcan.ca>. *468*

Statistics Canada. 2004h. Low income in census metropolitan areas. *The Daily*, April 7. <www.statcan.ca>. *109, 468*

Statistics Canada. 2004i. Births. *The Daily*, April 19. <www.statcan.ca>. *251, 281*

Statistics Canada. 2004j. Divorces. *The Daily*, May 4. <www.statcan.ca>. *390–392, 395, 403*

Statistics Canada. 2004k. Canada: A nation on the move. Accessed May 8, 2004. <www.statcan.ca>. *167*

Statistics Canada. 2004l. Household Internet use survey. *The Daily*, July 8. <www.statcan.ca>. *79*

Statistics Canada. 2004m. Aboriginal Peoples Survey: Children who live in non-reserve areas. *The Daily*, July 9. <www.statcan.ca>. *178, 182*

Statistics Canada. 2004n. General Social Survey: Social engagement. *The Daily*, July 6. <www.statcan.ca>. *14, 137, 149, 191*

Statistics Canada. 2004o. Study: Economic consequences of widowhood, *The Daily*, July 22. <www.statcan.ca>. *410*

Stein, N. 1995. Sexual harassment in school: The public performance of gendered violence. *Harvard Educational Review, 65*, 145–162. *446*

Stein, P. J. (Ed.). 1981. *Single life: Unmarried adults in social context.* New York: St. Martin's Press. *224*

Steinberg, L. 2001. We know some things: Parent/adolescent relationships in retrospect and prospect. *Journal of Research on Adolescence, 11*, 1–19. *476*

Steinberg, L., Brown, B. B., and Dornbusch, S. M. 1996. *Beyond the classroom: Why school reform has failed and what parents need to do.* New York: Simon and Schuster. *180, 334*

Steinberg, L., and Darling, N. 1994. The broader context of social influence in adolescence. In R. K. Silbereisen and E. Todt (Eds.), *Adolescence in context* (pp. 25–45). New York: Springer-Verlag. *333*

Steinberg, L., et al. 1995. Authoritative parenting and adolescent adjustment: An ecological journey. In P. Moen, G. H. Elder, Jr., and K. Lüscher (Eds.), *Examining lives in context* (pp. 423–466). Washington, DC: American Psychological Association. *153, 345, 457*

Steinberg, L., Dornbusch, S., and Brown, B. 1992. Ethnic differences in adolescent achievement in ecological perspective. *American Psychologist, 47*, 723–729. *337*

Steinmetz, S. K. 1993. The abused elderly are dependent: Abuse is caused by the perception of stress associated with providing care. In R. J. Gelles and D. Loseke (Eds.), *Current controversies on family violence* (pp. 222–236). Newbury Park, CA: Sage. *448*

Stenberg, S.-A. 2000. Inheritance of welfare recipiency: An intergenerational study of social assistance recipiency in postwar Sweden. *Journal of Marriage and the Family, 62*, 228–239. *467*

Stephan, W. G., and Stephan, C. W. 1991. Intermarriage effects on personality, adjustment, and intergroup relations in two samples of students. *Journal of Marriage and the Family, 53*, 241–250. *262*

Sternberg, K. J., et al. 1993. Effects of domestic violence on children's behavior problems and depression. *Developmental Psychology, 29*, 44–52. *434*

Stets, J. E., and Henderson, D. A. 1991. Contextual factors surrounding conflict resolution while dating: Results from a national study. *Family Relations, 40*, 29–36. *422*

Stevens-Simon, C., Nelligan, D., and Kelly, L. 2001. Adolescents at risk of mistreating their children: Part 1: Prenatal identification. *Child Abuse & Neglect, 6*, 737–751. *249*

Stevenson, K. 1999. Family characteristics of problem kids. *Canadian Social Trends, 55*, 2–6. *248, 334, 362*

Stewart, S. D. 1999a. Disneyland dads, Disneyland moms? How nonresident parents spend time with their absent children. *Journal of Family Issues, 20*, 539–556. *404*

Stewart, S. D. 1999b. Nonresident mothers' and fathers' social contact with children. *Journal of Marriage and the Family, 61*, 894–907. *404*

Stiers, G. A. 1996. *From this day forward: Love, commitment, and marriage in lesbian and gay relationships.* University of Massachusetts, Amherst, Ph.D. Dissertation. *321*

Stobert, S., and Kemeny, A. 2003. Childfree by choice. *Canadian Social Trends, 69*, 7–10. *250*

Stolzenberg, R. M., Blair-Loy, M., and Waite, L. J. 1995. Religious participation in early adulthood: Age and family life cycle effects on church membership. *American Sociological Review, 60*, 84–103. *197*

Stone, L. 1977. *The family, sex, and marriage in England, 1500–1800.* New York: Harper & Row. *396*

Stoneman, Z., et al. 1999. Effects of residential instability on Head Start children and their relationships with older siblings: Influences of child emotionality and conflict between family caregivers. *Child Development, 70*, 1246–1262. *168*

Stouffer, A. P. 1992. *The Light of nature and the law of God: Antislavery in Ontario, 1833–1877.* Baton Rouge, LA: Louisiana State University Press. *42*

Stouthamer-Loeber, M., et al. 2001. Maltreatment of boys and the development of disruptive and delinquent behavior. *Development and Psychopathology, 13*, 941–955. *434*

Strathern, M. 1995. New families for old? In C. Ulanowsky (Ed.), *The family in the age of biotechnology* (pp. 27–45). Aldershot, UK: Avebury. *254*

Straus, M. A. 1979. Measuring intrafamily conflict and violence: The Conflict Tactics (CT) Scales. *Journal of Marriage and the Family, 41*, 75–88. *426*

Straus, M. A., and Donnelly, D. A. 1994. *Beating the devil out of them: Corporal punishment in American families.* New York: Lexington Books. *338, 433*

Straus, M. A., and Gelles, R. J. 1990a. How violent are American families? Estimates from the National Family Violence Resurvey and other studies. In M. A. Straus and R. J. Gelles (Eds.), *Physical violence in American families: Risk factors and adaptations to violence in 8,145 families* (pp. 95–112). New Brunswick, NJ: Transactional Books. *428*

Straus, M. A., and Gelles, R. J. 1990b. *Physical violence in American families: Risk factors and adaptation to violence in 8,145 families.* New Brunswick, NJ: Transactional Books. *438*

Straus, M. A., Gelles, R. J., and Steinmetz, S. K. 1980. *Behind closed doors: Violence in the American family.* Garden City, NY: Anchor. *442*

Straus, M. A., and Smith, C. 1990. Family patterns and child abuse. In M. A. Straus and R. J. Gelles (Eds.), *Physical violence in American families.* New Brunswick, NJ: Transactional Books. *434*

Straus, M. A., and Ulma, A. 2003. Violence of children against mothers in relation to violence between parents and corporal punishment by parents. *Journal of Comparative Family Studies, 34*, 41–60. *447*

Strawbridge, W. J., et al. 1997. New burdens or more of the same? Comparing grandparents, spouse, and adult-child caregivers. *The Gerontologist, 37*, 505–510. *291*

Stromberg, B., et al. 2002. Neurological sequelae in children born after in-vitro fertilization: A population-based study. *Lancet, 359*, 461–465. *255*

Sturino, F. 1984. Contours of postwar immigration to Toronto. *Polyphony*, Summer, 127–130. *99–101*

Sturino, F. 1990. *Forging the chain: Italian migration to North America 1880–1930.* Toronto: Multicultural History Society of Ontario. *100*

Sugarman, D. B., Aldarondo, E., and Boney-McCoy, S. 1996. Risk marker analysis of husband-to-wife violence: A continuum of aggression. *Journal of Applied Social Psychology, 24,* 313–337. *424*

Sui-Chu, E. H., and Willms, J. D. 1996. Effects of parental involvement on eighth-grade achievement. *Sociology of Education, 69,* 126–141. *183*

Suitor, J. J., and Pillemer K. 2000. Did mom really love you best? Exploring the role of within-family differences on parental favoritism. *Motivation and Emotion, 24,* 104–119. *369*

Sullivan, A. 1995. *Virtually normal: An argument about homosexuality.* New York: Alfred A. Knopf. *222*

Surra, C. A. 1990. Research and theory on mate selection and premarital relationships. *Journal of Marriage and the Family, 52,* 844–865. *208*

Sutherland, N. 1997. *Growing up: Childhood in English Canada from the Great War to the age of television.* Toronto: University of Toronto Press. *67*

Swaim, P. 1995. Adapting to economic change: The case of displaced workers. In L. J. Beaulieu and D. Mulkey (Eds.), *Investing in people: The human capital needs of rural America* (pp. 213–234). Boulder, CO: Westview Press. *160*

Sweet, R., and Anisef, P. (Eds.). Forthcoming 2005. *Preparing for post-secondary education: New roles for governments and families.* Montreal: McGill-Queen's University Press. *174*

Swinford, S. P., et al. 2000. Harsh physical discipline in childhood and violence in later romantic involvements: The mediating role of problem behaviors. *Journal of Marriage and the Family, 62,* 508–519. *422, 434*

Swisher, R. R., et al. 1998. The long arm of the farm: How an occupation structures exposure and vulnerability to stressors across role domains. *Journal of Health and Social Behavior, 39,* 72–89. *161*

Szinovacz, M. E. 2000. Changes in housework after retirement: A panel analysis. *Journal of Marriage and the Family, 62,* 78–92. *311*

Talbani, A., and Hasanali, P. 2000. Adolescent females between tradition and modernity: Gender role socialization in south Asian immigrant culture. *Journal of Adolescence, 23(5),* 615–627. *88, 108, 113*

Talbott, S. L. 1995. *The future does not compute: Transcending the machines in our midst.* Sebastopol, CA: O'Reilly & Associates. *459*

Tamis-LeMonda, C. S., and Cabrera, N. 1999. Perspectives on father involvement: Research and policy. *Social Policy Report (Society for Research on Child Development), 12(2).* *140*

Tang, P. N., and Dion, K. 1999. Gender and acculturation in relation to traditionalism: Perceptions of self and parents among Chinese students. *Sex Roles, 41,* 17–29. *105*

Tarmann, A. 2002. International adoptions. In M. M. Kent and M. Mather, What drives U.S. population growth? *Population Bulletin, 57.* *262*

Tarver-Behring, S., and Barkley, R. A. 1985. The mother-child interactions of hyperactive boys and their normal siblings. *American Journal of Orthopsychiatry, 55,* 202–209. *339*

Tasker, F., and Golombok, S. 1995. Adults raised as children in lesbian families. *American Journal of Orthopsychiatry, 65,* 203–215. *243, 244*

Tasker, F. L., and Golombok, S. 1997. *Growing up in a lesbian family: Effects on child development.* New York: Guilford Press. *243*

Tatara, T. 1993. Understanding the nature and scope of domestic elder abuse with the use of state aggregate data: Summaries of the key findings of a national survey of state APS and aging agencies. *Journal of Elder Abuse and Neglect, 5,* 35–57. *448*

Taylor, A. 2002. Keeping up with the kids in a wired world. *Transition,* Autumn, 3–6. *79, 80*

Taylor, D. M., et al. 2004. "Street kids": Towards an understanding of their motivational context. *Canadian Journal of Behavioural Science, 36,* 1–16. *157*

Taylor, J. E., and Norris, J. A. 2000. Sibling relationships, fairness, and conflict over transfer of the farm. *Family Relations, 49,* 277–283. *161*

Teachman, J. 2003a. Premarital sex, premarital cohabitation, and the risk of subsequent marital dissolution among women. *Journal of Marriage and Family, 65,* 444–455. *397*

Teachman, J. 2003b. Childhood living arrangements and the formation of coresidential unions. *Journal of Marriage and Family, 65,* 507–524. *242*

Teachman, J. D. 2004. The childhood living arrangements of children and the characteristics of their marriages. *Journal of Family Issues, 25,* 86–111. *411*

Teti, D. M., et al. 1996. And baby makes four: Predictors of attachment security among preschool-age firstborns during the transition to siblinghood. *Child Development, 67,* 579–596. *360*

Thibaut, J. W., and Kelly, H. H. 1959. *The social psychology of groups.* New York: Wiley. *13*

Thoits, P. A. 1992. Identity structures and psychological well-being: Gender and marital status comparisons. *Social Psychology Quarterly, 55,* 236–256. *316*

Thomson, D. C. 1984. *Jean Lesage and the Quiet Revolution.* Toronto: Macmillan of Canada. *97*

Thorne, B. 1992. Feminism and the family: Two decades of thought. In B. Thorne and M. Yalom (Eds.), *Rethinking the family: Some feminist questions* (rev. ed., pp. 3–30). Boston: Northeastern University Press. *20*

Thornton, A., Axinn, W. G., and Hill, D. H. 1992. Reciprocal effects of religiosity, cohabitation and marriage. *American Journal of Sociology, 98,* 628–651. *198*

Thornton, A., Axinn, W. G., and Teachman, J. D. 1995. The influence of school enrollment and accumulation on cohabitation and marriage in early adulthood. *American Sociological Review, 60,* 762–774. *211, 213*

Thornton, A., and Lin, H.-S. 1994. *Social change and the family in Taiwan*. Chicago: University of Chicago Press. *378*

Thornton, A., and Young-DeMarco, L. 2001. Four decades of trends in attitudes toward family issues in the United States: The 1960s through the 1990s. *Journal of Marriage and the Family, 63*, 1009–1037. *231*

Thurow, L. C. 1999. Building wealth: The new rules for individuals, companies, and nations. *The Atlantic Monthly*, June, 57–69. *119*

Tian, G. 1991. *Chinese-Canadians, Canadian-Chinese: Coping and adapting in North America*. Lewiston, NY/Queenston, ON: Edwin Mellen Press. *104*

Tilly, L. A., and Scott, J. W. 2001. The family economy in modern England and France. In B. J. Fox (Ed.), *Family patterns, gender relations*, 2nd Ed. (pp. 78–107). Toronto: Oxford University Press. *38*

Timer, S. G., and Veroff, J. 2000. Family ties and the discontinuity of divorce in Black and White newlywed couples. *Journal of Marriage and the Family, 62*, 349–361. *397*

Tonry, M. 1995. *Malign neglect—race, crime, and punishment in America*. New York: Oxford University Press. *464, 470*

Totten, M. D. 2000. *Guys, gangs and girlfriend abuse*. Peterborough, ON: Broadview Press. *423*

Townsend, A. L., and Franks, M. M. 1997. Quality of the relationship between elderly spouses: Influence on spouse caregivers' subjective effectiveness. *Family Relations, 46*, 33–39. *319*

Townsend-Batten, B. 2002. Staying in touch: Contact between adults and their parents. *Canadian Social Trends, 64*, 9–12. *348, 349*

Tremblay, J., et al. 2002. Valeur prévisionnelle de la différenciation de soi et des stratégies religieuses d'adaptation dans l'étude de la satisfaction conjugale. *Revue Canadienne des Sciences du Comportement, 34*, 19–27. *196*

Treas, J., and Giesen, D. 2000. Sexual infidelity among married and cohabiting Americans. *Journal of Marriage and the Family, 62*, 48–60. *196, 215, 231*

Trocme, N., et al. 2003. Nature and severity of physical harm caused by child abuse and neglect: Results from the Canadian Incidence Survey. *Canadian Medical Association Journal, 169*, 911–919. *432*

Trovato, F. 1985. Implications for the Italian community in Canada. *Il Congresso, 2*, December 12. *102*

Trusty, J. 1998. Family influences on educational expectations of late adolescents. *The Journal of Educational Research, 5*, 260–270. *181*

Tubman, J. G. 1993. Family risk factors, parental alcohol use, and problem behaviors among school-age children. *Family Relations, 42*, 81–86.

Tucker, C. J., McHale, S. M., and Crouter, A. C. 2003. Dimensions of mothers' and fathers' differential treatment of siblings: Links with adolescents' sex-typed personal quality. *Family Relations, 52*, 241–248. *369, 370*

Tucker, C. J., Marx, J., and Long, L. 1998. "Moving on": Residential mobility and children's school lives. *Sociology of Education, 71*, 111–129. *167*

Turcotte, P. 2002. Changing conjugal life in Canada. *The Daily*, July 11. <www.statcan.ca>. *211, 213, 239, 460*

Turcotte, P., and Bélanger, A. 1997a. Moving in together: The formation of first common-law unions. *Canadian Social Trends, 47*, 7–10. *135, 398*

Turcotte, P., and Bélanger, A. 1997b. *The dynamics of formation and dissolution of first common-law unions in Canada*. Ottawa: Statistics Canada. *213, 405*

Turkheimer, E. 1998. Heritability and biological explanation. *Psychological Review, 105*, 782–791. *19*

Turner, R. J., Sorenson, A. M., and Turner, J. B. 2000. Social contingencies in mental health: A seven-year follow-up study of teenage mothers. *Journal of Marriage and the Family, 62*, 777–791. *246*

Twenge, J. M., Campbell, W. K., and Foster, C. A. 2003. Parenthood and marital satisfaction: A meta-analytic review. *Journal of Marriage and Family, 65*, 574–583. *252*

Tyler, T. 2004. Ottawa backs gay divorce. *Toronto Star*, July 22, A1, A19. *390*

Tyyskä, V. 2001. *Long and winding road: Adolescence and youth in Canada today*. Toronto: Canadian Scholars' Press. *341*

Tzeng, J. M., and Mare, R. D. 1995. Labor market and socioeconomic effects on marital stability. *Social Science Research, 24*, 329–351. *320*

Udry, J. R. 2003. How to string straw into gold. In A. C. Crouter and A. Booth (Eds.), *Children's influence on family dynamics* (pp. 49–54). Mahwah, NJ: Erlbaum. *383*

Uhlenberg, P., and Hammill, B. G. 1998. Frequency of grandparent contact with grandchild sets: Six factors that make a difference. *The Gerontologist, 38*, 276–285. *293*

Umberson, D. 1992. Relationship between adult children and their parents: Psychological consequences for both generations. *Journal of Marriage and the Family, 54*, 664–674. *348*

Umberson, D. 2003. *Death of a parent: Transition to a new adult identity*. Cambridge, UK: Cambridge University Press. *295*

Umberson, D., et al. 1998. Domestic violence, personal control, and gender. *Journal of Marriage and the Family, 60*, 442–452. *426*

Umberson, D., and Williams, C. L. 1993. Divorced fathers: Parental role strain and psychological distress. *Journal of Family Issues, 14*, 378–400. *403*

United Nations. 1998. *Demographic Yearbook*, 1996. New York: United Nations. *393*

United Way of Toronto. 2001. *A decade of decline: Poverty and income inequality in the City of Toronto in the 1990s*. <www.unitedwaytoronto.com>. *130, 151*

Updegraff, K. A., and Obeidallah, C. L. 1999. Young adolescents' patterns of involvement with siblings and friends. *Social Development*, 8, 52–69. *364*

Updegraff, K. A., et al. 2001. Parents' involvement in adolescents' peer relationships: A comparison of mothers' and fathers' roles. *Journal of Marriage and Family*, 63, 655–668. *344*

U.S. Bureau of the Census. 1997. Marital status and living arrangements, March 1997. *Current Population Reports*, Series P-20–506. Washington, DC: U.S. Government Printing Office. *393*

U.S. Commission on Civil Rights. 1977. *Window dressing on the set: Women and minorities in television.* Washington, DC: A report of the U.S. Commission on Civil Rights. *71*

U.S. Department of Health and Human Services. 2002a. *Trends in sexual risk behaviors among high school students—United States, 1991–2001.* Center for Chronic Disease, September 27. <www.cdc.gov/mmwr>. *78*

U.S. Department of Health and Human Services. 2002b. *HHS report shows teen birth rate falls to new record low in 2001.* June 6. *227, 246*

Uzzell, O., and Peebles-Wilkins, W. 1989. Black spouse abuse: A focus on relational factors and intervention strategies. *Western Journal of Black Studies*, 13, 10–16. *428*

van den Akker, O. B. A. 1994. Something old, something new, something borrowed, and something taboo. *Journal of Reproductive and Infant Psychology*, 12, 179–188. *255*

Van Galen, J. 1991. Ideologues and pedagogues: Parents who teach their children at home. In J. Van Galen and M. A. Pitman (Eds.), *Home schooling: Political, historical, and pedagogical perspectives* (pp. 63–76). Norwood, NJ: Ablex. *189*

Vangelisti, A. L., and Huston, T. L. 1994. Maintaining marital satisfaction and love. In D. J. Canary and L. Stafford (Eds.), *Communication and relational maintenance* (pp. 165–186). New York: Academic Press. *317, 321*

Vangelisti, P. G. 1956. *Gli Italiani in Canada.* Montreal: Chiesa Italiana di N.S. Della Difesa. *99*

Vanier Institute of the Family. 2000. *Profiling Canada's families. II.* Ottawa: Vanier Institute of the Family. *130, 131, 160, 393*

Vanier Institute of the Family. 2002. *Sources of diversity: geography, ethnicity, gender, kinship ties and technology.* Ottawa: Vanier Institute of the Family. Accessed December 8. <www.vifamily.ca>. *218, 257*

Vanier Institute of the Family. 2004. *Profiling Canada's families. III.* Ottawa: Vanier Institute of the Family. *264*

Varga, D. 1997. *Constructing the child: A history of Canadian day care.* Toronto: James Lorimer. *174, 344*

Veblen, T. 1899. *The theory of the leisure class.* New York: Modern Library. *128*

Veevers, J. E. 1979. Voluntary childlessness: A review of issues and evidence. *Marriage and Family Review*, 2, 1–26. *331*

Veevers, J. E., and Mitchell, B. A. 1998. Intergenerational exchanges and perceptions of support within "boomerang kid" family environments. *Intergenerational Journal of Aging and Human Development*, 46, 91–108. *289*

Villeneuve-Gokalp, C. 1997. Vivre en couple chacun chez soi. *Population*, 5, 1050–1982. *8*

Voisey, P. 1987. *Vulcan: The making of a Prairie community.* Toronto: University of Toronto Press. *45*

Volling, B. L. 1997. The family correlates of maternal and paternal perceptions of differential treatment in early childhood. *Family Relations*, 46, 227–236. *370, 372, 373*

Volling, B. L., and Belsky, J. 1993. Parent, infant, and contextual characteristics related to maternal employment decisions in the first year of infancy. *Family Relations*, 42, 4–12. *279*

Volling, B. L., and Feagans, L. V. 1995. Infant day care and children's social competence. *Infant Behavior and Development*, 18, 177–188. *175*

Vosko, L. F. 2002. Mandatory "marriage" or obligatory waged work. In S. Bashevkin (Ed.), *Women's work is never done* (pp. 165–199). New York: Routledge. *134, 266*

Votruba-Drzal, E., Coley, R. L., and Chase-Lansdale, P. L. 2004. Child care and low income children's development: Direct and moderated effects. *Child Development*, 75, 296–312. *176*

Voydanoff, P. 1988. Work role characteristics, family structure demands, and work/family conflict. *Journal of Marriage and the Family*, 50, 749–761. *311*

Vroegh, K. S. 1997. Transracial adoptees: Developmental status after 17 years. *American Journal of Orthopsychiatry*, 67, 568–575. *262*

Vuchinich, S., et al. 1991. Parent-child interaction and gender differences in early adolescents' adaptation to stepfamilies. *Developmental Psychology*, 27, 618–626. *415*

Waite, L. J. 1995. Does marriage matter? *Demography*, 4, 483–507. *220*

Waite, L. J., and Gallagher, M. 2000. *The case for marriage.* Cambridge, MA: Harvard University Press. *218, 398, 471*

Walby, S. 1990. *Theorizing patriarchy.* Oxford: Basil Blackwood. *266*

Walby, S. 1997. *Gender transformation.* London: Routledge. *266*

Waldfogel, J., Han, W.-J., and Brooks-Gunn, J. 2002. The effects of early maternal employment on child cognitive development. *Demography*, 39, 369–392. *125*

Waldo, C. R., Hesson-McInnis, M. S., and D'Augelli, A. R. 1998. Antecedents and consequences of victimization of lesbian, gay, and bisexual young people: A structural model comparing rural university and urban samples. *American Journal of Community Psychology*, 26, 307–554. *208*

Walker, A. J., and McGraw, L. A. 2000. Who is responsible for responsible fathering? *Journal of Marriage and the Family*, 62, 563–569. *313, 404*

Walker, J. 1976. *The Black Loyalists: The search for a promised land in Nova Scotia and Sierra Leone, 1783–1807.* London: Longman. *43*

Wall, C. S., and Madak, P. R. 1991. Indian students' academic self- concept and their perceptions of teacher and parent aspirations for them in a band-controlled school and a provincial school. *Canadian Journal of Native Education, 18,* 43–51. *187*

Wall, G. 2001. Moral construction of motherhood in breast-feeding discourse. *Gender and Society, 15,* 592–610. *274*

Wall, G. 2004. Is your child's brain potential maximized?: Mothering in an age of new brain research. *Atlantis, 28.2,* 41–50. *64, 182, 174, 273, 332*

Wallace, H. 1999. *Family violence: Legal, medical, and social perspectives,* 2nd Ed. Boston: Allyn & Bacon. *442*

Wallerstein, J. S. 1998. Children of divorce: A society in search of policy. In M. A. Mason, A. Skolnick, and S. D. Sugarman (Eds.), *All our families: New policies for a new century* (pp. 66–94). New York: Oxford University Press. *408*

Walsh, C., MacMillan, H., and Jamieson, E. 2002. The relationship between parental psychiatric disorder and child physical and sexual abuse: Findings from the Ontario health supplement. *Child Abuse and Neglect, 26,* 11–22. *433*

Walters, S. D. 1999. Sex, text, and context. In M. M. Ferree, J. Lorber, and B. B. Hess (Eds.), *Revisioning gender* (pp. 222–257). Thousand Oaks, CA: Sage. *70*

Waters, J. L. 2002. Flexible families? Astronaut households and the experiences of mothers in Vancouver, British Columbia. *Social & Cultural Geography, 3,* 117–134. *111*

Wang, H., and Amato, P. R. 2000. Predictors of divorce adjustment: Stressors, resources, and definitions. *Journal of Marriage and the Family, 62,* 655–668. *400*

Ward, C. 1998. Community resources and school performance: The Northern Cheyenne case. *Sociological Inquiry, 68,* 83–113. *187*

Warren, S. B. 1992. Lower threshold for referral for psychiatric treatment for adopted adolescents. *Journal of the American Academy of Child & Adolescent Psychiatry, 31,* 512–517. *260*

Wartella, E., Caplowitz, A. G., and Lee, J. H. 2004. From baby Einstein to leapfrog, from doom to the Sims, from instant messaging to Internet chat rooms: Public interest in the role of interactive media in children's lives. *Social Policy Report, 18,* 3–19. *75*

Wasik, B. H., et al. 1990. A longitudinal study of two early intervention strategies: Project CARE. *Child Development, 61,* 1682–1696. *176*

Watamura, S. E., et al. 2003. Morning-to-afternoon increases in cortisol concentrations for infants and toddlers at child care: Age differences and behavioral correlates. *Child Development, 74,* 1006–1020. *176*

Waters, H. F. 1993. Networks under the gun. *Newsweek,* July 12, 64–66. *74*

Weaver, S. E., Coleman, M., and Ganong, L. H. 2004. The sibling relationship in young adulthood: Sibling functions and relationship perceptions as influenced by sibling pair composition. *Journal of Family Issues, 24,* 245–263. *374*

Weedon, C. 1999. *Feminism, theory and the politics of difference.* Oxford: Blackwell. *21*

Wegar, K. 1992. The sociological significance of ambivalence: An example from adoption research. *Qualitative Sociology, 15,* 87–103. *455*

Wegar, K. 1997. *Adoption, identity, and kinship: The debate over sealed birth records.* New Haven, CT: Yale University Press. *70, 258*

Weinfeld, M. 2001. *Like everyone else ... but different.* Toronto: McClelland & Stewart. *209*

Weiss, A. J., and Wilson, B. J. 1996. Emotional portrayals in family television series that are popular among children. *Journal of Broadcasting and Electronic Media, 40,* 1–29. *72*

Wentzel, K. R. 2002. Are effective teachers like good parents? Teaching styles and student adjustment in early adolescence. *Child Development, 73,* 287–301. *180*

Wertheimer, R. 2001. Working poor families with children: Leaving welfare doesn't necessarily mean leaving poverty. *Child Trends,* May. <www.childtrends.org>. *133*

Weston, K. 1991. *Families we choose: Lesbians, gays, and kinship.* New York: Columbia University Press. *4*

Whalen, C. K., Henker, B., and Dotemoto, S. 1980. Methylphenidate and hyperactivity: Effects on teacher behavior. *Science, 208,* 1280–1282. *339*

Whitbeck, L. B., Hoyt, D. R., and Huck, S. M. 1993. Family relationship history, contemporary parent-grandparent relationship quality, and the grandparent-grandchild relationship. *Journal of Marriage and the Family, 55,* 1025–1036. *290*

White, C. O. 1994. Maintaining Anglo-Celtic cultural hegemony in Saskatchewan: Rev. E. H. Oliver, provincial educational policy, and the German Catholics. *Historical Studies in Education, 6,* 253–279. *45*

White, D., and Mill, D. 2000. The child care provider. In L. Prochner and N. Howe (Eds.), *Early childhood education and care in Canada* (pp. 236–251). Vancouver: University of British Columbia Press. *175*

White, J. M. 1999. Work-family stage and satisfaction with work-family balance. *Journal of Comparative Family Studies, 30,* 163–175.

White, J. M., and Klein, D.M. 2002. *Family theories,* 2nd Ed. Thousand Oaks, CA: Sage. *13, 15, 16, 17, 30*

White, J. M., and Marshall, S. K. 2001. Consciously inclusive family research: Can we get there from here? *Journal of Marriage and Family, 63,* 895–898. *26*

White, L. 2001. Sibling relations over the life course: A panel analysis. *Journal of Marriage and Family, 63,* 555–568. *374*

White, L., and Edwards, J. 1990. Emptying the nest and parental well-being: Evidence from national panel data. *American Sociological Review, 55,* 235–242. *318*

White, L., and Gilbreth, J. G. 2001. When children have two fathers: Effects of relationships with stepfathers and noncustodial fathers on adolescent outcomes. *Journal of Marriage and Family, 63,* 155–167. *416*

White, L., and Peterson, D. 1995. The retreat from marriage: Its effect on unmarried children's exchange with parents. *Journal of Marriage and the Family, 57,* 428–434. *350*

White, L. K., and Riedmann, A. 1992. When the Brady Bunch grows up: Step/half- and fullsibling relationships in adulthood. *Journal of Marriage and the Family, 54,* 197–208. *376*

Whiteman, S. D., McHale, S. M., and Crouter, A. C. 2003. What parents learn from experience: The first child as a first draft? *Journal of Marriage and Family, 65,* 608–621. *287, 369*

Whiting, B. B., and Edwards, C. P. 1988. *Children of different worlds.* Cambridge, MA: Harvard University Press. *273*

Whiting, J. B., and Lee, R. E. 2003. Voices from the system: A qualitative study of foster children's stories. *Family Relations, 52,* 288–295. *265*

Whittaker, T. 1995. Violence, gender, and elder abuse: Toward a feminist analysis and practice. *Journal of Gender Studies, 4,* 35–45. *447, 449*

Wickrama, K. A. S., and Bryant, C. M. 2003. Community context of social resources and adolescent mental health. *Journal of Marriage and Family, 65,* 850–866. *153*

Widmer, E. D. 1997. Influence of older siblings on initiation of sexual intercourse. *Journal of Marriage and the Family, 59,* 928–938. *365*

Widmer, E. D., Treas, J., and Newcomb, R. 1998. Attitudes toward nonmarital sex in 24 countries. *Journal of Sex Research, 35,* 349–358. *231*

Widom, C. S. 1990. The intergenerational transmission of violence. In N. A. Weiner and M. E. Wolfgang (Eds.), *Pathways to criminal violence* (pp. 137–201). Newbury Park, CA: Sage. *435*

Widom, C. S., and Morris, S. 1997. Accuracy of adult recollections of childhood victimization: Part 2: Childhood sexual abuse. *Psychological Assessment, 9,* 34–36. *442*

Wieke, V. R. 1997. *Sibling abuse: Hidden physical, emotional and sexual trauma,* 2nd Ed. Thousand Oaks, CA: Sage. *442*

Wilcox, B. L., and Kunkel, D. 1996. Taking television seriously: Children and television policy. In E. F. Zigler, S. L. Kagan, and N. W. Hall (Eds.), *Children, families, and government* (pp. 333–352). Cambridge: Cambridge University Press. *69*

Wilcox, K. L., Wolchik, S. A., and Braver, S. L. 1998. Predictors of maternal preference for joint or sole legal custody. *Family Relations, 47,* 93–101. *403*

Wilcox, W. B. 2002. Religion, convention, and parental involvement. *Journal of Marriage and Family, 64,* 780–792. *198*

Wiley, A. R., Warren, H. B., and Montanelli, D. S. 2002. Shelter in a time of storm: Parenting in poor rural African American communities. *Family Relations, 51,* 265–273. *197*

Wilkie, J. R., Ferree, M. M., and Ratcliff, K. S. 1998. Gender and fairness: Marital satisfaction in two-earner couples. *Journal of Marriage and the Family, 60,* 577–594. *309, 311*

Wilkins, R., Bertholet, J.-M., and Ng, E. 2002. *Trends in mortality by neighbourhood income in urban Canada from 1971 to 1996.* Supplement for Health Reports, Vol. 13, Cat. No. 82-003. *151*

Willetts, M. 2003. An exploratory investigation of heterosexual licensed domestic partners. *Journal of Marriage and Family, 65,* 939–952. *222*

Williams, C. 2001a. Connected to the internet, still connected to life? *Canadian Social Trends, 63,* 13–15. *79, 80*

Williams, C. 2001b. The evolution of communication. *Canadian Social Trends, 60,* 15–18. *81*

Williams, C. 2001c. Family disruptions and childhood happiness. *Canadian Social Trends, 62,* 2–5. *343, 405*

Williams, C. 2002. Time or money? How high and low income Canadians spend their time. *Canadian Social Trends, 65,* 7–11. *127, 128*

Williams, C. 2003. Finances in the golden years. *Perspectives on Labour and Income, 4,* November, 5–13. *465*

Williams, L. M., and Banyard, V. L. 1997. Gender and recall of child sexual abuse: A prospective study. In J. D. Read and D. S. Lindsay (Eds.), *Recollections of trauma: Scientific evidence and clinical perspective* (pp. 371–377). New York: Plenum Press. *442*

Willms, J. D. (Ed.). 2002a. *Vulnerable children.* Edmonton: University of Alberta Press. *26*

Willms, J. D. 2002b. A study of vulnerable children. In J. D. Willms (Ed.), *Vulnerable children* (pp. 3–22). Edmonton: University of Alberta Press. *248*

Willms, J. D. 2002c. Socioeconomic gradients for childhood vulnerability. In J. D. Willms (Ed.), *Vulnerable children* (pp. 71–103). Edmonton: University of Alberta Press. *141, 184*

Willms, J. D., and Corbett, B. A. 2003. Tech and teens: Access and use. *Canadian Social Trends, 69,* 15–20. *81*

Wilmoth, J., and Koso, G. 2002. Does marital history matter? Marital status and wealth outcomes among preretirement adults. *Journal of Marriage and Family, 64,* 254–268. *221, 412*

Willson, A. E., Shuey, K. M., and Elder, G. H., Jr. 2003. Ambivalence in the relationship of adult children to aging parents and in-laws. *Journal of Marriage and Family, 65,* 1055–1072. *354*

Wilson, S. M., Martoz-Baden, R., and Holloway, D. P. 1991. Stress in two-generation farm and ranch families. *Lifestyles: Family and Economic Issues, 12,* 199–216. *161*

Wilson, W. J. 1987. *The truly disadvantaged.* Chicago: University of Chicago Press. *135, 171*

Wilson, W. J. 1996. *When work disappears: The world of the new urban poor.* New York: Knopf. *153*

Winks, R. W. 2000. *The Blacks in Canada: A history,* 2nd Ed. Montreal, Kingston: McGill-Queen's University Press. *42*

Withrow, A. 2002. *Nova Scotia's ethnic roots*. Tantallon, NS: Glen Margaret. *39*

Wolfe, S. M., Toro, P. A., and McCaskill, P. A. 1999. A comparison of homeless and matched housed adolescents on family environment variables. *Journal of Research on Adolescence, 9*, 53–66. *158*

Wolff, E. N. 2001. The economic status of parents in postwar America. In S. A. Hewlett, N. Rankin, and C. West (Eds.), *Taking parenting public* (pp. 59–82). New York: Rowan & Littlefield. *127*

Wong, J., and Checkland, D. 1999. Introduction. In J. Wong and D. Checkland (Eds.), *Teen pregnancy and parenting* (pp. viii–xxiii). Toronto: University of Toronto Press. *245, 269*

Wood, D., et al. 1993. Impact of family relocation on children's growth, development, school function, and behavior. *Journal of the American Medical Association, 270*, 1334–1338. *167*

Wood, P. K. 2002. *Nationalism from the margins: Italians in Alberta and British Columbia*. Montreal, Kingston: McGill-Queen's University Press. *101*

Woodberry, R. D. 1998. Comment: When surveys lie and people tell the truth: How surveys oversample church attenders. *American Sociological Review, 63*, 119–122. *192*

Woodward, L., Fergusson, D. M., and Horwood, L. J. 2001. Risk factors and life processes associated with teenage pregnancy: Results of a prospective study from birth to 20 years. *Journal of Marriage and Family, 63*, 1170–1184. *248*

Wright, K. 1998. Human in the age of mechanical reproduction. *Discover, 19*, 74–81. *256*

Wrobel, G. M., et al. 1996. Openness in adoption and the level of child participation. *Child Development, 67*, 2358–2374. *263*

Wu, L. L. 1996. Effects of family instability, income, and income instability on the risk of a premarital birth. *American Sociological Review, 61*, 386–406. *405, 407*

Wu, Z. 1995. Remarriage after widowhood: A marital history study of older Canadians. *Canadian Journal on Aging, 14*, 719–736. *241, 410*

Wu, Z. 1999. Premarital cohabitation and the timing of first marriage. *Canadian Review of Sociology and Anthropology, 36*, 109–127. *238*

Wu, Z. 2000. *Cohabitation: An alternative form of family living*. Toronto: Oxford University Press. *213–216, 234, 269, 397, 398, 460*

Wu, Z., and Balakrishnan, T. R. 1995. Dissolution of premarital cohabitation in Canada. *Demography, 32*, 521–532. *397*

Wu, Z., and Hart, R. 2002. The effects of marital and nonmarital union transition on health. *Journal of Marriage and Family, 64*, 420–432. *213*

Wu, Z., and MacNeill, L. 2002. Education, work, and childbearing after age 30. *Journal of Comparative Family Studies, 33*, 191–213. *251, 252*

Wu, Z., and Schimmele, C. M. 2003. Childhood family experience and completed fertility. *Canadian Studies in Population, 30*, 221–240. *245*

Wu, Z., et al. 2000. Age-heterogamy and Canadian unions. *Social Biology, 47*, 277–293. *209, 216*

Wu, Z., et al. 2004. "In sickness and in health": Does cohabitation count? *Journal of Family Issues, 24*, 811–838. *219*

Wulczyn, F. 2004. Family reunification. *The Future of Children, 14*, Winter, 95–113. *265*

Yamaguchi, K., and Ferguson, L. R. 1995. The stopping and spacing of childbirths and their birth-history predictors: Rational-choice theory and event-history analysis. *American Sociological Review, 60*, 272–298. *250*

Yancey, G. 2002. Who interracially dates?: An examination of the characteristics of those who have interacially dated. *Journal of Comparative Family Studies, 33*, 179–190. *209*

Yee, S. 1994. Gender ideology and Black women as community-builders in Ontario, 1850–70. *Canadian Historical Review, 75*, 53–73. *44*

Yelsma, P. and Athappilly, K. 1998. Marital satisfaction and communication practices: Comparisons among Indian and American couples. *Journal of Comparative Family Studies, 19*, 37–54. *50*

Yip, A. K. T. 1997. *Gay male Christian couples*. Westport, CT: Praeger. *321*

Young, B. 2001. The 'mistress' and the 'maid' in the globalized economy. *The Socialist Register*, 287–327. *112*

Young, V. H. 1974. A Black American socialization pattern. *American Ethnologist, 1*, 415–431. *334*

Zabin, L. S., and Hayward, S. C. 1993. *Adolescent sexual behavior and childbearing*. Newbury Park, CA: Sage. *253*

Zack, N. 1997. "The family" and radical family theory. In H. L. Nelson (Ed.), *Feminism and families* (pp. 43–51). New York: Routledge. *61*

Zajonc, R. B. 2001. The family dynamics of intellectual development. *American Psychologist, 56*, 490–496. *360*

Zajonc, R. B., and Mullally, P. R. 1997. Birth order: Reconciling conflicting effects. *American Psychologist, 52*, 685–690. *362, 363*

Zelizer, V. A. R. 1985. *Pricing the priceless child: The changing social value of children*. New York: Basic Books. *251*

Zigler, E. F., and Styfco, S. 1996. Head Start and early childhood intervention: The changing course of social science and social policy. In E. F. Zigler, S. L. Kagan, and N. W. Hall (Eds.), *Children, families, and government* (pp. 132–155). Cambridge: Cambridge University Press. *469*

Zill, N. 1988. Behavior, achievement, and health problems among children in stepfamilies: Findings from a national survey of child health. In E. M. Hetherington and J. D. Arasteh (Eds.), *Impact of divorce, single parenting, and stepparenting on children* (pp. 325–368). Hillsdale, NJ: Erlbaum. *404*

Zill, N., Morrison, D. R., and Coiro, M. J. 1993. Long-term effects of parental divorce on parent-child relationships, adjustment, and achievement in young adulthood. *Journal of Family Psychology, 7*, 91–103. *343, 405*

Zill, N., and Nord, C. W. 1994. *Running the place: How American families are faring in a changing economy and an individualistic society.* Washington, DC: Child Trends, Inc. *182*

Zima, B. T., et al. 1996. Mental health problems among homeless mothers: Relationship to service use and child mental health problems. *Archives of General Psychiatry, 53*, 332–338. *159*

Zimmerman, J. 2003. *Made from scratch: Reclaiming the pleasures of the American hearth.* New York: Free Press. *124*

Zimmerman, S. L. 1995. *Understanding family policy,* 2nd Ed. Thousand Oaks, CA: Sage. *464, 474*

Zimmerman, T. S., and Fetsch, R. J. 1994. Family ranching and farming: A consensus management model to improve family functioning and decrease work stress. *Family Relations, 43*, 125–131. *161*

Zucchi, J. 1981. *The Italian immigrants of the St. John's Ward, 1875–1915: Patterns of settlement and neighbourhood formation.* Toronto: Multicultural History Society of Ontario.

Subject Index

Photo Credits

p. 2: Anne-Marie Ambert.; p. 15: Will Faller; p. 31: Anne-Marie Ambert; p. 40: From a painting by R.J. Tucker; p. 44: Library of Congress; p. 58: Will Hart; p. 67: Anne-Marie Ambert; p. 86: Courtesy of National Institute of Aging; p. 95: Anne-Marie Ambert; p. 107: © Joel Benard/Masterfile; p. 117: Nathan Benn/Corbis; p. 133: Tony Freeman/PhotoEdit; p. 146: PhotoEdit; p. 161: Anne-Marie Ambert; p. 172: Will Hart; p. 177: Anne-Marie Ambert; p. 198: Myrleen Ferguson Cate/PhotoEdit; p. 204: Anne-Marie Ambert; p. 219: Anne-Marie Ambert; p. 235: Laura Dwight/PhotoEdit; p. 243: Stone/Tamara Reynolds; p. 256: Will Faller; p. 270: Anne-Marie Ambert; p. 281: Deborah Davis/PhotoEdit; p. 287: Anne-Marie Ambert; p. 291: Anne-Marie Ambert; p. 300: Stone/David Hanover; p. 307: Anne-Marie Ambert; p. 322: Anne-Marie Ambert; p. 329: Laura Dwight/PhotoEdit; p. Will Yurman/The Image Works; p. 358: Anne-Marie Ambert; p. Will Hart; p. Anne-Marie Ambert; p. 388: Joel Gordon; p. 413: Michael Newman/PhotoEdit; p. 420: Michael Newman/PhotoEdit; p. 443: Courtesy of Pearson Education; p. 448: Courtesy of Pearson Education; p. 453: Nubar Alexanian/Stock, Boston; p. 466: Anne-Marie Ambert; p. 475: Library of Congress